Ways to Writing

LINDA C. STANLEY
DAVID SHIMKIN
ALLEN H. LANNER

Queensborough Community College
City University of New York

Ways to Writing

Purpose, Task, and Process

THIRD EDITION

MACMILLAN PUBLISHING COMPANY

NEW YORK

Editor: Eben W. Ludlow
Production Supervisor: Linda Greenberg
Production Manager: Paul Smolenski
Text and Cover Designer: Jane Edelstein
Cover photograph: © James Robinson Photography
This book was set in Meridien by V & M Graphics and printed and bound by Arcata
Graphics/Halliday. The cover was printed by Phoenix Color Corp.

Acknowledgments appear on pages 619–622, which constitute an extension of the
copyright page.

Macmillan Publishing Company
866 Third Avenue, New York, New York 10022

Macmillan Publishing Company is part of
the Maxwell Communication Group of Companies.

Library of Congress Cataloging-in-Publication Data
Stanley, Linda, 1940–
    Ways to writing: purpose, task, and process / Linda C. Stanley,
David Shimkin, Allen H. Lanner. — 3rd ed.
        p.   cm.
    Includes index.
    ISBN 0-02-415651-5
    1. English language — Rhetoric.   2. Exposition (Rhetoric)
I. Shimkin, David.   II. Lanner, Allen H.   III. Title.
PE1408.S684   1992
808′.042 — dc20   91-12128
                    CIP

Printing: 1 2 3 4 5 6 7   Year: 1 2 3 4 5 6 7 8

Preface

Through its first two editions, *Ways to Writing* has been received and used with an enthusiasm that confirms our original premise in writing it: Students best understand the writing process when it is presented through a series of integrated activities that take them through each stage of the process.

In this third edition, the premise and hence the essential character and structure of the book have not changed. *Ways to Writing* continues to offer a coherent, unified sequence of specific writing assignments intended to show students how their decisions as to purpose, invention, audience, arrangement, revision, and style are crucial to the effectiveness of their writing. The changes that we have made, in response to extensive feedback from our students, our peers, and our reviewers, are intended to improve on and refine both individual assignments and the sequence as a whole. We believe that in making these changes we have strengthened the book further. The most important of them are as follows:

- We have added two new chapters. In Chapter 6, students are given the opportunity to write about a family or cultural tradition as an exercise in explaining a subject with which they are familiar. In Chapter 11, they are encouraged to make meaning out of a short story.
- We have expanded the Introduction to include a student essay and the journal the writer kept as he made his various decisions about completing the task in order to introduce students more quickly and thoroughly to the dynamics of the writing process and its reflection in the flow of each chapter.
- We have moved the writing task to the front of each chapter so that all elements of the writing process can be considered in the context of this task.
- We have also rearranged the sequence of chapters, placing the research assignment near the end of the text so that students can apply to this complex task the persuasive and critical thinking skills they have learned previously.
- We have added nine new professional essays and six new student essays.

- We have appended to each chapter title the thinking activity demanded by the writing process for that chapter.
- Finally, we have added a revision checklist to each Rewriting section.

We have made other small changes to clarify concepts or facilitate the use of different parts of the book. Those familiar with the first and second editions will, we hope, find that the major change is simply that *Ways to Writing* is now more effective in initiating students to the process of writing college-level essays. For those who are using the text for the first time, a few more comments about its rationale and organization may be helpful.

In their effort to write more effectively, our students have taught us the urgency of starting with what the writer already knows. They remind us that even very good writers do not use personal experience or expressiveness merely as a springboard to writing about something outside themselves, namely, the world of ideas or abstractions, but that their work is in the fullest sense "expressive" of their own voice and vision. Thus, in Chapters 1–3 we emphasize the value of the journal, of free writing, of a first-person perspective on things, ideas, and institutions. Because we want our students to become more conscious of themselves as writers writing, we guide them first to what they can express or explain with the power that comes from having experienced the subject directly.

With increased ability to write about their perceptions, students can do better with the complex demands of expository writing. In Chapters 4–7 we ask them to examine and explore their environment and values by gathering, analyzing, and interpreting information. In Chapters 8–11 we introduce them to methods of argumentation, library research, and ways of responding to literature.

The central focus of *Ways to Writing* is the task that sets each writing assignment in motion. To plan for this task, we first lead the student writer through a series of prewriting activities that suggest ways of generating ideas as well as of analyzing audience considerations. Subsequent sections guide the writer through possible patterns of arranging the essay and, as models, present professional essays based on a similiar task and the rough draft of a student essay written in fulfillment of the task.

Concluding each chapter is, first, a "Focus" section that in the early chapters introduces matters of form or structure that students find useful to talk about in the early stages of writing. In later chapters, this section discusses more sophisticated stylistic concerns or matters of form or structure necessitated by the chapter task.

A section on rewriting follows, which suggests different approaches to revision and includes a set of peer response questions, a checklist for revision based on the chapter task, and a revised version of the student essay for the chapter.

"Becoming Aware of Yourself as a Writer" concludes the chapter with a series of questions on the chapter's writing process that encourages students to become more conscious of what they do when they write.

We have found many advantages for the student in this task-centered organization. First, the student benefits from a "hands-on" approach that provides concrete, specific assistance for an actual writing assignment. Second, the task itself enables the student to draw from a broad range of experiences and, through a sequence of self-designed strategies, to arrive at a conclusion that follows naturally from the student's own cognitive processes. Third, and probably most important for the student writer, each task builds on the skill and awareness acquired in completing the previous tasks. Beginning with expressive writing, the writer is encouraged to move beyond the personal narrative to tasks requiring more complex analytic and critical thought. In fact, it was our desire to help students make this transition that drew us to this cumulative, task-centered method.

We believe our task-centered approach will also be of practical advantage to the instructor, who can relate the writing strategies to the actual assignment at hand. The many rhetorical exercises, examples, and readings should also help the instructor focus on the problems that often arise in discussions of "good" and "bad" writing. The task format yields even greater benefits, we believe, in assignments that require the student to absorb, evaluate, and synthesize reading material—assignments such as the research paper or the essay exam. Here the student is guided through the difficult stages of writing such essays, from formulating the shaping idea to revising the rough draft.

We feel that both student and teacher will benefit from the unity of design and purpose that we have created in each chapter. Of course, no approach to teaching writing can or should presume to be prescriptive or definitive in its methods, and we encourage the users of this text to choose what they think useful and to modify what they think does not respond expressly to the needs of their own students. The "Generating Ideas" and "Audience" sections in each chapter can be used for tasks in other chapters or in class activities devised by the instructor. An instructor can quite easily restructure some of the tasks to suit a particular expressive or expository demand. Although the chapters cover most of the customary writing assignments undertaken in college writing classes, an instructor need not use every chapter, for each individual chapter provides the student with parallel purposive activities. One of our intentions has been to encourage instructors to modify or augment our tasks and activities with their own.

Ways to Writing offers instructor and student concrete direction through the process of writing but without the reductive "by-the-numbers" approach of many basic writing texts or the exhaustive minutiae of the all-encompassing rhetoric. By engaging student writers in activities that are both interesting and immediately useful, we hope to give them ways to gauge their own progress in expressing themselves effectively and to direct their vision beyond the classroom in exploring and explaining the world that they have already experienced and observed. We have also prepared the *Instructor's Manual* that introduces the pedagogy of the text, offers suggestions for approaching the tasks, includes a ten-week and fifteen-week syllabus, and lists sources for the instructor who seeks more information on both traditional and current approaches to the teaching of writing.

The authors wish to express their admiration for, and indebtedness to, James Moffett for his *A Student-Centered Language Arts Curriculum: K–13*, from which we have drawn the central role of the task in the formulation of a writing consciousness. We have constructed our tasks to reflect Moffet's perception that an interplay between the "concrete" and "abstract" is the basis for the development of sound thinking and writing. We are also most obviously indebted to James Kinneavy for his analysis of the different underlying purposes in writing: expressive, referential, persuasive, and literary.

The authors wish to thank the many students who over the ten-year gestation period of this book have good-humoredly submitted themselves to the trials and errors that we have put them through while developing both approach and materials in their classrooms. We wish to thank particularly the students whose work—both in rough and more polished stages—we have used as models for each task.

We are indebted to those reviewers who gave us valuable suggestions and comments throughout the process of writing this text: Valerie M. Balester, Texas A & M University; Richard Bullock, Wright State University; Theresa Enos, University of Arizona; Michael C. Flanigan, University of Oklahoma; James N. Laditka, Mohawk Valley Community College; Avise Nissen, George Washington University; Betty Jo Hicks Peters, Morehead State University; David W. Smit, Kansas State University; and Margaret Urie, University of Nevada, Reno.

At Macmillan we thank Eben Ludlow, Executive Editor for the College Division, for his intelligent guidance and patience; Linda Greenberg, our production editor, for seeing the manuscript through production; Scott Rubin, marketing manager, for his thorough approach to marketing; and Jane Edelstein, book designer.

L. C. S.
D. S.
A. H. L.

Contents

Preface   V

Introduction: Ways to Writing   1

Student Essay "Life in the Food Chain"   2
Choices in Writing   7
Rough Draft of Student Essay "Life in the Food Chain"   8
Purpose   12
Task   12
Generating Ideas   12
Audience   13
Writing the Essay   13
Rewriting   14
Focus on Form and Style   15
Becoming Aware of Yourself as a Writer   15

PART **I**

Self-Expression   17

Introduction   18

1 Writing About Yourself—Keeping a Journal   19

Purpose   19
Task: Writing a Journal   21
You keep a journal on a regular basis, examining the patterns of thought and feeling that emerge there. Audience for task: Yourself.

Writing Your Journal   21
  Generating Ideas: Free Writing   21
    Free Writing as a Source of Ideas   23
    Starting a Journal   27
    Keeping a Journal   35
    Using Your Journal as a Source of Ideas for Writing an Essay   36
  Addressing Your Audience: Private Voice   37
    Your Private Voice   37
    Discovering Your Own Voice   39
    How Others Hear Your   40
    Establishing Your Point of View   45
Becoming Aware of Yourself as a Writer   47

2   Writing About Yourself—Expressing Your Point of View
48

Purpose   48
Task: Writing an Essay Based on Your Journal   49
    *You write an expressive essay on a series of connected journal entries and
    what they reveal about you. Audience for task: A sympathetic reader.*
Writing Your Essay   49
  Generating Ideas: Tracing a Pattern in Your Journal   49
  Addressing Your Audience: The Sympathetic Reader   53
    Reacting to Another's Point of View   53
    Expressing Your Point of View   54
    Expressing Your Point of View About a Series of Journal Entries   57
  Arranging Your Essay   57
    Finding a Shaping Idea   57
    From *The Journals of Henry David Thoreau*   58
    From "Where I Lived, and What I Lived For," Henry David Thoreau   61
  Working in a Peer Group   64
  Writing Your Rough Draft   65
    From the Journal of Angela S.   65
    "Henry David Thoreau" (Rough Draft of Student Essay)   69
Focus on Form: Stating Your Thesis/Writing Your Introduction   72
  Conventions of Form and Style   72
  Stating a Thesis   72
  Stating a Thesis About a Series of Journal Entries   75
  Writing an Introduction   75
  Writing an Introduction for Your Essay on a Series of Journal
    Entries   80
Rewriting   80
  Obtaining Feedback on Your Rough Draft   80
  Working in a Peer Group on Revising   81
  Revision of Student Essay "Henry David Thoreau"   82

Revising   85
   Cutting   85
Revising Your Essay About Yourself   86
The Final Product   86
   Presentation   86
   Your Title   87
   Proofreading   87
Becoming Aware of Yourself as a Writer   87

3 Writing About an Incident — Reporting an Experience 89

Purpose   89
Task: Writing About an Incident   90
   You search your memory for an incident that you observed or were
   involved in that in some way affected your attitudes, thoughts, or
   feelings. Audience for task: Your peers.
Writing Your Essay   91
   Generating Ideas: The Journalist's Questions   91
      The 5 W's and How   91
      Using the Journalist's Questions in Writing an Essay   94
      Using the Journalist's Questions in Generating Ideas About an Incident   96
      Using Your Journal to Collect Details of an Incident   96
      Double-Entry Journal   96
   Addressing Your Audience: The "Intended" Reader(s)   97
      Making Inferences About Your Reader   100
      Determining Your Audience's Point of View for Your Essay on an
         Incident   102
   Arranging Your Essay: The Shaping Idea, Narration, and Exposition   102
      The Shaping Idea   103
      Narration   103
      Duration   103
      Model Essay: "The Angry Winter" by Loren Eiseley   103
      Details   105
      Working with Your Peer Group to Analyze an Essay   106
      Model Essay: "Momma's Private Victory" by Maya Angelou   106
      Arranging the Details of Your Essay   110
      Exposition in the Service of Narration   110
Writing Your Rough Draft   112
   "One night I was awakened by a phone call. . . ." (Rough Draft of
      Student Essay)   112
Focus on Form: Paragraph Structure/Making Transitions   114
   Paragraph Structure   114

Making Transitions   120
Rewriting   126
  Obtaining Feedback on Your Rough Draft   126
  Revision of Student Essay ("Approaching Life from a New
    Perspective")   127
  Adding   129
  Revising Your Essay on an Incident   130
  Editing   131
    Adding   131
    Topic Sentences   131
    Transitions   131
    Mechanics   131
Becoming Aware of Yourself as a Writer   132

PART **II**

Exploration   134

Introduction   134

4   Writing About a Place — Exploring Your Point of View   135

Purpose   135
Task: Exploring a Place   137

Exploring a place about which a myth may have been created for you by others, you write to explain your perceptions as fully and richly as possible. Audience for task: People interested in your findings about the place, such as other students in your curriculum or people with the same interest or hobby.

Writing Your Essay   138
  Generating Ideas: The Explorer's Questions   138
    Using the Explorer's Questions to Generate Ideas About a Place   140
    Using Your Journal in Answering the Explorer's Questions About a
      Place   142
  Addressing Your Audience: Depth of Information   143
    Determining Your Audience's Depth of Information for Your Essay on a
      Place   147
  Arranging Your Essay   149
    The Shaping Idea   149
    Narrative Patterns   150
    Patterns of Exposition   151
    Patterns of Description   152
    Dialogue   153

The Overriding Impression   154
Model Essay: "On a Kibbutz," Saul Bellow   154
Working with Your Peer Group to Analyze an Essay   157
Model Essay: "The Iowa State Fair," Paul Engle   158
Writing Your Rough Draft   161
"Paying for a Higher Education" (Rough Draft of Student Essay)   162
Focus on Form: Paragraph Development/Writing Your Conclusion   164
Paragraph Development   165
Writing a Conclusion   171
Rewriting   174
Obtaining Feedback on Your Rough Draft   174
Revision of Student Essay "Paying for a Higher Education"   175
Substituting   179
Revising Your Essay on a Place   180
Editing   180
Substitutions   180
Transitions   180
Paragraphs   181
Mechanics   181
Becoming Aware of Yourself as a Writer   182

5 Writing About a Prejudgment — Exploring Other Points of View

183

Purpose   183
Task: Writing About a Prejudgment   184
Choosing an ongoing event or situation that you have prejudged in some way, you write a case study in which you test your prejudgment or prejudice against the information that you have amassed. Audience for task: Your college newspaper, a newsletter at work, a local weekly newspaper, or a hobby magazine.
Writing Your Essay   186
Generating Ideas: The Classical Questions   186
The Classical Questions and the Explorer's Questions   186
Forming Subquestions   186
Using the Classical Questions in Writing About a Prejudgment   190
Addressing Your Audience: Writing for Publication   192
The Reader Common to a Publication   192
The Frame of Reference of a Publication's Reader   193
Selecting a Publication for Your Essay on a Prejudgment   195
Arranging Your Essay   197
The Shaping Idea   197
Cause and Effect   198
Comparison and Contrast   199
Process Analysis   200

    Model Essays: "Workers," Richard Rodriguez   201
                "A Second Look at Allen Ginsberg," Patrick Fenton   205
    Writing Your Rough Draft   210
    "A Classical Question" (Rough Draft of Student Essay)   210
  Focus on Form: Sentence Combining   212
    The Base Sentence   212
    Subordinate Clauses   213
    Free Modifiers   214
      Noun Cluster   214
      Verb Cluster   214
      Adjective Cluster   214
      Adverb Cluster   214
    Varying Sentence Length and Rhythm   216
    Punctuation   217
    Transitions   218
    Sentence Combining in Essays Using Narrative Patterns   219
  Rewriting   222
    Obtaining Feedback on Your Rough Draft   222
    Revision of Student Essay "A Classical Question"   222
    Distributing   224
    Revising Your Essay on a Prejudgment   225
    Editing   226
      Distributing   226
      Sentence Combining and Transitions   226
      Paragraphs   226
      Mechanics   226
  Becoming Aware of Yourself as a Writer   227

PART III

Explanation

                                                                         229

  Introduction   229

6 Writing About a Tradition—Explaining What You Know

                                                                         231
  Purpose   231
  Task: Writing About a Tradition   232

You write an essay about the structure and significance of a tradition, custom, ritual, rite, or customary way of doing things that you have observed in your family or cultural or religious group. Audience for task: Someone from outside the family or from a different cultural or religious group.

Writing Your Essay   234
    Generating Ideas: Brainstorming   234
        Listing   234
        Clustering   236
        Brainstorming and the Explorer's and Classical Questions   236
        Using Brainstorming to Generate Ideas for Your Essay on a Tradition   238
    Addressing Your Audience: Considering the Values and Attitudes of the
        Uninformed Reader   240
        Analyzing the Frame of Reference of the Uninformed Reader   241
        Addressing the Uninformed Reader's Values and Attitudes   241
        Addressing a Reader's Values and Attitudes in Writing an Essay on a
            Tradition   243
    Arranging Your Essay   245
        The Shaping Idea   245
        Explanation   246
        Definition   247
        Classification   247
        Narrative Examples   248
        Model Essays: "I Am a Catholic," Anna Quindlen   249
                from "On Being Black and Middle Class," Shelby Steele   251
    Writing Your Rough Draft   256
        "House of Delight" (Rough Draft of Student Essay)   256
Focus on Style: Eliminating Deadwood   258
    Pretentiousness   258
    Wordiness   259
    Qualifiers   260
    Awkward Sentence Structure   260
    Avoiding Deadwood in Writing Your Essay on a Tradition   262
Rewriting   263
    Obtaining Feedback on Your Rough Draft   263
    Revision of Student Essay "House of Delight"   264
    Rearranging   267
    Revising Your Essay on a Tradition   267
    Editing   268
        Rearranging   268
Becoming Aware of Yourself as a Writer   268

7   Writing About the Media—Explaining What You Think

269

Purpose   269
Task: Writing About the Media   270
From your experience with the media, you gather observations, make generalizations, and draw conclusions for your reader. Audience for

task: A group chosen from your school, community, or the larger culture who are familiar with the media and with the use of a public voice.

Writing Your Essay   272
   Generating Ideas Through Generalization   272
      Generalization   272
      Narrative Examples   272
      Generalization and the Classical Questions   273
      Generating Ideas for Your Essay on the Media   274
   Addressing Your Audience: Adopting a Public Voice   276
      Addressing a Public Audience   276
      Public Voice and Private Voice   277
      Appropriateness as a Characteristic of a Public Voice   278
      Assessing the Public Voice Appropriate to Your Publication   278
      Addressing the Public Audience of Your Essay on the Media   282
   Arranging Your Essay   284
      The Shaping Idea   284
      Arranging Your Generalizations and Narrative Examples   284
      Model Essays: "Teenage Films: Love, Death, and the Prom," Alice
                  McDermott   285
                  "Triumph of the Wheel," Lewis Grossberger   290
   Writing Your Rough Draft   298
   "Horrors" (Rough Draft of Student Essay)   298
Focus on Style: The Components of Style   302
   Ways of Adjusting Style   303
      Adjusting for Concreteness   303
      The Verbal Sentence   304
      Adjusting for Abstractness   305
      The Nominal Sentence   305
   How to Write More Eloquently   306
      Balanced Phrasing   306
      Loose and Periodic Sentences   306
      Figurative Language   306
      Irony   307
   Adjusting Your Style in Writing Your Essay on the Media   310
Rewriting   311
   Obtaining Feedback on Your Rough Draft   311
   Revision of Student Essay "Horrors"   311
   Consolidating   317
   Revising Your Essay on the Media   318
   Editing   319
      Consolidating   319
      Style   319
      Mechanics   319
Becoming Aware of Yourself as a Writer   320

PART **IV**

Persuasion 322

Introduction 322

8 Writing About an Issue — Arguing Your Point of View 323

Purpose 323
Task: Arguing Your Point of View on an Issue 325

> *You construct a life situation or "case" in which you take the role of one of the participants in the situation and write an argument to convince one or more other participants of your point of view about a controversy that has arisen. Audience for task: One or more other participants in your case.*

Writing Your Essay 326
  Generating Ideas: Strategies for Argument, Induction, Deduction, and the Classical Questions 326
    Strategies for Argument 327
    Induction, Deduction, and the Classical Questions 331
    Induction 332
    Deduction 339
    Deductive Fallacies 342
    The Classical Questions in Support of Persuasion 344
    Using the Principles of Induction and Deduction to Generate Ideas for Arguing Your Point of View 345
  Persuading Your Audience 348
    Establishing Credibility 349
    Adopting the Proper Tone 349
    Analyzing Your Audience 350
    Presenting an Ethical Appeal 350
    Using the Ethical Appeal in Arguing Your Point of View 353
  Arranging Your Essay 355
    The Shaping Idea: Stating Your Argument 355
    Building an Argument 355
    Model Essay: "The Declaration of Independence" 357
  Writing Your Rough Draft 360
    "Bodybuilding: The Shape of the Future" (Rough Draft of Student Essay) 360
Focus on Style: Persuasive Language and the Appeal to the Emotions 362
  Connotation 362

Figurative Language   364
Allusion   365
Repetition   365
Humor and Satire   366
Categorical Statements   367
Logical Terms   367
Tone and Audience   367
    "Letter From a Birmingham Jail," Martin Luther King, Jr.   367
Using the Emotional Appeal in Arguing Your Point of View   372
Rewriting   374
    Obtaining Feedback on Your Rough Draft   374
    Revision of Student Essay "Bodybuilding: The Shape of the
        Future"   374
    Revising Your Persuasive Essay   377
        Editing   378
Becoming Aware of Yourself as a Writer   378

9   Writing About an Issue — Joining a Debate   379

Purpose   379
Task: Joining a Debate on an Issue   380
        *You read three essays expressing varying points of view on a
        controversial issue and attempt to arrive at a new, broader point of
        view. Audience for task: An informed reader.*
Reading to Write   382
    I. Abortion Essays: 382
        "Is There a Middle Ground?" Ernest Van Den Haag   382
        "Giving Women a Real Choice," Rosalind Petchesky   387
        "Persuasion Preferred," John Garvey   392
    II. Euthanasia Essays: 395
        "Active and Passive Euthanasia," James Rachels   395
        "Active Euthanasia Violates Fundamental Principles," Samuel F.
            Hunter   400
        "The State as Parent," Sandra H. Johnson   402
    III. Pornography Essays: 407
        "Erotica vs. Pornography," Gloria Steinem   407
        "The First Amendment Forbids Censorship," Lois Sheinfeld   415
        "The First Amendment Does Not Protect Pornography," Janella Miller   418
Writing Your Essay   423
    Generating Ideas: Critical Thinking   423
        Arriving at a Broader Point of View   424
        Using Evidence   426
        Using Your Journal   428
        Brainstorming Groups   429
        Using Critical Thinking in Generating Ideas for Your Essay on a
            Debate   429

Addressing Your Audience: The Informed Reader   430
  Role-playing   431
  Addressing the Informed Reader of Your Essay on a Debate   432
Arranging Your Essay   433
  The Shaping Idea: Stating Your Broader Point of View   433
  Close-up on the Organization of Petchesky's Essay   434
Writing Your Rough Draft   435
  "Pornography and Me and You" (Rough Draft of Student Essay)   435
Focus on the Writer: Joining the Community of Discourse   437
Rewriting   440
  Obtaining Feedback on Your Rough Draft   440
  Revision of Student Essay "Pornography and Me and You"   441
  Editing   444
  Revising Your Essay on a Debate   444
Becoming Aware of Yourself as a Writer   445

PART **V**

Writing About Research, Writing About Literature

448

Introduction   448

10 Writing About Research—Testing a Hypothesis   449

Purpose   449
Task: Testing a Hypothesis   452
    *You formulate a hypothesis about a subject in the social or natural
    sciences with which you have some familiarity and through research
    attempt to determine the validity of that hypothesis. Audience for task:
    Students and professors interested in the writings of students on the
    sciences and social sciences.*
Writing Your Essay   453
  Generating Ideas Through Induction   453
    Thinking Inductively   453
    Using Evidence: The Writer as Observer   454
    Using Evidence: Evaluating Sources   455
    Using Evidence: Seeking Non-print Sources for Your Essay   456
    Using Induction to Generate Ideas for Testing Your Hypothesis   458
  Addressing Your Audience: The Lay Reader   459
    Addressing the Lay Reader of Your Essay Testing a Hypothesis   463
  Doing Research   464
    Finding a Topic   464

Gathering Sources: Preparing a Preliminary Bibliography   466
Taking Notes   468
Arranging Your Essay   473
The Shaping Idea: Stating Your Hypothesis   473
Outlining   474
Putting Your Notes Together   476
Writing the Introduction   478
Writing Your Rough Draft   479
"Not the Weaker Sex: A Comparison of Girls and Boys" (Rough Draft of
Student Essay)   479
Focus on Form: Documentation   484
Using the Citation Method   484
MLA and APA Styles of Documentation   485
Specialized Science Research   486
Using a Bibliography   486
Using Footnotes   487
Rewriting   490
Obtaining Feedback on Your Rough Draft   490
Revision of Student Essay "Not the Weaker Sex: A Comparison of Girls
and Boys"   491
Citation Method   492
Endnotes Method   497
Revising and Editing   503
Revising   503
Editing   504
Becoming Aware of Yourself as a Writer   505

11   Writing About a Short Story — Interpreting a Text

506

Purpose   506
Task: Interpreting a Short Story   508

*You write an essay in which you explore the meaning or significance
of a story to you, showing how and why you arrived at your
understanding of the story. Audience for task: Other readers of the
story whose understanding might be enhanced by your interpretation.*

Reading to Write   508
"Gooseberries," Anton Chekhov   508
"The Lesson," Toni Cade Bambara   515
Writing Your Essay   521
Generating Ideas: Reader Responses   521
The Active Reader   521
Double-Entry Journal   523
Question Sets   527
Brainstorming   528
Responding to a Short Story in Writing Your Essay   529

Addressing Your Audience: Reader Perspectives   529
   Reader Points of View   530
   Reader Frames of Reference   531
   Reader Perspectives: Angles on a Story   531
   Using Reader Perspectives in Writing Your Essay   533
Arranging Your Essay   533
   The Shaping Idea   533
   The Reader's Story   533
   The Writer's Repertoire   536
Writing Your Rough Draft   536
   "No Man Is an Island" (Rough Draft of Student Essay)   537
Focus on Form and Style: The Elements of the Short Story   539
   Beginnings   539
   Plot   540
   Character   540
   Point of View   541
   Theme   541
   Irony   541
Rewriting   543
   Obtaining Feedback on Your Rough Draft   543
   Revision of Student Essay "No Man Is an Island"   544
   Revising Your Essay on a Short Story   547
Becoming Aware of Yourself as a Writer   547

Handbook

Grammar

Parts of Speech   551
   The Noun   551
   The Pronoun   551
     Personal Pronouns   552
     Reflexive Pronouns   552
     Indefinite Pronouns   552
     Demonstrative Pronouns   552
     Relative Pronouns   552
     Interrogative Pronouns   553
   The Verb   553
     Tense   553
     Voice   554
     Mood   554
   The Adjective   555
   The Adverb   555
   The Conjunction   555
   The Conjunctive Adverb   556

The Preposition   557
The Article   558
Review Exercise — Parts of Speech   558
Parts of Sentences   558
The Subject   558
The Predicate   559
The Complement   559
Base Sentences   560
Phrases and Clauses   560
The Phrase   560
  The Noun Phrase   560
  The Verb Phrase   560
  The Prepositional Phrase   560
  The Infinitive Phrase   561
  The Participial Phrase   561
  The Gerund Phrase   561
  The Absolute Phrase   561
The Clause   562
Combined or Expanded Sentences   563
Review Exercise — Parts and Types of Sentences   563
Awkward Sentences   564
Faulty Coordination or Subordination   564
Incomplete Sentences   565
Mixed Sentences   566
Inconsistent Point of View   566
Review Exercise — Awkward Sentences   567
Common Grammatical Errors   568
Faulty Agreement   568
  Subject/Verb Agreement   568
  Pronoun/Antecedent Agreement   570
Faulty References   572
Case Errors   573
Misplaced and Dangling Modifiers   576
  Misplaced Modifiers   576
  Dangling Modifiers   577
Faulty Parallelism   578
Run-on Sentences and Comma Splices   579
Sentence Fragments   581
Review Exercise — Common Grammatical Errors   582

Punctuation

The Period   584
The Question Mark   585
The Exclamation Point   586
The Comma   586
The Semicolon   590

The Colon   591
The Dash   592
Parentheses and Brackets   593
  Parentheses   593
    Factual Information   594
    Examples   594
    Explanations   594
    Qualifications   594
  Brackets   594
The Ellipsis   595
Quotation Marks   596
The Apostrophe   599

Mechanics

Capitalization   601
Italics   604
Abbreviations   604
Numbers   606
Hyphenation   608
Spelling   608
  Commonly Confused Homonyms   610
Review Exercise — Punctuation and Mechanics   617

Index   623

RHETORICAL CONTENTS

PURPOSE

Self-Expression—Chapters 1–3
  Keeping a Journal—Chapter 1
  Expressing Your Point of View—Chapter 2
  Reporting an Experience—Chapter 3
Exploration—Chapters 4–5
  Exploring Your Point of View—Chapter 4
  Exploring Other Points of View—Chapter 5
Explanation—Chapters 6 and 7
  Explaining What You Know—Chapter 6
  Explaining What You Think—Chapter 7
Persuasion—Chapters 8 and 9
  Arguing Your Point of View—Chapter 8
  Joining a Debate—Chapter 9
Writing About Research—Chapter 10
Writing About a Short Story—Chapter 11

GENERATING IDEAS

Free Writing—Chapter 1
The Journal—Chapters 1–11
The Journalist's Questions—Chapter 3
The Explorer's Questions—Chapter 4
The Classical Questions—Chapters 5–8
Brainstorming—Chapters 6, 9, 11
Induction—Chapters 8, 9, 10
Using Evidence and Sources—Chapters 8, 9, 10

Deduction — Chapters 8, 9
Critical Thinking — Chapter 9
Reader Response — Chapter 11

AUDIENCE ANALYSIS

Private Voice — Chapter 1
The Sympathetic Reader — Chapter 2
The Intended Reader — Chapter 3
Depth of Information — Chapter 4
Writing for Publication — Chapter 5
The Uninformed Reader — Chapter 6
Public Voice — Chapter 7
Persuading Your Audience — Chapter 8
The Informed Reader — Chapter 9
The Lay Reader — Chapter 10
Reader Perspectives — Chapter 11

ARRANGEMENT

Narration — Chapters 2–4
Shaping Idea — Chapters 2–11
Exposition — Chapters 2–11
Description — Chapter 4
Cause and Effect — Chapters 5, 6, 8
Comparison and Contrast — Chapters 4, 5, 6, 8
Process Analysis — Chapters 4, 5, 6
Generalization and Specification — Chapters 5–11
Argumentation — Chapters 8, 9

FORM AND STYLE

Form — Chapters 2–5, 10, 11
Stating a Thesis — Chapter 2
Writing an Introduction — Chapter 2
Paragraph Structure — Chapter 3
Making Transitions — Chapter 3
Paragraph Development — Chapter 4
Writing a Conclusion — Chapter 4
Sentence Combining — Chapter 5
Style — Chapters 6–8
Eliminating Deadwood — Chapter 6
The Components of Style — Chapter 7

Persuasive Language and the Appeal to the Emotions — Chapter 8
Joining the Community of Discourse — Chapter 9
Documentation — Chapter 10
The Elements of the Short Story — Chapter 11

REVISING STRATEGIES

Self, Peer, or Instructor Feedback — Chapter 2
Cutting — Chapter 2
Adding — Chapter 3
Substituting — Chapter 4
Distributing — Chapter 5
Rearranging — Chapter 6
Consolidating — Chapter 7
Revising Persuasive Writing — Chapters 8, 9
Revising Scientific Writing — Chapter 10

Introduction: Ways to Writing

In his well-known poem "The Road Not Taken," Robert Frost speaks of choices. Of the two roads that "diverged in a yellow wood," he finally chooses one, keeping "the first for another day!" Because he knows that choices lead us in unforeseen directions, he adds,

> Yet knowing how way leads on to way,
> I doubted if I should ever come back.

He concludes his poem,

> Two roads diverged in a wood, and I—
> I took the one less traveled by,
> And that has made all the difference.

In this textbook, we hope to show you the many ways to writing that we as writing teachers have learned over the years and then to assist you in making the many choices necessary to discovering your own road to successful writing.

To illustrate these choices, we asked Scott, a student of ours, to write an essay, which he calls "Life in the Food Chain." We also asked him to keep a journal of what he was thinking about over the two weeks that he worked on the essay. By showing you first Scott's essay and then some selections from his journal that reveal his decision-making process, we hope to introduce you to ways of writing and the choices a writer must make. Here is "Life in the Food Chain."

LIFE IN THE FOOD CHAIN

Having been both born and raised here in New York City, I believe that I can say that I am fairly typical of middle-class New Yorkers in my age group, those in their mid-twenties. During the past few years I have been attending college here in Queens and working part-time in Manhattan. I consider myself to be at least moderately street smart, and because of this and a fair share of luck, I have yet to join the statistical ranks of many of my fellow New Yorkers who have become the victims of violent crime. This is not to say that I have been completely untouched by the less pleasant aspects of city life.

One Monday night last summer marked my closest brush with becoming a crime statistic. Having just gotten off work, I was waiting on a subway platform for an uptown train at about two in the morning. Given the hour, the only other people on the platform were a couple of older men, farther down towards the end of the platform. I was sitting on a bench reading a magazine when I noticed four guys walking towards me. Instantly, I became concerned: after all, it was two AM and this was the New York subway system. One guy sat down beside me and a second stood on my other side. The other two stood a few feet away. Of course, I had noticed them approaching, but there was no place to run (and running did not seem prudent at that point) so I continued to read the magazine. You will understand that I was no longer paying too much attention to the article; my mind was occupied by what seemed to be developing into a potentially dangerous situation. Sure enough, the one who sat next to me gave me a sharp nudge and demanded to know "What's in your pocket?" His question confirmed what I had suspected since I noticed them approaching the bench: if I were lucky, I was about to be mugged. If I were not so lucky, I might be in for worse.

Instead of being afraid, which would probably have been an intelligent response, I found myself to be angry. Despite the irrationality of the thought, I was angry at them for presuming to violate my rights, and at myself for the fact that I seemed about to become a victim. Even though I had no apparent control over their actions, I felt guilty about becoming a statistic. My luck had run out, and I felt angrier about that than about anything else.

Calmly, without moving my hands or my magazine, I responded. "Just some lifesavers" I said, knowing that what he had felt when he nudged me was a small can of mace that I often carry. Any attempt to use it at that moment would have been foolish. He was sitting right next to me and was considerably larger than I was, to say nothing of his companions, the smallest of whom outweighed me by at least 30 pounds. A series of questions followed; he wanted to know if I had a gun, if I was a cop, etc ... and finally, he demanded "How much money have you got?" At this, the one standing next to me stated: "Give us some money or we'll take it from you."

I had a few dollars with me, and given my position, I would have been only too happy to part with it, despite my indignation at having the odds catch up with me. However, I didn't think that they would be satisfied with what little I had, and might insist on something more. My mind raced, considering the possibilities. Running seemed out of the question, unless I made it to the edge of the platform and jumped onto the tracks. If I did jump onto the tracks, I didn't doubt that they could catch me if they decided to try. My blood was full of adrenaline, but there were simply too many of them to fight, not that I had even considered that as an option, for obvious reasons.

I decided that I must get some distance between them and myself so that I would have time to act if I had to. The only way that I could see to put some space between us without alarming them into action was to confuse them. I decided that the best way to do this would be to tell them how indignant I felt about becoming a victim. I thought that this, along with a verbal scolding for preying on other people, might surprise them long enough for me to get to the edge of the platform. I would take it from there, but I probably wouldn't jump unless a train was about to approach so that I might be able to get to the opposite platform before the train passed and they were able to follow.

Having resolved to take this particular course of action, I closed my magazine and put it into my pack without saying a word. I did this very slowly, so as not to alarm them. I then stood up, and with my back to them, I walked to within a few feet of the platform's edge. In doing so, I put my hands in my pockets and released the safety on the can of mace. Taking it out of my pocket as a defensive measure seemed foolhardy, as it would have raised the stakes. I still hoped that I might be able to resolve the situation with nothing more dangerous than words. It was at this point, when I had my back turned, that I felt most vulnerable. After a few steps, I turned, and looked at them. Addressing the one who had sat next to me and was doing the most talking, I said "Well, you know ... " but before I could really begin my hastily prepared speech of morals, human rights, and common decency, he stood and said "Forget it." He then approached me and offered me his right hand. In order to shake it, I had to leave the can of mace in my pocket. Warily, I did so and we shook hands, with me expecting violence at any second. He then gestured to his pals, and the four of them left the platform. Only later, when I was safe at home, did the impact of what had occurred really hit me. Recounting the events to my sister in the safety of our kitchen, I realized that my hands were shaking and there was little I could do to control it.

I believe that even without my speech, I gave them the impression that I was not about to willingly accept becoming a victim, and I suppose that they thought that pressing the point wasn't worth their trouble. I guess that they figured there were easier pickings elsewhere. Looking back, I can see that I was very fortunate that things turned out the way they had. Lest you think from my description of the event that I was or am a model of rational thought, I am no such thing. During the incident, I was busy suppressing panic and foolish actions. If I had not been so busy concentrating on that, my actions would probably have been different, which would have resulted in their actions being different as well. The outcome of this could only have been worse than what did actually happen. I think that I made some good decisions, but I was very lucky as well. They might have reacted differently, or they might have been high, and things could have gone much worse.

As you can see, life here is never boring. Unfortunately, it is often dehumanizing. Although I have yet to be seriously victimized myself, I have friends who have been less fortunate than I. I suppose that in a city of more than seven million people, it is inevitable that each night's newscast is filled with stories about murder, rape, and assault. Only a fraction of the crimes committed are actually covered by the media, which is probably for the best. If they were to make an attempt to cover all of the violent crimes committed each day, they'd probably need a 24 hour news channel exclusively for complete coverage, and suicide and emigration rates would undoubtedly increase beyond present levels. As it is, the evening news has been particularly rough during the past week. Four children under the age of ten have been killed by "indiscriminate" gunfire in the last eight days. "Indiscriminate" means that they were innocent bystanders unfortunate enough to be in the wrong place at the wrong time.

To a certain extent, a person becomes jaded by the constant reports of atrocity. However, once in a while a saturation point is reached and you find yourself aghast and in awe. You cannot help but ask: "How can people live like this? How can I keep living here?"

This time last year, a Daily News headline proclaimed "HER LIFE FOR HER KIDS." The article told the story of a pregnant young mother who gave her life to protect her children from an intruder who had broken into her apartment on the upper East Side. I'll spare you the graphic details, but this headline marked a saturation point for me. While reading the story at my kitchen table, I found myself sobbing freely. Something inside of me reached critical mass and I just let go. When I shared this experience with a couple of close friends, I learned that they too had had similar experiences. Apparently, a person can only take so much before a limit is passed and an outlet is sought for all of the emotions boiling inside.

By now, you are probably wondering, "If things are so bad here in New York City, why do people stay?" Well, as a matter of fact, some of them don't. Others (like myself) feel a certain attachment to this place, in spite of all its faults. I've visited most of the major cities in this country (except for those in Texas and Florida) and of all of them, none is even remotely as interesting a place as New York City. It is probably a cliche and a self-centered attitude, but to many people New York City is the center of the universe and they could not consider living any-place else.

To be sure, the number of resources, attractions, institutions, and facilities that can be found within city limits is far too numerous to list in the modest confines of this essay. The worlds of finance, fashion, publishing, theater are centered here, along with numerous colleges, sports stadiums, museums, gal-leries, shopping areas, and historical and cultural landmarks. Ours is a city of neighborhoods and cultural diversity, with doz-ens if not hundreds of ethnic and religious groups represented among New York's citizens. I find it difficult to imagine that there is another city in the world that has the sheer variety that New York has. For many, many New Yorkers, there simply is no other place.

In addition, certain aspects of the New York personality keep many of its citizens from pulling up their roots and moving else-where. These two factors are probably more unique to citizens of New York City than they are to citizens of any other major city in America.

One aspect concerns heritage. New York owes its stunning cul-tural and ethnic diversity to its position as a port city serving as a center for immigration since the United States was young. Families that have lived here for generations consider this to be home, regardless of what part of the globe their ancestors came from. They relish and revel in their individual heritage, be they Jamaican, Italian, Greek, Russian, Chinese, etc... but they are

New Yorkers as well, and this means a great deal to them. To leave would be to lose a part of their history, a part of what makes them who they are.

The other personality aspect that keeps many people from leaving has to do with survival. Here, survival in itself is something of a status symbol, and quite a few New Yorkers take a certain amount of pride in managing to live here, stay alive, and remain sane. New Yorkers know, better than anybody else, that this is a tough place to live. They know this, and because they are constantly and acutely aware of it, staying here and making a go of life within the city's borders carries with it a sense of honor and pride. Anyone can survive where life is easy and uncomplicated, but only a New Yorker can survive in New York. A real New Yorker can even manage to prosper. This feeling probably has a lot to do with why so many New Yorkers remain here by choice, despite the crime, crowds, dirt and noise.

If I wanted to, I could conceivably attend school elsewhere, but I've chosen to stay here, at least for the present. I have made this choice not only because the school that I am transferring to, New York University, is here, but also because life in the City offers so much despite the difficulties. I feel certain that last summer's encounter on the subway platform will not be my last close call. Despite this, I think that if I stay alert, am prepared for trouble, and have my fair share of luck, I cannot only survive here, but I can grow and prosper as well. Like so many of my fellow citizens, I'll stay here and take all that New York has to offer, both the good and the bad. As far as the near future is concerned, I'll take my chances living in the food chain that is New York City. With a little luck and perseverance, I won't get caught at the bottom.

Choices in Writing

Having read Scott's essay, you may be surprised to know that someone who prides himself on surviving in New York City writes in his journal of the many difficulties he had in selecting a topic for an essay. In his first entry, he writes, "I procrastinate a lot . . . I have a habit of starting the morning that the work is to be handed in. . . . This is my own method of self-motivation, I don't recommend it since it is fairly stressful."

Scott in fact made several false starts before selecting this topic. His initial thought was to write an essay about televised beer commercials that "misrepresent the place their product plays in personal interaction and enjoyment." Then he realizes that "The title is the only really firm idea that I have about the essay: 'Life Is Not a Beer Commercial'." He decides to write instead a "defense of alcohol consumption (in moderate quantities, of course)." He rejects this idea too: "The idea itself is somewhat vague and unsubstantial and I think that it would be difficult to properly support. Perhaps I'm just not up to the effort right now."

He next goes back to the beer commercial topic but not before writing an entry in his journal that indicates his final choice is beginning to percolate up from his subconscious:

I'm looking forward to living in Manhattan for the next few years, but I presently believe that I would not want to raise children in New York City.

Unhappy with the introduction he has written to "Life Is Not a Beer Commercial," Scott thinks of two more possible topics, one on "the complexities of a developing friendship" and the other on the lack of money. He doesn't like either of these much, however.

He misses the deadline for handing in the essay, is given an extension of three days, sits down and types a new essay "in one sitting. It's called 'Life in the Food Chain' and it's about living with crime in New York City."

Here is Scott's rough draft of "Life in the Food Chain." How do the two drafts differ?

LIFE IN THE FOOD CHAIN

Having been both born and raised in New York City, I believe that I can say that I am fairly typical of middle-class New Yorkers in my age group, those in their mid-twenties. During the past few years I have been attending college here in Queens and working part-time in Manhattan. I consider myself to be at least moderately street smart, and because of this and a fair share of luck, I have yet to join the statistical ranks of many of my fellow New Yorkers who have become the victims of a violent crime.

This is not to say that I have been untouched by the less pleasant aspects of city life. In the past three years alone, my car has been broken into on three separate occasions. Last summer, I talked my way out of being mugged by four guys on a subway platform late one evening. I believe that I gave them the impression that I was not about to willingly accept becoming a victim, and I suppose that they thought that pressing the point wasn't worth their trouble. I guess that they figured there were easier pickings elsewhere. Looking back, I can see that I was very lucky, since the smallest of the four outweighed me by at least thirty pounds. A few days before this incident, I was almost knocked over by some men running along 6th Avenue. The men were being chased by armed guards, and were eventually caught and frisked at gunpoint in front of a McDonald's, while a small crowd of people munched french fries and watched with mild interest. As recently as last month, I witnessed a gang of teenagers chase and beat a man just two blocks away from my house. After locating my can of mace, I moved to intervene, but after the victim was on the ground they apparently felt that a half dozen quick kicks were enough and moved off. Probably a good thing too, since these teens didn't look like they were in the mood to listen to reason, and my can of mace is pretty small. As it turned out, the guy was shaken up but not seriously injured. He declined my offer to call an ambulance and rose shakily to his feet and went off to find his girlfriend.

As you can see, life here is never boring. Unfortunately, it is often dehumanizing. Although I have yet to be seriously victimized myself, I have friends who have been less fortunate than I. And in a city of more than seven million people, it is inevitable that each night's newscast is filled with stories about murder, rape, and assault. Only a fraction of the crimes committed are actually covered by the media, and this is probably for the best. If they were to make an attempt to cover all of the violent crimes committed each day, they'd probably need a 24 hour news channel exclusively for complete coverage. As it is, the evening news has been particularly rough during the past week. Four children under the age of ten have been killed by "indiscriminate" gunfire in the last eight days. "Indiscriminate" means that they were innocent bystanders unfortunate enough to be in the wrong place at the wrong time.

To a certain extent, a person becomes jaded to the constant reports of atrocity. However, once in a while a saturation point is reached and you find yourself aghast and in awe. How can people live like this? How can I keep living here? This time last year, a Daily News headline proclaimed "HER LIFE FOR HER KIDS." The article told the story of a pregnant young mother who gave her life to protect her children from an intruder who had broken into her apartment on the upper East side. I'll spare you the graphic details, but this headline marked a saturation point for me. While reading the story at my kitchen table, I found myself sobbing freely. Something inside of me reached critical mass and I just let go. When I shared this experience with a couple of close friends, I learned that they too had had similar experiences. Apparently, a person can only take so much before a limit is passed and an outlet is sought for all of the emotions boiling inside.

You might wonder, if things are so bad here, why do people stay? Well, as a matter of fact, a lot of them don't. A steady exodus has been in progress for much of the past decade. According to some statistics I saw on the news, the population of the city has declined by something like 800,000 people in the last ten years. According to the same report, a record high was reached for murders in New York City last year, although both Washington and Detroit surpassed the figure. However, I think that many people have little choice in the matter. They either work or attend school here (as I do) and many of them probably can't afford to pick up their lives and just move. I'm sure that quite a few of them would if given the opportunity.

Others (also like myself) feel a certain attachment to this place, despite all of its faults. I've visited most of the major cities in this country (except for those in Texas and Florida) and of all of them, none is as interesting a place as New York City. The number of resources and attractions that can be found within city limits is far too numerous to list in the modest confines of this essay, to say nothing of the cultural diversity present. In addition, survival in itself is something of a status symbol here, and many New Yorkers take a certain amount of pride in managing to live here and remain sane. This fact probably has a lot to do with why so many New Yorkers remain here by choice. I could conceivably attend school elsewhere, but I've chosen to stay here, at least for the present. If I had a family to raise however, I am not certain that I would be willing to make the same choice. Until such a point in time as when I have children to worry about arrives, I'll continue to stay alert, and take my chances living in the food chain that is New York City. With a little luck, I won't get caught at the bottom.

Robert Frost begins his poem,

> Two roads diverged in a yellow wood,
> And sorry I could not travel both
> And be one traveler, long I stood
> And looked down one as far as I could
> To where it bent in the undergrowth;
>
> Then took the other, as just as fair,
> And having perhaps the better claim,
> Because it was grassy and wanted wear;
> Though as for that the passing there
> Had worn them really about the same, . . .

Scott, like Frost, looked down several roads, examining the possibilities for travel on each, before suddenly making his decision as to the one he would take. Both writers believe the choice they made was the right one for them.

You, like Scott, have choices to make about your writing, choices only you can make. You will need to choose one topic and not choose several others, you will need to choose your way of getting started and not someone else's, select your own way of generating ideas, your own attitude toward your topic and toward your reader, the words you alone would use and the sound your sentences make. In this textbook, we can begin to indicate the range of choices you have about all of these aspects of the writing process, but the ways to writing you eventually select will be your own.

Purpose

Every time you sit down to write, whether at a desk or, like Scott, at a computer, you have a *purpose* in doing so. Scott's purpose was to write an essay for this Introduction; for this course your purpose will be to complete an assignment. And people write for many other reasons as well: for pleasure, for communication, for work. But each writing assignment, regardless of its context, must have a specific purpose as well: it may be intended to explain, to explore, to persuade, to amuse, or to express the writer's feelings. We present writing tasks here that fulfill many of these different aims in writing, beginning with several that are personally expressive, moving on to some that ask you to explore a subject with which you are unfamiliar and then some that ask you to explain what you know well, and concluding with tasks that require persuasion on an issue and response to two short stories.

We didn't give Scott a purpose to fulfill in writing this essay, so he had to make a decision as to what that purpose would be. In his journal, he rejects writing to express personal thoughts and feelings when he says "I don't know if I am up to elaborating (on the complexities of a developing friendship)." The purpose he finally selects is to explain. As he says, "I know it's a cliché, but it really helps if you're writing about something you know. Ideally, write about something you know very well." Scott feels he knows New York City very well and decides to explain its good and bad features.

Task

We believe that writing is a dynamic process not only because it involves the writer in choices about completing an assignment but also because it provokes thought and learning. As a result, we have created for each chapter a broad and flexible writing *task* that not only requires you to exercise your ability to make choices about writing, including selecting a topic, but also provokes you to thought. As you move through the tasks, you will find yourself learning the power of language to express your thoughts and feelings—in a journal as well as in personal essays—to test preconceptions and prejudgments, to explain the significance of subjects you know well, to persuade another of your point of view, to test a hypothesis, and to examine what you as a person bring to the reading of a short story.

Generating Ideas

In his journal, Scott indicates some ways of writing that he has learned that assist him in making his choices. On *generating ideas* about a topic, he says,

Often, a title or sentence will germinate into an idea given the proper nourishment. I once had to write a short story for a (much procrastinated) college application and I couldn't think of a single thing. Never having written any fiction before, and with the application already late, I was very stressed out. At some point, the words "God is dead!" appeared on the screen and fairly rapidly, a story grew out of it.

At another point, he uses the journal itself as a source of ideas: "Haven't come up with any ideas yet, so I'll go back and read this log from the start to see if it helps me come up with anything new. . . ." Stream of consciousness writing, he also hopes, "might yield a workable idea."

Three of Scott's ways of generating ideas we present in *Ways to Writing*: stream of consciousness or free writing (Chapter 1) and brainstorming (Chapter 6); the journal (Chapter 1 and throughout the text); and writing about what you know well (Chapters 6 and 7), as well as several other methods of generating ideas, including various sets of questions you can ask about your material.

Audience

Scott says that "you have to know who the intended reader is so that you can tailor your writing for them." As an example, he adds, "If you were writing about a love affair on a cruise ship (not that I'd ever really want to write about that) and your audience was the romance novel set, you'd be foolish to go into detail about the ship's twin turbo diesel marine power plants."

We told Scott that he would be writing his essay for you, a college student. He believes that you like to read about things that are "evocative of reality" so he has written about real experiences that he has had: "I hope," he says, "that my readers will enjoy what I've written specifically because it is real."

We suggest that, like Scott, you write each essay to a specific audience. Some of the readers we suggest for the various tasks are sympathetic peers, a class in your major, the readership of a publication, an uninformed reader, your English teacher, and so forth. In each chapter, we also suggest ways to appropriately address your writing for this reader.

Writing the Essay

At this stage in the process of writing an essay, you may have yet to write a complete draft. Determining purpose and audience as well as generating ideas, the aspects of writing that we have discussed so far, are choices that you must find your own process for making. It is possible that, like Scott, ideas may be "bubbling quietly in (your) cranium" long before you sit down to write your rough draft.

Scott has ideas about getting this rough draft out. If he doesn't like something he's written, he suggests,

Rather than restart, however, I'm just going to keep going and get as much down as I can, so that I can cut it down and reshape it afterwards. It's always much easier to take the time to properly critique something if the core of it has already been written. Otherwise, you can find yourself rushing through the revision of individual sections because you know that more remains to be written. Besides, a grasp of the entire work is needed if you're going to tackle anything larger than minor corrections, since big changes must be viewed in the context of the entire work.

You may want to note that we are not alarmed that Scott did not make an outline before he began to write. In fact, many writers seem to write first and outline later, although some of course organize first. We suggest both options in this *Writing the Essay* section in the various chapters. Near the end of his journal, Scott does outline his essay and decides that it is well organized.

Rewriting

As the quote above indicates, Scott believes strongly in *rewriting* what he has written. His journal entries reveal his concerns about his rough draft:

Upon re-reading it, it strikes me that the essay ends sort of abruptly. I think that I may not have done enough to tie it in with the whole "food chain" idea, but I'm not certain. I will reread it again and give this some thought.

Scott also showed us his first draft at this point, and we suggested he balance his criticisms of New York with what he feels are its good points, the reasons why, as he says, he and others "feel a certain attachment to this place." You can see from comparing the two drafts that Scott has extended the ideas in his original conclusion to form the final six paragraphs of his final draft. While he answered our critique, do you think he answered his own—that this last paragraph does not tie the essay in with "the whole food chain idea"? He has also extended his original comment about "talking (his) way out of being mugged" into a three-page story. Why do you think he did so? Do you agree with his choice?

In this book, we will suggest that you, like Scott, get feedback on an early draft and revise your essay. This feedback may come from other readers, such as a group of fellow students, and from yourself as you reread and rethink what you have written.

Focus on Form and Style

Scott not only revised the ideas in his rough draft, but he also edited some of the words and sentences. Immediately after finishing the first draft, he wrote in his journal.

> I just finished and read back the first paragraph. I'm not very happy with it. As I re-read it, I changed a couple of words, nothing significant. For an introductory paragraph, it doesn't really grab the reader's attention the way that I hoped it would, and to be honest, it strikes me as sort of clumsy.

From comparing the first paragraph in each of the two drafts, do you think Scott has made significant changes in his choice of words? Do you agree with his assessment that his introduction was clumsy and did not grab the reader's attention? If so, have his changes improved his introduction? How would you have revised the meaning or edited his words?

In the *Focus on Form* or *Focus on Style* section of each chapter, we will discuss matters of form and style that will assist you in improving the organization of your sentences, paragraphs, and whole essay; in improving the sound of your words on paper; and, in later chapters, in documenting research and analyzing a short story. A grammar handbook concludes the book, should you want to refer to it at any point.

Becoming Aware of Yourself as a Writer

Finally, again as Scott did, we will encourage you to think about the essay you have just written, considering what you have learned about thinking and writing as you completed the process of writing, and to record these responses in your journal. *Becoming aware of yourself as a writer* will help you to become a better writer.

What, then, is successful writing? We would say that it is the writing that results from knowing what choices you as a writer must make, knowing the ways to writing from which to make these choices, and then selecting those ways that will best complete your purpose. In his journal entries above, Scott gives evidence that he has learned the ways of writing open to a writer and has chosen among them the road that he will follow. But the reader is always the final judge, the final arbiter of whether to accept a piece of writing or reject it for being the result of wrong choices. What do you think of "Life in the Food Chain"? Is it a successful piece of writing? Why do you think it is or isn't?

"What is successful writing?" We hope that you will have more knowledge and experience by the time you finish the tasks in this book as to how both to answer this question and to produce ways to successful writing of your own.

PART

I

Self-Expression

INTRODUCTION

Imagine yourself describing an incident to a close friend, a member of your family, or a schoolmate. Everything about you—your voice, your facial expressions, your body movements, even your dress—establishes a unique physical presence that gives force to your story. Like a musical instrument, your voice rises and falls, emphasizing key words at moments of high drama or anxiety. Every gesture of your hands, every arching of your eyebrows reveals to the other person the unity of your voice and being.

Now imagine yourself wishing to transform this spoken narrative into a written account. Immediately your hand freezes, your brain numbs, and your eyes gaze fixedly at pen and paper. What was so easy and spontaneous an act of language now becomes weighted with the difficulty of premeditation, the self-consciousness of beginnings.

Ironically, our membership in a literate culture further inhibits our powers of self-expression, because we so often experience events through the language of others, for example, the press, government, business, and artistic communities. How, we might ask, can we develop in our writing an honest expression of our own? If we write on a sports event, must we see it only through the television language of the "thrill of victory and the agony of defeat"? If we already have a cultural overlay of meaning to apply to experience, we do not express the world as *we* have seen and experienced it.

We hope to provide a context for writing in Part I that will encourage you to develop your own voice and perceptions, your individual sense of yourself. By reporting the world as you see and experience it directly, you will engage in what is fundamentally an act of self-expression, even as you begin to learn how to adjust your voice so that it is appropriate to your subject and understandable to your audience.

In Chapter 1, you can begin to experiment with self-expression in the privacy of a journal. As a journal writer, you do not need to worry if a reader will understand you or not. You are writing for yourself alone, and so you are free to examine in any way you choose your feelings and thoughts about yourself and your world, and about writing as well.

Chapters 2 and 3 introduce you to the challenge of self-expression as a way of writing for someone other than yourself. In Chapter 2, your task is to write an essay about one pattern of concerns that you can trace in your journal—to tell someone else about one thing that your journal reveals about you. In Chapter 3, your task is to write about the details of an incident so that a reader can experience the incident as you did.

We suggest that you try starting with the journal not only because of the opportunity it provides to express yourself openly, without feeling inhibited by rules or the expectations of others, but also because of the source it may turn out to be of ideas for many of the writing assignments that follow. Thus, once we have introduced you to journal writing in Chapter 1, we will continue to suggest that you keep up your journal and make use of it in each of the subsequent chapters in the book.

1

Writing About Yourself—Keeping a Journal

PURPOSE

When you write, you are engaging in an activity that might be graphically portrayed as a triangle:

Your purpose is to communicate about a subject to a reader. You have feelings, knowledge, ideas about both the subject matter and the reader, and you must take both into account if you are to communicate effectively. What your reader knows about your subject, for example, is important to consider, since no one is interested in being told what they already know.

Writing then is a process of negotiating among the three different corners of this "communications" triangle. When you write about yourself, however, this triangle collapses. The writer becomes the subject and, in some cases, such as in a journal, the audience for his/her writing as well.

What purposes can such "communication" about and even with the self serve? Really, quite a few.

There are occasions when it is necessary and appropriate to tell someone else about yourself. In a thank-you note, you express how much a gift means to you. In a college application, you express your reasons for wanting to attend a particular school. In a "living will," you express your private thoughts and feelings about a much-debated public issue. Although the subject in such cases is yourself, you write in order to affect or influence others.

There are also occasions when you may find it useful to write for yourself alone. For example, if you wish to set down your day-to-day experiences and observations and responses to life as directly, completely, and honestly as possible, you may seek a form of writing that is flexible enough so that you do not have to be overly concerned with the effect on others of what you write or how you write it. For many writers, this form has been the journal.

A journal is a record, often kept daily, of one's life, a kind of personal account book. In the privacy of your journal, you can write about your conflicts and pleasures with family, friends, and associates without worrying about offending or embarrassing anyone. You can try out your responses to events, people, and things without worrying about the critical eye of a teacher or the difficulty of writing without error. You can open up and express yourself without fear of being poorly understood or harshly judged by anyone other than yourself. In short, you can discover your own uniquely personal voice.

Sometimes, you may focus in your journal on your inner life: your private feelings, thoughts, memories, dreams. Sometimes, you may focus on your experiences in and perceptions of the world outside yourself, writing narratives of your day, details of your observations, or ideas, questions, and notes about the things you learn from listening to or reading someone else's words. Your journal may serve you as a diary, but it should be more than that as well. It should be a place in which you can collect and develop your thoughts as a student and a writer, serving possibly as a notebook, for example, in which you record details of a lecture or a reading assignment in school and then write down your reactions.

The journal acts for many writers as a means of testing the self in its confrontations with the world. In your journal entries, you can express your confusion and disillusionment, your whimsicality and curiosity toward all the eccentric shapes of daily experience. Often, writing in your journal about an experience you have had can reveal to you something about yourself or your perceptions that you might not have realized as clearly before.

In the composition class, there are a variety of reasons why students are asked to keep a journal. It can help make writing a more habitual process, something you grow used to and hence more comfortable doing. Also, since you sometimes don't know what you think until you write it down, keeping a journal can help you discover and develop your thoughts and opinions about any subject that might be on your mind. A story that you tell or a description you offer in a journal entry may invite additional writing to explore or explain more about it. Such entries may become the start or one part of a piece of writing for others. Further, as you read over your journal, you can examine your experiences and ideas with a critical eye and possibly see them from a new perspective.

In this chapter then, we ask you to keep a journal as a means of both learning about yourself and collecting material that you might use later in the course in writing a formal essay.

TASK: WRITING A JOURNAL

The task in this chapter is to begin keeping a journal. You may use your journal to write about yourself in any number of ways: narrating your experiences, perhaps, or recording your sense impressions or revealing your thoughts and feelings or experimenting with your voice. You may write entries about other things as well, other people, events in the news, classroom lectures, or reading assignments.

As you do so, begin to look for the subjects that you keep coming back to and the feelings that you keep focusing on, for the patterns of thought and interest that appear. We would like you to begin writing about these patterns too. Doing so should help you grow more conscious of and comfortable with your personal voice, the way of saying—and seeing—things that most clearly reflects who you are.

In the next section of this chapter, "Writing Your Journal," we discuss how to use free writing as you start keeping a journal. We also introduce you to ways of developing your private voice, of seeking personal authenticity in the entries you write.

WRITING YOUR JOURNAL

Generating Ideas: Free Writing

Peter Elbow, in his book *Writing Without Teachers* (Oxford, 1973), explained what free writing is and how it can help you to find something to say about your subject. Free writing is writing about a subject without restrictions, writing whatever comes into your head, without concern for grammar, spelling, or organization. It is not prepared writing; it is not intended for a reader. Its only purpose is for you to explore on paper whatever thoughts and feelings you might have about your subject.

For example, the two students who wrote the following free-writing exercises were given a lemon and were asked to spend ten minutes in writing whatever came into their heads about it.

WRITER 1

Lemon--a yellow lemon, the color of my bright yellow sweatshirt the color of yellow taxi cabs the color of the sun in a kid's coloring book my yellow paper on my test bananas are yellow. It feels smooth but has a soapy or waxy texture. The Lemon Ice King has good lemon ices. Lenny used to work at the Lemon Ice King, Lenny, Levy, and Mike used to rob a lot of money from Fat Pete. Lemons are yellow I had a yellow car that was a lemon. Bobby Pistilli's father used to call Bobby a lemon. He is a lemon driving in his Monte Carlo. I like lemons I hate the people who passed the lemon to me I don't want to see it. I like lemons, I like lemons in my iced tea. I like lemons over chicken cutlets, I like lemons raw, I like to take the lemon right out of the pitcher of iced tea and eat it raw. I love the sour taste, I love the expression on someone's face when they bite into a very sour lemon. I like lemon on seafood. My favorite is freshly squeezed lemon over freshly crumbed and baked shrimp or over fresh shrimp or over filet of any fish. Some lemons are round, others oval-shaped--most lemons have a nipple at either end which is very small. One way to use a lemon (probably the most common way) is to slice it in half and squeeze it. Another way which is better is to first squeeze the lemon before you cut it open and roll it on a flat surface.

Notice how this writer has relaxed and let his mind wander in any direction that the lemon has taken him; he touches on the appearance, the taste, and the feel of a lemon; its uses; and its emotional associations for him in the past and even in the present as he is writing. (Notice also that he has omitted much punctuation, perhaps in order to encourage the flow of his thoughts.)

Past associations engulf the second writer as she relaxes and writes about her subject.

WRITER 2

Sometimes when I see a lemon, it brings back memories of my childhood. I remember the lemon tree my family and I used to have in our backyard. There were other trees but the lemon tree was my favorite. No other house in the neighborhood had one. My mother had put nicely formed bricks around the trunk in a circle. It used to amaze me how those beautiful and nice smelling flowers turned into lemons. This may sound ridiculous, but when I remember that lemon tree, it brings back nostalgic feelings. This may be because of how pleasant life used to be at that time.

SOME PRACTICE WITH FREE WRITING

1. As a way of getting started in free writing, begin with a subject that emphasizes a particular sense, for example, begin with the taste of a favorite food or dish and let go all your associations with it. Then move on to the other senses — touch, sight, sound, smell — and write freely about the subjects and associations each evokes.

   As another way of stimulating free writing, write about one subject and try to include associations with all five senses.

2. Write for ten minutes about an impersonal object: a pencil, a pen, or a piece of chalk, for example. Then read the free writing that follows. Have you stretched your mind as much as or more than the student who wrote this piece?

   Pen is an object, invented and created by man. It can make peace or start wars with just a simple wave from its point. It can teach people and help write important papers it can invent books, technology and create a picture of the universe. But yet we see what is a simple object which permits us to write as a worthless thing when really it holds the destruction of man or the creation of peace and love in the world in a small little tip. Down through time there have been different types of pens and pencils but all they did was to record our history and carry it down to each generation. A pen can be noble or very bad it all depends on who uses it. It has been called the sword of man or the staff of peace.

   Free Writing as a Source of Ideas.   Free writing can serve as a way of generating ideas once your imagination has really expanded, for you can discover ideas about subjects that you never realized were even in your mind. Peter Elbow said, "Free writing is a way to end up thinking something you couldn't have started out thinking." By examining the free writing that you do in class and at home in your journal, you can find thoughts or feelings to expand into prepared essays.

For example, read over the following free-writing sample:

Well, trick or treat, it is Halloween today. How I used to love that saying. Well I guess that I am growing up because I really do not feel that way anymore. But of course that is normal.

The hoodlums on the corner were throwing eggs at everybody today. It was so much fun to observe the action. It was hilarious to see the dumb fools getting bombarded with eggs.

Nobody, of course, ever tried throwing an egg at me. If they had, I swear that I would definitely have flipped out. But I am a familiar face and one does not throw eggs at the people he knows.

At home, I packed the little candy bags and it was fun distributing candy to all the really cute little kids dressed in their costumes coming to the door. I felt sad for a while there, it reminded me of how much fun my sister and I used to have on Halloween.

Oh well, the advantages of being an adult beat anything--even the fun kids have on Halloween.

Well, it's Tuesday and it seems as though I am not going to go anywhere again. Last night I decided to sleep over at Aggie's house, me and that girl are so compatible that we have so much fun together.

I love Aggie, and she's been my best friend ever since I was little, and she'll always be. We have been friends ever since we were little and I have always thought of her as I would a sister.

Her parents really like me, they are always asking me about how I am doing and how my parents are doing. We've been through a lot of garbage together, and after all our messed-up years I really don't know how we are alive after all the drugs that we have done.

It is true that we had both flipped out once but now, thank god, we are all right.

Aggie though it seems to me is still a little shaky at times. I sometimes think that maybe the drugs did affect her more than any of us would ever care to admit to ourselves or of course to her.

Why do you think that the writer associated Halloween with her friendship with Aggie? What would you say was the primary topic, the main pattern of thought, that this writer had on her mind? What sort of thoughts and feelings might this writer expand into a formal essay, one that is organized, fully developed, and grammatically correct?

In the next passage, note how as the writer relives a "nightmarish" experience, the intense emotions that it aroused in her seem to take possession of her writing.

A nightmarish trip to Port Authority, our flight canceled, all planes grounded. At the bus terminal, down so many stairs, my knees want to buckle. I am afraid I will drop Margot onto these concrete steps. Jack parks us near the snack shop, by a wall; there are no seats available. He constructs a fortress of luggage around us, then leaves us with a caveat to stay put no matter what. If he does manage to get tickets for the last stretch of this interminable holiday journey home, we may have to leave very quickly. Keep everything packed up and stay put. He is gone. People all around and every person desperate, except Margot, peaceful on my lap. I hold her tightly as if I were clinging to her instead of my being the mother lion.

A few yards away from us, in the center of the room, a wild-eyed drunken ragged limping man is playing to the crowd, cajoling, confronting people for money and cigarettes. He has seen Margot, she is looking in his direction, and he is stumbling over to where we are. He reels before my eyes, speaks broken English, sings in Spanish, a lullaby, in a voice that once perhaps was beautiful but which now quakes and is off key, drunken. He is inside the barricade, he has shoved one foot in between two suit.cases, he wants to hold the baby. Do you mind, reaching down for her, do you mind, touching her, do you mind, we are both touching her, where can I go I mind I mind no you cannot hold her.

He is holding her, the dirty ragged filthy foul vile drunken bum animal he is holding her my sweet baby and my god I am standing here alone watching him with her. His cigarette what if she thinks it is food she will get burned he is holding her I must have said something because he has put his cigarette on the floor she will not get burned by it but oh god he is holding my only baby my sweet margot my and I have her back.

He had thought of <u>leche</u> <u>leche</u> when she had started to cry, the baby don't want cigarettes, baby want <u>leche</u> he had said not wanting her to cry and somewhere in between the cigarette and the <u>leche</u> i got her back and he was gone, into the coffee shop, to get <u>leche</u> for the baby, <u>leche</u> for the baby.

now jack is here we have no time he says we have to hurry i managed to get us tickets but the bus is leaving he says. he doesn't hear what i hear through the thick glass next to us, doesn't hear the cries for <u>leche</u> <u>leche</u>, doesn't feel the cigarette ash hot against flesh he can't see it burn deeply. we are running we will have no <u>leche</u> from this place this night.

—Mary Ann Lynch

Free writing is often a productive way of recalling personal experiences. It is also a good technique for getting down on paper all the material on a recently studied topic. It is a useful antidote to writer's block, or the "I don't know where to start" syndrome. If you have given considerable thought to, and perhaps even done some research on, an assigned topic but do not know where to begin in writing about it, free writing of your thoughts or your recollections of what you read will get your material on paper.

MORE PRACTICE WITH FREE WRITING

3. Write briefly for thirty to forty-five minutes about a holiday you went on and the memories that you associate with it. When you are finished, make a list of the aspects of your subject that you might develop into a prepared essay. How are these aspects related? What pattern of thought or feeling do they trace? Which of them fit the least well into the pattern? Might these aspects be the start of a different pattern?

4. Think of a subject that you have recently studied for one of your classes or one that you have read about rather extensively. Without thinking too hard about the subject, start writing freely about it. After writing for thirty to forty-five minutes, consider how many aspects of the subject you covered. Have you sufficient ideas for an essay? What pattern do these ideas form? Now that you have taken stock of what you have written, would more free writing serve a useful purpose?

Starting a Journal. In starting a journal, you are making a kind of contract with yourself. You agree to record your observations and reactions over an extended period of time and expect in return a writer's bounty: some usable glimpses of yourself or others that you can work into a finished essay, or perhaps some developing pattern of feeling or thought that reveals you in the act of resolving some personal conflict or perceiving a subject in a new way. Although you receive no guarantee that your entries will be more interesting, less common, or even less boring than your daily routine or your usual thoughts may seem to you, what is surprising is how often the bright hue of fresh observation emerges from the uniform gray of the workaday world.

But how do you start? What do you write about first? The answer, of course, is whatever you want. Still, it may be helpful to take a look at how others have gotten started.

Often in starting journals, writers focus first on themselves as writers, on how they feel about keeping a journal or about writing in general. Here are early entries from the journals of four students. Notice that each entry has the feel and appearance of a piece of free writing:

Feb. 4

10:00 P.M.--You know, I've always wanted to keep a diary but always put it off. Sometimes you just have more things to say than others. I think it could be interesting to read something you've written a long time ago. Surprisingly enough, you might even find certain values and attitudes have changed about yourself. Diaries are good for letting out your feelings. Writing them down, knowing no one will ever read them, is a good release. Diaries trace a person's emotional development.

Feb. 5, 1985

The teacher says to write and practically all the kids cringe about it. "Oh no, we have to write!" Writing--I love to write!

Sometimes writing is the only way I can express something or get some understanding. The words just flow faster than I can get them on the paper, there's so much to write about... The most wonderful thing about writing is that you can write anything, absolutely anything, and the paper doesn't talk back--

Moving along--to me, this journal is no hassle. In fact it will probably help.... I will just write how I feel when I feel it, and then I'll try to make sense of what it is I wrote later on.

2/9/85

When I first started thinking about writing this journal, I said to myself "I don't know what to write," and I still don't know what to write. When I think of writing I usually think that some important conclusion has to be reached. If not, then it is a waste. I am usually very opinionated and always have some important topic which I discuss with family and friends. But when it came down to writing this journal my mind kept going blank. I haven't had much time this first week to really get adjusted and get into the swing of academic life again.... At this point though, I'm thankful to have time to reflect, and to set new goals for the weeks ahead.

9th Feb '85

When the professor first said that we had to keep a journal for the semester I just accepted it since I thought that well it was one of the course's requirements. The problem started when she asked the class to write our first journal concerning characteristics about ourself which we would like our new classmates to know. Well, I didn't want my classmates to know anything except that I was a friendly person and easy to get along with, so I had to find a way to say those two lines in a page. Of course, I made a mess and decided to try again by talking about my family and status in the college. Now I have realized my problem is with expressing my feelings on paper, something I have never done. I know that the journal would help me to become a better writer but I still have to get accustomed to expressing my feelings on paper.

It is not only students who approach the task of starting a journal this way. Here are entries from the journals of two professional writers, Susan Kinnicutt and Sylvia Plath, each of whom is puzzling over the purpose of keeping a journal. As you read them, consider the degree to which these entries also exhibit a kind of spontaneity and free association that suggest each author simply wrote down whatever came into her head.

January 1, 1978. Vermont

This diary looked so inviting when I first bought it, just like all the enticing "Blue Horse" notebooks I hoarded in Carolina. And then left unfilled though I sniffed them a lot. The smell of books and paper used to be so wonderful. But this isn't big enough, for one thing; I feel limited by the short page. And it doesn't open up, bend nicely, invite me to write, like the first hole of a good golf course should invite you to play. It looks official, though, it demands I mention the day. If I used my old Blue Horse, I probably wouldn't start at all.

But "journal" sounds so formal, so egocentric. [Who cares?] It's supposed to warm you up for writing; maybe there'll be bits and pieces of possible stories. That thought is depressing. I never seem to get to write all the stories I want to. Life interferes, always, and I haven't solved that problem.

And I feel as if someone were looking over my shoulder. What is this book for? What I did? What happened? What I think and feel? What I did is on the engagement calendar, not much usually, small events and sometimes outlandish. More important, who is this book for? Posterity? What a sickly sweet Ladies' Home Journal picture I could paint of myself, but what a finicky, mouth-tightening chore that would be. I guess what I'll do is run on and if I use this book up on July 6, go out and buy another and keep going. I hope, reading back, I can remember happy times, learn from sad — or skip the whole day if it's desperate.

—Susan Kinnicutt

November 13, 1949

As of today I have decided to keep a diary again — just a place where I can write my thoughts and opinions when I have a moment. Somehow I have to keep and hold the rapture of being seventeen. Every day is so precious I feel infinitely sad at the thought of all this time melting farther and farther away from me as I grow older. *Now, now* is the perfect time of my life.

In reflecting back upon these last sixteen years, I can see tragedies and happiness, all relative — all unimportant now — fit only to smile upon a bit mistily.

I still do not know myself. Perhaps I never will. But I feel free — unbound by responsibility, I still can come up to my own private room, with my drawings hanging on the walls . . . and pictures pinned up over my bureau. It is a room suited to me — tailored, uncluttered and peaceful. . . . I love the quiet lines of the furniture, the two bookcases filled with poetry books and fairy tales saved from childhood.

At the present moment I am very happy, sitting at my desk, looking out at the bare trees around the house across the street. . . . Always I want to be an observer. I want to be affected by life deeply, but never so blinded that I cannot see my share of existence in a wry, humorous light and mock myself as I mock others.

I am afraid of getting older. I am afraid of getting married. Spare me from cooking three meals a day—spare me from the relentless cage of routine and rote. I want to be free—free to know people and their backgrounds—free to move to different parts of the world, so I may learn that there are other morals and standards besides my own.

—Sylvia Plath

In the second entry, Plath goes on to introduce herself. The pages of her journal become, in this sense, a kind of mirror in which she can see who she is. For many students, this is the first purpose a journal serves also. In the following entry, a student starts her journal by introducing herself:

Feb 4th, '88

I really cannot say definitely who I am, but I know I am a very stern person when it comes to my life. I have always set goals for myself and have always planned what I was going to do in life. I do not know if that's something good or bad. Sometimes I feel my life is too calculated and I set too high goals for myself and if I fail I am too hard on myself. I never had the courage to say to myself that I should just let what happens happen. Maybe it's because I am too scared that by not planning my life carefully I would make a great mistake which I would definitely regret. There are times when I am proud of myself and the ability to organize my self and my life style but sometimes I feel a great strain on me and the weight of everyday activities. But I know that I'll always organize my life possibly I hate to think that I waste any of it.

There are less direct ways to introduce yourself in your journal. You might simply record the events of a day, as the following writer did:

6/9/86

9:15 P.M.--After class this evening I was thinking about writing -

what was I going to write about? I was going to discuss the way my day began--that would be easy enough.

My first week of no longer working full-time and a day when I could sleep late and what happens? The phone rings at 7:50 A.M. My girl friend calls from Florida. Her brother is dying and she's very upset and there is nothing that I can say to make her feel better. He's 29 and he's dying. He's got AIDS and there's not a damn thing that anybody can do for him. There's nothing I can do for her and that hurts because I love her. I can't lie to her and say that everything is going to be OK. So we cry together. That's all I can do.

Now mind you that was the way my day began. I got a letter from Abe (my guy) and that made me happy. Then I went to class and that made me happy (sort of). Then the Mets were losing 1-0 to the Phillies in the 3rd or 4th inning and I wasn't very happy. Then I turned the game off because I had writing that I had to do.

First though I saw my brother's new motorcycle and he was happy so that made me happy (doesn't take much, does it!). Then I started to read those essays that we had been assigned. The "Autobiography" was interesting, but then I got to "Shooting an Elephant" and I found myself getting very upset. I think I understand the meaning of the story--you know, doing something not because you want but feel you have to due to the pressure from others. That's not what got to me. It was the actual shooting that made me sad. All I could think of was this poor animal suffering and dying slowly, frightened and alone. How very sad (my dog died alone in a hospital). It's kind of silly mentioning that now, but it just crossed my mind.

I guess the beginning of my day and the end were very similar--my girlfriend's brother and a silly elephant both dying and dying slowly. I've had enough.

Note how this writer includes her thoughts about a reading assignment and how these then lead to a perception about herself.

Or you might get started by simply describing a scene you observed or another person, as the writers of the following two entries did:

October 18, 1979. Napa Valley

Today I watched trucks pull orange gondolas filled with dark purple grapes along the road outside my office window. The workers were hurrying to get in the last of the Zinfandel. It is six in the evening now. A steady gray rain is falling. There are patterns of wet leaves on the lawn. Something is very emotional about this moment. Tears are squeezing out of the corners of my eyes. I am not sad. Perhaps I am feeling the seasons changing, my children growing, the skin at my elbows wrinkling.

—Eleanor Coppola

Mon., 2/10

That's what it was, it was time with Brian. He was a brand-new sponge soaking up a big new world and I was old and broken-down. Eventually, I was not broken down at all. Eventually, I was a human being again, and an uncle. A GOOD UNCLE. We spent a lot of good hours together.... I made a million silly noises for Brian. When he learned to crawl, I crawled with him. When he ran, I chased him. I fed him, burped him, changed him (AND HE CHANGED ME).

Before I met Brian, I hadn't any experience raising a kid. I'd seen 'em before but never so much as changed a diaper. Wasn't looking forward to such stuff, smelly and all that. Feeding an infant--HOLDING an infant is a thrill at first. "Oh, he's so tiny." "Look at those teeny little fingernails." "Can you believe those eyes?" Brian was fun to watch. Even when he was just sleeping he was fun to watch. It was so funny to watch him try to turn over, from his back to his chest. Looked like a bug, a fat bug. It was funny to watch Brian trying to pick the flowers off the wallpaper. He thought he was looking at solid objects and he was trying to pick them off the wall.

He took his socks off. He took his diapers off, wet or dry, and threw them out of the crib. By winter, he was strong enough to remove anything from the crib; clothes, toys, bottles, food--no not food. He only drank from the bottle. But when food came along a little later, he flung that out too.

Each of these writers, Eleanor Coppola in the first case and a student who had suffered a disabling injury in the second, offers a subtle insight into the self, by writing about the world outside the self. So does the writer who expressed her feelings about her psychology teacher in the next entry:

Tues., Feb.11

I cannot tolerate the Psych instructor. She is totally obnoxious. How can they have a woman with no children teach a child psychology course? And she's so adamant about everything! "Never, never discipline your children!" "Always, always speak to a child at his physical level!" "Believe me 'people'--it works!" Balony!--imagine poor Aunt Jeanine talking to 7 kids at their level--she'd be crawling around all day! I told John about her-- figured I'd get his professional opinion--he agreed--she doesn't know what she's talking about!

I have enough pressure as a single parent. I second guess myself enough, without some idiot with no kids and no idea of what she's talking about telling me that you don't discipline a child--"you guide them." I wonder how she thinks you can "guide" a child in a temper tantrum. I'm sure her answer would be that she'd never let it get as far as a temper tantrum. Idiot!

Commenting, like this student, on something that you have learned or listened to or read is another good way of getting started on your journal. You might take down a remark of a television personality, for example, or copy a quotation from a magazine article. Then write a few sentences in which you apply these comments to an experience you have had recently or to an idea that you have been thinking about.

Of course, you don't have to start by consciously writing about anything at all. If you give yourself over completely to free writing, if you simply let the pen move as spontaneously and automatically as possible without the intervention of rational thought and order, without pause and without lifting pen from paper, you may find an effective way of getting in touch with your most honest feelings and thoughts. The result may be something like the next two entries:

14th Feb. 1988

Valentine, when I think about valentine I think of love and a time for loved ones to be together. Valentine is not like Christmas where the whole family comes together, but it is particularly a time for lovers. I do not have a boyfriend and actually I am proud of myself and my capability to stay out of relationships, but when Valentine comes around I suddenly wish I did have a boyfriend, even if for just that day. I remember going to Junior High and having my first few infatuations and how wonderful I felt when guys would give me roses. Later on as I grew up I did not get any roses or chocolates since guys wanted too much out of a relationship when they became your boyfriend. So although I love Valentine and getting roses and chocolates I think I'd rather wait until I decide to get someone to buy them for me on valentine, until then I buy them for myself.

May 1st 1986

   8:30 A.M.--Good morning it's May Day to some people Mayday is the time to dance around the maypole an ancient ritual in the communist countries or is it more broad than that it's the workers holiday May 1st was the day I moved back to the Bronx after having lived in Manhattan for four years May 1st same year a friend of mine moved to America to some people May 1st is their birthday to a pilot "mayday" means an emergency but I don't think that's related to May 1st one thing that May 1st is to all people is Spring no that's not true south of the equator May is like our November

How long could one or the other of these entries have taken to write? Perhaps no more than a minute. Remember our language-making power never stops working, not even during sleep. In fact, in a way, free writing resembles the flow of language in dreams. There is no "correct" order of events in dreams, and rules of grammar and sentence structure are irrelevant. Try to tap this flow of verbal energy and put it to work for you. Free writing, for timed intervals, is a practical means of "priming the pump." It helps a writer to overcome that initial fear of beginning, and it is another way of discovering what is going on within your mind.

Keeping a Journal.   Begin now to keep a journal. Your instructor may have a preference, but otherwise use a notebook or blank diary available in bookstores or stationery departments. Perhaps you will want to discuss with your instructor just how to set the journal up, the type and range of subject matter that seem appropriate to include, and what role overall the journal will play in the course. Here are notes that one student took in her composition class about these things:

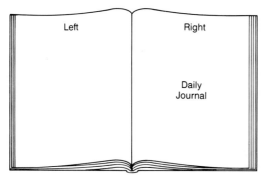

Left · Right

Daily Journal

Right side
5 days a week
date entries
time entries
15 minutes a day
write what you want (free write)

Grammar doesn't matter -- punctuation, etc. Only interested in words. Talking about yourself, your thoughts and inhibitions.
Left side: Write about the reading you do. Also, take class notes on left side. For each essay you read, write 5 minutes about your reactions. First "free write" about the essay -- write questions about the essay -- comments about the essay.

This is actually the first entry in the student's journal. It suggests a number of basic guidelines that are worth following. Starting each entry with a notation of the date, the time, and even the place that you are writing is a good idea. The regularity with which you write in your journal is important, and you may want to settle with your instructor on a set number of times that you will write each week. Also, you need not worry about grammar, punctuation, spelling, organization, or even necessarily about making much sense. Writing freely and honestly, no matter what your subject, may be the best way to make keeping a journal a productive experience.

Finally, note that another good way to get started writing in your journal is to use it as a notebook in class or when you read. Then, like the student who wrote about her psychology teacher, add your own comments and questions about what you are learning. This suggests, in fact, one further guideline you may decide to follow: read back over your entries at periodic intervals and write your thoughts and feelings about what you find there. Some writers even leave blank pages in their journal, so that when they do go back and read previous entries, they have the open space in which to write their comments and reactions.

SOME PRACTICE IN STARTING YOUR JOURNAL

1. Write an entry about your writing class. How do you feel about taking this class? What expectations do you have? What are your first impressions?

2. Write an entry about keeping a journal and/or about writing in general. Do you like to write? Why or why not? What difficulties does writing hold for you?

3. Write an entry in which you introduce yourself, either by describing the sort of person you are or by recording the events of a typical day in your life.

Using Your Journal as a Source of Ideas for Writing an Essay. Our reactions to people and events seldom occur in isolation. Usually, we can trace a thought or feeling through a series of journal entries and discover that seemingly random observations actually have a shape, an order, a logic. In other words, your private journal may reveal a pattern of ideas or emotions connected to one subject. This pattern can become the basis for a public piece of writing, a formal essay. As you continue to write in your journal, you may find yourself noting over a period of time sufficient ideas on enough different topics for all the formal writing you must do, whether the subject is personal experience or, more objectively, thoughts about the world you live in.

SOME PRACTICE IN USING YOUR JOURNAL

1. Reserve the same time each day for several days for writing in your journal. Note the difference in your attitude from day to day. What has caused you to have these differing feelings? Can you trace your feelings to a specific incident that occurred that day? Does any pattern of response emerge as you reread your entries for the preceding days?

2. Write a number of entries, preferably on successive days, that record your activities with, and feelings toward, one person. What do these comments reveal about the nature of your relationship to this person? Can you notice a change in this relationship or recognize a phase that you are going through with this person?

3. Forever, it seems, mankind has been afflicted by, and sometimes consumed by, boredom. In the Middle Ages, monks feared the onset of midday, the

"demon of noontide," when life seemed particularly empty and joyless. Is there any time of day when you feel the regular approach of the demon boredom? Select this time to record your response in your journal, preferably over a period of several days. Explain how you attempted to slay the demon. In addition, become an observer of others' boredom, writing down what you see of boredom in its public forms, namely, in shopping centers, in the student lounge, at airline terminals, or on mass transportation.

4. Over a period of time, note your reactions to a particular public personality: a television performer, a newspaper columnist, a sports figure, or an author. What do your reactions tell you about yourself? What do they tell you about the subject you have been studying?

Addressing Your Audience: Private Voice

Your Private Voice. Writing in a journal is like talking to yourself. Because there is no one around, you can say what you want to without worrying about whether anyone is listening to you, judging your sincerity, or evaluating your skill as a writer. You can test your thoughts and feelings, as well as your ability to express them openly and directly. You can listen to your most private and personal voice.

This is not necessarily easy to do. For one thing, you may not wish to hear your private voice, the honest and original expression of yourself; there may be feelings you wish to hide from, to keep out of your own conscious awareness. Keeping a journal can be a way of tapping those feelings, but only if you allow it to.

Even if you are uninhibited about revealing your feelings, you may find that the language you use to convey them has a false note to it, is not unique or original enough, does not really sound like you. When we write, we often imitate one or another public voice that seems to us to command wide attention, or we adopt the voice of a close associate or a friend or a parent, or we rely on trite, cliched expressions because they come readily to mind.

You may feel, for example, that it is a good idea to draw your ideas and language from the world of advertising, television, or popular journalism, for these media provide us with a stock of ready-made expressions and current attitudes. But in a way, allowing your voice to be an echo of someone else's is like wearing someone else's name on your clothes, applying to yourself a kind of designer's label of the mind. And this process may actually make you even more inhibited about expressing your most original ideas and observations.

For example, think of how often you, as a student, are tempted to imitate a teacher in order to make a good impression. In yielding to this temptation, you may feel uncomfortable, even guilty, about pretending to be someone that you're not. Feeling this way, you may reveal even less about yourself and hide your thoughts even more, rather than express them in an inauthentic way.

Consider the student who wrote the following note:

Dear Professor Ames,

Due to circumstances beyond my control, the paper on Hamlet was not submitted. I shall complete said paper and submit it as soon as possible prior to the final date of failure previously determined by the departmental authorities.

The student begins by sounding like a television announcer, then goes on to employ a pretentious, abstract style of phrasing that is perhaps meant to echo the academic language of the classroom. The effect is phony, unnatural, and unconvincing.

Nor would this student make a much better case if he or she tried to convey a false sense of familiarity that actually says little:

Dear Professor Ames,

I'm sorry I can't hand in my paper on Hamlet today. I've been having a rough time lately. But I'm getting myself together now, so I definitely should have the paper done by next week, OK?

Again the writing is unconvincing because it hides more than it tells. Phrases like "getting myself together" are so trite and commonplace that we use them most often as a way of avoiding telling what we really feel.

But what if the student wrote the following:

Dear Professor Ames,

I'm sorry that I don't have my paper on Hamlet for you today. I had a biology test yesterday and now I've got a math test today, and I'd fallen behind in my studying for both. So I didn't get the paper done. Would you still accept it if I write it tonight and get it to you first thing tomorrow?

Might this note have more success? Whether or not it would depends, of course, on the sort of person and teacher Professor Ames is. But at least the student sounds more forthright.

This might not always be the best strategy to take when you write. If you honestly feel that *Hamlet* is a rotten play and Professor Ames is a rotten teacher for making you write a paper on it, you probably would be wise to exercise a certain diplomacy and edit these feelings out of your note. Sometimes you will have thoughts and feelings that you rightly choose to keep to yourself. Often you will want to adjust your voice to the expectations and values of your audience (a subject we take up in Chapter 2 and examine in most of the audience sections thereafter). But you do want to develop a firm sense of your own most direct and original voice, because even when you edit this voice, it will remain the foundation of all the writing that you do.

Discovering Your Own Voice. Other than simply trying to write about your observations and experiences as freely and honestly as possible, what can you do to write in the voice that is most uniquely an expression of yourself?

Ken Macrorie, in his book *Telling Writing*, speaks of truthfulness in writing as a way to achieve this kind of personal authenticity. By *truthfulness* he does not mean simply the avoidance of lies and dishonesty; rather, he means the willingness to figure out what we really do want to say and to find a way of saying it. This approach recognizes, first, that we do not often know what we think unless we write about it and, second, that in order to express exactly what we think we need to find the words and the examples that will best convey it. We do not, in other words, think and then write. A process is involved in which thinking and writing are intertwined. This process is an arduous one; the right words do not always flow easily from the pen of even the greatest writer.

What you write about is less a problem than how you approach the subject. Taking an approach that allows you to learn something new from writing about the subject and to see the subject in a new, perhaps even contradictory, light will help you locate the truth.

Looking for unexpected perceptions that contrast with the perceptions of others or even with perceptions you have previously held yourself is, in fact, an excellent way of discovering something new, fresh, and original to say about a subject. If you feel there really is something rotten about a play that everyone tells you is a great classic, this feeling may be worth exploring in a paper. Perhaps the personality of one of the characters is offensive to you, and by writing about it, you may discover something new and vital about the character and about yourself as well. Macrorie suggests that the writer would be wise always to look for unexpected or opposing perceptions. Consider the positive aspects of a subject that strikes you as negative and vice versa. You thus treat a subject in all of its complexity and give yourself the opportunity to reveal the complexity of your own character.

Finding the words and phrases that reveal rather than mask this complexity is a challenge. By trying to be as concise and, at the same time, as detailed as possible in your own choice of words, you can at least avoid sounding overly imitative of others.

On the one hand, you do not want to waste words. A phrase may convey more than a sentence or even a paragraph. Try not to use more words than you need to make your point. Why write, "When a black cat crosses my path, I am a superstitious enough person to believe that it is apt to be prophetic of misfortune," when you can write, "When a black cat crosses my path, I feel it will bring me bad luck"? Why be long-winded when you can be direct and to the point?

But truthfulness in writing is not just bare-bones economy. Although empty phrases should be pared from your writing, details that convey the uniqueness of your observations and experiences should be included. Work to find the specific nouns and the active verbs, adjectives, and adverbs that will bring your thoughts and feelings to life. Why write, "I felt very uptight," when you can write, "My stomach was doing triple somersaults, and everytime I swallowed, I felt like a wad of cotton had been stuffed down my throat." Try to make your ideas more specific, more concrete, by offering detailed examples of what you mean. Try to re-create the feel of your experiences by telling the reader how they were like or unlike comparable experiences.

As you write in your journal then, aim for the sort of truthfulness that arises out of unexpected or opposing perceptions, concrete words and details, and short narrative examples. Try to avoid the pitfalls to which the best intentioned writer can succumb: substituting other voices for your own, feeling intimidated by your audience, or relying on vague, overused words and omitting vivid detail. Strive for a voice that is your own, that is unaffected by what you have heard or what you think others want to hear.

How Others Hear You.   One test of how truthful you have been will be the response of a reader. Have you expressed yourself clearly, colorfully, and concisely enough so that your reader believes in your experiences, trusts your feelings, and understands and respects your thoughts? Have you given the reader a good sense of who you are and what you are all about?

Once you are writing for an audience[1] and not just for yourself, you may feel reticent about expressing yourself openly and honestly. If your subject itself is very private, you may decide not to write about it for a particular audience or not to write about it at all. But when this is not the case, the chances are that your reader will draw you along the path to honesty by his or her interest in your subject, rather than putting up roadblocks that will inhibit you.

---

[1] We use *reader* and *audience* interchangeably here to mean either a group of readers or an individual. Each task will specify whether your audience is to be a group or a particular individual.

For example, a student wrote the following entry in her journal:

Sat., Sept. 25

12:00 noon--I just got out to lunch. The most terrible thing has just happened to me! I just got mugged. The two creeps that mugged me caught me off guard. I mean who would expect two clean-cut American kids to mug you on 86th St. and 3rd Avenue? I'm really shocked to hell! I think I've never been so afraid of New York City in all the 19 years that I've lived here.

The student followed this with a brief entry the next day saying that she had been robbed of her self-confidence as well as her money. In another entry two days after that, she wrote, "I am beginning to get over my feelings of bitterness about the mugging—my roommate's been quite a lot of help."

How honestly does she probe her feelings about being mugged? To what degree is her private voice hidden here behind pat phrases like "shocked to hell"? To what degree does she express the complexity of her feelings and especially the reality of her fear?

She decided to write more about the mugging, in order to see if she could convey her experience vividly enough so that a reader might feel what she did, and submitted the following paragraphs to other members of the class:

Just two hours ago I got mugged. The two muggers were pushy, and for the first time in my life, I was actually afraid. I was so angry not just at the muggers but at New York in general.

Before this incident occurred, I was very confident about living in New York. I mean for nineteen years, I lived in the Bronx and never had any problems whatsoever. I guess one can say that all the years in New York gave me some kind of instinct for distinguishing the good from the bad. It turned out to be wrong, at least in my case. I never thought that the two "gentlemen" that approached me would turn out to be two of the "bad" guys. I always pictured the "bad" guy as a shabbily dressed, dirty-looking being. However, my stereotyping cost me 150 bucks!

If I had been a lot wiser about who I allowed to come near

me (whether shabbily dressed or not), this would never have
happened to me. I should have applied caution to everything and
everyone. I should never trust anyone right off. My problem was
that I applied caution in only one area (bad neighborhoods and
shabby-looking people), instead of all neighborhoods and all
people.

I guess it's not fair to blame all of New York; however, for a
while there, I was really upset and I still carry a lot of the bitterness around with me. I blame the city because it disappoints
me to see and feel that I could be harmed in a place and an
area in which I've been brought up and have grown accustomed
to. It really hurts to feel afraid suddenly when you've never
known that feeling before; and it's really awful to have to think
that two people can make you fear a whole city.

When her classmates read her story, they felt that her concise style and use
of slang conveyed her anger and disappointment well. But they did not feel
that her fear came through fully, even though she refers to it repeatedly. To
be as convincing as possible, she may need to convey her fear more thoroughly.
How might she accomplish this?

Her classmates suggested that she describe her attackers and the mugging
incident in detail. They felt that a more concrete narrative of what actually
happened might capture more of her feelings and attitudes and might allow
a reader to get to know her more fully. Here, in response, is what the student
added between the second and third paragraphs:

I was on my way out to lunch from work when two creeps
caught me off guard. I mean, who would expect two clean-cut
American types to mug you on 86th St. and 3rd Avenue? Maybe
that made it worse. They were nice looking guys.

One minute they were walking past me; then before I knew
what was happening, the big one reached out and grabbed my
arm hard. His hand was so big, it fitted all the way around my
arm muscle. I must've looked shocked, 'cause all of a sudden he
laughed in my face. He didn't have his two front teeth. For some
reason, I keep remembering that.

The next thing I knew they'd pushed me against the wall of a
building. I'm not sure I ever felt it when the other one tore my

bag from off my shoulder. The next thing I knew, they were gone.

I was so shocked for a while I just stood there looking at the people walking by. It was like nobody even noticed. Then I got the shakes! I shook so hard, I thought I'd cry. I think I've never been so afraid of New York City in all of the nineteen years that I've lived here. Those two muggers robbed me of more than just my money: they robbed me of my self-confidence.

In this case, the student's consciousness of an audience may have helped her to convey her experience more honestly and originally than she might otherwise have, in a voice that more thoroughly captured the range of her emotions. In your journal, of course, you may be writing for yourself and not for a reader, but if you read your entries as an attentive reader would, you may find yourself including the telling detail, the precise word. (See pp. 80–81 on developing your ability to read critically what you write.)

SOME PRACTICE WITH VOICE

You can develop the following exercises in your journal, and you can comment on them there as well.

1. In the student's notes to Professor Ames on page 38, how does the choice of words affect the overall tone of the language? For example, how do the words *departmental authorities* function in the first note? What words create a vague, ambiguous feeling in the second note? What words clear up this ambiguity in the third note?

2. What can you conclude about the intentions and the character of the voices in the following quotations?

    a. I have resolved on an enterprise which has no precedent, and which, once complete, will have no imitator. My purpose is to display to my kind a portrait in every way true to nature, and the man I shall portray will be myself. . . . I am like no one in the whole world. I may be no better but at least I am different.

    —Jean Jacques Rousseau, *Confessions*

    b. When in the Course of human events, it becomes necessary for one people to dissolve the political bands which have connected them with another . . . a decent respect to the opinions of mankind requires that they should declare the causes which impel them to the separation.

    —Thomas Jefferson, *Declaration of Independence*

c. Psychopathology: Aimed at understanding obsessions and phobias, including the fear of being suddenly captured and stuffed with crabmeat, reluctance to return a volleyball serve, and the inability to say the word "mackinaw" in the presence of women. The compulsion to seek out the company of beavers is analyzed.

—Woody Allen, "Spring Bulletin"

d. It is a truth universally acknowledged, that a single man in possession of a good fortune must be in want of a wife.

—Jane Austen, *Pride and Prejudice*

3. Select a popular newspaper or magazine with a distinctive voice. Write an entry in your journal on some commonplace event for that day, but try to narrate it in the voice of the magazine.

4. Write a brief advertisement for an expensive perfume, but use the voice you would expect to hear in a beer commercial. What kind of voice is usually used for these products? What are some words that would most likely appear in these commercials to create a distinctive voice?

5. Select sentences from your journal that don't really sound the way you sound, that distort or mask your most private voice. How do you account for this writing? Rewrite the sentences so that they seem to be more "truthful." What changes did you make?

6. Collect examples of newspaper and magazine advertisements that take on a voice that you find to be manipulative, deceitful, or dishonest. What kind of language do these voices use? What kinds of audiences are addressed by these advertisements?

7. Working against the most individual self-expression is the tendency of student writers to rely on clichés—secondhand thoughts and feelings. For example, a reference at the beginning of the chapter to the "thrill of victory and the agony of defeat" suggests the abundance of clichés in the language of sports. Make a list of the sports clichés that you know. Collect clichés characteristic of other special-interest groups. What phrases can one substitute for the easily recognized expressions on your lists?

8. Change the following expressions into phrases that establish a more concrete voice in their description of objects or events:

Example
Fantastically beautiful autumn woodland.
An October forest of red- and golden-leafed oak and maple trees.

a. Wonderful beach of sun worshipers.

    b. Exciting marathon runners passing by.

    c. Laughing students hanging out on campus.

    d. Municipal hospital admissions room filled with people.

9. Restore the common expressions disguised by an inflated voice in these sentences.

   Example

   A rapidly accelerating glacial deposit accumulates zero spongy vegetation.
   A rolling stone gathers no moss.

    a. A military consortium peregrinates on its internal digestive organ.

    b. A feathered biped retained manually is cost-effectively superior to pairs inhabiting low-lying vegetation.

    c. Avoid enumerating domestic fowl prior to their postovum existence.

    d. Contemporaneously with the feline's exodus is experienced the diminutive rodent's ludic spontaneity.

Establishing Your Point of View. Think about the attitudes and feelings expressed by the student who was mugged. While you probably would not question her fear, anger, shock, how about her views of New York City? Do you think that she should have been more cautious in the first place? Do you agree with her when she says, "I should have applied caution to everything and everyone"? Or, is this an extreme, if understandable, reaction to her experience?

Possibly, your point of view on this writer's experience differs from hers. As she writes, she discovers how she feels about her subject. But how she feels and hence what she writes is a reflection of who she is. The same will be true of you, whenever you write.

You have a particular set of ideas and values because of where and how you have lived, whom you have known, what you have gone through, and what reading you have done. You come to your subject with a preconceived view of the world, and this view of the world, in turn, colors the way you perceive the subject: your frame of reference is your view of the world, which, in turn, determines your way of perceiving the subject, your point of view.

The way in which one's frame of reference influences one's point of view toward a subject can be illustrated by the following examples: If you are writing about space travel and are a socially concerned person, you might feel that tax dollars could be better spent on social programs. On the other hand, if you are a science major, you might support the point of view that space travel will contribute significantly to our expanding knowledge of the universe. Finally, if you are a science fiction fan, you might see space travel as providing an infinite range of exciting adventures. Your frame of reference will affect your view of your subject and hence how you write about it.

Or what if the topic is single parenthood? If you were a thirty-five-year-old divorced mother of three, had a good job in a social service agency that was funding your education, loved your children, and were too busy to marry again at the moment, your point of view might be that under favorable economic and emotional conditions, single parenthood is a viable option. On the other hand, if you were raised by one parent who worked a double shift to support the family and had no time or energy left over for personal contact with family members, you might feel that single parenthood is a burden to the parent and inadequate for the children.

One thing to look for as you write in and then read over your journal is an emerging point of view. Expressing yourself as directly as possible from that point of view is another way of achieving personal authenticity when you write.

The following ten questions will help you to determine your own frame of reference. Write out answers to them in your journal, then try the first exercise below to explore your point of view on a controversial subject.

1. How old are you?
2. Of what ethnic background are you? What economic or social class are you in?
3. Do you have a job or career? If so, what do you do? If not, what are your career plans?
4. Where were you born? Where do you live now?
5. What is your religious affiliation, if any?
6. Are you a member of a political party? If so, which one?
7. What roles do you play in your family?
8. What significant events have occurred in your life?
9. What are your hobbies or other leisure activities?
10. What are your goals for your life?

SOME PRACTICE WITH YOUR POINT OF VIEW

1. How would your frame of reference, based on your answers to the preceding questions, affect your point of view on the following topics?

   a. Legalization of drugs.

   b. Environmental conservation measures.

   c. Nuclear energy.

   d. Nursing homes for the elderly.

   e. Military spending.

2. In the following paragraphs, part of an incident is described. Complete the narrative from the point when the performers begin to play:

> The performers entered forty minutes late, buttoning their shirts and adjusting the slings on their instruments as they moved to center stage. They bowed nervously, turned awkwardly to one another, then got ready to play.
>
> The audience had restrained itself for the first thirty minutes but grew noticeably restless in the last few minutes before the performers appeared. Several people were throwing empty cans and boxes toward the stage. Others were standing directing their boos and cries to the absent performers.
>
> Several security police, hired for the occasion, paced the hall nervously, fearing an outburst of violence from the impatient crowd.

a. What does the ending that you have created reveal about your point of view toward the incident?

b. How might you have changed the ending you wrote if you were attempting to see the incident from the point of view of one of the performers, or of a member of the audience, or of a security police officer?

BECOMING AWARE OF YOURSELF AS A WRITER

Make use of your journal to record your thoughts and feelings about the task in Chapter 1. As you write in your journal, consider the following questions:

1. What effect does writing a journal entry have on you? What value have you found in the process so far?

2. Do you think that a writer's journals should be read by others? How would you feel if others read your journals? How would the presence of others affect what you write?

3. What kinds of subjects make keeping a journal useful to you?

4. Which are your most interesting journal entries so far? Why do you think so?

5. What connection at this point can you make between keeping a journal and writing an essay?

6. How successful were you in hearing and conveying your private voice? What methods contributed to your success?

7. Were you able to trace a distinct point of view emerging in your journal? How would you characterize this point of view?

2

Writing About Yourself— Expressing Your Point of View

PURPOSE

In Chapter 1, you wrote about yourself for yourself. You were both the subject of and the audience for your journal.

Perhaps, though, after reading over some of your entries, you felt motivated to show them to someone else or to tell someone else about them. You may have shown your close friends an entry that you felt would amuse or surprise or puzzle them because of what they already know about you. You may have told a classmate who was confused by an assignment about an entry in which you complained about or worked through a similar confusion.

How much more public might you go with your private voice? Some writers go so far as to publish their journals. Their point of view—the feelings, observations, opinions, ideas they express—proves interesting to others because it is unique enough to give readers something to think about and/or because it is typical enough to give readers something to identify with.

You will probably want to keep some entries in your journal private. But there may also be entries worth writing about because they express a point of view that a reader other than yourself would find interesting or useful or important to learn about.

When you express your point of view about any subject, you let a reader know where you are coming from and hence who you are. A reader with a personal interest in you will naturally be interested in your point of view. But so might a "sympathetic" reader—someone whose interest in your point of view is sparked by the fact that they share something in common with you: they have a similar background, or a similar major in college, or a similar role in their family; they have experienced a similar event or crisis or phase in their life; they hold similar attitudes or beliefs; in short, their frame of reference (see Chapter 1, pp. 45–46) coincides with yours in one or more ways.

In this chapter, we will ask you to express your point of view to such a "sympathetic" reader by writing about a pattern of thought or feeling that you have traced in your journal.

TASK: WRITING AN ESSAY BASED ON YOUR JOURNAL

The task for this chapter is to write an expressive essay on a series of connected entries and what they reveal about you, about how you see things and why you see them as you do. The revelation may surprise you in some way: perhaps the entries confirm something that you already knew but that you did not realize you would focus on so much when you began keeping your journal; perhaps the entries indicate something new about you of which you were unaware.

We suggest that, as you write, you use the private voice of your journal in order to offer a complete and characteristic expression of yourself. Write for an audience of readers who are sympathetic to and interested in your self-revelation because they too are involved in self-discovery.

In the remaining sections of this chapter, we discuss how patterns of thought and feeling can emerge in a journal; how you might clarify your point of view by tracing these patterns; how you might formulate a general statement about an emerging pattern, a statement that could point you to the subject of a possible essay; and how to move into your rough draft and then revise your essay.

WRITING YOUR ESSAY

Generating Ideas: Tracing a Pattern in Your Journal

When you read over your journal, you are likely to notice that certain concerns come up again and again, or certain moods recur, or certain ideas get examined, reexamined, and reexamined again. Maybe you enjoy a particular kind of music, and so you write about it regularly in your journal. Maybe you have been feeling down lately, and this is reflected in the way you perceive and write about your daily experiences. Maybe you are intrigued by what you are learning in a particular class, and so you repeatedly devote space in your journal to raising questions and formulating opinions about that subject.

The patterns that weave through your journal may be obvious or subtle. But even the most obvious will hold subtleties of meaning. It is one thing to note that you are an avid sports fan. It is quite another to puzzle out what this means about you, what a pattern of references to sports in your journal reveals about you as a unique individual.

Look, for example, at the following series of entries, written by a poet named Margaret Ryan during her pregnancy. There is an obvious pattern here in terms of subject; the writer was, naturally, preoccupied with being pregnant. But what are the more subtle patterns of thought and feeling? What kind of complexities of personality emerge? What might the writer conclude about herself and about her attitude toward being pregnant, after reading these entries?

As you read through her entries, make a list of the different things Ryan says about her body, or about her family, or about her work, or about her new baby. Note when and why she is positive and/or negative. What do these patterns reveal about the personal and the social implications of her pregnancy?

October 3

Odd, I haven't written since I learned I am pregnant. I've been withholding my mind from it, trying not to think about it, not to intellectualize it to death. Life does not all happen above the neck but happens in the belly, the breasts. Morning sickness since the third or fourth week—awful heaving, nausea; still, knowing I am not sick is a comfort. Breasts tender as bruises, swollen, my nipples darken, little nightfalls. Stretch marks. I fear the deformity of my body and the almost physical need I have to write.

My family is excited about the baby. Mother is prouder of this than of anything I have ever done—degrees, honors, publications, jobs. Timmy, who has two children of his own, is more excited than when Mary told him she was pregnant. "My baby sister is going to be a mother," he keeps saying. "My baby sister." Eileen, who had three children, is all unalloyed joy. But my other sister, Anne, who has no children, who has had her uterus removed because of cancer, is frankly envious. When she recovers enough to be civil, she asks me if I'm frightened, if I think I'm well enough.

The women in my husband's family have stopped asking me about my work. Though I am producing my first videotape, they talk to me only of my pregnancy. How much weight have I gained? Do I still throw up in the morning?

October 31

In Atlanta to attend a sporting goods meeting I produced. The baby is my carry-on-luggage, the size of my crooked thumb. It is lonely at night in my hotel, but I go to sleep thinking of the baby travelling with me, and I am comforted.

November 6

The cleaning woman is thrilled that I am pregnant. She tells me stories: about her daughter's breech birth, and how she was in labor for three days before finally having a Caesarean. About the birth of her own fourth child, who was coming before the doctor got there, and how the nurse tried to hold the child in with a towel, pressing against its head, and about the child's neck breaking.

November 8

I am working on a tedious project with a sweet but tedious old man. He wants me to come in at 7 A.M. to view football footage for his presentation. I don't want to so I tell him I am three months pregnant and don't feel so well in the mornings. He tells me his daughter has just given birth to his first grandchild, and that he has carefully monitored her pregnancy. He tells me I must be careful. He becomes sweet and tractable—apparently it's no longer necessary for me to view footage at all, much less at 7 A.M.

Another man I work with accuses me of wanting to have things both ways, of unfair tactics. He says, how can you be a feminist yet use pregnancy to get special treatment, to make your clients behave? I tell him that in baseball, anyone who doesn't steal a base when the chance arises is considered a fool.

November 23

Thanksgiving. My mother-in-law gives me a pat on the rump and says, Look at the little pregnant lady. You're carrying behind. It's going to be a girl. I feel like a herd of cattle. It angers and humiliates me to be treated like this. I tell my mother about it later on the phone, and she says, It'll get worse. Wait until the baby's born. It will have Steven's nose, her hair, his sister's eyes. You'll feel as if you had nothing to do with it. This news does not thrill me, but it does comfort me to know that my mother also went through it, and that she understands.

December 14

Christmas approaching, and the anniversary of my father's death. Nineteen years this year. I still wear the wool shirt I inherited from him when he died. Though I am 4 1/2 months pregnant, it still fits. Odd, how many of my clothes still fit—bras, slips, sweaters—though finally my jeans won't zip. It's as if I always bought everything a few sizes too large, as if I were still that fat unhappy eighth grader who wore a size 16 dark-brown tent. I look forward to getting my figure back—I miss being slim. My face seems more beautiful now—perhaps as a consolation for my lack of shape below. Round, Steven says, asked to describe my shape. And I am round, a pear. (I used to think of souls as pear-shaped when I was in first grade, white and pear-shaped, and black spots indicated sins.)

January 7

I am in the sixth month of my first pregnancy, and I feel like running away. I feel as I've not made good use of my (relative) freedom while I've had it, and sometime in early May, it's all going to disappear. I feel panicky and desperate. But what would running away solve? What does it ever solve? I would still be carrying this child with me, and perhaps more important, I would still be carrying this paralyzed will.

I would lack as much freedom in Paris as I do here—perhaps I would even be less free there, because my tongue would be tied. Here, at least, I can voice my distress, and am at least sometimes understood.

January 9

Last night I dreamt of loving and wanting to marry a very wealthy man. Apparently, the only difficulty was the fact that I was pregnant by another man. My pregnancy is interfering with my happiness, the union of myselves? Perhaps. But really, only if I let it. It is too late now to reconsider this child— and I think that if I could, I would probably choose to have it anyway. But it is certainly not too late to make myself happy, to take care of myself.

January 10

Carole has invited me to participate in a writer's conference at her college in Georgia, to read my poems, give workshops, talk about writing for money. The conference is in April—my ninth month. I said, Let me think about it, let me ask my doctor, not wanting to say no. This is the chance I've been waiting for, hoping for, for years. This morning I asked my doctor. He said, Going won't make anything happen, but if I were you, I wouldn't take the chance. I've spent the day feeling sorry for myself, talking to Sally, who thinks I shouldn't let anything stop me, and Steven, who definitely feels I shouldn't go. Already the child is impeding my career. But who can I blame? Not the child; not my husband; not the fates. I decided to have this baby, and like a responsible adult I now must live with the decision. I took a long walk by the river this afternoon, a continuity. And I realize that this child I carry, my health and safety, are more important to me than anything else. I spoke to Carole this evening, and told her I couldn't make it, to try me again next year.

—Margaret Ryan

Try rereading your journal now, with an eye to those entries that seem to form a pattern, an obvious pattern of subject, or some more subtle pattern of emotions, perhaps, or ideas. Once you begin to trace a pattern, you can look for other entries that fit into it or have a bearing on it in some way, that offer explanations about it, for example, or that even seem to contradict it. In order to generate some ideas for the essay in this chapter, you might try to look for a series of entries that surprise you, that teach you something new about yourself, or that reveal you to be more interested in or absorbed by something than you would have guessed you were.

It is possible, of course, that a pattern will fail to emerge clearly in your journal. In this case you might use one of the exercises below in "Some Practice in Tracing a Pattern in Your Journal" to develop a topic. Or, you could work with a single entry, completing the story of an event or experience, for example, and speculating about the causes that led you to write about it in your journal in the first place.

SOME PRACTICE IN TRACING A PATTERN IN YOUR JOURNAL

1. Reread the entries in your journal that relate different encounters that you have had with others during a period of at least a week, in school, at work, or at home. Is there any pattern to these encounters? For example, was there a kind of forced casualness with other students, an unexpected tenseness at home, or a pleasing sense of friendship at work? What do these various encounters say about you and your social relations? Is there anything inconsistent in your different responses to other people?

2. Select an entry that describes one experience you have had recently — a lucky occurrence, an accident, an unexpected encounter. Then reread your journal, looking for other entries that are related to the first, either because they comment on it directly or because they express feelings and thoughts that are comparable with the feelings and thoughts you expressed about the experience. What light does the pattern that you trace shed on the meaning of the first experience for you?

3. Has a public issue, local or national or even international, captured your attention lately? Trace your references to and comments on this issue in your journal. How has the issue affected you personally? What contributions might you make to general opinion about the subject?

4. How often have you written in your journal about a class you are taking this term: about the subject matter, the teacher, the reading assignments, the other students? Review any entries that refer to your schoolwork this term. What do these entries reveal about you as a student or about some aspect of your college experience so far?

Addressing Your Audience: The Sympathetic Reader

Reacting to Another's Point Of View.   Consider all that Margaret Ryan expresses about herself in her journal. Note, for example, her various and at times contradictory feelings — uncertainty, comfort, fear, humor, reluctance, vanity, acceptance. She does not fill the old stereotype of the mother-to-be, blushing with pride and happiness in anticipation of the new arrival. How might you characterize her frame of reference? How might you most accurately describe her point of view towards her pregnancy?

Give some thought as well to your own response to these entries. Were you a "sympathetic" reader of them? Why or why not? Certainly, you do not have to be pregnant to appreciate Ryan's journal entries. In what other ways might your frame of reference coincide with hers? Do you find her point of view unique, or is it one you can easily identify with?

Expressing Your Point of View.   Your own point of view towards one or another subject may emerge suddenly in a single journal entry or, as is perhaps the case with Margaret Ryan, subtly in the pattern of thought and feeling that weaves through many entries. Notice how, in the next example, a student explores her point of view towards a sociology class through a series of journal entries:

Feb. 5th '88

I wanted to start my journal later but chances are that I'll be busy so I'll do it now. I think I'll write my journal about my sociology class. I have more interesting classes, but I am hoping that things would happen in my sociology class so that I would no longer view it as somewhat boring but I'd look forward to it. Unlike my Biology, Human Growth and Development and other classes, I find it particularly difficult to concentrate in my Sociology class. Maybe it's the environment, or possibly, it's difficult for me to concentrate on the course simply because the teacher is boring. Also, there are many students in the class so there is a somewhat strained rather than a relaxed atmosphere. I'm expecting things to get better since sociology is an interesting course and I do look forward to studying it and learning as much as I can.

Feb 8th '88

There was not much improvement in my sociology class today, but I think I've come closer to the source of my problem. First of all my professor has a slight accent and a hiss ends his words. From where I sit in the middle of the class I hear the hiss more than I hear the actual words. In my sociology class tomorrow I have decided to sit further to the front of the class.

In addition, we change rooms for every sociology class so presently I cannot associate my class with a specific surrounding. A fact that is somewhat comforting is that very few questions are asked in the class and there are blank looks in the eyes of other students beside myself; so here I would like to assume that the problem is not with just me and my inability to understand the class, but it may be other factors which affect not only me but other students in the class.

Feb 12th '88

I've had two sociology classes since my last class entry. Well I have made attempts to improve my concentration on the course, and fortunately they help. Sitting at the front of the class has helped me to hear and understand the professor better and to concentrate on what he says. In my most recent sociology class, I heard a student saying that he thought that the class was difficult and his ability to understand the work was decreasing. He also said that he did not know what he'd do when the time comes for an exam. The student beside him agreed. I was honestly surprised, I mean, this guy asked the most questions in the class and I thought if anyone understood the teacher, it was him. Actually, I felt proud of myself since I was now learning quite a bit from the class and I found the way to help myself.

Feb 17th '88

My sociology class has become more interesting in that I can now understand the lectures better. Maybe I should try to figure out as much as I can about my professor from my observations. Well, I can say that he tries very hard to make himself understood. He gives good explanations and examples of some of the terms he uses. Sometimes he goes all out to try to make the student understand that which is being taught. I can remember in my last class he was trying to show us that even though we may not understand some foreign language we may be able to understand slightly what is being said by the facial expression, body posture, and tone of voice used by the person. I simply think that with a different voice, Dr. Jones would have been an excellent professor.

Feb 26th '88

My day started with a Biology exam which was not too bad. I hope I could get an A, but I'm not raising my hopes too high. I remember last semester in my psychology class I had always expected to make over 90, and my results were always in the 80's and I got only one 90. Anyway my day was fine. I enjoyed my classes, and was not as tired as I thought I would be. I have been able to concentrate better in my sociology class. I hope that I would be able to do so for the rest of the semester. Unfortunately, I have not been studying my sociology as I should. Maybe it's because of lack of motivation, but I intend to catch up by reading more of the textbook and studying the notes on a more detailed basis. I feel more confident about the class and my ability to make an "A," but I know that it would take a lot of input on my part, since I want to be prepared when I get my first exam which would not be for a couple of weeks yet.

This student has actually made her point of view one of the subjects of her entries. You may have done the same. Or you may find in reading over a series of journal entries that you could have expressed your point of view more fully and consciously.

SOME PRACTICE IN EXPRESSING YOUR POINT OF VIEW

1. Rewrite a previous journal entry so that it ends in a way that you find more satisfying or pleasing to your view of yourself. What kind of changes did you make? Would another reader be able to see through your deception?

2. Are there any previous entries that now appear to you false or inaccurate, either because you failed to observe carefully or because you willfully distorted the "facts"? Rewrite, this time giving a more reliable account and adding an explanation of the inaccuracies, along with a summary of the differences in the two versions.

3. After you write an entry about an experience, write another in which you see yourself as a writer would see you going through the same experience. Change the narrative point of view (the voice telling the story) from the personal "I" to the impersonal "he" or "she." What differences are there in the two versions? What possible advantages are there in this change?

Try now to write out a clear statement describing the point of view you seem to take in the series of entries you have chosen to write your essay about. Think about what sort of readers might prove a "sympathetic" audience for your essay, about how their frame of reference might coincide with yours. Doing so should help you not only to write more authentically but also to formulate the shaping idea of your essay more completely.

In order to generate your statement, you might need to combine two or more sentences from different entries, or you might have to write an entirely new sentence describing your overall point of view. In either case, the following exercises may help:

Expressing Your Point of View About a Series of Journal Entries

1. Write a commentary on one of your previous entries in which you related your feelings and thoughts about an emotional confrontation with another person, a recent experience you have had, a public issue that has captured your attention, or a class that you are taking this semester. Do you see the subject now in the same way you did when you first wrote about it? Explain why or why not, referring to other journal entries that might help illustrate or clarify your answer.

2. As you read through your journal, underline words or phrases that refer to one specific subject: a person, a place, a situation, an idea. Why have you been writing about the subject? What have you been saying about it? What does your focus on this subject express about yourself?

Arranging Your Essay

Finding a Shaping Idea. Margaret Ryan (see pp. 50–52) does not offer any overall assessment of what her journal entries reveal. But she might. In the contradictions of feeling that her private voice expresses, for example, she might find a key to the shape or structure that the pattern of her entries unfolds. Perhaps they tell us something about the ironies of modern motherhood. Perhaps they tell us about the ambiguities involved in pregnancy for an individualistic woman in any age.

Is there a sentence in Ms. Ryan's journal or one you could formulate yourself that captures, for you, the essential meaning of what she has written? Selecting or creating such a sentence about one or another pattern in your journal is a way of discovering what we will call a shaping idea. In writing the essay for this chapter, you will need to formulate such a shaping idea, one that can crystallize for you the main point of your essay.

Since different people approach the writing process in different ways, we cannot say that there is a single best time to come up with a shaping idea. Some people may put together a rough formulation before they begin writing out their first draft. Others may not settle clearly on a shaping idea until they are writing or even revising their draft. But, as you read over the material you have collected from your journals, you should start thinking about what your shaping idea might be. (See "Focus on Form: Stating a Thesis," pp. 72–75.)

Now take a look at the following series of entries from the journals of the nineteenth-century American essayist Henry David Thoreau. What kinds of patterns do you find tie the entries together? How thoroughly does Thoreau seem to reveal his private voice? What sort of shaping idea might you formulate about the significance of this set of entries? Consider how your answer to this last question accords with the main point of the essay by Thoreau that follows and that was in part structured out of the writer's journal entries.

From *The Journals of Henry David Thoreau*

[From Volume 1 (undated)]

Twenty-three years since, when I was five years old, I was brought from Boston to this pond, away in the country,—which was then but another name for the extended world for me,—one of the most ancient scenes stamped on the tablets of my memory, the oriental Asiatic valley of my world, whence so many races and inventions have gone forth in recent times. That woodland vision for a long time made the drapery of my dreams. That sweet solitude my spirit seemed so early to require that I might have room to entertain my thronging guests, and that speaking silence that my ears might distinguish the significant sounds. Somehow or other it at once gave the preference to this recess among the pines, where almost sunshine and shadow were the only inhabitants that varied the scene, over that tumultuous and varied city, as if it had found its proper nursery.

Well, now, tonight my flute awakes the echoes over this very water, but one generation of pines has fallen, and with their stumps I have cooked my supper, and a lusty growth of oaks and pines is rising all around its brim and preparing its wilder aspect for new infant eyes. Almost the same johnswort springs from the same perennial root in this pasture. Even I have at length helped to clothe that fabulous landscape of my imagination, and one result of my presence and influence is seen in these bean leaves and corn blades and potato vines.

[1841]

[Dec.] 15. Wednesday. A mild summer sun shines over forest and lake. The earth looks as fair this morning as the Valhalla of the gods. Indeed our spirits never go beyond nature. In the woods there is an inexpressible happiness.

. . .

The trees have come down to the bank to see the river go by. This old, familiar river is renewed each instant; only the channel is the same. The water which so calmly reflects the fleeting clouds and the primeval trees I have never seen before. It may have washed some distant shore, or framed a glacier or iceberg at the north, when I last stood here. Seen through a mild atmosphere, the works of the husbandman, his plowing and reaping, have a beauty to the beholder which the laborer never sees.

. . .

I seem to see somewhat more of my own kith and kin in the lichens on the rocks than in any books. It does seem as if mine were a peculiarly wild nature, which so yearns toward all wildness.

. . .

When I see the smoke curling up through the woods from some farm-house invisible, it is more suggestive of the poetry of rural and domestic life than a nearer inspection can be. Up goes the smoke as quietly as the dew exhales in vapor from these pine leaves and oaks; as busy, disposing itself in circles and in wreaths, as the housewife on the hearth below. It is contemporary with a piece of human biography, and waves as a feather in some man's cap. Under that rod of sky there is some plot a brewing, some ingenuity has planted itself, and we shall see what it will do. It tattles of more things than the boiling of the pot. It is but one of man's breaths. All that is interesting in history or fiction is transpiring beneath that cloud. The subject of all life and death, of happiness and grief, goes thereunder.

[1842]

Jan. 5, Wednesday. I find incessant labor with the hands, which engrosses the attention also, the best method to remove palaver out of one's style. One will not dance at his work who has wood to cut and cord before the night falls in the short days of winter; but every stroke will be husbanded, and ring soberly through the wood; and so will his lines ring and tell on the ear, when at evening he settles the accounts of the day. I have often been astonished at the force and precision of style to which busy laboring men, unpracticed in writing, easily attain when they are required to make the effort. It seems as if their sincerity and plainness were the main thing to be taught in schools, — and yet not in the schools, but in the fields, in actual service, I should say. The scholar not unfrequently envies the propriety and emphasis with which the farmer calls to his team, and confesses that if that lingo were written it would surpass his labored sentences.

Who is not tired of the weak and flowing periods of the politician and scholar, and resorts not even to the Farmer's Almanac, to read the simple account of the month's labor, to restore his tone again? I want to see a sentence run clear through to the end, as deep and fertile as a well-drawn furrow which shows that the plow was pressed down to the beam.

[1846]

July 5. Saturday. Walden. — Yesterday I came here to live. My house makes me think of some mountain houses I have seen, which seemed to have a fresher auroral atmosphere about them, as I fancy the halls of Olympus. I lodged at the house of a saw-miller last summer, on the Caatskill Mountains, high up as Pine Orchard, in the blueberry and raspberry region, where the quiet and cleanliness and coolness seemed to be all one,—which had their ambrosial character. He was the miller of the Kaaterskill Falls. They were a clean and wholesome family, inside and out, like their house. The latter was not plastered, only lathed, and the inner doors were not hung. The house seemed high-placed, airy, and perfumed, fit to entertain a travelling god. It was so high, indeed, that all the music, the broken strains, the waifs and accompaniments of tunes, that swept over the ridge of the Caatskills passed through its aisles. Could not man be man in such an abode?

July 6. I wish to meet the facts of life—the vital facts, which are the phenomena or actuality the gods meant to show us—face to face, and so I came down here. Life! who knows what it is, what it does? If I am not quite right here, I am less wrong than before; and now let us see what they will have. The preacher, instead of vexing the ears of drowsy farmers on their day of rest, at the end of the week,—for Sunday always seemed to me like a fit conclusion of an ill-spent week and not the fresh and brave beginning of a new one,—with this one other draggletail and postponed affair of a sermon, from thirdly to fifteenthly, should teach them with a thundering voice pause and simplicity. "Stop! Avast! Why so fast?" In all studies we go not forward but rather backward with redoubled pauses. We always study *antiques* with silence and reflection. Even time has a depth, and below its surface the waves do not lapse and roar. I wonder men can be so frivolous almost as to attend to the gross form of negro slavery, there are so many keen and subtle masters who subject us both. Self-emancipation in the West Indies of a man's thinking and imagining provinces, which should be more than his island territory,—one emancipated heart and intellect! It would knock off the fetters from a million slaves.

[July 7, 1846]

I am glad to remember to-night, as I sit by my door, that I too am at least a remote descendant of that heroic race of men of whom there is tradition. I too sit here on the shore of my Ithaca, a fellow-wanderer and survivor of Ulysses.

. . .

The Great Spirit makes indifferent all times and places. The place where he is seen is always the same, and indescribably pleasant to all our senses. We had allowed only neighboring and transient circumstances to make our occasion. They were, in fact, the causes of our distractions. But nearest to all things is that power which fashions their being. Next to us the grandest laws are being enacted and administered. Next to us is not the workman whom we have hired, but ever the workman whose work we are. He is at work, not in my backyard, but inconceivably nearer than that. We are the subjects of an experiment how singular! Can we not dispense with the society of our gossips a little while under these circumstances?

From "Where I Lived, and What I Lived For"

At a certain season of our life we are accustomed to consider every spot as the possible site of a house. I have thus surveyed the country on every side within a dozen miles of where I live. In imagination I have bought all the farms in succession. . . .

. . .

The nearest that I came to actual possession was when I bought the Hollowell place, and had begun to sort my seeds and collected materials with which to make a wheelbarrow to carry it on or off with; but before the owner gave me a deed of it, his wife—every man has such a wife—changed her mind and wished to keep it, and he offered me ten dollars to release him. Now, to speak the truth, I had but ten cents in the world, and it surpassed my arithmetic to tell, if I was that man who had ten cents, or who had a farm, or ten dollars, or all together. However, I let him keep the ten dollars and the farm too, for I had carried it far enough; or rather, to be generous, I sold him the farm for just what I gave for it, and, as he was not a rich man, made him a present of ten dollars, and still had my ten cents, and seeds, and materials for a wheelbarrow left. I found thus that I had been a rich man without any damage to my poverty. But I retained the landscape, and I have since annually carried off what it yielded without a wheelbarrow.

. . .

I have frequently seen a poet withdraw, having enjoyed the most valuable part of a farm, while the crusty farmer supposed that he had got a few wild apples only. Why, the owner does not know it for many years when a poet has put his farm in rhyme, the most admirable kind of invisible fence, has fairly impounded it, milked it, skimmed it, and got all the cream, and left the farmer only the skimmed milk.

The real attractions of the Hollowell farm, to me, were its complete retirement, being about two miles from the village, half a mile from the nearest neighbor, and separated from the highway by a broad field, its bounding on the river, which the owner said protected it by its fogs from frosts in the spring, though that was nothing to me; the gray color and ruinous state of the house and barn and the dilapidated fences, which put such an interval between me and the last occupant; the hollow and lichen-covered apple trees, gnawed by rabbits, showing what kind of neighbors I should have; but above all, the recollection I had of it from my earliest voyages up the river, when the house was concealed behind a dense grove of red maples, through which I heard the house-dog bark.

. . .

All that I could say, then, with respect to farming on a large scale, (I have always cultivated a garden,) was, that I had had my seeds ready. Many think that seeds improve with age. I have no doubt that time discriminates between the good and the bad; and when at last I shall plant, I shall be less likely to be disappointed. But I would say to my fellows, once for all, As long as possible live free and uncommitted. It makes but little difference whether you are committed to a farm or the county jail.

. . .

The present was my next experiment of this kind, which I purpose to describe more at length; for convenience, putting the experience of two years into one. As I have said, I do not propose to write an ode to dejection, but to brag as lustily as chanticleer in the morning, standing on his roost, if only to wake my neighbors up.

When first I took up my abode in the woods, that is began to spend my nights as well as my days there, which by accident, was on Independence day, or the fourth of July, 1845, my house was not finished for winter, but was merely a defense against the rain, without plastering or chimney, the walls being of rough weather stained boards, with wide chinks, which made it cool at night. The upright white hewn studs and freshly planed door and window casings gave it a clean and airy look, especially in the morning, when its timbers were saturated with dew, so that I fancied that by noon some sweet gum would exude from them. To my imagination it retained throughout the day more or less of this auroral character, reminding me of a certain house on a mountain which I had visited the year before. This was an airy and unplastered cabin, fit to entertain a travelling god, and where a goddess might trail her garments. The winds which passed over my dwelling were such as sweep over the ridges of mountains, bearing the broken strains, or celestial parts only, of terrestrial music. The morning wind forever blows, the poem of creation is uninterrupted; but few are the ears that hear it. Olympus is but the outside of the earth every where.

I was seated by the shore of a small pond, about a mile and a half south of the village of Concord and somewhat higher than it, in the midst of an extensive wood between that town and Lincoln, and about two miles south of that our only field known to fame, Concord Battle Ground . . .

. . .

Every morning was a cheerful invitation to make my life of equal simplicity, and I may say innocence, with Nature herself. I have been as sincere a worshipper of Aurora as the Greeks. I got up early and bathed in the pond; that was a religious exercise, and one of the best things which I did. They say that characters were engraven on the bathing tub of king Tching-thang to this effect: "Renew thyself completely each day; do it again, and again, and forever again." I can understand that. Mornings bring back the heroic ages. . . . The Vedas say, "All intelligences awake with the morning." Poetry and art, and the fairest and most memorable of the actions of men, date from such an hour. All poets and heroes, like Memnon, are the children of Aurora, and emit their music at sunrise. To him whose elastic and vigorous thought keeps pace with the sun, the day is a perpetual morning. It matters not what the clocks say or the attitudes and labors of men. Morning is when I am awake and there is a dawn in me. Moral reform is the effort to throw off sleep. Why is it that men give so poor an account of their day if they have not been slumbering? They are not such poor calculators. If they had not been overcome with drowsiness they would have performed something. The millions are awake enough for physical labor; but only one in a million is awake enough for effective intellectual exertion, only one in a hundred millions to a poetic or divine life. To be awake is to be alive. I have never yet met a man who was quite awake. How could I have looked him in the face?

We must learn to reawaken and keep ourselves awake, not by mechanical aids, but by an infinite expectation of the dawn, which does not forsake us in our soundest sleep. I know of no more encouraging fact than the unquestionable ability of man to elevate his life by a conscious endeavor. It is something to be able to paint a particular picture, or to carve a statue, and so to make a few objects beautiful; but it is far more glamorous to carve and paint the very atmosphere and medium through which we look, which morally we can do. To affect the quality of the day, that is the highest of arts. Every man is tasked to make his life, even in its details, worthy of the contemplation of his most elevated and critical hour. If we refused, or rather used up, such paltry information as we get, the oracles would distinctly inform us how this might be done.

I went to the woods because I wished to live deliberately, to front only the essential facts of life, and see if I could not learn what it had to teach, and not, when I came to die, discover that I had not lived. I did not wish to live what was not life, living is so dear; nor did I wish to practise resignation, unless it was quite necessary. I wanted to live deep and suck out all the marrow of life, to live so sturdily and Spartan-like as to put to rout all that was not life, to cut a broad swath and shave close, to drive life into a corner, and reduce it to its lowest terms, and, if it proved to be mean, why then to get the whole and genuine meanness of it, and publish its meanness to the world; or if it were sublime, to know it by experience, and be able to give a true account of it in my next excursion.

. . .

Our life is frittered away by detail. An honest man has hardly need to count more than his ten fingers, or in extreme cases he may add his ten toes, and lump the rest. Simplicity, simplicity, simplicity! I say, let your affairs be as two or three, and not a hundred or a thousand; instead of a million count half a dozen, and keep your accounts on your thumb nail. In the midst of this chopping sea of civilized life, such are the clouds and storms and quicksands and thousands-and-one items to be allowed for, that a man has to live, if he would not founder and go to the bottom and not make his port at all, by dead reckoning, and he must be a great calculator indeed who succeeds. Simplify, simplify. Instead of three meals a day, if it be necessary eat but one; instead of a hundred dishes, five; and reduce other things in proportion. . . .

. . .

The preacher, instead of vexing the ears of drowsy farmers on their day of rest at the end of the week, — for Sunday is the fit conclusion of an ill-spent week, and not the fresh and brave beginning of a new one, — with this one other draggletail of a sermon, should shout with thundering voice, — "Pause! Avast! Why so seeming fast, but deadly slow?" I perceive that we inhabitants of New England live this mean life that we do because our vision does not penetrate the surface of things. We think that that *is* which *appears* to be. If a man should walk through this town and see only the reality, where, think you, would the "Milldam" go to? If he should give us an account of the realities he beheld there, we should not recognize the place in his description. Look at a meeting-house, or a court-house, or a jail, or a shop, or a dwelling house, and say what that thing really is before a true gaze, and they would all go to pieces in your account of them. Men esteem truth remote, in the outskirts of the system, behind the farthest star, before Adam and after the last man. In eternity there is indeed something true and sublime. But all these times and places and occasions are now and here. God himself culminates in the present moment, and will never be more divine in the lapse of all ages. And we are enabled to apprehend at all what is sublime and noble only by the perpetual instilling and drenching of the reality that surrounds us. The universe constantly and obediently answers to our conceptions; whether we travel fast or slow, the track is laid for us. Let us spend our lives in conceiving then. The poet or the artist never yet had so fair and noble a design but some of his posterity at least could accomplish it.

Let us spend one day as deliberately as Nature, and not be thrown off the track by every nutshell and mosquito's wing that falls on the rails. Let us rise early and fast, or break fast, gently and without perturbation; let company come and let company go, let the bells ring and the children cry,—determined to make a day of it. Why should we knock under and go with the stream? Let us not be upset and overwhelmed in that terrible rapid and whirlpool called a dinner, situated in the meridian shallows. Weather this danger and you are safe, for the rest of the way is down hill. With unrelaxed nerves, with morning vigor, sail by it, looking another way, tied to the mast like Ulysses. If the engine whistles, let it whistle till it is hoarse for its pains. If the bell rings, why should we run? We will consider what kind of music they are like. . . .

. . .

Time is but the stream I go a-fishing in. I drink at it, but while I drink I see the sandy bottom and detect how shallow it is. Its thin current slides away, but eternity remains. I would drink deeper; fish in the sky, whose bottom is pebbly with stars. I cannot count one. I know not the first letter of the alphabet. I have always been regretting that I was not as wise as the day I was born.

Working in a Peer Group

A peer group is usually made up of four or five students who will work together throughout the semester and so come to know one another's thinking and writing fairly well. One function of a peer group is called collaborative learning. Members of a group join together in order to understand a subject better—to share one another's questions and answers; to look at the material from one another's point of view.

Try working with a group now on tracing a pattern in Thoreau's journal entries and identifying the shaping idea of his essay. One way to begin is by exchanging journal entries that each member of the group has written on Thoreau. Another is by *brainstorming*—working together to make a list of details from, comments on, and questions about Thoreau that the group can then discuss: Which details that attracted the notice of group members seem to form a pattern of thought or feeling? Which comments shed light on the main point of "Where I Lived, and What I Lived For"? (See "Generating Ideas: Brainstorming" in Chapter 6, pp. 234–240, for more information about brainstorming.)

It is not a bad idea to designate one member of the group as the recorder and have him/her take notes on these matters as the group discusses them. Having such a record to refer back to can help keep the group discussion focused and on track.

Writing Your Rough Draft

As Thoreau writes about his reasons for going off to live in a cabin in the woods, he also offers a critical point of view on his fellow New Englanders. His opinion of their life is as much a subject of his essay as his description of his own life.

When you begin writing your rough draft, you may find yourself narrating your daily experiences, like Margaret Ryan does in her journal. You may express yourself through your views on a subject of interest to you, like the student who wrote in her journal about her sociology class. You may, like Thoreau, find it useful to employ both strategies in putting together an essay based on a series of entries from your journal.

Before you start, take a look at the next series of entries from the journal of a student who chose to write her essay for Chapter 2 about Thoreau. What do these entries reveal about the student's frame of reference? What point of view do they suggest she might take toward Thoreau? Consider how well your answer accords with the shaping idea of the rough draft that follows and also how well this draft of the student's essay expresses the private voice of her journal entries.

FROM THE JOURNAL OF ANGELA S.

2/4

I think I will enjoy English 101. I thought it would be so structured, with grammar, spelling, punctuation etc. as in grammar school and high school. It seems this will not be so. The professor wants us to express our thoughts and feelings on paper as they come. I like that. It is like having a diary when I

was a little girl. I feel like a writer, writing a book. I look forward to reading the essays also. I never read Walden, although
I've heard people speak of it.

2/5

After class today I took my boys to lunch at Pizza Hut with a
friend Josie and her son. We had a great lunch. It is different at
Pizza Hut than going to a Pizzeria. Everyone liked the thick
crusted pies. We put the kids in one booth and we sat in
another. It was good to socialize with a friend. A little gossip, a
little about our kids, a little about work, school, homelife, etc.
Sometimes we get so caught up in our little worlds, we forget to
take time out for ourselves. As the saying goes, "Take time to
smell the flowers." I must learn to relax and stop being so busy.
Sometimes I have to be busy, social obligations, other times I
make myself busy so I just won't have time to think about
things.

2/6

I'm looking forward to going to bed tonight. I had a busy day,
went shopping in the morning and worked three hours in the
afternoon. When I came home, I drove my son to the Burger
King to eat with some friends and I picked him up when he
was through and drove everyone home. It is a tough life growing
up and being an adult. Plus I am an adult with two boys ages 7
yrs. and 11 yrs. I worry about them growing up to become mature adults and I worry about myself. The future seems so far
away and so uncertain. Take one day at a time.

2/15

I get a certain peace when I attend Mass on Sunday. I have
stayed away from the church about six months. A lot of things
happened over the summer and I felt angry at God so I stayed
away. I just felt I had to. Really as Catholics we are taught to
go to God when in trouble and doubt. I just felt angry and
stayed away. I returned two weeks ago because I felt ready. I felt

good to be there and participate with other people. I am not ready to receive Holy Communion. In time I will receive. Right now I am content with just going to Mass.

2/21

I am having a peaceful Saturday. My kids are at Grandma's house for the day. I am really enjoying the peace and quiet. I cleaned my house a little, listened to some albums, washed my car and ordered Chinese food for dinner. It is good to have time to be alone sometimes. I like it. Just cleaning and relaxing without the children running around. It is good for them to be away at their grandparents house too. Their grandparents enjoy them for the day too.

4/1

I read White's "Once More to the Lake" and enjoyed it very much. I like when White writes about nature. He writes about things I don't even notice in life and with such clarity. How do writers do that? I like the line about the minnows, "each minnow with its individual shadow, doubling the attendance." I remember looking into a lake, Lake George to be exact, and seeing minnows and thinking about the shadow giving the minnows a larger group. I could never put that into words. I like to read about White's experiences. They are not boring--they are light and gay and at the end he always puts in a deeper meaning to make you think, as his last line, "As he buckled the swollen belt, suddenly my groin felt the chill of death." White felt time catching up with him. He was once the boy pulling on icy trunks and probably his Dad was watching him. Now he was the Dad watching his son. Wasn't it yesterday... Where does time go? He remembers things and sights well when he was a boy and now he is a man experiencing pleasures of summer through his son. Pleasures still felt familiar such as the exact dragon fly on his fishing rod, the lake looking exactly the same, the cabin smelling the same as when he was a boy and the thunderstorm creating the same sensations of awe and fear. It couldn't be that so much time has passed since those summers. Everything felt the same and looked the same. Only White knew he was older and wiser, and not the better for it.

4/10

Finally the weekend is here. Time to relax a little and also to do some chores. It takes organization and routine to run a home and two boys. My boys have practice tomorrow for Little League. Joey is in the Midget division. Both boys love sports especially baseball and swimming. I hope that continues into the teenage years. Very important sports and children. Even if I had girls I would put them into sports and extra curricular activities. Children need something extra than going to school. They need a social life too. My boys are pretty active and sociable. Louis my seven year old makes friends instantly. He just goes over to a child and asks to play or to see the toy he is playing with. Joey who is 11 years old is more apprehensive about new friends. He approaches carefully.

My boys at least have each other. I am very proud of that. It is sad to be the only child in a family. Especially my family was just my Mom and me, no Dad. Dad was on the road most of the time. He was to become a country-western singer and guitarist. But in reality, my Mom and Dad had problems and my Dad preferred not to be home much. I missed him a lot. I was quite lonely also with no brothers or sisters. My boys have each other but they always like a friend to come along with us. I don't mind. When a friend comes along, they fight less.

4/27

I returned to school today. It was good to be back. The professor is into Thoreau and we are discussing his works. Very interesting person. I don't particularly enjoy his work. It is hard reading, not quite as entertaining as E.B. White. I don't chuckle much reading Thoreau. He is always criticizing the world in which we live, always scrutinizing. He does get you thinking though. I have no idea what kind of paper I will write. This is going to be a hard one.

THOREAU

village	pond
society	nature
corrupt	find yourself
dirty	escape to the country
polluted	clean air
	get lost--lose your way

Paradoxical--conflicts in himself
pattern of life destroys you
not fulfilling yourself.

HENRY DAVID THOREAU
(Rough Draft of Student Essay)

I have just experienced my first glimpse of Thoreau through his writings in his journal, essays and his famous "Walden." I can now see why he is cited as a famous writer, philosopher and naturalist. In the twentieth century, professors and students are still analyzing and discussing his work. Thoreau was a profound man with deep thoughts and feelings.

I knew when I read White's review of Thoreau it would be favorable. In some aspects Thoreau and White are alike; both men loved nature, animals and the beauty and naturalness of the land. The future of the world with her hopes of prosperity and inventions did not appeal to them. The moment did.

I do not agree fully with White's praise of Thoreau. In his sentence, "To reject the book because of the immaturity of the author and the bugs in the logic is to throw away a bottle of good wine because it contains bits of cork." If you have ever tasted wine with bits of cork in it you will find the wine flavorful, but the bits of cork annoying. That is how I find Thoreau. Some of his philosophies are tasteful and entertaining like the wine, but his methods are eccentric, contradictory and annoying as in the cork.

Thoreau's drum does not beat for me and I will attempt to explain why through White's review. White said, "I think it is of some advantage to encounter the book at a period in one's life when the normal anxieties and enthusiasms and rebellions of youth closely resemble those of Thoreau, etc." I agree. Thoreau writes for the young, the adventurer, the rebel. A person who has nothing to lose, someone who can follow his dreams with no one to worry about but himself. He can afford to fight society. Thoreau's followers to me must be self-centered and selfish. They can say, "I am unhappy with life and its problems and I am going off somewhere (to the woods) to find myself and be happy, to hell with the rest of you." How many men and woman can really do this? Can you totally disengage yourself from your family, friends and the world? I for one cannot. I am an adult with a goal, responsibilities and people depending on me. I cannot go off to the woods, nor do I want to. I like to live in a house with more than one room, a door with a lock on it, gas heat, electricity and all the comforts therein. I enjoy learning new things and getting an education. I cannot picture living in a world without a president, a government, religion and rules and regulations. I enjoy reading my newspaper, talking on the phone and the news these inventions bring me is never boring. Alas, Thoreau would say I am truly lost, brainwashed and conditioned by my society. Maybe I am, but I am happy. I have felt life's dance and it is a fast step, but I am determined to keep up the pace and make it my way. All of us cannot be Thoreaus. His readings, excerpts and journal entries sound pleasant, but are they realistic and can his philosophies endure? Thoreau only lived in the woods for two years and then he returned to live out the rest of his life in the civilized world. Why? His answer to us is this: "Perhaps it seemed to me that I had several more lives to live and could not spare any more time for that one." I find that very contradictory to his philosophies. Maybe Thoreau too was consumed by tradition and conformity and had had enough of "Walden" after two years.

On the positive side, a lot of his writings are God-like and I feel are good examples in which to live. For example, Thoreau said, "Rather than love, than money, than fame, give me truth"; "Goodness is the only investment that never fails." He goes on in different passages to praise the poor, oppose the rich, gratify working with one's hands at a hard day's labor, eating and living simply. Thoreau wanted to be a simple man. I find some of Thoreau's philosophies basic to life, others are non-traditional, far-fetched, contradictory and an attempt to change society to his liking. Thoreau does get readers thinking about their lives and what they want out of it. I find that is the key to "Walden." Each one of us finding our own niche and our own inner peace and happiness. I have found my "Walden," and I do try to stop and smell the flowers along the way.

In the section on "Rewriting" (see pp. 80–87), we will look at the response to this draft by other students in the writer's class and then at how the writer revised her essay. Now, you should get ready to write your rough draft of the essay assignment in this chapter.

First, like a professional writer, choose an appropriate time and place to write. Set aside a specific place for writing: a quiet area of your home that has a table or desk, a special part of your dorm room, or the least distracting desk in your local or school library. Also set aside a block of two or three hours, possibly the same time each day, when you do not have to worry about other responsibilities. This kind of regularity — call it discipline, if you wish — can help you to create a mood for writing. Now, all you need are the tools of the trade: lots of paper, pencils, pens, and/or a typewriter or word processor.

Once you have written through to the end of your first draft, stop writing and take a long break — twenty-four hours, if time permits.

FOCUS ON FORM: STATING YOUR THESIS/ WRITING AN INTRODUCTION

Conventions of Form and Style

It is a matter of convention that, in general, English speakers agree to use the letters CAT to spell a word designating a small, furry house pet that meows and catches mice. There are groups of English speakers who, operating under a specialized or localized set of conventions, mean something different by the word: a nurse speaking to a doctor may use CAT to refer to a piece of X-ray equipment; on some parts of the Mississippi River, a CAT is a fish!

Like vocabulary and even, to some degree, grammar, the form and style with which we express ourselves are matters of convention—agreed upon standards for facilitating communication. You may be quite used to adopting a more formal, less colloquial style in school or at work than at home or among your peers. You probably would not take leave of a prospective employer with a high five and a "Later, Dude!"

As there are conventions which work best among friends, so there are among academics. Each discipline—each subject of study in the academic world—generates its own specialized conventions: thus, chemists write lab reports while sociologists write case studies; yet both tend to adopt a scientific style, using inductive logic to test their hypotheses. At the same time, there are general conventions that seem to facilitate communication between students in any discipline.

The Focus section in this and subsequent chapters will introduce you to some of these more general academic conventions. We begin with matters of form that should help you emphasize the unity and coherence of your ideas.

Stating a Thesis

As part of this chapter's task, we asked you to review your journal as a source of ideas about yourself. In order to write an essay about what you learned from your review, you need to formulate a main point around which to organize your ideas. We suggested that you look for a pattern of thought or feeling in your journal entries, then produce a single statement expressing what this pattern is and what significance it holds. Doing this, you are employing one possible strategy for developing a main or shaping idea.

Let's look, for example, at how the student who wrote about Thoreau employed this strategy. Rereading her journal, she noticed the following things about herself:

1. She had looked forward to reading Thoreau at the start of the semester, but then found him hard reading.
2. She wrote repeatedly about her family obligations, the pressures and demands but also the pleasure and self-satisfaction she felt in raising her two sons.
3. She expressed a need to take time out from her busy schedule for herself.
4. She holds quite traditional values. She deeply appreciates religious, social, family life.
5. She did not enjoy reading Thoreau, who is critical of "the world in which we live" and advises a kind of escape in order to fulfill ourselves.

What patterns are there in the entries that express these things about her? Probably a number of significant ones. As the student began to write her rough draft, she focused on the contrast between her values and Thoreau's, her way of life and his. She did not find a single statement about this in her journal. She worked towards such a statement by writing a draft about her journal entries as well as other reading she had done in Thoreau and E. B. White.

A clearly stated shaping idea may leap out at you from an entry in your journal. But if not—and this is more likely to be the case—you also may need to begin writing a rough draft in order to generate such a statement.

A good shaping idea—the main point or *thesis*, as some writers call it—defines the subject and expresses what the author wants us to understand about that subject, what the writer's point of view towards the subject is. Which sentence or sentences might you choose from the student's rough draft on Thoreau as the shaping idea? Here are some possibilities:

1. Thoreau was a profound man with deep thoughts and feelings.
2. In some aspects Thoreau and White are alike; both men loved nature, animals and the beauty and naturalness of the land.
3. I do not fully agree with White's praise of Thoreau.
4. Thoreau's drum does not beat for me and I will attempt to explain why through White's review.
5. All of us cannot be Thoreaus. His readings, excerpts and journal entries sound pleasant, but are they realistic and can his philosophies endure?

The first sentence is perhaps too vague. It fails to explain what Thoreau's "deep thoughts" are. Nor does it express what the writer wants to say about Thoreau's thoughts. Sentence 2 is better in the first respect. But the writer's point of view towards her subject does not really come out until sentence 3 which, like sentence 4, is phrased in the first-person singular and so directs our attention to the expressive purpose of the essay. Sentence 4 not only indicates the author's attitude but also lets us know something about how the essay is organized to make its point.

Statement 5 is perhaps the most specific version—in question form—of what the author wants us to understand about her subject. But since she does qualify her criticism of Thoreau at the end of the draft, sentence 3 may finally be the most accurate way to phrase her shaping idea—a simple, concise, direct expression of her purpose, subject, and point of view.

Once you determine your shaping idea for a paper (note that you may need to write a number of drafts before you settle on a shaping idea), you will want to state this idea in a single declarative sentence (not a phrase, not a question) that contains both your subject and the main point that you are making about it. Your statement of your shaping idea should be precise, unambiguous, and grammatically correct. We advise that, as an apprentice writer, you place this statement in the first paragraph or two of your essay (although, as you will see, many skilled writers state the shaping idea elsewhere in the essay). By writing your main thought in one sentence and placing it at the beginning of your essay, you will be better able to keep focused during additional drafting stages, and you will give your reader a clear sense of the purpose of your essay at the outset.

SOME PRACTICE WITH STATING A THESIS

1. From the following ideas, select the one that you think will create a sharply focused and organized essay and explain why you think so:

   a. Major league baseball is boring.

   b. Fast food is dangerous to your health.

   c. I don't like science fiction movies.

   d. My high school biology teacher's persistent encouragement helped me to overcome my learning disabilities.

2. From the following related statements, form a clear thesis statement that will explain what they refer to:

   a. The neighborhood bars have been turned into "eating boutiques."

   b. Old, established small businesses have been driven out by high rents.

   c. Young executives and trendy singles have displaced the original ethnic mix of immigrant families.

   d. Tenements and row houses are being replaced by luxury high-rise condominiums.

   e. Schools and playgrounds are in need of restoration and expansion.

   f. Traditional political alignments are being revised.

3. Expand the following subjects to form thesis statements. For example, "teenage alcoholism" to "Teenage alcoholism can be reduced if the drinking age is raised to twenty-one."

a. Nuclear energy plants . . .

b. The decline of the American automobile industry . . .

c. Television soap operas . . .

d. The nursing profession . . .

Stating a Thesis About a Series of Journal Entries

Try now to put together a thesis statement for your essay for Chapter 2. Pick the five sentences from your rough draft that come closest to summarizing the overall pattern of thought and feeling that is expressed by your journal entries. Perhaps one of these sentences expresses the pattern well. Perhaps you want to combine two or more of these sentences in order to describe the pattern fully. Once you have made this sentence as clear as possible, combine it with the sentence that you wrote describing your point of view toward the pattern you have traced in your journal (see "Expressing Your Point of View," pp. 54–57), in order to put together your thesis statement.

Writing an Introduction

The first paragraph or two in a final draft should do more than simply note the writer's shaping idea. In the introduction to a paper, a writer has the chance to use his or her imagination to attract the interest of an audience and lead them to read on. There is no one right way to do this. But it can be helpful to keep the following things in mind.

A good introduction should take into account the intended audience — who they are and what their point of view towards the subject might be. (See "Addressing Your Audience: The 'Intended' Readers" in Chapter 3, pp. 97–102 for more about this.) For example, consider this introduction:

Yo, Bro, who would ever figure that I would ever attend college--a place of higher education. Certainly not I for one. I mean, I didn't even pass or graduate from high school. But to my and everybody else's amazement, here I am, studying in a college.

The informal, chatty tone might draw the interest of the student's peer. But would it lead a corporate employment officer to read on?

By contrast, the next introduction might appeal to a more general audience. The style is less colloquial—less typical of the relaxed conversation of a particular group. Also, the story-like invitation to find out what happened is hard to resist:

On March 3, 1990, the day of my sister's Bat Mitzvah, I had a catharsis. I finally revealed the true story of Harry Apricot. But wait, I'm getting way ahead of myself.

Let me take you back to a warm May day in 1982, when Harry became a member of the family. It was carnival time at ye olde nursery school. My sister, ping pong ball in hand, deftly hauled it into a waiting plastic cup.

"Ah!" said the teacher running the booth, "You have just won a goldfish; you can go pick it out from the tank."

More often than not, a brief piece of narration or description will work to hook the reader:

I was sixteen years old. It seems so long ago. A lifetime. I woke every morning to look her in the eye and tell her just how much I hated her. One morning I actually spit in her face. I've never felt such pure hate for anyone in my life. I was totally consumed by it.

I can understand why she didn't have any friends. She was such a miserable person. Always depressed, always angry. She felt guilty, she was sorry for ruining my life. She was an ugly, fat slob of a person.

Things are different now. Every morning I rise and go in the bathroom to brush my teeth and there she is staring back at me from the mirror. Her face is the same -- but different. She smiles now.

Note here how the shaping idea is, at best, hinted at in the surprise twist of the third paragraph. If the writer's purpose is simply to recall a personal experience, there may be no need to do more. At the same time, a clear, precise statement of the main point may be another means of raising a reader's curiosity, even in the most personal of essays:

"Hi! Whats up?" That's the way that most of my journal entries begin. My journal has become a place for me to let my pen and feelings be free and to run wild. I was really surprised to see some of the things that got into my journal.

Considering the fact that my journal started out as an English assignment, it was really fun. In a very short time, my journal turned into so much more.

Ed called me up one Saturday morning, asking me to drive upstate with him and watch him skydive. I'd been wanting to go with him for a while, but I never had the chance, and since it was a nice spring day and I wasn't planning on doing anything else, I went. I didn't know it at first, but this was one trip that would make me reevaluate my views on life and death.

There are as many effective introductory strategies as your imagination can create. A time-tested one is to begin with a question that the rest of the essay will then answer:

"I want you to keep a journal," the professor said. What is a journal? Why keep one? The idea of writing a paragraph or two every day was scary to say the least. If you haven't noticed by now, I'm not exactly Russell Baker or E.B. White. I'm not even Dr. Seuss. But I did it. My first entry dated 2-7-90 was a brief summary on a piece of writing entitled "Murder in Baltimore." It was so brief that I did not include the author's name. What's the point?

Another effective strategy is to start with a strongly voiced opinion:

Recently, I was informed that my seven-year-old daughter, Geri-Anne, was having difficulty in school. Her trouble stemmed from her inability to grasp learning how to read by the use of phonics. My initial reaction was to take the child out of public school and place her in a private one. I had always believed that the teachers employed by the New York City Board of Education were only overpaid and overglorified baby-sitters. This idea was reinforced when I visited my daughter's class last year, and the teacher calmly walked out of the class to go to the bathroom, neglecting to separate two little boys who had their hands around each other's throats.

In totalitarian countries the ordinary citizen has no problem with his government, he simply does what he is told. Paradoxically, in a free society, one is often worried and frustrated by government policy. For E.B. White in 1941, the issue was segregation; for Henry Thoreau in 1845, it was slavery and the war in Mexico; and for me today, it is Central America. Thus two essays, White's "On a Florida Key" and Thoreau's "On the Duty of Civil Disobedience," held a special impact for me, leading me to decide that discretion is the better part of valor.

In the above two examples, the writers introduce their ideas about subjects beyond themselves—about the quality of New York City teachers in one case, the issue of civil disobedience in the other. Each offers a well-stated thesis that a reader may expect the body of the essay to explain or argue. There is a formal quality about such an introductory strategy. It is typical of writing addressed to members of groups that communicate in highly conventionalized formats—scientific researchers, for example, or members of the business community, or students and teachers.

At times, such introductions may take on a programmatic quality, telling a reader not only what the essay's subject is but also how the essay will develop that subject:

In this paper I will discuss the theme of birth and death in Oedipus Rex. I will explain how Oedipus experienced being born to things he had never known and then destroyed by the things he had just found out. By way of conclusion, I will show how in one day Oedipus lived his whole life over and saw what was to become of him and his family.

This strategy of letting the reader know, step-by-step, how the paper will unfold can be useful especially when introducing a lengthy research paper. But for shorter papers it may be heavy-handed, in which case an introduction that simply explains the shaping idea in some detail is probably a better alternative:

> Everyday we look at people and make generalizations about them. We judge them by their appearance. But this is wrong. In "The Song of the Banana Man," the speaker was very anxious to tell who he is, due to the remarks of the tourist. This poem is about how a tourist saw the Banana Man and how the Banana Man saw himself. It made me understand how one should be proud of what they are and what they have.

Like the shaping idea, the introduction may develop at any point in the writing process. But it is always a good idea to finalize the introduction last, after you have written and revised the rest of the essay.

SOME PRACTICE IN WRITING AN INTRODUCTION

1. Select a topic that you are studying in another course. From your class notes or journal entries, write down several ideas that you have on this subject and begin to develop them into a shaping idea. For example, in business you are studying the Federal Reserve Board and its role in controlling the money supply. You might write down some of its duties and then formulate a statement that would work these ideas into a shaping idea ready to be developed into an essay. Write a possible introduction for such an essay.

2. Read the following two versions—rough draft and revision—of a student's introduction. Explain what changes the student made, why you think she made them, and how effective they are in your view.

> When I looked over a series of journal entries, I found that I worry about everyone else's troubles as if they were mine. I worry so much, I often end up feeling miserable about my own life. When I finally devote time to my own problems, they are usually huge or they seem minute compared to the worries of my friends.

> After reviewing a series of journal entries I found that I often worry about other people's problems as if they were mine. I found that I devote so much time to other's troubles, I end up neglecting my own until they become huge, or until I realize that my problems are minute compared to many other people's. It seems to me that my friends, their friends, casual acquaintances, and even total strangers have always sought me out to play their "Dear Abby."

Writing an Introduction for Your Essay on a Series of Journal Entries

Read over your rough draft, then either revise your opening paragraph or write a new one in order to introduce your thesis statement in a way that will hook your readers, arousing their curiosity and motivating them to read on. Try writing an introduction by using one of the following strategies: beginning with a brief piece of narration or description, telling an anecdote or setting a scene; beginning with a question that the rest of the essay will answer; beginning with a strongly voiced opinion.

As your audience for this assignment are readers who are sympathetic to and interested in your self-revelation, you probably can make your introduction fairly informal. But you do want your readers to appreciate you *as a writer*, so you should work to create as imaginative a hook as possible.

In the section on "Rewriting" that comes next, examine the final draft of the student essay on Thoreau. Note how the writer has revised both the introduction and the conclusion of her rough draft. How has she improved these important parts of her paper in revision? How well does her revised introduction convey the shaping idea and create an imaginative hook for the reader?

REWRITING

Obtaining Feedback on Your Rough Draft

After you have written your rough draft and have taken a break, you can resume the writing process by revising what you have written. Of course, you may have already made changes as you were writing the first draft, and in fact, your copy may look much worked-over already. However, looking again at what you have written after a rest period will help you to read your paper as your audience will read it: more or less objectively.

In a sense, another self will take over, a self that may have been looking over your shoulder as you wrote the rough draft, keeping track of what you were doing, evaluating how each part fits in with the whole, noting problems and possible solutions, criticizing, and encouraging. This other self needs to be given full permission to comment at this point, because it has a distance that you didn't have while immersed in writing the essay.

Your teacher may also wish to play the role of the "other self" at this point and to comment on your first try. And a third source of feedback is your peers. Your instructor may ask a group of your classmates to react to your paper, or if not, you may select a group yourself to do this job. Do not be afraid to show your work to your classmates. You can assume that most students have passed through similar periods of self-discovery and will be sympathetic to you.

Regardless of who provides the feedback — you, your instructor, your peers, or any combination — your paper should receive an evaluation that answers the following four questions of the "Audience Response Guide."

AUDIENCE RESPONSE GUIDE

1. What do you think the writer wanted to say about him/herself in this paper? What is his or her purpose in writing? What does he or she want the paper to mean?

2. How does the paper affect a sympathetic reader?

3. How effective has the writer been in expressing his or her point of view? What are the strengths of the paper? What are the weaknesses?

4. How should the paper be revised to better fulfill its purpose and meaning?

Working in a Peer Group on Revising

It is important that you take your role as commentator on your peer's writing seriously. The more thoughtful the feedback you can give to your peers, the better they will be able to revise their work. But there will be a benefit to you as well — for if you can learn to be an effective reader of others' writing, you may also become a more effective reader of your own writing and hence better able to revise, when necessary, on your own.

There are a number of different ways the group may critique one another's work. Each student may read his/her paper to the group. The paper should be read slowly, two times. Then the members should answer the questions of the Audience Response Guide to the best of their ability. If a specific audience is designated by the task, try to assume the role of that audience and listen to the paper from its point of view.

Alternatively, writers may xerox enough copies of their paper so that each group member has one to read. Everyone then will read, rather than listen to, the same paper at the same time and again write out answers to the Audience Response Guide questions.

In either case, the group may choose additionally to discuss a draft after writing down their comments about it and giving them to the author of the draft; or the group may discuss possible revision strategies after everyone's draft has been read.

A third alternative is to have each member of the group give a draft to the person on his or her right, who reads the draft, answers the Audience Response Guide questions about it, then passes it on to the group member on his/her right.

The group should devote a solid twenty minutes to reading and commenting on each paper. Use the full twenty minutes. If you finish with a paper in less time, go back and elaborate on your answers to the Audience Response Guide.

One last point: To make the most of this sort of feedback, a writer probably should not be concerned with responding to the comments of a reader; rather the writer should consider whether or not each comment he/she receives can be useful in revising his/her paper.

Revision of Student Essay "Henry David Thoreau"

The following is a peer evaluation of the rough draft of the student essay "Henry David Thoreau" (pp. 69–71) in response to the four questions of the Audience Response Guide.

1. The writer wanted to express how her views are different from Thoreau's. Although at the end she said she likes some things about Thoreau, she can't live her life as he did. Also she thought he contradicts himself.

2. The essay was impressive for the way the writer made a strong stand about who she is and what is important to her. Her private voice really came through--her sense of responsibility and the way she enjoys society. She also has interesting ideas about Thoreau.

3. She conveyed her differences from Thoreau well because she made her own point of view so clear. One strong point was the way she used specific examples of what she likes about her own life and how she compares herself to the sort of people Thoreau writes for. But she could make her overall view of Thoreau clearer. Her introduc-

tion really doesn't say anything. Her last paragraph doesn't explain well what she does like about Thoreau.

4. The shaping idea should be emphasized at the start. The ideas of the last paragraph could be expressed more clearly.

Here is a revised version of "Henry David Thoreau." In what ways has the writer responded to the group's suggestions, as well as to her own sense of how the paper should be improved?

HENRY DAVID THOREAU

I knew when I read White's review of Thoreau it would be favorable. In some aspects Thoreau and White are alike. Both men loved nature, animals, and the beauty and naturalness of the land. The future of the world with her hopes of prosperity and inventions did not appeal to them. The moment did.

I do not agree fully with White's praise of Thoreau. He writes, "To reject the book because of the immaturity of the author and the bugs in the logic is to throw away a bottle of good wine because it contains bits of cork." But if you have ever tasted wine with bits of cork in it you will find the wine flavorful but the bits of cork annoying. That is how I find Thoreau. Some of his philosophy is tasteful and entertaining like the wine, but his methods are eccentric, contradictory, and annoying as the cork.

Thoreau's drum does not beat for me and I will attempt to explain why through White's review. White said, "I think it is of some advantage to encounter the book at a period in one's life when the normal anxieties and enthusiasms and rebellions of youth closely resemble those of Thoreau." I agree. Thoreau writes for the young, the adventurer, the rebel. A person who has nothing to lose, someone who can follow his dreams with no one to worry about but himself. He can afford to fight society. Thoreau's followers, to me, must be self-centered and selfish. They can say, "I am unhappy with life and its problems and I am going off somewhere (to the woods) to find myself and be happy, to hell with the rest of you."

How many men and women can really do this? Can you totally disengage yourself from your family, friends, and the world? I for one cannot. I am an adult with a goal, responsibilities, and people depending on me. I cannot go off to the woods, nor do I want to. I like to live in a house with more than one room, a door with a lock on it, gas heat, electricity, and all the comforts therein. I enjoy learning new things and getting an education. I cannot picture living in a world without a president, a government, religion, and rules and regulations. I enjoy reading my newspaper, talking on the phone, and the news these inventions bring me is never boring. Alas, Thoreau would say I am truly lost, brainwashed and conditioned by society. Maybe I am, but I am happy. I have felt life's dance and it is a fast step, but I am determined to keep up the pace.

All of us cannot be Thoreaus. His writings sound pleasant, but are they realistic and can his philosophy endure? Thoreau only lived in the woods for two years and then he returned to live out the rest of his life in the civilized world. Why? His answer to us is this: "Perhaps it seemed to me that I had several more lives to live and could not spare any more time for that one." I find that very contradictory to his philosophy. Maybe Thoreau too enjoyed tradition and conformity and had had enough of Walden after two years.

On the positive side, a lot of his work offers good advice. For example, Thoreau said, "Rather than love, than money, than fame, give me truth" and "Goodness is the only investment that never fails." He goes on in different passages to praise the poor, oppose the rich, gratify working with one's hands at a hard day's labor, eating and living simply. Thoreau wanted to be a simple man, and I find some of his philosophy basic to life.

In any case, Thoreau does get his readers thinking about their lives and what they want out of life. That may be the key to Walden. Each one of us has to find our own niche and our own inner peace and thus happiness.

One obvious change that the writer made was to cut her first paragraph from the paper. Does this help give more emphasis to her shaping idea? She also breaks her final paragraph into two paragraphs and revises the phrasing to make it less wordy, more concise. How do these changes improve the essay? What other changes has she made in the body of the essay? Are they effective?

In this and subsequent chapters, once you have feedback from your other self, your instructor, or your peers, you can revise your rough draft.

Revising

Revising affects the content and organization of your essay. The revising that your other self, your instructor, or your peer group suggests you do will no doubt be one or more of six activities: cutting, adding, substituting, rearranging, distributing, or consolidating. The writer of "Henry David Thoreau," for example decided both to cut material out of her rough draft and to rearrange material in her final draft. Such revisions affect the meaning of the essay, some to a greater extent than others.

Each of these activities will receive a full discussion in a subsequent chapter, but in case you wish to move ahead when revising, we list the pages for each discussion:

Cutting, the following section

Adding, pp. 129–130

Substituting, pp. 179–180

Distributing, pp. 224–225

Rearranging, p. 267

Consolidating, pp. 317–318

Additional sections on revising in Chapters 8–11 focus on revision techniques for persuasive writing (pp. 377–378), to sharpen critical thinking (p. 444), for writing on research (pp. 503–505), and for writing about literature (p. 547).

Cutting.   When you write for yourself in your journal, you can be wordy or vague or irrelevant if it suits you. But when you write for others, for an audience, it is helpful to be concise, detailed, and to the point. Cutting or deleting words and phrases from a rough draft that are redundant, for example, that are needlessly repetitious, should make the writing more readable. Why write "in this day and age" when you can simply write "today"? Why begin a sentence with the phrase, "Personally, in my opinion," when you can give your opinion directly?

You may decide while revising a paper to cut out whole passages that you originally included, less because they contributed to the point of the paper, than because you simply liked what you said or sounded like in them. Might this be the case, for example, with the first paragraph in the rough draft of "Henry David Thoreau"?

The student writer of this essay did more than cut her opening paragraph when she revised her work. She rearranged the material by breaking her very long final two paragraphs into five shorter paragraphs; she substituted shorter, more direct phrasing for lengthy, poorly focused phrasing; and she clarified her conclusion. In each case, she worked to communicate in a more straightforward manner with her reader, to reveal herself and her thoughts as directly as possible.

When you revise, try to cut out vague, overused, and imitative words or phrases, as well as material that does not really help your reader understand the point you want to make, material that leaves your reader asking, "Why did the writer include this?" Such cutting can be as important to the success of your work as adding, substituting, or any of the other revisions you might choose to make.

Revising Your Essay About Yourself

Finally, recheck your paper for Chapter 2 by asking the following questions about it:

 Checklist to Consider in Revising an Essay About Yourself

1. **Do I express myself as directly and accurately as possible? How might I rephrase parts of the paper to better reflect my private voice?**
2. **Have I stated my shaping idea succinctly enough? Where does it appear in the paper? Is this the most effective placement?**
3. **Have I expressed my point of view in a way that might hold a sympathetic reader's interest? Do I need to clarify how such a reader's frame of reference coincides with mine?**
4. **Is my introductory strategy effective? How could my introduction offer a better hook for my reader?**

The Final Product

Presentation.   After taking a break, reread your revised essay for mechanical errors such as spelling, grammar, punctuation, and capitalization. Refer to the Handbook if you are uncertain about how to correct a mechanical error.

Appearance is the key at this final stage. Write neatly on good-quality lined paper, such as that from a loose-leaf notebook or a pad of lined paper. If you type your essay, choose a good-quality bond paper.

Write or type on one side of the page, leaving margins of one inch on all four sides. Number the pages after page 1 (which is not numbered) in the upper right-hand corner or in the middle of either the top or bottom of the page.

If you use a word processor, format the print-out so that there are one-inch margins on all four sides, the text is double-spaced, and the pages following page 1 are numbered.

Include a cover page, with your title in the middle, and your name, teacher, class and date in the lower right-hand corner.

Your Title.   A title fulfills two functions: it attracts your readers' attention and gives them some indication of your subject, although often the meaning of a title is not clear until the essay is read. Titles are fun to write: you can be as creative as you like. The title of the student essay here, "Henry David Thoreau," could be more attractive, although it does indicate the subject. With your class or your group, brainstorm some more interesting versions.

Proofreading.   By now, you might expect that your work is over. Not quite. One final step is necessary. You must now proofread.

Proofreading is reading your final copy to check for mistakes, omissions, and typos that might have occurred in the transcription from the revised essay to the final copy that will be submitted to your instructor. This process is a tedious one and should be undertaken at a time when you are alert and calm. It is advisable, if time permits, to proofread the draft at least three times. Make your corrections neatly and clearly.

1. Read slowly what is on the page, not what you think is on the page. Correct mistakes as you see them: spelling, punctuation, and so on.
2. Read again, out loud. Sometimes you will hear mistakes that you cannot see.
3. Read your essay backward from end to beginning, sentence by sentence. This procedure will relieve you of analyzing the content and will help focus on words and punctuation.
4. Skim from right to left and top to bottom, looking for misspellings and other errors.

BECOMING AWARE OF YOURSELF AS A WRITER

Make use of your journal to record your thoughts and feelings about the task for Chapter 2. As you write in your journal, consider the following questions:

1. Which parts of the essay that you wrote for Chapter 2 were generated by writing in your journal? Did you use any other means of generating material for your essay?

2. What effects did writing for an audience have on your attempts to be honest and authentic? What did you express about yourself in your essay? Did you change or hold back parts of your journal that contributed to the essay?

3. At what point in the process of writing did you come up with your shaping idea? What steps did you go through to do so? Did this idea change at all after you first formulated it?

4. In what ways did your shaping idea affect what you said and how you said it? In what ways was your shaping idea effective or ineffective? What did it make your audience feel or do? Was this result intended by you?

5. How do you feel about the peer feedback you received on your draft? Did it help you revise your essay in any significant ways? What were the most important revisions you made?

6. How much work did you do before you began to write your first draft? How long did it take you to actually write the draft? To revise it ? At what stages of the process did the work go smoothest for you? Can you explain why?

3

Writing About an Incident—Reporting an Experience

PURPOSE

When you write expressively, you focus on yourself as the subject. But depending on what you intend to express about yourself, the focus will broaden to take in other subjects as well. If you write about your experience of an event, for example, or your observation of an incident, you bear witness to what you saw and heard as well as to what you felt and thought. You may, in fact, express your feelings and thoughts more clearly to others; the more thoroughly you try to recapture an experience that gave rise to them, the more exactly you try to tell what happened.

One reason for this is that your audience will probably never share your attitudes and perspectives completely. There will always be a gap between you and even your most sympathetic reader. But if you convey the facts of your experience along with your impressions, reactions, and interpretations; if you report on what happened as vividly and concretely as a journalist reporting a news story, you offer a reader the opportunity to see and hear as you did and so share your responses with you.

The purposes behind such self-expression are often private—you share your experiences and observations with a reader so that he or she might know, or understand, or appreciate you better. But such writing can serve public aims as well. You might tell your side of a story, for example, to express your dissatisfaction with a product to its manufacturer; to recommend someone who did a job well for you; to process an accident claim with an insurance company.

Beyond such practical reasons, you may relate your experience of a particular incident because it holds a valuable insight into human experience in general. If you discover something about your individual self in writing about your experiences, you may also be discovering something that you hold in common with many other people.

We will ask you in your writing for this chapter to order a series of impressions, a group of details about a meaningful event in your life, so that a reader other than yourself can experience them in much the same way that you did. It will be helpful, in addition, to consider your reader's point of view along with your own, particularly as you try to determine what selection and arrangement of details will convey the essence of your experience most effectively.

TASK: WRITING ABOUT AN INCIDENT

To begin the task for this chapter, search your memory for an incident that you observed or were involved in that abruptly changed your mood or your thoughts, that suddenly caused you to reassess your feelings toward or attitudes about something, and that thus in some way affected your life. This may be an event that impressed you when you were younger, or it may be a more recent event. Try to focus on an incident that occurred over the course of a few hours, or a few days, but not beyond a week; then record the incident in detail, clarifying for the reader the important aspects of the experience, as well as what you think its significance was for you.

We suggest that you devote special attention to specific details in order to make your account of the incident vivid and authentic. You will want to collect as many details as possible, to gather the facts. Also, you will want to pay attention to the arrangement of your details, so that you can offer your readers a clear sense of the chronology of the incident, of the order in which the events of your story unfolded.

Your peers are the most likely audience for this essay. They may have experienced an incident similar to yours and therefore are likely to prove both interested and sympathetic readers. But even though you will be writing to an audience whose frame of reference is similar to your own, you cannot expect the group as a whole to understand all of your perceptions and feelings automatically. Subtle differences in point of view will have to be bridged, as they always must be, even between the closest of friends.

In the remaining sections of this chapter, we will discuss how you, as an essayist, can generate ideas with the tools that professional reporters use when they investigate the facts of a newsworthy incident, how to build bridges between you and your intended reader, how to arrange the details of your incident, how to move into your rough draft, and how to revise your essay.

WRITING YOUR ESSAY

Generating Ideas: The Journalist's Questions

The 5 W's and How. The news reporter often gets started on a story by asking six questions about whatever incident he or she is covering. The six questions are introduced by the following words:

who   when
what   how
where   why

If you examine the following article which was taken from the *New York Times* of February 21, 1962, you will notice how the answers to the journalist's questions are integrated into it.

50,000 on Beach Strangely Calm as Rocket Streaks Out of Sight

"He's in the Hands of the Lord Now," Woman Says — Hilarity Erupts at Word of Recovery — 900 Pound Cake Is Cut

by Gay Talese
Special to the New York Times

COCOA BEACH, Feb. 20 — At 9:47 A.M. today the rocket rose slowly over the beach like a high infield fly, but moments later it was streaking out of sight, leaving a thin, white and fluffy vapor trail.

Fifty thousand spectators stood along the beach watching the climbing Atlas carrying Lieut. Col. John H. Glenn Jr. into orbit. Some cheered, some clapped. An elderly woman said solemnly: "He's in the hands of the Lord now." Most remained silent.

They watched the sky until there was nothing left to see except pelicans and sea gulls, and until the rocket's vapor trail had lost its shape and become a floating, upside-down question mark.

Then they slumped on the beach to hear the rest by radio, or returned to homes, motels or taverns to watch on television, as millions were doing around the country.

Not until 3:01 P.M., when the astronaut had gone thrice around the earth and had been safely retrieved from the Atlantic by the destroyer Noa, did the hilarity begin. Faces lost their looks of concern.

Cheers Go Up

A 900-pound cake, the size and shape of the Mercury capsule, was sliced. And a huge movie-type marquee along the main road lighted up to say: "Our Prayers Were Answered."

There were cheers around poolsides when it was reported that President Kennedy would come here to honor Colonel Glenn. By twilight, Cocoa Beach's jazz bands and cash registers were swinging and ringing in merry syncopation.

"Oh, he done it, buddy, he done it, so let's have a drink," John Godbee of Deland called to the crowd around him at the Vanguard Bar.

"I said 'go, go, go,' and seeing it go gave me a glorious feeling," John Pellegrino, the Vanguard's bass player, said.

"It was just undescribable," said Mrs. Thomas J. Knight of Baltimore, relaxing on the beach.

"Undescribable is right," Mrs. Howard Balliet of Orlando agreed with a nod.

Though the countdown was halted a few times, there was an undefinable feeling of optimism. People seemed to sense that this was finally the big day, that after ten postponements the orbital shot would leave the launching pad.

At 9:23, radios in cars, on people's shoulders and in their pockets could be heard everywhere saying "T Minus 22, and counting . . . T minus 20 minutes, and counting . . . T minus 17 minutes . . . T minus 13 minutes."

Now there was a vast quiet along the beach. People stood on sand dunes, motel porches, trucks and trailers, all with eyes fixed on the missile gantries, towering like a mirage eight miles north over the waves.

"Rosemary!" screamed a mother, almost hysterically, grabbing her fleeing child. "Get over here."

"T Minus 3 minutes," went the radio. "T minus 30 seconds . . . 20 seconds . . . 10 seconds . . . 5 . . . 4 . . . 3 . . . 2 . . . ."

"Lift off!" somebody yelled.

"Look, it's up!"

"Go, baby go!" a man cried, clenching his fist. But the great majority watched silently as the missile moved slowly skyward. There was a red flame behind it as it began to climb. Then it was just a blazing speck, rising higher and higher, with only the vapor trail marking the ascent for those without binoculars.

Pensiveness Noted

The lack of delirium, the pensiveness of the thousands who stared toward the sky were hard to interpret. The flights of Comdr. Alan B. Shepard and Capt. Virgil I. Grissom here had brought rousing demonstrations. Each had evoked cheers usually heard after a game-winning world series home run.

Perhaps the crowd was quieter because it had been let down by the postponements, or maybe it thought there was no cause for cheering until Colonel Glenn was safely returned.

There was noticeable excitement at 2:30 P.M. when somebody at the Holiday Inn's television set shouted, "He's coming down, he's on his way down!"

Nine-year-old Michael von Fremd of Bethesda, Md., jumped up and down.

"I knew things would go right today," said Mrs. Marion Fega of Los Angeles.

A few hours later, the happy trailer caravans began to leave the beach, where some had been entrenched more than a week. The drivers shook hands and promised to write.

"Today was the highlight of my life," said Ernest Perkins, gunning his motor and heading back to Toledo.

We can reconstruct the six questions asked by the writer of this article, as well as the answers:

1. Who (or what) was involved in the incident? (Fifty thousand spectators and Lieut. Col. John H. Glenn Jr.)
2. What was the incident? (The lift-off of the Atlas rocket carrying Glenn into orbit; the journalist examines the reaction of the spectators.)
3. Where did the incident occur? (Cocoa Beach, Florida.)
4. When did the incident occur? (February 20, 1962, at 9:47 A.M.)
5. How did the incident occur? (The rocket rose slowly, then streaked out of sight; the spectators watched silently, for the most part, with looks of concern.)
6. Why did the incident occur? (The journalist speculates that the crowd might have been quiet because they had been let down by postponements or because they thought that there was no cause to cheer until Glenn had returned safely.)

Notice how the six questions generate additional questions, which contribute more details to the report:

1. Who were some of the spectators, by name and age?
2. What were the spectators doing during the liftoff? What did they do and say afterward?
3. Where did the spectators come from? Where did they go after the lift off?
4. When did the crowd leave the beach?
5. How did the crowd's reaction compare to the reaction of the spectators at previous space shots? How did the crowd's reaction change after Glenn had landed?

Note: Although in this chapter's task we ask you to use the journalist's questions to report on an incident, you can also use these questions to develop ideas and information about many different topics. For example, if you were asked in an economics course to write an essay on a topic such as inflation, you might use the journalist's questions to develop information about what inflation is, who it affects and how, when and why it occurs, and so forth. Furthermore, although you may use all six questions in writing the narrative task for this chapter, other topics may require that you emphasize or focus on answers to only one or two of the questions. We encourage you, then, to use this method of generating ideas, along with others that we will introduce you to in later chapters, not only to complete the task at hand but also to develop ideas and information for other assignments in this and other courses.

SOME PRACTICE WITH THE JOURNALIST'S QUESTIONS

1. Read a newspaper article (preferably one that reports an event — a happening) and identify the answers to the journalist's six questions.

   a. Who?

   b. What?

   c. Where?

   d. When?

   e. How?

   f. Why?

2. Reread the article by Gay Talese and then analyze the reporter's impressions. Was his information about the thoughts and feelings of the spectators factual? To what degree did Talese include his own subjective thoughts and feelings in the article?

3. Using the journalist's questions, develop an account of an historical event. The event may have occurred in the recent past, such as the explosion of the space shuttle Challenger, or in a distant time such as the trial and sentencing of Socrates.

4. a. Use the journalist's questions in order to gather information about an incident that you either observed as an outsider or acted in as a participant. Choose an incident that is limited in time and space, a distinct piece of action.

   b. Either with your class, your peer group, or on your own, analyze the details that you have gathered: How concrete, how specific, are they? Which aspect of the incident did you gather the most information about: The who? The what? The where? The when? The why? Or the how? Are there any questions that you have left unanswered? Did you describe actions and objects only, or did you also describe thoughts and feelings?

   Using the Journalist's Questions in Writing an Essay. The journalist's questions can be used for writing essays as well as newspaper or magazine articles. The responses of the essayist, however, may differ in form and substance from those of the journalist. Whereas the traditional journalist usually writes under the pressure of a deadline, the essayist often has more time for contemplation and hence the opportunity to find longer and more fully developed answers to the six questions. Also, whereas a journalist is expected to record the facts as objectively as possible, an essayist is free to offer the most subjective insights into and interpretations of the facts.

The following questions are among those that an essayist may generate from the six basic ones:

Who What must the reader know about the person or persons involved in order to understand what happened? What objective details must be included: age, appearance, social status, economic status, family relationships? What subjective elements about the person(s) should be supplied: background, philosophy, values, emotions?

What What led up to the event? In what order did the stages of the event occur? Were there any foreshadowings of what was to come? What effect(s) did the event have, both immediate and long-range? What details must be included to convey the drama of the event to someone who was not there?

Where How many locations are involved? How much description of the location(s) does the reader require? What details will convey the scene?

When What time of day, what week, what year did the event occur? Of what significance was the date, the time of day, the weather?

How In what way did the incident happen? How involved a description of the process is necessary? What details are required?

Why Is the cause known for sure? Was there more than one cause? Was one person or thing more responsible than others? Can immediate causes be distinguished from distant ones? If there was no known cause, what interpretation can you bring to bear on the event? What general conclusions can be drawn?

Another major distinction between the essayist's responses and those of the journalist is the style in which they are written. The journalist tends to use a spare style, one stripped of those elements that personalize the essayist's work. Whereas the journalist tries consistently to sound direct, straightforward, and factual, the essayist may play more freely with such elements as tone of voice (see Chapter 1, pp. 37–45); complex and varied sentence structuring (see Chapter 5, pp. 212–222; Chapter 6, pp. 258–263; and Chapter 7, pp. 302–311); and comparisons such as metaphors, similes, and analogies (see Chapter 7, pp. 306–307; and Chapter 8, p. 364).

Whereas the journalist, then, is usually concerned simply with reporting an event, the essayist may utilize fuller, more subjective responses and stylistic embellishments to dramatize the event, inviting the reader to participate in it vicariously. Put another way, whereas the journalist usually *tells* what happened, the essayist often *shows* what happened.

Using the Journalist's Questions in Generating Ideas About an Incident.   Once you have decided on an incident to write about, begin recalling and recording as much specific and related information as possible about your subject. Use the six questions of the news reporter to discover relevant and telling details about the event. After you have generated information from the six basic questions, see if further questions arise, those subquestions that it is the luxury of the essayist to answer. Answer these as well. Do not worry if you seem to have a lot of information; when you begin to arrange your essay, you will probably discard some of it. If, however, you find that you lack specifics, that is cause for worry; you might need to go out and gather more information from other sources, such as relatives, friends, diaries, journals, and photographs.

Using Your Journal to Collect Details of an Incident.   Your own journal can be helpful here. It can be used, for example, as a reporter's notebook in which you gather details of incidents that you observe during the next few days and that seem like potentially good subjects for your essay. Or you can use the journal like a diary to probe your memory for incidents from the past worth writing about. In either case, if you collect details in your journal, you then can go back and read over them in order to assess your thoughts and feelings about how an incident affected you.

Double-Entry Journal.   One technique for assessing your thoughts and feelings recorded in a journal is to make *double-entries:* Divide each page of the journal into two columns. In the left-hand column, record the details of the incident: what happened, to whom, when, where, why, and how. In the right-hand column write about how particular details affected you and what role they played in the overall meaning of the incident for you.

Addressing Your Audience: The "Intended" Reader(s)

Because the purpose of most writing, with the exception of the personal journal, is to communicate something to another person, you may find that you can write more effectively when you know, as well as you can, with whom you are communicating. Your audience — the people you write for — can affect both what you write about and the way in which you write about it. Just as you have attitudes toward your subject, so will your audience, and unless you consider your potential readers' attitudes as well as your own, you may be unable to keep your readers' attention; you might even offend them.

For example, pretend that you are going to write an essay entitled "The Facts of Life." Your audience is a class of first-graders and their mothers. What sort of essay would you write? What material would you include? What material would you exclude? What sort of tone would you adopt?

Now change your audience. Pretend that you are writing the essay for a class of teenagers. Obviously, such an audience would be bored by the essay that you wrote for the class of first-graders. How might you write so as to capture the interest of the teenage students?

Your knowledge of either audience will, inevitably, be incomplete. How fully can you share a first-grader's frame of reference (see Chapter 1, pp. 45–46)? You may feel closer in age, experience, and attitude to a teenager. But how can you be certain that the point of view of individual teens will match your assumptions about a teenage point of view in general?

The truth is that in many cases you write less for an actual or "real" reader than for what we will call an "intended" reader — an imagined version of the audience that you want to communicate with. You should not be surprised if it turns out that some of the first-graders you write for show no interest in your essay or that some of the teenagers know more about your subject than you do. You should expect there to be a gap between the audience that you think you are writing for and the audience who actually reads your text.

Sometimes you can find out a lot about your potential readers by questioning them directly or learning about them from others. An article by a prominent sociologist, for example, about the increasingly conservative outlook of today's teenagers might lead you to reassess your own assumptions about a teenage audience.

There are other times, though, when you can only know your readers through the assumptions and inferences you make about them. And even if you are well acquainted with an audience, you cannot know everything about them and so must rely to some degree on inferences that may not always prove correct. If you are writing for a group of your peers, for example, as in the assignment for Chapter 3, chances are that despite similarities in age, occupation, even social status, the point of view of some members of the group will prove surprising because of the cultural and ethnic diversity of our society.

Nevertheless, thinking about your "intended" readers is useful. It may prompt you to seek more information about their frame of reference, to clarify what their point of view towards your subject might be. It often will lead you to make adjustments—some fine, some major—during the course of writing a paper.

One student, for example, about to write an essay for her classmates on her recently acquired ethnic pride in being a Lithuanian, came to realize that few of her readers had any notion of what this meant. She had to alter her expressive purpose by providing some exposition on what it meant to be a Lithuanian. Because the class did understand what it meant to become aware of one's ethnic identity, the writer could use this frame of reference to build on, and she gained some new understanding of her experiences by learning how others had responded to theirs. Perhaps she learned more about her subject and its relation to her life by having to see it as others would. She was able to gain a certain distance from her subject, to see it from the perspective of others, and finally to see where she could meet her readers on a common ground. These are essential advantages in considering your audience's point of view. They send you back to your writing with a sharpness and a clarity of purpose that you might not have gained otherwise.

SOME PRACTICE WITH A READER'S FRAME OF REFERENCE

1. **a.** Choose a classmate and construct his or her general frame of reference by asking the ten frame-of-reference questions:

      (1) How old are you?

      (2) Of what ethnic background are you? What economic or social class are you in?

      (3) Do you have a job or career? If so, what do you do? If not, what are your career plans?

      (4) Where were you born? Where do you live now?

      (5) What is your religious affiliation, if any?

      (6) Are you a member of a political party? If so, which one?

      (7) What roles do you play in your family?

      (8) What significant events have occurred in your life?

      (9) What are your hobbies or other leisure activities?

      (10) What are your goals in life?

    b. Using the information you gather, construct a brief biography of your classmate. If the responses to the frame-of-reference questions are not sufficient to construct a narrative, reinterview your subject in order to obtain fuller information. If necessary, prepare additional questions to ask.

    c. Have your classmate critique the biography you wrote. How accurate a portrait did you paint, in your subject's eyes? How might you explain any "inaccuracies" that your classmate points out?

2. What can you find out about the frame of reference of someone to whom you would feel uncomfortable asking some of the ten frame-of-reference questions, about a teacher, for example, to whom it might be tactless to ask questions about age, or economic background, or religious affiliation? Choose a course you are taking and phrase a set of questions you could ask the instructor about his or her knowledge of, attitude toward, and feelings about a topic discussed in the course. Which of the ten frame-of-reference questions might you also ask? How much can you learn about another's frame of reference this way?

SOME PRACTICE WITH A READER'S POINT OF VIEW

1. a. From the answers that you received when you interviewed your classmate, attempt to determine your classmate's attitude toward the following topics:

    Legalization of drugs.

    Environmental conservation measures.

    Nuclear energy.

    Nursing homes for the elderly.

    Military spending.

If the answers are not helpful, perhaps they were not specific enough. How might you reformulate your questions to elicit the information you need?

b. Now attempt to determine your classmate's attitude toward the incident you plan on writing about in your essay for Chapter 3. Have your classmate and/or your peer group critique the assessment you have made.

2. Each of the following passages offers a different impression of the same incident. Describe the point of view of the speaker in each case. What point of view might each take toward an incident you observed or were involved in recently? In each case, how would it compare with the point of view that you took?

a. This crazed maniac walked into the college cafeteria, picked up a boiling-hot plate of soup, and dropped it over the head of this gorgeous, innocent blonde. Everyone was simply mortified by this sickie's routine. He should get twenty years.

b. You should have seen the hysterical performance in the college caf yesterday. This clown poured some red stuff on his girlfriend's goofy bleached head and broke the whole place up. They should do their act on the stage — they were a riot.

c. A riot call placed from the Holbrook College Cafeteria was responded to immediately by Patrolman Hodges, who found Jack Jenkins, the alleged perpetrator, with an empty plastic dish standing next to the plaintiff, Betty Lou Jones, a student at the college. Several witnesses were questioned. An investigation is under way.

d. If you want some idea of today's college student, you should see what goes on in the cafeteria. Two students, I am told, acted in the kind of barbaric manner suggested in the movie *Animal House*. What can you expect with the kind of music they play over the loudspeakers there?

Making Inferences About Your Reader.   We regularly make inferences about other people, assumptions about what they are like or how they will react to us. We base these inferences on our observations of their appearance, conversation, and other aspects of their behavior. For example, you may decide that you want to make friends with one person but not with another, because of the first impression each makes on you. Based on what is undoubtedly partial evidence, you infer that one will be worth having as a friend yet the other will not.

As a writer, the inferences you make about your potential readers will help you adjust what and how you write so that others will understand and appreciate you better. Inference, in fact, may be the only way that you can easily and quickly determine vital information concerning the frame of reference and point of view of a large group of potential readers. With most groups, you can go a long way in inferring the answers to the ten frame-of-reference questions. You will, of course, have to generalize about the group and not record data about individual members. The general frame of reference of a group would include the following information:

1. Age
2. Ethnic background, education, and economic and social class
3. Occupation (or career plans)
4. Place of habitation
5. Religious affiliation
6. Political affiliation
7. Family structure
8. Significant experiences (shared by the group)
9. Leisure interest and activities
10. Goals

Of course, even when you don't think about it consciously, you are making assumptions about your readers whenever you write. Take a look at the information you generated with the journalist's questions about the incident that you intend to write about for this chapter's task. What sort of unconscious assumptions about your audience did you make in putting this information together? What parts of the incident did you assume they would be most interested in? Why? Did you assume that they already knew anything that, in reality, they might not? Did you focus on details that would appeal to some readers more than others, to your teacher, for example, more than to your classmates, or vice versa? What details might you need to explain more fully, so that someone who did not witness the incident will really be able to follow your narration?

SOME PRACTICE WITH INFERENCE

1. **a.** A certain student in your English class has freely voiced her opinions that children should be strictly disciplined, that marijuana use should remain illegal, and that juvenile offenders should be prosecuted as adults. Therefore it would be reasonable, if you were writing to her, to infer that she believes that society needs strict discipline. What do you think her point of view would be on the following issues? Formulate one or more statements on each topic that you think would represent her point of view:

   Alimony.
   A worker's right to strike.
   The draft.
   Children's rights.

   b. Now write a statement that assesses what her point of view might be toward the incident you are writing about for Chapter 3.

2. **a.** Using your class that has the largest enrollment this semester, infer the class's frame of reference. Then determine the point of view of the majority of the students on the following topics:

   Teacher-student relationships.
   Coed dormitories.
   The student newspaper.
   Abortion.

   On what basis have you inferred the group's attitude in each case?

b. Now write a statement summarizing your assessment of the group's point of view toward the incident you are writing about in your essay for Chapter 3.

Determining Your Audience's Point of View for Your Essay on an Incident.   As indicated in the description of the task (p. 90), you are writing this essay to be read by your peers—probably the members of your freshman composition class. Now using either direct questioning or inference, determine the frame of reference of your peers and hence how their point of view toward the incident that you are writing about might differ from yours. An incident that you found shocking, for example, they may feel more blasé about. Consider a student who wrote about the upsetting effect of finding her car vandalized on the city street outside her own house. She needed to find ways to bridge the gap between her point of view and that of an audience of her fellow students, most of whom, on the one hand, had not been similarly victimized and, on the other hand, were used to hearing about such acts of random violence both in the news and from their neighbors and acquaintances. For these reasons, they felt less shocked reading about the incident than the victim herself felt experiencing it firsthand. She had to look at the incident from their perspective as well as her own, in order to begin finding ways to help them understand and appreciate her response.

Your analysis of your audience should lead you to make adjustments not only in what you write but also in how you write it. Answering the following questions of the "Audience Analysis Guide" will help:

——— AUDIENCE ANALYSIS GUIDE ———

1. Who is my audience?
2. What is the frame of reference of this audience?
3. What point of view is my audience likely to have on my subject?
4. How do my own frame of reference and point of view differ from those of my audience?
5. How can I bridge any gap that exists between my audience's point of view and my own?

Arranging Your Essay: The Shaping Idea, Narration, and Exposition

Once you have discovered, through the journalist's questions, something to say about your subject and have formulated your answers to the "Audience Analysis Guide," you are faced with the problem of selecting and arranging the material in the order that best serves your purpose. You will want to formulate a shaping idea that indicates what significance the incident had for you. Then, in telling your story, you can select from the details that you have gathered those that are most relevant and memorable and omit those that are unimportant and unnecessary. The next step is to arrange your material in such a way that you clearly convey the event to your readers, emphasizing its most important aspects and what it means to you.

The Shaping Idea.   In devising a shaping idea for this task (see Chapter 2, "Focus on Form: Stating a Thesis," pp. 72–75), one of the key questions that you need to address is "What is the particular significance of this event?" Your statement of your shaping idea will embody the answer to this question, an answer that may explain not only how the incident affected you but also why.

   Of course, many writers do not know precisely how to organize their thoughts until after they have written the rough draft, and you may find that your shaping idea isn't clear to you until this later stage. The final version of your essay, however, should be clearly guided by one well-defined idea.

Narration.   The narrative mode is a natural method of telling a story step by step, one that the material you generated by answering the journalist's questions should readily lend itself to. You, of course, need to describe and explain as well, in order to answer these questions. But because you are focusing on an event, you are likely to use the descriptions and explanations that you generated in the service of narration.

Duration.   How do you decide on a particular order or arrangement of ideas for this chapter's essay? You are being asked to write about an event that took place in the past. You are being asked to elaborate on the journalist's question "What happened?" You can answer this question in several ways, depending on the purpose that you have in mind. First you might decide to write a straightforward chronological narrative that describes the event just as it occurred in time: an A-to-Z arrangement, with A as the beginning of the event and Z as the end. In the following selection, "The Angry Winter," Loren Eiseley used an A-to-Z arrangement, taking us through a series of steps in an incident that began when he laid a fossil bone on the floor of his study.

The Angry Winter
Loren Eiseley

> As to what happened next, it is possible to maintain that the hand of heaven was involved, and also possible to say that when men are desperate no one can stand up to them.
> — XENOPHON

A time comes when creatures whose destinies have crossed somewhere in the remote past are forced to appraise each other as though they were total strangers. I had been huddled beside the fire one winter night, with the wind prowling outside and shaking the windows. The big shepherd dog on the hearth before me occasionally glanced up affectionately, sighed, and slept. I was working, actually, amidst the debris of a far greater winter. On my desk lay the lance points of ice age hunters and the heavy leg bone of a fossil bison. No remnants of flesh attached to these relics. The deed lay more than ten thousand years remote. It was represented here by naked flint and by bone so mineralized it rang when struck. As I worked on in my little circle of light, I absently laid the bone beside me on the floor. The hour had crept toward midnight. A grating noise, a heavy rasping of big teeth diverted me. I looked down.

The dog had risen. That rock-hard fragment of a vanished beast was in his jaws and he was mouthing it with a fierce intensity I had never seen exhibited by him before.

"Wolf," I exclaimed, and stretched out my hand. The dog backed up but did not yield. A low and steady rumbling began to rise in his chest, something out of a long-gone midnight. There was nothing in that bone to taste, but ancient shapes were moving in his mind and determining his utterance. Only fools gave up bones. He was warning me.

"Wolf," I chided again.

As I advanced, his teeth showed and his mouth wrinkled to strike. The rumbling rose to a direct snarl. His flat head swayed low and wickedly as a reptile's above the floor. I was the most loved object in his universe, but the past was fully alive in him now. Its shadows were whispering in his mind. I knew he was not bluffing. If I made another step he would strike.

Yet his eyes were strained and desperate. "Do not," something pleaded in the back of them, some affectionate thing that had followed at my heel all the days of his mortal life, "do not force me. I am what I am and cannot be otherwise because of the shadows. Do not reach out. You are a man, and my very god. I love you, but do not put out your hand. It is midnight. We are in another time, in the snow."

"The *other* time," the steady rumbling continued while I paused, "the other time in the snow, the big, the final, the terrible snow, when the shape of this thing I hold spelled life. I will not give it up. I cannot. The shadows will not permit me. Do not put out your hand."

I stood silent, looking into his eyes, and heard his whisper through. Slowly I drew back in understanding. The snarl diminished, ceased. As I retreated, the bone slumped to the floor. He placed a paw upon it, warningly.

And were there no shadows in my own mind, I wondered. Had I not for a moment, in the grip of that savage utterance, been about to respond, to hurl myself upon him over an invisible haunch ten thousand years removed? Even to me the shadows had whispered — to me the scholar in his study.

"Wolf," I said, but this time, holding a familiar leash. I spoke from the door indifferently. "A walk in the snow." Instantly from his eyes that other visitant receded. The bone was left lying. He came eagerly to my side, accepting the leash and taking it in his mouth as always.

A blizzard was raging when we went out, but he paid no heed. On his thick fur the driving snow was soon clinging heavily. He frolicked a little— though usually he was a grave dog—making up to me for something still receding in his mind. I felt the snowflakes fall upon my face, and stood thinking of another time and another time still, until I was moving from mid-night to midnight under ever more remote and vaster snows. Wolf came to my side with a little whimper. It was he who was civilized now. "Come back to the fire," he nudged gently, "or you will be lost." Automatically I took the leash he offered. He led me safely home and into the house.

"We have been very far away," I told him solemnly. "I think there is something in us that we had both better try to forget." Sprawled on the rug, Wolf made no response except to thump his tail feebly out of courtesy. Al-ready he was mostly asleep and dreaming. By the movement of his feet I could see he was running far upon some errand in which I played no part.

Softly I picked up his bone—our bone, rather—and replaced it high on a shelf in my cabinet. As I snapped off the light the white glow from the win-dow seemed to augment itself and shine with a deep, glacial blue. As far as I could see, nothing moved in the long aisles of my neighbor's woods. There was no visible track, and certainly no sound from the living. The snow contin-ued to fall steadily, but the wind, and the shadows it had brought, had vanished.

Eiseley narrated the incident in a step-by-step fashion. He omitted few steps between the beginning and the end, perhaps because the incident took a relatively short time. Are there moments in the incident that you would like to know more about? To what degree did Eiseley record objective facts? To what degree is the focus of his essay more on his subjective insights into and interpretations of the facts?

The longer the incident about which you are writing, of course, the more decisions you must make about which steps should be omitted from your narrative, which should be given only passing attention, and which should be emphasized with detail. Both your own point of view and that of your audi-ence should be taken into consideration when you determine what parts of your narrative to emphasize or de-emphasize.

What is Eiseley's shaping idea? Where does it occur in the essay?

What is Eiseley's point of view in his narrative? Is he serious, reasonable, scientific? What does he express about himself? How would you compare his voice to that of Gay Talese in his article about spectators who witnessed John Glenn's space shot? How do you account for any differences? What sort of assumptions did Eiseley seem to make about his audience's frame of reference and point of view?

Details.   As we have suggested, in writing your narrative it will help you to keep in mind that your readers want to become a part of what happened; they want to see and hear what you did. This is one reason for you to include memorable and relevant details conveyed in vivid language, including details of dialogue. Further, analogy might be used to help your readers share your thoughts and feelings about the incident.

Every detail included should contribute to what you want your readers to know and feel about the event. These details should elaborate the who, where, when, and how of your incident. The why and what may be answered through more direct statement. At the same time, irrelevant details should be omitted.

Working with Your Peer Group to Analyze an Essay.   Reread the essay by Loren Eiseley, paying close attention to how the author used details to retell an event.

Now meet with your peer group and, either by exchanging journal entries or by brainstorming, answer the following questions (see "Working in a Peer Group," in Chapter 2, pp. 64–65):

1. What role do the following details play in the essay?
   • winter
   • wind
   • fire and light
   • midnight
   • snow
   • shadows
2. The author mentioned in the first paragraph that the dog "glanced up affectionately." What role does this detail play in the story? Why did he add that the dog was big?
3. What details did Eiseley include to convey the dog's metamorphosis into a fierce beast? What further details dramatize the ambivalence that the dog feels about his new ferocity?

In the next selection, Maya Angelou does not begin to narrate her incident until the fifteenth paragraph. What does she write about first, and why? How does her long introduction help to bridge the gap between her point of view and that of her readers? What assumptions does she make about her readers' frame of reference and point of view? How has her own point of view changed since that time in her childhood when she experienced the incident?

Momma's Private Victory

Maya Angelou

"Momma's Private Victory" (editor's title) is the fifth chapter of Angelou's book *I Know Why the Caged Bird Sings.* Since their early childhood, she and her brother who was a year older, had lived with their grandmother ("Momma" of the narrative), who operated a store in the front of her home in the black section of their small Arkansas town.

"Thou shalt not be dirty" and "Thou shalt not be impudent" were the two commandments of Grandmother Henderson upon which hung our total salvation.

Each night in the bitterest winter we were forced to wash faces, arms, necks, legs and feet before going to bed. She used to add, with a smirk that unprofane people can't control when venturing into profanity, "and wash as far as possible, then wash possible."

We would go to the well and wash in the ice-cold, clear water, grease our legs with the equally cold stiff Vaseline, then tiptoe into the house. We wiped the dust from our toes and settled down for schoolwork, cornbread, clabbered milk, prayers and bed, always in that order. Momma was famous for pulling the quilts off after we had fallen asleep to examine our feet. If they weren't clean enough for her, she took the switch (she kept one behind the bedroom door for emergencies) and woke up the offender with a few aptly placed burning reminders.

The area around the well at night was dark and slick, and boys told about how snakes love water, so that anyone who had to draw water at night and then stand there alone and wash knew that moccasins and rattlers, puff adders and boa constrictors were winding their way to the well and would arrive just as the person washing got soap in her eyes. But Momma convinced us that not only was cleanliness next to Godliness, dirtiness was the inventor of misery.

The impudent child was detested by God and a shame to its parents and could bring destruction to its house and line. All adults had to be addressed as Mister, Missus, Miss, Auntie, Cousin, Unk, Uncle, Buhbah, Sister, Brother and a thousand other appellations indicating familial relationship and the lowliness of the addressor.

Everyone I knew respected these customary laws, except for the powhite-trash children.

Some families of powhitetrash lived on Momma's farm land behind the school. Sometimes a gaggle of them came to the store, filling the whole room, chasing out the air and even changing the well-known scents. The children crawled over the shelves and into the potato and onion bits, twanging all the time in their sharp voices like cigar-box guitars. They took liberties in my Store that I would never dare. Since Momma told us that the less you say to white-folks (or even powhitetrash) the better, Bailey and I would stand, solemn, quiet, in the displaced air. But if one of the playful apparitions got close to us, I pinched it. Partly out of angry frustration and partly because I didn't believe in its flesh reality.

They called my uncle by his first name and ordered him around the Store. He, to my crying shame, obeyed them in his limping dip-straight dip fashion.

My grandmother, too, followed their orders, except that she didn't seem to be servile because she anticipated their needs.

"Here's sugar, miz Potter, and here's baking powder. You didn't buy soda last month, you'll probably be needing some."

Momma always directed her statements to the adults, but sometimes, Oh painful sometimes, the grimy, snotty-nosed girls would answer her.

"Naw, Annie . . ." — to Momma? Who owned the land they lived on? Who forgot more than they would ever learn? If there was any justice in the world,

God should strike them dumb at once! — "Just give us some extra sody crackers, and some more mackerel."

At least they never looked in her face, or I never caught them doing so. Nobody with a smidgen of training, not even the worst roustabout, would look right in a grown person's face. It meant the person was trying to take the words out before they were formed. The dirty little children didn't do that, but they threw their orders around the Store like lashes from a cat-o'-nine-tails.

When I was around ten years old, those scruffy children caused me the most painful and confusing experience I had ever had with my grandmother.

One summer morning, after I had swept the dirt yard of leaves, spearmint-gum wrappers and Vienna-sausage labels, I raked the yellow-red dirt, and made halfmoons carefully, so that the design stood out clearly and mask-like. I put the rake behind the store and came through the back of the house to find Grandmother on the front porch in her big, wide white apron. The apron was so stiff by virtue of the starch that it could have stood alone. Momma was admiring the yard, so I joined her. It truly looked like a flat redhead that had been raked with a bigtoothed comb. Momma didn't say anything but I knew she liked it. She looked over toward the school principal's house and to the right at Mr. McElroy's. She was hoping one of those community pillars would see the design before the day's business wiped it out. Then she looked upward to the school. My head had swung with hers, so at just about the same time we saw a troop of the powhitetrash kids marching over the hill and down by the side of the school.

I looked to Momma for direction. She did an excellent job of sagging from her waist down, but from the waist up she seemed to be pulling for the top of the oak tree across the road. Then she began to moan a hymn. Maybe not to moan, but the tune was so slow and the meter so strange that she could have been moaning. She didn't look at me again. When the children reached halfway down the hill, halfway to the Store, she said without turning, "Sister, go on inside."

I wanted to beg her, "Momma, don't wait for them. Come on inside with me. If they come in the Store, you go to the bedroom and let me wait on them. They only frighten me if you're around. Alone I know how to handle them." But of course I couldn't say anything, so I went in and stood behind the screen door.

Before the girls got to the porch I heard their laughter crackling and popping like pine logs in a cooking stove. I suppose my lifelong paranoia was born in those cold, molasses-slow minutes. They came finally to stand on the ground in front of Momma. At first they pretended seriousness. Then one of them wrapped her right arm in the crook of her left, pushed out her mouth and started to hum. I realized that she was aping my grandmother. Another said, "Naw, Helen, you ain't standing like her. This here's it." Then she lifted her chest, folded her arms and mocked that strange carriage that was Annie Henderson. Another laughed, "Naw, you can't do it. Your mouth ain't pooched out enough. It's like this."

I thought about the rifle behind the door, but I knew I'd never be able to hold it straight, and the .410, our sawed-off shotgun, which stayed loaded and was fired every New Year's night, was locked in the trunk and Uncle

Willie had the key on his chain. Through the fly-specked screen-door, I could see that the arms of Momma's apron jiggled from the vibrations of her humming. But her knees seemed to have locked as if they would never bend again.

She sang on. No louder than before, but no softer either. No slower or faster.

The dirt of the girl's cotton dresses continued on their legs, feet, arms and faces to make them all of a piece. Their greasy uncolored hair hung down, uncombed, with a grim finality. I knelt to see them better, to remember them for all time. The tears that had slipped down my dress left unsurprising dark spots, and made the front yard blurry and even more unreal. The world had taken a deep breath and was having doubts about continuing to revolve.

The girls had tired of mocking Momma and turned to other means of agitation.

One crossed her eyes, stuck her thumbs in both sides of her mouth and said, "Look here, Annie." Grandmother hummed on and the apron strings trembled. I wanted to throw a handful of black pepper in their faces, to throw lye on them, to scream that they were dirty, scummy peckerwoods, but I knew I was as clearly imprisoned behind the scene as the actors outside were confined to the roles.

One of the smaller girls did a kind of puppet dance while her fellow clowns laughed at her. But the tall one, who was almost a woman, said something very quietly, which I couldn't hear. They all moved backward from the porch, still watching Momma. For an awful second I thought they were going to throw a rock at Momma, who seemed (except for the apron strings) to have turned into stone herself. But the big girl turned her back, bent down and put her hands flat on the ground—she didn't pick up anything. She simply shifted her weight and did a hand stand.

Her dirty bare feet and long legs went straight for the sky. Her dress fell down around her shoulders, and she had on no drawers. The slick pubic hair made a brown triangle where her legs came together. She hung in the vacuum of that lifeless morning for only a few seconds, then wavered and tumbled. The other girls clapped her on the back and slapped her hands.

Momma changed her song to "Bread of Heaven, bread of Heaven feed me till I want no more." I found that I was praying too. How long could Momma hold out? What new indignity would they think of to subject her to? Would I be able to stay out of it? What would Momma really like me to do?

Then they were moving out of the yard, on their way to town. They bobbed their heads and shook their slack behinds and turned, one at a time:

"'Bye, Annie."

"'Bye, Annie."

"'Bye, Annie."

Momma never turned her head or unfolded her arms, but she stopped singing and said, "'Bye, Miz Helen, 'bye, Miz Ruth, 'bye, Miz Eloise."

I burst. A firecracker July-the-Fourth burst. How could Momma call them Miz? The mean nasty things. Why couldn't she have come inside the sweet, cool store when we saw them breasting the hill? What did she prove? And if they were dirty, mean and impudent, why did Momma have to call them Miz?

She stood another whole song through and then opened the screen door to look down on me crying in rage. She looked until I looked up. Her face was a brown moon that shone on me. She was beautiful. Something had happened out there, which I couldn't completely understand, but I could see that she was happy. Then she bent down and touched me as mothers of the church "lay hands on the sick and afflicted" and I quieted.

"Go wash your face, Sister." And she went behind the candy counter and hummed, "Glory, glory, hallelujah, when I lay my burden down." I threw the well water on my face and used the weekday handkerchief to blow my nose. Whatever the contest had been out front, I knew Momma had won.

I took the rake back to the front yard. The smudged footprints were easy to erase. I worked for a long time on my new design and laid the rake behind the wash pot. When I came back to the store, I took Momma's hand and we both walked outside to look at the pattern.

It was a large heart with lots of hearts growing smaller inside, and piercing from the outside rim to the smallest heart was an arrow. Momma said, "Sister, that's right pretty." Then she turned back to the store and resumed, "Glory, glory, hallelujah, when I lay my burden down."

Like Eiseley, Angelou relies on details of scene, action, and dialogue to recreate the incident for her readers. Which details stand out most vividly for you as a reader? What effect does the incident have on you? What effect did it have on Angelou?

Like Angelou you may decide to offer background information first, to help the reader see the incident from your point of view. The latter tactic also may help to heighten the drama of the narration. So might the use of a flashback technique, in which you begin at the end, perhaps with the overall effect of the incident on you, or in the middle, and then flash back to earlier events. Thus, you may go from Z to A or from M to A to Z.

Arranging the Details of Your Essay. Try the following procedure in organizing your essay: make a list of the stages in your incident, arranging them in the order that you think is most effective: A to Z, Z to A to Z, to M to A to Z; asterisk those aspects of the incident that you think are the most important; cross out those aspects that do not contribute much to what you wish to convey about your incident; beside each stage, jot down those details that you feel are necessary to convey the importance of each stage and the overall significance of the event.

Exposition in the Service of Narration. Unlike the purely narrative mode, the expository mode, when used in a narrative framework, does not recount events in chronological order; rather it summarizes, explains, or interprets them. Narration shows what your experience was like; exposition tells about it. Both have their place.

The technique of summarizing is not something new to you. In our day-to-day activities, we all constantly condense experiences, conversations, and happenings, because doing so allows us to extract the essence of an experience from all of the unnecessary details. Thus, when we summarize, we engage in heavy editing by asking ourselves, "What information can I omit without significantly changing the experience I am telling about?"

As an example, what is your favorite spectator sport? Have you ever noticed the difference between the sportscaster's on-the-air report on the action of a sporting event while it is occurring and the report of the event prepared for a newspaper the next day? The first is a blow-by-blow account, detailed and unedited, and if recorded, it would take up as much time as the game itself. The second account is condensed. It is likely to be heavily edited, with details only of highlights, and will probably also include interpretation or explanation. The impulse to comment (explain or interpret) is one that comes almost automatically from the writer's attempt to fuse highlights with selected details.

The opportunity to have some distance (time) between the actual event and the reporting of the event is valuable in the use of exposition for it forces you to ask yourself how you felt about the event when it happened and how you feel about it now. The differences between the two sets of feelings can provide the basis for a dynamic interpretation of the event. During narration, you are getting close to the action, capturing its immediacy through sensory details. During exposition, you are getting away from the action and applying your powers of interpretation and analysis to the event.

There are then several forms that exposition can take in the service of narration: (1) straight summary, which retains narration's effect of placing the reader in the scene and which is a condensed telling of what happened, and (2) explanation and interpretation, which remove the reader from the action and ask him or her to contemplate its meaning or significance. Explanation and interpretation both clarify, increasing our understanding of an event; but the former is more emphatically objective and factual, whereas the latter tends to have a greater element of subjectivity and hence is more open to argument.

By way of example, think again of a sportswriter. If when reporting on a track meet, the sportswriter tells you that Smith beat Jones in the mile, that the race was close, and that the winning time was 3:58, he or she is summarizing the event. If the sportswriter tells you that Smith, who was expected to break the record, failed, he or she is explaining. If the sportswriter suggests that the poor condition of the track was the main reason that Smith failed to set a new record, he or she is interpreting.

Both Eiseley and Angelou blend expository passages into their narratives. How important is summary to each of them? Explanation? To what degree does either interpret the details of their story?

As you arrange the details of your essay for this chapter, consider whether or not some exposition might heighten your reader's understanding of one or more stages of the incident.

Writing Your Rough Draft

Before you begin writing the rough draft, take a look at the following draft that a student wrote in response to the task for Chapter 3:

"One night I was awakened by a phone call...."

One night I was awakened by a phone call. The troubled voice on the line belonged to a sister of a friend. She pleaded with me to come to Elmhurst General, she said there was something terribly wrong with her brother and the family needed me to translate what the doctor had to say.

I drove to the hospital in a hurry, expecting the worst. I finally spotted them in a corner of the emergency room. Like any other emergency room, this one too was made up of small partitions. You could tell that it was a busy night because every one of the beds was full.

As I walked across and to the other side of that huge room, I could hear people scream and moan, as the doctors and nurses were working on them. I tried to look away with my eyes to the floor stained with blood, away from the naked bodies. My friend's family stood motionless holding hands, with their eyes glued to a drawn curtain.

Then I saw his mother's eyes and I felt my stomach turning cold. She said nothing, but with her hand, she motioned me to look inside the divider. I couldn't; I was too scared. My hands were numb as if full of lead. She asked me, in Russian, to go inside and to see how was her son. I didn't have to: The curtain had opened, and a nurse with a doctor came out, and approached us, and the doctor asked me to translate to the family that they did everything they could, and that my friend has died--o.d. cocaine.

His parents buried my friend the next day as the Jewish tradition dictates. I was there, as were many of his other friends. His mom wept when the rabbi was finished with the ceremony and the coffin was lowered into the ground. I kept seeing my friend's smiling face.

Weeks later, when my mind had adjusted a little better to what had happened to my friend, I asked myself many questions. There was guilt and anger. Guilt for not being there for my friend. Anger toward my friend for doing this to himself and his family. His death seemed so senseless to me.

Which details of this narrative most effectively convey the writer's point of view? Are there parts of his story that you need to know more about? Where might some additional exposition be helpful?

In the "Rewriting" section (pp. 126–131), you can read the peer response to this draft and the writer's subsequent revision. But now it's time for you to write a draft of your essay on an incident.

In Chapter 2, we suggested that different people go about writing in different ways. Just how you go about writing your rough draft, just what process you employ in getting the words down on paper, is a personal matter. Perhaps you are beginning to find that the words come more easily to you if you write freely at first, without stopping to edit your sentence structure or the arrangement of your details. Perhaps you do better if you focus on one paragraph at a time, working each paragraph into as final a shape as you can before moving on to the next.

Perhaps you will want to start your rough draft by writing down your shaping idea and then reviewing the list of concrete details that you put together by answering the journalist's questions. By now, you may also have decided on a rough pattern of arrangement, both details and arrangement chosen with the audience's point of view in mind. Now place yourself in your chosen spot for writing and begin.

Once you start, keep on going. Refer to your notes on details, audience, and arrangement as often as you need to. Bear in mind the need for chronological sequencing and specific details; build your essay with paragraphs that move the reader smoothly through the incident in a step-by-step fashion. Write through to the end in one sitting.

Once you finish your draft, look at the Focus section below on paragraph structure and transitions, both of which may help you clarify the sequence of events and their effect on you.

FOCUS ON FORM: PARAGRAPH STRUCTURE/MAKING TRANSITIONS

Paragraph Structure.   Essays are divided into paragraphs as an aid to both the reader and the writer. The paragraph breaks in an essay help the reader to follow the flow of thought from point to point and of conversation from speaker to speaker. In addition, some paragraphs serve to emphasize for the reader the writer's major points, others to illustrate and/or elaborate a point, and still others to make a transition or bridge between different points or parts of the essay.

Dividing an essay into paragraphs helps the writer to develop the shaping idea sequentially throughout the essay. The writer of narrative may wish to use paragraph breaks to separate the major stages of the event, whereas the writer of exposition will use paragraphs to develop the primary aspects of his or her subject. Reexamine the student draft in the previous section (pp. 112–113) for the paragraph structure. What rationale had the writer for his paragraph breaks?

Different writers will approach paragraphing in their own way. In writing a rough draft, you may start a new paragraph without thinking about it each time you move from one stage or point to another, as the student who wrote "One night I was awakened by a phone call" seems to have done. You may also write a whole draft without many — or any — paragraph breaks, adding them only as you begin to revise, as the student who wrote on Thoreau in Chapter 2 (pp. 69–71) did.

You may decide to begin a new paragraph because you are making a new point. Or you may do so simply because the previous paragraph was getting too long. The indentation that begins a new paragraph is essentially an aid for the reader's eye. Reading a page without any paragraph breaks, you only need to blink in order to lose your place — and if you do, you will likely have trouble finding it again.

Because of the importance of the paragraph, in writing your essay you will want to pay attention to the length and structure of each paragraph.

If your reader is going to be unwilling or unable to give full attention to what you write, you may keep your paragraphs short. Think, for example, of someone who is trying to read a set of instructions and put together a child's swing set at the same time — such a reader will appreciate concise paragraphs that guide him or her step-by-step through the construction process.

If, on the other hand, you are writing about a complex subject for readers whose levels of interest and concentration are probably going to be high, your paragraphs may necessarily be long and involved. Even in such a case, however, a paragraph of no more than a single sentence or two, particularly if it comes between two lengthy paragraphs, may provide the reader with a useful moment of rest and reflection as well as give the writer a means of emphasizing the importance of a particular point.

You can be as flexible and creative with paragraph structure as you can with length. Just as essays have a beginning, a middle, and an end, so many effective paragraphs will have a beginning, a middle, and an end.

You may state the point of the paragraph at the start in what may be called a *topic sentence* and then develop that point or topic in several other sentences. If the paragraph is sufficiently long, or if you want to add emphasis, you may want a concluding sentence as well. You might also begin (or end) the paragraph with one or more transition sentences that serve as links to a previous (or following) paragraph.

Notice in the paragraph below that the third sentence introduces the paragraph (after two initial background sentences), the next six develop the topic, and the last concludes emphatically by restating the topic sentence.

> I have long wondered just what my strength is as a writer. I am often filled with tremendous enthusiasm for a subject, yet my writing about it will seem a sorry attempt. Above all, I possess a driving sincerity, that prime virtue of any creative worker. I write only what I believe to be the absolute truth — even if I must ruin the theme in so doing. In this respect, I feel far superior to those glib people in my classes who often garner better grades than I do. They are so often pitiful frauds, artificial, insincere. They have a line that works. They do not write from the depths of their hearts. Nothing of theirs was ever born of pain. Many an incoherent yet sincere piece of writing has outlived the polished product.
>
> —Theodore Roethke, *On the Poet and His Craft*

But paragraphs do not have to be this neatly structured in order to be effective.

The next example begins with a topic sentence but has no conclusion, as the writer was more interested in the details of his day than he was in emphasizing the general idea of how he passed his time.

> Do you want to know how I pass my time? I rise at eight or thereabouts — & go to my barn — say good morning to the horse, & give him his breakfast. (It goes to my heart to give him a cold one, but it can't be helped.) Then, pay a visit to my cow — cut up a pumpkin or two for her, & stand by to see her eat it — for its a pleasant sight to see a cow move her jaws — she does it so mildly & with such a sanctity. — My own breakfast over, I go to my workroom & light my fire — then spread my M.S.S. on the table — take one business squint at it, & fall to with a will. At 2½ P.M. I hear a preconcerted knock at my door, which (by request) continues till I rise & go to the door, which serves to wean me effectively from my writing, however interested I may be. My friends the horse & cow now demand their dinner — & I go & give it

them. My own dinner over, I rig my sleigh & with my mother or sisters start off for the village — & if it be a Literary World day, great is the satisfaction thereof. My evenings I spend in a sort of mesmeric state in my room — not being able to read — only now & then skimming over some large printed book.

—Herman Melville

In the next paragraph, the writer has only a conclusion, or one could say that he placed his topic sentence at the end. This arrangement creates a dramatic, climactic effect.

When I first began to describe the little world of yesterday that lives again in my books, that small corner of a French province, scarcely known even to Frenchmen, where the vacations of my school days were spent, I had no idea that I would attract the attention of foreign readers. We are all quite convinced of our utter singularity. We forget that the books which we ourselves found enchanting, those of George Eliot or of Dickens, of Tolstoy or Dostoevsky, or of Selma Lagerlof, describe countries very different from our own, people of another race and another religion; and yet we loved them, because we recognized ourselves in them. All humanity is in this or that peasant back home, and all the landscapes in the world coalesce in the horizons familiar to our childish eyes. The novelist's gift is precisely his power to make plain the universal quality concealed in that sheltered world where we were born, and where we first learned to love and suffer.

—Francois Mauriac

Joan Didion's topic sentence in the following paragraph asks a question, and her conclusion summarizes the answers given in the developing sentences. This arrangement also creates a climactic effect:

Why did I write it down? In order to remember, of course, but exactly what was it I wanted to remember? How much of it actually happened? Did any of it? Why do I keep a notebook at all? It is easy to deceive oneself on all those scores. The impulse to write things down is a peculiarly compulsive one, inexplicable to those who do not share it, useful only accidentally, only secondarily, in the way that any compulsion tries to justify itself. I suppose that it begins or does not begin in the cradle. Although I have felt compelled to write things down since I was five years old, I doubt that my daughter ever will, for she is a singularly blessed and accepting child, delighted with life exactly as life presents itself to her, unafraid to wake up. Keepers of private notebooks are a different breed altogether, lonely and resistant rearrangers of things, anxious malcontents, children afflicted apparently at birth with some presentiment of loss.

—Joan Didion, "On Keeping a Notebook"

The following paragraph has no distinct topic sentence. The writer's point is understandable, however. Her topic sentence might have been, "Because the eyes can communicate in an instant, communication between two people in our fast-paced technological age is possible, but how can we learn to communicate in this way?" The topic sentence has been omitted because the writer was following a line of thought — delineating the aspects of a problem — rather than making a point:

> Messages are conveyed by the eyes, sometimes by no words at all. It is no excuse to say that technology has accelerated our life to the point where we pass others without noticing them, without contacting, or without a real meeting. A real meeting can take place in one instant. But how does that come about? How do we reach a moment when in one instant we can communicate with another human being?
>
> —Marya Mannes, "Television: The Splitting Image"

SOME PRACTICE WITH PARAGRAPH STRUCTURE

1. Three topic sentences are given for each of the paragraphs below. Can you decide which one is the actual topic sentence written by the author of the paragraph? Explain your choice in each case.

   a. _____

      _____

   My mother passed away three years ago, and now I'm the only one living at home with my father. I'm there to make sure he eats, takes his medicine, and has clean clothes. I know these things aren't much but I can tell by the way he talks to me and by what is said that he sometimes confuses me with my mother. He's even called me by my mother's name a couple of times. I can't really think anything of it. I know he just gets confused sometimes, because the things I do for him are the same things my mother used to take care of.

      1. Loss is always hard to accept, no matter what kind of loss it is.

      2. I too am experiencing some sort of role confusion, only I'm not the confused one.

      3. You can never go back in time to regain what has already been lost.

b. _____

_____

Up ahead on the road we caught sight of two baby deer trying to cross. They were on the opposite side of the road so we had enough time to slow down, but the lady coming in the opposite direction didn't. The first deer made it across okay, but when the other tried to follow it was hit and killed instantly. We pulled over and dragged the poor thing off the road. There wasn't much more we could do. The funny thing was that the lady was more worried about how she was going to explain the broken head-light on her husband's car than anything else.

      1. Later that night we were driving back home and I was tel-ling Ed how scary it was to actually see someone have a close call, especially if you don't expect it.

      2. There was a certain feeling of danger in the air all day, but I didn't realize it until the last incident.

      3. I don't know if the events of that day were meant to be an omen, but it did strike me a little strange to be ending the day with death making its mark.

c. Suddenly, I noticed how content my sister was with her new pet, Harry, and how discontent I was with no new pet. _____

_____

And then it happened. There Harry swam and here, in my hand, was the big, white, fluffy tissue. This wasn't just a plain white tissue. It had little pink flowers printed on it. I don't know what came over me. It was somewhat like the dark ominous clouds engulfing the blue sky before a storm. I eased my way over to the bowl and sprinkled tissue, oh so lightly, over the water's edge.

1. Jealousy can make you do inexplicable things.
2. I could feel the jealousy escalate inside of me.
3. I didn't know whether to scream or cry.

2. Write a topic sentence for each of the following paragraphs.

a. _____

_____

After a few runs I let myself go and picked up speed. I got a feeling of flying that would have to be experienced to grasp. It may have only been five degrees out, but the wind wisping in my face felt great. There is so much energy pumping through the body that the bitter cold goes unnoticed. To take even the slightest jump into the air is something else. Just thinking about it excites me. I never loved winter more than I do now. In fact, up until I went skiing I didn't care for winter at all.

b. _____

_____

Suddenly the engine was cut and six bodies came spilling out the side door. Watching them leave the plane for the first time was a thrill in itself because I didn't know what to expect. You could hear the engine restart as we watched them fall. The idea of this jump was to create a circle, which they did, locking arms and holding it for about ten seconds. It was hard to watch them as they fell because of the speed at which they were travelling. I thought they wouldn't have enough time to open their chutes before they hit the ground, but at the last second they exploded from the circle and popped open their chutes.

c. _____

_____

After talking for a while and skimming through a few magazines, we decided it was time for a walk. We walked down the beach, away from everyone. We were playing in the water and looking around for shells. We were just having fun. Then all of a sudden, out of the corner of my eye, I spotted something in the water. I couldn't really tell what it was. It could have been a fish jumping or a piece of wood floating. I wasn't really fazed by it. I never even thought it might be a person because we were past the red flags and you can't swim there.

3. Which paragraphs in Exercises 1 and 2 have concluding sentences? Why has a conclusion been added in each case?

SOME PRACTICE WITH PARAGRAPH STRUCTURE IN YOUR ESSAY ON AN INCIDENT

1. Write a paragraph describing in detail one scene from the incident that is the subject of your essay for this chapter. First write the paragraph without any topic or concluding sentence. Rewrite it with a topic sentence. Add a concluding sentence if it seems effective. Which version might work best in your essay? Why?

2. Identify by number or some other mark each major step in your narrative of an incident, each key stage of your story from start to finish. Mark the high point or climax of your story. Also mark those places where you describe or explain in the service of narration. Which of the places that you marked begin a new paragraph? Which do not but should? Are there some places where you might combine separate paragraphs?

Making Transitions.   Transitions are words and phrases that establish connections between words, sentences, and paragraphs. Through the use of transitions, the writer emphasizes the coherence of the essay for the reader. The most common form of transition is the conjunction. Conjunctions form such connections between thoughts as addition (and), contrast (but), comparison (as), causation (for), choice (or), process (after), and chronology (before). Transitional phrases can also be employed to make the same connections, for example, "in addition," "on the other hand," "as well as," "as a result," and "after a while."

A second means of creating transitions between thoughts is to refer to the shaping idea throughout the essay by repeating the key words that you have used to express it (or synonyms or pronouns clearly referring to it). The repetition of key words assures the reader of the unity of the paper and of its development of one main point.

In Passage 1, following, most of the transitions have been omitted. After reading the first passage, read Passage 2. Does the writing in the second version seem much clearer with the transitions (underlined) restored?

Passage 1

I think I was in the first press bus. I can't be sure. Pete Lisagor of the *Chicago Daily News* says he was in the bus. He describes things that went on aboard it that didn't happen on the bus I went in. I think I was in the bus.

Confusion is the way it was in Dallas in the early afternoon on Nov. 22. No one knew what happened, or how, or where, much less why. Bits and pieces fell together. A reasonably coherent version of the story was possible. I know no reporter who was there who has a clear and orderly picture of the afternoon; it is a matter of bits and pieces thrown hastily into something like a whole.

Passage 2

I think I was in the first bus. But I can't be sure. Pete Lisagor of the *Chicago Daily News* says he knows he was in the first press bus and he describes things that went on aboard it that didn't happen on the bus I was in. But I still think I was in the first press bus.

I cite that minor confusion as an example of the way it was in Dallas in the early afternoon of Nov. 22. At first no one knew what happened, or how, or where, much less why. Gradually, bits and pieces began to fall together, and within two hours a reasonably coherent version of the story began to be possible. Even now, however, I know no reporter who has a clear and orderly picture of that surrealistic afternoon; it is still a matter of bits and pieces thrown hastily into something like a whole.

—Tom Wicker, *Times Talk,* 1963

In analyzing Tom Wicker's use of transitions in Passage 2, you might notice first that he used words like *but, and, or,* and *however* to form very specific connections (addition, choice, and contrast) between his words, phrases, sentences, and even paragraphs.

Second, as Wicker was narrating the events on the day of the assassination of John F. Kennedy, he used many conjunctive words and phrases that indicate chronology, thus clarifying the sequence of events: "at first," "gradually," "within two hours," "even now," and "still."

Finally, he inserted key words in every sentence. This repetition of key words builds bridges by establishing that his sentences and paragraphs cluster around his shaping idea, the confusion surrounding the president's assassination. This shaping idea is conveyed through the use of the key word *bus* in the first paragraph and the use of the word *confusion* and its synonyms *bits and pieces* and *surrealistic afternoon* in the second. Even the demonstrative adjective *that* is used several times to refer to the confusion of that afternoon. (The demonstrative adjectives *this, that, these* and *those* also act as transitions.)

As a further example, notice the use of transitional words and phrases in the following paragraphs:

William Wolcott died and went to heaven. Or so it	—*Shaping key idea*
seemed. Before being wheeled to the operating table,	—*Conjunction indicating*
he had been reminded that the surgical procedure would	*beginning of*
entail a certain risk. The operation was a success, but just	*chronology*
as the anesthesia was wearing off, his heart went into	*Conjunction*
fibrillation and he died. It seemed to him that he had	*establishing a*
somehow left his body and was able to look down upon	*contrast of ideas*
it, withered and pathetic, lying on a hard and unforgiv-	*Repetitition of key idea*
ing surface. He was only a little sad, regarded his body	
one last time—from a great height, it seemed—and con-	*Conjunctions and other*
tinued a kind of upward journey. While his surroundings	*words that establish*
had been suffused by a strange permeating darkness, he	*chronology*
realized that things were now getting brighter—looking	
up, you might say. And then he was being illuminated	
from a distance, flooded with light. He entered a kind of	
radiant kingdom and there, just ahead of him, he could	
make out in silhouette, magnificently lit from behind, a	*Repetition of key idea*
great godlike figure whom he was now effortlessly ap-	
proaching. Wolcott strained to make out his face. . .	
And then awoke. In the hospital operating room, where	—*Conjunction of*
the defibrillation machine had been rushed to him, he	*chronology*
had been resuscitated at the last possible moment. Ac-	
tually, his heart had stopped and, by some definitions of	*Conjunction word*
this poorly understood process, he had died. Wolcott	*indicating contrast*
was certain that he *had* died, that he had been vouch-	
safed a glimpse of life after death and a confirmation of	*Repetition of key idea*
Judaeo-Christian theology.	

—Carl Sagan, "The Amniotic Universe," *Atlantic,* April 1974

SOME PRACTICE WITH TRANSITIONS

1. Underline the transitional words in each of the following paragraphs. Indicate whether each word (or phrase) underlined is a conjunction or a key word. Be specific about what type of relationship each conjunctive word and phrase has formed (causal, contrast, and so on).

   a. I got in the plane and the first thing the pilot did was to make me put on a parachute—just in case. The ride up was nice, but my ears felt like they were going to explode from the lack of pressure. The plane was a single engine Cesna, which can hold about six to eight people. It took us about fifteen minutes to get up to twelve thousand feet, by which time my ears were screaming because of the change in pressure. But after a couple of minutes my ears popped and I was okay. The pilot signaled that we were approaching jump run. One guy opened the door to the plane and told the pilot they were ready to go. Ed smiled at me and said, "See you on the ground," and jumped out like Superman, followed by everyone else. I lost sight of them after a few seconds, but I was having fun sitting on the floor of the plane with my feet hanging out the door at twelve thousand feet.

b. It was my first day in Sugarbush, Vermont. I knew that skiing wouldn't be easy right away, but no one told me I'd have to learn to walk all over again. There I was strapped into these ankle high boots, weighing a ton each, immobilized. Because of the shape of the boots, I couldn't even straighten my legs. Walking in them, I did a great impression of a funky chicken. Then came the skis themselves. After putting them on, it was as if I had lost all coordination of my legs and feet. At least all of the coordination I had to begin with. What did I know? I'm used to sneakers.

2. Insert transitional words and phrases in the following student essay:

THE HALLOWEEN PARTY

My friend decided to have a Halloween party on the Saturday before Halloween. I was invited. I had to decide on what costume I would wear. I went to Rubie's Costume Rental and picked out a Minnie Mouse costume.

I was especially excited about this party. Everyone would be wearing costumes. Costume parties always seem to be lively. The disguises are usually amusing, funny, scary, or creative, making the party interesting. It can be fun to be surrounded by imaginative figures. Each person's identity is disguised, and it's easy to play practical jokes on each other. My costume disguised me from head to toe. No one would know my real identity.

Saturday night came. I got dressed in my costume and headed over to the party. The house was full of people in their Halloween costumes. My friends could not recognize me under my mask. I had to identify myself to each one of them.

I noticed someone wearing a Mickey Mouse costume. He was taking pictures of some of the people at the party. He noticed me in my Minnie Mouse costume and motioned for me to come over. He handed his camera to someone wearing a Peter Pan costume so that Peter Pan could take a picture of Mickey and me together. After all, Mickey and Minnie Mouse are a pair. He thanked me for being in the photograph with him. I left the picture-taking scene to find my friends. I wondered who it was wearing the Mickey Mouse costume. He'd said only two words to me. I hadn't recognized his voice.

I saw an old friend of mine who happened to look really cute in a Little Bo-Peep outfit. I went over to talk to her for a while. We decided to look for more of our friends. We found them on the dance floor and joined them. Mickey Mouse happened to be dancing away on the dance floor. He spotted me, came over, and we danced together. Everybody was working up a good sweat. I got tired after dancing to a couple of songs. I went to get something to drink.

The movie <u>Halloween</u> was being played on a VCR in the TV room. I decided to watch it. By the time the movie was over, it had got rather late. I started to clean up the house while my friend broke up the party. I happened to turn around and catch Mickey Mouse without his mask on. He was saying goodnight to some people. To my surprise, I found that the man under the Mickey Mouse mask was my ex-boyfriend--the same ex-boyfriend that I usually feel so uncomfortable around and try to avoid.

Our relationship had been a good one until he had to move to Florida with his family. The day he left for Florida was a sad one. We wrote each other letters twice a week. We called each other on the phone at least once a week. After the first month, our communication grew less frequent.

Four months passed. I had received only two short letters from him. Then I got a call from him. He told me that he would be moving back to New York within the next few months. I was extremely happy to think that I would be with him again. I counted the days until he moved back to New York.

After he had moved back here, I realized that our relationship had changed. He treated me as a friend instead of as a girlfriend. I realized that we no longer had a romantic relationship. I felt foolish. I decided to avoid him whenever possible.

My experience with him at the Halloween party made me realize that there is no need for me to feel foolish or uncomfortable with him. The masks we wore helped me to relate to him as a person rather than as an ex-boyfriend. Feeling foolish was no longer an excuse for me to avoid him. It is okay to feel for him as a friend. I looked back at our relationship and was able to accept the change that had taken place.

Ending my relationship with him as a girlfriend did not end my relationship with him as a friend. I had not been a friend to him because of fear that rejection of me as a girlfriend had affected his attitude toward me as a person. It did not mean rejection of friendship. I now want a friendly relationship, like the one we had the night of the party.

Images, impressions, fears, perceptions, and feelings toward others affect our relationships. We may see only one side of a situation or a person. The outside world can be very misleading about the real inside world that we live in and know. When we are disguised, our fears and anxieties, perceptions and worries, are put aside. We can be ourselves and learn to see another side of the world we live in or of the people we know. If we look closely enough, we can see ourselves.

SOME PRACTICE WITH TRANSITIONS IN YOUR ESSAY ON AN INCIDENT

1. Brainstorm with your peer group to come up with a list of as many conjunctive words and phrases that indicate chronology as possible. Which words on the list might you add to your essay on an incident, in order to help clarify the sequence of events?

2. Read one or two paragraphs of the essay you are writing on an incident to the members of your peer group. As they listen to you, your group members should write down each transition they hear. Based on what they write down, discuss what additional connections you might establish or emphasize, in order to strengthen the coherence of the paragraph(s).

REWRITING

Obtaining Feedback on Your Rough Draft

After you have written your rough draft, take a break for a period of time. This period should be long enough for you to be able to return to your essay refreshed. Once you have rested, your "other" self can emerge, the self that can see your essay objectively and make any necessary revisions. You may also want to obtain peer feedback at this point. Because your peers are your audience for this essay, the responses of your classmates should be particularly useful in determining how well you have written for your readers.

Regardless of who provides the feedback—you, your instructor, your peers, or any combination—your paper should receive an evaluation that answers the four questions of the "Audience Response Guide."

AUDIENCE RESPONSE GUIDE

1. What was the writer's purpose in reporting about an incident?
2. How does the paper affect the writer's peers?
3. How effective has the writer been in narrating the incident and conveying its effect? What are the strengths of the paper? What are the weaknesses?
4. How should the paper be revised to better fulfill its purpose and meaning?

Revision of Student Essay "One night I was awakened by a phone call. . . ."

Following is a peer evaluation of the rough draft of the student essay on an incident (pp. 112–113). Compare your own evaluation of the draft to that of the peer group by answering the four questions of the "Audience Response Guide" yourself before reading their answers.

1. The writer was trying to say how hurt and angry he felt because of his friend's death. His purpose is to let the reader know what kind of person he is and what he thinks about the way his friend wasted his life.

2. The way that the essay tells what happened, it's almost like reading a newspaper story. The reader learns a lot about where the incident happened but not enough about why or about who was involved. Although the writer expressed his feelings, he seems more like an onlooker than a participant. We know what it's like to see a friend hurt himself or herself and be unable to help, but a reader feels distant from the writer's story here.

3. The paper is visually effective in its use of detail to picture the scene and describe the events. The step-by-step narrative creates a certain suspense. One weakness is that the paper doesn't tell enough about the kind of person the friend was and how his death affects the writer. There is no clearly stated shaping idea, and the conclusion leaves the reader wondering.

4. The writer should try to think back and relive the incident, explaining what really went through his mind as he walked in the ER and how he felt when the doctor spoke to him. He could also tell what questions he asked at the end and why he felt guilt and anger. He also might give some background about himself and the family.

A revised version of the student essay, now titled "Approaching Life from a New Perspective," follows. How were the group's suggestions incorporated? What changes did the writer make himself? Do his expanded introduction and conclusion improve the essay? How successfully does he incorporate expository passages? How do these additional passages affect his paragraph structures? Do you notice improvements in the transitions from paragraph to paragraph as well? What other additions might the writer have made? How, for example, might the addition of some dialogue have improved this final draft?

APPROACHING LIFE FROM A NEW PERSPECTIVE

Sometimes a single occurrence changes your whole outlook towards life and the way you perceive things. One such incident happened to me, and it changed my way of looking at life.

One night I was awakened by a phone call. The troubled voice on the line belonged to a sister of a friend. She pleaded with me to come to Elmhurst General; she said there was something terribly wrong with her brother and the family needed me to translate what the doctor had to say. She hung up before I was able to question her.

I drove to the hospital in a hurry, expecting the worst. I finally spotted them in a corner of the emergency room. Like any other emergency room, this one, too, was made up of small partitions. You could tell that it was a busy night because every one of the beds was full. As I walked across and to the other side of that huge room, I could hear people scream and moan as the doctors and nurses were working on them. I tried to look away.

My friend's family stood motionless, holding hands, with their eyes glued to a drawn curtain. I saw his mother's eyes, and I felt my stomach turn cold. With her hand she motioned me to look inside the divider. I couldn't; I was too scared. My hands were numb, as if full of lead. She asked me, in Russian, to go inside and to see how was her son. I didn't have to.

The curtain had opened, and a nurse with a doctor came out and approached us. The doctor said to the family that he did everything he could but that my friend had died of a cocaine overdose.

My mind went blank. I felt someone pulling my arm, and I heard my friend's father asking me something in Russian. At that moment, I realized that my friend's parents didn't understand what the doctor had said. With horror, I realized that I was the one who had to tell them that their son had died.

I will never, as long as I live, forget their faces that night. It was not easy for me to explain to them the cause of their son's death. I did not understand it myself.

His parents buried my friend the next day as the Jewish tradition dictates. There were many of his other friends there. His mom wept when the rabbi was finished with the ceremony and the coffin was lowered into the ground. I kept seeing my friend's smiling face.

Weeks later, when my mind had adjusted a little better to what had happened to my friend, I asked myself many questions. I felt guilt and anger: guilt for not being there for my friend, anger toward my friend for doing this to himself and his family. His death seemed so senseless to me. He was a really nice guy, a good friend, someone you could count on. He had big plans for himself. He just got off the right track. I miss my friend.

I cannot help but think how his death affected my life. I do not take things for granted anymore. I enjoy life every second. I do what I want in my life, and I do not want to go off the right track.

Adding

Adding—of words, phrases, or whole passages—is required when you neglect to put on paper information that the reader needs to know. Subconsciously, you may have assumed that because what you wrote was clear to you, it would be clear to the reader. Or some facets of your subject may simply not have occurred to you when you wrote your rough draft. However, your "other self," your peer group, or your instructor may now suggest that important additions be made.

Details may need to be added that will make your writing more concrete; perhaps you wrote something like "The experience was terrifying" without indicating to the reader what the terrifying elements of the experience were. Or perhaps you wrote something like "The situation impinged on me in a negative fashion," thinking that you were writing impressively, but not realizing that your language was very abstract and did not present an actual picture to the reader of how you felt about what was happening to you.

Revising such sentences in order to add details to an essay can result in much more vivid writing: "With her hand she motioned me to look inside the divider. I couldn't; I was too scared. My hands were numb, as if full of lead"; or "My mind went blank. I felt someone pulling my arm, and I heard my friend's father asking something in Russian. At that moment, I realized that my friend's parents didn't understand what the doctor had said."

You may also need to add details that define the relationships between the ideas in your draft, as the writer of "Approaching Life from a New Perspective" added details about the kind of person his friend was in order to clarify why his friend's death seemed senseless and left him feeling angry.

You may have neglected an important feature of your subject and now need to expand the essay to include it. Might the writer of "Approaching Life from a New Prospective" have improved his draft by adding information about cocaine addiction?

In addition to considering the information that the reader needs to know, think also of his or her point of view on your subject. Does your voice build a bridge between your point of view and that of your reader, or should words and phrases be added that will create this rapport? For example, if you, as a college student, wrote to your younger brother about your new appreciation of Picasso and did not take into account his disparagement of those "funny figures" in Picasso's work, you might want to add phrases that would bring your attitude and his closer together. To the following sentence in your draft, "Picasso introduced the twentieth century to new perceptions of time and space," you might add, "as Einstein did in physics," as your brother is currently taking that subject in high school.

Whether you are adding information or building bridges between you and your reader, adding words, phrases, and even paragraphs is an important part of revision.

Revising Your Essay on an Incident

In adding to the rough draft of your essay for this task, decide whether you have enabled your audience to experience the incident as you did. If not, add details to make your narrative as vivid as possible or, as did the writer of "Approaching Life from a New Perspective," to enable your reader to see the relationships between your ideas. Also, if any important aspect of the incident has occurred to you belatedly, add that aspect. Further, create a tone of voice that indicates that you are responsive to your audience by adding analogies or explanations that will encourage your reader to see your point of view.

Finally, recheck your paper for Chapter 3 by asking the following questions about it:

Checklist to Consider in Revising an Essay About an Incident

1. What strategy do I employ to hook my reader? Are there additional ways I can stimulate a reader's interest in my report on an experience?

2. Have I narrated my experience of the incident in vivid and concrete enough detail to allow my reader(s) to share my perceptions and responses? Have I included any background information that is necessary for the reader(s) to understand my point of view?

3. Does my arrangement effectively recount the most vital stages of the incident? Do I include sufficient exposition to clarify my shaping idea? Do my paragraph structures and transitions convey the sequence of stages and ideas effectively?

4. Have I informed myself adequately about my audience's frame of reference? What additional adjustments do I need to make, in order to bridge any gaps between myself and my audience?

Editing

Editing is different from revising in that revising affects content and organization, whereas editing affects the surface features of the essay, such as transitions, word choice, and mechanics. Editing should be done only when your revisions are complete. Editing changes include the same processes, however, as revisions: adding, substituting, rearranging, distributing, consolidating, and cutting.

Adding. Add words that further clarify the meaning of your phrases and sentences. These words, such as adjectives and adverbs, can provide additional details as well.

Topic Sentences. Once again, review your topic sentences. Should transitions be added to relate the paragraph to the essay? Should any other words or phrases be added to make this important sentence as precise a summary of the paragraph as possible?

Transitions. Make sure to add transitions to your rough draft so that your peers can easily grasp the connections between your thoughts and also follow your chronological sequence.

Mechanics. At this point, forget *what* you are saying and concentrate on *how* you are saying it. Reread your first draft solely for mechanical errors such as spelling (use a good dictionary); grammar (refer to the handbook at the end of this text); punctuation (again, the handbook); and capitalization (handbook once again).

Now, revise and edit your rough draft.

BECOMING AWARE OF YOURSELF AS A WRITER

Make use of your journal to record your thoughts and feelings about the task for Chapter 3. As you write in your journal, consider the following questions:

1. How useful were the journalist's questions in generating ideas for the task? Did you rely on any other means of generating information? In what ways were these means useful?

2. Do you understand the concept of the "Intended" Reader? Under what writing circumstances do you think that you must analyze your reader's frame of reference?

3. What are the limitations of inference in trying to determine your audience's point of view?

4. How did you feel about writing for your peers? How helpful was it for you to evaluate the differences between their point of view and your own?

5. How did the writing process described in this chapter help or hinder the writing of your essay?

6. How helpful was the feedback you received on your rough draft? Did it lead to any significant improvements in your final draft?

7. What was the single most difficult aspect of the writing task for you? How did you resolve it?

P A R T

II

Exploration

INTRODUCTION

It is a close play at the plate. The runner starts his slide just as the catcher gets the throw from second. The two players meet in a cloud of dust. The catcher is certain that he has tagged the runner out. The runner is equally certain that he has slid safely underneath the catcher's outstretched mitt. Each man looks toward the umpire . . .

Someone is likely to disagree with the umpire's decision. Whichever way he calls the play, someone in the stands or on the field is likely to say he is blind.

Yet the umpire's view is taken as final, because it is his role to play an objective observer. Unlike the fan or the manager or the second baseman, he has nothing to gain or lose as a result of his decision. His decision is always more impartial and less prejudiced, even if his perspective is often equally limited.

The umpire's view is limited: he attempts only to call the play as *he sees it*. Similarly, when you as a writer attempt simply to describe the world as you see it, as it appears from your personal angle of vision, you offer a limited perspective, a perspective that perhaps tells as much about you as it tells about whatever you describe.

But what if you want to broaden your angle of vision and see the world more fully, not only as it looks to you but as it actually is in all its richness and complexity? What if you are interested in *exploring the close play at the plate from various vantage points:* in explaining why that decision is controversial, in comparing the play at the plate to other close plays you have seen, in speculating about the effect of the umpire's call on the outcome of the game, in evaluating the power of the second baseman's throwing arm or the agility with which the runner executed the mechanics of a slide into home plate. In each of these cases, you are exploring the world beyond any single self, any single perspective.

Exploratory writing, such as case studies and progress reports, is writing to learn what you do not already know about a subject. It is writing that probes and questions, analyzes and evaluates. It is the writing of the dedicated learner. Janet Emig, a writing theorist, says writing is a "unique mode of learning" because it is active, and because it provides for reseeing what has been already learned or noted and thus encourages new connections between information and between ideas.

Your goal in tasks that follow will be to explore the world from a perspective broader than that open to you when your concern is primarily self-expression, and then to inform your audience of the discoveries you have made. In Chapter 4, you will explore a place to see if it merits its good reputation. In Chapter 5, you will explore a prejudgment you have made to see if multiple observations bear out your initial impression.

4

Writing About a Place— Exploring Your Point of View

In completing the task for Chapter 3, you wrote not only about yourself but also about the details of an incident that you experienced. In order to reconstruct what happened, you had to stand back—at least a step or two—and try recalling everything you saw and heard.

But what if you were to describe the incident with the objectivity of a news reporter? You probably would have to distance yourself a good deal further from what happened. As much as possible, you would have to make the incident itself—rather than your experience of it—the subject of your writing.

Put another way, the writer and the subject would have to become emphatically separate corners of the communications triangle that we introduced you to in Chapter 1:

Writer

Reader   Subject

In this chapter, we ask you to begin stepping back from your subject in this way, so that you can try your hand at a more objective kind of writing. Your role will shift from participant to interested observer as you explore the world of experience beyond the self. Your purpose will no longer be expressive but expository — to seek information about a subject that you may then pass on to others.

To explore a subject is to broaden your point of view on that subject. This is a common motive for writing; you might need to test out what you know or find out more about a subject for personal reasons. If, for example, you want to buy a car and see an ad for Honest Sam's Used Cars that promises the best deal in town, you might decide to investigate whether or not Honest Sam's is all that its ad claims. You could visit the used car lot, of course, and talk to the employees and possibly to other customers too. You could also visit other used car lots and compare their deals to Sam's. You might check with your local mechanic to see if he/she knows anything about the cars Sam sells. You might even visit the local department of consumer affairs and ask them about Sam's reputation as a businessman.

It is possible that as you conduct your exploration, you will keep notes on your findings and put them in some kind of summary order to help you decide whether you should buy from Sam. You surely would write up your findings if you were exploring Honest Sam's for more public or professional reasons: as an investigator for the consumer affairs department, for example; or as a marketing consultant for a group of investors interested in opening a new car dealership across the street from Sam's.

In Chapter 4, we will ask you to explore a place and write up your findings. In moving on to this more objective, expository writing, you will continue to use, of course, the skills developed in the first chapters, such as keen observation of what you see, a sense of ordering an experience chronologically, and an ability to analyze the significance of that experience. To these skills, now directed towards the world of others, you will begin to add other techniques to be learned here, such as describing people, places, and objects and interviewing people to learn of their knowledge about your subject. Your focus will shift from narration and exposition in the service of narration (Chapters 2 and 3) to exposition and narration in the service of exposition.

Because you will be seeking information about your subject, your method of generating ideas will be that of an explorer who asks, "How shall I learn about this subject?" Your audience, too, will be seeking information, and therefore the most important audience question for you to answer will become "What information about my subject does my audience both want and need?"

TASK: EXPLORING A PLACE

The task for this chapter asks you to visit a place closely or tangentially related to your major, to a hobby, or simply to an interest, a place you have not visited before, one that you know about only through the opinion of others. This should be a place for which you have high regard because of its reputation. You will want to observe its appearance and what is going on there, and to interview the people you meet so that you can come to some overall impression of the place that does or does not justify your initial good opinion.

The purpose of this assignment is to give you the opportunity to explore a place about which a myth may have been created for you by others. Essentially you will be answering the question "What do I perceive and how can I explain my perceptions to others as fully and richly as possible?" You can do so by asking yourself a more specific writing question: "Is this place as vital as everyone led me to believe?" or "What can I discover about this place that will either support or negate my earlier opinion?"

You might, for example, plan to be a children's librarian, and you may always have wanted to visit the main branch of the public library in your city. The local librarians have cited as their models the procedures followed in the main branch, and you wish to visit to see if efficiency does indeed reign there. Or, as a future aerospace engineer, you may have read about Grumman or Boeing or McDonnell Douglas as the giants in the field. A visit might confirm your sense of admiration, but the industry is facing strong competition from abroad, and a visit might also explain why the once-proud aircraft industry is faltering. By asking yourself the question "Does this place justify my regard?" you leave yourself open to an honest evaluation of what you have discovered.

The audience for this task should be someone like you who is interested in your findings about this place, so we suggest that you write for a group of like-minded people, such as a class in your curriculum or a group of people who share your hobby or interest. This audience will know more about your subject than either a random selection of college students or your English class or possibly your English teacher.

In the sections that follow, we will introduce you to the "Explorer's Questions" that can help you gather information and broaden your point of view about a place; to a method of evaluating the depth of information your audience possesses about the place and determining what about your subject they need to learn; to an arrangement strategy of weaving chronology, description, exposition, and dialogue together to create an overriding impression of your subject; and to the drafting and revising process of putting your essay together.

WRITING YOUR ESSAY

Generating Ideas: The Explorer's Questions

To generate ideas when exploring almost any subject, whether it is an object, a place, a person, an experience, or an idea, you can ask yourself the following five questions:

1. What features characterize it? In other words, what is it, and what does it look like?
2. How does it differ from others in its class? How is it similar to them?
3. How does it fit into larger systems of which it is a part: a larger category, an enterprise, a neighborhood, or a community?
4. How does it change? How has it changed since its inception? What was its high point? What will it be like in the future?
5. What are its parts, and how do they work together?

The first question asks for a description of the subject, whether it is a physical description of a place, an object, or a person, or the characterization of an idea or an abstract object, such as a poem. The intent in answering this question is to describe the thing in itself, the object in its unique existence. In describing a particular classroom on campus, for example, you might describe the old wooden desk tops on which past students have carved their initials, the poor ventilation that results in a stuffy atmosphere, the green color of the blackboards, and the other characteristics of this particular classroom.

Question 2 asks for a comparison of your subject with others like it—others in the same class. To continue with the example of the classroom, Question 2 asks how it compares with other classrooms, or perhaps with other places of study, such as a library. Is it a typical example of a classroom, or does it distinguish itself in some way? Is it, for example, smaller and more intimate than the typical classroom, perhaps having a large table around which students sit rather than individual desks? Or is it a room in which only science classes are held? Or is it a room in which you have been more bored or more stimulated intellectually than in other classrooms you have entered?

Question 3 wants to know about the many systems that most subjects fit into. Any classroom fits into a number of different systems. It is a part of a campus building, a reflection of the architectural and engineering systems of the building. It is a part of an educational system, a reflection of the philosophy and techniques of educating students at a particular school. It is a part of a college community, a reflection of the professional and social relationships at the school, a place where learning occurs but also where friendships are formed, ambitions are tested, and so forth.

Question 4 investigates the subject as dynamic—as it changes or has changed or will change. A classroom may seem a very different place at different times of the day or of the semester. It ages, of course, over time and may be subject to renovation on occasion. Its high point might have been when it was brand new or when a particularly effective teacher taught in it. Its future may be dark or bright, depending perhaps on the fate of the school of which it is a part.

Finally, Question 5 asks how the subject works—what parts it is composed of, which together comprise its whole and perform its function. Classrooms are composed of tables, desks, chairs, blackboards, chalk, and erasers, of course, but also of books, students, teachers, and so forth.

To cite another example, let's look at an idea that might be discussed in a classroom. Suppose that in a political science class you are studying the constitutional principle of free speech. Finding answers to the explorer's questions can help you to learn and write about this principle.

What is this principle? It is a right guaranteed to Americans by the First Amendment. It prohibits the government from censoring or in any other way limiting our right to say what we think whenever and to whomever we want. But it does not give us blanket permission to speak out: the right to free speech does not include, for example, a sanction to shout "Fire!" in a crowded place when there really is no fire or a right to commit libel against someone else.

How does our right to free speech compare with other rights enjoyed by American citizens? It can excite as much controversy as our right to bear arms. It can conflict with our right to privacy. It also can be compared with the principle of free speech as practiced (or not) in other nations.

This principle is a part of the system of government by which we live, but it is also a part of other systems. You might write about the role that free speech plays in our philosophy of individualism or in our capitalist economic system or in our artistic community.

Although the actual wording that guarantees the right to free speech in the Constitution has not changed over time, our attitudes toward this right have changed. At some points in our history, for example, the Supreme Court has interpreted this right less broadly than at other times. Private attitudes toward this right, toward who should be allowed to speak freely about what, often change. Have Americans enjoyed this right more or less thoroughly in the past? How strong will this right remain in our future? Answers to these questions can help you explore the meaning of the principle, as can an examination of the parts that compose it.

Of what parts is a principle or an idea composed? The right to free speech is composed, to a degree, of the laws passed by Congress over the years to defend it. It is also composed of the moral and political ideals used by its defenders to justify their position.

SOME PRACTICE WITH THE EXPLORER'S QUESTIONS

1. As you write in your journal, select a simple object—a lamp, a book, a picture—and analyze it according to the explorer's five questions.

2. Using the five explorer's questions, construct a dialogue between two people whose questions and answers provide information about a subject. For example, in the following dialogue, one person is trying to learn about the other by asking these questions:

   Lou: Who are you? I've never seen you here before.
   Sue: That's for you to find out.
   Lou: That's pretty funny. It's dark in here. Do you have red hair or is that the lights?
   Sue: I'm six feet tall and look like Brooke Shields.
   Lou: Are you like all the other girls who come to this place?
   Sue: Of course. They're beautiful and so am I. But I'm also brilliant.
   Lou: Boy, you're pretty high on yourself. What are you doing here if you are so terrific?

   Most likely, you can also guess where they are. In your dialogue, try to create a situation that will allow the characters to arrive at an understanding of a subject of your choice. Some suggestions: landing on the moon, the first day of the semester, choosing a teacher at registration, arguing about a team's prospects for the new season.

3. Create a riddle by having the subject define itself by giving information that answers the five explorer's questions. For example:

   I am long and blond, but that's not the point. Some think that I'm too soft, others think I'm hard enough but that I snap under pressure. Although I look like a lot of others in my class, I often have a distinctive name tattooed all over my body. Many people say I'm not as important as I was years ago, that I've been made obsolete. But let me tell you, buddy, I can still go a long way. Get the message?
   Answer: a pencil

4. Select from one of your courses a topic that you have been asked to investigate. For example, in history you may have been asked to explain the changes in American attitudes towards politics in the 1960s. How could you use the explorer's questions to find an approach to this subject?

   Using the Explorer's Questions to Generate Ideas About a Place. To generate information and ideas for this assignment, try using your powers of observation to answer as many of the explorer's questions as time and access permit. You might want to take some notes about your observations, for example, a description of some unusual object or procedure that caught your attention or some person whose appearance or manner struck you as unusual. An old office building might have some unusual decorative feature that seems to you to contrast with the high-tech architectural design of the employees' work area. Although you might not see the immediate practical use of small details, when you begin to write your essay, some of these details can be useful in characterizing the place, revealing some interesting feature, or highlighting an important process.

Another method for answering the explorer's questions is to seek help from others who already know the way the place works, how it may have changed or plans to change, or the systems that it fits into. Don't be intimidated at the thought of engaging strangers in a question-and-answer conversation. Most people are flattered that you think they have information worth imparting. It would be helpful for you to try to anticipate questions ahead of time. Therefore, you might want to prepare a list of questions that would elicit information you need in order to answer each explorer's question. Be specific—a question like "Can you tell me how your job task contributes to the overall process here?" is more effective than "Can you tell me about this place?"

Further, depending upon the place you visit, brochures may be available as sources of information. Often a publicity piece will provide some information in answer to some or all of the explorer's questions. However, the information may be too general for your purposes and it may be slanted in favor of the place, so you will want to use brochures with these drawbacks in mind.

Some explorer's questions may generate fuller answers than others, and some may be more crucial to the particular place you are writing about than others. For example, a place not similar to others in its class may require more description than a place comparable to others. A unique place will demand the most description of all.

In general, ask yourself which questions are the most important in writing about your place, which you can answer yourself, which you will need to interview people to answer, and how full an answer your reader requires in each case. Note that you may want to reshape the five questions to elicit the most appropriate information about your subject. You may want to add questions, make them more specific, or redirect them in some way.

Following is the approach of a student who plans to write about the geology exhibit of a museum.

Question 1
What does this geology exhibit look like?

Question 2
How does it differ from the other exhibits in the museum? Why has the

museum arranged it in this way? How does it compare with other geology exhibits I have seen?

Question 3

How does it fit into the layout of the museum? As this is a museum of natural history, how does a geology exhibit fit into the overall purpose of the place? What role does the exhibit play in the education of those who view it?

Question 4

How has the exhibit changed since the museum first created it? How will it change in the future, based on what I know or can learn about geological findings? Was the acquisition of moon rocks the high point of the exhibit? If not, what was?

Question 5

How is the exhibit arranged? What specific categories are there? What special exhibits exist?

Like this student, you may need to reshape the explorer's questions to suit the needs of your task.

SOME PRACTICE WITH USING THE EXPLORER'S QUESTIONS TO GENERATE IDEAS ABOUT A PLACE

1. Recall a place that you visited recently where people were involved in some mutual experience or enterprise. Analyze this place using the five questions as your guide.

2. You have been sent by your employer in marketing research to do some field research for Dr. Fu's Spicy Hot Chicken, a new fast-food chain that is thinking of opening up a branch in your neighborhood. You are to do an analysis of their chief competitors, located across the street on a busy intersection in your community. Write a brief report using the explorer's five questions on two restaurants in your neighborhood that would be competitors for Dr. Fu's.

Using Your Journal in Answering the Explorer's Questions About a Place.   You can use your journal again as a kind of reporter's notebook (see Chapter 3, p. 96), to record the answers you generate to the explorer's questions as you visit the place you plan to write your essay on for Chapter 4. As you do so, try making use of the double-entry technique as a means of examining the different perspectives or angles on the place that the explorer's questions generate. Dividing the pages of your journal into two columns, try one or more of the following exercises:

1. In the left-hand column, list the answers to one explorer's question that you get from your own observation and from interviews with one or more other people. In the right-hand column, write about the similarities and/or differences in these answers.
2. In the left-hand column, write the answers to two different explorer's questions. In the right-hand column, compare the information that each question generates, commenting on the significance of the similarities and/or differences in this information.
3. Once you have completed your exploration, reread all the information that you collected. As you do so, write in the right-hand column about what different pieces of information add to your overall assessment or impression of the place.

Addressing Your Audience: Depth of Information

Some audiences require more information; some require different information. As we suggested in Chapter 3, if you were writing to a group of grade-school children, you would write differently from when you were addressing teenagers. In this section, we will discuss how you might analyze the frame of reference of your intended readers in order to determine how much "depth of information" you should supply. We will discuss how to answer the question, "What information about my subject does my audience both want and need?"

Here are two passages on the same subject written for two different audiences, one (A) a class of college English students, the other (B) an English professor:

A. *Preparation.* For writers, there are probably two parts to the preparation stage. The first includes just about everything a person has engaged in before he or she starts on a writing assignment—education, personal experiences, sports, work, reading, family life. All these areas of one's life provide potential writing material, and the more alert and thoughtful one is about his or her experiences, the better prepared that person is to write.

The second part of the preparation stage in writing begins when the writer identifies the writing task. This stage may include choosing and narrowing a topic or clarifying an assignment made by someone else. It also requires identifying audience and purpose: for whom are you writing and why are you writing? When the writer has answered those questions, he or she can begin to employ various strategies for generating material. The writer may also start to develop it. The activity at this stage of the process might be compared to feeding information into a computer from which one will later write a program or solve a problem.

B. In preparation, the starting point for a writer is recognizing a problem worthy of honest inquiry. There must be reasonably substantial personal experience, observation, education or reading to supply the subject matter or situation within which the student can recognize, formulate, and explore such a problem. Original thinking may grow out of recalling old and comfortable knowledge and integrating it with new or previously separate elements in a new combination. Students probably will demonstrate greater motivation and originality in their writing if they aim at something they find worth investigating on their own. But even that supposition needs qualifying, in that too many students seem conditioned to look for easy answers instead and avoid problems if they can. Students typically choose an idea acquired from someone else to write about, perhaps because they like it, not because there is any problem in it for them and not because they have anything original to say about it, at least at the moment of choosing. The most common curricular approach, to include challenging reading materials in a writing course, whether poetry by Dickinson and Plath or essays by Bruner and Eiseley, offers opportunities for problems, but only if the student reads attentively and competently enough to see the difference between a problem worthy of exploration and rather easily resolved factual ignorance. Richard Young, following John Dewey, suggests that the source of a problem lies in a clash of some sort contributing to an "uneasy feeling" in one's personal reaction to a situation. The clash may be explained as a logical inconsistency or a conflict with one's cultural values or educational training. But whatever the cause, awareness, curiosity, and a sort of discomfort usually stimulate strong motivation to correct or clarify the situation. The starting point, at any rate, is not with problems patiently waiting for any qualified researcher to come and seize them; rather it is with particular individuals recognizing and creating their own problems in the material they are working with. But students must not only be taught to look for problems; even at this early stage, they should define their problems so that the problems look potentially solvable and so that students will know when, and if, they have solved them.

> —David V. Harrington, "Encouraging Honest Inquiry
> in Student Writing," *College Composition and
> Communication* (May 1979)

The first paragraph of Passage A, written for college students, roughly corresponds to Sentences 2 and 3 of Passage B, written for a professor. However, the second paragraph in Passage A offers much less information than the corresponding section in Passage B (the rest of the paragraph), which includes a more detailed discussion of selecting a writing task, generating material for writing about it, and planning the evolution of the paper. (Other characteristics of the two passages indicate their differing audiences as well, such as language level and paragraph length, but we are concerned here only with differences in depth of information.)

Note how the material that is presented as new in Passage A serves as background material that the writer of Passage B then develops in greater depth:

A. Background

1. The first part of the preparation stage includes personal experience.

2. The second part involves identifying the writing task.

New Material
1. Students must be alert and thoughtful about their experience.

2. Identifying the task includes choosing and narrowing a topic, identifying audience and purpose, generating material.

3. Preparing to write might be compared to feeding information into a computer.

B. Background
1. A student writer needs "reasonably substantial personal experience" to supply subject matter "within which the student can recognize, formulate, and explore" a problem worthy of honest inquiry.

2. The most common curricular approach includes challenging reading material that offers "opportunities for problems."

New Material
1. The supposition that students will be more motivated and original if they write about something worth investigating needs qualifying, in that "too many students seem conditioned to look for easy answers instead."

2. Challenging reading material is useful only if students see "the difference between a problem worthy of exploration and rather easily resolved factual ignorance."

3. According to Richard Young, awareness, curiosity, and "a sort of discomfort" stimulate writing within individuals who recognize and create "their own problems in the material they are working with."

4. Students should be taught to define their problems so that the problems are potentially solvable.

Points 2 and 3 listed under *New Material* in Passage A are not directly mentioned in Passage B, presumably because a professor would already be familiar with such information. Point 2 listed under *Background* in Passage B never comes up in Passage A, presumably because a student in an English Composition class does not need information about "common curricular approaches" in general, but rather information in depth about the specific approach to writing he/she is being introduced to.

In order to analyze the information needs for your intended audience, make an exhaustive list of the aspects of your subject. Then, using your audience's frame of reference as a guide, try to determine which aspects your audience is familiar with and which represent unfamiliar territory. Group those in the first category under the heading "Familiar" or "Background" and the second under the heading "Unfamiliar" or "New." If you have more aspects grouped under "Familiar" than under "Unfamiliar," you know you are writing for an informed audience that will not require much in the way of a general introduction to your subject and that you can therefore concentrate on giving new, in-depth information about the unfamiliar aspects. If, on the other hand, you have very few aspects of your subject grouped under the heading "Familiar," your audience is uninformed, and you will give basic background on your subject and present little specialized information.

Suppose, for example, that you are writing about an exploration that you made of a nearby campus of the state university you were considering transferring to. If your audience was composed of seniors in your high school class who were also thinking about applying to this school, you might begin to analyze their information needs in the following way:

Familiar

1. Reputation of campus.
2. Location (and possibly appearance) of campus.
3. Relationship between students at campus and neighboring community.

Unfamiliar

1. Life of students on campus: courses of study; dormitory and social life; financial obligations.
2. Activities in particular buildings.
3. History of campus as part of community and/or state university system.

Might you add anything to either list? How would your lists change, if your audience instead was made up of students at other colleges who were considering transferring to your branch of the state university?

SOME PRACTICE WITH AUDIENCE DEPTH OF INFORMATION

1. You are the head of the art history department at your school, and one art history course is required in the first semester for all incoming freshmen. However, most freshmen are not art majors, and you want to write them a letter at the end of the first semester, hoping to get them interested in taking other art courses in addition to the required one. How much depth of information would you include? You want to write a letter to declared art majors at the same time informing them of second-semester course offerings. How would this letter differ in depth of information?

2. Prepare to write two letters on some aspect of college life, one to your college classmates and one to some friends still in high school. How do the frames of reference of the two audiences differ? With what aspects of your subject is each group familiar? Unfamiliar? What background information must you give each group? What new material can you present? Once you have determined the answers to these questions, write the letters.

3. List the information you would classify as familiar and unfamiliar to your audience if you were going to write about a visit you made to some sort of annual event — the yearly state fair or circus, a local pageant or championship game, a class picnic, or street fair — for each of the following group of readers:

a. Children who have never been to the event.

b. Your contemporaries who usually go with you but missed the event this year.

c. Older people who used to attend regularly but have not been to the event in recent years.

Determining Your Audience's Depth of Information for Your Essay on a Place.   In working through the task for this chapter, you will want to compose a frame of reference for your audience and analyze how much depth of information this audience will need. Answer the questions: "What points can I skim over?" "What knowledge can I take for granted?" and "Where and how much can or should I go into depth?"

In answering these questions, refer to the material you have generated through the explorer's method of inquiry. Ask yourself if any of the answers to the explorer's questions, or parts of the questions, should be given to your audience as necessary background. If so, should the answers be detailed or brief? Which questions, or parts of questions, should be answered in depth for this audience? How much depth can the audience absorb?

For example, the student writing about the geology exhibit composed the following frame of reference for her audience:

- **Audience:** A Geology I class.
- **Characteristics:** Interested in geology, although not necessarily planning to major in it.
- Did well in high-school science courses.
- Two are creationists; the rest are evolutionists.
- Most have not visited the geology exhibit.

The frame of reference helped her to understand the depth of information that her audience required:

Background (Brief)
1. What does the exhibit look like?
2. How does it differ from the other exhibits in the museum? From geology exhibits in other museums?
3. How does it fit into the museum? Into the interests of geologists and geology students in the area?

New Material (In Depth)

4. How has the exhibit changed over the years since it was first introduced into the museum? What was its high point? How might it change in the future?

5. What method of arrangement of exhibits has been used? What special exhibits are there?

Answering the following questions of the "Audience Analysis Guide" should help you to write more effectively for your audience.

——————— AUDIENCE ANALYSIS GUIDE ———————

1. Who is my audience?
2. What is the frame of reference of this audience?
3. What point of view is my audience likely to have on my subject?
4. How do my own frame of reference and point of view differ from those of my reader?
5. How can I bridge any gap that exists between my reader's point of view and my own?
6. How much depth of information does my audience need and want on the background of my subject? On the new material I wish to present?

SOME PRACTICE IN DETERMINING YOUR AUDIENCE'S DEPTH OF INFORMATION FOR YOUR ESSAY ON A PLACE

1. The nursing student who wrote the following paragraphs was addressing an intended audience of fellow nursing students who, she assumed, would share her interest in Planned Parenthood:

The walk from the subway seemed long, and a strong, cold wind was at my back, pushing me down Twenty-third Street. It was a nice part of the city, however, as there were lots of auxiliary cops around from the nearby Police Academy and lots of kids with portfolios were coming from the School of Visual Arts. The wind kept pushing me toward Second Avenue. From a distance, I could see my destination. A dirty, blue and white banner hung from the second story of 380 Second Avenue, proudly announcing the Margaret Sanger Center of Planned Parenthood.

Planned Parenthood has quite a reputation. It is where young women and men can go to get information about birth control, pregnancy, abortion, and venereal disease. The outstanding feature is its promise of confidentiality. Although other women's health organizations also offer confidentiality, Planned Parenthood was the first to do so.

I entered the reception area and asked for an appointment. Without looking up, the secretary told me to "Go down the hall, turn right and pick up one of the beige phones on the wall to make an appointment." Although I was taken aback by her indifference, I did as she said. The woman on the phone said I could have an appointment that morning and told me to return to the reception desk.

This time, the woman looked up. She gave me forms to fill out and said I would have to pay in advance. A pelvic exam would be fifty dollars. I filled out the forms, paid the money, and waited.

a. What other inferences has the writer appeared to make about her readers?

b. How might she have rewritten these paragraphs, had she asked herself one or more of the following questions:

    (1) What if some of my readers have already visited a branch of Planned Parenthood?

    (2) What if some of the people who will read my essay are opposed to abortion?

    (3) What if my essay is read by someone who has never been to New York City?

2. Review the information you have collected about a place with the help of the explorer's questions, then write an introductory paragraph for your essay for this chapter. What inferences does your introduction make about your readers' depth of information?

Arranging Your Essay

The Shaping Idea. The answers that you generate to the five explorer's questions should help you to answer one further question: "What is my *overriding impression* about this place?" Your overriding impression may point out some vital connection among the different pieces of information that you have gathered about the place. You might want to write an initial statement of your impression of the place before you begin arranging your rough draft; then, as you write, reconsider your statement in light of the way you shape your material. Or, you might want to wait and write your overall impression last.

As you answer the explorer's questions, you will find yourself using different patterns of paragraph development. Question 1 calls for description; Questions 2–4 suggest patterns of exposition, such as comparison, contrast, classification, and analysis; and Question 5 requires a form of narration that describes a process. You will therefore be weaving together patterns of narration, description, and exposition.

Narrative Patterns.   Although in this chapter you are writing about a place involving others, you should not disappear from the essay entirely, as you have chosen this place to write about because of its vital interest to you. As an observer of the place and the activities there, you can put yourself in the essay by giving a chronological account of your visit as an unobtrusive narrative framework to the essay. The question of arranging the essay then becomes "How can I frame the essay with a narrative account of my visit so that I can convey my considerable interest and at the same time keep the atmosphere and action of the place in the foreground?"

One way to answer this question is to develop a second narrative that, in answer to the fifth question of the explorer's method of inquiry, relates the process by which the systems of the place work together. Process analysis is a type of chronology that indicates how a person or mechanism accomplishes a task from the beginning of the operation to its completion. Whenever one discusses how anything works—from a simple can opener to the writing of an essay—one is dealing in time; in beginnings, middles, and endings.

A narrative account of the operation may be most effective in answering the question "How does this place operate?" The period of time covered, of course, will depend on the cycle or cycles of operation. Processes can be completed in an hour, in a day, on a weekly basis, monthly, annually, or seasonally. Once you have determined what processes need explanation, the objective is to narrate them sequentially (see Chapter 5, pp. 200–201 for more on process analysis).

Here is an example of a process:

It's seven in the morning and the day shift is starting to drift in. Huge tractors are backing up to the big-mouthed doors of the warehouse. Cattle trucks bring tons of beef to feed its insatiable appetite for cargo. Smoke-covered trailers with refrigerated units packed deep with green peppers sit with their diesel engines idling. Names like White, Mack, and Kenworth are welded to the front of their radiators, which hiss and moan from the overload. The men walk through the factory-type gates of the parking lot with their heads bowed, oblivious of the shuddering diesels that await them.

Once inside the warehouse they gather in groups of threes and fours like prisoners in an exercise yard. They stand in front of the two time clocks that hang below a window in the manager's office. They smoke and cough in the early morning hours as they await their work assignments. The manager, a nervous-looking man with a stomach that is starting to push out at his belt, walks out with a pink work sheet in his hand.

—Patrick Fenton, "Notes of a Working Stiff"

Patterns of Exposition. The answers to the Explorer's Questions 2, 3, and 4 call for exposition. As we saw in Chapter 3, exposition is the presentation and explanation of ideas. In contrast to narration, which presents the world of time, and to description (which we will discuss below), which presents the world of space, exposition presents the world of the mind as it exists apart from time and space, interpreting their relationships and analyzing their meanings.

The ideas presented by exposition may be concrete: an analysis of a beaver dam, a comparison of race tracks, a classification of the foods eaten by the athletes in various sports. They may also be abstract: a classification of the psychologies of different groups in America, an analysis of the international banking system, a comparison of Eastern and Western philosophies of religion. Whether concrete or abstract, or a mixture of the two, exposition classifies, analyzes, and compares ideas about objects, places, people, and emotions. (These and other purposes of exposition will be explained more fully in subsequent chapters.)

In fulfilling the task for this chapter, you will want to use exposition in answering the explorer's Question 2, which asks you to compare your subject with others like it; Question 3, which asks you to analyze what larger systems it is a part of; and Question 4, which requires you to analyze how it has changed, does change, and will change.

Understanding the differences between comparison and analysis will help you to organize your answers. Comparison and its corollary, contrast, ask you to point out the similarities and differences between two objects or among three or more objects. You can do this either (1) by presenting the similarities and then the differences or (2) by comparing and contrasting your subject point by point (see Chapter 5, pp. 199–200 for further discussion of comparison and contrast). An example of comparison and contrast follows. Which method of arrangement does it use, (1) or (2)?

We know from our work hundreds of outstanding competitors who possess strong character formation that complements high motor skill. But we found others who possessed so few strong character traits that it was difficult on the basis of personality to account for their success. There were gold-medal

Olympic winners at Mexico and Japan whom we would classify as overcompensatory greats. Only magnificent physical gifts enabled them to overcome constant tension, anxiety, and self-doubt. They are unhappy, and when the talent ages and fades, they become derelicts, while someone like Roosevelt Grier just goes on to bigger mountains. We often wonder how much higher some of these great performers might have gone if they had, say, the strong personality structure that characterized our women's Olympic fencing team.

—Bruce C. Ogilvie and Thomas A. Tutjo, "Sport: If You Want to Build Character, Try Something Else"

Analysis calls for a breaking down of the subject into parts. It calls for probing beneath a solid surface to discover what a thing is composed of or how it changes (has changed or will change). Analysis also seeks to discover the larger pattern to which a thing belongs. The arrangement pattern of analysis is the presentation of the parts in a systematic order. What parts does the author of the following passage delineate in the origin of **Y'know?**

We know less about the origin of *Y'know* than about the origin of *Boola boola*, but there is some reason to believe that in this country it began among poor blacks who because of the various disabilities imposed on them, often did not speak and for whom *Y'know* was a request for assurance that they had been understood. From that sad beginning it spread among people who wanted to show themselves sympathetic to blacks, and among those who saw it as the latest thing and either could not resist or did not want to be left out.

—Edwin Newman, "A Protective Interest in the English Language"

Note how the author of the next paragraph fits a current "misuse" of the word *momentarily* into a larger pattern of linguistic change:

Who says that *momentarily* shouldn't mean *soon?* After all, *clown* once meant *farmer.* A *villain* was someone who lived in the country. *Gay* used to mean *carefree.* "Linguistic change is going on all the time," says Read, who spent years tracking down the origin of the ultimate Americanism: *O.K.* "It isn't necessary for us to feel hot and bothered about it."

—John Powers, "Bitespeak"

Patterns of Description.   Description presents the appearance of things that occupy space, whether they be objects, people, buildings, or cities. The aim of description is to convey to the reader what something looks like. It attempts to paint a picture with words.

In order to clarify the appearance of your subject for your reader, you should develop the tools of the visual artist and describe shapes, colors, positions, and relationships. Following a particular order — left to right, top to bottom, inside to outside — also aids the reader. Selecting your details with an eye to creating a main impression simplifies your task and at the same time enhances the description.

The question to be answered in description is "How can I best describe my subject so that my readers can visualize what I want them to see?" Here is an example of description:

> In winter, the warehouse is cold and damp. There is no heat. The large steel doors that line the warehouse walls stay open most of the day. In the cold months, wind, rain, and snow blow across the floor. In the summer, the warehouse becomes an oven. Dust and sand from the runways mix with the toxic fumes of forklifts, leaving a dry, stale taste in your mouth. The high windows above the doors are covered with a thick, black dirt that kills the sun. The men work in shadows with the constant roar of jet engines blowing dangerously in their ears.
>
> —Patrick Fenton, "Notes of a Working Stiff"

Description may be used as an end in itself but it often serves other purposes. In fulfilling this task, in fact, you will describe your place in answering Question 1, but you will combine description with process narration in answering Question 5, as the reader will better understand the process if she or he knows what the machinery, equipment, props, uniforms, and so on look like.

Dialogue.   *Dialogue* literally means the conversation of two people. In fulfilling this task, you will be interviewing one or more people in the place visited, and therefore dialogue will be a part of your arrangement. In writing the paper, you may want to include part of an exchange you had with someone, or you may want simply to quote the person interviewed. Your guide will be to select comments that highlight an aspect of your subject. The question you will be answering is "What comments were made that are particularly useful to my purposes because they succinctly state the answers to the explorer's questions?"

Following are two examples of quotation, one including only one speaker, the second the dialogue of two speakers. Notice the use of paragraphs for each speaker in the dialogue and the use also of quotation marks:

> "Some of these activities are very appealing to people who've been turned off by team sports," William H. Monti, a physical education reform leader at San Raphael High, explained. "A number of students who rebelled against all forms of physical education have gravitated toward rock climbing. These were the types who said that they didn't like team sports of any kind. Later,

of course, they found out that rock climbing involves as much teamwork as the traditional team sports, or more. They still love it."

—George Leonard, "Why Johnny Can't Run"

Banke, a red-haired, red-faced man, takes a special interest in the Elmhurst tanks because he lives in Maspeth, which borders Elmhurst.

"This is a natural landmark," he said. "It's our version of the Statue of Liberty."

"Anything goes wrong here, I yell at him," said Trieste.

"I get the neck of the chicken," said Banke. "But being a local resident, I make sure things go right."

—"Tanks," *The New Yorker*

The Overriding Impression.   So far you have been asking and answering questions about the parts of this task: the five explorer's questions, the four types of arrangement spelled out. If you have not already done so, you now need to answer the question, "What is my overriding impression about this place? What ties all these parts together?" Included in your overridding impression will be no doubt be an answer to the specific question of the task: "Is this place as vital as everyone has led me to believe?" A sentence clearly stating this impression will serve as the shaping idea of your essay (see Chapter 1) and will help you write the rough draft.

Following is a professional essay that attempts to answer the same questions that you are answering in terms of the description of place, narration of visit and the place's processes, and exposition of the more abstract facts about systems and dynamics, including dialogue between the observer and people in the place. Most important, the author, Saul Bellow, explored the question "How vital (and how safe) is a kibbutz?"

Developed in Israel, the kibbutz is an autonomous, self-sustaining communal settlement usually engaged in agriculture. All its members participate in the many duties of the kibbutz, even the elected leaders. The children are generally reared and educated apart from their parents, although recently this practice has changed in many kibbutzim.

On a Kibbutz

Saul Bellow

On a kibbutz.

Lucky is Nola's dog. John's dog is Mississippi. But John loves Lucky too, and Nola dotes on Mississippi. And then there are the children—one daughter in the army, and a younger child who still sleeps in the kibbutz dormitory. Lucky is a wooly brown dog, old and nervous. His master was killed in the Golan. When there is a sonic boom over the kibbutz, the dog rushes out, growling. He seems to remember the falling bombs. He is too feeble to bark, too old to run, his teeth are bad, his eyes under the brown fringe are dull, and he is clotted under the tail. Mississippi is a big, long-legged, short-haired, brown-and-white, clever, lively, affectionate, and greedy animal. She is a "child dog"—sits in your lap, puts a paw on your arm when you reach for a tidbit to get it for herself. Since she weighs fifty pounds or more she is not welcome in my lap, but she sits on John and Nola and on the guests—those who permit it. She is winsome but also flatulent. She eats too many sweets but is good company, a wonderful listener and conversationalist; she growls and snuffles when you speak directly to her. She "sings" along with the record player. The Auerbachs are proud of this musical yelping.

In the morning we hear the news in Hebrew and then again on the BBC. We eat an Israeli breakfast of fried eggs, sliced cheese, cucumbers, olives, green onions, tomatoes, and little salt fish. Bread is toasted on the coal-oil heater. The dogs have learned the trick of the door and bang in and out. Between the rows of small kibbutz dwellings the lawns are ragged but very green. Light and warmth come from the sea. Under the kibbutz lie the ruins of Herod's Caesarea. There are Roman fragments everywhere. Marble columns in the grasses. Fallen capitals make garden seats. You have only to prod the ground to find fragments of pottery, bits of statuary, a pair of dancing satyr legs. John's tightly packed bookshelves are fringed with such relics. On the crowded desk stands a framed photograph of the dead son, with a small beard like John's, smiling with John's own warmth.

We walk in the citrus groves after breakfast, taking Mississippi with us (John is seldom without her); the soil is kept loose and soft among the trees, the leaves are glossy, the ground itself is fragrant. Many of the trees are still unharvested and bending, tangerines and lemons as dense as stars. "Oh that I were an orange tree/That busie plant!" wrote George Herbert. To put forth such leaves, to be hung with oranges, to be a blessing—one feels the temptation of this on such a morning and I even feel a fibrous woodiness entering my arms as I consider it. You want to take root and stay forever in this most temperate and blue of temperate places. John mourns his son, he always mourns his son, but he is also smiling in the sunlight.

In the exporting of oranges there is competition from the North African countries and from Spain. "We are very idealistic here, but when we read about frosts in Spain we're glad as hell," John says.

All this was once dune land. Soil had to be carted in and mixed with the sand. Many years of digging and tending made these orchards. Relaxing, breathing freely, you feel what a wonderful place has been created here, a homeplace for body and soul; then you remember that on the beaches there are armed patrols. It is always possible that terrorists may come in rubber dinghies that cannot be detected by radar. They entered Tel Aviv itself in March 1975 and seized a hotel at the seashore. People were murdered. John keeps an Uzi in his bedroom cupboard. Nola scoffs at this. "We'd both be dead before you could reach your gun," she says. Cheerful Nola laughs. An expressive woman—she uses her forearm to wave away John's preparations. "Sometimes he does the drill and I time him to see how long it takes to jump out of bed, open the cupboard, get the gun, put in the clip, and turn around. They'd mow us down before he could get a foot on the floor."

Mississippi is part of the alarm system. "She'd bark," says John.

Just now Mississippi is racing through the orchards, nose to the ground. The air is sweet, and the sun like a mild alcohol makes you yearn for good things. You rest under a tree and eat tangerines, only slightly heavy-hearted.

From the oranges we go to the banana groves. The green bananas are tied up in plastic tunics. The great banana flower hangs groundward like the sexual organ of a stallion. The long leaves resemble manes. After two years the ground has to be plowed up and lie fallow. Groves are planted elsewhere — more hard labor. "You noticed before," says John, "that some of the orange trees were withered. Their roots get into Roman ruins and they die. Some years ago, while we were plowing, we turned up an entire Roman street."

He takes me to the Herodian Hippodrome. American archaeologists have dug out some of the old walls. We look down into the diggings, where labels flutter from every stratum. There are more potsherds than soil in these bluffs — the broken jugs of the slaves who raised the walls two thousand years ago. At the center of the Hippodrome, a long, graceful ellipse, is a fallen monolith weighing many tons. We sit under fig trees on the slope while Mississippi runs through the high smooth grass. The wind is soft and works the grass gracefully. It makes white air courses in the green.

Whenever John ships out he takes the dog for company. He had enough of solitude when he sailed on German ships under forged papers. He does not like to be alone. Now and again he was under suspicion. A German officer who sensed that he was Jewish threatened to turn him in, but one night when the ship was only hours out of Danzig she struck a mine and went down, the officer with her. John himself was pulled from the sea by his mates. Once he waited in a line of nude men whom a German doctor, a woman, was examining for venereal disease. In that lineup he alone was circumcised. He came before the woman and was examined; she looked into his face and she let him live.

John and I go back through the orange groves. There are large weasels living in the bushy growth along the pipeline. We see a pair of them at a distance in the road. They could easily do for Mississippi. She is luckily far off. We sit under a pine on the hilltop and look out to sea where a freighter moves slowly toward Ashkelon. Nearer to shore, a trawler chuffs. The kibbutz does little fishing now. Off the Egyptian coast, John has been shot at, and not long ago several members of the kibbutz were thrown illegally into jail by the Turks, accused of fishing in Turkish waters. Twenty people gave false testimony. They could have had a thousand witnesses. It took three months to get these men released. A lawyer was found who knew the judge. His itemized bill came to ten thousand dollars — five for the judge, five for himself.

Enough of this sweet sun and the transparent blue-green. We turn our backs on it to have a drink before lunch. Kibbutzniks ride by on clumsy old bikes. They wear cloth caps and pedal slowly; their day starts at six. Plain-looking working people from the tile factory and from the barn steer toward the dining hall. The kibbutzniks are a mixed group. There is one lone Orthodox Jew, who has no congregation to pray with. There are several older gentiles, one a Spaniard, one a Scandinavian, who married Jewish women and settled here. The Spaniard, an anarchist, plans to return to Spain now that Franco has died. One member of the kibbutz is a financial wizard, another was a high-ranking army officer who for obscure reasons fell into disgrace. The dusty tarmac path we follow winds through the settlement. Beside the undistinguished houses stand red poinsettias. Here, too, lie Roman relics. Then we come upon a basketball court, and then the rusty tracks of a children's choochoo, and then the separate quarters for young women of eighteen, and a museum of antiquities, and a recreation hall. A strong odor of cattle comes from the feeding lot. I tell John that Gurdjiev had Katherine Mansfield resting in the stable at Fontainebleau, claiming that the cow's breath would cure her tuberculosis. John loves to hear such bits of literary history. We go into his house and Mississippi climbs into his lap while we drink Russian vodka. "We could live with those bastards if they limited themselves to making this Stolichnaya."

These words put an end to the peaceful morning. At the north there swells up the Russian menace. With arms from Russia and Europe, the PLO and other Arab militants and the right-wing Christians are now destroying Lebanon. The Syrians have involved themselves; in the eyes of the Syrians, Israel is Syrian land. Suddenly this temperate Mediterranean day and the orange groves and the workers steering their bikes and the children's playground flutter like illustrated paper. What is there to keep them from blowing away?

Working with Your Peer Group to Analyze an Essay. Before meeting with your peer group, answer the following questions in the left-hand column of your double-entry journal:

1. Bellow provides a loose narrative framework by telling the story of his morning tour of the kibbutz. What features of the kibbutz does he describe during his exploration? How complete a picture does he paint? Does he offer any points about the philosophy on which the kibbutz operates?
2. Bellow does not compare this kibbutz to others that he may have visited. Where does he make comparisons that help us to understand the nature of life on this kibbutz better? What do you make, for example, of the opening contrast that he draws between the two dogs?
3. How does the kibbutz fit into the larger system of Mideast politics? How does the answer to this question alter Bellow's view of the kibbutz?
4. In what ways have the kibbutz and the life of its inhabitants changed over time? What do the answers to this question reveal about the inhabitants of the kibbutz?
5. What overriding impression of the kibbutz does Bellow finally offer? How does the dialogue in Paragraph 5 contribute to this impression?

When you meet with your group, exchange journals so that members can read each other's answers and add their comments in the right-hand column. Discuss how and why group members agreed and/or disagreed in their answers.

In the next essay, Paul Engle uses many descriptive details to convey an overriding impression of an Iowa state fair as the "best of all possible worlds." How do these details contribute to Engle's overriding impression? What unusual organizing device does he use to express many of the sense impressions one might encounter at the fair? Engle's enthusiasm for the fair contrasts with Bellow's objectivity. How would you account for the difference?

The Iowa State Fair

Paul Engle

If all you saw of life was the Iowa State Fair on a brilliant August day, when you hear those incredible crops ripening out of the black dirt between the Missouri and Mississippi rivers, you would believe that this is surely the best of all possible worlds. You would have no sense of the destruction of life, only of its rich creativeness: no political disasters, no assassinations, no ideological competition, no wars, no corruption, no atom waiting in its dark secrecy to destroy us all with its exploding energy.

There is a lot of energy at the Fair in Des Moines, but it is all peaceful. The double giant Ferris wheel circles, its swaying seats more frightening than a jet plane flying through a monsoon. Eighty thousand men, women, and children walk all day and much of the night across the fairgrounds. Ponies pick up their feet in a slashing trot as if the ground burned them. Hard-rock music backgrounds the soft lowing of a Jersey cow in the cattle barn over her newborn calf, the color of a wild deer. Screaming speeches are made all around the world urging violence; here there are plenty of voices, but they are calling for you to throw baseballs at Kewpie dolls, to pitch nickels at a dish which won't hold them, to buy cotton candy, corn dogs, a paring knife that performs every useful act save mixing a martini.

Above all, you would believe there was no hunger in the world, for what the Iowa State Fair celebrates is not only peace but food. It walks by you on the hoof, the Hereford, Angus, Charolais, Shorthorn steer, the meat under its hide produced by a beautifully balanced diet more complicated than a baby's formula. These thousand-pound beef animals look at you with their oval, liquid eyes, not knowing that in human terms they are round steak, rib roast, tenderloin, chuck, and hamburger.

The Fair has always specialized in show-ring competition for swine and cattle, but in recent years this has been extended to the slaughtered and dressed carcass. Often the animal which won on the hoof will not actually be as good a meat specimen as one graded lower on its "figure." Probably the most important single event at the Fair is also the quietest and most hidden: the judging of the carcass by experts in white coats in a refrigerated room. The months of elaborate feeding, of care to prevent injuries, all have their meaning when the loin eye is measured and the balance between fat and lean is revealed. At the 1974 Fair, Roy B. Keppy's crossbred hog placed second in the live competition, but first in the pork carcass show. It yielded a chop which measured 6.36 square inches, one of the largest in the history of the Fair. A little more than an inch of fat covered the rib (loin-eye) area.

If you saw close up the boys and girls of 4-H, you would also believe that this world was lived in by the best of all possible people. These are not the drugged youth of the newspapers. They are intelligent and sturdy and have carried into the present the old-fashioned and sturdy ideas: the four-H concept means thinking HEAD, feeling HEART, skilled HAND, and strong HEALTH. They walk with the ease of the physically active and the confidence of people who have done serious and useful projects. They understand animals, machines, fibers.

Nor are they the "hicks" of rural legend. Newspapers, radio, television have brought the world into their home; before their eyes they see what is happening not only in the nearest city but in a country five thousand miles away. Nor are they dull. Often a 4-H boy and girl will work together washing down their steers, shampooing the tails and polishing the hooves, and then go off to spend the evening dancing or at a rock concert.

One of the great sights in 4-H at the Fair is the weeping face of a bright, attractive farm girl whose steer has just won a championship. She has raised the animal herself. She has kept a daily record of how much she fed it each day, of how many pounds of feed it took to make pounds of grain (a corn-fed beef steer's daily growth is frightening and fattening). She has washed and brushed and combed it, taught it to lead with a halter, to stand still on order.

The final moment of truth comes when she leads it into the show ring and the judge examines it with a hard and expert eye. If a Blue Ribbon is awarded, tears of joy on the cheeks of the 4-H girl, after her months of loving care and the tension of competing. Then the auction, for which she receives much more per pound than the average because she has the champion, with tears of sadness because the creature who had become a pet at home is led off to be slaughtered. Head, Heart, Hand and Health of that devoted girl went into the profitable health of that sexless steer.

One of the dramatic examples of energy at the Fair is in the tractor, draft team and pony "pulls," in which the machine and the animals rear up as they try to pull a weighted sledge. The tractor is the usual case of a souped-up engine performing a task it would never do on a farm, with a great snorting and straining. The fun is in the horse and pony pulls, where the animals dig into the turf and drive themselves beyond their real strength, as if they understood the nature of competition.

Above all, the Fair gives a workout to the body's five senses they could get nowhere else in the U.S.A. Apart from the fact that most people walk far more than they realize in their four-wheeled daily life, one reason for the healthy tiredness at the end of a morning-afternoon-evening at the Fair is that eye, hand, ear, tongue, and nose are exercised more than in all the rest of the year.

Eye sees the great, full udders of Holstein cows swaying between those heavy legs, the rounded bellies of hogs unaware that the symmetry will lead to an early death, the sheep struggling under the shearer's hand as he draws red blood on their pink skin in his haste, the giant pumpkin glowing orange as an autumn moon, the Ladies' Rolling Pin Throw contest (you wouldn't argue with one of them), the blue-purple-white stalks of gladioli from home gardens, the harness horses pulling goggled drivers as they trot and pace frail sulkies in front of the grandstand.

Hand touches surfaces it never meets at home unless it belongs to a farmer: softness of Guernsey hide or of the five-gaited saddle horse sleek from the currycomb, the golden feel of new oat straw, the fleece of Oxford Down or Shropshire lambs, the green surface of a John Deere eight-row corn picker, smooth as skin and tough as steel, the sweet stickiness of cotton candy.

Ear has almost too much to take in: the hog-calling contest with its shrill shrieks, the husband-calling contest combining seduction with threats, the whinnying of Tennessee walking horses, the lowing of cattle bored with standing in the showring, the male chauvinist crowing of roosters at the poultry barn, loudest at daybreak (the champion crowed 104 times in half an hour), the merry-go-round playing its old sentimental tunes, the roar of racing cars, the barkers praising the promised beauty to be revealed at the girlie show, the old fiddler's contest quivering the air with "Buffalo Gal," "Texas Star" and "Tennessee Waltz," the clang of horseshoes against each other and against the stake.

Tongue learns the taste of hickory-smoked ham, the richness of butter on popcorn with beer, the tang of rhubarb pie, sour elegance of buttermilk served ice cold, the total smack of hamburger with onion, pickle, mustard and horseradish, many-flavored ice cream, chicken fried in sight of their live cousins in the poultry barn, barbecued pork ribs spitting their fat into the fire as fattened hogs waddle by on their way to be judged.

Nose has an exhausting time at the Fair. It smells the many odors rising from the grills of men competing in the Iowa Cookout King contest, grilling turkey, lamb, beef, pork, chicken, ham with backyard recipes which excite the appetite, the delicate scents of flowers in the horticulture competition, the smell of homemade foods, the crisp smell of hay. People drive hundreds of miles in airconditioned cars which filter out smells in order to walk through heavy and hot late summer air across the manure-reeking atmosphere of the hog, cattle, horse and sheep barns, to sniff again the animal odors of their childhood.

You can watch the judging of home-baked bread or listen to the latest rock group. You can watch free every day the teenage talent search or pay money to hear the same nationally known acts you can watch free on television. The 4-H sewing contest, in which contenders wear the clothes they made, was startled in 1974 to have a boy enter himself and his navy blue knit slacks and jacket with white trim (he grew up on a hog farm, but wants to design clothes). A girl won.

The Iowa State Fair is a great annual ceremony of the sane. Young girls still stand all night behind dairy cows with pitch forks to keep the freshly washed animals from getting dirty before being shown in the morning. Boys milk cows at 10 P.M., 2 A.M., and 3 A.M. to be sure their udders are "balanced" when judges look at them. This is hardly the view of teenagers we often hear. A six-year-old boy wins the rooster crowing contest. There is Indian Wrestling (arm-hand wrestling) with a white and black sweating in immobile silence; the judge was John Buffalo, a real Indian from the Tama reservation.

Year after year this rich and practical ritual of life is repeated. Animals whose ancestors competed many Fairs ago come back. So do people, returning by plane and automobile to the grounds their grandparents visited by train and buggy. Three-hundred-and-fifty horsepower internal-combustion gines have replaced the one-horse hitch or the two-horse team, but the essential objects of life are the same: the dented ear of corn, the rounded rib of steer and pig, that nourishment of the human race which is the prime purpose of the plowing and harvesting State of Iowa.

To some, the Fair seems corny. To others, the world still needs to catch up to the human and animal decency which each year dignifies a corner of this corrupt world. A few hundred acres of human skill and animal beauty in Des Moines, Iowa, prove to the space capsule of Earth how to live.

Like Bellow, Engle uses descriptive details to reveal the process of his subject. What does he wish to emphasize about the process of the fair? Why does Engle refer to the fair as a "ritual of life"? What does this explain about his attitude toward the fair? How does Engle combine narrative, exposition, and description in his essay?

Writing Your Rough Draft

The question at this point is how to weave together the various answers to the explorer's questions and the elements required by the task: narration, exposition, description, and dialogue.

One approach, of course, is to use the explorer's questions as an outline for your essay, working description in naturally in answering Question 1, exposition for the answers to Questions 2 through 4, and process narration for Question 5. Appropriate dialogue or quotations can be tucked in at any point. And the chronological account of your visit can frame the essay, providing the content of the introduction and the conclusion.

You might want to follow the method of Saul Bellow and weave a more intricate design by interspersing the elements throughout the essay. Or, like Paul Engle, you could emphasize the process of the place by focusing your reader's attention on the many sense impressions you observed. Notice, however, that Bellow did use a narrative framework and that Engle found narrative generally unnecessary for his purpose.

To begin organizing your essay, write down the overriding impression that you wish to convey about the place you visited. This shaping idea may also suggest a pattern of arrangement. If not, this pattern will occur to you as you forge an outline before beginning to write, or you may need actually to immerse yourself in writing for a pattern to emerge. Regardless of your method —preoutlining or immersion outlining—you will want to arrive at a coherently presented essay.

Here is one student's rough draft. What patterns of arrangement did the student use?

PAYING FOR A HIGHER EDUCATION

I got off the N train at 8th street and climbed up the stairs
into the hazy sunlight of a Monday Morning in July. Traffic was
light, but the streets and sidewalks were thick with people of
every color, shape and size. I felt confident that there were few
places in the world that could equal downtown New York City
for ethnic diversity at any given moment. I checked the street
signs to get my bearings, and once situated, I headed west towards Washington Square Park and the campus of New York
University.

I had been accepted for admission into the fall class of the
film program at NYU's Tisch School of the Arts, and today was
the last possible due date for housing fees. Despite the fact that
I was still many thousands of dollars short of covering my total
expenses for the first year, I had no choice but to come to the
campus and pay the housing fee today if I wanted to be sure of
having a room come September. With me I had brought a knapsack full of papers, forms and brochures that NYU had sent
since my acceptance, along with my checkbook and a roll of peppermint lifesavers. I didn't doubt that it was going to be a long
morning.

Heading towards the park from the subway stop, I walked
briskly as New Yorkers do, deftly avoiding other pedestrians and
the occasional taxi. Having been born and raised here, I felt relatively comfortable despite the crowds and the smell of garbage
warming in the morning sun. As always, I looked at the people
on the street although I made an effort to avoid prolonged eye
contact, as people here do. You're never sure who might object
to your glance and decide to do something about it. It happens
more often than you might think.

After a few minutes, I reached the area surrounding the park,
the heart of the NYU campus. The buildings here bristled with
the purple and white banner of the school. I entered the nearest
one, and asked the first person I saw for the location of the
bursar's office. A friendly gentleman standing in the lobby di-

rected me to the "big white building just up the block." I thanked him and left, heading up the block as he indicated.

The omnipresent banner sat atop the entrance of the large white building, hanging listlessly in the bright, heavy air. I entered, stepping into a cool hallway that seemed dark in contrast to the hazy sunlight outside. Affixed to the wall was a directory. On it, the bursar's office was listed as being on the second floor. I looked around, spotted a stairwell, and climbed towards my goal.

Entering the office, I was surprised to find that it wasn't nearly as crowded as I had expected. To be sure, it was a large area, with many windows and desks, along with the obligatory posts and ropes forming aisles for lines of waiting customers, much as you'll find in any bank. However, this morning the office seemed sparsely populated. Glancing at the wide variety of signs proclaiming the functions of specific desks and windows, I joined a small line and withdrew some papers and my checkbook from my pack. I looked around at the other people who had come to pay bills like myself. Most seemed to be tired and none too happy to be parting with such large sums of money. I realized that I felt the same way, and for the hundredth time since being accepted, I wondered whether I was doing the right thing by coming to NYU.

Despite the school's excellent reputation, and its long list of notable graduates now working in the film industry, the cost of attending school here was daunting. I had received far less financial aid than I had expected, and there was no doubt whatsoever that I would be completely broke and deeply in debt before I had finished my first year of study. To add to my concern was the fact that the film program is a five semester commitment, not including graduate work. I knew that if I did attend school here, I'd be a few years older by the time I graduated. Even my most conservative estimates of my projected total debt were staggering. All of this ran through my mind, and all too quickly, I found myself to be first on line, with a clerk motioning me towards an available window.

I stepped up to the window, and the woman sitting there looked at me in a disinterested fashion. Checkbook in hand, I stood there for a moment, with no coherent thought in my head. The woman said nothing, so for lack of a better idea, I smiled and said "Good morning, is this where I pay the housing fee?" She nodded and wordlessly tapped a few keys on her terminal. I then wrote out a check for more than half of my savings and handed it to her with the bill I had received in the mail. Moments later, it was over. She handed me a receipt and looking over my shoulder, she called "next!"

I stepped away from her window, but no one took my place. There was no one waiting on line just then. Putting the receipt in my pocket, I closed my checkbook and returned it to my pack. I now had a place to live for one semester. I headed down the stairs and into the cool hallway. As far as I could tell, I felt no different. Not better, not worse, not different at all. I stepped outside into the sun, stood there for a moment, and then started on the long trip home.

Now begin writing your rough draft. When you have completed it, take a day's rest, then read over the focus section below on paragraph development and writing a conclusion.

Paragraph development will be important to you as you write about a place — you will need to develop paragraphs that enumerate details of the place and also paragraphs that explain the impression these details made on you. Your conclusion also may prove significant in helping you focus the reader's attention on the overall impression that resulted from your exploration.

FOCUS ON FORM: PARAGRAPH DEVELOPMENT/ WRITING YOUR CONCLUSION

As individual paragraphs have beginnings, middles, and endings, so do these paragraphs take their place in the structure of the essay as a whole. If the experience of many writers is any guide, some of the most difficult moments of the writing process center around writing introductions and conclusions. The reasons seem clear: We're not sure how to begin and we're reluctant to say we have finished. We could look at the practice of many writers and point to countless strategies for creating beginning and concluding paragraphs.

Since this would be impractical, we can offer a few general suggestions and examples here.

Because the introductory paragraph is your first encounter with your readers, you want to interest them, to set in motion some energy current of an idea, incident, or issue that will be completed only by reading the rest of the essay. This might take the form of an anecdote, a question, a statement of a problem or a contradiction, the background of an issue or event, or a striking image or impression. The scope and depth of your topic will also influence the extent of your introduction. As the introduction is so vital to a good essay, you might feel more at ease by writing it after you have finished the body of your essay. Many writers do this, for it is often only when we have completed expressing an idea that we have an overall grasp of how we should approach it. (For a fuller discussion of writing an introduction, see Chapter 2, pp. 75–80.)

Concluding paragraphs generally work in the opposite direction of introductions. Rather than narrowing the readers' focus towards the specific topic of the essay, conclusions try to open them up to the larger context or possibilities of ideas and issues, to lead them to the connections that might exist between your specific topic and some larger generalization that might be inferred from it. This will remind readers of the importance of your topic and send them back to your essay with a larger perspective on the topic. For example, the concluding paragraph of Paul Engle's essay suggests that we look upon the Iowa State Fair as a model of decency and beauty for human beings to follow. For Engle, the fair has a moral quality that contrasts with "this corrupt world."

Paragraph Development

Whether we look at paragraphs that function as beginnings, middles, or endings, there is another way of examining how paragraphs are developed—the way they are formed to express ideas. Just as sentences are structured to coordinate ideas or subordinate them, so are most paragraphs. Coordination occurs when two or more equal ideas are enumerated or an idea is repeated for emphasis. Subordination offers one idea in explanation of another. Coordination enumerates or emphasizes; subordination explains. In developing your topic sentence, therefore, determine the needs of your readers. Do they require you to enumerate or list points about your subject, or do they need an explanation of it? This method of inquiry should help you to develop any topic into a paragraph once you have determined your readers' needs.

For example, the following paragraph utilizes coordination:

When a society's values and institutions are seriously questioned, life transitions become anxious and traumatic. What does it mean to face the time of marriage when divorce is so common and alternative living arrangements, such as communes and cohabitation, are so widely explored? What does it mean to choose a vocation when all forms of work, and the idea of work itself, are so severely criticized? What does it mean to grow up when adulthood implies being locked into support of a violent, directionless culture? What does it mean to grow old when old people are isolated, put off by themselves in "homes" or institutions, apart from family and ongoing community? What does it mean to die when science has challenged sacred religious beliefs and in the place of spiritual comfort has left only the "scientific method"?

—Robert Jay Lifton and Eric Olson,
"Death—The Lost Season," from *Living and Dying*

An outline of this paragraph follows:

Topic sentence: When a society's values and institutions are seriously questioned, life transitions become anxious and traumatic.

1. What does it mean to face the time of marriage when divorce is so common and alternative living arrangements, such as communes and cohabitation, are so widely explored?
2. What does it mean to choose a vocation when all forms of work, and the idea of work itself, are so severely criticized?
3. What does it mean to grow up when adulthood implies being locked into support of a violent, directionless culture?
4. What does it mean to grow old when old people are isolated, put off by themselves in "homes" or institutions, apart from family and ongoing community?
5. What does it mean to die when science has challenged sacred religious beliefs and in the place of spiritual comfort has left only the "scientific method"?

Note the use of the repetitive "What does it mean" phrase to emphasize the equality of all five points. Coordination often employs repetition, thus creating a dramatic effect.

The following is an example of subordination, in that Sentence 3 develops the topic sentence by explaining why the order of the city streets is complex, and Sentence 4 compares city street life to a ballet, explaining the topic sentence further. Sentence 5 continues the analogy:

Under the seeming disorder of the old city, wherever the old city is working successfully, is a marvellous order for maintaining the safety of the streets and the freedom of the city. It is a complex order. Its essence is intricacy of sidewalk use, bringing with it a constant succession of eyes. This order is all composed of movement and change, and although it is life, not art, we may fancifully call it the art form of the city and liken it to the dance—not to a simple-minded precision dance with everyone kicking up at the same time, twirling in unison and bowing off en masse, but to an intricate ballet in which the individual dancers and ensembles all have distinctive parts which miraculously reinforce each other and compose an orderly whole. The ballet of the good city sidewalk never repeats itself from place to place, and in any one place is always replete with new improvisations.

—Jane Jacobs, *The Death and Life of Great American Cities*

Outlined, the paragraph looks like this

Topic sentences: Under the seeming disorder of the old city, wherever the old city is working successfully, is a marvellous order for maintaining the safety of the streets and the freedom of the city. It is a complex order.

I. Its essence is intricacy of sidewalk use, bringing with it a constant succession of eyes.
  A. This order is all composed of movement and change, and although it is life, not art, we may fancifully call it the art form of the city and liken it to the dance—not to a simple-minded precision dance with everyone kicking up at the same time, twirling in unison and bowing off en masse, but to an intricate ballet in which the individual dancers and ensembles all have distinctive parts which miraculously reinforce each other and compose an orderly whole.
    1. The ballet of the good city sidewalk never repeats itself from place to place, and in any one place is always replete with new improvisations.

Most paragraphs are a mixture of coordination and subordination because most lists need explanation and explanations often require lists of examples. In the following paragraph, subordination follows coordination, as the first four sentences following the topic sentence are coordinate, and the fifth is subordinate to the fourth.

This man made no flourishes to attract anybody. He never drove a fast horse. He never wore trousers with checks any larger than an inch square— which, for the time, was conservative. His house never got afire and burned down just after the fire insurance had run out. Not one of his boys and girls ever got drowned or run over by the steamcars. The few that died growing up died of diphtheria or scarlet fever, which were what children died of then, the usual ways.

—Robert P. Tristram Coffin, "My Average Uncle," from *Book of Uncles*

An outline of Coffin's paragraph clearly shows the mixture of subordination with coordination:

Topic sentence: This man made no flourishes to attract anybody.

1. He never drove a fast horse.
2. He never wore trousers with checks any larger than an inch square—which, for the time, was conservative.
3. His house never got afire and burned down just after the fire insurance had run out.
4. Not one of his boys and girls ever got drowned or run over by the steamcars.

    a. The few that died growing up died of diphtheria or scarlet fever, which were what children died of then, the usual ways.

The following paragraph, on the other hand, illustrates the mixture of coordination with subordination. Two parallel examples in Sentences 4 and 5 provide the coordination in an otherwise subordinate organization.

> I have an increasing admiration for the teacher in the country school where we have a third-grade scholar in attendance. She not only undertakes to instruct her charges in all the subjects of the first three grades, but she manages to function quietly and effectively as a guardian of their health, their clothes, their habits, their mothers, and their snowball engagements. She has been doing this sort of Augean task for twenty years, and is both kind and wise. She cooks for the children on the stove that heats the room, and she can cool their passions or warm their soup with equal competence. She conceives their costumes, cleans up their messes, and shares their confidences. My boy already regards his teacher as his great friend, and I think tells her a great deal more than he tells us.
>
> —E.B. White, "Education," from *One Man's Meat*

Again, an outline reveals the pattern:

Topic sentence: I have an increasing admiration for the teacher in the country school where we have a third-grade scholar in attendance.

1. She not only undertakes to instruct her charges in all the subjects of the first three grades, but she manages to function quietly and effectively as a guardian of their health, their clothes, their habits, their mothers, and their snowball engagements.
2. She has been doing this sort of Augean task for twenty years, and is both kind and wise.

    a. She cooks for the children on the stove that heats the room, and she can cool their passions or warm their soup with equal competence.

      b. She conceives their costumes, cleans up their messes, and shares their confidences.

      (1) My boy already regards his teacher as his great friend, and I think tells her a great deal more than he tells us.

    When composing a paragraph, of course, a writer is also choosing a pattern of exposition. In a subordinate paragraph, he or she may be listing reasons, examples, definitions, or effects. In a coordinate paragraph, he or she may also use definition, example, cause and effect to explain the points. And in a mixed paragraph, lists and explanations may be based on any combination of patterns (see Chapter 5, pp. 198–201, for further discussion of patterns of exposition).

    For example, Robert Jay Lifton's coordinate paragraph, preceding, lists causes, or reasons why; Jacobs uses analogy to explain her point; Coffin uses a list of examples followed by a contrastive explanation; and White combines a cause-and-effect explanation ("She has been doing this sort of Augean task for twenty years, and is both kind and wise.") with a list of reasons and concludes with an explanation that is an example.

SOME PRACTICE WITH DEVELOPING PARAGRAPHS

1. Analyze the following paragraphs to determine whether their organization is coordinate, subordinate, or mixed. Outline the paragraph, if an outline is helpful.

    a. Besides, aren't commercials in the public interest? Don't they help you to choose what to buy? Don't they provide needed breaks from programming? Aren't many of them brilliantly done, and some of them funny? And now, with the new sexual freedom, all those gorgeous chicks with their shining hair and gleaming smiles? And if you didn't have commercials taking up a good part of each hour how on earth would you find enough program material to fill the endless space/time void?

           —Marya Mannes, "Television: The Splitting Image," from
The Saturday Review of Literature (Nov. 1970)

    b. The mother wasp goes tarantula-hunting when the egg in her ovary is almost ready to be laid. Flying low over the ground late on a sunny afternoon, the wasp looks for its victim or for the mouth of a tarantula burrow, a round hole edged by a bit of silk. The sex of the spider makes no difference, but the mother is highly discriminating as to species. Each species of Pepsis requires a certain species of tarantula, and the wasp will not attack the wrong species. In a cage with a tarantula which is not its normal prey, the wasp avoids the spider and is usually killed by it in the night.

—Alexander Petrunkevitch, "The Spider and the Wasp,"
from *Scientific American* (Aug, 1952)

c. Tell General Howard I know his heart. What he told me before I have in my heart. I am tired of fighting. Our chiefs are killed. Looking Glass is dead. Toohoolhoolzote is dead. The old men are all dead. It is the young men who say yes or no. He who led on the young men [Ollokot] is dead. It is cold and we have no blankets. The little children are freezing to death. My people, some of them, have run away to the hills, and have no blankets, no food; no one knows where they are — perhaps freezing to death. I want to have time to look for my children and see how many of them I can find. Maybe I shall find them among the dead. Hear me chiefs! I am tired; my heart is sick and sad. From where the sun now stands I will fight no more forever.

—Chief Joseph, U.S. *Secretary of War Report,* 1877

d. It is thus no exaggeration to say that Americans have taken to mechanical cooling avidly and greedily. Many of them become all but addicted, refusing to go places that are not air-conditioned. In Atlanta, shoppers in Lenox Square so resented having to endure natural heat while walking outdoors from chilled store to chilled store that the mall management enclosed and air-conditioned the whole sprawling shebang. The widespread whining about Washington's raising of the thermostats to a mandatory 78°F suggests that people no longer think of interior coolness as an amenity but consider it a necessity, almost a birthright, like suffrage. The existence of such a view was proved last month when a number of federal judges sitting too high and mighty to suffer 78°F, defied and denounced the government's energy-saving order to cut back on cooling. Significantly, there was no popular outrage at this judicial insolence; many citizens probably wished that they could be so highhanded.

—Frank Trippett, "The Great American Cooling Machine,"
Time (1979)

2. What patterns of exposition — definition, contrast, comparison, exemplification, cause and effect, analogy, and so on — did each writer of the paragraphs above use?

SOME PRACTICE WITH DEVELOPING PARAGRAPHS IN YOUR ESSAY ON A PLACE

1. To what degree does the information generated by a particular explorer's question lend itself to coordination or subordination in a paragraph? Organize the information you have collected in response to one explorer's question into

both a coordinate and a subordinate paragraph; which seems best to you? Why? Try it again with the information you have collected in response to a different explorer's question.

2. As you work on your rough draft, step back and analyze the patterns of exposition that you are using to develop your paragraphs. Jot down next to each paragraph when you have used definition, comparison, analysis, and so forth. Are you relying primarily on one or two patterns, or is there variety in the patterns you are using? To what degree should you try to develop paragraphs with more varied patterns of exposition, when your purpose is to explore?

Writing a Conclusion

Just as there is no right way to begin an essay, so there is no right way to conclude. Your goals should be to indicate clearly that the essay has come to an end and, at the same time, encourage the reader to think more about what you have written. But especially in a short paper, you want to rely on your creativity and imagination in putting together a conclusion that accomplishes these goals.

You do not want to trail off, to leave the readers with the expectation that there is more to follow; nor do you want to sound too abrupt — "The End." You do not want to introduce an entirely new topic; nor do you want to sound repetitious — "In conclusion, the main point of this essay has been. . . ." While it is often appropriate and useful to conclude a long paper by reminding a reader of the thesis, part of the challenge in concluding a short essay is to come full circle by, if possible, saying something new.

If you are writing a story, of course, the conclusion may simply tell what happened last:

Upon his death Harry was given a first-class funeral, a flush to fish heaven. On this somber day we all gathered around the commode, flipped poor Harry into the bowl, said a small fish prayer and watched him be sucked away to new life.

Harry, rest in peace. You were my first confidant.

An alternative strategy might be to comment on the significance of the story, as the writer of the next conclusion does:

A man was drowned and washed to shore right at our feet. I still get chills when I think about it. I'm not saying I'll never

go to the beach again or swim in the ocean. I went the next
day. I'm just trying to say that this is something that from time
to time pops into my head. It doesn't haunt me--it just kind of
reminds me.

Notice how in the next example, the writer also concludes by focusing on
the personal significance of her topic. But she also connects her topic — skiing — to a larger context — the importance of having something to escape to:

My first ski trip introduced me to a great sport. I have gone
since that trip and plan to go as often as I can. Skiing is now
something that makes me happy, and I have it to look forward
to. It is so important to have something to escape to--to forget
about everything going on around you and just enjoy yourself.
I've found that skiing is a great way to do this.

In each of these examples, the reader is left with something to think about —
the first writer's relationship with Harry; the second writer's distinction between feeling haunted and being reminded; the third writer's generalization
about the value of escape. Also in each, this amounts to a subtly new twist
or variation on the writer's subject.

In a more expository paper, a writer may elaborate more fully and explicitly on his/her thesis as an effective way of concluding. Thus, a writer who
began her essay with the following introduction,

"Once More to the Lake" is a story of a man who appears to be
trying to go back to his past. He is a middle-aged man who
seems to be going through some sort of mid-life crisis,

ended by offering her thoughts about the meaning of the man's story along
with her analysis of his problem:

I think what all this is about is that loss is always hard to accept, no matter what kind of loss it is. Whether it's the loss of
a loved one, the loss of a home, or even the loss of a favorite

time. The latter is what seems to be the man's loss in "Once More to the Lake." He seems to be trying to regain something he lost. The problem is you can never go back in time to regain what has already been lost.

The writer of the next conclusion also offers an analysis of a problem — in this case his own — and then, in his last sentence, draws a larger generalization about the effects of such a problem on anyone, including the reader:

Laziness--my biggest enemy. It seems that laziness has contributed a lot to my relatively unsuccessful life. I think that there is a lesson to be learned here. If one is lazy and doesn't do something to be rid of this accursed disease, then it may rule your life. Because of it, you may be restricted in life. You may fail in school because you didn't study. Your job prospects may be limited because of substandard academic achievement. Thus you cannot taste the fruits of life.

Depending on the subject and structure of an essay, you may find that it is as effective to conclude as it can be to begin with a brief anecdote or quotation, a question, or a challenging opinion (see Chapter 2, pp. 75–80) — as the writer of the last example does:

When the doctor called me in, I sighed with relief. She introduced herself as Irma and smiled. We discussed the advantages and disadvantages of different methods of birth control, and I began to feel at ease. I then told her of how disappointed I was with Planned Parenthood, and she didn't seem surprised. She said that up to a year ago they had heard no complaints. However, as they've become increasingly popular over the past year, they have more patients than they're equipped to handle. "Yet," she defended, "we do our best."

Given a choice, I would go back to my usual doctor. He's closer to home, cheaper, and much faster. I spent over two and a half hours at Planned Parenthood--I'm not impressed.

In concluding then, try to sum up your essay without simply repeating what you have already written: change the focus, so that you are looking at your subject from a different angle; challenge your reader to ponder the larger implications of your point of view; give some hint at the end of a possible new beginning.

SOME PRACTICE WITH WRITING A CONCLUSION FOR YOUR ESSAY ABOUT A PLACE

1. Develop the following topic sentences into concluding paragraphs.

   a. It's beyond my comprehension how any critic who had actually eaten here could give the restaurant a four-star rating.

   b. All things considered, you really can appreciate the game better being at the stadium than watching it on TV at home.

   c. So the pristine lake of my father's childhood was something we would never get to know—except as another victim of our gradual pollution of the planet.

   What arrangement pattern did you use in each paragraph you wrote?

2. Review the material you have collected in your exploration of the place that you are writing about for this chapter's task: your journal entries; your introduction; your rough draft. Then do the following:

   a. Write a narrative in which you tell the story of your exploration from start to finish. Write a conclusion that explains your final overall impression—what it is and why you came to hold it.

   b. Next, turn this conclusion into an introduction, offering what you say about your overall impression as a thesis statement. Now, write a new conclusion that sums up your essay without repeating what you have already written: comment on the broader significance of your exploration; relate a closing anecdote; offer a challenging opinion.

REWRITING

Obtaining Feedback on Your Rough Draft

By now, you should have developed one or more successful channels for obtaining responses to your rough draft: your "other self," your peers, or your teacher. Again, use these channels for obtaining answers to the "Audience Response Guide" about your draft of your essay on a place.

─────────── AUDIENCE RESPONSE GUIDE ───────────

1. What is the writer's purpose in writing about this place? What overriding impression does the writer wish to convey?
2. How does the paper affect the audience for whom it is intended?
3. How effective has the writer been in conveying an adequate and accurate impression of the place through observation and interviews?
4. How should the paper be revised to better convey a sense of the place and its significance?

The following is a peer evaluation of the rough draft of the student essay "Paying for a Higher Education," in response to the four questions above:

1. The writer wanted to tell us about his impressions of NYU, how he went there to pay his housing fee and how anxious he felt about it. While the film school has an excellent reputation, the cost seems overwhelming to him. But the ending is vague when he says that he felt "no different," so it is unclear exactly what he wants the paper to mean or what his overall impression is.
2. The paper gives the reader a good feel for the neighborhood and the bursar's office although if the audience is other film students, some of whom may never have been to New York, he might go into more detail. But his audience should identify easily with his concern about the high cost of college.
3. The paper is effective in conveying the look and feel of the campus and the emptiness of the bursar's office. The narrative structure and detailed descriptions are its strengths. But the writer needs to explain more about why he wrote the essay, what the visit meant to him. The weakest part of the paper is that it doesn't convey well enough what the writer felt and especially why.
4. The writer should clarify what his initial expectations and his final impressions were. He might tell more about why he chose NYU. Explaining more about why he felt no different at the end would help.

Revision of Student Essay: "Paying for a Higher Education"

Here is a revised version of "Paying for a Higher Education." How has the writer responded to the group's suggestions that he explain more about his final impressions and feelings? How effective are the additional details he includes? What other changes has he made?

PAYING FOR A HIGHER EDUCATION

I got off the N train at 8th street in New York's Greenwich Village and climbed up the stairs into the hazy sunlight of a Monday morning in July. Traffic was light, but the streets and sidewalks were thick with people of every color, busily rushing about their business. I felt confident that there were few places in the world that could equal downtown New York City for both ethnic diversity and sheer energy at any given moment. I checked the street signs to get my bearings, and once situated, I headed west towards Washington Square Park and the campus of New York University.

I had been accepted for admission into the fall class of the film program at NYU's prestigious Tisch School of the Arts, and today was the last possible due date for housing fees. Despite the fact that I was still many thousands of dollars short of covering my total expenses for the first year, I had no choice but to come to the campus and pay the housing fee this day if I wanted to be sure of having a room come September. With me I had brought a knapsack full of papers, forms and brochures that NYU had sent since my acceptance, along with my checkbook and a roll of peppermint lifesavers. I had no doubt that it was going to be a long morning.

Heading towards the park from the subway stop, I walked briskly as New Yorkers do, deftly avoiding other pedestrians and the occasional taxi. Having been born and raised here, I felt relatively comfortable despite the crowds and the smell of garbage warming in the morning sun. As always, I occupied myself by looking at the people on the street, although I made an effort to avoid prolonged eye contact, as New Yorkers customarily do. You're never sure who might object to your glance, and decide to do something violent about it. So, it's better not to be caught staring.

After a few minutes, I reached the neighborhood surrounding the park, the heart of the NYU campus. Many of the older, stately brick and stone buildings here bristled with the purple and white banner of the school. I entered the nearest one, and asked the first person I saw for the location of the bursar's office. A friendly older gentleman standing in the lobby directed me to the "big white building just up the block." He then asked me if I was a student at the university. I replied, "I suppose I will be, come September." He smiled and said, "Well, then, let me welcome you in advance to NYU." I thanked him and left, heading up the block as he indicated.

The omnipresent banner sat atop the entrance of the large white building, hanging listlessly in the bright, heavy air. I stepped into a cool hallway that seemed dark in contrast to the hazy sunlight outside. A directory was affixed to the wall, listing the bursar's office as being on the second floor. I looked around, spotted a stairwell, and climbed towards my goal.

Entering the office, I was surprised to find that it wasn't nearly as crowded as I had expected. To be sure, it was a large area, with many windows and desks, along with the obligatory posts and ropes forming aisles for lines of waiting customers, much as you'll find in any bank. However, this morning the office seemed sparsely populated. Glancing at the wide variety of signs proclaiming the functions of specific desks and windows, I joined a small line, reached into my pack, and withdrew some papers and my checkbook. I looked around at the other people, who had apparently come to pay bills like myself. Most seemed to be tired, and none too happy to be parting with such large sums of money. With some anxiety, I realized that I felt the same way, and for the hundredth time since being accepted, I wondered whether I was doing the right thing by coming to NYU.

NYU's film school has facilities and instructors befitting its excellent reputation, and its long list of notable graduates now working in the film industry includes Martin Scorsese, Oliver Stone, Susan Seidelman and Spike Lee, among others. Although I was looking forward to the idea of studying here, the cost of actually attending school here was daunting, to say the least. The seeds of doubt had been planted in my mind when I had first learned what the total cost of attendance would be, and the bill that I had come to pay was keeping those seeds well watered. I had received far less financial aid than I had expected, and there was no doubt whatsoever that I would be completely broke and deeply in debt before I had finished my first year of study here. To add to my concern was the fact that the film program is a five semester commitment, not including graduate work. I knew that if I did attend school here, I'd be a few years older by the time I graduated. Even my most conservative estimates of my projected total debt were staggering. These facts ran through my mind, and all too quickly, I found myself to be first on line, with a clerk motioning me towards an available window.

I stepped up to the window, and the woman sitting there looked at me in a disinterested fashion. Checkbook in hand, I stood there for a moment, with no coherent thought in my head. The woman said nothing, so for lack of a better idea, I smiled and said "Good morning, is this where I pay the housing fee?" She nodded and wordlessly tapped a few keys on her terminal. I then wrote out a check for more than half of my savings and handed it to her with the bill I had received in the mail. Moments later, it was over. She handed me a receipt and looked over my shoulder, wordlessly dismissing me.

I stepped away from her window, but no one took my place. There was no one waiting on line just then. Putting the receipt in my pocket, I closed my checkbook and returned it to my pack. I now had a place to live for one semester. I headed down the stairs and into the cool hallway. As far as I could tell, I felt no different. I think that I had expected to feel more confident about my choice to go to school here once I had committed myself financially. If not more confident, then perhaps I had hoped to feel just a little less anxious and uncertain about my decision. However, this did not seem to be the case. I felt no better or worse than I had before, not any different at all. I stood in the hall and considered this for the better part of a minute. I then stepped outside into the sun, stood there for a moment, and then started on the long trip home.

Note how the writer has revised his conclusion by adding a more complete explanation of the effect of his visit on him. He has added explanatory sentences to the body of the essay, like the one about the "seeds of doubt" in the seventh paragraph, that also help clarify his overall impression, as do additional details, like the modifiers "older, stately brick and stone" that describe the buildings in the fourth paragraph. Overall, do you find his revisions help him in accomplishing the purpose of the task? Consider whether your draft might benefit from one or more similar revisions.

Substituting

A third method of revision, in addition to cutting (pp. 85–86) and adding (pp. 129–130), is substituting. Substituting means trading words, phrases, and/or whole passages that do not contribute to the meaning of your essay for those that do.

Substitutions may be desirable for several reasons. One is that a word you have used may seem, when you are reading your essay over, to be not concrete enough: Why say the sky is "gray" when you can say it is "leaden"? Another is that a word may be inexact: you may have told your parents that your campus is "far" from the airport, leaving them to draw their own conclusions as to how much time they should leave for the taxi drive; to say that it is "thirty minutes away" is much more exact. You may also decide that one word conveys your tone of voice more successfully than another: "Teachers are stern" may convey the tone you want to establish more successfully than "Teachers are mean."

You may also want to substitute details if you find that your original detail does not create the impression that you wish to convey of your subject to your audience: When you are delineating the problems you are having with your car, for example, a description of its good features is out of place and should be replaced with further complaints, especially if your audience is the mechanic whom you paid to fix the car in the first place.

The structure of your essay may require substitutions as well. Whole paragraphs may be substituted if you discover that one point serves your purpose better than another. An item erroneously classified, for example, may be replaced with an item that does belong in the class you are writing about: Were you to classify the Kodak Instamatic as one of the types of 35mm cameras and omit the Leica, then a substitution would clearly be in order.

The student writer of "Paying for a Higher Education" has substituted the sentence "So, it's better not to be caught staring" for the sentence "It happens more often than you think" at the end of the third paragraph, and a more detailed sentence about NYU film school's "excellent reputation" for the first sentence of the seventh paragraph. Can you point out other substitutions that the writer has made, more exact for less exact words, for example, or more appropriate for less appropriate details?

In writing the task for this chapter, you may want to substitute some dialogue that is especially pertinent for some that is lackluster. Some description may be extraneous to the operation of the place, and you may want to trade that for description that clarifies the process of the place. Or perhaps you have included too much narration of your visit and wish to substitute more information about the place.

Revising Your Essay on a Place

As a last step in revising your essay for this chapter's task, answer the following questions about what you have written:

 Checklist to Consider in Revising an Essay About a Place

1. Have I explored this place thoroughly enough so that my overall impression represents a new, broader point of view? What additional information might I seek about the place, in order to test out its reputation?

2. Have I adequately assessed the "depth-of-information" needs of my intended readers? Might they require more detailed information about either the place itself or my perspective on it?

3. Have I arranged my essay to convey as effectively as possible the reputation of the place, how I went about testing that reputation, and my final impression? How clearly have I stated and how strategically have I placed my shaping idea? Have I used coordination effectively in paragraphs that enumerate details of the place and subordination in paragraphs that explain my impression of these details?

4. Will my introduction interest my audience in reading about the place? What does my conclusion add to my reader's understanding of the significance of my visit to this place?

Editing

Substitutions. Substitutions can also be made when you are editing. A word or a phrase can be traded for another word or phrase for a number of reasons: More formal language is needed, more precise words are available, more colorful expression is desirable, or a different grammatical construction is required.

Transitions. You are now combining your sentences nicely with conjunctions and conjunctive words and phrases. Scan your draft for these transitions. Are you using too many *and*'s and *but*'s? Try substituting more precise transitions — those that convey the exact relationship between ideas. *And* and *but*, particularly, are easily overdone.

For this particular assignment, substitute transitions of place when you are describing: "in the right-hand corner," "above me," "to my left," "on top." These prepositional phrases visually orient your readers and lead them from space to space.

Paragraphs.   Although rewriting paragraphs is usually a revising chore affecting meaning, paragraphs can also be edited. On the surface, in other words, does each paragraph have a clear structure, or does the topic sentence need a few additions or substitutions to clearly characterize the content of the paragraph? Are transitions included between thoughts? Are they, moreover, precise?

Mechanics.   By now, you know what mechanical errors you are inclined to make. Proofread your rough draft for these habitual mistakes and for any others that may have crept in.

Now revise and edit your rough draft.

BECOMING AWARE OF YOURSELF AS A WRITER

Make use of your journal to record your thoughts and feelings about the task for Chapter 4. As you write in your journal, consider the following questions.

1. How did the explorer's method of inquiry aid you in thinking about your subject? For what other subjects might this be a useful inquiry method?

2. How did writing for a class in your curriculum differ from writing for your peers in general (or your English class) in the task for Chapter 3? To what extent do you think your audience affects the way you write?

3. Was interweaving the exposition, narration, description, and dialogue difficult for you? Do you understand the differing functions of exposition, narration, and description? Can you think of other writing assignments in which you have interwoven or might interweave the three?

4. What more have you learned about your own writing process from completing the task in this chapter? For example, are you more comfortable outlining before writing, or does an outline emerge only after you have completed your rough draft? Or does some other method of arranging your essay work for you?

5. What did you learn from writing about a place that was meaningful to you when you began the assignment? How did exploring the subject affect your perception of the place? What other subjects might you explore in the same way?

6. What kind of feedback are you receiving from your evaluators? Is it helpful? How could it be more helpful?

7. How are you as an evaluator of the writing of others? To what extent does your reading of the writing of others affect your own writing?

8. What problems are you facing as a writer at the present? What steps have you plotted to solve them?

9. What are you satisfied with in your writing?

5

Writing About a Prejudgment — Exploring Other Points of View

PURPOSE

In this chapter, you will continue the exploratory activity of the previous chapter by seeking the answer to a question. Whereas in Chapter 4 you asked, "Is my visit to this place going to corroborate the high opinion others have of it?" here you will be asking, "After frequent observation of a situation that I have prejudged, will I prove my prejudgment or prejudice to be, in fact, an accurate evaluation, or will I find that I must discard it in favor of a new conclusion?"

Observing a situation—an ongoing event or a person—over a period of time is called *casing the subject,* much as, in the popular use of the term, a thief "cases a joint" before breaking in to determine employee or resident patterns of behavior, or police "case" a location to observe and hopefully catch criminals. Probably the most common use of the term *case* is found among social workers, who write case studies about the families they visit to explain their financial, physical, and emotional needs. And psychiatrists use the term to refer to their written narratives about the lives of their patients. The task for this chapter will be to observe a situation of some kind over a period of time and to write your own case study.

The main thrust of the chapter lies in testing a prejudice about a subject by acquiring facts about it. Prejudice is by definition an evaluation of a situation arrived at before one knows all the facts. Although we form these hasty conclusions all too often throughout our lives, thoughtful people attempt to decrease their tendency to prejudge and seek instead to form a conclusion based on a thorough examination of the subject.

In the first four chapters, we presented four methods of generating ideas: the journal and free writing (Chapters 1 and 2), the journalist's questions (Chapter 3), and the explorer's questions (Chapter 4). In this chapter, we are going to present another series of questions, the classical questions, as further probes into your material.

The classical questions were devised by Aristotle during the Classical Age of Greece. As Athenians needed material for oral presentations at court and on ceremonial occasions, Aristotle devised a list of "topics" that would provide various ways of looking at any subject and generating ideas about it. These classical topics have been used in the study of rhetoric — both speech and writing — ever since. They have thus influenced Western patterns of thought for over two thousand years. You will discover that they are familiar to you.

As you observe your situation, you may find some of the classical questions helpful in generating material for your case study. These questions, as used over the years, have also generated corresponding methods of arrangement of the material they generate, and they thus become a primary tool for the writer at various stages in the writing process.

After testing a prejudice through actual and frequent observation, and after writing about it with the aid of the classical questions, you should consider publishing your essay. In order to affect others' opinions about the situation that you observed, we suggest that you select an audience that would be most interested in the outcome of your case and an appropriate vehicle for publishing your findings — your student newspaper, for example.

TASK: WRITING ABOUT A PREJUDGMENT

As the writing task for this chapter, choose an ongoing situation — an event, a person, a process, or a condition — about which you have made a prejudgment of some sort, and through a series of visits, observations, and/or interviews, write a case study in which you test your prejudgment or prejudice against the information that you have amassed. Your subject must be one that you have not observed sufficiently to form a legitimate conclusion about and that you have prejudged for one reason or another, either because of past experience with similar subjects, because of hearsay, or because you judged hastily. This subject must be one that you can frequently observe while you are preparing to write the essay.

Logical areas in which to search for the subject of your case study are school, work, or your neighborhood. You might, for example, observe a sports team at practice or in the first two weeks of play to determine if the players are as bad as your prejudice tells you they are; a class after a difficult exam to determine if they will, as you suspect, blame only the teacher; a new arrangement at work that you believe will prove counterproductive; a noisy group in the local library who you think cannot possibly be accomplishing any work; public transportation that you have always assumed to be inefficient although you have never used it; or a person with whom your first encounter was unpleasant.

In order to successfully test your prejudice, you will want to observe your situation frequently and with objectivity. You will be following much the same procedure that a scientist engages in when testing a hypothesis: Through the gathering of many facts, she or he either corroborates the hypothesis or rejects it. Because a prejudice, like a hypothesis, precedes the acquisition of actual knowledge, testing it is absolutely essential for the thoughtful, educated person. As you embark on this task, play the role of the scientist — that of a disinterested, objective observer who is always willing to reject her or his own hypothesis if the facts demand it.

Use the questions of the classical method of inquiry in generating material for your case study. Different questions will be useful for different topics, so you will want to choose those that seem like they are going to prove most useful for you in gathering information and evaluating your reaction.

Obviously, other people may share your prejudice about your subject, and you may want to prove to them that you and they have been either wrong or completely justified. Choose a publication whose readership would be interested in your case study and that would actually consider publishing your essay. You might try for the school newspaper, for example, or a newsletter at work or the neighborhood weekly. Because most such publications are addressed to an homogeneous audience, the discussion on pp. 192–197 should be helpful in determining what your readers' background and point of view are and what depth of information they require. If you are not serious about publication at this point, then select any magazine that you are familiar with and do your best to analyze and write for its audience.

In the sections that follow, we will discuss how to choose the most appropriate classical questions for your topic, how to construct a frame of reference and evaluate the depth of information needs of the reader common to a particular publication, and how to arrange your essay according to the arrangement patterns that correspond to the classical questions you have asked.

WRITING YOUR ESSAY

Generating Ideas: The Classical Questions

As we indicated in the Purpose section of this chapter, Aristotle and other classical rhetoricians devised several "topics" to generate ideas on subjects about which they had to speak. Ten of these topics are in frequent use today for both speeches and writing. Framed as questions, they are the following:

1. What is it?
2. What class does it belong to, or what classes can it be divided into?
3. How is it like or unlike other objects, events, or ideas?
4. What caused it?
5. What did (will) it cause?
6. What process does it go through (has it gone through)?
7. What general ideas and values does it exemplify?
8. What examples are there of it?
9. What can be done about it?
10. What has been said about it by others?

In this chapter, we will consider Questions 3 through 6. Questions 1 and 2 will be discussed in Chapter 6; Questions 7 and 8, in Chapter 7; Question 9, in Chapter 8; and Question 10, in Chapter 10.

The Classical Questions and the Explorer's Questions.   One way to illustrate the use of the classical questions is to compare and contrast them with the explorer's questions from Chapter 4 to see how each set of questions yields different results. Let's say that you are thinking of writing about your prejudice toward your uncle, a person you have always disliked because he embarrasses you with his comic remarks and silly behavior. What can your uncle be compared to? The explorer's questions ask how your uncle compares and contrasts with others in his class. For example, you might always have envied your friend's uncle, who always behaves so properly and brings her presents. Or you might compare your uncle with other relatives or adult friends of the family.

The classical questions also generate this material but allow for analogy as well. Analogy, which discovers the similarities between two unlike things, creates a tension and interest by going beyond the limits of a specific object to reveal its hitherto unnoticed connections to other abstract or concrete things. For example, your uncle might seem to you like a blemished, irregularly shaped, tart Macintosh apple sitting in a bowl of perfectly shaped, glossy, sweet Delicious apples. As a child, this difference disturbed and embarrassed you, but now your mental and emotional maturity suggest to you that the "misfit apple" of your childhood might be more interesting and valuable than you previously thought. An analogy can reveal to the writer subtle and complex relationships that might not otherwise be disclosed.

Another example of the difference between the classical and explorer's questions is illustrated by the classical question "What caused it?" The explorer's questions do not search for a causal relationship. They do not help us to see, for example, that your uncle's comic behavior might be his way of facing some personal setbacks encountered in his life, or that his intention might be to encourage you to develop your own sense of humor. The classical questions are not only concerned with such immediate causes but also with ultimate or more general causes or purposes. Using the example of your uncle, you might be struck with the universal need of children for adult models outside the immediate family, or the significance of comic language as a means of revealing the causes of behavior.

"What will it cause?" The explorer's method does not look for effects, and so it isn't very helpful to you in demonstrating how your uncle's outlook on life has helped you to deal with any of your own failures or misfortunes. Nor can it suggest that you will want to carry over to your own children some of his playfulness and distrust of conventions.

A further difference is that the classical approach adds an evaluative dimension in asking, "How well does it fulfill its intention or purpose?"

The classical and the explorer's questions can also explore the same questions: "How does it work?" "What is it?" and "What class does it belong to?"

From the comparison and contrasts between the two sets of questions, their differing thrusts should be clear: the explorer's questions seek out new facts about the subjects—as a static entity, as a dynamic entity, and as part of a larger system—whereas the classical questions relate the subject to past or current knowledge and values by comparing and contrasting it with unlike subjects, by explaining its causes and effects, and by evaluating it. Both sets of questions, used separately or together, can aid you in generating an almost infinite number of ideas about your subject.

Forming Subquestions.   In order to explore a subject fully, you will want to inquire into it at as many points as possible. By analyzing each classical question you choose to ask, you can form subquestions that will help you generate fuller answers. Some possible subquestions for Questions 3 through 6 are these:

Question 3. How is *X* like or unlike other objects, events or ideas?

A. Am I equally interested in the other objects, events or ideas, or am I using comparison and contrast as a device to describe *X* alone?
B. If I am interested in all, then what points do they have in common? How are they different? (See "whole-by-whole" paragraph example, p. 200.)

C. If I am interested in describing *X* alone, then what objects, events, or ideas can I compare it with?
  1. Is there an analogy that usefully conveys *X*?
  2. How is *X* like *Y*, or like *Y* and *Z*?
D. What can I contrast *X* with? How are these objects or ideas unlike *X*? (See "part-by-part" sample paragraph, p. 200.)

Question 4. What caused *X*?

A. What is the most probable cause(s)?
B. How far can I push the cause-and-effect relationship without committing one of the following logical fallacies? (See also Chap. 8, pp. 342–343.)
  1. Oversimplification
      a. Is it reasonable to assume *X* caused *Y*? Am I linking *X* and *Y* only because *X* happened just before *Y*?
      b. Is *X* the only cause of *Y*?
  2. Scapegoating
      a. Am I unfairly blaming an individual or a group for causing an effect that they did not actually cause?

Question 5. What will *X* cause?

A. Is the effect inevitable?
  1. Will *X* lead to this effect and this effect alone?
  2. Has *X* been the only cause of this effect?
B. What reasonable effect(s) can I predict?
C. What analogies can I devise to show what the outcome might be?

Question 6. How does *X* work? (See sample paragraphs, pp. 150–151, and 201.)

A. What does *X* do?
B. How is *X* put together?
C. What was *X* intended to do?
D. How well does *X* fulfill its intention or purpose?

SOME PRACTICE WITH THE CLASSICAL QUESTIONS

1. Choose an everyday event, process or condition — for example, travelling to school, working on a computer, feeling hungry — and generate ideas in your journal using the classical questions. Compare your ideas with the ideas members of your group generated and compose a master list of results. Write a paragraph utilizing all the ideas you and your group generated.

2. Identify the logical fallacies of the following causal statements. Which are examples of oversimplification and which of scapegoating?

   a. The size of Cleopatra's nose caused the fall of the Roman Empire. If her nose had been longer, she would have been less beautiful, and Marc Anthony would not have fallen in love with her. He would not then have neglected his military duties and lost the battle of Salamis, thus setting in motion the decline in might and authority of Roman rule.

   b. Johnny caused his teacher to go crazy. When he accidentally hit her with a board eraser he had thrown across the room, Mrs. Gorp became hysterical and had to leave school. She never returned. It was later reported that she had been institutionalized.

   c. The headline read, "Pac Man Kills. Enraged Youth Kills Friend After Losing at Video Game."

   d. The student was asked, "Why did you fail math?" The student replied, "Because the teacher was boring. If the class had been more interesting, I'd have been more attentive to my work."

3. Which pairs of items seem most promising as subjects for comparison or contrast? Explain why some are promising but not others. How do comparison and contrast help you to understand each item in the pair better than if it were described alone?

   a. The Persian Gulf War/Vietnam War

   b. Rental apartment/private home

   c. The Beatles/the Marx Brothers

   d. Compact discs/video cassettes

   e. NHL hockey games/street fighting

   f. Cigarette smoking/drug addiction

4. Complete the following statements by devising an analogy to fit each example. How does each analogy help to describe the subject?

   a. My love is like . . .

   b. This politician was as smooth as . . .

   c. He captained the basketball team like . . .

   d. Her hamburger tasted like . . .

   e. He strode down the street like . . .

Using the Classical Questions in Writing About a Prejudgment. Before beginning to case the subject about which you have made a prejudgment, you might want to decide how best to use the classical questions in deciding what to look for while you observe. Although all of the listed questions are at your disposal, and one subject will suggest answers to some questions better than to others, questions 3 through 6 seem to be most useful in completing this task. Each of these four questions generates subquestions in response to the task in general and may generate still others in response to your particular subject.

Question 3. How is my subject like or unlike other objects, events, or ideas?

How is it like or unlike other similar situations?
How is it like or unlike the ideal of its situation?
How is it like or unlike what I thought of it before observing it?

Question 4. What caused it?

What brought about the situation or an aspect of the situation?
What caused the prejudgment that I originally had about the situation?

Question 5. What did (will) it cause?

What effect(s) has this situation I am observing caused?
What effect(s) do my observations suggest it might cause in the future?

Question 6. What process does it go through (has it gone through)?

What process is the situation going through as I am making my observations?
How is the situation changing from observation to observation?

Jot down any other variations on these questions that occur to you to ask about your subject. A student writing about the Soho Soccer Club, which he felt lacked cohesion, asked the following subquestions:

1. How is it like or unlike other objects, events, or ideas?

How does the Soho Soccer Club compare and contrast with a
professional soccer team?
How does the coach compare with professional coaches?
2. What caused it?

Why does the team lack cohesion?
Why is the coach unable to achieve this cohesion?

3. What did (will) it cause?

Will the team improve in the next two weeks under this coach's supervision?

Will the team suffer loss of morale?

Will team discipline be affected?

4. What process does it go through (has it gone through)?

What will the coach encourage his team to do in the practices that I observe?

Will he teach transition before he teaches the proper passing techniques? Will he teach them how to kick properly?

Do his players like and respect him?

As in Chapter 4, you may wish to interview someone knowledgeable about the situation you are casing in order to obtain complete answers to your questions. To the extent that your subject is one about which many people form prejudgments, however, you will want to determine the objectivity as well as the knowledgeability of your source. Interviewing the coach of a team you are observing may result in biased or guarded answers at best.

SOME PRACTICE WITH USING THE CLASSICAL QUESTIONS IN WRITING ABOUT A PREJUDGMENT

1. Select one of the following subjects about which you have formed a prejudgment. Which classical questions might you ask in casing the subject? How would you adapt each question to this particular subject? What information would you expect to generate?

Classical, rap, or house music

The value of joining clubs

Skinheads

Other students' attitudes toward your school

A particular food that you do not like

2. Select the prejudgment about which you plan to write for the chapter task and phrase the questions that you will ask in casing the subject of your prejudgment. Ask any of the journalist's and explorer's questions that appear helpful as well.

3. Because you write in your journal regularly, noting down the date, time, and place of each entry, your journal is an excellent place to keep track of your observations of the subject about which you are testing your prejudgment.

The double-entry format can be especially useful in a number of ways for this assignment:

a. Ask different classical and explorer's questions about your subject at the same time, noting your observations in the left-hand column of a page, then in the right-hand column comparing the information that each question generates. *Note:* skip a page each time you do this, so a blank page always follows a page with written entries. This page will be used for step C below.

b. Ask the same questions about your subject repeatedly over a series of days, keeping track of your observations in dated left-hand column entries. Each day, note in the right-hand column any similarities and/or differences between your observations from one day to the next. *Note:* again skip a page each time you do this.

c. Once you feel you have collected sufficient data, read over the right-hand columns of your entries. Use the blank pages you have left to explain what you think about the similarities and differences that your observations raised. How do you account for them? How do they finally support or challenge your prejudgment?

Addressing Your Audience: Writing for Publication

The Reader Common to a Publication.   When writers write for publication, they usually write for one of two audiences. Either the magazine or journal is directed toward a very specific audience, or it has a general readership. In the last chapter, we discussed writing for a specific audience, one that is interested in your subject matter and knowledgeable about it. In this chapter, we are going to discuss how to write for a very general audience, an audience that may or may not be interested in your subject and may or may not know much about it.

The writer who writes for a large audience that is comprised of many different groups of people must therefore extrapolate those interests and qualities that these readers share and use this composite frame of reference in deciding how to write for this audience. How this can be done is the subject of this section.

No matter what magazine or newspaper you may read, none is written for everyone, no matter how unspecialized the content may appear to be. Each publication has a readership that can be fairly well defined, even though it may not be a technical journal, an entertainment rag, or a musician's bible. The reader of one publication is not necessarily the reader of another.

Think, for example, of the newspapers that are sold on the newsstands in your town. Newspapers with national circulations like the *Wall Street Journal* and even the *New York Times* have audiences that can be fairly well defined.

Businesspeople probably read the *Wall Street Journal*, and many people who buy the *New York Times*, with its sections on cultural affairs and informed opinion, are college educated. Consider next the paper with the largest distribution in your state. Its readership may include these two audiences, but it may also number many who read neither the *Journal* nor the *Times*. And when you add your local neighborhood daily or weekly to the list, you find still another reader emerging, one who may read none of the other newspapers, one interested only in news that is close to home, like local marriages and births, sports, and politics. Finally, the reader of your college newspaper is still another composite, based on the interests and knowledge shared by the students on your campus.

The Frame of Reference of a Publication's Reader.   How does one determine the frame of reference of the readership common to a particular publication? The following aspects of the publication should provide some guidelines: the types of subjects covered, the depth of the information given, the editorial perspectives delineated, the level of vocabulary used, the number and type of visuals printed (such as photographs and comics), and the advertisements included.

Take the *New York Times*, for example, which is available in all college libraries if not on your local newsstand. Why do we assume that it is for a reader who has a college education? Look first at the subjects covered. We find in Section 1 world and U.S. news and two pages of editorials, usually of a liberal bent, and informed opinions; in Section 4, we find extensive treatment of the stock market; and there are various daily supplements on sports, business, science, education, and entertainment. Although the types of information do not necessarily set the *Times* aside as aimed at the educated reader, the depth of information clearly does so. Also, the vocabulary level is high (it is estimated to be at a 12th-grade reading level). The number and type of visuals are a further indication, because the headlines are small, the pictures are few, and no comic strips are included. And although middle-priced items are advertised in its pages, luxury items tend to predominate.

At the other extreme are the tabloids. The topics covered in their pages are news, sports, and entertainment, with an emphasis in each case on their sensational aspects. The size of the headlines is very large, as are the pictures. The articles, on the other hand, are very short, and their depth of information is shallow. They are written on about an 8th-grade reading level. The advertisements are for products that are in a low to middle price range.

Once a writer has scanned his or her chosen publication from these angles, he or she can begin to assemble a reader frame of reference. The typical reader of the tabloid, we can assume, has perhaps a high-school education but often less; has a lower to middle income; is interested in the easily understood, often flamboyant aspects of the news rather than an in-depth analysis; and spends as much time on the sports, human interest, and comic sections as on the news. The reader of the *New York Times*, we can assume, not only is educated but is also inclined to be fairly prosperous, interested in understanding the news as well as in keeping abreast of it, liberal in political views, and willing to read the news on a daily basis. Anyone writing for either publication must take all of these factors into account if he or she wishes to reach the intended readership.

SOME PRACTICE WITH WRITING FOR PUBLICATION

1. Analyze the audiences of the following publications. What groups in America are excluded by the audience appeal of any of these magazines? Which magazines are addressed to the same audiences?

   Life Magazine   *TV Guide*
   Time Magazine   *People Magazine*
   National Enquirer   *Atlantic Monthly*
   Reader's Digest

2. Compare the audiences of the *New York Times*, your state's largest daily newspaper, and your hometown newspaper. To what extent do their audiences overlap? How are they different?

3. Take the frame of reference assembled above for the readers common to the *New York Times* and determine how they would best be approached on the following topics in terms of their attitude toward the subject and the depth of information they would require.

   The CIA in Central America

   Glasnost

   The New York Yankees

   Disarmament

   Princess Di

   Unemployment

4. Select one of the following topics, find a shaping idea for it, and determine what audience you would best like to reach. Then choose a publication that reaches that audience, explaining why you think it does:

   The American auto industry

   Cable television

   The value of an education in America

Young people and the job market

Automation

5. Analyze the frame of reference of the audience for your college newspaper suggested by a perusal of a few issues. How similar is this frame of reference to that you devised for your peers in Chapter 3? On the basis of any dissimilarities, what suggestions would you make to the editors about the appropriateness of the newspaper for its audience?

Selecting a Publication for Your Essay on a Prejudgment. Of course, a writer does not always know what publication a given piece of writing should best be directed toward. Often one must select a publication after a piece has been written. The question then becomes "What publication has an audience similar to the one I have written for?" The first step in the process of finding an appropriate home for your writing is to make a list of the publications with which you are familiar. In addition to newspapers on the national, state, local, and campus levels, consider newsletters as a likely vehicle for publication. Newsletters are published by most agencies—by libraries, schools, department stores, homeowners' associations, athletic associations, and theater groups. The advantages of writing for a newsletter are many: The audience in most cases is specialized, and if you are yourself familiar with the specialization, their frame of reference will be easy for you to discover. Also, newsletters will be more likely than a more professional publication to publish the work of a beginning writer. Finally, the editor might work with you in shaping your piece for publication.

After you have considered the most likely vehicles for the publication of your essay such as newspapers and newsletters, begin to think also of magazines that might publish your work. If you are serious about being published, think realistically about which magazines, such as small specialty magazines, might be likely to publish the work of a student writer. You can arrive at the frame of reference of the readers common to magazines by analyzing the same features as were analyzed above for newspapers and newsletters.

If you are not well versed in the particulars of your publication, then browse through it at some length now, looking at the types of articles and reading some of them to determine the depth of information they contain; examining the editorials, if any, for the editors' point of view; noting the products advertised and any other visuals (how large are the headings, are pictures or photographs included, are there any cartoons and, if so, of what nature: political, comic strip, other?); and surveying the feature columns for subject and focus. Ask yourself throughout this get-acquainted period whom each article and editorial is intended for: Are the readers being addressed educated, and if so, how much education do they have? Is a special hobby or career being presupposed? What social class does the publication seem aimed at? Is religion or sex or political persuasion being appealed to?

Once you have a knowledge of the publication you are writing for, answer the questions of the "Audience Analysis Guide" developed for this task.

―――――――――――― **AUDIENCE ANALYSIS GUIDE** ――――――――――――

1. What is the frame of reference of the readers common to this publication for which I am writing?

2. What will be their point of view of my subject? Will they share my initial prejudice?

3. What voice am I selecting as I write this essay? How can or will my voice selection affect my audience's point of view? If through observation I have decided that I no longer believe what I once did about my subject, but I suspect that my audience is still prejudiced about it, what voice can I use to bridge the gap?

4. What depth of information about my subject does my audience need and want: (a) are they prejudiced as I was; (b) have we both observed the situation sufficiently to form a valid conclusion; or (c) have they formed no opinion on my subject at all. In each case, a different depth of information will be needed: The first reader will need much depth of new material gleaned from your observations; the second reader will be interested in both why you formed the prejudice in the first place (background) and why you subsequently changed your mind (new information); and the third reader will need to know both what the situation is and why you formed a prejudice about it (mainly background).

For example, a student interested in the Thalia Spanish Theater wrote about its "innovative" director, who "encourages the creativity of the actor." The publishing "home" for his essay was the Thalia Program, which audiences receive at the beginning of each performance. He decided that the frame of reference of his readership was that they were Catholic, were of Spanish descent (although some might be simply devotees of the Spanish theater), were middle class, had received a secondary education in their native countries or had a background in the performing arts, and were of both sexes and all ages.

He felt that his audience loved the theater and would share his excitement about the director. The role he was playing was that of a student of the Spanish theater who hoped one day to be a leading actor in the Thalia Company. He felt that the audience would respond to the voice of someone who shared their love of the theater and knew something about it.

Because his audience was familiar with his subject, at least in its general outlines, he knew he could devote his essay to an in-depth discussion of the techniques employed by the director which he observed over a period of time.

SOME PRACTICE IN ADDRESSING THE READER OF THE PUBLICATION FOR WHICH YOU WILL WRITE YOUR ESSAY ON A PREJUDGMENT

1. Make a list of all the publications with which you are familiar that publish the writing of unprofessional writers. Some examples might be, in addition to your student newspaper, a weekly newspaper; a newsletter of the place where you work, of your church, or of an organization to which you belong; the letter-to-the-editor or op-ed pages of a daily newspaper. Analyze the frame of references of the readers of these newspapers as suggested by question 1 of the Audience Analysis Guide.

2. Select one publication that you would consider sending your essay to once you have completed it. Your criteria may be that you feel this publication would be most likely to publish an essay by a student, that its readers would be most interested in your prejudgment, or both.

3. Answer questions 2–4 of the Audience Analysis Guide about the readers of your selected publication.

Arranging Your Essay

The Shaping Idea.   There are several patterns you might use in arranging your essay, each corresponding to a classical question you might have asked: cause and effect, comparison and contrast, and process analysis. These may be used separately or in combination, depending on the shaping idea that you have chosen for your essay. If you have not yet chosen a shaping idea, you will want to compose one now, one that reflects the situation that you are casing, your prejudice toward it, and the classical questions that you chose to answer in generating ideas for your paper. Here are some examples of students' shaping ideas:

1. I have heard that the process of creating a character is always challenging when working with Mr. Davila, who has developed a number of innovations on the Stanislavsky method that have proven stimulating to the creativity of the actor.

2. Although some of the players have a good sound knowledge of the game, the team lacks cohesion because of the coach's poor tactical methods.

3. I have always thought that the public library is like a zoo and that students cannot accomplish very much there.

4. Fifteen years is a long time to hold a grudge against food.

The student writing on the first shaping idea will no doubt discuss the process that Mr. Davila goes through in directing his actors, perhaps also discussing why this approach is so stimulating to the actors, and perhaps comparing him with other directors as well. The second shaping idea calls for a discussion of the coach's poor process of teaching tactical methods, of the effects of this proceess on the players, and of the ways in which he compares with other coaches. The third shaping idea intends to present the effects on students of studying in the public library and perhaps to contrast this place of study with other, quieter ones. The last idea suggests the writer will analyze the causes of her prejudice against certain foods as well as the effects of testing it.

These classical questions all have corresponding patterns of arrangement, and we will now discuss cause and effect, comparison and contrast, and process analysis.

Cause and Effect.   The pattern of arranging your material when discussing causes and effects depends entirely on your subject matter and how many causes and effects you are discussing. The basic patterns are these:

- A caused B (and C and D, depending on the number of effects).
- A is caused by B (and C and D, depending on the number of causes).
- A caused B, B caused C, and C caused D.

These patterns can be used to apply to a single paragraph or to an entire essay. When applied to a paragraph, A, B, C, and D may each be contained in one or two sentences; when applied to an essay, each pattern may be developed over an entire paragraph. Here are two student paragraphs each developed according to one of these causal patterns:

A is caused by B and C.

Eight books were assigned from the course, and I found myself reading from four at a time. As if that wasn't difficult enough, the reading material never seemed to be fully explained in class.

Something was always left hanging. For a while, I figured that perhaps it was just I who was having difficulty and that I wasn't putting enough effort into my work. No one asked questions as "Mrs. Doe" went along through the battles between lords and vassals, popes and kings. Thus I figured that everyone else understood the work, and that I just had to devote more time and effort to my studies. So read and study I did, until I was down to four hours' sleep per night.

A caused B; (testing) B caused C, D, E.

I next tried mayonnaise, which I was always a little wary of due to the fact that it looks like a big gob of phlegm. And when it goes bad, the color changes to a real cheesy-looking yellow. I don't even know what mayo is made of; I really don't want to know. But I was adventurous this time. I ate two deviled eggs-- not only was there the mayo but the much-hated egg yolk as well. I survived the deviled egg episode and graduated to potato salad, which wasn't too bad so long as I avoided the clots of mayo sitting nonchalantly on the potatoes. I figured it was now time for the big one … sandwiches! I was actually going to spoon out mayonnaise and plop it onto my sandwiches. I cheated at first by eating tuna and mayo on toast but moved swiftly into the ham and lettuce on white category where I would be able to taste it more. The bread was not toasted, I was going to risk soppy, mayo-soaked bread for this experiment. I surprised myself by liking it. The sandwich was a little sweeter, that's all. I was getting myself stressed over nothing apparently. For twenty-two years I had avoided mayo because of its appearance only.

Comparison and Contrast. Two basic patterns are available when you are comparing and contrasting subjects. One is the "whole-by-whole" method, in which each subject is presented separately, and then comparisons and contrasts are delineated; the other is the "part-by-part" method, in which the two subjects are compared and contrasted point by point throughout the paragraph or essay.

When applied to a paragraph, the whole-by-whole method requires that two or three sentences at the beginning of the paragraph be devoted to the first subject, two or three in the middle deal with the second subject, and the final third of the paragraph point out the similarities and differences. The part-by-part method for a paragraph calls for every sentence or two to explore a different point at which the two subjects either compare or contrast.

When applied to an entire essay, the whole-by-whole method would suggest that the first section of the essay discuss one subject, the middle section present the other, and the final section directly compare and contrast the two. In using the part-by-part method for an essay, one would probably assign to each paragraph a different point on which the two subjects would be compared and/or contrasted.

Below are two student paragraphs illustrating these two methods of comparison and contrast:

Part-by-part

The roles of the candidates' wives finally convinced me who would win. Louise Lehrman sent a "woman-to-woman" message telling of the faith she had in her husband. This may have been a good idea, but unfortunately Matilda Cuomo beat her to the punch. Days earlier, Mrs. Cuomo was seen on TV giving virtually the same message. Also, Matilda Cuomo was on the campaign trail with and without her husband. Louise Lehrman's lack of involvement in her husband's campaign may have hurt him very much.

Whole-by-whole

When the public library is busy, which is most of the time, all the tables are full, and the majority of people are engrossed in conversation. The smaller kids are running around wildly. High-school kids are noisily putting the books back on the shelves. The elderly talk louder because many of them are hard of hearing. Long lines have formed at the reference desk and checkout counters. On the other hand, the library at the local college has lots of space for students who want to study. It is equipped with several small, comfortable, soundproof rooms for people who need peace and quiet. These rooms have glass all around them, and you can see people talking but you can't hear them. The college library is more spacious, more quiet, and more accommodating.

Process Analysis. As we discussed in Chapter 4 (pp. 150–151), process analysis combines elements of narration and exposition: narration because a process usually occurs in chronological order, exposition because one is explaining how something is done. The logical pattern for process analysis is to break up the stages of a process into their proper or logical order: Step A, Step B, Step C, Step D, and so on. If you are describing a process that others must attempt to follow, you'll want to take care in presenting the correct order of the steps in the process as well as in describing what takes place at each step.

Again, as in the cause-and-effect and the comparison-and-contrast patterns, if you are writing a paragraph on a process, each sentence or so will depict a different step; if you are writing an essay, each paragraph will describe a step or a unified series of steps. Here is a paragraph developed according to the process pattern:

Our defense is an intelligent and coordinated one. I drop back ten yards to break up a pass over the middle. Danny Romero, a solid defensive player, moves to the deep right side as safety. Left-side safety Eddie Dietrick, who leads the team in interceptions with four, tears across his side of the field. Short left-side safety Jimmy White, who has the reactions of a cat, watches the opposing quarterback intently. On the short right-hand side, John Sullivan, the most physical player on the team, prepares for a receiver foolish enough to run into his orbit. Jeff Marconi and Frank Roberto, two solid backup defensive players, dig their cleats in and tense their bodies. This is the way our shifting zone defense works.

Model Essays.   The first essay that follows, "Workers," from Richard Rodriguez's autobiographical *Hunger of Memory* (1982), exemplifies the chapter task in many significant ways. The author recounts his experiences as a manual laborer at a summer construction job. Expecting at first that his work would gain him "admission to the world of the laborer," he finds instead that a wide gap separates him from the lives of *los pobres*, the real working poor he will never come to know because of his education and class difference. He "cases" his subject by showing us his reactions to the work over a short period of time, his attitude changing as he becomes familiar with his fellow workers and the demands of physical labor.

Workers

Richard Rodriguez

It was at Stanford, one day near the end of my senior year, that a friend told me about a summer construction job he knew was available. I was quickly alert. Desire uncoiled within me. My friend said that he knew I had been looking for summer employment. He knew I needed some money. Almost apologetically he explained: It was something I probably wouldn't be interested in, but a friend of his, a contractor, needed someone for the summer to do menial jobs. There would be lots of shoveling and raking and sweeping. Nothing too hard. But nothing more interesting either. Still, the pay would be good. Did I want it? Or did I know someone who did?

I did. Yes, I said, surprised to hear myself say it.

In the weeks following, friends cautioned that I had no idea how hard physical labor really is. ("You only *think* you know what it is like to shovel for eight hours straight.") Their objections seemed to me challenges. They resolved the issue. I became happy with my plan. I decided, however, not to tell my parents. I wouldn't tell my mother because I could guess her worried reaction. I would tell my father only after the summer was over, when I could announce that, after all, I did know what "real work" is like.

The day I met the contractor (a Princeton graduate, it turned out), he asked me whether I had done any physical labor before. "In high school, during the summer," I lied. And although he seemed to regard me with skepticism, he decided to give me a try. Several days later, expectant, I arrived at my first construction site. I would take off my shirt to the sun. And at last grasp desired sensation. No longer afraid. At last become like a *bracero.* "We need those tree stumps out of here by tomorrow," the contractor said. I started to work.

I labored with excitement that first morning — and all the days after. The work was harder than I could have expected. But it was never as tedious as my friends had warned me it would be. There was too much physical pleasure in the labor. Especially early in the day, I would be most alert to the sensations of movement and straining. Beginning around seven each morning (when the air was still damp but the scent of weeds and dry earth anticipated the heat of the sun), I would feel my body resist the first thrusts of the shovel. My arms, tightened by sleep, would gradually loosen; after only several minutes, sweat would gather in beads on my forehead and then — a short while later — I would feel my chest silky with sweat in the breeze. I would return to my work. A nervous spark of pain would fly up my arm and settle to burn like an ember in the thick of my shoulder. An hour, two passed. Three. My whole body would assume regular movements, my shoveling would be described by identical, even movements. Even later in the day, my enthusiasm for primitive sensation would survive the heat and the dust and the insects pricking my back. I would strain wildly for sensation as the day came to a close. At three-thirty, quitting time, I would stand upright and slowly let my head fall back, luxuriating in the feeling of tightness relieved.

Some of the men working nearby would watch me and laugh. Two or three of the older men took the trouble to teach me the right way to use a pick, the correct way to shovel. "You're doing it wrong, too hard," one man scolded. Then proceeded to show me — what persons who work with their bodies all their lives quickly learn — the most economical way to use one's body in labor.

"Don't make your back do so much work," he instructed. I stood impatiently listening, half listening, vaguely watching, then noticed his work-thickened fingers clutching the shovel. I was annoyed. I wanted to tell him that I enjoyed shoveling the wrong way. And I didn't want to learn the right way. I wasn't afraid of back pain. I liked the way my body felt sore at the end of the day.

I was about to, but, as it turned out, I didn't say a thing. Rather it was at that moment I realized that I was fooling myself if I expected a few weeks of labor to gain me admission to the world of the laborer. I would not learn in three months what my father had meant by "real work." I was not bound to this job; I could imagine its rapid conclusion. For me the sensation of exertion and fatigue could be savored. For my father or uncle, working at comparable jobs when they were my age, such sensations were to be feared. Fatigue took a different toll on their bodies—and minds.

It was, I know, a simple insight. But it was with this realization that I took my first step that summer toward realizing something even more important about the 'worker.' In the company of carpenters, electricians, plumbers, and painters at lunch, I would often sit quietly, observant. I was not shy in such company. I felt easy, pleased by the knowledge that I was casually accepted, my presence taken for granted by men (exotics) who worked with their hands. Some days the younger men would talk and talk about sex, and they would howl at women who drove by in cars. Other days the talk at lunchtime was subdued; men gathered in separate groups. It depended on who was around. There were rough, good-natured workers. Others were quiet. The more I remember that summer, the more I realize that there was no single *type* of worker. I am embarrassed to say I had not expected such diversity. I certainly had not expected to meet, for example, a plumber who was an abstract painter in his off hours and admired the work of Mark Rothko. Nor did I expect to meet so many workers with college diplomas. (They were the ones who were not surprised that I intended to enter graduate school in the fall.) I suppose what I really want to say here is painfully obvious, but I must say it nevertheless: The men of that summer were middle-class Americans. They certainly didn't constitute an oppressed society. Carefully completing their work sheets; talking about the fortunes of local football teams; planning Las Vegas vacations; comparing the gas mileage of various makes of campers—they were not *los pobres* my mother had spoken about.

On two occasions, the contractor hired a group of Mexican aliens. They were employed to cut down some trees and haul off debris. In all, there were six men of varying age. The youngest in his twenties; the oldest (his father?) perhaps sixty years old. They came and they left in a single old truck. Anonymous men. They were never introduced to the other men at the site. Immediately upon their arrival, they would follow the contractor's directions, start working—rarely resting—seemingly driven by a fatalistic sense that work which had to be done was best done as quickly as possible.

I watched them sometimes. Perhaps they watched me. The only time I saw them pay me much notice was one day at lunchtime when I was laughing with the other men. The Mexicans sat apart when they ate, just as they worked by themselves. Quiet. I rarely heard them say much to each other. All I could hear were their voices calling out sharply to one another, giving directions. Otherwise, when they stood briefly resting, they talked among themselves in voices too hard to overhear.

The contractor knew enough Spanish, and the Mexicans—or at least the oldest of them, their spokesman — seemed to know enough English to communicate. But because I was around, the contractor decided one day to make me his translator. (He assumed I could speak Spanish.) I did what I was told. Shyly I went over to tell the Mexicans that the *patrón* wanted them to do something else before they left for the day. As I started to speak, I was afraid with my old fear that I would be unable to pronounce the Spanish words. But it was a simple instruction I had to convey. I could say it in phrases.

The dark sweating faces turned toward me as I spoke. They stopped their work to hear me. Each nodded in response. I stood there. I wanted to say something more. But what could I say in Spanish, even if I could have pronounced the words right? Perhaps I just wanted to engage them in small talk, to be assured of their confidence, our familiarity. I thought for a moment to ask them where in Mexico they were from. Something like that. And maybe I wanted to tell them (a lie if need be) that my parents were from the same part of Mexico.

I stood there.

Their faces watched me. The eyes of the man directly in front of me moved slowly over my shoulder, and I turned to follow his glance toward *el patrón* some distance away. For a moment I felt swept up by that glance into the Mexicans' company. But then I heard one of them returning to work. And then the others went back to work. I left them without saying anything more.

When they had finished, the contractor went over to pay them in cash. (He later told me that he paid them collectively — "for the job," though he wouldn't tell me their wages. He said something quickly about the good rate of exchange "in their own country.") I can still hear the loudly confident voice he used with the Mexicans. It was the sound of the *gringo* I had heard as a very young boy. And I can still hear the quiet, indistinct sounds of the Mexican, the oldest, who replied. At hearing that voice I was sad for the Mexicans. Depressed by their vulnerability. Angry at myself. The adventure of the summer seemed suddenly ludicrous. I would not shorten the distance I felt from *los pobres* with a few weeks of physical labor. I would not become like them. They were different from me. . . .

That summer I worked in the sun may have made me physically indistinguishable from the Mexicans working nearby. (My skin was actually darker because, unlike them, I worked without wearing a shirt. By late August my hands were probably as tough as theirs.) But I was not one of *los pobres*. What made me different from them was an attitude of *mind*, my imagination of myself.

I do not blame my mother for warning me away from the sun when I was young. In a world where her brother had become an old man in his twenties because he was dark, my complexion was something to worry about. "Don't run in the sun," she warns me today. I run. In the end, my father was right — though perhaps he did not know how right or why — to say that I would never know what real work is. I will never know what he felt at his last factory job. If tomorrow I worked at some kind of factory, it would go differently for me. My long education would favor me. I could act as a public person — able to defend my interests, to unionize, to petition, to speak up — to challenge and demand. (I will never know what real work is.) I will never know what the Mexicans knew, gathering their shovels and ladders and saws.

Their silence stays with me now. The wages those Mexicans received for their labor were only a measure of their disadvantaged condition. Their silence is more telling. They lack a public identity. They remain profoundly alien. Persons apart. People lacking a union obviously, people without grounds. They depend upon the relative good will or fairness of their employers each day. For such people, lacking a better alternative, it is not such an unreasonable risk.

Their silence stays with me. I have taken these many words to describe its impact. Only: the quiet. Something uncanny about its. Its compliance. Vulnerability. Pathos. As I heard their truck rumbling away, I shuddered, my face mirrored with sweat. I had finally come face to face with *los pobres*.

1. How does Rodriguez's use of comparison and contrast help the reader to understand the meaning of his experience with physical labor?

2. What prejudgment of workers had Rodriguez made before he started the job? What accounts for his change in attitude?

3. Why does the author devote almost half his essay to the Mexican workers he doesn't even know? How does he contrast himself with them?

4. How does the knowledge that Rodriguez has gained by his concluding paragraph contrast with the expectation about work that he expresses in his introductory paragraphs?

5. How may the author's summer experience have significance later in his life with regard to what he calls his "imagination of myself"?

In this essay, Patrick Fenton, a free-lance writer, writes of an episode in which he had to interview the well-known poet of the Beat Generation, Allen Ginsberg. Because Ginsberg has become notorious, the writer was not sure he would find the interview a pleasant experience, despite his admiration for the poet as a young man.

A Second Look at Allen Ginsberg

by Patrick Fenton

The 38th Parallel is simply a geographic line, a dotted map marker that shows the division of South Korea and North Korea, but when I was growing up in the fifties it was the name of some mysterious border the mention of which always drove the men of my Brooklyn neighborhood into a patriotic rage. And that was because in the summer of 1950, while the off-duty cops and trolley car drivers of the neighborhood were sitting in McNulty's Bar and

Grill on Seventeenth Street listening to prize fights and baseball games coming over the radio, the Communists of North Korea invaded South Korea, and the Korean War began.

And in my old neighborhood it never ended. Well into the 1960's the old-timers of the "Hill," a blue-collar area that starts a few blocks past the recognized borders of well-to-do Park Slope, still argued about the war. Every Saturday night the roaring sound of men arguing in high-pitched saloon voices could be heard coming out of the open doors of the bars of Ninth Avenue.

And while this patriotic talk of old wars was going on, Bob Rice, a friend of mine, and I would be sitting on benches in the darkness above the Prospect Expressway, a sunken highway that ran next to the rows of red-brick factories that lined the neighborhood like a wall, and we would be reading the poems of the Beat Generation poet, Allen Ginsberg.

One of Ginsberg's poems was called "America," and part of the words to it were "It's true I don't want to join the Army or turn lathes in precision parts factories, I'm nearsighted and psychopathic anyway." As we stood in the moonlight, Bob would read the words, a nervous twist coming to his lips. And as he read them, we would carefully look around, waiting for some beefy, campaign-hat-tilted member of the local American Legion hall, McFadden Brothers Post, to come and throw the two of us down onto the expressway.

Bob and I came from a blue-collar neighborhood in Brooklyn where poets like Allen Ginsberg were looked upon as trouble. Few people went off to college, so there was little talk of writers or poets, except for what the nuns in Holy Name Parochial School had taught us about poets like Robert Frost. I don't remember ever hearing anyone in the neighborhood saying they wanted to be a writer. Most of us were encouraged to study for the city bus driver's exam—either that or work in the factories. A few of the more pious boys just disappeared from the neighborhood and went off to become priests after their parents proudly announced that they had "the calling."

And if you had any dreams of becoming something else, you wouldn't get much inspiration from Joe Lang, or one of the Williams brothers, as you stood on the corner of Seventeenth Street, watching one of them as they steered the hulking body of the Smith Street bus down Ninth Avenue, going through the same run that men before them had once driven trolley cars on. You wouldn't get much inspiration watching the night crews as they marched, heads bowed, into the paint factories of Nineteenth Street. Reading the rebellious poems of Allen Ginsberg made it possible for Bob and me to not go off willingly to this inevitable blue-collar fate.

In the summer of 1989, over three decades later, after I had worked my share of factory jobs (and Bob Rice had made it to Wall Street), I had an opportunity to interview Allen Ginsberg while I was doing some free-lance writing for the Sunday Magazine section of the New York newspaper, *Newsday*. I was working on a story about a friend of his, the late Beat Generation writer, Jack Kerouac, author of *On the Road*. By now his poetry had gone through several generations, and I was no longer sure why I had liked him in the first place.

As I prepared for the interview, taking notes, calling up people who knew him, I thought back to those fifties nights when Bob Rice and I used to sit along the expressway, reading word after word of Ginsberg's poems in the illuminated glare of a street light. I also thought of what I had learned of him since the fifties. I had only seen him read his poems once, and that night he read them all in a rapid voice, full of an exhausting emotion that made the veins in his head stand out. He came across as an intense man, a man so caught up in his work that I felt he would not be easy to talk to. And there were other things I learned about him as I prepared for the interview, pictures and stories about him that led me to believe that he would turn out to be an eccentric poet with little time or patience for questions about his life.

In the 1960's he was kicked out of Czechoslovakia after spending several wild nights in Prague at parties and chanting "Hare Krishna" whenever the police would stop to question him in the street. That same year he danced naked at London parties thrown by the rock group, the Beatles, and he became friends with Timothy Leary, a radical professor who introduced the drug LSD to the hippies of the Love Generation.

Now, at fifty, I decided I was no longer as comfortable with the ideas of Ginsberg as I had been when I was younger.

A writer friend of mine helped me set up the interview by giving me Allen Ginsberg's personal home phone number, but I had to promise him that I would not tell Ginsberg's people where I got the number from. I was told if I called the number, I would reach an office that he works out of in his apartment. "But you'll have to go through several people before you get to him," he told me. "If they don't think you're sincere about what you want to write about him," he warned, "they won't put him on."

After getting by a woman who questions me about why I want to talk to Allen Ginsberg, I am passed on to Bob Rosenthal, a close associate of the poet. "Allen is not feeling well right now. He can't talk to you. He's doing too much, and now he's trying to take care of his health," he tells me. I persist, and he says that if I call again in the morning he might be able to set it up so that Allen Ginsberg can give me a quote for my article.

"That won't help me," I tell him. "I need more than a quote. I need an interview for *Newsday*."

"Patrick, there are always too many people trying to see Allen. He has to take care of his health."

The next morning, I call and I'm told by a young woman to hang on. As I wait, I look down at my notes scattered about my basement desk, and I read one from a recent biography by Barry Miles that describes Ginsberg as "a man whose rebellious life style fueled the counter cultural revolution of the 1960's." On another piece of paper I have written the first line of "Howl," his most famous poem: "I saw the best minds of my generation destroyed by madness, starving hysterical naked. . . ." I can visualize in my mind Allen Ginsberg standing screaming on the edge of a stage somewhere in the fifties, rocking back and forth as he reads this line, and I brace myself for the few minutes of madness that I expect will soon be coming over the phone.

Then I hear a voice say, "Hang on, Patrick, I'm going to transfer you to Allen."

At first he sounds a little tired. "What do you want to know?" he asks.

"Is 'Howl' your favorite poem?"

"No," he says. "Most people think it is, but it's not. 'Kaddish,' a poem I wrote about my mother, is my favorite."

I ask him about the writer, Jack Kerouac. Then his voice starts to change. It becomes calm and rich, a voice that has the softness of voices you hear coming down from priests on altars, coming down from rabbis in temples. He reads to me from a part of a Kerouac book called *Visions of Cody*, a book that he appeared in as the character, Irwin Garden: "Around the pool halls of Denver during World War II. . . ."

He recalls the house in which his friend, Jack Kerouac, lived in Richmond Hill in the New York borough of Queens. He describes the room that Kerouac wrote in as "brown, gloomy, lamp in room, old wooden banister leading up to it. His room was on the second floor with a window that faced the street." He describes it to me as if he were going through some type of literary exercise for the writing of a poem. Then a sound of awe comes into his voice as he says, "One day he gave me a writing lesson in that room. He sat me down at his typewriter and told me to type onto the page the words of a poem I was working on exactly as I'm thinking of them. He taught me spontaneous prose, straight to the page as it comes into your mind. Jack was brilliant — he was a genius."

"The way he explained it to me affected my whole way of writing. Jack became my guru — my teacher," he said. I'm surprised at the patience in his voice as he explains this technique to me. "The idea," he says, "is to take words as they come into your mind and to form them into ideas, and to move them from mind to page in one swift act of completed prose. It's easy," he says with a playful laugh. "Anyone can do it." And then he left me to ponder the cosmic writing lesson he had just passed along to me from Jack Kerouac.

After that, he allowed me to interview him about five times on the phone. Once when he was going out on the road, he promised me that he would call me from out of state. And much to my surprise he did. The phone rang one night at about eight o'clock, and Allen Ginsberg's voice was asking me what else I needed to know for my piece on Jack Kerouac.

He granted me permission to go through his personal papers, which are stored in the Ginsberg Deposit at the Rare Book and Manuscript Room of the Butler Library at Columbia University. It is here that all the personal things of his life have been stored.

I had not expected to see anything that would show him as a saver of childhood memorabilia — the documents and things that we keep to remind us of our first innocent journeys into the world, but according to a catalog, box #501 holds "memorabilia" of his school years at Public School Number 6 in Paterson, New Jersey, from which he graduated in 1939. Inside it there is an autograph album, a class pin and one of his first diplomas. Box #502 holds his 1949 diploma from Columbia University as well as his freshman notes. Box #581 lists an old pocket knife, some road maps, a walking stick, even a pair of his sneakers.

I'm surprised that these things that serve as evidence of the innocence of his youth, evidence of his meteoric rise as poet for several generations were simply not left behind, scattered about somewhere in motel rooms across the America he had wandered through so long ago with Jack Kerouac.

A librarian produces box #44–01. I slide my hand into it and pull out a small, brown, weathered notebook. On the front of it in a circle in bold black letters there is the brand name "Junita." Below the circle he has penciled the name "Ginsberg." It is full of bits and pieces of his first poems — the first evidence of the shaping of his craft. There is nothing here of the apparition of the young Ginsberg I had expected to find, the wild Ginsberg thumbing his nose at society. Instead, there is page after page of his rough drafts, brilliant works in progress, some with the tone of the nineteenth century poet, Walt Whitman, alive with a feel for the common people of America.

On page three there is one of the first penciled entries he made in the early forties as a young poet: "Society bleeds geniuses." I turned the notebook over in my hand, and I thought about how few geniuses come along in any one time — I thought about how important it is not to misjudge them.

In the eight hours I had spent in the Rare Manuscript Room of the Butler Library, I had flipped through over a hundred letters and watched the Beat Generation come alive again before my eyes, I watched Ginsberg and Kerouac sadly grow old on the pages of their personal letters, and I realized a little more clearly now that the reason I had spent so many years reading Thomas Wolfe and Sherwood Anderson, reading Whitman and Ginsberg and Kerouac, and all the other free thinkers that come out of each American generation was because I was constantly attempting to free myself from the prejudice that you take with you from out of the small town, the prejudice that you take with you from out of the neighborhood of the city. And of course as I walked out onto the great stone steps of Columbia University, I realized I still had a way to go.

1. Why does Patrick Fenton begin his essay by describing both the Brooklyn environment in which he grew up and his early admiration for Allen Ginsberg's poetry?

2. What does Fenton's essay add to your knowledge about the Beat Generation of the 1950's and to what you may know about Allen Ginsberg's role in the Beat Movement?

3. What observations does Fenton make that alter his judgment of Ginsberg? To what extent do you agree that these observations justify his implication that Ginsberg is a genius and that he should not be misjudged?

4. What experiences of your own coincide with the author's assertion that both town and city breed prejudices from which we must constantly strive to free ourselves?

5. What do you think of Fenton's style in this essay? Why, for example, does he shift at some points into the present tense? What would have been the

effect of his introducing the essay by informing the reader that he wanted to interview Allen Ginsberg and then flashing back to his own childhood, rather than pursuing the chronological order that he uses here?

6. Kerouac's method of "spontaneous prose" is similar to free writing. Reading "Howl" or "America," two of Ginsberg's most famous poems, will give you an idea of how free writing can be utilized as a stylistic device for poetry as well as a means of generating ideas for essays.

Writing Your Rough Draft

Once you have made your observations with the aid of the classical questions, have decided what audience you are addressing, and have planned what arrangement patterns you will use, you are about ready to begin your rough draft. At this point, if you have not already done so, you will also want to decide whether your observation of your subject has supported your prejudice. Although your shaping idea has announced your prejudice, it will not necessarily indicate your final decision about it, especially if you have changed your mind in the course of your observations. Your verdict can emerge in your essay at various junctures: in the introduction, in the course of presenting your observations, in your conclusion, or in all three. Knowing your verdict about your situation is important before beginning to write: Whether or not your reader agrees with your conclusion will shape what you say and how you say it.

Following is the rough draft of a student's essay in fulfillment of this task. Where did she state her shaping idea? At what point do you know whether she felt her initial prejudice was justified or not? What questions did she ask in generating material? How did she arrange her paragraphs? What type of publication do you think she might be writing for?

A CLASSICAL QUESTION

(draft)

It was always the part of the day I dreaded. I could put up
with almost anything else the work day handed out; I could
clean 30 bloody filets, debone 20 smelly fish and peel apples for
9 hours but the one thing I could not put up with was Jim's
turn to pick the radio station. In the kitchen where I work

there are about 15 people so to be fair everyone gets a chance to pick what kind of music we listen to. Most of us like a wide variety of music so it's not often a problem. Except for Jim. He always seems to wait until the end of the day when we've just worked 10 hours and are desperately trying to finish up, and then he insists on putting on the classical music station.

Instantly my mind would rebel. That was for "old people" (like my mother) and besides it would put me to sleep. Jim said he liked it because it relaxed him but that's exactly what I had against it! At that hour of the day I didn't need to be relaxed, I needed something to get my pulse going so I could finish the work.

Anyway, to add insult to injury, Jim, who is also a musician, was performing in a recital which we were all invited to. Of course we all went to show support even though they were play-ing—classical music!

The funny thing was sitting there in person and watching someone I knew performing it, I actually found myself enjoying the music. Somehow it didn't sound so much like it belonged in an elevator. Hmm, I thought, maybe there is something to this.

A few days later another co-worker mentioned that he was nervous about dancing at his upcoming wedding, so we had an impromptu social dancing lesson to classical music.

Alright, I thought, I'll give this stuff a try. I went home and put on one of my mother's tapes while I cooked dinner. There I was humming and swaying around. It wasn't Madonna but it was still pretty good.

I figured I was cured. The next time Jim put on that station I wouldn't just grin and bear it I'd actually enjoy it. I might even put it on when it was my turn. Unfortunately it didn't hap-pen that way. He put it on, it was 9:00, we had 2 more hours to go and it slowed me down, made me sleepy and generally ag-gravated me.

Oh well Rome was not built in a day. At least I have discov-ered that classical music can be enjoyable in the right place and at the right time. At work, I'll take Madonna!

FOCUS ON FORM: SENTENCE COMBINING

The sentence, like the paragraph, is a basic unit of thought. How one phrases one's sentences — their language, their structure, their punctuation, and even their length — indicates one's level of maturity as a writer. In this section, we suggest exercises that will help you to improve the structure and therefore the maturity of your sentences by giving you options for shaping them with which you may be unfamiliar. The first exercises work with the simple base sentence. These exercises gradually lead into longer, combined sentences. Other exercises show the relationship of punctuation to sentence structure. Still others show how sentence structure can help build transitions between thoughts, on both the sentence and paragraph levels.

The Base Sentence

The base sentence is a simple sentence that includes a subject, a verb, and often either an object, a predicate nominative, or a predicate adjective. Examples of these four base sentence patterns are the following:

The girl cried. (SUBJECT AND VERB)

The girl takes calculus. (SUBJECT, VERB, AND OBJECT)

The girl is a mathematics major. (SUBJECT, VERB, AND PREDICATE NOMINATIVE)

The girl is smart. (SUBJECT, VERB, AND PREDICATE ADJECTIVE)

SOME PRACTICE WITH BASE SENTENCES

1. Write a paragraph on any subject, using only simple sentences. Formulate your sentence patterns using the four base sentences above.

2. Rewrite the paragraph from Exercise 1, placing each sentence on a separate line and leaving three spaces between each sentence. Then list three adjectives, three adverbs, and three prepositional phrases that will add information to each base sentence. Finally, combine all the new elements with each simple sentence and rewrite the four sentences as a paragraph.

   Example
   Base sentence: The boy eats chocolates.
   Adjectives: plump, young, expensive
   Adverbs: slightly, hastily, greedily

Prepositional phrases: in the cafeteria, of his school, during lunchtime

Combined: The slightly plump young boy hastily and greedily eats expensive chocolates in the cafeteria of his school during lunchtime.

3. Write a second paragraph on any subject. Again, write in simple sentences based on the four simple patterns above. Combine two or more base sentences with coordinating conjunctions such as *and, or, but, for,* and *yet,* adding adjectives, adverbs, and prepositional phrases where appropriate as you go along (see Handbook, pp. 558–564).

Subordinate Clauses

You can turn a base sentence into a subordinate clause by adding subordinating conjunctions before it, such as *although, as, because, since, when, that, after, before, how, if, though, unless, until, what, where, while, in order that, provided that, as long as, as though,* and *so (that).*

Example

Base sentence 1: Television is no longer slavishly watched.

Base sentence 2: The network executives are becoming worried.

Combined: Because television is no longer slavishly watched, the network executives are becoming worried. (The addition of the subordinating conjunction *because* creates a subordinate clause out of the first base sentence, and the second sentence remains "independent." Note: subordinate clauses cannot stand alone as sentences; they must be joined to an independent base sentence for the completion of their meaning.)

SOME PRACTICE WITH SUBORDINATE CLAUSES

1. Combine the sentences in the paragraph in Exercise 3 above so that some base sentences become subordinate clauses.

Example

Base sentence 1: The husky coach calmly and quietly announced the lucky winner of the first prize for boxing at the college.

Base sentence 2: My usually courageous brother shook.

Combined: As the husky coach calmly and quietly announced the lucky winner of the first prize for boxing at the college, my usually courageous brother shook.

Free Modifiers

Base sentences can also be turned into "clusters" of words that act as free modifiers coming before, after, or in the middle of base clauses and set apart by punctuation. These clusters can act as nouns, verbs, adjectives, or adverbs in reference to another base sentence.

Noun Cluster

Example
Base sentence 1: Wally is a jokester.
Base sentence 2: His pranks are funny only to him.
Combined: A jokester, Wally's pranks are funny only to him.

Verb Cluster

Example
Base sentence 1: Wally hooted with laughter at the absurd dilemma of his friend.
Base sentence 2: He was not appreciated.
Combined: Hooting with laughter at the absurd dilemma of his friend, Wally was not appreciated.

Adjective Cluster

Example
Base sentence 1: Wally is disliked.
Base sentence 2: Most of his fraternity brothers avoid him whenever possible.
Combined: Disliked, Wally finds himself avoided by most of his fraternity brothers whenever possible.

Adverb Cluster

Example
Base sentence 1: Wally is scarcely aware of their antipathy.
Base sentence 2: This is hard to believe.
Combined: Unbelievably, Wally is scarcely aware of their antipathy.

Subordinate clauses are also free modifiers.
When two or more free modifiers modifying the same word are used in a sentence, they should be in the same or parallel form.

Example

Base sentence 1: The April sun shone *weakly*.

Base sentence 2: An intermittent source of light, the sun shone.

Base sentence 3: The sun, *the rain falling all the while,* shone.

Base sentence 4: While storm clouds threatened to eclipse it, the sun shone.

Combined: Weakly and intermittently, the April sun shone while the rain fell and storm clouds threatened to eclipse it.

SOME PRACTICE WITH FREE MODIFIERS

1. Write three sentences, each of which contains parallel free modifiers. Use a different type of free modifier in each sentence.

2. Rewrite the paragraph from Exercise 3 on page 213, turning each subordinate clause into another type of free modifier.

    Example

    Subordinate Clause: Because television is no longer slavishly watched, the network excutives are becoming worried.

    Verb Cluster: Noticing that television is no longer slavishly watched, the network executives are becoming worried.

3. Write as long a sentence as you can by adding all types of free modifiers to the base clause. Remember to keep the free modifiers in parallel form. Structure the sentence so that it does not sound strung together. As an example, examine the sentences in the paragraph that follows, some of which continue for five or six lines, but none of which sounds tedious or run-on:

    > About ten years ago a well-known literary critic and essayist, a good friend of long standing, told me that a wealthy widely-circulated weekly pictorial magazine had offered him a good price to write a piece about me — not about my work or works, but about me as a private citizen, an individual. I said No, and explained why: my belief that only a writer's works were in the public domain, to be discussed and investigated and written about, the writer himself having put them there by submitting them for publication and accepting money for them; and therefore he not only would but must accept whatever the public wished to say or do about them from praise to burning. But that, until the writer committed a crime or ran for public office, his private life was his own; and not only had he the right to defend his privacy, but the public had the duty to do so since one man's liberty must stop at exactly the point where the next one's begins; and that I believed that anyone of taste and responsibility would agree with me.
    >
    > — William Faulkner, "On Privacy," *Harper's Magazine,* July 1955

Varying Sentence Length and Rhythm

Base or simple sentences need not always be combined; they remain useful to the mature writer, usually to introduce a new topic, to emphasize a point or to make a dramatic statement. Examine the use of varying sentence structures in the following paragraphs, paying attention to the rationale with which the writers used simple sentences as well as combined sentences. How are both sense and rhythm affected in each case?

It is the traffic that makes it all unique. A traffic in trams grinding round corners, a traffic in approximately London buses whose radiators seem ready to burst, in gypsy-green lorries with "Ta-ta and By-by" and other slogans painted on the back, in taxis swerving all over the road with much blowing of horns, in rickshaws springing unexpectedly out of sidestreets, in bullock carts swaying ponderously along to the impediment of everyone, in sacred Brahmani cows and bulls nonchalantly strolling down the middle of the tram-tracks munching breakfast as they go. A traffic, too, in people who are hanging on to all forms of public transport, who are squatting cross-legged upon the counters of their shops, who are darting in and out of the roadways between the vehicles, who are staggering under enormous loads, who are walking briskly with briefcases, who are lying like dead things on the pavements, who are drenching themselves with muddy water in the gutters, who are arguing, laughing, gesticulating, defecating, and who are sometimes just standing still as though wondering what to do. There never were so many people in a city at seven o'clock in the morning. Patiently the driver of the limousine steers his passage between and around them, while they pause in mid-stride to let him through, or leap to get out of his way, or stare at him blankly, or curse him roundly, or occasionally spit in the path of his highly polished Cadillac. Presently, and quite remarkably, he comes to the end of the journey without collision and deposits the traveler and his luggage upon the pavement in front of an hotel. And here the traveler has his first encounter with a beggar. He had better make the best of it, for beggary is to be with him until the end of his days in Calcutta.

—Geoffrey Moorhouse, *Calcutta*

Now when I had mastered the language of this water and had come to know every trifling feature that bordered the great river as familiarly as I knew the letters of the alphabet, I had made a valuable acquisition. But I had lost something, too. I had lost something which could never be restored to me while I lived. All the grace, the beauty, the poetry, had gone out of the majestic river! I still kept in mind a certain wonderful sunset which I witnessed when steam-boating was new to me. A broad expanse of the river was turned to blood; in the middle distance the red hue brightened into gold, through which a solitary log came floating, black and conspicuous; in one place a long, slanting mark lay sparkling upon the water; in another the surface was broken by boiling, tumbling rings that were as many-tinted as an opal; where the ruddy flush was faintest was a smooth spot that was covered with graceful circles and radiating lines, ever so delicately traced; the shore on our left was densely wooded, and the somber shadow that fell from this forest was broken in one place by a long, ruffled trail that shone like silver; and high above the forest wall a clean-stemmed dead tree waved a single leafy bough that glowed like a flame in the unobstructed splendor that was flowing from the sun. There were graceful curves, reflected images, woody heights, soft distances, and over the whole scene, far and near, the dissolving lights drifted steadily, enriching it every passing moment with new marvels of coloring.

—Mark Twain, *Life on the Mississippi*

SOME PRACTICE WITH SENTENCE LENGTH AND RHYTHM

1. Now write a paragraph, again on a subject of your own choosing, in which you use a variety of sentence structures: simple sentences, sentences with a variety of free modifiers, including subordinate clauses, and base sentences joined with coordinating conjunctions. What function does each type of sentence play in conveying the meaning of the paragraph?

Punctuation

Once you understand the concept of base clauses, subordinate clauses, and verb, noun, adverb, and adjective clusters, the punctuation of sentences becomes much clearer (see Handbook, pp. 584–600). Below are four rules for sentence punctuation.

1. A comma either separates elements in a series or sets off a base clause from a free modifier. With a conjunction, it can separate two base clauses.

   ### Examples

   The rain, fog, and humidity did not deter them from making the trip.

   Quietly and furtively, he approached the abandoned car.

   Children are growing up very fast, and their parents must be partly responsible.

   Because children are growing up very fast, their parents must be partly responsible.

2. A semicolon can separate two base clauses.

   ### Example

   Children are growing up very fast; their parents must be responsible.

3. A colon can appear only at the tail end of a base clause; it introduces either a list or a restatement of the base clause.

Examples

The economy has been sluggish in many ways: employment, construction, and trade.

I would like to invite you to dinner: I would like to see you very much.

4. A dash acts as a strong comma, setting off middle- and final-position free modifiers from a base clause.

Examples

The man left the office—at once.

The man—who could scarcely wait to don his coat—left the office.

Transitions

Free modifiers are also useful as transitions between thoughts, whether these thoughts occur in sentences or in paragraphs. When placed at the beginning of a sentence, the free modifier connects the sentence to the preceding one.

Example

Farm prices are down from what they were five years ago. As a result, farmers are angry.

Notice in the following paragraphs the use of free modifiers to connect thoughts between parts of sentences, between sentences themselves, and between paragraphs.

Why is that woman laughing so early in the morning? I keep trying to put myself in her place, but she always surprises me. From somewhere else in the building, sound waves echoing around the courtyard to disguise their origin, comes a brutal argument. So I must wonder what makes that couple fight so furiously and, even more, what makes them continue living together despite their rage.

I live in an apartment, but not totally apart. I can tell a body not to enter my space, but I cannot command the sound waves. They enter as they will. And not only that, but they force their way into my head and, with no regard for my own volition, tie me into the lives of my neighbors.

Accosted also by sounds from the street, I am pulled into the activity there. A youngster tries to call his friend down from a high floor, and calls and calls his name, unaffected by lack of response. Soon I yearn for Henry to come down as much as the caller does. A transistor blares with a volume that bothers my ears. Drawn to the window, I marvel that the teenage boy, dancing alone on a stoop, can stand it right beside him. The sound must anesthetize like a drug. Now someone double parked is blocking a man who wants his car out. He honks, and makes me turn from whatever I'm thinking about to share his frustration, which is intense.

Back inside, I hear a young woman in an apartment next to mine practicing her clarinet. She is pretty good, beginning a professional career, I've learned, getting jobs with an orchestra here and there. Her practice hours give the building a cool, classical sound. I'm also brought into the anxieties of her young career. I hear the answering machine she has installed, asking whoever it is please to leave a message. Maybe it will mean another break for her.

> —Tracey Early, "Sounds That Bring Us Closer Together,"
> *Christian Science Monitor, Jan. 1980*

SOME PRACTICE WITH SENTENCE COMBINING

1. Write two paragraphs in which you use free modifiers to connect the thoughts within sentences, between sentences, and between paragraphs. Use the appropriate punctuation.

2. Combine the following sentences into an effectively written essay. The breaks between sentence groups represent paragraphs in the student's original essay, but ignore them if you think it is advisable. Add words when necessary to combine the sentences but do not change the meaning. This exercise can also be done in groups, but whether completed individually or in groups, comparing the different versions that result will indicate the variety of sentence combinations possible.

Imaginary Jane

1. I moved into the house I am living in now.
2. I was only three years old.
3. We bought the house from my grandfather.
4. We have been living there for about fifteen years now.
5. There were no other children on my block.
6. There were no children to play with.
7. The other families were mostly old people.
8. The other families lived on my block.
9. Their children were already grown up.
10. This left me with no choice.
11. I had to play by myself.

12. I found many things to do on my own.
13. I would play house alone and dolls alone also.
14. I played with my parents.

15. My parents were often too busy.
16. The day was really long and boring.
17. This went on for a couple of years.
18. Then kindergarten started.

19. School was a relief.
20. I made new friends.
21. I had a lot of classmates.
22. This did not, of course, help me with my problem of staying alone.
23. I continued to stay by myself at home.

24. I became six years old.
25. A little girl named Diane moved next door.
26. I did not like to play with her.
27. I was so used to staying alone.
28. I did not want her to touch any of my things.
29. I was afraid.
30. She was going to take my toys away from me.

31. Staying alone was not such a good idea.
32. I started to make things up.
33. I started to pretend.
34. I had an imaginary friend.
35. My friend's name was Jane.
36. I have no idea where the name came from.
37. I do not know anyone with that name.
38. Jane lived in the bathroom and in many of the closets.
39. I used to talk to her.
40. I pretended that she answered me.

41. We would play house together.
42. My mother used to give me cookies and milk.
43. I, of course, ate my cookies.
44. So did Jane.
45. I ate her cookies.
46. I pretended she ate her cookies.
47. This went on for about a whole year.
48. I would play with Jane.
49. I went to bed in the evening.

50. My parents began to get worried.
51. They asked my doctor about Jane.
52. They asked my doctor about this imaginary friend.
53. The doctor said it was normal.

54. A lonely child creates an imaginary friend.
55. He made a recommendation.
56. I should play with a real friend.
57. I should play with Diane.

58. My mother would make me play with Diane.
59. I would call for Diane.
60. Diane and I would play together.
61. We would play for a little while.
62. I forgot about Jane little by little.
63. I played with Diane all the time.

64. This was not an unusual phase to go through.
65. This went on for a whole year.
66. I rarely thought about Jane again.
67. That is, until now, for this essay.

Sentence Combining in Essays Using Narrative Patterns

You probably have used narrative in arranging your essay for each of the tasks in Chapters 2–5. Whether writing about your journal, an incident, a place, or a prejudgment, you used either a narrative arrangement for the entire essay or organized individual paragraphs according to a chronological pattern. Narrative, more than any other form of arrangement, seems to lend itself to short, choppy sentences and to a need for sentence combining.

The problem of short sentences in narrative writing occurs when the writer strings incidents together as beads on a string: this happened and then that happened and then that and then that. A good example is "Imaginary Jane" in Exercise 10 above, where the pattern is perfunctory and repetitious. What is needed are subordinate clauses and free modifiers that describe and explain the action, lengthening the sentences and creating an even rhythm at the same time.

SOME PRACTICE WITH SENTENCE COMBINING IN WRITING AN ESSAY ON A PREJUDGMENT

1. Notice that the writers of the professional and student essays in this chapter use a narrative framework in exploring their prejudices. Examine the formulation of their sentences for the effect of narration on the rhythm of their essays. Do you notice any choppy, repetitive sentences that need combining? How might they be combined? Where the sentence rhythm is more sustained, analyze how the writer accomplished this rhythm through sentence combining.

2. What sentence combining techniques did you or your group use in revising "Imaginary Jane"?

3. Reread the essays you wrote for Chapters 2, 3, and 4. Have you used a narrative framework for one or more of these essays? Read the essay aloud. Does the rhythm sound staccato? If so, how might you combine sentences for variety and a more even rhythm? How does any additional combining of sentences affect the meaning of the narrative?

4. Reread your rough draft on a prejudgment for the sound your sentences make. Combine those sentences that sound abrupt or repetitive. Review the different patterns of sentence combining presented above for variety in combining.

REWRITING

Obtaining Feedback on Your Rough Draft

In order to give you the proper response to your rough draft, your evaluators will want to role-play the reader to whom your essay is directed. Your "Audience Analysis Guide" should give them sufficient information about your audience to successfully look at your essay from your readers' point of view. If you yourself are evaluating your rough draft, then you too will want to role-play your audience as you do so.

The "Audience Response Guide" can then be filled in.

———————— AUDIENCE RESPONSE GUIDE ————————

1. What do you think the writer wanted to say about a prejudgment in this paper? What is his or her purpose in writing? What does he or she want the paper to mean?

2. How does the paper affect the reader of the publication for which it was intended?

3. How effective has the writer been in conveying his or her purpose and meaning? What are the strengths of the paper? What are the weaknesses?

4. How should the paper be revised to better fulfill its purpose and meaning?

Revision of Student Essay "A Classical Question"

Below are peer responses to the rough draft of "A Classical Question" (pp. 210–211), using the questions of the Audience Response Guide. How does their evaluation compare with yours?

Question 1. The writer had made a prejudgment about classical music, and her purpose in writing the paper was to see if her prejudgment was right. She was open-minded about the process of observation, concluding that classical music could be enjoyable, although not all of the time.

Question 2. The paper was intended for a group of young working students; this essay could definitely be found in the student newspaper. It was humorous and detailed, which provided a real glimpse into the idiosyncrasies of the work world.

Question 3. The writer was very effective in conveying her purpose and meaning in the paper. The use of humor while providing specifics gives the reader a clear idea of the writer's ideas and the process by which she arrives at her conclusion.

Question 4. Neither reader believed any revising was necessary. They felt, however, that some editing was required: the upgrading of her vocabulary, the tightening of her sentences, the combining of some paragraphs.

As you read the writer's revision of "A Classical Question" below, decide how she has responded to her readers' comments. What comments of her "inner self" also appear to have influenced her revision? Did she make any revisions that you would have recommended? What other revisions might she have made?

A CLASSICAL QUESTION

It was the part of the day that I always dreaded. I could put up with almost anything else the work day handed out: I could clean dozens of bloody filets, debone a school of smelly fish, and peel potatoes for nine hours straight, but the one thing I could not abide was Jim's turn to choose the radio station.

In the kitchen where I work there are fifteen people, so, to be fair, everyone gets a chance to pick the radio station. Most of us like a wide variety of music so it's not often a problem--except with Jim. At the end of the day, when the rest of us are desperately downing coffee in an effort to remain standing while we finish our work, Jim always insists on putting on a classical music station. He says it relaxes him. I say it puts me to sleep.

I had always had a sort of mental block against classical music anyway. As soon as I heard it my body tensed and my mind closed. It was boring, it put me to sleep, it was for "old" people, as my mother listened to it. I had plenty of excuses for not listening to it.

My excuses did me no good, however, when Jim, who is also a musician, invited all of us to a recital that he was performing in. Of course we went to show our support even though it meant three hours of classical music. I went prepared. I popped a couple of No-Doz and practiced stifling yawns and looking interested. The funny thing was that I actually found myself enjoying the music. Hearing it live and watching someone I knew performing it added a great deal for me. Somehow it didn't sound so much like it belonged in an elevator. Still, I considered it an isolated incident and didn't think much more about it.

A few days later at work, we staged an impromptu social dancing lesson for a soon-to-be-married colleague who was worried about dancing at his wedding. Before I knew it we were all waltzing around the kitchen to classical music and having a great time. It was fun! So, I thought, maybe there is a place for this kind of music.

I decided to really give it a chance. I went home and put on one of my mother's tapes while I cooked dinner. I liked it. I was swaying and humming along. I mean it wasn't Madonna, but it was still kind of nice.

I decided I was cured. The next time Jim put on that station I would not only grin and bear it, but I would also enjoy it. I might even put it on when it was my turn! I was sure that was how it would happen. I was wrong. Jim put on that station, it was late, we had just worked nine hours and we still had two more to go. I found it irritating, boring, slow, and basically useless.

Well, Rome was not built in a day. At least I have developed a certain appreciation for and even an enjoyment of classical music in the right place and at the right time. At work, however, I'll have to stick with Madonna.

Distributing

Distributing is a form of revision in which material on the subject is added to more than one segment of the original draft, usually as a means of achieving unity. A key word or concept may bear repeating, as, for example, when the writer of the student essay in this chapter, "A Classical Question," mentions Madonna at two different points in her essay. See also Chapter 3 on Transitions (pp. 120–122).

By examining the early paragraphs of a piece that you are writing, you may discover structures that should be distributed throughout; for example, a metaphor worked out early in the essay might well be extended throughout in order to create a coherent and unified pattern. If at one point in your essay, you compare your car to an old friend because it is so reliable, you might consider extending the comparison to your entire description of your car.

In general, you will probably not want to start an approach to your subject and then drop it. Rather, distribute that approach throughout your work, just as Patrick Fenton does in referring to his childhood environment in Brooklyn at the beginning of his essay, in the middle, and again at the end.

Revising Your Essay on a Prejudgment

Before revising your essay, your "other self" may find it helpful to ask the following questions.

A Checklist of Questions to Consider in Revising an Essay About a Prejudgment

1. Do I state my prejudgment clearly as my shaping idea? Is my final conclusion about the subject stated with clarity?

2. How thoroughly have I cased my subject? Have I clearly indicated to my reader the instances during which I made my observations? Has my evidence been convincingly distributed throughout my essay? Have I justified my conclusion with sufficient evidence from these observations?

3. How thoroughly have I analyzed the readers common to the publication for which I am writing? What aspects of their frame of reference have shaped their point of view on my prejudgment? How have I recognized their point of view and met their depth of information needs?

4. Have I chosen a clear pattern of organization in answering each classical question that I ask? What pattern have I used in organizing the whole essay? How clear is this pattern? Is evidence of this pattern distributed throughout the essay?

5. Are my sentences combined to reflect the length and varied structures of the mature writer? Are there sentences I can combine or recombine for better effect?

Now you should be ready to revise your essay.

Editing

Once you have gone through the steps of revising your essay — cutting (Chapter 2); adding (Chapter 3); substituting (Chapter 4); rearranging (Chapter 6); or distributing (above) — you should turn to editing to determine correct word choice and grammatical precision.

Distributing. Distributing can be an editing exercise also. For example, if you decide to alter your word choice, you may decide to distribute that alteration throughout the essay wherever you have used that word. Or you may need to distribute a change in verb tense or pronoun reference. Distribution, whether in revising or in editing, asks that you look at the larger picture, at the total essay, rather than tinkering with isolated parts only.

Sentence Combining and Transitions. A very important part of editing, as we have stressed in each chapter so far, is the use of transitions. To combine sentences is another way to establish connections between thoughts. Sentence combining also keeps your essay from having the "choppy" rhythm of strung-together simple sentences and achieves instead the flowing rhythm of the mature combined sentence. Reviewing your writing from the point of view of sentence combining is one of the most important of the editing techniques.

Paragraphs. Continue to regard your paragraphs closely. Are they structured tightly around some clearly defined unit of thought? Have you developed them with sufficient coordinate accumulation of detail or subordinate provision of example and explanation? How well do your first and last paragraphs fulfill their purposes to introduce and conclude your essay? Review as often as you need to the paragraph sections in Chapters 3 and 4.

Mechanics. What mechanical errors of grammar or spelling have persisted in your writing? Perhaps it is time now to make a list of those errors that have constantly defied your attempts to correct them. Now turn this list into a chart by indicating next to each error a definition of the problem and then a method of solution. Finally, in a fourth column, analyze why the method of solution has escaped you. As you go about editing the rough draft for this task, develop this analysis further in the hope of finding a way of implementing the solution.

Now, revise and edit your rough draft.

BECOMING AWARE OF YOURSELF AS A WRITER

You might want to make use of your journal to record your thoughts and feelings about the tasks for this chapter. As you write in your journal, consider the following questions.

1. In what future situations can you foresee writing cases? What appear to be the important features of case writing?

2. Do you feel satisfied that you know how to analyze the frame of reference and the point of view of the readers common to a particular publication? When in the future can you imagine yourself writing to the reader of another publication? How did you analyze your reader's frame of reference when you wrote the essay for this chapter?

3. How useful is the sentence-combining approach to your own writing? Are your clauses and ideas combined already, or do you feel that you need to pay attention to this aspect of your writing?

4. Did you enjoy learning about your subject as you tested a prejudice while writing? How important do you think writing is or should be as a way of learning, as well as of expressing what you already know?

5. How often in the past have you used the classical questions without being aware of having used them? Have you observed others using them (your teachers, for example)? The explorer's questions have been devised in this century out of a need to supplement the classical ones. What roles can you foresee both sets of questions playing in your thinking and writing in the future?

PART

III

Explanation

INTRODUCTION

In Part II, writing as an interested observer, you invited your readers to explore a subject along with you, to experience your own curiosity and the broader perspective that it led to. Now we are going to ask you to write essays in which you explain to your readers subjects that you have already explored at some length and in some depth.

The difference between exploration and explanation is often subtle. It may be a difference, in part, of tone and emphasis. In the former case, you are likely to adopt the attitude of a peer as you share your discoveries with your audience. In the latter case, you may take on a more knowledgeable, authoritative tone, drawing conclusions based on your broadened perspective and offering information that has a general application and validity.

The conventions of explanatory writing also differ from those of both expressive and exploratory writing. For example, while expressive writing emphasizes the writer and exploratory writing emphasizes the subject—even while the writer remains in the foreground as the one exploring—in explanatory writing, the subject is the clear focus, and in order to appear objective, the writer moves further to the background. Also, the organization of expressive and exploratory writing is often narrative; in explanatory writing, narrative is usually reduced to short, yet vital examples.

One subject that we all have explored sufficiently well to render us experts is a tradition that we observe within our family or within our culture. Another subject with which we are familiar is the media. The tasks for Chapters 6 and 7 will be to select from your own experience general and specific narratives about a family or cultural tradition and about the media and explain their significance to your readers.

Your own ideas about a subject may gain more validity, of course, the more you take into account the ideas of others who are knowledgeable about the subject. To explain a subject well, it is often helpful to inform your audience not only of your own explorations but also of the explorations and discoveries, the observations and conclusions of others. For the tasks in this section, you will want to brainstorm with your class their opinions on your tradition, interview family members or others in your cultural group, and read what others have said about the media. Further, you will want to distinguish between what the segment of the public for whom you are writing about knows and needs to know about your media experience.

Explanation is a common aim in writing, both for college and on the job. In the writing that they assign, your professors will usually require you to explain what you have learned. Whether they ask you to compare and contrast, describe, discuss, assign causes, or give examples, they are asking you to explain what they assume you already know, both from attending course lectures and from doing assigned reading. Likewise, many professions require their workers to write manuals explaining how something is done or how it works; to write reports that explain a situation, a new procedure, the lines of communication within the company; or to write news articles for company newsletters or for newspapers. Learning how best to explain a subject is a vital asset both in school and in the workplace.

6

Writing About a Tradition—Explaining What You Know

In fulfilling the aim of explanation in this chapter, you will utilize all that you have learned about expressive and exploratory writing, about understanding yourself and about exploring your world, in order to explain a subject which you have already both experienced and explored to a reader or group of readers who are unfamiliar with what you are writing about.

In the task for this chapter, you will be asked to utilize personal experience for an explanatory purpose. In writing about a family or cultural tradition, you will explain your knowledge of its structure and significance to a group of readers who have little knowledge or appreciation of it. You will express both what the tradition is and how observing the tradition has affected you, your family, and culture.

You will no doubt be called upon often to explain a family or cultural tradition to someone unfamiliar with it. The United States is becoming increasingly multicultural, and as we attempt to understand our cultural diversity, we seek explanations from others of their values and customs and seek in turn to explain our own traditions. These uncomprehending others may be as near as our friends or as distanced from us as officials from whom we might seek permission to use public facilities for a cultural festival.

The writing strategies in this chapter include brainstorming as a means of generating ideas. Both individuals and corporations have found the various brainstorming techniques useful in obtaining ideas and solving problems. Because all members of your English class have observed family and cultural traditions, brainstorming as a group will provide ideas and perspectives from which to write for each of you.

While most of your writing in school has been for informed readers—your teachers and professors—much writing on the job is done for the uninformed reader. Understanding how to write for the unknowledgeable reader, the audience for this chapter's task, will prove a useful tool for your writing kit.

In moving from the essay as narrative to the essay with narratives, we will continue to focus on the value of telling a good story. Explanatory writing that tells stories as examples of what is being said is vivid writing, and vividness engages the reader in the writer's message. The quality of your stories will be a measure of the success of your explanation.

TASK: WRITING ABOUT A TRADITION

The task for this chapter will be to write an essay explaining the structure and significance of a tradition, of information, beliefs, and customs that have been handed down to you by your family or your cultural or religious group. In addition to explaining the primary features of this tradition, you will want to include some narratives or stories that illustrate these attributes. The audience for your essay will be one from outside the family or from a different cultural or religious group; you may choose a group within a culture or an entire culture as long as its members are unfamiliar with your subject.

Selecting a tradition about which to write may be an easy process—or an extremely difficult one. If you or your family comes from another country, for example, you may easily recognize traditions about which to write: religious or national observances such as Divali, an important Hindu holy day; Bakari-idd, a Muslim holy day; Cofradia, a West Indian celebration to honor the saints; Jamaican or Dominican independence days; or traditional values such as that placed on the closeness of the extended family by Italian Americans, and the reverence for age by those from Asian cultures.

Even if your family has been in America for several generations, you may still celebrate traditions that many if not most Americans would be unfamiliar with such as Sukkot and Passover, two Jewish holy days; an Italian Sunday family dinner; and the reunions that many African American families hold in the South each summer.

If you are not in any of these groups, if you think of yourself as simply "an American," you may find it difficult to isolate a tradition that your family or all Americans share, other than some obvious ones like celebrating the Fourth of July or Columbus Day or learning about the ideals of the Constitution. Americans, in fact, have long prided themselves on having fled the heavy weight of old-world tradition. But every culture has customary ways of thinking and acting that separate it from other cultures, and every family has traditions that separate it from other families. The noted anthropologist, Margaret Mead, wrote that "Every (American) home is different from every other home, every marriage, even within the same class, in the same clique, contains contrasts between the partners as superficially striking as the difference between one New Guinea tribe and another." She then goes on to say that American families "will be alike in their very difference" and this alikeness arises from cultural traditions — information, beliefs, and customs — that Americans share in common.

If you are not convinced that America is a unique culture with unique traditions and that your family has its own traditions even within the common culture, then you might consider how your family or culture observes traditions that anthropologists believe differ from culture to culture and from family to family: growing up, expectations of the opposite sex, the use of language, religious observances, getting to know people, courtship, marriage, raising children, growing old, dying.

Brainstorming, the method for generating ideas in this chapter, may be helpful both in selecting a tradition about which to write and in generating ideas for your paper. Brainstorming is a group activity in which every member contributes ideas on a chosen subject rapidly, without pause and without constraint. Brainstorming is equivalent to an oral, collective form of free writing. Particularly if your class includes students from many countries or students whose families immigrated to America, learning their more objective viewpoints on your own culture through a brainstorming exercise should assist you in selecting a topic and learning how to present it.

You may want to use also methods of generating ideas that you experimented with in earlier tasks such as the explorer's questions, which will assist you in describing the features of your tradition, and the classical questions, which will help you probe the significance of this tradition to you and others in your family or culture. You may also want to generate ideas through interview and observation. And too, your journal may be a source of ideas for this essay.

The "Audience" section will discuss how to write for an uninformed reader, and the "Writing the Essay" section will help you both to explain the features of your tradition and to include stories that will serve to illustrate for the reader the significance of that tradition.

WRITING YOUR ESSAY

Generating Ideas: Brainstorming

Brainstorming is the simplest method of generating ideas, the most versatile, and probably the most commonly used — it is popular with students, committees, and corporations. We include it here because it is a group process (although it can be used individually as well), and you may find that preparing the task for this chapter will be easier if you obtain feedback from a group.

Essentially, brainstorming is just what the word suggests: a rapid production of ideas on a subject through free association. Listing and clustering are two different types of brainstorming.

Listing. Some rules for group brainstorming to produce a list of ideas should be helpful:

1. Work on one person's topic at a time, until the group or class has brainstormed for each topic.
2. Select a recorder who will write the ideas on the blackboard or perhaps on paper.
3. The recorder writes as many ideas, both sensible and silly, as the group can produce.
4. Each person says whatever comes into her head, as in free writing.
5. No idea is censored or rejected. This rule will encourage the flow of ideas to continue; also, a silly idea one minute may seem a sensible one the next.
6. Ideas already mentioned can be improved or added to.
7. Allow five minutes only for each topic.
8. The writer copies the list and considers which ideas are valuable, which need some rethinking, and which are unusable.

Here is an example of a list of ideas generated by brainstorming:

Topic: Relationships Between Men and Women

at work	family	care of children
courtship	nuclear family	division of work
rituals	extended family	division of responsibility
marriage	subservient wife	rape
mourning	multiple wives	macho
romantic love	divorce	affairs
violence	economics	generational differences
patriarchal	class	stereotypes

matriarchal	caste	morality
arranged marriages	sexual	legality
equality	friendship	feminist
roles	beauty	chauvinist
breaking down of roles	housework	living together

When a group is not available or when the subject is not appropriate for groupwork, you can of course brainstorm a list by yourself.

SOME PRACTICE WITH LISTING

1. With your class or group, brainstorm about traditions that your families observe, even if they seem as boring to you as Charlie Brown's does to him.

Reprinted by permission of UFS, Inc.

2. Families are tied together because they share the same memories. Traditions would not exist, in fact, if families did not share memories of how they do things on specific occasions or in certain contexts. Brainstorm by yourself or with family members, including as many generations as possible, the memories you have of customary ways you do various things in your family.

3. Leaf through a family photo album. Then, brainstorm a list of all the poses, attitudes, activities, and locations that you associate with family traditions.

4. Ella Taylor, who teaches courses in cultural theory and popular culture at the University of Washington, says, "The shared experience of tele-history has

become one of the major ways in which we locate ourselves in time, place, and generation, and at the heart of that history lies television's obsession — the family." Brainstorm about her comment that family shows on television tell us who we are and (by extension) what our traditions are.

5. "Ancient people perceived the world and themselves within that world as part of an ancient continuous story composed of innumerable bundles of other stories" — Leslie Marmon Silko. Brainstorm about America's "ancient" story and the "innumerable bundles of other stories" that reveal our traditions to us. The class might want to include personal stories as well, such as what they were doing during the bicentennial celebrations or the Persian Gulf War.

Clustering.   A variation on brainstorming is clustering, which has the added advantage of visually representing the relationship among the brainstormed ideas. In group clustering, the topic is written in the middle of the board, and as brainstorming occurs, the ideas are clustered in related groups around it. You can also cluster by yourself.

Opposite is a cluster on the same topic as the brainstorming list on pp. 234–235. Notice the three levels of ideas: topic, major ideas, and supporting ideas.

Clustering, while seemingly simple, is based on right brain/left brain research, which indicates that visual brainstorming unlocks the intuitive and creative capacities of the right brain, while outlining and even listing are more structured and appeal to the more orderly functions of the left brain. If listing or outlining inhibits your thinking, then you may be a "right brain" person, and clustering may be more useful for you.

SOME PRACTICE WITH CLUSTERING

1. Arrange one of your brainstorming lists from the exercise above as a cluster.

2. Choosing a holiday observed in the United States, cluster the traditions that have evolved in celebrating it. Cluster details around each tradition.

3. Interview a member of the older generation about a tradition observed in your family. Using this tradition as a core word, cluster around it their perceptions and recollections as well as your own.

Brainstorming and the Explorer's and Classical Questions.   You may find it helpful to direct your brainstorming by asking the explorer's and the classical questions about your subject and then brainstorming the answers. The explorer's questions will be helpful in analyzing the subject itself: its unique features, its relationship to other similar subjects, its evolution. The classical questions will assist you in analyzing the significance of your tradition — its causes and its effects, for example.

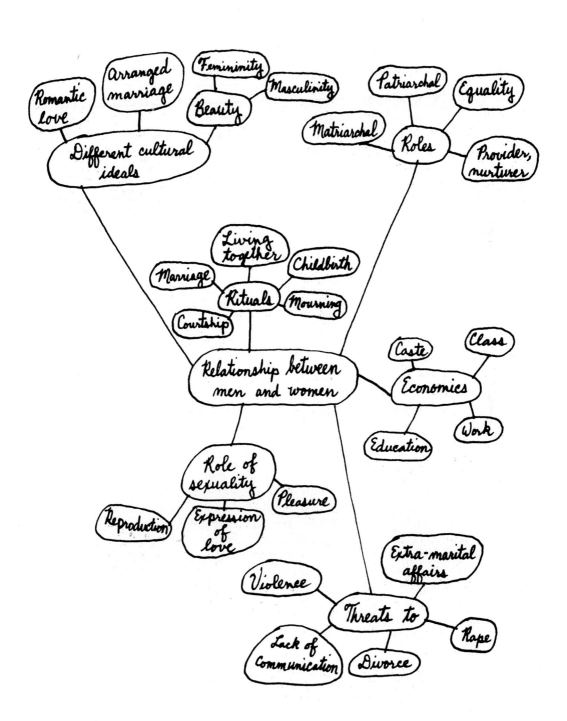

SOME PRACTICE WITH USING THE EXPLORER'S AND CLASSICAL QUESTIONS IN BRAINSTORMING

1. Cluster a tradition that you or your family has broken. Brainstorm a series of classical questions about this tradition as your second set of circles, and then a series of answers for each question. You may want to develop a further set of details for each answer for a four-level cluster.

2. Select one of the following areas of family life about which your family has formed a tradition and brainstorm a list of the classical questions that apply to it. Then brainstorm a list of answers to each of the questions:

   food or eating

   relations between several generations

   observance (or nonobservance) of privacy in the home

   division of housework

3. Generate ideas about one of the American educational traditions listed below through directed brainstorming—clustering or listing—using one or all of the explorer's questions.

   pledging allegiance to the flag

   multiple-choice exams

   graduation ceremonies from nursery school through college

   the emphasis on sports

Using Brainstorming to Generate Ideas for Your Essay on a Tradition. Once you have chosen the tradition about which you will write the essay for this chapter's task, you can brainstorm about as many aspects of the tradition as seem fruitful to you. If you are writing about a tradition of Sunday family dinners, for example, you may want to brainstorm lists about each of the following: each generation's role in the preparation of the dinner, about Sunday dinners that were special or unusual for some reason, about your feelings about these dinners. Or each of these ideas may form the second level of ideas in clustering.

Those classical questions that students have found helpful in completing the essay on a tradition are both the four discussed in Chapter 5: "How is it like or unlike other objects, events, or ideas?", "What caused it?", "What will it cause?", "What process does it go through?", as well as the first two listed on p. 186: "What is it?" and "What class does it belong to, or what classes can it be divided into?" The classical question "What is it?" may in fact shape your entire essay, with the other questions asked as both specific and far-ranging approaches to defining your tradition and analyzing its significance (see the "Arranging Your Essay" section below for more information on answering the questions "What is it?" and "What classes can it be divided into?").

You can brainstorm lists in answer to each question, or you can use the questions as the second level of ideas in a cluster. A student uses the classical questions to brainstorm a cluster on the topic, Bakari-idd, a Muslim holiday:

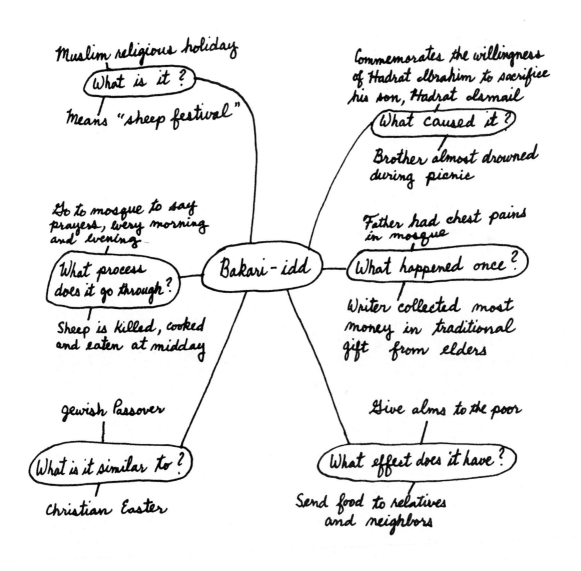

SOME PRACTICE WITH BRAINSTORMING TO GENERATE
IDEAS FOR YOUR ESSAY ON A TRADITION

1. You may want to use your journal as a source of ideas about which you can then brainstorm, either with your peer group or on your own. A narrative entry remembering a childhood holiday, or a family tradition, or a neighborhood ritual may prove a good starting point for a list or a cluster.

2. List everything that occurs to you about the tradition you have selected as the subject of the essay for this chapter. Remember not to censor any ideas for any reason. Encourage the ideas to come with machine-gun rapidity.

   If you know or suspect that family members have important information that you will need for your essay, encourage them to brainstorm with you, either in person or via the telephone.

3. Arrange the items on the list in the form of a cluster, relegating some ideas to subheadings and others to lesser headings. Once you have clustered your list, other ideas may occur to you that you will want to add.

4. Try another cluster, this time using the classical questions as your secondary or subheadings. Use the ideas from your list for Exercise 1; add others that the questions themselves suggest. Again, interview family members to fill in gaps in the cluster. Or, if the tradition is an ongoing one, try observing your family in the enaction of this tradition for further ideas or details about which to write.

5. You might use your journal as a place to analyze and generalize about the material you produce by brainstorming. Consider the list or cluster you generated, for example, as if it were the left-hand side of a double-entry page. Write a series of right-hand entries tracing a pattern in the list, or elaborating on the connections between ideas in a cluster in order to explain the significance of the tradition that you plan to write about.

Addressing Your Audience: Considering the Values
and Attitudes of the Uninformed Reader

In the "Addressing Your Audience" section in Chapter 3, we discussed how to determine your reader's frame of reference in order to know his values in general and his attitudes toward your subject in particular. In the "Audience" section in Chapter 4, we discussed how to use the reader's frame of reference in assessing the depth of information he requires. Here, we will discuss how frame of reference can be used to gauge the knowledge, values, and attitudes of the uninformed reader.

Analyzing the Frame of Reference of the Uninformed Reader. For example, we can surmise a good deal about the frame of reference that the writer of the following information about buying and assembling an unfinished armoire has constructed for her reader:

The best part about buying our home was selecting new furniture. Since we had to watch our budget, I decided I could save if I tried a Yield House kit.

I was a bit apprehensive about how complicated it might be, so I called their customer service line.

The woman I spoke with was very helpful. She assured me that all I needed was a phillips screwdriver, a hammer and my finishing supplies. Everything else was included with the kit.

When I received my armoire kit, I discovered the illustrated instructions were easy to follow, and everything I needed to assemble my kit was included, even tips on sanding, staining and applying topcoat.

My armoire went together quickly, and I chose the new Yield House Canterbury Blue stain with a white glaze for my finish. My armoire has received so many compliments that I'm planning to start a new kit soon: a Bradford Desk for the den.

I'll save up to a third off the price of the finished furnishing, and I can stain or paint it exactly the way I want.

I'm especially happy with my armoire because I built it myself, and it's an heirloom my daughter will be proud to own.

As she writes in the role of a woman who has found the procedure simpler than she expected, the writer has obviously determined that her audience is the uninformed woman. The frame of reference of this woman, the writer has decided, includes a lack of experience in assembling furniture, a concern about cost, a concern that her home be attractive, a desire to express herself, and a pleasure in having her daughter proud of her.

Based on this frame of reference, the writer provides background information on both the tools that will be required and some of the procedures that will need to be followed. Also, she writes in a reassuring tone about the procedure and its costs and in a glowing tone about its attractiveness, her freedom to choose her own colors, and her and her daughter's pride in her accomplishment.

Addressing the Uninformed Reader's Values and Attitudes. The writer of the passage above has clearly determined who the reader is, what her frame of reference is, including how much information she needs, and what her values and her attitudes toward the subject are. This information is key to selling the product to an uninformed woman.

As another example of how to use frame of reference to determine values and attitudes, after reading below the introductory paragraphs to a travel article, we can determine who the writer's intended reader is, what frame of reference the writer constructed for this reader, what depth of information she decided was required, and what tone she thought best to use.

> At 7 a.m. in the restaurant at the New Woodlands in Madras, more than 10 people are already waiting in line for breakfast. The scent of coconut drifts through the air as barefoot waiters race past bearing trays loaded with steaming white patties and large, fragrant pancakes. Madrasis and visitors pore over their morning papers, washing down patties and pancakes with small cups of sweet, milky coffee. As sure as the sun rises over the Bay of Bengal, another day begins with *idlis* and *dosas*, the all-purpose snack foods of south India.
>
> Although they have no real Western equivalent, *idlis* and *dosas* are similar to many of our foods. *Idlis*, which resemble spongy dumplings, are always served in pairs. *Dosas* are crepelike pancakes served neatly rolled. Both are widely available throughout south India—and difficult to find anywhere else.

These first two paragraphs of "The Vegetarian Snacks of South India" (Travel section, *New York Times*, July 15, 1990) reveal that the reader is intended to be an American whose frame of reference includes never having had the inclination to visit India but valuing travel and good food and having the income to make so extensive a journey. Based on this frame of reference, the writer supplies an initial description of *idlis* and *dosas* and, in the second paragraph, a further description. In order to assist the reader in finding the thought of travel to India attractive, the writer's tone is alluring and suspenseful in the first paragraph, building up to the climax of the last sentence. In the second paragraph, the writer's tone reassures the reader that these new foods are not really so different from some that he is familiar with.

While supplying adequate information is clearly an aim in writing for the uninformed reader, addressing the reader's values and bridging any gaps between the reader's and writer's attitudes about the subject are equally important. The uninformed reader has no experience with the subject, has possibly not sought that experience, and consequently may be skeptical about its value or fearful of involvement. Appealing to the reader's values and reassuring her that knowing about the subject will benefit her are key aims for the writer addressing the uninformed reader, whether the writer's aim is persuasion, explanation, or a combination of both.

SOME PRACTICE WITH WRITING FOR AN UNINFORMED READER

1. Write the directions for completing a procedure that your reader will find unfamiliar. Appeal to the reader's values and select a reassuring tone in explaining why and how he should proceed.

2. Write a short news article on a subject that your reader will find unfamiliar.

While remaining true to the journalist's need to be objective in presenting the news, present your details in such a way that the reader will both understand your subject and relate positively to it.

Addressing a Reader's Values and Attitudes in Writing an Essay on a Tradition. Bear in mind that the reader's values and attitudes are particularly important when explaining the traditions and customs of those outside our own family and cultural groups. Values differ from culture to culture, and often from family to family. Even when we share values, and we often do, deep-seated attitudes toward the new and the strange may preclude us from appreciating the traditions of others. Building bridges by referring both to the reader's values and to what she finds familiar and adopting a reassuring tone will go a long way toward cross-family and cross-cultural understanding. Asking yourself the following questions of the "Audience Analysis Guide" for this chapter may help you decide how wide the gap in understanding may be.

─── AUDIENCE ANALYSIS GUIDE ───

1. Who are my readers?
2. What is their frame of reference? Do they value tradition in general? What traditions do they observe?
3. What attitude will they have toward my tradition?
4. What bridges can I build to eliminate any gaps through the way I present my content and through the tone I adopt?

SOME PRACTICE IN WRITING ON A TRADITION FOR AN UNINFORMED READER

1. Read the following introductions students have written to essays about their family and cultural traditions. How successful have the writers been in addressing the uninformed reader? Answer in terms of the depth of information supplied, the values addressed, and the tone used.

   a. Living in Silver Beach, you would be crazy to miss the festivities held during the Labor Day weekend. Even though everyone hates when the summer is ending, especially me, everyone loves Labor Day weekend. This weekend is one of my family's favorite traditions and no one ever misses it! One year I remember my sister even flew all the way in from a business trip to the Middle East. We are always together on Labor Day!

b. Every Sunday, I wake up to the smell of fresh tomato sauce simmering in a pot on the stove. The reason for this is that each Sunday my family sits at the table together and eats the traditional Italian Sunday lunch, consisting of pasta, ravioli, meat balls, and lamb soaked in tomato sauce. To most non-Italian people, eating such a meal for lunch is kind of bizarre. I remember one time in particular when I invited a German friend of mine over to the house for Sunday lunch, he couldn't believe how much food there was at the table. He was also shocked that my whole family was there. I was very surprised at his reaction because I thought everyone carried out this tradition. I guess that's because most of my friends are Italian and carry out the same traditions that we do.

c. Black fraternity parties are beach parties, picnics, and step shows thrown by black fraternities and sororities. The classes that these parties can be divided into are spring break parties, summer vacation beach parties, and college fraternity get-togethers. These parties, like the big get-togethers in Daytona every spring, find college students assembling together from all over the country to have fun. The only difference is that these parties are attended by a majority of black students; even though you will see a couple of kids from other ethnic backgrounds, mostly students of African descent attend.

d. The trees are green again, flowers are growing, and there is a distinct scent in the air. It is spring time, and Pesach is approaching. "Pesach" is the Hebrew word for Passover. In Hebrew, the word means "to jump." We call the celebration this because when the plagues were delivered by G-d upon the Egyptians, the

Jews were spared. During the tenth plague, when every Egyptian first-born died, the Jews' homes were "jumped over" or passed over by the Angel of Death. Passover also commemorates the liberation of the Jewish people from Egypt.

e. The men in the village get together on this particular day to show their artistic skills. They take the stems from the bamboo grass and split them down the center, leaving about one foot unsplit. The unsplit end is then buried in the ground, and the loose ends are formed into beautiful arches on which are placed the deyas or tiny clay pots, which will later be filled with oil and lit. "Divali" or the festival of lights is a ritual celebrated once a year by Hindus globally.

2. Based on your answers to the "Audience Analysis Guide," draft an introduction to your essay that incorporates the suggestions you have made for building bridges between you and your reader. Work on the tone that you will want to use throughout the essay as well as suggest the approach you will take to your material and the depth of information you will include. Then, read the section on the "The Shaping Idea" below, and revise your introduction.

Arranging Your Essay

The Shaping Idea.   Once you have decided what family or cultural or religious tradition you will write about, you will want to determine what you want your reader to understand about its features and about its significance for you and others who observe it. You also will want to decide what tone you will adopt. Your shaping idea will reflect both of these decisions.

In the students' shaping ideas below, notice that, regardless of their culture, the writers have happy memories of their family traditions, an attitude that bridges all cultural differences:

Passover is a tradition filled with memories, wonder-filled memories of my grandfather and of my childhood.

I not only look forward to being with my family on Sunday, but I also have many good memories because of this great Italian tradition.

When I lived in the West Indies, a tradition that my family and I regularly enjoyed was called "Cofradia"--a celebration to honor the saints.

Here are some shaping ideas from professional writers who are also writing on a tradition. Can you discern from these passages what the writer is going to say about the tradition and what his or her attitude is toward it?

> But Las Vegas seems to exist only in the eye of the beholder. All of which makes it an extraordinarily stimulating and interesting place, but an odd one in which to want to wear a candlelight satin Priscilla of Boston wedding dress with Chantilly lace inserts, tapered sleeves, and a detachable modified train.
>
> —Joan Didion, "Marrying Absurd"

> A few weeks ago this feeling got so strong (of a desire for the placidity of a lake) that I bought myself a couple of bass hooks and a spinner and returned to the lake where we used to go, for a week's fishing and to revisit old haunts.
>
> —E. B. White, "Once More to the Lake"

> The other Chinese girls did not talk either, so I knew the silence had to do with being a Chinese girl.
>
> —Maxine Hong Kingston, *The Woman Warrior*

> How could it be that I was I and now was now when in four months it would be Christmas, wintertime, cold weather, twilight and the glory of the Christmas tree?
>
> —Carson McCullers, "Home for Christmas"

Explanation.   As we indicated in the Introduction to Part III, the differences between exploration and explanation are partly matters of tone and emphasis and partly the use that the writer gives to narrative and the distance the writer keeps from the subject. In explaining your tradition, you will want to sound knowledgeable and emphasize that you have given the reader fairly complete information about the subject. You will also want to convey objectivity about your tradition by avoiding overly personal reactions to your subject. While you may certainly include your own reactions to your tradition, you will want to do so as a representative of your group. The use of narrative in explanatory writing is discussed on pages 248–249.

In arranging your essay, the patterns that you used in Chapter 5 to answer the Classical Questions can be used here: comparison and contrast, process analysis, and cause and effect (pp. 198–201). Two additional arrangement patterns we wish to discuss are definition and classification, which help to organize the answers to the classical questions discussed on pp. 238–239: "What is it? and "What class is it in?" or "What classes are there of it?"

Definition.   A definition may be as brief as that found in the dictionary, or you may extend it through attributing characteristics, analyzing the parts, stating functions, giving examples, and comparing and contrasting with other subjects. In writing about a tradition, you may very well write an extended definition.

The arrangement pattern for definition may follow any ordering of these answers to various classical questions. In the definition of friendship below, the writer uses comparison and contrast and analogy ("What is it like/unlike?"), quotation ("What has been said about it?"), and causation ("What caused them to say it?").

> Friendship is by its very nature freer of deceit than any other relationship we can know because it is the bond least affected by striving for power, physical pleasure, or material profit, most liberated from any oath of duty or of constancy. With Eros the *body* stands naked, in friendship our *spirit* is denuded. Friendship, in this sense, is a human condition resembling what may be humanity's most beautiful and necessary lie—the promise of an afterlife. It is an almost celestial sphere in which we most resemble that society of angels offered us by Christian theology, in which we can sing the truth of our inner thoughts in relative freedom and abundance. No wonder then that the last contemporary writers whose essays on friendship may remain classics are those religiously inclined, scholars relatively unaffected by positivism or behaviorism, or by the general scientificization of human sentiment. That marvelous Christian maverick, C. S. Lewis, tells us: 'Friendship is unnecessary, like philosophy, like art, like the universe itself (since God did not *need* to create). It has no survival value; rather it is one of those things that give value to survival.' And the Jewish thinker Simone Weil focuses on the classic theme of free consent when she writes: 'Friendship is a miracle by which a person consents to view from a certain distance, and without coming any nearer, the very being who is necessary to him as food'.
>
> From Francine Du Plessix Gray, "On Friendship," from *Adam and Eve and the City*, 1987, *Vogue.*

In arranging the elements of classification, you may define the class, usually by analyzing its various components, or discuss how your subject fits into that class by comparing and contrasting your subject with other members of the class. Here are examples of classification:

(1) Fitting a subject into a class. Into what class is the writer attempting to fit superstitions?

In a religious context, where truths cannot be demonstrated, we accept them as a matter of faith. Superstitions, however, belong to the category of beliefs, practices and ways of thinking that have been discarded because they are inconsistent with scientific knowledge. It is easy to say that other people are superstitious because they believe what we regard to be untrue. "Superstition" used in that sense is a derogatory term for the beliefs of other people that we do not share. But there is more to it than that. For superstitions lead a kind of half life in a twilight world where, sometimes, we partly suspend our disbelief and act as if magic worked.

—Margaret Mead, "New Superstitions for Old"

(2) Defining a class by comparison and contrast.

I watched *Gone With the Wind* on television recently. It's my favorite movie. It's hokey, it's predictable, the color's lurid, I throw balled-up tissues at Olivia de Havilland when she's on screen. I love it. Each time I see it I notice something new.

This time, I noticed that in some ways it perfectly illustrates one of the great truths about men. Most men fall into one of two categories for the purpose of relationships: Husband or Boyfriend. These are not literal classifications based on marital status, just the best I can do. (I once classified them as the Good Guy and the Louse, which was an oversimplification made when I was depressed, menwise, and before I had admitted that I found the Lice much more interesting than their nobler brothers.)

Ashley Wilkes is a classic Husband: upright, dependable, prone neither to wild partying nor to gross flirtation. He will show up for dinner on time and be the kind of father a kid can depend on for lots of meaty talks about life and honor.

Rhett Butler is, of course, vintage Boyfriend: entertaining, unprincipled, with a roving eye and a wickedly expressive brow above it. I've watched Scarlett turn around and see him for the first time at the bottom of the staircase at Twelve Oaks plantation at least a hundred times. "He looks as if—as if he knows what I look like without my shimmy," she says, one of the few insightful things she says in the first half of the film, before she eats the radish and swears that she'll never be hungry again. And still my heart stops and I have trouble breathing. Give a damn? You bet I do.

—Anna Quindlen, "Husbands and Boyfriends"

Narrative Examples.   While much of expressive and exploratory writing is narrative—tells a story of an event or of a series of events in which the writer's emotions or perceptions are engaged—explanatory writing is analytical of a subject that usually is not embedded in one event. Good explanatory writing does not reject the story, however, but instead uses the narrative example to illustrate its analysis. For your task here, these stories may be of what happened once during the observance of the tradition or of what often happened.

In the professional essays below, notice how the writers' use of stories works to more clearly explain their tradition. Answering the questions after each essay will help you understand how to use the essays to exemplify the task for this chapter.

I Am a Catholic

by Anna Quindlen

Dominus vobiscum. Et cum spiritu tuo. These are my bona fides: a word, a phrase, a sentence in a language no one speaks anymore. *Kyrie eleison. Confiteor dei.* I am a Catholic. Once at a nursing home for retired clergy, I ate lunch with a ninety-year-old priest, a man who still muttered the Latin throughout the English Mass and ate fish on Fridays. When he learned how old I was, he said with some satisfaction, "You were a Catholic when being a Catholic still meant something."

What does it mean now? For myself, I cannot truly say. Since the issue became material to me, I have not followed the church's teaching on birth control. I disagree with its stand on abortion. I believe its resistance to the ordination of women as priests is a manifestation of a misogyny that has been with us much longer than the church has. Yet it would never have occurred to my husband and me not to be married in a Catholic church, not to have our children baptized. On hospital forms and in political polls, while others leave the space blank or say "none of your business," I have no hesitation about giving my religion.

We are cultural Catholics. I once sneered at that expression, used by Jewish friends at college, only because I was not introspective enough to understand how well it applied to me. Catholicism is to us now not so much a system of beliefs or a set of laws but a shared history. It is not so much our faith as our past. The tenets of the church which I learned as a child have ever since been at war with the facts of my adult life. The Virgin Birth. The Trinity. The Resurrection. Why did God make me? God made me to know Him, to love Him, and to serve Him in this world and to be happy with Him forever in the next. I could recite parts of the Baltimore Catechism in my sleep. Do I believe those words? I don't know. What I do believe are those guidelines that do not vary from faith to faith, that are as true of Judaism or Methodism as they are of Catholicism: that people should be kind to one another, that they should help those in need, that they should respect others as they wish to be respected.

And I believe in my own past. I was educated by nuns, given absolution by priests. My parents were married in a Catholic church, my grandparents and mother buried from one. Saturday afternoons kneeling on Leatherette pads in the dim light of the confessional, listening for the sound of the priest sliding back the grille on his side. Sunday mornings kneeling with my face in my hands, the Communion wafer stuck to the roof of my dry mouth. These are my history. I could no more say I am not Catholic than say I am not Irish, not Italian. Yet I have never been to Ireland or Italy.

Some of our Jewish friends have returned to the ways of their past, to Shabbat without automobiles and elevators, to dietary laws and the study of

Hebrew. We cannot do the same. There is no longer a Latin Mass, no Communion fast from midnight on. Even the inn is gone from the Bible; now Mary and Joseph are turned away from "the place where travelers lodged."

The first time my husband and I went to midnight mass on Christmas Eve in our parish church, we arrived a half-hour early so we would get a seat. When the bells sounded twelve and the priest came down the center aisle, his small acolytes in their child-size cassocks walking before him, the pews were still half empty. We were thinking of a different time, when the churches were packed, when missing Mass was a sin, when we still believed that that sort of sin existed—sins against rules, victimless sins.

There are more families coming to that church now, families like us with very small children who often have to leave before the Gospel because of tears, fatigue, temper tantrums. (I remember that, when I was growing up, my family's parish church was shaped like a cross, and one of the short arms was for the women with babies. It had a sheet of glass walling it off and was soundproof. And through the glass you could see the babies, as though in a movie with no audio, their little mouths round, their faces red. Inside that room, the noise was dreadful. But missing Mass was a sin.)

I think perhaps those families are people like us, people who believe in something, although they are not sure what, people who feel that in a world of precious little history or tradition, this is theirs. We will pass down the story to our children: There was a woman named Mary who was visited by an angel. And the angel said, "Do not be afraid" and told her that though she was a virgin she would have a child. And He was named Jesus and was the Son of God and He rose from the dead. Everything else our children learn in America in the late twentieth century will make this sound like a fairy tale, like tales of the potato famines in Ireland and the little ramshackle houses with grape arbors on hillsides in Italy. But these are my fairy tales, and so, whether or not they are fact, they are true.

I was born a Catholic and I think I will die one. I will ask for a priest to give me Extreme Unction, as it was given to my mother, and to her mother before her. At the end, as in the beginning, I will ask for the assistance of the church, which is some fundamental part of my identity. I am a Catholic.

1. What is Anna Quindlen's shaping idea? Where is it placed in the essay? Is her point of view on her tradition clear from this statement? Does she indicate its significance? What effect does her concluding paragraph have on the reader's perception of her shaping idea?

2. What features of Catholicism does Quindlen mention? Does she appear to be writing for an uninformed reader in explaining her faith? To some other reader? Explain.

3. What narrative examples or stories does she include? What contribution does each story make to her explanation of the significance of her tradition?

4. What does Quindlen mean by saying "I am a cultural Catholic"? Why does

she think it is important to be one, even though she has ceased to believe in much of Catholic teaching? How representative of other Catholics are her views in her opinion? In yours?

from **On Being Black and Middle Class**
by Shelby Steele

Not long ago a friend of mine, black like myself, said to me that the term "black middle class" was actually a contradiction in terms. Race, he insisted, blurred class distinctions among blacks. If you were black, you were just black and that was that. When I argued, he let his eyes roll at my naiveté. Then he went on. For us, as black professionals, it was an exercise in self-flattery, a pathetic pretension, to give meaning to such a distinction. Worse, the very idea of class threatened the unity that was vital to the black community as a whole. After all, since when had white America taken note of anything but color when it came to blacks? He then reminded me of an old Malcolm X line that had been popular in the sixties. Question: What is a black man with a Ph.D.? Answer: A nigger.

For many years I had been on my friend's side of this argument. Much of my conscious thinking on the old conundrum of race and class was shaped during my high school and college years in the race-charged sixties, when the fact of my race took on an almost religious significance. Progressively, from the mid-sixties on, more and more aspects of my life found their explanation, their justification, and their motivation in race. My youthful concerns about career, romance, money, values, and even styles of dress became a subject to consultation with various oracular sources of racial wisdom. And these ranged from a figure as ennobling as Martin Luther King, Jr., to the underworld elegance of dress I found in jazz clubs on the South Side of Chicago. Everywhere there were signals, and in those days I considered myself so blessed with clarity and direction that I pitied my white classmates who found more embarrassment than guidance in the fact of *their* race. In 1968, inflated by my new power, I took a mischievous delight in calling them culturally disadvantaged.

But now, hearing my friend's comment was like hearing a priest from a church I'd grown disenchanted with. I understood him, but my faith was weak. What had sustained me in the sixties sounded monotonous and off the mark in the eighties. For me, race had lost much of its juju, its singular capacity to conjure meaning. And today, when I honestly look at my life and the lives of many other middle-class blacks I know, I can see that race never fully explained our situation in American society. Black though I may be, it is impossible for me to sit in my single-family house with two cars in the driveway and a swing set in the back yard and *not* see the role class has played in my life. And how can my friend, similarly raised and similarly situated, not see it?

Yet despite my certainty I felt a sharp tug of guilt as I tried to explain myself over my friend's skepticism. He is a man of many comedic facial expressions and, as I spoke, his brow lifted in extreme moral alarm as if I were uttering the unspeakable. His clear implication was that I was being elitist and possibly (dare he suggest?) anti-black—crimes for which there might well be no redemption. He pretended to fear for me. I chuckled along with him, but inwardly I did wonder at myself. Though I never doubted the validity of what I was saying, I felt guilty saying it. Why?

After he left (to retrieve his daughter from a dance lesson) I realized that the trap I felt myself in had a tiresome familiarity and, in a sort of slow-motion epiphany, I began to see its outline. It was like the suddenly sharp vision one has at the end of a burdensome marriage when all the long-repressed incompatibilities come undeniably to light.

What became clear to me is that people like myself, my friend, and middle-class blacks generally are caught in a very specific double bind that keeps two equally powerful elements of our identity at odds with each other. The middle-class values by which we were raised—the work ethic, the importance of education, the value of property ownership, of respectability, of "getting ahead," of stable family life, of initiative, of self-reliance, etc.—are, in themselves, raceless and even assimilationist. They urge us toward participation in the American mainstream, toward integration, toward a strong identification with the society—and toward the entire constellation of qualities that are implied in the word "individualism." These values are almost rules for how to prosper in a democratic, free-enterprise society that admires and rewards individual effort. They tell us to work hard for ourselves and our families and to seek our opportunities whenever they appear, inside or outside the confines of whatever ethnic group we may belong to.

But the particular pattern of racial identification that emerged in the sixties and that still prevails today urges middle-class blacks (and all blacks) in the opposite direction. This pattern asks us to see ourselves as an embattled minority, and it urges an adversarial stance toward the mainstream, an emphasis on ethnic consciousness over individualism. It is organized around an implied separatism.

The opposing thrust of these two parts of our identity results in the double bind of middle-class blacks. There is no forward movement on either plane that does not constitute backward movement on the other. This was the familiar trap I felt myself in while talking with my friend. As I spoke about class, his eyes reminded me that I was betraying race. Clearly, the two indispensable parts of my identity were a threat to each other.

Of course when you think about it, class and race are both similar in some ways and also naturally opposed. They are two forms of collective identity with boundaries that intersect. But whether they clash or peacefully coexist has much to do with how they are defined. Being both black and middle class becomes a double bind when class and race are defined in sharply antagonistic terms, so that one must be repressed to appease the other.

But what is the "substance" of these two identities, and how does each establish itself in an individual's overall identity? It seems to me that when we identify with any collective we are basically identifying with images that tell us what it means to be a member of that collective. Identity is not the same thing as the fact of membership in a collective; it is, rather, a form of self-definition, facilitated by images of what we wish our membership in the collective to mean. In this sense, the images we identify with may reflect the aspirations of the collective more than they reflect reality, and their content can vary with shifts in those aspirations.

But the process of identification is usually dialectical. It is just as necessary to say what we are *not* as it is to say what we are—so that finally identification comes about by embracing a polarity of positive and negative images. To identify as middle class, for example, I must have both positive and negative images of what being middle class entails; then I will know what I should and should not be doing in order to be middle class. The same goes for racial identity.

In the racially turbulent sixties the polarity of images that came to define racial identification was very antagonistic to the polarity that defined middle-class identification. One might say that the positive images of one lined up with the negative images of the other, so that to identify with both required either a contortionist's flexibility or a dangerous splitting of the self. The double bind of the black middle class was in place.

The black middle class has always defined its class identity by means of positive images gleaned from middle- and upper-class white society, and by means of negative images of lower-class blacks. This habit goes back to the institution of slavery itself, when "house" slaves both mimicked the whites they served and held themselves above the "field" slaves. But in the sixties the old bourgeois impulse to dissociate from the lower classes (the "we-they" distinction) backfired when racial identity suddenly called for the celebration of this same black lower class. One of the qualities of a double bind is that one feels it more than sees it, and I distinctly remember the tension and strange sense of dishonesty I felt in those days as I moved back and forth like a bigamist between the demands of class and race.

Though my father was born poor, he achieved middle-class standing through much hard work and sacrifice (one of his favorite words) and by identifying fully with solid middle-class values—mainly hard work, family life, property ownership, and education for his children (all four of whom have advanced degrees). In his mind these were not so much values as laws of nature. People who embodied them made up the positive images in his class polarity. The negative images came largely from the blacks he had left behind because they were "going nowhere."

No one in my family remembers how it happened, but as time went on, the negative images congealed into an imaginary character named Sam, who, from the extensive service we put him to, quickly grew to mythic proportions. In our family lore he was sometimes a trickster, sometimes a boob, but always possessed of a catalogue of sly faults that gave up graphic images of everything we should not be. On sacrifice: "Sam never thinks about tomorrow. He wants it now or he doesn't care about it." On work: "Sam doesn't favor it too much." On children: "Sam likes to have them but not to raise them." On money: "Sam drinks it up and pisses it out." On fidelity: "Sam has to have two or three women." On clothes: "Sam features loud clothes. He likes to see and be seen." And so on. Sam's persona amounted to a negative instruction manual in class identity.

I don't think that any of us believed Sam's faults were accurate representations of lower-class black life. He was an instrument of self-definition, not of sociological accuracy. It never occurred to us that he looked very much like the white racist stereotype of blacks, or that he might have been a manifestation of our own racial self-hatred. He simply gave us a counterpoint against which to express our aspirations. If self-hatred was a factor, it was not, for us, a matter of hating lower-class blacks but of hating what we did not want to be.

Still, hate or love aside, it is fundamentally true that my middle-class identity involved a dissociation from images of lower-class black life and a corresponding identification with values and patterns of responsibility that are common to the middle class everywhere. These values sent me a clear message: be both an individual and a responsible citizen; understand that the quality of your life will approximately reflect the quality of effort you put into it; know that individual responsibility is the basis of freedom and that the limitations imposed by fate (whether fair or unfair) are no excuse for passivity.

Whether I live up to these values or not, I know that my acceptance of them is the result of lifelong conditioning. I know also that I share this conditioning with middle-class people of all races and that I can no more easily be free of it than I can be free of my race. Whether all this got started because the black middle class modeled itself on the white middle class is no longer relevant. For the middle-class black, conditioned by these values from birth, the sense of meaning they provide is as immutable as the color of his skin.

.   .   .   .

The discomfort and vulnerability felt by middle-class blacks in the sixties, it could be argued, was a worthwhile price to pay considering the progress achieved during that time of racial confrontation. But what may have been tolerable then is intolerable now. Though changes in American society have made it an anachronism, the monolithic form of racial identification that came out of the sixties is still very much with us. It may be more loosely held, and its power to punish heretics has probably diminished, but it continues to catch middle-class blacks in a double bind, thus impeding not only their own advancement but even, I would contend, that of blacks as a group.

The victim-focused black identity encourages the individual to feel that his advancement depends almost entirely on that of the group. Thus he loses sight not only of his own possibilities but of the inextricable connection between individual effort and individual advancement. This is a profound encumbrance today, when there is more opportunity for blacks than ever before, for it reimposes limitations that can have the same oppressive effect as those the society has only recently begun to remove.

It was the emphasis on mass action in the sixties that made the victim-focused black identity a necessity. But in the eighties and beyond, when racial advancement will come only through a multitude of individual advancements, this form of identity inadvertently adds itself to the forces that hold us back. Hard work, education, individual initiative, stable family life, property ownership — these have always been the means by which ethnic groups have moved ahead in America. Regardless of past or present victimization, these "laws" of advancement apply absolutely to black Americans also. There is no getting around this. What we need is a form of racial identity that energizes the individual by putting him in touch with both his possibilities and his responsibilities.

It has always annoyed me to hear from the mouths of certain arbiters of blackness that middle-class blacks should "reach back" and pull up those blacks less fortunate than they—as though middle-class status were an unearned and essentially passive condition in which one needed a large measure of noblesse oblige to occupy one's time. My own image is of reaching back from a moving train to lift on board those who have no tickets. A noble enough sentiment—but might it not be wiser to show them the entire structure of principles, effort, and sacrifice that puts one in a position to buy a ticket any time one likes? This, I think, is something members of the black middle class can realistically offer to other blacks. Their example is not only a testament to possibility but also a lesson in method. But they cannot lead by example until they are released from a black identity that regards that example as suspect, that sees them as "marginally" black, indeed that holds *them* back by catching them in a double bind.

To move beyond the victim-focused black identity we must learn to make a difficult but crucial distinction: between actual victimization, which we must resist with every resource, and identification with the victim's status. Until we do this we will continue to wrestle more with ourselves than with the new opportunities which so many paid so dearly to win.

1. What function does the story Shelby Steele tells about his and his friend's conversation have in the essay? What does the story contribute to his shaping idea? Where does the sentence containing his shaping idea appear?

2. What role does Steele's phrase "victim-focused black identity" play in his essay? What are the features of this identity? To what extent does Steele believe it has become a tradition? What group shares this tradition?

3. What features does the author ascribe to the middle-class tradition in America? In what ways and to what extent does Steele think the values of the black middle class are different from those of the white middle class?

4. Whom do you think Steele is writing to? To what extent is this audience uninformed? What attitudes and values does he believe this group of readers has?

5. What function does his story about "Sam" play in his explanation of his subject?

6. How does Steele propose that the class and race double-bind be resolved, for both poor and middle-class black people?

Writing Your Rough Draft

Before completing your rough draft, you may want to examine the following rough draft of a student essay on a tradition. Ask yourself questions similar to those asked above about the professional essays: What and where is the writer's shaping idea? What features of her tradition does she describe? How thorough is this explanation for an uninformed reader? What arrangement patterns does she use? What is the effect of any stories that she included? Finally, what revisions do you think she might make of this essay?

HOUSE OF DELIGHT

Christmas is the time for poinsettias, evergreens, ornaments, carols, and lights--but most of all, it is a time for home baked goods and scrumptious dinners. Of all of the holidays I can remember, none impressed me more than the ones spent at my paternal grandparents' house when I was a child. Not only did they serve holiday dinners in grand Italian style, but they made it seem like Christmas every Sunday all year round.

As you approached Grandma's house, the first thing you would notice was an overwhelming hedge which surrounded the entire house. This reminded me of the thorny enclosure around Sleeping Beauty's Castle, yet the real mystery lay within. When you entered, the aroma of sauce and meat cooking immediately made you hungry, but there was another odd smell. On the dining room dresser seven statues of saints stood in a row, and in front of each one incense burned. Out of reverence for God, each Sunday my grandparents prayed and carried out this ritual.

The kitchen was off limits to the children, and I thought of it as grandma's private sanctum. Both walls were lined with huge pots, which looked like caldrons, and every one was shining. The cupboards, which stretched from ceiling to floor, held jars of pickled and preserved oddities such as pickled pig's knuckles. In this room, she whipped up everything from homemade pasta, ravioli, and lasagna noodles to mouth watering pastries and zeppolas.

Most people might be sickened by some of the foods my grandparents prepared. Everyone except my mom, my brother, and me spoke Italian, and you never quite knew what you were eating or where it came from, but it smelled so good that you devoured it--only to find out later that the entrée was tripe, frog's legs or brains. The most unusual dish was one eaten solely by my grandfather called capozella or lamb's head. One Sunday, he consumed everything but the teeth and skull, and he laughed and spoke in Italian as we all stared at him! In Naples, Italy it was common to eat capozella especially around Eastertime.

Once grandpa took me shopping on Ralph and Utica Avenues in Brooklyn, where there were large farms and numerous slaughterhouses. You would look into a chicken's eyes one minute and he would be dinner on someone's plate in the next minute. All the meat and produce used in their cooking was purchased fresh, and I remember once that we brought two live hens home for fresh eggs! Grandma had her own unique ideas about obtaining food. Many times she took me to fields near her house where we could pick mushrooms and dandelion greens. Grandma turned these ingredients into delicious soup. I remember a time when a cat followed us home, and afterwards I never saw it again. I wonder?

Even though the menu could be peculiar, every Sunday grandma would serve course after course of some of the best tasting food I have ever eaten. The table was set casually, and the plates and silverware didn't match, but four hungry men and their families sat at a long wooden table with grandpa at its head, and they ate all day long. The meal began with soup and an antipasta, followed by pasta topped with a special sauce. Finally, a roast and assorted vegetables would be served all seasoned just right. We ate until we were stuffed, and the adults drank wine as well. After dinner, the men would doze and watch T.V. with us, and the women would clean up the remains of dinner.

On one particular Sunday, my grandfather prepared the meal and he rivaled my grandmother in the cooking department. The fish feast he prepared included fried calamari (squid), boccala (cod fish), octopus salad, shrimp, scallops and pasta with clam sauce, of course. Grandma's homemade zeppolas and pastries added a special touch to the occasion and I remember enjoying the meal thoroughly!

Sadly, this tradition died with my grandmother on my Communion day, May 30, 1956, when I was seven years old. There can be no replacement for the time and effort my grandparents put into preparing food, nor the love they showed us by serving it. Even though they spoke very little English, we understood that Sundays were very special--and I will always remember their house and cherish the special times I spent with them.

Once you have completed your rough draft, consider those elements of a mature style discussed in the following "Focus" section that you might want to apply in revising your essay.

FOCUS ON STYLE: ELIMINATING DEADWOOD

The term *deadwood* is a general label for language that obscures the meaning of a sentence. By cutting deadwood, we sharpen and clarify our language. We learn to be more direct with our audience, more accurate in our choice of words and less tentative about our assertions. As writers we do not intend to write deadwood; rather, it is a reminder to us all how difficult it is to write clearly and concisely. Many types of deadwood clog our sentences.

Pretentiousness

Original. In my considered opinion, in the area of accuracy of steering, this driving machine performed in an erratic manner due to the fact that the road was of a wet condition. It is recommended by the inspector that in such a definitely damp and humid weather situation, the vehicle operator act in a manner that exercises extreme caution.

What is wrong with this language? Doesn't it have the sound of authority, of some official writing a report in an official style? If so, isn't it adequate for its intended audience, probably another official? But would the intended reader of such prose, even another inspector, make sense of it? Writers who use such language are really placing a barrier to communication between themselves and their audience. Part of the problem with this kind of writing is that we don't hear the *person* behind the language. Instead there is a mask of pretentiousness disguising a simple statement with lengthy connective expressions ("in the area of," "due to the fact that"); wordy substitutes for common nouns ("weather situation," "vehicle operator"); and the passive voice ("is recommended," "caution is exercised"). The writer wishes to sound important and to appear an expert by avoiding simple, clear language.

Revised: Because the road was wet, the car was hard to steer. The driver should be careful when it rains.

Here is another example:

Original: This mandatory curfew is largely inequitable for the minors who haven't been in any serious trouble or haven't done anything deviant. Therefore, why should all young teenagers have to pay the consequences for a minority of a special group?

Revised: Minors who haven't been in any serious trouble should not have to pay the consequences for the minority of teenagers who have broken the law.

Wordiness

Wordiness, the adding of unnecessary words or phrases, is one of the most common types of deadwood.

Original: Independence Day in Jamaica is a time when all business places are closed and school students are given the week off from school.

Revised: On Independence Day in Jamaica businesses are closed and students are given the week off from school.

Original: On Chinese New Year, many owners of businesses invite the dragons to dance on their property for good luck and in return the owner will give the dragon a good luck envelope.

Revised: On Chinese New Year, many owners of businesses invite the dragons to dance on their property for good luck and in return give the dragon a good luck envelope.

Original: There is no way that we can completely drift away from religion. There are too many compelling reasons to believe.

Revised: We cannot completely drift away from religion because of the many compelling reasons to believe.

Often, by writing a series of short sentences, the writer repeats words and phrases. As we discussed in Chapter 5, by combining sentences the writer not only improves the sound of the sentence but also avoids wordiness:

Original: I gathered the facts that I found on obese people in my health book. I found that obese people have a statistically higher risk of developing many types of health problems. They have to deal with numerous psychological and practical problems as well.

Revised: My health book stated that obese people have a statistically higher risk of developing health problems as well as experiencing numerous psychological and practical difficulties.

Original: I walked past each room slowly. I could feel the pain and anguish of the people through the doors. After what seemed like hours, we reached the room. I hesitated at the door.

Revised: After walking slowly past each room, feeling the pain and anguish of the people within, I came to one door and hesitated.

Qualifiers

The writer who says, "In my opinion, I feel that abortion on demand can be considered counterproductive," is avoiding a direct commitment to a point of view. Instead of saying, "Abortion on demand is wrong," the writer tries to hide behind weak, unconvincing language that qualifies every assertion. This deadwood must be cleared out if the sentence is to be effective. Here is another example:

Original: I am of the mind that capital punishment would serve justice well.

Revised: Capital punishment would be just.

Awkward Sentence Structure

Deadwood can be the result of awkward sentence structure as well as poor word choice. In this case, the writer must be more analytical, revising the sentence fully. The following sentences show how to revise statements whose awkwardness hinders communication between writer and audience:

Original: This woman who was boisterous and unruly was thrown out of the restaurant, which was French and therefore elegant, and in which we were eating dinner.

Revised: While we were eating dinner in an elegant French restaurant, a boisterous, unruly woman was thrown out.

This sentence was improved by the use of subordination and the omission of unnecessary modifying clauses.

> *Original:* His car, which was an antique black Ford, moved in a creeping fashion toward the other cars.
>
> *Revised:* His antique black Ford crept toward the other cars.

The modifying clause *"which was an antique black Ford,"* is replaced by adjectives attached directly to the noun. *Car* is replaced by the more specific *Ford*.

> *Original:* Another theory has been set forth by Sally Langendoen, who has based her theory on the works of Dr. Joseph Stolkowski.
>
> *Revised:* Another theory, based on the works of Dr. Joseph Stolkowski, has been set forth by Sally Langendoen.
>
> *Revised:* Sally Langendoen has set forth a theory based on the works of Dr. Joseph Stolkowski.

In this example, the elimination of repetitive phrasing more clearly emphasizes the subject.

SOME PRACTICE WITH ELIMINATING DEADWOOD

Rewrite the following sentences, eliminating the many unnecessary and awkward words, phrases, and clauses.

1. Every Sunday I wake up to the smell of fresh tomato sauce simmering in a pot on the stove. The reason for that is that each Sunday my family sits at the table together and eats the traditional Italian Sunday dinner.

2. This so-called "house music" usually involves an intensely passionate and hard beat which I find to be acceptable.

3. It seems apparent that in today's society murderers have the run of the city.

4. Naturally, even the opponents of pornography agree that this type of absolute censoring could eventually lead to other impositions on our freedom of speech and serious infringements or complications thereof.

5. It is not always fun eating lunch with the entire family. Sometimes, major fights break out and this will tend to ruin our entire Sunday.

6. I personally think that the majority of right-wing conservatives lack compassion, aren't openminded, and are quite ignorant in their way of thought.

7. I have always thought that joining a club or organization clashed with school and work so that the little time you end up with as a result is in other words a waste of my time.

8. As humans we can live together but when it comes to the suffering and death of a loved one it is difficult to deal with and results in the loved one being left to die alone.

9. In the medical community, doctors seem to have divided views on the issue of euthanasia.

10. Although I find myself in the aforementioned category of older women, I would like to note the following observation. There are many students, despite age or marital status, whose differing responsibilities restrict them to the same limited time schedule as myself, thereby facing similar difficulties.

11. There are some people who do not believe that pornography should be tolerated in this society.

12. I never took the time to really listen to rap music. The sound of rap always repulsed me. My boyfriend listens to rap, once in a while, and a couple of my friends showed some interest in it. This surprised me. I couldn't understand what they found so interesting about rap.

Avoiding Deadwood in Writing Your Essay on a Tradition

When in conversation we attempt to explain a subject to an uninformed listener, especially if the subject is one we care about, we tend to overexplain. In our eagerness to make our reader understand and appreciate the subject as we do, we may add a lot of deadwood to our writing as well. In addition to being wordy, we may be pretentious if we feel defensive about our tradition: using high-flown language protects us from the imagined scorn of our readers. Or, conversely, our defensiveness may lead us to use qualifiers so that we do not appear to think too highly of this tradition or to have invested too much of ourselves in it should the reader disapprove. Defensiveness may also entangle us in awkward sentence structure. Eliminating deadwood takes considerable work if we have a vested interest in its use.

SOME PRACTICE IN ELIMINATING DEADWOOD IN YOUR ESSAY ON A TRADITION

1. Look again at the essays that you have handed in thus far this semester. Have your evaluators—your peers or your instructor—indicated that your writing

contains deadwood? Have they commented, in other words, about wordiness, awkwardness, pretentiousness or high-flown jargon, the use of qualifiers? If so, and you have not yet edited these essays to eliminate this deadwood, try your hand at doing so now.

2. Examine the rough draft you have written on a tradition for examples of deadwood. Can you locate any? One tried-and-true method of finding and eliminating deadwood is to cut your material. Set a goal for yourself of eliminating, say, 100 words, and then do so without eliminating content as well. The chances are that in cutting 100 words you will be cutting deadwood.

3. Decide the reason you used the deadwood you found. Did your reason have to do with your relationship with your reader or with your subject? If you think any pretentiousness or qualifiers result from a feeling of defensiveness about your tradition, as best you can, attempt to revise your attitude both toward your subject and toward your reader, just as you revised your style. Then, reread again for any deadwood you may have missed.

REWRITING

Obtaining Feedback on Your Rough Draft

Once again, you are ready to hand a rough draft of an essay you have written to your peers. At this point, you might ask yourself how effective your peers' critiques are proving to be. Are they identifying the aspects of your essays that most require revision from your point of view or from that of your instructor? If not, how can you obtain more useful critiques? You might ask yourself if you are perhaps unwittingly discouraging your peers from honest evaluation by being defensive or by arguing with their comments. A solution might be to ask them specific questions about concerns that you have about your draft.

Here is the Audience Response Guide for this chapter:

AUDIENCE RESPONSE GUIDE

1. **What do you think the writer wanted to say about his or her tradition? What is his or her purpose in writing about it? What does he or she want the paper to mean?**

2. **How does the paper affect the uninformed reader?**

3. **How effective has the writer been in conveying his or her purpose and meaning? What are the strengths of the paper? What are the weaknesses?**

4. How should the paper be revised to better convey the writer's intention in writing about a tradition?

Revision of Student Essay "House of Delight"

Before revising your own rough draft of your essay on a tradition, you may want to read the critiques of the readers of "House of Delight." In responding to the questions of the "Audience Response Guide," did her readers make suggestions for revision of her rough draft (pp. 256–258) similar to those you would make?

1. Her readers felt that she wanted to convey the delight she and her family experienced when eating at her grandparents' home, both for the food itself and the loving preparation that went into serving it. She also wanted to convey the mystery that the house behind the hedges with its candle-burning ritual and peculiar food held for her as a young child.

2. Her readers were able to understand her tradition and experience it through her stories and vivid details. One of them said he felt envious of this Italian family tradition.

3. Her readers appreciated her descriptiveness, but were surprised that the essay wasn't about Christmas, as the first sentence of the essay led them to believe that it would be. They also felt the essay didn't sustain the theme of mystery throughout.

4. They suggested that she revise her introduction to prepare the reader better for her purpose in writing.

Below is the student's revision of "House of Delight." What changes has the writer made in her revised draft? Has she made the changes recommended by her readers? Has her "other self" suggested further revisions?

HOUSE OF DELIGHT

Do certain events in your childhood remain vivid in your mind? Do these spans of time stir feelings within you? The memories of Sunday meals at my paternal grandparents' house in my early years, are alive in me. During these visits, I felt like a foreigner in their strange land, and the emotions that stirred in me ranged from fear, to curiosity and on to belonging. There can be no replacement for the time and effort they put into preparing food, nor the love they showed us by serving it.

As you approached grandma's house, the first thing you would notice was an overwhelming hedge which surrounded the entire house. The hedge reminded me of the thorny enclosure around Sleeping Beauty's Castle, yet the real mystery lay within. When you entered, the aroma of meat and sauce cooking immediately made you hungry, but there was another strange smell. On the dining room dresser seven statues of saints stood in a row, and in front of each one incense burned. Out of reverence for God, each Sunday my grandparents prayed and carried out this ritual.

The kitchen was off limits to the children, and I thought of it as grandma's private sanctum. Both walls were lined with huge pots, which looked like caldrons, and every one was shining. The cupboards, which stretched from ceiling to floor, held jars of pickled and preserved oddities such as pickled pig's knuckles. In this room she whipped up everything from homemade pasta, ravioli, and lasagna noodles to mouth watering pastries and zeppolas. Her meals were served promptly at noon, and the amount of time spent leisurely consuming the feast came close to the long hours spent preparing it.

Most people might be sickened by some of the foods my grandparents prepared. Everyone except my mom, my brother, and me spoke Italian, and you never quite knew what you were eating or where it came from, but it smelled so good that you devoured it--only to find out later that the entrée was tripe, frog's legs or brains. The most unusual dish was one eaten solely by my grandfather called capozella or lamb's head. One Sunday, he consumed everything but the teeth and skull, and he laughed and spoke in Italian as we all stared at him! In Naples, Italy it was common to eat capozella especially around Eastertime.

Once grandpa took me shopping on Ralph and Utica Avenues in Brooklyn, where there were large farms and numerous slaughterhouses. You would look into a chicken's eyes one minute and he would be dinner on someone's plate in the next minute. All the meat and produce used in their cooking was purchased fresh, and I remember once that we brought two live hens home for fresh eggs! Grandma had her own unique ideas about obtaining food. Many times she took me to fields near her house where we could pick mushrooms and dandelion greens. Grandma turned these ingredients into delicious soup. I remember a time when a cat followed us home, and afterwards I never saw it again. I wonder?

Even though the menu could be peculiar, every Sunday grandma would serve course after course of some of the best tasting food I have ever eaten. The table was set casually, and the plates and silverware didn't match, but four hungry men and their familes sat at a long wooden table with grandpa at its head, and they ate all day long. The meal began with soup and an antipasta, followed by pasta topped with a special sauce. Finally, a roast and assorted vegetables would be served all seasoned just right. We ate until we were stuffed, and the adults drank wine as well. After dinner, the men would doze and watch T.V. with us, while the women would clean up the remains of dinner.

On one particular Sunday, my grandfather prepared the meal, and he rivaled my grandmother in the cooking department. The fish feast he prepared included fried calamari (squid), boccala (cod fish), octopus salad, shrimp, scallops and pasta with clam sauce, of course. Grandma's homemade zeppolas and pastries added a special touch to the occasion, and I remember enjoying the meal thoroughly!

Although they spoke very little English, their exaggerated movements, gestures and facial expressions communicated feelings that words could not, and I felt loved and protected there. Sadly, my grandma passed away when I was seven years old, and none of the surviving children or my grandpa held Sunday gatherings again. My grandparents, particularly my grandma, were the glue that bound our family together. My father can come close to duplicating some of their cooking, but the strong family unity died along with grandma. If you could have looked through my impressionable eyes at that time, you would have experienced a style of life which was both unusual and unforgettable.

Rearranging

In revising your rough draft, you will want to decide whether the pattern of arrangement you have devised is effective. You can start by rereading your introduction: does it suggest a pattern of organization for your essay, and if it does, does your arrangement of your essay parallel this pattern? If it does not, you might want to rephrase your introduction to reflect the organization you want to use.

Next, you will want to examine the sequence of paragraphs to see if they follow each other in the most effective order. Read your essay through from beginning to end. If some paragraphs now seem to be out of a logical sequence, then you will want to rearrange them. In the revised student essay on pp. 264–266, the writer of "House of Delight" shifted material from her conclusion to her introduction.

Now, you may want to inspect the structure of your paragraphs. Reread each paragraph. Are the sentences in a logical order? For example, do they proceed from most to least important or from least to most important, depending on your purpose? Or do they discuss causes and then effects or similarities and then differences? To answer this question of order, you can analyze the pattern for each of your paragraphs. You will want to rearrange any sentences that do not contribute to the over-all organization.

Revising Your Essay on a Tradition

Before beginning the process of revising your own essay, answering the following questions may prove helpful.

A Checklist of Questions to Consider in Revising an Essay About a Tradition

1. **What is my shaping idea for this essay? Have I stated it clearly so that the reader knows what my tradition is, what significance I believe that it has for those who observe it, and what my own point of view on it is? If not, how can I revise it?**
2. **Do I explain its features and significance fully enough so that my reader will understand both my tradition and the reasons for my point of view? If not, what can I add to my explanation?**
3. **Have I bridged any gap between my reader's values and point of view and my own? If not, how can I now do so?**
4. **Have I added any stories that would help exemplify my tradition? Should other more effective stories be substituted?**
5. **Have I presented my ideas both among and within paragraphs in the most logical manner? Do I need to rearrange any ideas to assist my reader in understanding my explanation?**

Now you should be ready to revise your essay.

Editing

Rearranging. Reread your essay for the rhythm of your sentences. Do you still hear some choppiness where you have used too many short sentences? Would rearranging these sentences in the various patterns suggested in the sentence combining section in Chapter 5 add to their length and improve their variety? Would rearranging some words and phrases eliminate dead-wood and improve the naturalness of your style and the directness of your communication? Before handing in your final draft, reread it once more, seeking to fine tune the style. Finally, reread for mechanical errors.

BECOMING AWARE OF YOURSELF AS A WRITER

1. How difficult did you find explaining your tradition to a reader to whom it was unfamiliar? What other subjects are you familiar enough with to explain to a reader?

2. While writing the essay for this chapter, what techniques, other than those discussed here, did you discover for explaining a subject? What would you say is the key ingredient in a successful explanation?

3. How effective did you find brainstorming lists and clusters as a means of generating ideas? Had you used brainstorming before? In what other contexts can you imagine using it again?

4. What problems, if any, did selecting stories to illustrate your subject pose for you? Do you agree that telling stories is an effective method of explaining? Which of your stories do you feel was most effective? Why?

5. What have you learned about writing sentences in Chapter 5 and in this chapter? Do you combine your sentences effectively? Is your writing free from deadwood?

7

Writing About the Media — Explaining What You Think

PURPOSE

To the extent that your discoveries as an explorer of the world beyond yourself broaden your perspective on that world, you gain a greater capacity to understand and appreciate widely different patterns of behavior and thought. In a sense, you learn to look with new eyes, to comprehend what once might have puzzled you, and to see the value in what you once might have thought valueless. It is a natural impulse to seek to tell others what you have learned in this fashion, broadening their knowledge by explaining a subject to them so that they understand and appreciate it more fully than they otherwise might. You will continue to write with an explanatory aim in this chapter.

One common way of understanding and explaining our experience is to assume a separation between our private and our public lives. We say we live one life at school, work, or wherever we act in a formal or official capacity, and another life with our family and friends or by ourselves. But in a real sense it is no longer possible to make a clear distinction between our private and public lives, for as soon as we enter our homes we are met with all the signs of our involvement with the public world — more specifically, the world of the media. Newspapers, magazines, books, television, film, videos, tapes — how could we possibly turn off their influence on us even if we wanted to?

Few consumers of these media remain neutral about the nature and quality of the products that result. Whether we love them or loathe them, we are fascinated by their hold on us and by the ways they provoke us to respond. We often move quickly from an attraction to the "what" of the media, i.e., our observations and experiences with them, to an interest in the "how," the methods and ideas that comprise them. Thus we try to arrive at an understanding of the media for ourselves and others. In this chapter, we shall direct your attention to the media and how your already impressive knowledge of the subject can be focused toward writing an essay that interprets and explains your encounters with the media for a broad audience that shares your experience but has not analyzed it.

In writing this essay, you can continue to rely on your personal experiences and observations in order to gather information. You will want to generalize, to point out the broader, more universal interest inherent in your specific observations and knowledge of the media. We will suggest in this chapter that you attempt to answer the classical questions "What have I seen or heard that can offer support as examples?" and "How can I generalize about what has been said?" (See "Generating Ideas: the Classical Questions," Chapter 5, pp. 186–192.)

Because the audience for the media is so broad, encompassing your school, community, and culture, we shall ask you to write for one possible group of this large media-consuming public. Because you are no longer writing from personal experience for an unfamiliar audience as in Chapter 6 but from a public experience to an audience nearly as familiar with that experience as yourself, you will be asked here to develop a more formal, more public voice with which to express your generalizations and narrative examples.

TASK: WRITING ABOUT THE MEDIA

Your task for this chapter is to write an essay on your experience of the popular media. You are asked to explore some aspect of television, film, video, radio, books, newspapers, and/or magazines and to explain your findings to your audience. You will gather observations you have made about this aspect of the media, make generalizations about these observations, and draw a conclusion for your reader.

The best way to begin this task might be to take a brief inventory of your own reading and viewing habits in order to determine where your areas of interest and knowledge lie: you know best what kinds of television programs you respond to, the newspapers and magazines in your home, the films that

have moved or entertained or dismayed you. Because of your extensive experience with these media, you already possess a large storehouse of images,
scenes, characterizations, stories, points of view, and ideas drawn from a variety of sources.

Your task as a writer is to create from these materials a coherent pattern
of connection—a theme. This theme will emerge from your demonstration of
some significant general observation or conclusion, e.g., the difficult role of
the television game show host or the changing image of the working woman
in fashion magazines. You will want to explain what your theme is, how it
is present in the examples you have chosen to discuss, and what its signfi-
cance is. You may also want to read the analyses of others in articles and
books on aspects of the media with which you are familiar.

In writing this essay, you will want to seek a balance between the broad
generalization and the narrative incidents you offer as examples for your
theme. A pattern of arrangement may emerge from this alternation of the
general with the specific, or one or more of the classical patterns of arrangement may prove an effective way of developing your explanation (see Chapter 5, pp. 197–201).

In choosing how to address your audience, you may find it helpful to
consider how pervasive the media are in our lives. In a sense, you will be
writing to everyone, for few in our society choose to ignore the interest or
power of the media. We suggest, however, that you try to imagine your audience as one group within your school, community, or larger culture. The
audience you choose may to some extent be determined by your subject, e.g.,
the homemakers in your community who, like you, watch afternoon soap
operas or sports fans in your school who, along with you, read local newspaper coverage of sports events. You may want to write to the readership of
a publication with national circulation, on rock music for *Rolling Stone* or
Circus, for example. Your audience may or may not be familiar with the narrative incidents you use as examples, and you will have to decide how much
of your own media experiences you will need to relate in order to provide
support for the generalizations at which you arrive.

The two professional essays are intended to offer you examples of public
voices writing on the media. Both essays are rich with narrative examples
drawn from the authors' viewing experiences. Both essays arrive at generalizations that give significance to these specific examples. As did the authors of
these essays, you will try to provide answers to the classical questions "What
have I seen or heard that can offer support as examples?" and "How can I
generalize about what has been said?"

In the "Arranging the Essay" and "Focus" sections, we discuss how to
create generalizations for your narrative examples, how best to arrange your
pattern of generalization and examples, and what kind of stylistic concerns
enter into your developing a public voice.

WRITING YOUR ESSAY

Generating Ideas Through Generalization

Generalization.   In thinking about our experiences and observations, we generalize about them; that is, we attempt to see a linked significance to them, a common meaning that connects them. When something happens to us or we observe an event, we attempt to relate the experience or observation to others that we have had or seen and to see a pattern. Without the ability to generalize, our lives would appear to be a series of random events, with no significant connections. We would not be able to learn anything about ourselves or about the world; in fact, the ability to form generalizations is crucial to our survival and growth. A child who cannot learn after touching a hot stove three times that hot stoves should not be touched is doomed to a life of suffering, just as is the unemployed mill worker who observes that mills are closing down but does not conclude that there will be no job for him and that he should look for a different type of occupation.

On the other hand, we often make generalizations that we cannot find adequate experience or observation to justify. Of what real use is it to make an assertion when it cannot be supported? As we saw in fulfilling the task for Chapter 5, we may be guilty of a prejudgment, or we may lose our argument or at the very least bore our audience. Who, for example, is impressed with the generalization that someone is a good cook when the speaker cannot cite one good dish that that person has produced? And who wants to know that a film or book is a good one if the speaker cannot support this claim with exciting episodes or thrilling commentary?

Narrative Examples.   Generalizations and their supporting examples must be part of the same process. A writer who wishes to write an essay on how black children are represented on TV sitcoms must point to specific incidents on these programs and then attempt to generalize about the meaning and significance of these incidents. He may begin by asking questions such as "What happened?" and "How did it turn out?" but he will then try to answer questions that impose a pattern of coherence on the narrative, such as "What do these incidents mean?" "What do they have in common?" and "What are they all about?"

In a sense it is our attraction to narrative examples or stories that gets us started in the process of explaining ourselves to others in the first place. TV news anchor persons refer to their news items as "stories," i.e., events that contain strong narrative interest and have clearly distinguishable beginnings, middles, and endings. Listen to a friend tell a personal story or relate a joke, and you will recognize something of the same narrative strategy: the teller selects to relate only the essential plot elements of the story; characterization is given only if it is directly connected to the outcome of the story. Television commercials are also examples of economical story telling that selects those incidents and images that produce the anticipated ending.

Generalization and the Classical Questions.   In response to the classical question "What have I seen or heard that can offer support as examples?" your experiences and observations in life have provided you with a large repository of material. In writing about the popular media, for example, your knowledge would provide you with a storehouse of images, stories, references to contemporary fashions, ideas, persuasive methods and language. You might determine from your viewing of television soap operas that women are portrayed in stereotype—they are either wonderfully warm and good or hopelessly cold and evil. You will surely want to relate some examples to your readers who, although they may not have seen these incidents, will be informed by your brief narratives.

But you will probably also want to tell your readers what larger generalization you think this all adds up to. Why are women represented in this way? What effect does this representation have on the viewer? How does it compare to your real life experience? How do these characters compare to women characters in other media? By answering these classical questions discussed in previous chapters, you will also be answering the classical question "How can I generalize about what has been said?" An ability to explain the general significance of information is important to writers who would inform their audience. For one thing, it is often intelligent generalization that gives relevance and significance to the specific details that you have just related. Without a generalization that is adequate, reasonable, and convincing, you are left with a headless body of prose, an essay without coherence or purpose.

Suppose you wrote an essay about the persuasive, manipulative techniques of television commercials and print advertising. In this paper, you gave examples of advertisements for different products, showing how each makes its appeal to the apparently unknowing viewer. But suppose also that you failed to tell your readers what this all adds up to? Is it bad to advertise this way? What does it suggest about the psychology of viewers or readers? What does it reveal about American consumers? In other words, what do your examples tell us about such advertising? We already know it is manipulative; what we want to know is the general significance of the information you have given us. Here are some questions to keep in mind when creating a generalization:

1. Does the generalization seem too broad (or narrow) for the examples given?
2. Are there sufficient examples to support this generalization?
3. Does the generalization follow logically from your examples?
4. Does the generalization create a pattern of coherence for the supporting examples?

SOME PRACTICE WITH GENERALIZATION AS A WAY OF GENERATING IDEAS

1. Read every article on the front page of your daily newspaper, then write a paragraph about one general condition of contemporary life that the information you have read illustrates. In what way might information from other sources change the generalization that you have made?

2. Take a survey of the reading habits of your friends, family, and classmates. Inquire as to the kinds of material they read regularly, the articles and books they find most appealing and/or informative, and the criticism they have of those they find less worthwhile. Generalize about their reading habits: Are their responses typical? What effect have their reading habits had on you? How do their preferences compare to yours?

3. Joan Didion generalized about John Wayne that he symbolized "the inarticulate longings of a nation wondering at just what pass the trail had been lost." What specific things do you know about Wayne that might support this generalization? What general ideas and values does Wayne symbolize in your eyes? What stories from his films might exemplify your generalization?

4. Ben Franklin, writing in his *Autobiography* about his difficulty in correcting his moral faults, compared himself to a man who goes to a blacksmith to buy an ax. The man, Franklin wrote,

   > desired to have the whole of its surface as bright as the edge; the smith consented to grind it bright for him if he would turn the wheel. He turned while the smith pressed the broad face of the ax hard and heavily on the stone, which made the turning of it very fatiguing. The man came every now and then from the wheel to see how the work went on; and at length would take his ax as it was, without further grinding. "No," says the smith, "turn on, turn on; we shall have it bright by and by; as yet 'tis only speckled." "Yes," says the man, *"but I think I like a speckled ax best."*

   What generalizations about human nature might you draw from Franklin's tale of the man and his ax? How might you incorporate the general ideas represented by the tale into a paper of your own?

Generating Ideas for Your Essay on the Media. Setting out to write on the media can confront you with a formidable task. There is so much material surrounding you that you might wonder where to begin. As you move through this task, you might think of yourself as a media researcher, who, although expert in some ways on the images and strategies of the media, is not yet experienced with the formal methods of conducting and presenting research (see Chapter 10). From earlier tasks, you may recognize an important first step as gathering information relevant to your purpose.

You might begin with your own reading and viewing practices. Describe in your journal the kinds of television programs that interest you. What magazines or periodicals do you read regularly? What recent or past films have you seen or read about? Examine your journal for references to your attitudes toward the media and what you like or dislike about it. If you work in a group, you and your group members might brainstorm lists or clusters of striking media images or present trends (see Chapter 6, pp. 234–240). You might list also the subject matter you associate most with a particular medium, e.g., the television miniseries on historical events like the Civil War, the business magazine's treatment of Japanese competition with American industry, or the sports magazine's attitude toward the commercialization of college football.

You might also want to find publications on the media to assist you in selecting a topic, locating stories, and generalizing about them. One approach is to go to your college or public library to obtain articles on the media that appear in periodicals like *Harper's,* the *Atlantic Monthly,* the *New Republic,* and the *New Yorker.* Or you can refer to Chapter 10, p. 466 for information on the *Reader's Guide to Periodical Literature,* a reference work that will direct you to many articles on a wide variety of topics from many different periodicals. If you use the information from articles or books in writing your essay, then you will want to cite and list them in your paper. (See Chapter 10, pp. 484–490 for proper documentation form.)

Primarily, though, you can write your paper from your own media experiences, using any additional materials as supplementary to your own examples. What is it that you are looking for? Most likely, you want to discern some recurring or prevalent theme in your favorite media or among several media. If you are discussing television or film drama, what kinds of stories or characters have you observed? Because the media seem often to rely on narrative formulas or stereotypical characters, such as we find in crime shows and sitcoms, you might explain them or discuss their implications for the audience. If you are drawn to narrative situations and characters that go against type, you might ask yourself what developments in television and film seem to be going in interesting or imaginative directions? Of course, you can also explain what you perceive as unfortunate and misguided developments as well.

You might find that you hold views on some media images or ideas that are different from other people's. Your paper could then be built around showing how you perceive your topic differently from the way it is usually perceived. For example, you might find "The Simpsons" to be a destructive influence on the American family. Another approach you might want to use is to trace the development of some media work that you are knowledgeable about. For example, if you have watched a television program since its inception, you might be able to explain how and why certain changes in format or character have been undertaken. Or perhaps you have followed a rock or jazz group's development in subject matter or approach through several record albums. This approach answers the explorer's question "How has it changed?" that you might have used in an earlier task (see Chapter 4, pp. 138–143).

SOME PRACTICE WITH USING GENERALIZATION IN WRITING ABOUT THE MEDIA

1. For a few days, keep a record in your journal of your reading, viewing, and listening experiences with the popular media. What experiences particularly impressed you, either positively or negatively? Why? Is there a thread running through these experiences that might form the subject of your essay?

2. With your group or class, brainstorm the media experiences that have impressed all of you the most. What do you think these experiences have in common? A generalization might give you a subject for your essay.

3. Cluster around a particular television program that you are addicted to, a film that you have seen more than once, a comic strip that you have read since childhood, an advertising campaign that you found entertaining or enlightening. What secondary clusters did you form? What generalization about each of these secondary clusters can you make? Would one of them be suitable for your essay? If so, have you added sufficient supporting data in further clusters to support your generalization?

4. Read several articles in periodicals about media experiences with which you are familiar. Using a double-entry journal page, list the examples included in the articles in the left-hand column and the generalizations the authors draw in the right-hand column. On the next journal page, analyze your own responses to the examples. Does a new generalization about one or more of the media experiences occur to you?

Addressing Your Audience: Adopting a Public Voice

Addressing a Public Audience.   For a writer who intends to explain a subject for a large audience, there is an important point to consider: What voice will I adopt in presenting my ideas to my readers? Writing in your journal encouraged you to practice developing an expressive personal voice. Writing about personal experiences, observations, and attitudes made more demands on your personal voice as you moved outward to an audience that most likely shared your experiences and outlook. Your readers required you to think more deeply about what ideas to express and how they could be arranged more effectively. In short, you became more aware of what we might call the conventions of public discourse — what is expected of a writer who intends to reason and explain to a large audience.

In deciding how to address such a readership for the task in this chapter, you might think first of yourself as a writer reaching out to communicate with an ever-increasing audience: from your school to your community to the larger general culture of readers and viewers. These readers will have little direct personal knowledge of you or your experiences; they will be able to judge the worth of your thought and expression only by the power of your "argument" — a word used here to refer to the coherent pattern of generalization and narrative incident explained in the "Generating Ideas" section. Acquiring this "public voice" does not mean your voice will lack personal feeling or opinion, but it suggests that the writer must demonstrate to readers that her point of view is valid and convincing because of the way it is presented, not merely because she is sincere and well-intentioned.

Public Voice and Private Voice.   A public voice is not a substitute for a private voice; it is really different in degree rather than in kind. All the qualities that you associate with good personal writing — authenticity, truthfulness to your experiences, self-revelation and understanding — hold true for writing directed to a broader public purpose. It is mainly a matter of emphasis: a public voice generally leads the audience to observations and reasoned conclusions that have relevance to broader, more socially significant questions and concerns than the writer's own limited personal experiences and opinions. For example, note the subtle difference in voice between Anne Morrow Lindbergh's account of her busy life in her journal and in her essay "Channelled Whelk."

> Why can I not write as much as (my husband), when he is holding down a war job as well? It is four children and a household to run, I explain. But I have people to help. Yes, and they fight. I sometimes feel it would be better to do it all oneself. (I shall have to no doubt before long.)
>
> *War Within and Without: Diaries and Letters 1939–1944*

> With a new awareness, both painful and humorous, I begin to understand why the saints were rarely married women. I am convinced it has nothing inherently to do, as I once supposed, with chastity or children. It has to do primarily with distractions. The bearing, rearing, feeding and educating of children; the running of a house with its thousand details; human relationships with their myriad pulls — women's normal occupations in general run

counter to creative life, or contemplative life, or saintly life. The problem is not merely one of *Woman and Career, Woman and the Home, Woman and Independence.* It is more basically: how to remain whole in the midst of the distractions of life; how to remain balanced, no matter what centrifugal forces tend to pull one off center; how to remain strong, no matter what shocks come in at the periphery and tend to crack the hub of the wheel.

—*Gift from the Sea*

Note the complaining, self-pitying tone in her journal, as compared with the more objective, even humorous, tone of the passage from her essay. In the journal, furthermore, she refers only to her own life, while in the essay she considers the lives of all women. Finally, in the journal she does not document as thoroughly as she does in the essay the duties and "distractions" of a working woman.

Appropriateness as a Characteristic of a Public Voice.   Another characteristic of an effective "public voice" is one we might call appropriateness, i.e., an attitude or tone that is appropriate for the subject being explained. Anne Morrow Lindbergh's tone in her essay is generally serious because her subject is serious. The writers of the passages below realize that on a scale of relative importance the advertising for an antacid and the contents of drugstore novels are not matters of grave national security. Their language often takes on an ironic, slightly comic tone of voice that intends to entertain as much as inform the reader:

Where they (Alka-Seltzer's commercials) once leaned toward the ridiculous, they now seem headed for the sublime.
   —Bernice Kanner, "The Fizz Bizz: Tiny Bubbles," *New York Magazine,* 16 Jan. 1984

In stark contrast, the virtuous virginals generally feature saccharine-sweet, submissive heroines, chaste unto their inevitable marriages when, in a euphemism for sexual intercourse, the heroes transport them "up to the stars."
   —Carol Thurston and Barbara Doscher,
   "Supermarket Erotica," *The Progressive,* April 1982

Assessing the Public Voice Appropriate to Your Publication.   Of course, this tone of voice is also due in part to the publications these passages originally appeared in, and to the audience that might read them. Here is an example of a writer who has adopted a public voice for the large educated audience of the *New York Times.* How effectively does the writer present his views on television for the *Times* reader? (See Chapter 5, Addressing Your Audience: "Writing for Publication," pp. 192–195.) What characteristics of a public voice does the writer exemplify?

What Effect Is TV Having on the Evolution of English?
by Edwin Newman

Tomorrow evening at 9 on Channel 13, "The Story of English" will begin; the nine-part series, with Robert MacNeil as host, traces the history of the language from its beginnings to the present day. To one who has made a career in broadcast news, and a companion career in seeking to preserve the language in a reasonable state of health, it is encouraging that such a series should find its way onto television. It might also be taken as encouraging that the programs reflect the view that worry about the decline of English is unwarranted and misplaced. English, so Mr. MacNeil has concluded after three years of work on the series, is a mighty river that grows ever wider and richer.

If this is so, then television, which is so vastly influential, must itself contribute to the growing width and richness. Unfortunately, there's a good deal of evidence that points in the opposite direction. Television provides much that is informative and entertaining, and occasionally something that is splendid and notable. It does not, however, do much for the language.

Consider the "chat show." The name—chat is easy, informal, familiar—could not be more accurate. I know from my own experience that once you find yourself on camera, with a beaming host and an expectant studio audience, the pressure to tell an anecdote becomes almost irresistible. The exposition of ideas is frowned on. There isn't time. Besides, the audience isn't interested in talking heads.

Consider, then, "talking heads." You might think that what mattered was how well a head talked, whether it did any productive thinking before it talked. Yet, the very term is pejorative, dismissive.

That leads to something else television dislikes—"dead air," meaning the absence of talk and chat. There is a connection between thought and useful speech, between thought and interesting language. A period of silence would permit that, for both broadcaster and audience. Television has made periods of silence unacceptable. In the early days of radio, the World Series would be broadcast by one man. A second might be called in briefly. Now, on television, where far less description and explanation ought to be necessary, the job is done by four or five or half a dozen. The drone is incessant.

The fear that television would homogenize American speech has not been borne out. Anyone who travels around the United States knows that regional accents and expressions are as strong as ever. Television does, however, spread fashionable words and phrases across the country and make them tiresome. And not only across this country. Go to England and you will hear someone described as for real, an expert talking about a dynamic-type environment, and someone else referring to a pre-planned effort by a person who had everything going for him.

An opposition politician will tell a government minister to get his act together, and the minister will warn against a quick fix even though there are Brownie points to be had for giving it his best shot within a given time frame, because that is how he wants to play it. All of this is far too easy. Catch phrases are used as a labor-saving device: Nobody need be explicit.

Some critics make weightier charges against television. One is that staring at the screen has replaced conversation, and that it has replaced storytelling by parents, with predictable consequences for the language. There is something in this. Children are led to speak as characters in animated cartoons do, a horrifying thought. Nor is that all. On local news programs, "happy talk" passes for wit. In sitcoms, wit is represented by a gag line followed by a burst from a laugh track. On cops-and-gangsters programs, a battle of wits is a car chase. Soap-opera characters, explaining their problems, speak a popularized version of psychiatric jargon, another blight on the language. And commercials, by making exaggerated claims, devalue the language, as do the claims that networks and stations put forward in promoting their programs.

Come now to the mistakes advertisers make deliberately, so as to seem friendly and not "elitist." Here is a rent-a-car commercial: "Even us bigshots like Budget's low prices." Indeed us do. Here is quarterback Dan Marino of the Miami Dolphins in a glove commercial: "How can I pass, laying on my back?" Chevrolet had former Chicago Bears linebacker Dick Butkus opening a commercial with "Me and my buddies. . . ." Apparently, "my buddies and I" would depress sales. Jordache—this list of advertisers could go on for pages—had a young woman saying that she hated her mother. Why? "She's so much prettier than me." Burger King uses "Ain't nothing like the real thing" and "Don't it feel good?" though it also put on this:
"Who has the best darn burger in the whole wide world?"
"Burger King and I."
Evidently, correct English can be used without causing immediate bankruptcy.

Not all the mistakes on television are deliberate. "That should expire the clock," a football broadcaster may say. And another: "It's a race between he and Michael Downes." One may spot the ball "laying on somebody's head," another may venture the opinion that "next time he won't get so hard of a rush," and still another suggest that "it looks like he might could have had it." When members of the British royal family turned up at Wimbledon, they became "the sinecure of all eyes."

It isn't only the mistakes. There is also the level of English used. In a remarkable demonstration of devotion to duty, I once listened to John Madden for not quite the entire second half of an N.F.L. game. He repeatedly misused like, as in "he gets like five or six snaps a week." He said "I tellya" 11 times, "see" or "you see" 13 times, and "y'know" 39 times. That sets a fairly deplorable example for those listening.

Newsmen and newswomen on television? CNN reported: "The President said the bombing would not deter he or the United States." It described a group of demonstrators as "not large but noisome." Noisome means foul-smelling. One of the mightier members of NBC's Washington bureau came up with a new word: perplexion. A CBS correspondent, speaking of President Reagan and Mikhail Gorbachev before Geneva, said, "Neither one have met each other." A station in St. Louis offered advice on what to do when "it's lightning out." The advice was: "Lie yourself as low as possible."

A trivial matter? Not really. The language of television news and public affairs is generally correct, but television is a teacher, whether it intends to be or not. So, when a mistake is made, it may appear to millions to have been ratified. It is quickly picked up and widely used.

Television affects language also by what it does not do. The programs rest heavily on teamwork; the best language — by which I do not mean English that is inflated, obscure, and intended to impress and intimidate — usually comes from a single mind. Moreover, language needs time and space to make its effect. Television does not often provide them. It also tends to exclude the odd, the out-of-the-ordinary.

Perhaps it is as well that television provides no home for old-fashioned political oratory (although it does for evangelists) and that it has shortened the political speech. Still, many politicians, and businessmen, receive training in being comfortable before the cameras and in achieving the best, i.e., most sincere effect. The result? Similarity bordering on uniformity in manner and in language. In addition, television is a thing of snippets and of images, often compelling. Hence, the rise of "media advisers" and political commercials, with an accompanying reduction in the use of the candidate's own words and an increased use of words supplied by others.

Is television, then, to be condemned? Of course not. There would in any case be no purpose in condemning it. Television is part of the march of technology that is transforming our lives, and it does offer a form of education for those who would not read or write on their own.

There are also welcome signs that, apart from "The Story of English," television is beginning to understand that mass illiteracy and semi-literacy place the nation in peril. But sporadic bouts of conscience are not enough. Broadcasters owe the language more.

— *New York Times* (September 14, 1986, Sec. 2, pp. 27, 31)

SOME PRACTICE WITH A PUBLIC VOICE

1. Write a brief narrative of a personal experience or take one of your previous journal entries that narrate an experience. Rewrite the incident from an objective point of view and write a generalization that explains the meaning of this experience. How does this rewritten account take on a different voice? What kinds of changes were necessary?

2. Take an op-ed article from the *New York Times* or another newspaper and explain to what extent the author has adopted an effective public voice for this readership. Is there evidence of both private and public voices in the essay? Is the voice appropriate for its subject? Its intended audience? How would you evaluate its objectivity?

3. Examine the public voice in class of one of your instructors. What characteristics of this voice are determined by the requirements of the lecture or discussion format? To what extent does the subject of the class influence the kind of voice you observe? To what extent does a private voice also come through?

4. How would you describe the public voices of the prominent television network news anchor reporters? What characteristics do they appear to have in common? How successfully do they convey their credibility and authoritativeness to their audience? What do they do to accomplish this?

5. Obtain copies of *New York Magazine* and *The Progressive*. From analyzing the approach to the audiences of these magazines taken by several of the writers, would you say that the above excerpts by Bernice Kanner for *New York Magazine* and Carol Thurston and Barbara Doscher for *The Progressive*, indicate a similar assessment of reader tastes? How would you characterize the audiences of these publications?

Addressing the Public Audience of Your Essay on the Media.   Writing on the media to a specific audience of your school, community, or culture suggests that you have thought about the level of interest and the degree of understanding of your readers. There are many specific audiences for the media, and the public voice you choose for one may be inappropriate or confusing for another. In writing on the recent appearances of a rock group for a college audience, for example, you can assume that your readers will grasp your comparisons to other musical styles or performing techniques. If, however, your purpose is to explain this music to college or university faculty, your voice will adapt to this fact; you will make fewer assumptions about their knowledge and attempt to direct them to a different attitude toward music they may find strange or distasteful by means of reasoned explanation and examples. (See "Audience" sections in Chapter 3 and 4 on audience frame of reference and depth of information needs.)

Perhaps the most difficult decision to make with regard to addressing your audience is how much of your private voice should be expressed here. In other words, just where is the boundary between a personal and a public voice? Of course, there can be no precise dividing line, but you can generally assume that in an essay like this, your main objective is to explain some aspect of the media to your audience, perhaps to get them to see their own reading or viewing in a new, more satisfying or knowledgeable way. If you let your own strong feelings intrude too much, you direct your reader more to your emotions than to, say, what books of how-to advice for career women suggest about their success in the male-dominated business world.

A public voice usually means a moderate, objective, restrained approach to a subject; the writer possessing this voice shows a secure grasp of the topic, has generalized in a convincing way and provided sufficient specific examples as support for any generalizations. Expressions of irony, sarcasm, enthusiasm, disdain, even anger are not out of place, but they should be justified by the subject matter and supported by the examples you offer as evidence for these emotions. After all, everyone has strong opinions on the media; we certainly would not want it otherwise. Let your own understanding of your audience determine just how this public voice is to be adapted to the topic you choose. Answering the questions of the "Audience Analysis Guide" may help you in shaping your essay for your reader.

———————— AUDIENCE ANALYSIS GUIDE ————————

1. To what public audience have I chosen to address my essay on the media?
2. What is the frame of reference of this audience?
3. What point of view is my audience likely to have on my subject?
4. How do my own frame of reference and point of view differ from those of my reader?
5. How can I bridge any gap that exists between my reader's point of view and my own?

SOME PRACTICE WITH ADDRESSING THE PUBLIC AUDIENCE FOR YOUR MEDIA ESSAY

1. For your audience for this task, select a large group of readers from the general public that will be interested in your generalization about your media experiences. This group may be one that is formed through your imagination, or you may want to address the readership of a particular publication.

2. Give shape to this group in your mind by analyzing its frame of reference and depth of information needs.

3. Answer the remaining questions of the "Audience Analysis Guide" on point of view, contrasts between your frame of reference and theirs, and how you can bridge any gap that exists between your point of view and that of your reader.

4. In your journal, experiment with the mixture of public and private voices you want to use in writing to this audience. If writing for the readership of a

publication, experiment in your journal with imitating the voice of one or more of the writers published there.

Arranging Your Essay

The Shaping Idea. As you begin to write, you may by now have a small collection of notes detailing the media experiences you wish to describe and the generalizations that follow from them. These generalizations in turn form parts of one larger general statement, some overall pattern of significance that you derive from your reading or viewing encounters with the media. This theme — your shaping idea — might run through a series of TV dramas or a group of articles on the technological future you found in popular science magazines. Whatever the source, your purpose is to show how these materials embody this theme — both as examples and as narrower, more specific generalizations.

Your shaping idea might be, for example, that workplace shows — dramas, like "In the Heat of the Night," and comedies, like "Murphy Brown" and "Cheers" — have some of the most finely drawn characterizations on television. Episodes from each show might form your examples and lead to a specific generalization for that program. Or, as a further example, you might find that a group of articles on the future of technology do not take into account any of the social or economic changes that could affect the use of technology in the future; you may have examples of how society and the economy will affect technology and may make generalizations for each of these forces. Your shaping idea in either case will provide a manageable pattern with which to contain your examples and the generalizations about them that you wish to make.

Although we discuss the shaping idea first, you may not be certain what shaping idea will emerge from the generalizations and examples that you have put together until you actually begin writing. Often writers do not really know what they want to say until they begin to see a larger pattern form from the sequence of generalizations and examples that they set in motion. You might look over your observations and ideas for the dominant idea or ideas that were most important to you. After examining these for awhile, you will most likely see the direction in which you want to go.

Arranging Your Generalizations and Narrative Examples. As you write down the results of your media research, you are faced with some of the same questions facing any other researcher engaged in the writing process: "What comes first? How much space do I give to each example? In what order should I place my examples?" The answers to such questions cannot be given as rules or formulas. They really follow directly from your own research materials, the generalizations, and narrative examples you wish to offer your audience. As possible models, you might examine the media essays that follow to see how the authors arranged their generalizations and narrative examples into a coherent pattern of meaning. Answering the questions at the end of each essay may assist you in understanding how you can use it as a model in writing your own paper on the media.

Teenage Films:
Love, Death, and the Prom
by Alice McDermott

New York Times/August 16, 1987

Before I became a teenager in the mid-60s, my clearest vision of what it would be like to be one was taken from the movies, and while I thought Andy Hardy adorable and Annette and Frankie clearly self-satisfied, the one image that seemed to me to define what life then would entail was the final scene in "West Side Story," where the dying Tony sang with the tear-filled Maria "There's a Place for Us."

The message, of course, was that there wasn't. Or that the place for them was only the tragic dark night of the deserted schoolyard. The message was one that loomed over the ordinary threats of adolescence: that your body might grow, or might not stop growing where and when you wanted it to, that you'd wear the wrong clothes and make the wrong friends and screw up the parallel park on your driver's test. It was the larger threat that you would not make it through adolescence at all—that it would kill you.

And it was not Tony's last breath on the hard asphalt alone that fostered this image. For those of us of that pre-video cassette generation who learned our teenage movie history from late-night television, the two teenage deaths in *Rebel Without a Cause* assured us that high school would indeed be a mine field of desperate, startling emotion and random violence. It showed us how the simple teenage dilemmas that Gidget and Tammy handled with such aplomb might also lead any one of us to the same senseless end that came to Sal Mineo, who died, the picture seemed to say, only because he had been young and afraid and—we sensed the possibility ourselves—unloved.

These were serious matters. But in their seriousness, they were as much a part of the teenage fantasy as any of the beach party movies' endless summers. Andy Hardy's shows in the barn, or even the triumph of true love and rock-and-roll over parental prejudice and the merengue in . . . *Dirty Dancing*; for surely among the standard teenage daydreams—of wealth and popularity, of triumph and revenge—reigns the dream of strict attention, of being taken seriously by the rest of the world. Given the shower rooms, the nerds, the adventures in baby-sitting, the days off and risky business that have inspired this decade's movies about teenagers, it seemed, at least until the recent *River's Edge*, to be a dream abandoned by the makers of contemporary films about adolescents.

By the time I actually approached my teens, the melodrama or merry empty-headedness of those earlier films about teenagers had begun to be re-placed by what seemed a new realism. During those years, movies like *To Sir With Love* and *Up the Down Staircase* did nothing to alleviate my sense of high school as a tough and dangerous place (my own experience at genteel Sacred Heart Academy on Long Island notwithstanding). They did, however, offer an adult figure who seemed to understand, or at least to suffer with, the angry students. The teachers portrayed in those films by Sidney Poitier and Sandy Dennis seemed to offer to their students the possibility that there could be a chink in the isolation. The deserted schoolyard was still the place for us, but, they seemed to say, it was possible for someone to know you were there. Other films about teenagers offered a similar solace but in a different way. Both *Summer of '42* and *The Heart Is a Lonely Hunter* dwelled in fond detail on the ordinary difficulties of teenage life, first dates and obnoxious younger brothers, the longing to be popular and the urgent need to be un-burdened of your virginity, but they placed these small and mostly comic adolescent struggles into stories that also dealt with the death of a young husband in war, or the desperate isolation of the deaf mute.

The effect for us was startling. For rather than trivialize what we recognized as our own adolescent dilemmas, or reinforce our isolation in them by re-minding us that adults had larger concerns, these films showed us that our all-too-familiar problems existed in a world of adult sorrow that was no less unfair, no less angering than our own.

In my third year of high school, a story went around about a film that had just been released. It was 1970 and films about teenagers were scarce. We'd had Zeffirelli's *Romeo and Juliet* (another reminder of the tragic possibilities of young love which our parents and teachers urged us to see for the Shake-speare and which we returned to for the nude scenes), and an outlandish futuristic piece about our belligerence called *Wild in the Streets*, but for the most part teenagers by then had been abandoned as a subject for film.

Perhaps it was because we were getting enough air time on the evening news, or because we were changing our music and hair length and skirt length too rapidly to keep any film about us from becoming dated before its final cut. Or perhaps it was that the idea of teenagers dying simply because they were teenagers was no longer a dramatic fantasy but an uncomfortable fact. Whatever the reason, we had yet to see ourselves or our times portrayed in film.

The movie we were talking about that year was not about teenagers per se, but the story we first told about it had, we thought, everything to do with us.

It was the first Saturday night the film had been shown in our area, the story went, and when it ended and the lights went on, not one member of the audience got up to leave. No one spoke or even applauded. Not one person in that audience of Saturday night dates moved a muscle. And then, down in front, one boy stood, slowly, and raised a fist into the air. "Oh, God," he bellowed. "Oh, God!" He slumped back into his seat. There was some sporadic applause, some weeping. Slowly, quietly, the audience left the theater.

The movie was *Easy Rider*, and the story no doubt was as much a fable as the film itself, yet we repeated it eagerly, reminded by both the film and the story we told about it that we were the most vulnerable victims of a dangerous age: that nothing less than our lives was at stake.

The movies about teenagers that followed this era made some use of that threat. In *American Graffiti*, a 1973 movie about high school students in the 60s, it lent a subtle significance to the characters' debate over going to "J.C." or college in the East and gave the film's comedy a sharp edge: we knew even before we were told what the future of each male character would be (a writer in Canada, missing in action, killed by a drunk driver) that this long night would be the end of something more significant than their high school years. That in 1962 a young man who dreamed of going to Washington to work for President Kennedy was being delivered into a world far more dangerous that he could ever, at that moment in his youth, even imagine.

But *American Graffiti* and *The Last Picture Show* demonstrated then that films about teenagers did not have to be tragic to be serious or simpleminded to be funny. Later, *Breaking Away* proved they did not have to be cloaked in nostalgia either. *Saturday Night Fever* further showed that it was possible to make a movie about contemporary teenagers that had serious moments and comic moments and a beat you could dance to.

The genre seemed to have lost its boundaries. Films about teenagers could involve anything, could appeal to anyone. And yet, without melodrama, without the context of adult pain, without compromising their humor, they could also continue to demonstrate, as the best of their predecessors had done, the true and important emotions at the heart of a teenager's concerns. They could discover what sense of the dark night in the deserted schoolyard lingered in us all.

When I was young, I planned my weeks around what movie was on, when and where or what channel and how I could skip school or get out of the house to catch it. I'm not that kind of moviegoer anymore. Still, I've seen a fair selection of this decade's flood of films about teenagers, the raunchy comedies like *Porky's* and *Risky Business* and *Revenge of the Nerds*, John Hughes's sweet romances, the controversial *River's Edge*. Many of them are updated versions of the fantasy films of the 50s; some, like *Racing with the Moon*, are more thoughtful; all are marked by an exactness of detail, a faithfulness to the dress and language and looks of their subjects that can make the realism of the past seem as sweet and foggy as a Doris Day close-up.

Yet, for all their accurate reproduction of the way teenagers look and talk, for all their awareness of the quality of certain teenage daydreams (Your parents are away on vacation, you're alone in the house with a beautiful whore . . .), these films for the most part steer clear of that other teenage fantasy so exploited in the past: the fantasy of strict attention, of being taken with utter seriousness by a larger world.

There is never any sense that the emotions of the characters in these films surpass the immediate object of their desire or the brief circumstances of their young lives. That anything more than what they are certain they want is at stake.

In *Rebel Without a Cause*, the gang leader who challenges the James Dean character to a chicken race tells him just before the race begins, "I like you." "Then why are we doing this?" Dean asks. The leader shrugs and holds out his arms, "Got to do something."

Had he been a character in any one of a number of recent movies, had he been a character in *The Breakfast Club* for instance, he would have said, "Because of my parents."

Without a context, without a sense of the world beyond themselves, the characters in many of these contemporary teenage movies must lay all blame for their unhappiness, for the nameless rage that teenagers, and so many movies about them, have always dealt with, on their parents alone.

There is no universal condition, the pampered and pouty children in *The Breakfast Club* seem to say, there is only my condition, and my condition is the direct result of my rich/driving/brutish parents. What the movie builds to, then, cannot be cathartic. The teenagers don't come to see their difficulties as only a part of the same difficulties that plague most adults, or as the seeds of something that may indeed change, even cost them, their lives—they come only to see themselves in one another and leave the experience portrayed in the film with nothing more than a smug glimpse of their own reflections.

The place for us, the dark night of the deserted schoolyard, is well populated and so as far as we're concerned (and who else matters?) the only place to be.

The recent *River's Edge* would seem to illustrate just what this kind of teenage myopia can lead to. In the film, a slack-mouthed, beer-guzzling high school boy strangles his girl and then invites his friends, who were also her friends, to come to the river to view her nude body. The friends move around her (or more precisely it) like Neanderthals. They poke her flesh, laugh nervously, feel kind of creepy. One of the boys rallies the others to help protect the murderer. The girls vaguely consider calling the police. A few of them wonder, briefly, why they don't feel anything.

The death of a teenager, once the greatest tragedy a film about teenagers could offer, the saddest fulfillment of their most stirring fantasy, has become in the 80s one with everything else. The world view of these dulled products of divorce and drugs and day care has so narrowed that as long as they themselves are alive no other death matters—a frightening culmination of the entire teenage genre if, for a minute, any of it seemed true. But it doesn't.

For despite the accuracy of its detail (the teenagers look like teenagers, their language is the language you'll hear in any shopping mall, the body stiffens and draws flies as it should), the world in which the events of this movie take place is a false front. The dead girl's parents are never seen grieving at her funeral; the teenagers are not only unaffected by the murder, they are equally nonplused when a friend's father lifts a shotgun and blows out the living room window they have just tapped on; two ten-year-olds with murder as their goal tool around town in a huge car, their eyebrows just clearing the dashboard; the hermit drug dealer who puts a pistol to the head of anyone who knocks on his door gets a newspaper delivered (some paper boy!).

With this unbelievable world as a backdrop, the events of the movie are not tragic and horrifying, they are merely made up. The film becomes a fantasy of the worst kind; one that lies about the reality it pretends to reveal, that can make no distinction between what is real (the story is based on an actual incident) and what is true.

And it is this very distinction and so many current film makers' failure to see it that plagues this decade's movies about teenagers, where the precision with which their imitation characters are portrayed is time and again mistaken for the truth about their lives. Where the surface of a teenager's complex world is mistaken for its substance.

It is difficult to determine why this has occurred. It could be argued that teenagers today are only getting what they ask for, that the rate at which they consume these films is proof enough that they want no more from them, or that they are incapable of distinguishing anything they get; but the popularity of all these similar movies might also indicate a greater hunger: it's just as likely that teenagers go from one movie to the next looking for something they have not yet seen rather than to see the same thing repeated.

Some of Hollywood's, and this country's, own attitudes about youth, might be better taken into account. It is significant that many of the kindest, most thoughtful films about teenagers that have appeared in this decade are not about contemporary teenagers at all but about teenagers as they used to be. *Racing with the Moon*, *The Outsiders*, *Stand by Me*, and . . . *Dirty Dancing* all turn an affectionate eye on teenagers of another time and are among the few current films that treat their subjects with some seriousness. Perhaps this is because these film makers remember that some seriousness was what they most desired when they were teenagers in that time. Perhaps other film makers need to give the teenagers of this time as much credit.

Twenty years ago I was just beginning my life as a teenager, and in twenty more I'll just be over my time as the parent of one. What the movies told me about those years between thirteen and twenty was of very little use once I got there, and I doubt that they'll offer much practical help to my son. But still I like to think that there will be films then that will show him that his defeats are tragic, that his triumphs rock the universe; films that will make him both laugh at himself and shake his head sadly as he realizes it is all too true, there is no place for us, no place at all—even as he leaves the theater and makes his way home.

1. What generalization forms the shaping idea of this essay? Where does it appear? Why has McDermott placed it here?

2. What narrower generalizations does the writer use? How does she organize these generalizations into an overall pattern?

3. What examples does McDermott include to support these generalizations? Which examples would you consider stories? Which are merely details? Why

has she chosen to include stories about some films and give only details about others?

4. Explain the writer's distinction between "real" and "truthful." Do you agree with her analysis of these films? What other films might exemplify her point or, conversely, negate it?

5. Likewise, can you think of other films that either support or refute her point that teenagers today blame their parents and therefore cut themselves off from the adult world?

6. Who is McDermott's reader? Why does she think it important to explain this subject to this reader? How objective and convincing is her explanation?

Triumph of the Wheel

by Lewis Grossberger

Rolling Stone/December 4, 1986

The first time I saw "Wheel of Fortune," I thought it was a vapid piece of fluff that could appeal only to brain-dead TV zombies. Five minutes of this tedious dreck was all it took to waft me sleepward.

But the second time my reaction was different. The second time I realized—having been assigned meantime to write an article on the show that would bring a much-needed fee—that "Wheel of Fortune" was, in fact, a fascinating, deeply significant national phenomenon, the comprehension of which was essential to any proper understanding of our era.

Thank God I'm open-minded.

Soon I was wafting westward on an urgent sociophilosophical inquiry, clutching an envelope fat with press clippings that further impressed upon me the importance of my subject. The *Washington Post*'s TV critic said, "Wheel" is watched by 42 million people a day. *Time* said "Wheel" is the highest-rated syndicated series in television history. The *New York Times* said "Wheel" is so popular it has become a dominant factor in TV scheduling, sometimes wreaking havoc with local and network news. *People* said that Vanna White has blond hair, weighs 107, measures thirty-six—twenty-three—thirty three, and adores greasy hamburgers from White Castle.

Vanna White is the hostess on "Wheel of Fortune," which should not be confused with the master of ceremonies, who is Pat Sajak, although he is not called the MC but the host. Despite the fact that Vanna's function is mainly decorative and that she is rarely permitted to utter more than a parting "bye," she has become, *People* assured me, a bigger cult sensation that Paul Shaffer, Max Headroom, or even Willard Scott.

The only thing the press failed to tell me was *why*.

Why a silly game show based on a simple children's spelling game and a cheesy carnival wheel so captivates the mightiest nation on earth. Now here was a journalistic challenge worthy of Murrow, of Woodward and Bernstein, perhaps even of the great Geraldo Rivera. Immune to the show's mysterious allure, I could operate with scientific detachment. By God, I would take up the gauntlet. I would find out why—or doze off trying.

"I swear on the grave of every game-show host who ever lived that I have no idea," said Pat Sajak.

Pat Sajak is overqualified for his job in that he is capable of wit. A former TV weatherman, he sounds a little like Bob Newhart and looks like . . . well, if Dick Clark went through that teleportation gizmo from *The Fly* and this time a chipmunk sneaked in, out would come Pat Sajak.

I talked with Pat Sajak in his dressing room and found him a personable and modest man who readily admits that game-show hosting "is kind of a dopey way to make a living." I talked as rapidly as possible. When I arrived at the NBC studios in fabled Burbank, the publicity lady who collected me said that the staff would be taping five half-hour shows that night and that I could examine Pat and Vanna only during the fifteen-to-twenty-minute breaks between shows. She was very apologetic, but, you know, everyone wants them, it's so exhausting, we have to protect them. I groused a bit—journalistic reflex—but, it truth, it didn't matter. Both host and hostess had been asked to explain the *why* before. They never could.

"I mean, I know why it's successful," said Pat. "It's an easy game to play—you know, the people at home, unless you're a total moron, can generally solve the puzzles ahead of the people in the studio, so you feel kind of superior. It's a compelling game. You walk by the set and the puzzle's on and you tend to play along. But that just explains why it's a successful game show. Why it has gone beyond success to become—I don't know—part of the pop culture, I haven't the foggiest idea. I don't think anyone knows."

I assured him that I would know. Soon. For that was my quest. My Grail. He responded politely enough, but I could see he was skeptical. It seemed like we'd been talking only a few minutes when a pounding on the door commenced, and a voice demanded Pat's presence, and he went forth to hostify.

The "Wheel of Fortune" set looks like that of most eighties game shows, decorated in feel-good Vegas. Gaudy with the bright splashes of color, flashing lights, and revolving mounds of, as the announcer usually describes them, "fantastic prizes, fabulous and exciting merchandise." The studio and audience of close to two hundred well-behaved androids was stashed safely out of the way behind a sideline array of cameras, electronic gear, crew, and staff. As the taping began, I noticed that the rousing "Wheel . . . of . . . Fortune!" chant that kicks off each show is canned, and that the gold curtain Vanna White waltzes through so fetchingly when introduced has no other function whatever. It drops magically from the ceiling for her big entrance, then quickly reascends.

The actual gaming consists of a word puzzle and, naturally, a wheel. Large, multicolored, divided into slim wedges, each marked with a different dollar amount, the wheel is set horizontally in front of the three contestants, so they can lean forward and spin it. By doing so, they may accumulate a dollar account to be later spent on prizes.

Between twirls, they take whacks at the word puzzle, which is basically that old childhood chestnut, hangman. The puzzle is mounted on a big vertical display board on a platform that's hauled on and off the set by crewmen at alarming speeds, usually with the courageous Vanna aboard. A display of blank tiles tells the contestants how many words and letters there are in a mystery phrase. As the contestants guess at the letters and Vanna rushes purposefully about, uncovering those correctly called out, the mystery phrase (usually something as banal as "walking on air" or "curiosity killed the cat") gradually emerges until someone identifies it. The winner then may go shopping among the price-tagged prizes until his or her account is exhausted. At the end of the proceedings, the champion tackles a bonus-round puzzle for a grand prize.

Viewed at home, the whole ephemeral affair slips by in a smooth, slick, seamless blur, leaving no shadow or aftertaste. Conditioned as I was to somnolence, it was all I could do to stay alert. Fortunately, I was allowed to roam.

I watched one show from the control room, where the personnel debated whether a contestant on an earlier show got a fair shake when he correctly guessed "the patience of Job" but was disqualified for mispronouncing "Job." Then I spied on the letter lighters, two staffers who sit backstage and illuminate the tiles that show Vanna what to flip. A serene crewman named Vern pressed buttons, and a serious young research coordinator named Cheryl indicated which buttons. Over Vern's control board were crayoned the words WHEEL OF TORTURE.

"They all use the same letters," said Vern, indicating a contestant. "Watch, she'll say *t*." He was right.

During one break I was taken to meet the hostess. Vanna was in her dressing room, snacking from a take-out dish and wearing a snappy off-the-shoulder number. (She changes costume and hairdo for each show.) She was very energetic and cheerful and was able to maintain, under close interrogation, not only that Vanna White was her real name but also that she had known four other Vannas while growing up in South Carolina.

A small-town girl, Vanna, who is now twenty-nine, drove to Hollywood in a U-Haul truck six years ago, because it was a childhood dream. Hollywood, not trucks. After landing some bit parts in movies, she heard that "Wheel of Fortune" needed a new hostess, and she beat out two hundred other young women, even though in her final on-air audition she was so nervous her knees shook and she couldn't talk. Fortunately, speech was not a job qualification.

Laboring under the cloud of bimbosity imposed by the alternately fawning and smirking media, Vanna told me what she always tells interviewers: "It's a lot harder than it looks. It really is."

It seemed to me the wrong tactic. Were I her media adviser, I'd counsel this approach, "Hey, I look great, I walk sexy. For this they pay me a hundred big ones and put me on the cover of *People*. I should turn them down? Is it my fault I live in a society that accentuates superficial values?"

Too soon came the inevitable pounding, and Vanna vanished, leaving me back on the set, watching a woman named Ruth win a Toyota by guessing

"League of Women Voters." I talked to a contestant from Fresno named Bill. Bill told me that his family watches "Wheel of Fortune" all the time and that he was so good at it his wife got after him to become a contestant. He did. But he hadn't won a Toyota, and he seemed a little tense.

I was not to meet "Wheel's" biggest winner. Who is that? Why, Merv Griffin. Yes, the same Merv Griffin who has spent the last twenty-three years demonstrating what Johnny Carson would be like without jokes. Merv always did seem a bit dazed, as though his mind were on something else. Now we know what. Puzzles. It was Merv who invented "Wheel of Fortune," hired Pat Sajak and Vanna White, and still approves every single puzzle. It was Merv who recently sold Merv Griffin Enterprises, which produces "Wheel" (not to mention "Jeopardy" and "Dance Fever") to Coca-Cola for—my fingers go numb as I type this—a reported $250 million. According to Tom Shales, TV critic for *The Washington Post*, Merv was rumored to have run around his office waving his quarter-of-a-billion-dollar check in the air, joking that he couldn't find anyone to cash it.

Puzzles. All this from puzzles. The man is a lifelong puzzle junkie. "You would think," said Sajak, "that a man who's worth $84 billion, or whatever he is, would have better things to do than make up puzzles—but he does. If you have lunch with Merv, the waiter comes over and says, 'May I take your order?' and Merv goes, 'Ooo! "May I take your order?" What a great puzzle!' And he writes it down."

People, we underestimated Merv Griffin. We dismissed him as some kind of welfare agency for the Gabor sisters. But Merv figured out what America wanted, and he provided it. And became very, very rich. Much too rich to talk to the likes of me. But Nancy Jones, "Wheel's" producer, a woman who actually has puzzle meetings with Merv, did. Her take on *why* was family. "It's a show the whole family can enjoy. Anybody from six to a hundred can watch 'Wheel.'" Interesting, I thought, but not convincing. Not incisively all-encompassing. After all, there are plenty of family shows that don't have 42 million viewers.

If stats like 42 million or a quarter of a billion haven't sufficiently defined the scope of "Wheel's" triumph for you, surely Pat Sajak's parking spot will. It was one away from Johnny Carson's. Now *that's* success. I discovered this when Pat gave me a lift back to my hotel, a nice gesture. But he voiced a depressing vision. "This could literally be a show that is never canceled," he said. "You know, my grandkid will be up there, spinning the wheel, saying silly things and putting on hair spray."

Considerably sobered, I retired and the next morning flew away. I'd already spent an evening on this investigation—in my view more than enough. En route to the airport, a chatty cabby pointed out an evocative sight: a new, exclusive real-estate development on a hill where, he said, the houses start at $1 million. The hill had previously served as a garbage dump, and the driver indicated a pumping station built to clear away the methane gas constantly seeping forth. So scarce is land in L.A. there had been no problem finding wealthy people to reside on top of Old Stinky.

Soon afterward I was on the plane thinking about "Wheel of Fortune," which, as always, acted as a soporific. I dreamed of the lovely Vanna. She's in a terrific gold lamé jump suit, and she's starring in a big-budget disaster movie (a silent, oddly) about a gassy mountain threatening to explode and bury a nervous populace neck deep in putrid lava. Desperately trying to avert panic, Mayor Merv announces that the mountain, with its shining edifices concealing a rotten nether world, is merely a metaphor for an overly materialistic society, but then he whispers to me that only I can save the day—if I can complete this common everyday phrase:

V-C-R---THR-LLS

Then Pat Sajak's grandkid spins the wheel. The pointer falls on BANKRUPT, and Swill Hill erupts, burying me neck deep in lethal sludge. I woke high over the Jersey swamps, and I had the answer. I knew *why*.

Start with the game show revival. Game shows have been with us since the days of old-time radio. When TV arrived in the late forties, they proved easily adaptable to the new medium, taking various forms. There were celebrity-panel shows like "What's My Line" and "I've Got a Secret!" humiliation shows like "Truth or Consequences," and oddities like "You Bet Your Life," on which Groucho Marx posed the classic consolation-prize question "Who's buried in Grant's Tomb?"

Then arose the big-money quiz show, a world unto itself. Programs like "The $64,000 Question" and "Twenty-One" became phenomenal hits, and contestants like Charles Van Doren, a handsome young Columbia University professor, became national heroes. Even before the scandal broke, it was one of the strangest episodes in TV history. Imagine millions of Americans riveted by the spectacle of brain athletes struggling with impossible multipart questions whose answers not one viewer in a million had a clue to. (A student then, I always suspected that the secret appeal was the joy of watching someone else sweat out a vicious final exam from which you were exempt.)

When the news came in 1958 that some of the winners had been fed answers, a gullible nation reeled. Careers were destroyed, innocence was lost, legislation was passed to ensure that such a tragedy could never again be visited upon our land. And game shows disappeared. Temporarily. In television, nothing successful ever dies. Producers like game shows because they're cheap. There's one set and a few performers; you can tape a week's worth of shows in a day; and many of the prizes are donated by manufacturers. Sponsors have to love game shows, too. Their products in the commercials blend right into the endless parade of prizes.

By the sixties, game shows were back, though largely confined to the nine-to-twelve morning ghetto, with more modest prizes and a party atmosphere of easygoing fun. And now it's the eighties and the game show is king. Why? Just look to your politico-economic Big Picture.

As in the fifties, a conservative Republican is ensconced in the White House, and the nation prospers. But it's a nervous prosperity. The economy is stagnant, and there's a whiff of trouble ahead with our national debt ballooning, farms in crisis, banks at the mercy of tottering banana republics, our

industry looking anemic and backward compared to Japan's, and droves of
nomads roaming the streets. Lots of families are doing well (with two people
working), but many middle classers and blue collars are having trouble making ends meet. Those who have wealth are encouraged to flaunt it. Consuming runs amok. Yuppies graze. The media fling the rich and famous in your
face. The unrelenting message is that if you haven't made it big, you're a
schmuck. Increasingly, the American dream seems to coalesce into a narrow
vision of mere wealth. And people seem willing to do anything for it: wheel
and deal, rig stocks, sell national secrets, peddle crack, anything to score. So
what's a poor would-be entrepreneur to do who hasn't the guts or opportunity for any of that? Well, he can turn to the little man's last resorts — lotteries
and sweepstakes (bigger than *ever*), the track, the numbers, Vegas, Atlantic
City, and . . . on a fantasy level, game shows.

Game shows are part of the wish-fulfillment machine that helps left-out
Americans maintain the hope that anyone can hit it big, even if he has no
navy codes to sell the Russians. But of all the game shows, why "Wheel of
Fortune"? It gives away no cash. Its prizes are no more opulent than those
of other shows. It lacks gunshots and nudity.

"Wheel of Fortune" has been on the air since 1975. With Chuck Woolery
(whom Sajak replaced in 1981) as host, "Wheel" became a fixture on NBC's
morning schedule and eventually television's highest-rated syndicated game
show. It was the only one at the network to escape the ax when the legend-
ary Fred Silverman became convinced that game shows were dead.

In the fall of eighty-three, "Wheel's" producers decided to spin off a syndicated nighttime version. It was a momentous decision. Syndicated shows are
sold directly to local stations by independent distributors. This is attractive to
station owners, who get to keep a bigger chunk of advertising revenue than
they do from network shows. The new "Wheel" was aimed at the so-called
prime-access slot. That's the hour before prime time, which the FCC requires
to be set aside for nonnetwork programming, believing, in its charmingly
idiotic way, that this will stimulate diversity.

When the nightime "Wheel of Fortune" debuted, the slot was occupied by
magazine shows like "Entertainment Tonight" and "PM Magazine." The conventional wisdom was that only older women — not the bigger-spending eigh-
teen-to-forty-five mixed audience advertisers drool for — watched gamers. But
"Wheel" took off. Soon it was on 163 stations, in many cities twice a day. It
was huge.

Obviously, night gave "Wheel" bigger audience potential than day had.
More sets are on at night. (Daytime "Wheel" pulls a measly 8 million faces.)
But night alone doesn't explain the show's hegemony. What does explain it
is the subtle but powerful wonder ingredient all successful game shows have,
but none so purely as "Wheel of Fortune." It starts with a V, like Vanna. It's
called Vicariousness.

Vicariousness. "Wheel of Fortune" creates the illusion for the hard-work-
ing, treadmill-trotting Middle American yearner (the show's greatest strength
is outside the major media markets) that he or she is in the big game. Viewers don't exactly identify with the contestants; they *become* the contestants.

Look at the elements of the show.

The Players: Unlike the dramatized big names of the fifties, "Wheel" contestants are ordinary folk who serve as the viewers' surrogates. In the whoopee-cushion seventies, game-show contestants screamed, bounced, and wet themselves, but in the we-mean-business eighties, Americans are cooler and less likely to appear in public dressed as yams. "Wheel" subtly de-emphasizes its contestants, who seem interchangeable. Pat introduces these undemonstrative, low-profile types with the briefest possible questioning, then the camera quickly moves off them and zooms in on the game. With the contestants relegated to the background, the viewer can put himself in their place and play. And when a winner goes prize picking, we see only a small head shot in a corner of the screen; the main focus is on the merchandise. Even if undefeated, a contestant is booted out after three days. No stars are born here. (Which is why there's no chance "Wheel of Fortune" is rigged—the producers don't care who wins.) In your fantasy, you are the star.

The Game: Both games promise easy success, one through luck, the other skill. The wheel—hypnotic, alluring, symbolic of nearly everything—is luckier than a roulette wheel, since it can yield only two bad outcomes: BANKRUPT or LOSE A TURN. Any other spin wins. Nice odds. The word puzzle is simple but compelling—it gets easier as you play, because more letters fill in. (No Gloomy Gus, Merv discarded the morbid scoring system of the original hangman, which utilizes a stick figure dangling from a gallows. Like casino owners, game-show proprietors want you to be cheery.) As Pat Sajak noted, viewers often solve the puzzle before contestants. With the whole family watching, someone at home is almost bound to. The result: You feel happy, excited, superior. You're chalking up wins. You're on a roll.

The Payoff: During play, the wheel-whirling contestants (and, by extension, the viewers) are given credit. A nice touch. Who doesn't love credit? It's like betting on someone else's tab. And when you win, you don't win mere cash or some preordained prize. You go *shopping!* A brilliant touch. Shopping may be the ultimate thrill in this commodity-crazed era, an actual addiction for some. And it doesn't hurt "Wheel," in the yuppie department, either. Merv himself once said, "It's like being let loose on Rodeo Drive." As the winner shops, the camera lovingly roves around the prize showcase, as though the viewer's own eyeballs have been let loose amid the VCRs, Isuzu pickups, Tahitian vacations, and ceramic Dalmatians. "Wheel's" ambiance blends the organized excitement of the casino with the primal pull of the department store.

The Cast: Game-show hosts are permitters and forgivers. Their benign presence signals that it's okay to indulge your greed, just in case some shred of conscience or old-fashioned values intrudes to make you feel guilty for craving wealth without work. Pat Sajak is today's kind of authority figure: casual, low-key, jocular, even a bit irreverent. Dignified and well dressed, he could be a yuppie cleric, lawyer, or doctor. He could switch jobs with Ronald Reagan and little would change. Merv has said Pat is like everyone's son-in-law. He must have meant everyone's *fantasy* son-in-law.

And Vanna? Pat Sajak likes to say that Vanna's silence gives her a mysterious air. But there isn't any mystery. Her personality shines through without benefit of speech. She's a *cheerleader.* Your own personal cheerleader. Her most vital function is not really her letter turning (artistic though it is) but her clapping! She is forever clapping for the contestants (all of them—Vanna is impartial). Despite her glitzy outfits, which sophisticates find tacky but most Americans probably find glamorous, she's a throwback to the kind of simple, sunny, apple-pie-sexy, all-American girl next door who'd be content to stay on the sidelines cheering for someone else. Vanna knows what she's doing, sort of. When I asked if she'd been a cheerleader in high school, she said, "Of course. Who would have *ever* thought I'd still be a cheerleader?"

And that's *why*. Now you know. Let me just add, before taking a well-deserved nap, that I doubt that Merv and his minions set out to design "Wheel of Fortune" around the Big V Principle or analyzed the economy. I think they just happened, by instinct, experience—and good luck—to hit on a formula that would make it the state-of-the-art eighties game show. A formula that sucks the viewer through the screen and into that dazzling dreamscape— Vanna's Nirvana—where he is transformed from a nullity, a hapless anonymous bozo, a nobody from nowhere, to the only being now worth being: a Winner. Someone possessed of wealth, luck, and, maybe more important, television exposure. Someone, in short, who finally exists. You know, a big wheel.

1. What is the shaping idea of this essay on "Wheel of Fortune"? What other generalizations does the writer include in support of his shaping idea? What is his overall pattern of organization?

2. What examples does the writer include? Which of his examples are stories and which are details? Why is each example included?

3. Why does Grossberger mention being sleepy throughout the essay? What role does his dream play in his analysis of the success of "Wheel of Fortune"?

4. What is the writer's point of view in the essay—toward the show, toward its hosts, toward its viewers? How would you characterize the writer's tone? Do you think his tone is appropriate for his subject?

5. Who is Grossberger's intended reader? How familiar does he assume the reader is with "Wheel of Fortune"? What relationship does he develop with his reader; for example, do you think his tone is appropriate for this reader?

6. What is Grossberger's analysis of the reasons why "Wheel of Fortune" is successful? Is his analysis convincing?

Now that you have studied these essays, you might have some idea how to arrange your own. Perhaps you have already decided on a cause-and-effect pattern of generalization and example. Or a pattern of narrative incidents that lead to a conclusion about a major theme in one of the media. Whatever the pattern you choose, it is the alternation of generalization and incident that will drive your essay forward and create the interest and significance you wish to convey to your audience.

Writing Your Rough Draft

It is now time to write your rough draft. Once you have completed it, take a break. Before you begin to think about rewriting, look at the following essay written by another student in response to this chapter's task:

HORRORS

The evolution of horror films certainly doesn't compare to the wondrous and lengthy evolution of humankind. In fact, horror films might merely be a reflection of the twentieth century's ever-changing morals, values, and fears. Indeed, horror films have certainly changed over the years; however, whether yesteryear's horror films are better than today's is as arguable as stating that modern humans are better than their ancestors. Do we not commit the same atrocities (rape, thievery, murder) that our ancestors did?

The year 1931 marked the coming age of the horror genre. Although there had previously been scattered examples of films that dramatized the horrible and the grotesque, the horror film did not flourish until the high-budgeted Frankenstein, based loosely on Mary Shelley's novel, was released by Universal amid tremendous fanfare.

Audience reaction proved so favorable that the major Hollywood studios (chiefly RKO and Universal) loosely adapated many other classic horror novels and certain legends to the silver screen in films such as Dr. Jekyll and Mr. Hyde (with Spencer Tracy as Robert Louis Stevenson's schizoid novel creation); Dracula (with Bela Lugosi as the irrespressible count of Bram Stoker's novel); Island of the Lost Souls (with Charles Laughton in this adaptation of H. G. Wells's novel); The Mummy (Karloff in tape); The Invisible Man (with Claude Rains); The Wolf Man (with Lon

Chaney, Jr.); and <u>King Kong</u>. Not only was this new genre very successful, but it spawned a plethora of new stars who would become known as "horror stars" (such as Karloff, Lugosi, and Chaney, Jr.).

Curiously, Dracula, Frankenstein, and other assorted monsters achieved a weird kind of commercial immortality with their sudden success. It was necessary to resurrect them, no matter how thoroughly they had been killed off in the preceding film. They returned as themselves or as "sons," "daughters," and "ghosts" in such films as <u>Son of Kong</u>, <u>The Invisible Man Returns</u>, <u>The Mummy's Ghost</u>, and <u>The Bride of Frankenstein</u>.

However, there's a limit to human invention, if not human credulity. Horror films came out with the regularity of a monthly magazine. By the mid-1940s, Hollywood had gorged the public past horror satiety. In a desperate attempt to rejuvenate horror's sagging box office, Hollywood united horror filmdom's monsters (<u>Frankenstein Meets the Wolf-Man</u>), a move that slowed down the erosion of box-office dollars but didn't stop it. Feeling that the imaginary horror of a film couldn't possibly compete with the true horror tales of Nazism and World War II circulating in the United States, Hollywood lamely blamed World War II for the continuing plummet of horror's box-office popularity. Finally, horror expired in self-parody as it was exploited for cheap laughs: <u>Abbott and Costello Meet Frankenstein</u>, <u>The Dead End Kids Meet the Spook</u>, and so on. Ironically, a genre in which death was a constant staple had died the most unkind of deaths itself by 1945.

In 1952, like a Phoenix rising from its own ashes, the horror genre entered its second cycle, but it took on a vastly different appearance. With the major studios generally abandoning horror, the small, independent film companies (ranging from the fairly big American International Pictures to the ultracheap Astor) became the most consistent suppliers of horror films. These independents specialized in making quick, contemporary horror films, all of which had assured profit potential because of minuscule budgets and sensationalized advertising. Indeed, AIP, in many cases, just made up an advertising campaign, and if they liked the campaign's look, they would make the film in three to six days.

From old myths of vampires, werewolves, and inhuman monsters, the horror genre veered into new angles as it married with science fiction in such films as I Married a Monster from Outer Space, It Conquered the World, and The Incredibly Strange Creatures Who Stopped Living and Became Mixed-Up Zombies. If one replaces the words monster, zombie, and it with Communist and the words outer space with Russia in the preceding film titles, it becomes evident that with these films, the independent shrewdly exploited the prevalent fear in the United States of being "taken over" by subversives.

The public's fear of imminent nuclear disaster was also skillfully exploited. Thus were born the "atomic age monsters," who were either normal living organisms turned into mutants by incessant human dabbling in the atomic field (Colossal Man, Attack of the Crab Monsters) or supposedly extinct dinosaurs unleashed from their "dormancy" deep below the oceans or ice caps because of atomic testing (The Beast from 20,000 Fathoms). The independents also keenly sensed that with the advent of fast cars and rock 'n' roll, the mood of their basically youthful audience was shifting. Thus began the recycling of old horror monsters into romantic villains (I Was a Teen-Age Werewolf, I Was a Teen-Age Frankenstein)--misunderstood and inarticulate but sympathetic to the underdogs (i.e., the young audience) and irritants to authority (i.e., the establishment).

It was during this reincarnation of "old-time" monsters that the genre was ushered into its third cycle as it looked on its old saviors to return it to the prosperity that it had once tasted. In 1958, Hammer Films, a small, fledgling independent film company, released Horror of Dracula (with Christopher Lee and Peter Cushing). It was essentially a remake of the 1932 Dracula with an authentic gothic look (which became a Hammer trademark). Buoyed by the film's enormous success, Hammer recycled other horror films of the 1930s (Evil of Frankenstein, Curse of the

Mummy, Curse of the Werewolf). AIP also delved into gothic horror with the release of The Pit and the Pendulum (very loosely
based on Edgar Allan Poe's story and featuring Vincent Price) as
a counterpunch to Hammer. The success of this movie compelled
AIP to go through a wild rummage of Poe: Masque of the Red
Death, The Oblong Box, The Raven, and others (all with Price).
Interestingly, horror was once again spawning its own stars, as
the names of Price, Lee, and Cushing became synonymous with
horror.

Besides Hammer's "British invasion" (which, incidentally, was
not only similar in popularity to the Beatles' but preceded them
by six years), Japan sent us Godzilla, who was actually a rem-
nant of the "atomic-age monster" period. Released in 1958, the
film did so well that Godzilla returned in numerous sequels with
a slew of foes and allies to accompany him. The Japanese even
reincarnated King Kong, who inevitably did battle against Godzilla.

It was during the third cycle that the major studios returned,
opting for a more bold type of horror, which often paralleled re-
ality--Whatever Happened to Baby Jane? (mental illness), The Collector (sexual perversion), and Repulsion (sexual obsession)--
rather than the costumed period pieces of the independents. It
was also during the third cycle that blood and fairly explicit violence were used or, as director Don Sharp said in a recent interview on the subject of Hammer Films, "They'd got into the pattern of making each film a bit bloodier than the one before it."
It was with Alfred Hitchcock's Psycho in 1960 that horror
achieved a new permissiveness in the limits on screen violence,
as that film would forever shatter the invisible line of what was
and was not acceptable on the screen. In 1968, that line was
further annihilated when a small independent, Lavrel, released the
ultragraphic Night of the Living Dead, a film which was unrated
by the Motion Picture Association of America.

This film signified the beginning of the fourth cycle, a period
in which both the major studios and the independents prospered
and screen violence was given a new definition because the

newly imposed film ratings freed movies from their hitherto self-imposed censorship. The major studios continued to reject such previously traditional subjects as vampires, werewolves, and mad scientists and now relied on common earth critters to provide ample terror (Jaws, Orca, The Swarm) and became fixated on the supernatural (The Exorcist, The Omen, Carrie). The burgeoning expansion of independents also continued in the fourth cycle, as they forayed into the unusual (Ilsa: She-Wolf of the SS, Gore, Gore Girls, I Dismember Mama). It was in 1974, as the independents continued to create unusual formulas for success, that the highly successful ultraexplicit Texas Chainsaw Massacre was released. This film not only set a new precedent in screen violence but created a formula (the indestructible killer) that still saturates the independent horror-film market today (Friday the 13th, Maniac!, Madman). Today independents in the fourth cycle continue to follow the "deranged slasher" theme (affectionately dubbed splatter film by its fans), while the major studios continue to opt for new formulas. In recent years, the major studios have returned to the "bankable stars," as can be witnessed by the current spate of werewolf movies (The Howling, American Werewolf in London) and vampires (The Hunger). It is evident that, like most of their monsters, horror films never die.

What media experiences provided the subject for this essay? What was the writer's shaping idea? What examples did he use? How did he move between the general and the specific?

FOCUS ON STYLE: THE COMPONENTS OF STYLE

A writer's style, according to E. B. White, might be defined as "the sound his words make on paper." Writers may sound proper and formal or relaxed and colloquial. They may write lyrically and poetically or logically and scientifically. Their words may seem simple and forthright or satirically double-edged. Although one's style changes, clarity is most often the key to an intelligent style in any age. The question for writers is rarely whether they want to be clear or unclear, but whether they want to achieve clarity through simplicity or complexity, through plainness or eloquence. In *The Elements of Style*, White advised inexperienced writers to write about their subject as directly, simply, naturally, and sincerely as they can. By doing so, they may develop a clarity of expression often sacrificed by those who use the extremes of ornate, pretentious locution or breezy, offbeat slang.

Style is shaped by the writer's purpose in writing and by his or her audience. For example, a writer who has information to convey is likely to seek a plainer, less eloquent style than one who is writing to entertain or to argue. Thus, the author of a cookbook would be well advised to avoid writing like a poet: telling a reader to bake a cake in an oven "as hot as a jealous heart" would create pointless confusion. At the same time, a writer who is attempting to explain Einstein's theories of relativity will need to sound more erudite, and perhaps more poetic as well, than one who is explaining how to bake a cake.

Style is also shaped by the audience. For example, writing for a young, uneducated audience will affect the "sound your words make on paper" in a different way from writing for a peer audience (see Chapter 3) and from writing for an informed audience (Chapter 9). Your style in writing for a sympathetic audience would be different from your style in writing for an unsympathetic audience.

Perhaps, the key word is *adjust*. Writers do not usually use radically different styles in different situations; rather they make subtle adjustments in the style that comes most naturally to them. They try to be a bit more concrete for one audience, a bit more abstract for another. Often a writer is wise to introduce some variety, a simple sentence in a paragraph of complex ones, a metaphor in a sea of scientific facts.

Ways of Adjusting Style

What sort of adjustments in sentence structure and diction can one make in order to simplify or embellish the sound of one's prose? Perhaps we can seek a few basic answers to this question.

Often simplicity of style stems from concreteness, complexity from abstraction.

Adjusting for Concreteness.　To simplify your style and to make it easier to follow, write about your subject in concrete, specific terms. You may try using a narrative mode, for example, even when you are explaining a principle or a concept, as a dramatic situation is often more accessible than an abstract explanation. Compare the following two passages, each of which explains why Thoreau, the author of *Walden*, chose in 1845 to leave his home in the town of Concord, Massachusetts, and to go off to live alone in a hut in the woods by Walden Pond:

The principle of turning one's back on unpleasant facts—unpleasant, because they were so deeply inessential, so foreign, in a way, to our essential Nature—is one *naturally* congenial to the American mind. Thoreau gave this principle its classic utterance. In his spirit, if not in his name, we still take to such woods as we can find.

I think one reason he went to the woods was a perfectly simple and commonplace one. . . . [He was a] young man, a few years out of college, who had not yet broken away from home. He hadn't married, and he had found no job that measured up to his rigid standards of employment, and like any young man, or young animal, he felt uneasy and on the defensive until he had fixed himself a den. Most young men, of course, casting about for a site, are content merely to draw apart from their kinfolks. Thoreau, convinced that the greater part of what his neighbors called good was bad, withdrew from a great deal more than family.

The second passage, by White, is a bit easier to follow than the first, by Wright Morris, because White dramatized the "principle of turning one's back on unpleasant facts." At the same time, in writing more abstractly, Morris offered a more cogent summary statement of the general significance of Thoreau's action.

The Verbal Sentence.   When you narrate in order to explain, you involve your reader in an action that illustrates the ideas you want your reader to understand. You also write more concretely when you employ short sentences that emphasize persons or things as their subject and active verbs as their predicate. Look at the following three sentences:

The boy knew every trick.

He grew up in the ghetto.

He was tough and streetwise.

Each one is what we call a verbal sentence: the focus is on a subject that is an actor, a verb that tells what the action is, and modifiers that tell something more about who the actor is and/or what he is doing. Each one is in the active voice, which many style manuals argue is more direct than passive constructions, in which the actor becomes the object of the sentence and the verb is turned into a past participle ("Every trick was known by the boy"). You may not necessarily write more clearly if you favor short, active, verbal sentences, but your style will sound simpler and more concrete.

Of course, a piece of writing composed only of short, simple sentences is apt to be choppy and monotonous. Even the most concise and direct stylist wants to include longer, more complex sentence structures in her or his writing. In the "Focus" section of Chapter 5, you received some practice in sentence combining as a way of making your style more complex. A possible combination of the three sample sentences might be "Growing up tough and streetwise in the ghetto, the boy knew every trick." In this sentence, the noun *boy* is modified by the cluster "Growing up tough and streetwise in the ghetto," a cluster in which the verbal component "Growing up" is itself qualified by "tough and streetwise in the ghetto."

Adjusting for Abstractness. In the combined sentence above, attention has been directed to the ghetto toughness of the boy. The sentence is thus more abstract, focused as much on a concept, "ghetto toughnesss," as on an action. By modifying a noun or a verb, either with a string of adjectives and/or adverbs or with clusters of subordinate clauses, you draw the reader's attention to the distinctive qualities of the subject and/or the action you are writing about.

The use of modifiers and of long, involved sentences will not guarantee an intelligently complex style. But, especially in the service of abstract explanation, these rhetorical tools can lend clarity to the expression of complicated ideas. Thus, in the first sentence of the passage about Thoreau by Wright Morris, the subordinate clause, with its modifying adjectives *inessential* and *foreign*, does help to explain the concept of *unpleasant facts* and thus clarifies a reader's understanding of the subject of the sentence, the "principle of turning one's back on unpleasant facts."

The Nominal Sentence. Let's take the combined sentence about the boy in the ghetto and make one more alteration: "His growing up tough and streetwise in the ghetto is what taught the boy every trick." Note that "the boy" is no longer the subject of the sentence. We have nominalized the verbs and adjectives of the modifying cluster; that is, we have turned them into nouns that can function as the subject.

Nominal sentence structures, because they tend to create abstract subjects of verbs and adjectives, can be effective tools for the stylist interested in analyzing ideas. If you change the verbal construction "He loved the woods and felt free there and so went camping often" into a nominal construction, "His love of the woods and the freedom he felt there led him to go camping often," you are directing the reader's attention more emphatically to the idea that explains why the person went camping.

If you work in a more abstract, idea-oriented style, however, your writing will not necessarily be more profound than if you write in a more concrete, verbal style. Nor will you necessarily sound more eloquent. You may, in fact, choose plain, direct words because you want to explain a complex idea as clearly as you can.

How to Write More Eloquently

Whether your style is simple or complex, concrete or abstract, there are a few guidelines you might follow in attempting to write with more eloquence.

Balanced Phrasing.   Balanced phrasing is an effective means of lending an eloquent sound to your style. "He ate scrambled eggs, buttered toast, and fresh-squeezed orange juice" would sound less polished if it were written, "He ate scrambled eggs, toast with butter, and orange juice that had been freshly squeezed." Particularly when you are writing long, complicated sentences, phrasing similar grammatical units and similar ideas in similar ways is an important means of achieving clarity. Note how repetition lends balance to the following sentence: "The difference between living today and living at any time in the past is the difference between living in fear of nuclear destruction and living free of such fear." This would be a more difficult sentence to understand without such a balanced effect: "The difference between living today and at any time in the past is fear of nuclear destruction."

Loose and Periodic Sentences.   As you seek balance in your phrasing, seek variety in your sentence structuring. It is sometimes argued, for example, that periodic sentences, in which the modifiers precede the base, sound somehow better than loose sentences, in which the modifiers follow the base. But writing only periodic sentences is as dull as writing only short, simple sentences. The periodic sentence "having gone to the woods, he camped out" does place more dramatic emphasis on the subject than would a loose version of the same sentence. "He camped out, having gone to the woods." But there is really no justification for preferring one type of sentence over the other. A loose sentence may prove as effective as a periodic sentence, depending on what element in the sentence a writer wishes to emphasize and whether the emphasis will be best achieved by the placement of that element first or last. The context must always be taken into consideration.

Figurative Language.   Skillfully and judiciously used, similes, metaphors, irony, understatement, and similar figures of speech will lend eloquence to your style.

A metaphor is an implied comparison between dissimilar things. To write "Our world is a ship without a helmsman on the dark sea of space" is to imply that our world, like a ship drifting on the sea, needs someone to guide and steer it. In a simile, the comparison is made explicitly by the use of *like* or *as*.

There are a number of dangers in using metaphors and similes. They may end up sounding trite, as does the example above. If they are used too frequently, they may actually distract a reader's attention from the point that the writer wishes to make instead of making the point more memorable. Also, novices who try to extend a metaphor often mix it up, with ludicrous results. Thus, if the writer who compared the world to a ship goes on to write, "If we are not careful, our ship may sink in the flames of a third world war," the "sea" has gone through a most awkward transformation. Arthur Miller, who wrote *Death of a Salesman*, uses a similar figure of speech but expresses it much more naturally when he describes Willy Loman as "a little boat looking for a harbor." In general, use the occasional metaphor that comes to you naturally in the course of writing.

Irony.   Irony involves undercutting a reader's expectations. To write "After Adam and Eve ate the apple, they found life a bit tougher" is to create an ironic effect through understatement. The reader expects you to say and knows that you mean that Adam and Eve found life very much tougher. Like any form of verbal humor, irony requires subtlety. The ironist is always in danger of falling flat on his or her face. Irony should not be overdone.

You may find yourself most eloquent when your language is as simple and direct as you can make it. Take the following advice from E. B. White:

> The beginner should approach style warily, realizing that it is himself he is approaching, no other; and he should begin by turning resolutely away from all devices that are popularly believed to indicate style—all mannerisms, tricks, adornments. . . .
>
> Style takes its final shape more from attitudes of mind than from principles of composition, for, as an elderly practitioner once remarked, "Writing is an act of faith, not a trick of grammar." This moral observation would have no place in a rule book were it not that style *is* the writer, and therefore what a man is, rather than what he knows, will at last determine his style.
>
> —William Strunk, Jr. and E. B. White, *Elements of Style*

SOME PRACTICE WITH STYLE

1. Identify each of the following sentences as verbal or nominal. Restructure each verbal sentence into a nominal one, each nominal sentence into a verbal one:

   a. You take the high road, I'll take the low road, and I'll get to Scotland before you.

   b. Keeping physically fit has become a major preoccupation of many people today.

   c. Our capacity for wonder at the news has been lost because of television.

   d. I like the essay, have always like it, and even as a child was at work, attempting to inflict my young thoughts and experiences on others by putting them on paper.

2. Identify each of the following sentences as periodic or loose. Recast each periodic sentence into a loose one, and each loose sentence into a periodic one. What are the differing effects?

   a. Having a thick coat of fur, the animal survived.

   b. Mercilessly goading the bully, our hero saved the day.

   c. Snowstorms make driving hazardous and thus endanger lives, even as they give countless children hours of gleeful play.

   d. Newsmagazines are popular, offering an artful combination of news, popular opinion, and gossip.

3. Identify each of the following sentences as active or passive. Restructure each active sentence into a passive one, each passive sentence into an active one:

   a. Paradoxically, in a free society, one is often worried and frustrated by government policy.

   b. The house was torn apart by the swirling winds of the tornado.

   c. The hard day's work at the factory tired him out.

   d. Don't count your chickens before they hatch.

4. Simplify the style of the following paragraph by rewriting in order to dramatize its central idea:

   > The mass of men lead lives of quiet desperation. What is called resignation is confirmed desperation. From the desperate city you go into the desperate country and have to console yourself with the bravery of minks and muskrats. A stereotyped but unconscious despair is concealed even under what are called the games and amusements of mankind. There is no play in them, for this comes after work. But it is a characteristic of wisdom not to do desperate things.
   >
   > —Henry David Thoreau, *Walden*

5. Write a paragraph of abstract generalizations that summarize the interactions between the media and Americans according to the essays in this chapter.

6. Analyze the following passages for their style: identify sentences as verbal or nominal, periodic or loose, simple or complex; indicate whether verbs are passive or active; determine how phrasing has been balanced, what figures of speech have been used, and if irony is a component. Finally, has clarity been maintained throughout? What would you say is the chief means by which the writer's style gave eloquence and meaning to each passage?

Springtime in the heyday of the Model T was a delirious season. Owning a car was still a major excitement, roads were still wonderful and bad. The Fords were obviously conceived in madness: any car which was capable of going from forward into reverse without any perceptible mechanical hiatus was bound to be a mighty challenging thing to the human imagination. Boys used to veer them off the highway into a level pasture and run wild with them, as though they were cutting up with a girl. Most everybody used the reverse pedal quite as much as the regular foot brake—it distributed the wear over the bands and wore them all down evenly. That was the big trick, to wear all the bands down evenly, so that the final chattering would be total and the whole unit scream for renewal.

The days were golden, the nights were dim and strange. I still recall with trembling those loud, nocturnal crises when you drew up to a signpost and raced the engine so the lights would be bright enough to read destinations by. I have never been really planetary since. I suppose it's time to say good-bye. Farewell, my lovely!

—E. B. White, "Farewell, My Lovely!"

In a newsreel theater the other day I saw a picture of a man who had developed the soap bubble to a higher point than it had ever before reached. He had become the ace soap bubble blower of America, had perfected the business of blowing bubbles, refined it, doubled it, squared it, and had even worked himself into a convenient lather. The effect was not pretty. Some of the bubbles were too big to be beautiful, and the blower was always jumping into them or out of them, or playing some sort of unattractive trick with them. It was, if anything, a rather repulsive sight. Humor is a little like that: it won't stand much blowing up, and it won't stand much poking. It has a certain fragility, an evasiveness, which one had best respect. Essentially, it is a complete mystery. A human frame convulsed with laughter, and the laughter becoming hysterical and uncontrollable, is as far out of balance as one shaken with the hiccoughs or in the throes of a sneezing fit.

—E. B. White, "Some Remarks on Humor"

7. Take a passage from your journal or from an essay that you have written, and recast the sentences to make your writing more abstract and complex. Assume, for example, that you are writing for the *New York Times*. If your original passage was a narrative, you can summarize it as an abstract statement. You might recast your sentences into the nominal form and combine the various elements into sentences of greater length. Do not, of course, sacrifice clarity in your revision.

8. Now, revise the passage again, this time aiming for concreteness. You might begin by developing a narrative to support the main point of the piece. Employ any figures of speech that seem to you to add vividness. Balance your complex sentences with shorter verbal structures in the active voice that give emphasis to the action.

9. Examine the passage for ways in which you can make your writing more eloquent. What balanced phrasing can be added, and what variations in sentence structure, to achieve both periodic and loose sentences? Would it be possible to revise your passage once again, aiming for an ironic slant toward your subject?

Adjusting Your Style in Writing Your Essay on the Media

In moving from generalization to narrative example, you will want to move also from abstract writing to the more concrete and specific, from nominative sentences to verbal sentences.

Likewise, in writing for a public audience, you may want to become more eloquent, using balanced phrasing and varying your sentence structure between loose and periodic forms. To make your writing more vivid, you will also want to strive for picturesque figures of speech as well as the precise tone you wish to take toward your subject matter.

In general, writing for a public audience requires a greater repertoire of stylistic approaches from which to select so that the reader both understands your approach to your subject and is impressed with the means by which you convey it.

SOME PRACTICE WITH WRITING ON THE MEDIA FOR A PUBLIC AUDIENCE

1. Reread the first draft of your essay, paying particular attention to your narrative examples. Edit sentences with passive verbs by substituting active verbs. What effect does your editing have on the story you have told?

2. Cast each generalization you have developed in your essay as a nominal sentence. Then, recast as a verbal sentence. Consider the appropriateness for your purpose of both. Which seems better suited to expressing a generalization?

3. Next, reread the introduction and conclusion to your essay, considering the structure of each sentence as you proceed. In each case, have you used a nominal or verbal, loose or periodic sentence? Revise for appropriateness (verbal, nominal) and variety (loose, periodic).

4. In addition to forming verbal sentences in your narrative examples, you might consider where a figure of speech will assist you in vividly explaining your example to your reader. If a metaphor or simile comes to you that is natural and appropriate, you might want to include it.

5. What tone have you developed toward your media subject? Ironic, enthusiastic, sarcastic, satirical? Are you consistent in using this tone? If not, you may want to distribute this tone evenly throughout the essay.

REWRITING

Obtaining Feedback on Your Rough Draft

Once you have taken sufficient time away from your rough draft so that you can review it with a measure of objectivity, turn to one or more of the channels you have developed for obtaining feedback on what you have written: your "other self," your peers, or your teacher. Again, use these channels for obtaining answers to the "Audience Response Guide" about your draft.

——————— AUDIENCE RESPONSE GUIDE ———————

1. What do you think the writer wanted to say about the media? What is his or her purpose in writing? What does he or she want the paper to mean?
2. How does the paper affect the public audience for which it is intended?
3. How effective has the writer been in conveying his or her purpose and meaning? What are the strengths of the paper? What are its weaknesses?
4. How should the paper be revised to better fulfill its purpose and meaning?

Revision of Student Essay "Horrors"

Consider at this time the following peer evaluation of the rough draft of the student essay "Horrors." Compare your own evaluation of the draft to that of the peer group by answering the four questions of the "Audience Response Guide" before reading their answers.

1. The readers disagreed on the purpose of the essay. One felt that the writer intended to give a historical survey of the development of horror films and its later offshoots, but the other said that the purpose was unclear, that the paper provided a lot of information but failed to explain why it was doing so.

2. The first reader believed that the paper was intended for an uneducated film audience--one that had not seen most of these films and wasn't aware of the horror film's origins. The other reader felt a bit overwhelmed by the information.

3. Both readers agreed that the essay included too much information and too little assimilation, and that the information lacked supplemental explanations of its intended purpose. Both were very impressed by the extent of the writer's knowledge.

4. The readers agreed that the writer should narrow his focus, concentrate more on some representative films, and explain his purpose further.

Here is a revised version of "Horrors." How well were the readers' suggestions incorporated? Did the writer make any additional changes himself? What additional changes might he have made?

HORRORS

The evolution of horror films certainly doesn't compare to the wondrous and lengthy evolution of humankind. Horror films are, however, a vivid reflection of the twentieth century's ever-changing morals, values, and fears. Although horror films have certainly changed over the years, saying that yesteryear's horror films are better than today's is as arguable as stating that humans are better now than they were a half century ago. Do we not commit the same atrocities (rape, thievery, murder) as our grandparents or our great grandparents did?

The year 1931 marked the coming of age of the horror genre. Although there had previously been scattered examples of films that dramatized the horrible and the grotesque, the horror film did not flourish until Universal released <u>Dracula</u>, featuring Bela Lugosi as the irrepressible Transylvanian count of Bram Stoker's classic novel; shortly after, Universal released <u>Frankenstein,</u> featuring Boris Karloff as Mary Shelley's monstrous novel creation. As the genre prospered, in 1932 Karloff appeared in <u>The</u>

Mummy; in 1933 Claude Rains was <u>The Invisible Man</u>, and <u>King Kong</u> made a monkey of himself; and in 1940 Lon Chaney, Jr., was transformed into <u>The Wolf Man</u> to add to horror's growing assemblage of monsters and spooks. Interestingly, this new genre, in which all of the major Hollywood studios were involved, spawned a plethora of new stars who would become known as "horror stars" (such as Karloff, Lugosi, and Chaney, Jr.).

The horror genre's sudden success was indeed puzzling because these films succeeded during the economic depression that occurred after 1929. In fact, audiences relentlessly flocked to this macabre new genre. Perhaps the audiences of that era equated the grim stories of countless people and villages being destroyed by various creatures with the Great Depression, which in reality destroyed many people and cities. Perhaps they hoped that, like the films in which the creature dies at the end and a sense of balance is restored to the village, the poverty and despair induced by the Depression would also be conquered and a sense of order would be restored.

Curiously, Dracula, Frankenstein, and other assorted monsters achieved a weird kind of commercial immortality with their sudden success. Thus the studios set out on a steady and profitable progress through a series of sequels in which the creatures returned as themselves or as "sons," "daughters," and "ghosts" in such films as <u>Son of Kong</u>, <u>The Invisible Man Returns</u>, <u>The Mummy's Ghost</u>, and <u>The Bride of Frankenstein</u>.

However, there's a limit to human invention, if not human credulity. Horror films came out with the regularity of a monthly magazine. By the mid-1940s, Hollywood had gorged the public past horror satiety. In a desperate attempt to rejuvenate horror's sagging box office, Hollywood united horror filmdom's monsters (<u>Frankenstein Meets the Wolf Man</u>), a move that slowed down the erosion of box-office dollars but didn't stop it. Feeling that the imaginary horror of a film couldn't possibly compete with the true horror tales of Nazism and World War II circulating in the United States, Hollywood lamely blamed World War II for the continuing plummet of horror's box-office popularity. Finally, horror expired in self-parody as it was exploited for cheap laughs: Abbott and Costello Meet Frankenstein, The Dead End Kids Meet the Spook, and so on. Ironically, a genre in which death was a constant staple died the most unkind of deaths itself by 1945.

After the war, little was heard of horror until the advent of science fiction in 1950, when the genre, like a Phoenix rising from its own ashes, entered its second cycle. With the big Hollywood studios generally abandoning horror like a wounded, dying animal, various small, independent film companies, ranging from the fairly big American International Pictures (AIP) to the ultra-cheap Astor, became the most consistent suppliers of horror films. The independents shrewdly manipulated and exploited the prevalent fears and changing values of that era. The independents' skillful exploitation of the public's fear of imminent nuclear destruction, for example, gave birth to the "atomic-age monsters," who were either normal living organisms, transformed into mutants by incessant human dabbling in the atomic field (in such films as Colossal Man and Attack of the Crab Monsters), or supposedly extinct dinosaurs unleashed from their centuries' long "dormancy" deep below ocean floors or ice caps because of atomic testing, as in Beast from 20,000 Fathoms.

More subtle was the independents' shrewd, artful exploitation of McCarthyism for a generally unknowing audience. Such films as The Incredibly Strange Creatures Who Stopped Living and Became Mixed-Up Zombies, It Conquered the World, and I Married a Monster from Outer Space, although seemingly only crude productions dealing with aliens conquering us and/or infiltrating our very human existence, purposely paralleled (if somewhat indiscreetly) the shocking real-life aspects of McCarthyism. Indeed these films' menacing fictional aliens served as metaphors for the McCarthyite vision of Communists infiltrating and conquering our land.

The second cycle of horror was a time of high exploitation as the independents specialized in making quick contemporary horror films, all of which had an assured profit potential because of minuscule budgets and sensationalized advertising. In fact, AIP, in many cases, just made up an advertising campaign, and if they liked the campaign's look, they then made a film (usually in three to six days) pertaining to the poster's theme. As noted film historian Leslie Halliwell claimed, in The Film Goer's Companion, "Such crude and shoddy productions cheapened the genre considerably." Perhaps they were "crude and shoddy," but they were attuned to their audience's whims, and the independents keenly sensed that with the advent of fast cars and rock 'n' roll, the mood of its basically youthful audience was undergoing a drastic shift. Thus began the recycling of familiar horror-film monsters into "romantic villains" in such films as I Was a Teen-age Werewolf and I Was a Teen-age Frankenstein, whose heroes were misunderstood and inarticulate but, not uncoincidentally, sympathetic and identifiable to these films' chiefly youthful audiences, who had the same problems as these monsters; even less uncoincidentally, these monsters were irritants to authority, just as their youthful audiences were. By shrewdly exploiting this new significance of the teen-ager, these independents helped establish the now famous "youth market."

It was during this reincarnation of "old-time" monsters that the genre was ushered into its third cycle as it looked on its old saviors to return it to the prosperity that it had once tasted. In 1958, Hammer Films, a small, fledgling independent film company, released Horror of Dracula (with Christopher Lee and Peter Cushing). It was essentially a remake of the 1932 Dracula with an authentic gothic look, a bold style, and a new permissiveness in "screen blood." Buoyed by the film's enormous success, Hammer recycled other horror films of the 1930s (Evil of Frankenstein, Curse of the Mummy, Curse of the Werewolf). AIP also delved into gothic horror with the release of The Pit and the Pendulum (very loosely based on Edgar Allan Poe's story and featuring Vincent Price) as a counterpunch to Hammer. The success of this movie compelled AIP to go through a wild rummage of

Poe: Masque of the Red Death, The Oblong Box, The Raven, and others (all with Price). Interestingly, horror was once again spawning its own stars, as the names of Price, Lee, and Cushing became synonymous with horror. An explanation for this new and sudden fixation on "old" values might be linked to the presidency of that era. Just as America saw in the JFK administration the past pleasant virtues of Camelot, so may people have sought in Hammer's films the past virtues of the old horror "look."

It was during the third cycle that the major studios returned, opting for a more bold type of horror that often paralleled reality--Whatever Happened to Baby Jane? (mental illness), The Collector (sexual perversion), Repulsion (sexual obsession)--rather than the costumed period pieces of the independents. It was also during the third cycle that blood and fairly explicit violence were used or, as director Don Sharp said in a recent interview in Fangoria on the subject of Hammer Films: "They'd got into the pattern of making each film a bit bloodier than the one before it." It was with Alfred Hitchcock's Psycho in 1960 that horror achieved a new permissiveness in the limits on screen violence, as that film would forever shatter the invisible line of what was and was not acceptable on the screen.

In 1968, that line was further annihilated when a small independent, Laurel, released the ultragraphic Night of the Living Dead. This film, which went unrated by the Motion Picture Association of America, signified the beginning of the fourth cycle, a period in which both the major studios and independents prospered and screen violence was given a new definition because the newly imposed film ratings freed movies from their hitherto self-imposed censorship. Perhaps this new permissiveness mirrored the fact that our society at the time equated carnage with horror, what with television daily invading living rooms showing the grisly effects of the Vietnam War. After seeing such real-life bloody carnage in their homes, perhaps the public could no longer accept the quaint gothic horrors of the past.

During the mid-1970s, the major studios seemed intent on reflecting our ecological worries in such tales of ecological revenge as Jaws, Orca, and The Swarm and became fixated on the supernatural (The Exorcist, The Omen, Carrie). Meanwhile the independents successfully forayed into a variety of unusual subjects, including the return of Dracula and Frankenstein in the most unlikely of vehicles, such as Blacula, Andy Warhol's Frankenstein, and Ilsa: She-Wolf of the SS. It was in 1974, as the independents continued to create unusual formulas for success, that the highly successful, ultraexplicit Texas Chainsaw Massacre was released. This film not only set a new precedent in screen violence but created a formula (the indestructible killer) that still saturates the independent horror-film market today (Friday the 13th, Maniac!, Madman). This type of film has been affectionately dubbed splatter film by its fans, for obvious reasons.

One thing is certain: whether the monsters come from graveyards, outer space, or oceans, or are just plain homicidal psychotic killers, horror films, like the monsters they dramatize, will not die, and as the twentieth century continues to evolve, horror films will reflect our changing preoccupations.

Consolidating

Words, sentences, and whole passages often need consolidating to make a stronger impact. Consolidating occurs when the writer brings together ideas that in the rough draft were scattered throughout a sentence, a paragraph, or the entire essay. This scattering weakens the effect that the writer wishes to make by diluting the impact, whereas consolidating the material strengthens it by creating a concentrated effect.

Consider this sentence: "The health effects of all the different chemicals ingested by animals are well documented by impartial M.D.s., so this is not just hearsay from ASPCA people or the like." This is not a bad sentence as it is, but consolidating the two clauses on the health effects creates a more focused effect: "That animals' health is affected by all the different chemicals they ingest is not just hearsay from the ASPCA but is well documented by impartial M.D.s." (Refer also to the section on sentence combining on pages 212–222 for the different ways in which sentence elements can be consolidated.)

Consider the following introductory paragraph to an essay on fraternal orders:

As a youngster, I remember watching such shows as The Honeymooners and The Flintstones, during which, on many occasions, the main characters tried to deceive and lie to their wives in order to go bowling or play cards with their brother lodgemen. The lodges or fraternities that these men belonged to had funny names like "The Raccoons," which Ralph belonged to in The Honeymooners, and "The Loyal Order of Waterbuffaloes," which Fred was a member of in The Flintstones. All the members wore funny hats and had ridiculous handshakes. Unfortunately, that is where my education and that of many others about fraternal organizations began.

Although this first version presents some effective details, consolidating the information makes a stronger impact on the reader:

In order to go bowling or play cards, Fred Flintstone lied to his wife about his destination. Then he donned a funny hat and, with a ridiculous handshake, joined his brother lodgemen at "The Loyal Order of Waterbuffaloes." Ralph, in The Honeymooners, also had to stoop to deceit in order to participate in the activities of "The Raccoons." Unfortunately, these shows were where my education and that of many others about fraternal organizations began.

Look again at the final draft of "Horrors," the student essay on pages 312–317. Although on the basis of his peer-group analysis, the writer had consolidated much of the material that appeared in his rough draft (pp. 298–302), what additional consolidation might he have made? What segments of his sentences, paragraphs, and the whole essay might he have brought together to make his point more strongly?

Revising Your Essay on the Media

As you begin to revise your own essay, ask yourself the following questions:

Checklist of Questions to Consider in Revising an Essay About the Media

1. Do I clearly state the shaping idea of my essay? How might I rephrase it for greater impact? Would consolidation of words or phrases improve it?

2. Do I cite enough examples, whether stories or details, to justify any generalizations that I make? Will they convince my reader that my explanation is reasonable and thorough?

3. How have I organized the essay? Is the organization logical? Would any points benefit from rearrangement or consolidation? Do I use transitions to indicate the pattern I have used?

4. Have I adopted an objective and convincing public voice? Am I too personal or too emotional at any points? Have I written with a clear reader or group of readers in mind? If so, how has their frame of reference and point of view affected my writing?

5. How effective is my style? Have I developed my examples concretely? Are my generalizations intelligently abstract? Have I varied my sentence patterns? Is my tone appropriate for both my subject and my reader? Have I consolidated my phrasing and my ideas for greater impact?

Now you should feel ready to revise your essay.

Editing

Consolidating.   Consolidate words and phrases that ramble aimlessly in order to achieve a stronger impact. Why say "thin and sickly" when you can write "emaciated"? Or why write "Carrying the football, I lunged forward, the ball tucked snugly under my arm," when "I lunged forward, the football tucked snugly under my arm" consolidates your material for a sharper effect?

Style.   Review your essay with an eye to adjusting your style so that you have presented you ideas as clearly as possible. Are there sentences or phrases or words that you need to simplify? Might you turn a verbal sentence into a nominal one in order to focus your reader's attention on an abstract point? If you have employed figurative language, have you done so judiciously?

Mechanics.   Once again, review earlier samples of your writing in which mechanical errors have been noted, then check your draft for spelling, punctuation, and grammatical errors common to your writing. Work with the handbook in the back of the text, if necessary, to make corrections.
   Now review and edit your essay.

BECOMING AWARE OF YOURSELF AS A WRITER

You might want to make use of your journal to record your thoughts and feelings about the task for this chapter. As you write in your journal, consider the following questions.

1. How did you use your media experiences in generating ideas for this essay? How did you obtain your sources of information?

2. Was the information you provided sufficient for your audience to understand your subject? What kind of information could you have added? If you had offered more information, how would it have helped your audience?

3. Did you find that the ability to generalize was of help to you when you sought to convey information to your audience? What purpose did the generalization serve?

4. How specifically were you able to support the generalization on which you based your essay? What concrete examples or details did you use?

5. What would you say are the major characteristics of a public voice? How would you differentiate your public voice from the private voice you use in writing about yourself?

6. How would you characterize the style of writing that comes most naturally to you? Did you find it necessary to make adjustments in your style in order to write an effective explanatory essay? What kind of adjustments did you make?

PART

IV

Persuasion

INTRODUCTION

Argumentation is perhaps the oldest form of discourse. Before our ancestors were able to form a clear enough sense of their own identity to express it, had time free from their efforts to survive to explore the world, or knew enough about what they discovered to explain their experiences to others, they would have engaged in rudimentary forms of verbal persuasion: this tool over that tool, this method of hunting over that one, my territory not your territory.

By the time of the Greeks, persuasion, which was still the primary form of public discourse, had become very sophisticated, and it is to the Greeks and to the Romans who followed that we owe much of what we know about persuasive techniques today. Aristotle articulated three areas in which persuasive speakers and writers must appeal to the audience: they must appeal to their logic, their sense of ethics, and their emotions.

In this section on persuasion, we will study these three persuasive appeals. In Chapter 8, we will analyze each of them and present a task in which you are asked to utilize them in supporting an argument of your own. In Chapter 9, you will be asked to analyze several arguments which utilize these appeals in presenting the varying positions on an issue that is particularly controversial in our culture at the present time. You can then apply your critical thinking skills to the issue and attempt to formulate a broader point of view than any of the groups involved in the issue have so far espoused. Your task will be to convince them to accept your broader approach.

While various persuaders have emphasized the emotional appeal over the ethical and logical (advertisers come first to mind) or sincerity over the emotional and the logical (politicians often make this appeal), we can perhaps say that the logical appeal is a necessary ingredient in any successful argument. The Greeks developed the syllogism, a formula for developing logical thinking that provides a litmus test for the logic of any argument we might wish to make. A syllogism is a series of generalizations on a controversial issue to which various tests are applied to determine whether one generalization follows logically from the other and hence whether the argument is valid. The most famous syllogism is

> All men are mortal.
> Socrates is a man.
> (Therefore,) Socrates is mortal.

It is impossible to argue that Socrates is immortal because all men in human history have died; therefore, this is a logical argument.

In Chapter 8, we will discuss how to construct a syllogism that will test the validity of the argument you have chosen for your task; in Chapter 9, we will ask you to think critically about the varying viewpoints on a controversial issue in order to arrive at a broader point of view.

8

Writing About an Issue — Arguing Your Point of View

In Chapter 8, we turn to a third type of writing, writing that has an aim and purpose different from those of both expressive writing and expository writing. The primary aim in writing to persuade is neither to express the writer nor to explain the subject but to convince the reader of the writer's point of view on a particular issue. In terms of the triangle diagram from Chapter 1, the focus is on the reader rather than on the writer or the subject.

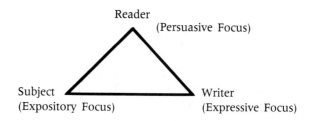

Reader
(Persuasive Focus)

Subject
(Expository Focus)

Writer
(Expressive Focus)

Persuasion, or argumentation, is a common aim in our society. Newspaper editorials aim to persuade, politicians argue their positions in speeches, preachers persuade from the pulpit, advertisers lure their readers in the pages of magazines and newspapers. And in our everyday communication with others, we often wish to convince them of our point of view. To learn how to persuade or argue effectively in writing is the purpose of Chapter 8.

The tools of persuasion are the abilities to reason well and to use language effectively. But as you develop these abilities, you should take some care in how you use them to influence others. Often, in our society, the tools of persuasion are wielded as weapons, to influence the public through illogical reasoning and seductive language, as in many political speeches and in much advertising. In its extreme form, persuasion can become propaganda, in which a cause is supported or attacked regardless of the merits of the arguments used.

When studying persuasive techniques, then, it is important to distinguish, as Aristotle himself did, among the different means of argumentation: You can appeal to an audience's logic, emotions, or sense of ethics. (In fact, a distinction is often made between persuasion and argumentation; the former is defined as an appeal to the emotions, and the latter, as an appeal to reason.) When appealing to the logic of your readers, you should be careful to be indeed logical and not to mislead them; when appealing to their emotions, you should be careful not to manipulate them; when appealing to their ethical or moral sense, you should be ethical yourself and not lead your readers astray. Perhaps the best argument includes all three appeals, each a counterbalance for the other. In the "Generating Ideas" section of this chapter, we will discuss the forms of logical appeal, including induction and deduction.

Because the emphasis in persuasive writing is on the audience, we will concentrate in the "Audience" section on how you, as a writer, can establish a relationship with your readers so that you can best persuade them to adopt your point of view. From the outset, you must take care to respect your readers even if they differ from you, and especially if they are ignorant of the subject altogether. You should have their attitude uppermost in your mind throughout or seek to foster a positive attitude if none exists.

It is also important that you seek to establish your own credibility as an authority on the subject, as well as your sincerity in presenting your point of view. All the facets of writing to an audience that we have discussed thus far should be brought to bear: understanding the audience's frame of reference, role playing the audience to understand their attitude, determining your voice, and finally, ascertaining how much depth of information the audience needs about the subject.

The "Audience" section culminates in a discussion of how to appeal to your readers' sense of ethics, and the "Focus" section concentrates on how to phrase your essay in words that will appeal to your audience's emotions.

In the "Arranging Your Essay" section of this chapter, we present one of the most powerful arguments in American history, the American colonists' "Declaration of Independence" and, in the "Focus" section, Martin Luther King, Jr.'s support of his nonviolent tactics in "Letter from a Birmingham Jail." Studying these documents in the light of what you know about their effect on history will dramatize for you the mighty force wielded by an effective argument.

TASK: ARGUING YOUR POINT OF VIEW ON AN ISSUE

Your task for this chapter is to write a persuasive essay about a controversy that has arisen. Through your use of the strategies of argumentation, you should generate support for your point of view on an issue and present a well-reasoned, well-organized argument to your readers.

The issue, the audience, and your purpose in writing are to be selected by you. In order to give your task a context, we would like you to create a life situation or "case" in which you take the role of one of the participants in the situation and write an argument to convince one or more other participants, or some other more neutral reader, of your point of view about an issue. In creating your case, you will devise the context, the participants, the issue, your purpose in writing the argument, and the audience for whom it is intended.

Thus, in this task, you are to write not as yourself but as one of the participants in the case that you set up. For example, you might take the role of the manager of a local chemical plant that is considering the installation of costly pollution-control devices. You have been asked by the president of the company to present to the other employees the company's arguments for installing these devices. You know that many of your readers may suffer pay reductions as a result of the high costs that the company will incur. How can you best argue your proposal?

The length of the case and its complexity are up to you. However, you should give your instructor and your peer evaluation group enough details about your role and that of your intended audience so that they can construct both frames of reference, and you should also give them enough information about the situation in general and the problem in particular so that they will know as much about your case as you do.

The audience that you select will be either undecided or hostile to your point of view; there is no point in selecting an audience that already agrees with you, as in that case you have no one to convince. Whether hostile or undecided, however, your audience should be interested in your subject and to some extent knowledgeable about it.

In constructing your case, you can proceed in one of two ways: (1) choose an issue that interests you and then build around it a situation containing a specific audience and a purpose for addressing that audience; or (2) choose a situation with which you are familiar, analyze the issues involved, and then select one issue to argue about.

For example, suppose that you want to argue that we should rely more than we do at present on nuclear power for local energy needs. By constructing a case around this issue, you can focus more sharply on whom you are addressing your argument to and why your argument is necessary. Your case might go something like this: You are a homeowner with a family to support in an area where energy costs are high. The local electric company has proposed building a nuclear facility that will lower energy costs to its customers, you and your neighbors. Many of your neighbors, however, are concerned about the dangers of such a facility, and some have formed an antinuclear group. You decide to attend a meeting of this group to try to convince its members to see your side of the issue. First, you must write out your argument so that you can present it clearly in what you realize will be a hostile setting. What do you write?

If you choose the second method, start with a situation that you know something about, perhaps one having to do with a job that you hold or with a subject that you are studying; decide what your role is to be; and then select your issue. You might, for example, be studying the period of the American Revolution in a history course, a period in which many important issues were fought over. Adopt a role for yourself from that era, say, the role of a merchant who has decided to back the rebel cause. The Boston Tea Party has just taken place. Write an essay for the local newspaper in which you state why your fellow citizens, many of whom feel that such an act of insurrection is immoral, should support those responsible for the Boston Tea Party.

Construct your case before proceeding further. In the section "Writing Your Essay," we discuss how to generate ideas for your argumentative essay, how best to address your audience, and how the arrangement patterns that correspond to the classical questions that you have asked can be used to help organize different sections of your essay. Most important, we present patterns of arranging a persuasive essay as a whole. In the "Focus" section, we discuss various considerations in choosing the language of your argument in order to best involve the emotions of your reader.

WRITING YOUR ESSAY

Generating Ideas: Strategies for Argument, Induction, Deduction, and the Classical Questions

Can you recall when people smoked in waiting rooms, restaurants, and even airplanes, without causing even a hint of disagreement? Why is it that today the smoker has become a decidedly unpopular character, banned from many public and private facilities? The answer seems obvious: smoking is dangerous to the health of smoker and nonsmoker alike. But how do we know this? Most would answer by pointing out the various scientific claims that have emerged in recent years.

However, as a result of these claims, smoking has also become a controversial issue in our society. Smokers clamor for their personal rights to smoke; nonsmokers argue for their right to a smoke-free environment. Who is right? What are the facts? What should be done?

By answering these questions we try to convince our audience that our views on this issue carry validity, that we have reasoned clearly and carefully and have constructed an argument that we hope is watertight. Before we can do this with confidence, however, we need to know more about the basic components and strategies of arguing an issue, such as making a claim, using evidence, and considering the limits of our claim.

Strategies for Argument

Making claims. When you argue, you make certain assertions that you believe will establish your point of view forcefully. These assertions or general claims can be broadly classified as the following:

Claims of fact. Example: The Surgeon General has determined smoking to be dangerous to one's health.

Claims of value. Example: The rights of nonsmokers exceed the rights of smokers.

Claims of policy. Example: Smoking should be prohibited in all public places.

You may argue these claims separately or include them as parts of a larger argument depending on how broad your issue is and what frame of reference you can expect from your audience. How do you support your claims? With evidence you judge to be ample and effective.

Evidence. What kinds of evidence would be convincing for supporting the claims stated above? *Facts*, certainly. The Surgeon General's report on smoking, in addition to other studies conducted by impartial scientists or experts, would seem to offer verifiable support for a claim relating to smoking and health.

Statistics also provide numerical support for many different kinds of claims. Statistics alone, however, rarely offer adequate support for an argument because of the real possibility of using numbers in a way that confuses or even deliberately misleads the audience. Thus research and argument that depend solely on a statistical foundation are often challenged.

Another source of evidence in making your claim is the *expert knowledge or judgment of authorities.* A legal scholar's point of view on whether smokers' rights are less valid than nonsmokers' can help establish a claim because of the likely probability that the writer has experience with and knowledge of the field of constitutional rights.

One source of evidence that might offer particularly convincing firsthand knowledge and observation of a subject is *the experience of the writer* making a claim. The writer's experience in a college dining hall where smoking was unrestricted might offer convincing evidence for why a ban on smoking should be instituted. Or the writer's recollection of a family member who suffered poor health from the effects of sidestream smoke in the home would also contribute to the validity of the claim. (For more on evidence, see the "Focus" section of Chapter 9, pp. 437–439).

Warrants. In general, evidence can be drawn from a variety of useful sources. You must be the judge of how reliable the evidence is and whether it is relevant and adequate for supporting your claim. In addition, whenever you create your argument by putting forward a claim and supporting evidence, you are making certain assumptions about your audience's ability to understand and share your concerns. For example, you can assume that your readers will believe in the importance of a healthy environment or in the need to consider the rights of a minority. These shared yet unexpressed principles are often referred to as the warrants for a claim. Warrants need not be stated for they are implicit in the facts or expert testimony the writer uses to demonstrate a claim.

Qualifiers. However, the use of warrants and evidence may lead the writer to make a bolder claim than the evidence justifies. Thus the need for some kind of *qualifier*, or recognition that the claim is probably but not necessarily absolutely supported by the evidence supplied. For example, one might need to qualify a claim that all toxic substances should be banned from use. Some toxic substances are clearly important in scientific research and commercial use.

Summarizing the overall strategy to follow for creating an argument, you will most likely need to do the following:

State your claim:	Take a stand for or against a controversial issue (value), make a proposal on a problem that you know the facts about (fact), or argue for a course of action or change of policy (policy).
Provide evidence:	Cite facts or statistics that argue to the point of your claim. Offer expert support or testimony. Relate a personal experience or observation.
Consider warrants:	Understand the basic assumptions and values of your audience.
Qualify your claim:	Don't go beyond your evidence and claim what you cannot support.

SOME PRACTICE WITH THE STRATEGIES OF ARGUMENT

1. Identify the kinds of claims in the following arguments:

a.
In Cities, Who Is the Real Mugger?
by Kenneth B. Clark

New York Times, Jan. 14, 1985

Bernhard Hugo Goetz has become a folk hero. Respectable citizens have identified with his shooting of four teen-agers who "harrassed" him on the subway and asked him for $5. In so dealing with these potential "muggers," Mr. Goetz personified and aroused the pervasive fears, anger and sense of personal powerlessness of a larger segment of the public faced with rising urban crime. The outrage over lawlessness in our cities has masked the lawless act of an individual. But this incident cannot be understood in isolation.

In our cities, fear of crime is valid. Almost everyone, without regard to race, becomes anxious about the possibility of being mugged when approached by a group of seemingly aimless teen-agers. The media cover the more sensational incidents, dramatizing the victims as well as the criminals and muggers. There are outraged cries for retaliation and punishment, demands for a more severe criminal justice system and more prisons, suggestions that outraged citizens protect themselves by whatever means necessary. The muggers are perceived as animals or, at best, as "creatures" who must be caged or destroyed. They are not seen as socially distorted humans.

But this ignores some significant problems. Our society does not ask itself, "How do so many young people become mindlessly antisocial and, at times, self-destructive?" A painfully disturbing answer to this core question is that "mugged communities," "mugged neighborhoods" and, probably most important, "mugged schools" spawn urban "muggers." Given this fact , a more severe criminal justice system, more prisons and more citizen shootings will not solve the problem of urban crime. These are selective forms of anger directed toward the visible "muggers." The educationally rejected and despised "muggers"—the pool of the unemployed and unemployable from which they come—will increase in numbers, defiance and venom. Not able to express their frustrations in words, their indignation takes the form of more crime. Having been robbed of the minimum self-esteem essential to their humanity, they have nothing to lose.

As a society adjusts to, or rewards, its accepted cruelties and continues to deny their consequences, it makes heroes of lawless "respectables" and in so doing develops a selective form of moral indignation and outrage as a basis for the anomaly of a civilization without a conscience.

b.
Ignorant Drug Policy
by Lester C. Thurow

New York Times, May 8, 1988

The United States' war on drugs has led to the attempted ouster of Panama's leader, the virtual kidnapping of a Honduran, new efforts to burn crops in Bolivia and a proposed Congressional resolution accusing Mexican officials of accepting bribes. A short time ago, similar actions were directed at Pakistan, Colombia, Peru, Turkey and Thailand.

Before we further damage our foreign relations, we should admit the failure of efforts to interdict drug supplies abroad and focus instead on reducing demand at home.

The current approach has led us to demand actions of others that we would not for a moment tolerate if asked of us. Consider what we would do if a foreign government kidnapped one of our citizens or if its parliament passed a resolution accusing us of complicity with drug dealers.

Drug sellers face what in the jargon of the economics profession is known as an inelastic demand curve. This means that if supplies are cut back by 10 percent, prices rise by more than 10 percent, leaving the seller with higher profits than before the cutback.

If our goal is to deprive criminals of large profits from selling drugs, economic theory and history teach us that legalization is the only answer. When liquor sales were legalized after Prohibition, criminals left the bootleg liquor industry because the huge profits available while the Government was attempting to stop liquor sales vanished.

If we do not legalize products for which there is a huge demand, profits will remain enormous and suppliers will always come forward. Individual sellers can be arrested, but others will take their place.

A demand-side solution would be expensive. Jailing buyers, educating addicts and changing the conditions that lead to pathological behavior—none of these are cheap. But effective interdiction of drugs at our borders would require an army of guards. Foreign interdiction is often advocated as a cheap alternative to expensive, politically divisive policies at home, but that view is a mirage.

c.   **Useless 'Japan-Bashing'**

by Paul H. Kreisberg

New York Times, Aug. 5, 1985

There are several possible things to do when you don't know what else to do about a problem. You can rant and rave, kick a door, look for a Communist or—the latest fad—jump on Japan.

The last, now commonly called "Japan-bashing," involves using blunt instruments as a substitute for clear thought. It has been heard with mounting intensity for the last year or so and is now taking on a shrill, almost warlike tone.

In fact, no one in or out of Government really has any good way of reversing the huge unfavorable tides of Japanese imports and capital. American consumers will inevitably lap up high-quality consumer and producer goods from Japan, and the Japanese clearly have a knack for identifying an unending variety of new products that will sell on our markets.

Nor would it solve the problem to adjust the exchange rate—for even with a more equitable rate American producers would have a hard time meeting the price and quality competition.

It is only a modest exaggeration to say that the essence of much American criticism of the Japanese is that they should behave more like Americans.

The critics would like Japanese businesses to imitate us when borrowing money, investing, dealing with suppliers, setting profit levels, marketing goods and dealing with their Government. They would like the Japanese to save and consume like Americans and to spend a lot more on defense, even if they have to change their Constitution to do so.

In the end, of course, this would add up to a transformation in Japanese society and culture. It should come as no surprise that the Japanese have preferred to adjust their policies at the margin and now bristle with increasing anger at the fundamental changes we seem to be asking for.

Yet American businessmen, Congressmen and others continue to fan flames of hostility. Resentment and anger toward America is beginning to seethe below the political surface in many parts of Japan.

It may be difficult for the United States and Japan to work together as friends, but Americans who think it would be easier dealing with Japan as an adversary really need to think again.

2. Describe what kinds of evidence are used in these arguments.

3. What warrants or generally agreed upon assumptions does each argument employ?

4. What additional evidence could be used for each argument? Write a paragraph in which you explain what you would add to make each argument more persuasive.

5. Create a case from the claims and evidence provided by one of the arguments.

6. Write a brief counterargument on one of the three issues. What personal experience or observation could you include as support for your argument?

7. Based on one of the arguments above, create a proposal that would either support or refute its claim.

8. Examine your recent journal entries to see what kinds of claims you may have made. What kinds of evidence have you used? What warrants do you assume in your own writing?

Induction, Deduction and the Classical Questions. In preparing your case you need to consider how you (the character you create) can support your argument in the most effective way. Clearly your evidence must strike your audience as convincing — based on fact, reliable sources, and relevant personal experiences. Your claim should be limited to what your evidence can support. And you should be able to meet your audience in a common understanding of the values and beliefs you share with them.

In order to prepare your case more efficiently, you can also benefit from an explanation of the reasoning that has traditionally been part of argumentation: *induction, deduction, and the classical questions.* These patterns of thinking are basic to our means of learning about the world around us and conveying our knowledge to others. Moving from particulars to generalizations and from generalization to specifics gives us a structure for our arguments. As their Latin roots indicate (*inducere*, to lead in; *deducere*, to lead down), they show us the way to or from our conclusions by means of an ordered path of evidence and assertion.

Induction.   In the task for Chapter 10 you will use induction — reasoning from example to conclusion — as a way of arriving at scientific probability, answering the classical question "What examples are there of it?" Because the use of induction as a process for arriving at a scientific conclusion is usually referred to as the "scientific method," more attention will be paid to it there (see pp. 449–451 and 453–455). Induction as a method for supporting a claim for a persuasive case follows from our discussion of evidence.

The evidence for an inductive argument is drawn from the various examples of individual experiences and observations you offer in support of a claim. For example, you can use evidence gathered from a survey of a group providing that it offers a representative sampling of that group. Sampling is used to arrive at a conclusion about a group through reference to a certain percentage of that group rather than the entire membership, as discussing or even knowing about every member of a group would be impossible.

But if you use too few examples or samples, you may not prove your position. Hasty generalizations — for example, we will have a recession every eight years because we had one in 1975 and another in 1983, and another in 1991 — tend to be unconvincing. Atypical examples tend to undercut the effectiveness of an argument; thus it may not help much to interview those not on welfare if you wish to argue that the welfare system is working. Moreover it is unfair to ignore examples that contradict your line of reasoning; if some people on welfare feel that the system is not too much help to them, there is a way of admitting this contrary evidence (see section on "Arranging Your Essay," pp. 355–356).

When you argue inductively, it is best to avoid claiming more for your examples than they merit and to avoid making sweeping generalizations as did the cigarette commercial "Everyone who knows smokes Kools."

The criteria for successful inductive reasoning, then, include the following:

1. Your examples should be of sufficient quantity.
2. They should be randomly selected.

3. They should be accurate and objectively presented.
4. They should be relevant to the conclusion drawn.
5. They should disprove the evidence of the opposition.

SOME PRACTICE WITH INDUCTION

1. Show how the authors of the following passages have used inductive reasoning. How accurate and relevant are the examples used in these passages? How can a reader determine their accuracy?

    a. "Beasts abstract not," announced John Locke, expressing mankind's prevailing opinion throughout recorded history. Bishop Berkeley had, however, a sardonic rejoinder: "If the fact that brutes abstract not be made the distinguishing property of that sort of animal, I fear a great many of those that pass for men must be reckoned into their number." Abstract thought, at least in its more subtle varieties, is not an invariable accompaniment of everyday life for the average man. Could abstract thought be a matter not of kind but of degree? Could other animals be capable of abstract thought but more rarely or less deeply than humans? . . .

    There is by now a vast library of described and filmed conversations, employing Ameslan and other gestural langauges, with Washoe, Lucy, Lana and other chimpanzees studied by the Gardiners and others. Not only are there chimpanzees with working vocabularies of 100 to 200 words; they are also able to distinguish among nontrivially different grammatical patterns and syntaxes. What is more, they have been remarkably inventive in the construction of new words and phrases.

    On seeing for the first time a duck land quacking in a pond, Washoe gestured "water bird," which is the same phrase used in English and other languages, but which Washoe invented for the occasion. Having never seen a spherical fruit other than an apple, but knowing the signs for the principal colors, Lana, upon spying a technician eating an orange, signed "orange apple." After tasting a watermelon, Lucy described it as "candy-drink" or "drink fruit," which is essentially the same word form as the English "water melon." But after she had burned her mouth on her first radish, Lucy forever after described them as "cry hurt food." A small doll placed unexpectedly in Washoe's cup elicited the response "Baby in my drink." When Washoe soiled, particularly clothing or furniture, she was taught the sign "dirty," which she then extrapolated as a general term of abuse. A rhesus monkey that evoked her displeasure was repeatedly signed at: "Dirty monkey, dirty monkey, dirty monkey." Occasionally Washoe would say things like "Dirty Jack, gimme drink." Lana, in a moment of creative annoyance, called her trainer "You green shit." Chimpanzees have invented swear words. Washoe also seems to have a sort of sense of humor; once, when riding on her trainer's shoulders and, perhaps inadvertently, wetting him, she signed: "Funny, funny."

    Lucy was eventually able to distinguish clearly the meanings of the phrases "Roger tickle Lucy" and "Lucy tickle Roger," both of which activities she enjoyed with gusto. Likewise, Lana extrapolated from "Tim groom Lana" to "Lana groom Tim." Washoe was observed "reading" a magazine — i.e., slowly turning the pages, peering intently at the pictures and making, to no one in particular, an appropriate sign, such as "cat" when viewing a photograph of a tiger, and "drink" when examining a Vermouth advertisement. Having learned the sign "open" with a door, Washoe extended the concept to a briefcase. She also attempted to converse in Ameslan with the laboratory cat, who turned out to be the only illiterate in the facility. Having acquired this marvelous method of communication, Washoe may have been surprised that the cat was not also competent in Ameslan. . . .

I would expect a significant development and elaboration of language in only a few generations if all the chimps unable to communicate were to die or fail to reproduce. Basic English corresponds to about 1,000 words. Chimpanzees are already accomplished in vocabularies exceeding 10 percent of that number. Although a few years ago it would have seemed the most implausible science fiction, it does not appear to me out of the question that, after a few generations in such a verbal chimpanzee community, there might emerge the memoirs of the natural history and mental life of a chimpanzee, published in English or Japanese (with perhaps an "as told to" after the byline).

If chimpanzees have consciousness, if they are capable of abstractions, do they not have what until now has been described as "human rights"? How smart does a chimpanzee have to be before killing him constitutes murder? What further properties must he show before religious missionaries must consider him worthy of attempts at conversion? . . .

The long-term significance of teaching language to the other primates is difficult to overestimate. There is an arresting passage in Charles Darwin's *Descent of Man*: "The difference in mind between man and the higher animals, great as it is, certainly is one of degree and not of kind. . . . If it could be proved that certain high mental powers, such as the formation of general concepts, self-consciousness, et cetera, were absolutely peculiar to man, which seems extremely doubtful, it is not improbable that these qualities are merely the incidental results of other highly-advanced intellectual faculties; and these again mainly the results of the continued use of a perfect language. . . ."

— Carl Sagan, *The Dragons of Eden*

b. When Lincoln at last determined, in July 1862, to move toward emancipation, it was only after all his other policies had failed. The Crittenden Resolution had been rejected, the border states had quashed his plan of compensated emancipation, his generals were still floundering, and he had already lost the support of great numbers of conservatives. The Proclamation became necessary to hold his remaining supporters and to forestall — so he believed — English recognition of the Confederacy. "I would save the Union," he wrote in answer to Horace Greeley's cry for emancipation.

"... If I could save the Union without freeing any slave, I would do it; and if I could do it by freeing all the slaves, I would do it." In the end, freeing all the slaves seemed necessary.

It was evidently an unhappy frame of mind in which Lincoln resorted to the Emancipation Proclamation. "Things had gone from bad to worse," he told the artist F. B. Carpenter a year later, "until I felt that we had reached the end of our rope on the plan of operations we had been pursuing; that we had about played our last card, and must change our tactics, or lose the game. I now determined upon the adoption of the emancipation policy. ..." The passage has a wretched tone; things had gone from bad to worse and as a result the slaves were to be declared free!

The Emancipation Proclamation of January 1, 1863, had all the moral grandeur of a bill of lading. It contained no indictment of slavery, but simply based emancipation on "military necessity." It expressly omitted the loyal slave states from its terms. Finally, it did not in fact free any slaves. For it excluded by detailed enumeration from the sphere covered in the Proclamation all the counties in Virginia and parishes in Louisiana that were occupied by Union troops and into which the government actually had the power to bring freedom. It simply declared free all slaves in "the States and parts of States" where the people were in rebellion — that is to say, precisely where its effect could not reach. Beyond its propaganda value the Proclamation added nothing to what Congress had already done in the Confiscation Act.

Seward remarked of the Proclamation: "We show our sympathy with slavery by emancipating the slaves where we cannot reach them and holding them in bondage where we can set them free." The London *Spectator* gibed: "The principle is not that a human being cannot justly own another, but that he cannot own him unless he is loyal to the United States."

But the Proclamation was what it was because the average sentiments of the American Unionist of 1862 were what they were. Had the political strategy of the moment called for a momentous human document of the stature of the Declaration of Independence, Lincoln could have risen to the occasion. Perhaps the largest reasonable indictment of him is simply that in such matters he was a follower and not a leader of public opinion. It may be that there was in Lincoln something of the old Kentucky poor white, whose regard for the slaves was more akin to his feeling for tortured animals than it was to his feeling, say, for the common white man of the North. But it is only the intensity and not the genuineness of his antislavery sentiments that can be doubted. His conservatism arose in part from a sound sense for the pace of historical change. He knew that formal freedom for the Negro, coming suddenly and without preparation, would not be real freedom, and in this respect he understood the slavery question better than most of the Radicals, just as they had understood better than he the revolutionary dynamics of the war.

For all its limitations, the Emancipation Proclamation probably made genuine emancipation inevitable. In all but five of the states freedom was accomplished in fact through the thirteenth amendment. Lincoln's own part in the passing of this amendment was critical. He used all his influence to get the measure the necessary two-thirds vote in the House of Representatives, and it was finally carried by a margin of three votes. Without his influence the amendment might have been long delayed, though it is hardly conceivable that it could have been held off indefinitely. Such claim as he may have to be remembered as an Emancipator perhaps rests more justly on his behind-the-scenes activity for the thirteenth amendment than on the Proclamation itself. It was the Proclamation, however, that had psychological value, and before the amendment was passed, Lincoln had already become the personal symbol of freedom. Believing that he was called only to conserve, he had turned liberator in spite of himself:

"I claim not to have controlled events but confess plainly that events have controlled me."

—Richard Hofstadter, "Abraham Lincoln and the Self-made Myth"

c. We should not conclude, either, that the child who has strong ties to his parents is insured against neurosis. We can only say that he will have the best possible measures within his personality to deal with conflict, which may then provide greater resistance to neurotic ills. But a neurosis is not necessarily an indictment of the parent–child relationship; a neurotic child is not necessarily an unloved child, or a rejected child. The child who has never known love and who has no human attachments does not develop a neurosis in the strict clinical meaning of the term. The unattached child is subject to other types of disorders. He might develop bizarre features in his personality, he might be subject to primitive fears and pathological distortions of reality, he might have uncontrollable urges that lead to delinquency or violence, but he would probably not acquire a neurosis because a neurosis involves moral conflicts and conflicts of love which could not exist in a child who had never known significant human attachments. The merit of a neurosis—if there is anything good to be said about it all—is that it is a civilized disease. The child who suffers a disturbance in his love relationships or anxieties of conscience offers proof of his humanity even in illness. But the sickness of the unattached child is more terrible because it is less human; there is only a primitive ego engaged in a lonely and violent struggle for its own existence.

Indeed, it can be argued that the real threat to humanity does not lie in neurosis but in the diseases of the ego, the diseases of isolation, detachment and emotional sterility. These are the diseases that are produced in the early years by the absence of human ties or the destruction of human ties. In the absence of human ties those mental qualities that we call human will fail to develop or will be grafted upon a personality that cannot nourish them, so that at best they will be imitations of virtues, personality facades. The devastating effects of two world wars, revolution, tyranny and mass murder are seen in cruelest caricature in the thousands of hollow men who have come to live among us. The destruction of families and family ties has produced in frightening numbers an aberrant child and man who lives as a stranger in the human community. He is rootless, unbound, uncommitted, unloved and untouchable. He is sometimes a criminal, whether child or adult, and you have read that he commits acts of violence without motive and without remorse. He offers himself and the vacancy within him to be leased by other personalities—the gang leaders, mob-ruler, fascist leaders and the organizers of lunatic movements and societies. He performs useful services for them; he can perform brutal acts that might cause another criminal at least a twinge of conscience, he can risk his life when more prudent villains would stay home, and he can do these things because he values no man's life, not even his own. All that he asks in return is that he may borrow a personality or an idea to clothe his nakedness and give a reason, however perverse, for his existence in a meaningless world.

We have more reason to fear the hollow man than the poor neurotic who is tormented by his own conscience. As long as man is capable of moral conflicts—even if they lead to neurosis—there is hope for him. But what shall we do with a man who has no attachments? Who can breathe humanity into his emptiness?

—Selma H. Fraiberg, *The Magic Years*

2. Evaluate Sagan's claim that chimpanzees, because of their acquisition of language, possess "human rights." Are there any claims that require qualifiers in this passage? Does Sagan's evidence justify his conclusions about chimpanzees?

3. How does the discussion of the Emancipation Proclamation serve as evidence for evaluating claims about Lincoln's character?

4. What claim does Fraiberg make about the child that fails to develop human ties? What is the purpose of the comparison between the neurotic child and the unattached child? Can you support Fraiberg's argument with an experience or observation of your own?

5. Create a life situation or case using one of the three passages. For example, you might imagine Sagan acting as an advocate for giving human rights to chimpanzees because of their advanced animal skills.

6. How persuasive is the use of induction as a method of reasoning? How can we know these writers are expressing the truth?

7. In preparing a case built on inductive reasoning, how can you be certain your audience will think you are telling them the truth? What kinds of examples do you need to provide?

8. Observe the use of induction in the following essay. Does the essay meet all of the criteria for effective induction?

I knew a man who went into therapy about three years ago because, as he put it, he couldn't live with himself any longer. I didn't blame him. The guy was a bigot, a tyrant and a creep.

In any case, I ran into him again after he'd finished therapy. He was still a bigot, a tyrant and a creep, *but* . . . he had learned to live with himself.

Now, I suppose this was an accomplishment of sorts. I mean, nobody else could live with him. But it seems to me that there are an awful lot of people running around and writing around these days encouraging us to feel good about what we should feel terrible about, and to accept in ourselves what we should change.

The only thing they seem to disapprove of is disapproval. The only judgment they make is against being judgmental, and they assure us that we have nothing to feel guilty about except guilt itself. It seems to me that they are all intent on proving that I'm OK and You're OK, when in fact, I may be perfectly dreadful and you may be unforgivably dreary, and it may be—gasp!— *wrong*.

What brings on my sudden attack of judgmentitis is success, or rather, *Success!*—the latest in a series of exclamation-point books all concerned with How to Make it.

In this one, Michael Korda is writing a recipe book for success. Like the other authors, he leapfrogs right over the "Shoulds" and into the "Hows." He eliminates value judgments and edits out moral questions as if he were Fanny Farmer and the subject was the making of a blueberry pie.

It's not that I have any reason to doubt Mr. Korda's advice on the way to achieve success. It may very well be that successful men wear handkerchiefs stuffed neatly in their breast pockets, and that successful single women should carry suitcases to the office on Fridays whether or not they are going away for the weekend.

He may be realistic when he says that "successful people generally have very low expectations of others." And he may be only slightly cynical when he writes: "One of the best ways to ensure success is to develop expensive tastes or marry someone who has them."

And he may be helpful with his handy hints on how to sit next to someone you are about to overpower.

But he simply finesses the issues of right and wrong—silly words, embarrassing words that have been excised like warts from the shiny surface of the new how-to books. To Korda, guilt is not a prod, but an enemy that he slays on page four. Right off the bat, he tells the would-be successful reader that

- It's OK to be greedy.
- It's OK to look out for Number One.
- It's OK to be Machiavellian (if you can get away with it).
- It's OK to recognize that honesty is not always the best policy (provided you don't go around saying so).
- And it's always OK to be rich.

Well, in fact, it's not OK. It's not OK to be greedy, Machiavellian, dishonest. It's not always OK to be rich. There is a qualitative difference between succeeding by making napalm or by making penicillin. There is a difference between climbing the ladder of success, and macheteing a path to the top.

Only someone with the moral perspective of a mushroom could assure us that this was all OK. It seems to me that most Americans harbor ambivalence toward success, not for neurotic reasons, but out of a realistic perception of what it demands.

Success is expensive in terms of time and energy and altered behavior — the sort of behavior he describes in the grossest of terms: "If you can undermine your boss and replace him, fine, do so, but never express anything but respect and loyalty for him while you're doing it."

This author — whose *Power!* topped the best-seller last year — is intent on helping rid us of that ambivalence which is a signal from our conscience. He is like the other "Win!" "Me First!" writers, who try to make us comfortable when we should be uncomfortable.

They are all Doctor Feelgoods, offering us placebo prescriptions instead of strong medicine. They give us a way to live with ourselves, perhaps, but not a way to live with each other. They teach us a whole lot more about "Failure!" than about success.

—Ellen Goodman, "It's Failure, Not Success"

Deduction. Deductive reasoning works quite differently from inductive reasoning: Rather than working from evidence to a conclusion, as does induction, deduction works from an assumption — a generalization that is generally accepted as true — to a specific conclusion. This assumption, called a *premise* in formal logic, leads to a specific conclusion with the help of a "linking statement." Here is an example of deductive thinking:

Assumption:	All college students should drink beer.
Linking Statement:	John is a college student.
Conclusion:	John should drink beer.

Of course, most of us usually do not think according to this process, called a *syllogism* in formal logic. Usually, we think only according to the last two steps of the process (formally called an *enthymeme*). For example, we might argue that because John is a college student, he should drink beer, taking for granted the assumption that all college students should drink beer.

If you decided to argue that we are going to war because we are having an army buildup, your argument similarly would rest on an unspoken assumption, in this case that an army buildup necessarily leads to war.

Assumption:	All army buildups lead to war.
Linking Statement:	We are having an army buildup.
Conclusion:	We are going to war.

You might find it a good idea to construct this syllogism to determine if the assumption on which your argument rests is a sensible (or valid) one. If it is valid that all army buildups lead to war (or that all college students should drink beer, for that matter), then your argument itself makes sense. To say that Peter is cold because he has no coat on is to assume that all people who have no coats on are cold. If the weather is cold, if the people are outdoors, and if they have no heavy sweaters on either, then your assumption is probably valid. And if your assumption is valid, then your argument is probably valid also.

Deduction is useful when you are trying to persuade your readers of a highly controversial conclusion because, if you can get them to agree with your assumption, you have a good chance of getting them to agree with your conclusion. It is worthwhile, therefore, to learn how to construct an informal syllogism. (Courses in logic instruct one in formal constructions.)

Each of the three statements in a syllogism has two parts, each of these parts appearing in one of the other statements according to the following pattern:

Assumption:	All that has a tendency to become stale needs renewing. 3 2
Linking Statement:	Slang has a tendency to become stale. 1 3
Conclusion:	Slang needs to be renewed. 1 2

Because your conclusion is usually your shaping idea, begin here to construct your syllogism. By adding a causal conjunction to your conclusion, you can usually arrive at your linking statement: *Slang needs to be renewed* because *it has a tendency to become stale.* You now have all three parts of your syllogism and can construct the third statement accordingly, as the assumption always contains Parts 3 and 2, in that order.

For example, suppose your shaping idea for your argument is "Our involvement in Vietnam was a no-win situation." By adding *because* to this sentence, you can arrive at your linking statement: "Our involvement in Vietnam was a no-win situation because it was a guerilla war." Diagramming your enthymeme will give you your assumption:

Conclusion:	Our involvement in Vietnam was a no-win situation (because) 1 2
Linking Statement:	Vietnam was a guerilla war. 1 3
Assumption:	Guerrilla wars are no-win situations. 3 2

We should add here that sometimes it is necessary to construct a series or string of syllogisms, in order to clarify just what general assumption lies behind a point that you wish to argue. For example, in a discussion of deductive logic in one class, the students decided to construct an argument in support of handgun control. They found that they had to put together the following series of syllogisms before they could determine the general assumption behind their feeling that handgun possession is immoral:

Syllogism 1:
All persons who kill except in self-defense or in defense of others are immoral.

He killed neither in self-defense nor in defense of others.

He is immoral.

(This syllogism does not establish that he has a handgun, so the students added Syllogism 2 to their argument.)

Syllogism 2:
All in possession of guns are readily equipped to kill in all situations (self-defense, defense of others, and nondefense).

He is in possession of a gun.

He is readily equipped to kill in all situations.

(This syllogism does not establish that the person equipped to kill is likely to kill, so the students added Syllogism 3.)

Syllogism 3:
All men readily equipped to kill are more likely to kill in nondefense situations, as well as in self-defense or in defense of others.

He is readily equipped to kill.

He is more likely to kill in nondefense situations.

(This syllogism does not establish the charge of immorality, so the students added still another syllogism.)

Syllogism 4:
All men more likely to kill in nondefense situations are immoral.

He is more likely to kill in nondefense situations.

He is immoral.

(With Syllogism 4, the students felt that they had clarified the logic behind their argument that handgun possession is immoral.)

Do you think the students' assumptions are valid?

SOME PRACTICE WITH DEDUCTION

Reconstruct the assumptions on which the following arguments (enthymemes) are based. In each case, does the argument seem to rest on a valid assumption?

1. Business is a good major because you can get a job.

2. Toxic waste disposal is a vital issue because undisposed-of poisons can affect our health.

3. The government should continue to subsidize student loans because college tuitions can no longer be afforded by a sizable percentage of the middle class.

4. Playing video games should not be ridiculed because they encourage mind–body coordination.

5. Because high-technology firms promise employment, Americans should train or retrain to enter a high-technology profession.

6. The sexual revolution has been harmful because so many people are contracting sexually transmitted diseases.

7. Bilingualism should not be encouraged because studies show that students in bilingual classes do not learn English well.

8. Advertising should not be considered worthless because buying an advertised product makes people feel good.

9. Women should resist the return to ultrafeminine fashions because this trend repudiates the philosophy of the women's movement.

Deductive Fallacies.   As we indicated previously, the reason for constructing a syllogism is to determine if your assumption is logical. Following are some of the problems that you might encounter as you try to make this determination.

1. *Faulty analogy:* There are not enough important similarities between the two subjects being compared to really support the conclusions that are being drawn. Although it is often said that the generation of the 1990s is just like that of the 1950s because both are silent, the differences between the two decades are greater than any similarities.
2. *False cause:* The ascribed cause is not really a cause at all or is just one

of many factors. Although the women's movement has been blamed for the disintegration of the family, other societal factors are the chief causes.

3. *Begging the question:* The assumption takes for granted what ought to be established by proof. You cannot assume, for example, that a person cannot be believed because he has a reputation as a liar. You must establish proof that he is lying in a particular argument.

4. *Ad hominem:* An argument is formulated on the basis of a person's personal life rather than on the issue itself. To argue that because one is a Catholic one has no business talking about abortion is to stray from one's ideas about abortion to one's religious beliefs.

5. *Ad populum:* An argument is based on appeals to popular biases such as an advertisement urging buyers to purchase an American car so that the United States won't be overrun by Japanese-made products.

6. *Either/or:* The implication is made that there are only the two options when, in fact, there may be several others. The argument of antiabortionists that one is either for life or against it is a well-known example of the either/or fallacy.

7. *Red herring:* The audience is diverted from the real issue. Faced with laws insisting on the installation of pollution controls, a company might warn that employees will lose their jobs if the costly controls are installed, thus diverting attention from the legal and environmental issues.

8. *Genetic fallacy:* The class that a person is from, and not the person's own qualifications, becomes the focus of the argument. For example, some people argued in the 1988 election that George Bush could not understand the needs of ordinary people because he had a privileged upbringing.

because "everybody" is doing it. Advertisements often commit this fallacy: "*Atlantic* Subscribers Never Miss" or "All Over the World People Have One Thing in Common: They Start the Evening with Red" (Johnnie Walker Red).

10. *Slanting:* Arguers sometimes use language unfairly to encourage the reader to take their view of the subject. To claim that over 30 percent of a class failed an exam when in fact nearly 70 percent had passed it for the highest percentage of passes ever is an example of slanting because it emphasizes the small percentage that failed rather than the vast majority that passed.

SOME PRACTICE WITH IDENTIFYING DEDUCTIVE FALLACIES

1. Which assumptions in the exercise on the previous page can be categorized by one of the logical fallacies?

2. Identify the fallacy in each of the following assumptions:

   a. He is an Italian; he must belong to the Mafia.

   b. Students, if you continue to protest this regulation, you will be encouraging anarchy in the schools.

   c. People who know use Product X.

   d. Ted doesn't use deodorant; how could he possibly be a good student-body president?

   e. The candidate has been divorced; therefore his qualifications for political office are questionable.

   f. If you do not learn computer languages, you will find yourself unemployed.

   g. His preposterous suggestion insults all red-blooded Americans.

   h. Foreign imports are destroying the U.S. economy.

   i. I cannot take this political speech seriously because politicians cannot be trusted.

   j. The politicians are at it again; first they want a pay raise and now the savings and loan mess.

The Classical Questions in Support of Persuasion. Whether you develop an argument through inductive or deductive thinking, you need proof to support your position. The classical questions are useful in generating ideas that will supply proof for your argument. Because most arguments combine deduction and induction, we direct your attention here to questions that generate proof for both types of argument.

The classical question "What examples are there of it?" can generate a sampling to support an inductive argument. Other inductive questions are "What is it like?" (analogy or analogies) and "What factor not characteristic of others in its class may have caused it?" (causal generalization).

Deductive arguments or portions of arguments can be supported by the material generated by the classical question "What is it?" which may help you argue that your subject, as defined, has certain properties: characteristics, parts, and functions. For example, if you argue that "This gun is a product of human hatred and fear because it is a weapon," then you can base your argument on the assumption that "Weapons are products of human hatred and fear," and that the ownership of guns therefore should be abolished.

Another classical question to ask in support of deduction is "What is it like or unlike?" A variation on this question asks, "How does it compare with the ideal?" If, for example, the ideal is in your assumption that "All good deeds deserve rewards," then you can argue that what you have just done compares favorably with a good deed (and therefore you deserve a reward). Another variation on this question is "How does it compare with my opponent's view?" Explain why she or he disagrees either that you have done a good deed or that good deeds deserve rewards. Still another variation: "How does it compare with the alternatives?" Remind your reader that being rewarded will produce further good behavior, whereas being unacknowledged will lead to indifferent behavior.

A third classical question in the service of deductive proof asks, "How can it be classified?" Corresponding questions are "How can this group be defined?" "What characteristics of the group does my subject show?" and "How does it compare with others in its class?" Because we know that our recent purchase was made by a designer, we classify it as a designer fashion. We also assume that "All designer fashions are well made," and we can therefore argue that this purchase, which has a flaw in it, should be replaced.

SOME PRACTICE WITH THE CLASSICAL QUESTIONS AS MEANS OF GENERATING IDEAS FOR AN ARGUMENT

Which of the classical questions might be useful in generating ideas for the following arguments (deductive and/or inductive)?

1. Natural foods are healthier than processed ones.
2. Dogs are better pets than cats.
3. Crack is America's Number One social problem.
4. America should adopt more vigorous measures for feeding the hungry people of the world.

Using the Principles of Induction and Deduction to Generate Ideas for Arguing Your Point of View. In order to generate proof for your argument, we suggest that you take the following four steps:

1. Construct a logically sound argument using deduction and/or induction; summarize your main points. Research your issue if necessary to obtain the best proof. If you can find an argument developed by the opposition or one supporting your own point of view, such material should be helpful in constructing your own argument and in acquiring supporting proof.
2. Reevaluate your summary in the light of any conflict between your frame of reference and that of your audience and/or your opponent (your audience may not necessarily be opposed to your point of view, it may be neutral instead). Once you have understood how your audience and/or your opponent would view your argument, you have some idea of what the issues really are.

3. Weigh the merits of the various points of view underlying both sides of the issue, and make a case for the higher priority of the values of your case over those of your opponent. In order to do so, you may have to locate a new assumption that your opponent must agree with. Incorporate your new perspective into your argument by writing a new summary.

4. Use this final summary to write your argument.

For example, a student arguing against coed dormitories might work through the four steps in the following way:

1. Formulate an Argument: He formulates his main points using a combination of deduction and induction:

- **Shaping Idea:** Coed dormitories should be abolished because they introduce distractions and tensions into students' lives.
- **Inductive Proof by Example:**

   a. Ned, whose girlfriend lived on his floor, flunked math because he did not want to study.

   b. Jim, who organized nightly dormitory parties, had to leave school for a semester because he was suffering from exhaustion.

   c. Sarah, who developed a nervous condition because her boyfriend moved to another girl's dormitory, withdrew from her classes and her social relations as well.

- **Assumption:** Anything other than their studies that distracts and preoccupies students should be abolished.
- **Conclusions:** Coed dormitories should be abolished.
- **Argument Stated as a Syllogism:**
  Assumption: Anything that distracts and preoccupies students should be abolished.
  Linking Statement: Coed dormitories distract and preoccupy students.
  Conclusion: Coed dormitories should be abolished.

2. Analyze Audience Frame of Reference: His readers are new freshmen who either have no opinion on coed dorms or are anxious to try their social wings and are stongly in favor of them. The strongest argument of those supporting these dorms is that they encourage students to gain valuable social experience and thus help them to mature faster. Proof of their argument comes from examples supplied by their older brothers and sisters who have experienced living in coed situations.

   a. Susan, who had always felt awkward and unsure of herself on dates, learned to relax with the opposite sex by coming in contact with them in everyday situations.

    b. John gradually removed the pedestal from beneath women, stopped breaking up with every girl he went out with, and accepted Dorothy even though she didn't meet his ideal.

    c. Carol, who had attended an all-girl high school, enjoyed learning what men thought of her.

- **Assumption:** Anything that encourages maturity should be maintained.

3. Consider a Higher Priority: Our writer recognizes that maturity is an important value and now knows that he must maintain that students have more to gain by doing well in their studies than by spending their study time in social pursuits, because this is a very competitive world, and a good education is a vital necessity.

4. Reconstruct Your Argument: He now reconstructs his argument in the following way:

- **Assumption:** In a competitive world, education must be students' first priority, and anything that interferes with that priority should be abolished.
- **Linking Statement:** Coed dorms interfere with education.
- **Conclusion:** Coed dorms should be abolished.

SOME PRACTICE WITH GENERATING IDEAS TO ARGUE YOUR POINT OF VIEW

1. Using your journal to brainstorm, write down as many characteristics of the person whose role you wish to play in your case that might have relevance to your argument. Example: Rachael McLish: strong physically and mentally independent, self-reliant, informed about her topic, dedicated to self realization.

2. Write a paragraph stating how you propose to argue your point of view: name the participants and context of your case, state what evidence you intend to use, and explain why this should persuade your audience for the task.

3. If you intend to argue a case based on a claim, state the following elements of your argument: (1) your claim; (2) the evidence you expect to use in support of your claim; (3) the warrant, or implied understanding about the case that your audience will also hold; (4) how you expect to limit or qualify the extent of your claim.

4. Examine the data you intend to use for your inductive argument. Ask your peer group to (1) evaluate how relevant your examples are to your conclusions; (2) determine how representative they are of the subject you have chosen to generalize about; (3) judge whether you have presented your data in an accurate and objective way. What suggestions did they have for selecting and presenting your evidence?

Persuading Your Audience

As the aim of persuasion differs from the aims of expressive and expository writing, so the role of the audience differs as well. When you engage in expressive writing, although you may wish to make yourself appealing to your audience and therefore may attempt to understand your readers through constructing their frame of reference, your purpose is not primarily to persuade your readers; you do not want your readers to adopt your point of view, but simply to accept you enough to enter into your experience.

In expository writing, your aim as a writer is to convey your subject matter, and your concern with your audience leads you to accommodate yourself to any disparity between their background and your own — in education generally and in the subject matter specifically. In order to be aware of any disparities, you must also construct a frame of reference and determine your own voice in writing — as an expert writing to a lay audience, for example.

For the most part, as a writer of persuasion, you can expect that your audience will be familiar with the subject matter already, although they may need some repetition of the basic facts and perhaps some in-depth treatment; what you want is for them to form an opinion about the subject matter, either their first opinion or a replacement opinion. In addition, you may want your readers to act on this newly formed opinion, either in a manner of their own choosing or in a very specific way determined by you. Thus you are demanding more of the audience than you might if you were writing expressive or expository prose, and you must use all the means at your disposal to accomplish your persuasive aim.

You must first of all establish a relationship with your audience — you must establish your credibility, your role, and your voice. Then you must build bridges by establishing that you are aware of the attitude or the frame of reference of the audience and that you esteem your readers despite any differences in their point of view and your own. You must also be aware of how much depth of information your readers need. Although, of course, you must pay a considerable amount of attention to the subject matter itself and to the rational arguments for your point of view, you will also want to consider how to appeal to the emotions of your audience through your use of language and whether you have handled the ethical implications well: those of your own approach as well as those of the situation.

Establishing Credibility.   How do you go about building a relationship with your audience? How do you establish bridges between your points of view? Whether your audience is neutral or hostile, a common ground can be established. The first thing that you will want to do is establish your credibility as someone who knows enough about the subject to have a worthwhile opinion about it. Professional writers, of course, have much less difficulty with this part of the task than does the average citizen or the college student. The editorial writers of the *New York Times* or of magazines with national circulation, like *Time* and *Newsweek,* have a built-in credibility by virtue of their position. Likewise, those in the professions arguing about issues in their fields are established authorities.

But how does the average citizen writing a letter to the editor or a student writing to a friend or speaking to his or her classmates establish credibility? One way is to indicate considerable experience with the subject. By narrating your encounters with the issue, you show yourself to be someone who has received firsthand knowledge. Another way is to research your subject thoroughly and to present this research to the reader. By giving background information, on the one hand, and inductive examples from research, as well as experience, on the other, you show yourself to be well versed in your subject matter.

Sometimes the role you choose to play will help you to establish your credibility. You should decide in which of your many roles you will appear most knowledgeable about your subject and select a voice that expresses that role. If you are presenting to your classmates the merits of soccer over lacrosse as a member of both teams, then the voice of a well-rounded athlete gives you added authority. If no knowledgeable voice is available to you, select a voice that indicates that you are involved in your subject.

You might, for example, want to argue about state politics, and the voice that would best indicate that you are involved in the subject would be that of concerned citizen. The most typical voice for writers of argument to adopt is that of concerned citizen because it allows them to identify with their audience, who will no doubt want to be considered concerned citizens also.

Adopting the Proper Tone.   Once you have chosen your issue and your voice in arguing that issue, you will also want to decide what tone—your attitude toward your subject matter—you should adopt. In most cases, your tone should be reasonable as opposed to strident or hostile. But once that is said, there are many combinations possible. As well as reasonable, you can be firm, distant, sarcastic, urgent, moral, full of righteous indignation, weary, chastising, disgusted, humorous, ironic, and so forth. The soccer and lacrosse player, for example, writing to his or her classmates on the merits of soccer, will adopt a tone consistent with his or her own attitude toward the two sports. After all, how much can one dislike lacrosse? His or her tone might, in fact, be humorous. And, too, this writer must take into account the audience's attitude toward lacrosse. Should they enjoy the sport, he or she must adopt a tone that will not offend them.

Thus your subject matter and your voice will help to determine your tone, and so will your audience. When arguing with politicians, for example, editorial writers often feel freer to adopt more extreme tones, such as sarcasm and disgust, than when writing to persuade private citizens. When persuading common citizens to change an opinion on a subject that is dear to their hearts, the writer often chooses a reasonable tone or combines it with humor or a "we're-all-in-this-together" camaraderie.

Analyzing Your Audience.   This discussion leads us to the importance of analyzing your audience. You should know your audience's frame of reference in order to proceed. Once you have analyzed that, you can evaluate their point of view on the issue. If the audience has not yet formed a point of view, one strategy that you might take is to foster for them a perception of themselves as concerned, reasonable citizens who are willing to act in a reasonable way. If, however, the audience has a point of view, take it into account at all junctures in writing your argument: in deciding on your premises, in adopting your tone, in deciding what action you want the audience to take, and in choosing the language through which you phrase your appeals.

Often your best strategy in arguing is to show esteem for your audience, and to convey this esteem throughout. If you attack your opponents as ignorant or wrong, they probably won't listen to your argument. Instead, adopt the attitude that they are concerned citizens just as you are, and that you "are all in this together." Assume that they want to act in the right manner, just as you do. Be willing to compromise, above all. Very seldom are opposing positions on an issue right and wrong: both sides are right in certain ways and wrong in certain ways. Be willing to recognize this fact as you proceed.

Finally, analyze the depth of your audience's information needs. Do they require background because of lack of acquaintance with the issue? Are they lay readers who can absorb only so much in-depth information? Or are they willing to follow a long, detailed argument? How detailed an argument need you prepare? Analyzing their frame of reference should help you answer this question.

Presenting an Ethical Appeal.   In the "Generating Ideas" section, we discussed how to appeal to your audience through the logical means of induction, deduction, and the classical questions. Two other appeals can be made. One is the ethical appeal, which depends on the writer's sincerity in approaching the topic; the writer seeks to involve his or her readers in the ethics of the situation as well. How can you establish your sincerity and honesty—your ethics—in approaching your issue?

Many professional writers have a reputation that establishes their ethics for them, just as it establishes their credibility. On the other hand, no one quite believes in the honesty or the sincerity of politicians because they usually feel obliged by their party affiliation to argue an issue from the party's point of view. They may sound sincere, sometimes to the point of making people believe in them, but the more dubious audiences often remain just that.

But as an average citizen or a student writer, you have no such baggage either to prove or to disprove your sincerity. You must rely on internal indications, such as your writing carefully, reasonably, and in a straightforward and clear style, making sure to support your points through careful research. Although these internal signs do not prove your honesty, they should appeal to most readers as honest attempts to present a credible argument.

The other appeal is to the emotions, which is made largely through your choice of language. The language of persuasion is discussed in the "Focus" section of this chapter.

SOME PRACTICE WITH PERSUADING YOUR AUDIENCE

Read the following argument and analyze who the writer's audience might be. How aware was the writer of his audience? What appeals has he made to his audience? Once you have read the essay, answer the questions at the end.

We are told that the trouble with Modern Man is that he has been trying to detach himself from nature. He sits on the topmost tiers of polymer, glass, and steel, dangling his pulsing legs, surveying at a distance the writhing life of the planet. In this scenario, man comes on as a stupendous lethal force, and the earth is pictured as something delicate, like rising bubbles at the surface of a country pond, or flights of fragile birds.

But it is illusion to think that there is anything fragile about the life of the earth; surely this is the toughest membrane imaginable in the universe, opaque to probability, impermeable to death. We are the delicate part, transient and vulnerable as cilia. Nor is it a new thing for man to invent an existence that he imagines to be above the rest of life; this has been his most consistent intellectual exertion down the millennia. As illusion, it has never worked out to his satisfaction in the past, any more than it does today. Man is embedded in nature.

The biologic science of recent years has been making this a more urgent fact of life. The new, hard problem will be to cope with the dawning, intensifying realization of just how interlocked we are. The old, clung-to notions most of us have held about our special lordship are being deeply undermined.

Item. A good case can be made for our nonexistence as entities. We are not made up, as we had always supposed, of successively enriched packets of our own parts. We are shared, rented, occupied. At the interior of our cells, driving them, providing the oxidative energy that sends us out for the improvement of each shining day, are the mitochondria, and in a strict sense they are not ours. They turn out to be little separate creatures, the colonial posterity of migrant prokaryocytes, probably primitive bacteria that swam into ancestral precursors of our eukaryotic cells and stayed there. Ever since, they have maintained themselves and their ways, replicating in their own fashion, privately, with their own DNA and RNA quite different from ours. They are as much symbionts as the rhizobial bacteria in the roots of beans. Without them, we would not move a muscle, drum a finger, think a thought.

Mitochondria are stable and responsible lodgers, and I choose to trust them. But what of the other little animals, similarly established in my cells, sorting and balancing me, clustering me together? My centrioles, basal bodies, and probably a good many other more obscure tiny beings at work inside my cells, each with its own special genome, are as foreign, and as essential, as aphids in anthills. My cells are no longer the pure line entities I was raised with; they are ecosystems more complex than Jamaica Bay.

I like to think that they work in my interest, that each breath they draw for me, but perhaps it is they who walk through the local park in the early morning, sensing my senses, listening to my music, thinking my thoughts.

I am consoled, somewhat, by the thought that the green plants are in the same fix. They could not be plants, or green, without their chloroplasts, which run the photosynthetic enterprise and generate oxygen for the rest of us. As it turns out, chloroplasts are also separate creatures with their own genomes, speaking their own language.

We carry stores of DNA in our nuclei that may have come in, at one time or another, from the fusion of ancestral cells and the linking of ancestral organisms in symbiosis. Our genomes are catalogues of instructions from all kinds of sources in nature, filed for all kinds of contingencies. As for me, I am grateful for differentiation and speciation, but I cannot feel as separate an entity as I did a few years ago, before I was told these things, nor, I should think, can anyone else.

Item. The uniformity of the earth's life, more astonishing than its diversity, is accountable by the high probability that we derived, originally, from some single cell, fertilized in a bolt to lightning as the earth cooled. It is from the progeny of this parent cell that we take our looks; we still share genes around, and the resemblance of the enzymes of grasses to those of whales is a family resemblance.

The viruses, instead of being single-minded agents of disease and death, now begin to look more like mobile genes. Evolution is still an infinitely long and tedious biologic game, with only the winners staying at the table, but the rules are beginning to look more flexible. We live in a dancing matrix of viruses; they dart, rather like bees, from organism to organism, from plant to insect to mammal to me and back again, and into the sea, tugging along pieces of this genome, strings of genes from that, transplanting grafts of DNA, passing around heredity as though at a great party. They may be a mechanism for keeping new, mutant kinds of DNA in the widest circulation among us. If this is true, the odd virus disease, on which we must focus so much of our attention in medicine, may be looked on as an accident, something dropped.

  Item. I have been trying to think of the earth as a kind of organism, but it is no go. I cannot think of it this way. It is too big, too complex, with too many working parts lacking visible connections. The other night, driving through a hilly, wooded part of southern New England, I wondered about this. If not like an organism, what is it like, what is it *most* like? Then, satisfactorily for that moment, it came to me: it is *most* like a single cell.

—Lewis Thomas, "The Lives of a Cell"

1. How did the writer establish his credibility with the audience?
2. What role was the writer playing throughout?
3. What tone would you say he was taking in regard to the issue?
4. What attitude did the writer assume the audience has? To what extent do you think the writer created that attitude for the audience?
5. In what ways has the writer shown esteem for the reader?
6. How much depth of information has the writer supplied?
7. To what extent has the writer appealed to the ethics of the reader? To her or his sense of right and wrong?
8. What role does the writer's use of language play in making his point? What function, for example, does his use of analogy have?

Using the Ethical Appeal in Arguing Your Point of View. As you have constructed a case, you virtually have the script for both playing your own role and role-playing that of your audience. Through role playing, you should be able to reconstruct your audience's frame of reference even more fully than you have done in writing the case. Know as thoroughly as you can their point of view on the issue, their education, their values, and the amount of information they have on the subject.

  You will also want to analyze the frame of reference and the point of view of the character you are playing, of course, in order to clarify his or her role as well. If this role does not immediately establish your credibility, you might decide to do research on your subject to bolster your authority. Finally, you will want to select a voice that is consistent with your role, the subject, and your knowledge of your audience.

  To the extent that the character you are playing is not yourself, keep in mind that you are writing as this character and use his or her voice consistently; as you write, make sure not to lapse into playing yourself at any point in the essay. Rather, develop the argument honestly and sincerely in this voice that you have selected, establishing how the subject engages your values, and remembering as well to relate your argument to the values of the audience.

The "Audience Analysis Guide" summarizes the questions you will want to ask in determining how best to approach your reader:

——————— AUDIENCE ANALYSIS GUIDE ———————

1. Have I established credibility with my audience through my knowledge of the subject?
2. Have I adopted the proper tone for addressing my audience?
3. Have I adequately gauged the frame of reference of my audience so that I can be sure I understand their point of view?
4. Have I communicated my sincerity to my audience?

SOME PRACTICE WITH USING THE ETHICAL APPEAL IN ARGUING YOUR POINT OF VIEW

1. Using the journal entry in which you brainstorm about the characteristics of the person whose role you intend to play (see p. 347), choose those characteristics you think will be most likely to persuade your audience. Rank these qualities on the scale of most important to least important, then write a brief paragraph explaining how these qualities can be most effectively conveyed to your audience.

2. Decide what the weakest part of your argument is, then match this with the specific characteristic of your role that you think best matches up with this deficiency. What can you do to enhance this personal trait and thus build up your argument? Address your attention to the following possible sources of examples to use: (1) past experiences or observations of your role, (2) reading about actions your role has done that might bolster this character trait, (3) what others have said about the characteristics of your role (4) examples of your character's authentic involvement in the issue being argued or in other related issues.

3. What experiences can your role draw on that you can expect your audience to have experienced as well? How can you arrange these experiences in your argument so that they have their maximum effect on your audience?

4. How might your role use some of the evidence you have accumulated in an ironic or humorous way? Although your issue may be a serious one, how could you still use humor to effect?

Arranging Your Essay

The Shaping Idea: Stating Your Argument. By now you have spent a lot of time thinking about the subject of your argument. You probably have chosen an issue or problem you feel pretty strongly about, and you want to argue your point of view in the most effective way possible. Most likely you have developed some extensive evidence to use in your case, such as printed sources, the views of people whose opinions you value, or your own experience with knowledge of a given situation. What you need to create is a shaping idea that clearly and forcefully expresses what you think: whether a situation is "good" or "bad"; what course of action should be followed; what will be the consequences of a proposed solution to a problem; what an issue means to those affected by it.

You should be able to state your shaping idea in a single sentence: "The college biological research laboratory should stop using live animal subjects in conducting its research." Because you are developing your argument in the form of a case, with a specific cast of participants and a limited focused issue, you run less risk of arguing on an issue that is too large and requires evidence that you probably could not acquire in the week or two you have to work on your paper. If you are proposing a solution to a specific problem, for example, you should be able to state in a sentence what that solution is: "Increasing the size of the city's police force by 50 percent will effectively reduce the crime rate and not require higher taxes." Your case will be built around this shaping idea, with the participants and audience determining what evidence will be necessary to support this claim.

Your careful inductive or deductive reasoning should provide you with a shaping idea that logically follows from your evidence. Your shaping idea should also reflect the frame of reference and point of view of your audience. How you marshal and present your evidence will, of course, determine the overall success of your argument. But it is with a shaping idea that makes a reasonable, limited claim that you should begin.

Building an Argument. Since classical times, the method for arriving at logical truth or certainty has been the formal argument, developed over centuries as a means for conducting public discussion and debate. Although public oratory is rarely heard today outside of debating societies or legislative bodies, the method for preparing a formal argument is still valid. Consisting of introduction, proof, refutation and conclusion, it gives you help where you need it: it provides a way to proceed through an argument so that it has the greatest impact. It allows you to organize your material and build to the conclusion you hope will win the assent and belief of your audience.

Introduction. The introduction to an argumentative essay fulfills the same function as does any introduction (see Chapter 2, pp. 75–79), although special care must be taken in developing some of its features. It must first of all establish your identity as the writer—what role you are playing and how the role helps establish your credibility.

You cannot introduce yourself, however, without knowing precisely who your audience is and how best to present yourself to them. At the outset, you must set the right tone for your subject and your audience in order to engage them. And then, of course, you must announce your shaping idea: the issue and your point of view on it.

Proof. The body of the paper should contain the proof of your argument and your refutation of your opponent's point of view. As we have discussed, you may garner proof through obtaining support for your arguments, whether inductive or deductive, by asking such classical questions as "What examples are there of it?" "What caused it?" "What is it?" "How can it be classified?" and "How does it compare with the ideal, with the opposing argument, with any alternatives, and with others in its class?" The arrangement of this proof thus should correspond to the patterns that we have discussed in previous chapters: cause and effect, comparison and contrast, and process in Chapter 6 and exemplification in Chapter 7 (general to specific) and Chapter 10 (induction).

Refutation. Once you have established proof of your shaping idea, your next step is to refute the opposition. Refuting those factors that detract from your argument can gain you further credibility. Not only are you recognizing that another point of view exists, but if that point of view happens to be shared by your audience, then you are also giving them credit for their viewpoint. By stating the objections fairly and then refuting them fairly, you make your own argument convincing.

Construct your opposing statements by concentrating on what you know about your audience. If your audience is hostile, then you will not want to further arouse their hostility; even a neutral audience will not respond well to a scathing attack. The most useful refutation may well be one that shows the opposition that a higher priority exists, as we discussed in the "Generating Ideas" section.

Sometimes it is also possible to deny the opposing argument by declaring it untrue or invalid under the circumstances. If an opponent has an erroneous grasp of the facts or if his or her facts do not apply in the situation, then you can point this out, remembering to do so tactfully.

Conclusion. The fourth section of an argumentative essay is the conclusion. In this final section, you will want to summarize your proof and restate your major conclusion.

The Declaration of Independence is certainly one of the most famous arguments ever presented in America. An analysis will indicate how the writers went about organizing this important document.

The Declaration of Independence, July 4, 1776

The Unanimous Declaration of the Thirteen United States of America

When in the Course of human events, it becomes necessary for one people to dissolve the political bands which have connected them with another, and to assume among the powers of the earth, the separate and equal station to which the Laws of Nature and of Nature's God entitle them, a decent respect to the opinions of mankind requires that they should declare the causes which impel them to the separation.

We hold these truths to be self-evident, that all men are created equal, that they are endowed by their Creator with certain unalienable Rights, that among these are Life, Liberty, and the pursuit of Happiness. That to secure these rights, Governments are instituted among Men, deriving their just powers from the consent of the governed. That whenever any Form of Government becomes destructive of these ends, it is the Right of the People to alter or to abolish it, and to institute new Government, laying its foundation on such principles and organizing its powers in such form, as to them shall seem most likely to effect their Safety and Happiness. Prudence, indeed, will dictate that Governments long established should not be changed for light and transient causes; and accordingly all experience hath shown, that mankind are more disposed to suffer, while evils are sufferable, than to right themselves by abolishing the forms to which they are accustomed. But when a long train of abuses and usurpations, pursuing invariably the same Object evinces a design to reduce them under absolute Despotism, it is their right, it is their duty, to throw off such Government, and to provide new Guards for their future security. Such has been the patient sufferance of these Colonies; and such is now the necessity which constrains them to alter their former Systems of Government. The history of the present King of Great Britain is a history of repeated injuries and usurpations, all having in direct object the establishment of an absolute Tyranny over these States. To prove this, let Facts be submitted to a candid world.

He has refused his Assent to Laws, the most wholesome and necessary for the public good.

He has forbidden his Governors to pass Laws of immediate and pressing importance, unless suspended in their operation till his Assent should be obtained; and when so suspended, he has utterly neglected to attend to them.

He has refused to pass other Laws for the accommodation of large districts of people, unless those people would relinquish the right of Representation in the Legislature, a right inestimable to them and formidable to tyrants only.

He has called together legislative bodies at places unusual, uncomfortable, and distant from the depository of their Public Records, for the sole purpose of fatiguing them into compliance with his measures.

He has dissolved Representative Houses repeatedly, for opposing with manly firmness his invasions on the rights of the people.

He has refused for a long time, after such dissolutions, to cause others to be elected; whereby the Legislative Powers, incapable of Annihilation, have returned to the People at large for their exercise; the State remaining in the mean time exposed to all the dangers of invasion from without, and convulsions within.

He has endeavoured to prevent the population of these States; for that purpose obstructing the Laws of Naturalization of Foreigners; refusing to pass others to encourage their migration hither, and raising the conditions of new Appropriations of Lands.

He has obstructed the Administration of Justice, by refusing his Assent to Laws for establishing Judiciary Powers.

He has made Judges dependent on his Will alone, for the tenure of their offices, and the amount and payment of their salaries.

He has erected a multitude of New Offices, and sent hither swarms of Officers to harass our People, and eat out their substance.

He has kept among us, in times of peace, Standing Armies without the Consent of our legislatures.

He has affected to render the Military independent of and superior to the Civil Power.

He has combined with others to subject us to a jurisdiction foreign to our constitution, and unacknowledged by our laws; giving his Assent to their acts of pretended legislation;

For quartering large bodies of armed troops among us:

For protecting them, by a mock Trial, from Punishment for any Murders which they should commit on the Inhabitants of these States:

For cutting off our Trade with all parts of the world:

For imposing Taxes on us without our Consent:

For depriving us in many cases, of the benefits of Trial by Jury:

For transporting us beyond Seas to be tried for pretended offences:

For abolishing the free System of English Laws in a neighbouring Province [Quebec], establishing therein an Arbitrary government, and enlarging its Boundaries so as to render it at once an example and fit instrument for introducing the same absolute rule into these Colonies:

For taking away our Charters, abolishing our most valuable Laws, and altering fundamentally the Forms of our Governments:

For suspending our own Legislatures, and declaring themselves invested with Power to legislate for us in all cases whatsoever.

He has abdicated Government here, by declaring us out of his Protection and waging War against us.

He has plundered our seas, ravaged our Coasts, burnt our towns, and destroyed the Lives of our people.

He is at this time transporting large armies of foreign mercenaries to compleat the works of death, desolation and tyranny, already begun with circumstances of Cruelty & perfidy scarcely paralleled in the most barbarous ages, and totally unworthy the Head of a civilized nation.

He has constrained our fellow Citizens taken Captive on the high Seas to bear Arms against their Country, to become the executioners of their friends and Brethren, or to fall themselves by their Hands.

He has excited domestic insurrections amongst us, and has endeavoured to bring on the inhabitants of our frontiers, the merciless Indian Savages, whose known rule of warfare, is an undistinguished destruction of all ages, sexes and conditions.

In every stage of these Oppressions We have Petitioned for Redress in the most humble terms: Our repeated Petitions have been answered only by repeated injury. A Prince, whose character is thus marked by every act which may define a Tyrant, is unfit to be the ruler of a free People.

Nor have We been wanting in attention to our British brethren. We have warned them from time to time of attempts by their legislature to extend an unwarrantable jurisdiction over us. We have reminded them of the circumstances of our emigration and settlement here. We have appealed to their native justice and magnanimity, and we have conjured them by the ties of our common kindred to disavow these usurpations, which would inevitably interrupt our connections and correspondence. They too have been deaf to the voice of justice and of consanguinity. We must, therefore, acquiesce in the necessity, which denounces our Separation, and hold them, As we hold the rest of mankind, Enemies in War, in Peace Friends.

We, therefore, the Representatives of the United States of America, in General Congress, Assembled, appealing to the Supreme Judge of the world for the rectitude of our intentions, do, in the Name, and by Authority of the good People of these Colonies, solemnly publish and declare, That these United Colonies are, and of Right ought to be Free and Independent States; that they are Absolved from all Allegiance to the British Crown, and that all political connection between them and the State of Great Britain, is and ought to be totally dissolved; and that as Free and Independent States, they have full Power to levy War, conclude Peace, contract Alliances, establish Commerce, and to do all other Acts and Things which Independent States may of right do. And for the support of this Declaration, with a firm reliance on the Protection of Divine Providence, we mutually pledge to each other our Lives, our Fortunes and our sacred Honor.

1. Discuss the assumptions made in the second paragraph. Are they valid? Under what conditions can such assumptions be considered not valid?
2. On what assumption does the argument for independence rest? Reconstruct the argument as an informal syllogism.
3. Does the Declaration conform to the four-part organization of introduction, proof, refutation, and conclusion? Explain.
4. What are the arguments of the opposition? How does the Declaration refute them and/or appeal to a higher authority?
5. Why have so many examples of America's grievances against the British king been listed? Does this appear to be a sampling or is it presented as an exhaustive list? To what extent do you think it was meant to inform the audience as well as to prove the argument?
6. How did the writers establish their credibility? In what voice did they speak and how did it affect their credibility?
7. Who was the audience for the Declaration? What was their frame of reference and point of view on the issue? What effect do you think the

Declaration had on them? What effect does it have on present-day readers?

8. What was the attitude of the writers toward their audience? How did this attitude affect the tone of the piece? How did it affect the writer's ethical appeal?

Writing Your Rough Draft

Once you have thought out your argument and assembled your proof for your audience, you are ready to begin writing your essay. Following is the case created by a student and the rough draft of her argument.

Case. I am Rachel McLish, two-time Miss Olympia, and a fervent believer in and practitioner of bodybuilding. You probably saw me on the Diet Rite commercials with Lee Majors. I have recently been asked by the editors of Redbook Magazine to write an article for their readers arguing that bodybuilding is good for women. I have agreed to do so because I think their readers can be persuaded of my point of view. If I were to write for some other women's magazines, on the other hand, I might not be able to convince their readers, who are more traditional. Of course, I know that there are still other magazines for women whose readers, like me, are already working out in the gym. Redbook readers are adventurous without being in the avant-garde, and I should be able to win them over.

BODYBUILDING: THE SHAPE OF THE FUTURE

I am a female bodybuilder who has been actively engaged in the sport for many years. When you hear the word bodybuilding, the first thing that comes to your mind is probably a masculine man who is said to be clumsy or muscle-bound. Or a woman who looks manly. Most people's attitudes toward bodybuilding have come a long way, but there are still some who are unaware of its benefits. It is now a respected sport for men and women. A woman bodybuilder does not lose any of her femininity; she gains sexuality.

What would you rather have--fat or muscle? A shapely, firm

body or a spongy, saggy one? I am sure everyone would pick muscle and a shapely, firm body. You don't gain large rippling muscles like the manly woman athletes whom you have seen unless you want them. But you will gain a strong, sleek, sexy body. If you lead a sedentary life, your youthful curves will quickly lose their shape and turn into fat. But if you choose the body-building lifestyle, you will stay young and firm.

Bodybuilders have long had a reputation for being muscle-bound and clumsy. But in reality, bodybuilders build their agility along with their muscles. It is important for a bodybuilder to be agile and flexible in order to help prevent injuries. That is why all professional bodybuilders do stretching exercises as part of their exercise routine.

Another part of their routine is aerobic exercise. This is running, swimming, and cycling. This form of exercise strengthens your heart and lungs.

The most essential part of their routine is weightlifting. This exercise increases your strength and power and gives you a defined, firm body.

Bodybuilders eat only the most nutritious foods. They live on a high-protein diet. The foods that they are allowed, especially when in training for competition, are very restricted.

Bodybuilding is becoming more widely accepted. Because of the American Federation of Women Bodybuilders, women's bodybuilding especially is a fast-growing sport. I am sure everyone knows Lou Ferrigno and Arnold Schwarzenegger, thanks to their total dedication to the sport.

Bodybuilders are specimens of perfect health. They are fit in all areas, such as strength, agility, flexibility, and muscular and cardiovascular endurance. Let's think of total physical fitness as a chair. One of the chair legs is stretching exercises, the second is aerobic exercises, the third is weight training, and the fourth is nutrition. Each leg needs the other to hold up the chair. If one element is missing, the chair falls. Bodybuilders do not confine themselves to lifting weights. They do all the exercises to keep themselves in the highest physical condition possible.

1. On what assumption did "Rachel McLish" base her argument? What did she hope to accomplish?
2. What proof did she offer to support her argument? What arrangement patterns did she use?
3. What is the view of the opposition? Has she refuted it? What method of refutation did she use, higher priority or denial?
4. How did she take her audience into account? Did she seem to understand *Redbook* readers well? How would she have changed the essay if she were writing to the readers of *Family Circle* or *Ladies' Home Journal?* How would she have changed it if she were writing to *Cosmopolitan* subscribers?
5. What voice and tone did she adopt? Was she sincere in her advocacy of bodybuilding? Explain.
6. How would you revise this draft?

FOCUS ON STYLE: PERSUASIVE LANGUAGE AND THE APPEAL TO THE EMOTIONS

In an effective argument, the writer's words and phrases play an important part because they form the foundation of the emotional appeal. Whereas the logical and ethical appeals are based on content (presenting facts and conclusions based on valid assumptions and establishing one's credibility through research), the emotional appeal evolves largely from how one phrases that content. Of course, in advertising and in propaganda, the words and even the content may be manipulated to convince the reader emotionally to accept as valid a half-truth or false conclusion, but in honest persuasion, the writer works out a logical argument and then heightens the reader's response through language. In some situations, the writer's audience might not respond to such language, of course; sometimes the members of the scientific community, for example, will be persuaded only by factual content. But in most arguments, the emotional appeal is a significant component.

The tools of persuasive language are many: connotation, figurative language, allusion, repetition, humor, categorical statements, and logical terms. The writer's language must also, of course, be appropriate for the audience and reflect his or her tone (see pp. 349–350).

Connotation

Connotative language is most commonly used to appeal to the emotions. *Connotation* refers to the overlays of meaning that our culture or segments of our culture attach to a word regardless of its denotation, or strictly literal meaning. The denotative meaning of a word is usually the first definition in the dictionary; the connotative meanings follow. Often, as words are so mercurial in our society, the writers of dictionaries cannot keep abreast of the current associations that words have for people. On the other hand, many words that once had fresh connotations have been used so frequently that they have become clichéd and have lost their excitement.

The astute writer is aware of the connotations of words and singles out from a group of possible choices the word that most clearly and freshly states her or his meaning. How many among us, for example, would not prefer to be called *slim* rather than *thin* or *skinny*? Although these words have similar denotations (or literal meanings), their connotations (or associated meanings) are quite different. And if *slim* seems to you to have been overworked, perhaps *slender* seems fresher.

Notice the writer's use of connotation in this paragraph from *Time* magazine that introduces an essay on the acquisition of former President Jimmy Carter's briefing papers by Ronald Reagan's campaign staff before the 1980 debate.

> There are moments in American life when events lurch out of context, when the public is hurtled from dim awareness of a seemingly trivial news item into a maelstrom of moral reappraisal. That appears to be happening in the affair that the Washington press corps has predictably dubbed "Debategate."

Words like *lurch, hurtled,* and *maelstrom* create turbulence in us, and when we see them immediately coupled with *American life* and *moral reappraisal,* we may feel fear and insecurity. Although other words and phrases like *moments, seemingly trivial, news item,* and *predictably dubbed* suggest that the cause of the turbulence is trivial, the language of this introduction implies that an apparently unimportant issue may possess real legal or moral significance. In this paragraph, no facts or assumptions are stated directly, but the language has strongly involved the reader's emotions.

The American novelist William Faulkner also made use of connotation in one of the most famous speeches of our time, given when he accepted the Nobel Prize for Literature. Referring to the human fear of being "blown up" in war, he said about the writer:

> Until he relearns these things, he will write as though he stood among and watched the end of man. I decline to accept the end of man. It is easy enough to say that man is immortal simply because he will endure; that when the last ding-dong of doom has clanged and faded from the last worthless rock hanging tideless in the last red and dying evening, that even then there will still be one more sound: that of his puny inexhaustible voice, still talking. I refuse to accept this. I believe that man will not merely endure; he will prevail. He is immortal, not because he alone among creatures has an inexhaustible voice, but because he has a soul, a spirit capable of compassion

and sacrifice and endurance. The poet's, the writer's, duty is to write about these things. It is his privilege to help man endure by lifting his heart, by reminding him of the courage and honor and hope and pride and compassion and pity and sacrifice which have been the glory of his past. The poet's voice need not merely be the record of man; it can be one of the props, the pillars, to help him endure and prevail.

Some of Faulkner's phrases have vividly negative connotations: "ding-dong of doom," "the last worthless rock hanging tideless in the last red and dying evening," "his puny inexhaustible voice." These images are contrasted with words with strong moral, even religious, positive connotations: "man is immortal," "man will not merely endure; he will prevail," "he has a soul, a spirit capable of compassion and sacrifice and endurance," "courage and honor and hope and pride and compassion and pity and sacrifice." Faulkner was not offering a strongly logical argument; rather, through the sheer impact of his words, he hoped to enlist our emotions in affirming that humans will not only endure but prevail.

Figurative Language

Metaphors and similes also aid the writer of persuasion. As we noted in the "Focus" section of Chapter 7, both figures of speech compare one's subject to another that is not really like it in kind but is like it in some other way that the writer has determined. "That car is a monster" is a metaphor in which two unlike things are compared because they both create fear. "The child waddles like (or as) a duck" is a simile because of the injection of the word *like* or *as*. The point of similarity is obvious: both children and ducks waddle. Whereas the comparison in similes is always clearly stated, the comparison may be submerged in metaphor; in "the car growled," the comparison between car and monster is only implied. Figurative language is used in persuasion because it is highly connotative.

These figures of speech abound in the speeches of our presidents and of other leaders. Abraham Lincoln's speeches during the Civil War used and created metaphors that are still famous: he quoted the Bible in asserting that "A house divided against itself cannot stand" and asked that Americans "bind up the nation's wounds." In a speech on the night of Mahatma Gandhi's death, Indian Prime Minister Jawaharlal Nehru said:

> The light has gone out, I said, and yet I was wrong. For the light that shone in this country was no ordinary light. The light that has illumined this country for these many years will illumine this country for many more years, and a thousand years later that light will still be seen in this country and the world will see it and it will give solace to innumerable hearts. For that light represented the living truth . . . the eternal truths, reminding us of the right path, drawing us from error, taking this ancient country to freedom.

Allusion

Allusion, especially to cultural heroes and myths, is another effective use of language in presenting arguments. Many writers allude to the Bible, because it has always been a cornerstone of our own national mythology. We have already quoted a figure of speech from the Bible used by Abraham Lincoln. And Adlai Stevenson, in accepting the nomination as Democratic Party candidate for president in 1952, alluded to Jesus's agony in the Garden of Gethscmane: "I have asked the merciful Father, the Father to us all, to let this cup pass from me. But from such dread responsibility one does not shrink in fear, in self-interest, or in false humility. So, 'If this cup may not pass from me, except I drink it, Thy will be done.'"

Repetition

One of the most frequently used language patterns in persuasion is repetition. Although repetition, if not handled well, can be boring, when handled skillfully, it can achieve quite impressive effects. In one of the most famous speeches of World War II, given after the Battle of Dunkirk, Winston Churchill concluded:

> Even though large tracts of Europe and many old and famous states have fallen or may fall into the grip of the Gestapo and all the odious apparatus of Nazi rule, we shall not flag or fail. We shall go on to the end, we shall fight in France, we shall fight on the seas and oceans, we shall fight with growing confidence and growing strength in the air, we shall defend our island, whatever the cost may be, we shall fight on the beaches, we shall fight on the landing grounds, we shall fight in the fields and in the streets, we shall fight in the hills; we shall never surrender, and even if, which I do not for a moment believe, this island or a large part of it were subjugated and starving, then our Empire beyond the seas, armed and guarded by the British fleet, would carry on the struggle, until, in God's good time, the New World, with all its power and might, steps forth to the rescue and the liberation of the old.

And Franklin Delano Roosevelt, after the bombing of Pearl Harbor by the Japanese, asked Congress for a declaration of war against Japan. In strikingly effective repetition, he said:

> Yesterday the Japanese government also launched an attack against Malaya.
> Last night Japanese forces attacked Hong Kong.
> Last night Japanese forces attacked Guam.
> Last night Japanese forces attacked the Philippine Islands.
> Last night the Japanese attacked Wake Island.
> And this morning the Japanese attacked Midway Island.

Humor and Satire

Humor can often accomplish for the writer what straight logical argument can not. Woody Allen, in a speech to a graduating class of 1979, argued that science has failed us:

> Put in its simplest form, the problem is: How is it possible to find meaning in a finite world given my waist and shirt size? This is a very difficult question when we realize that science has failed us. True, it has conquered many diseases, broken the genetic code, and even placed human beings on the moon, and yet when a man of 80 is left in a room with two 18-year-old cocktail waitresses nothing happens. Because the real problems never change. After all, can the human soul be glimpsed through a microscope? Maybe— but you'd definitely need one of those very good ones with two eyepieces. We know that the most advanced computer in the world does not have a brain as sophisticated as that of an ant. True, we could say that of many of our relatives but we only have to put up with them at weddings or special occasions. Science is something we depend on all the time. If I develop a pain in the chest I must take an X-ray. But what if the radiation from the X-ray causes me deeper problems? Before I know it, I'm going in for surgery. Naturally, while they're giving me oxygen an intern decides to light up a cigarette. The next thing you know I'm rocketing over the World Trade Center in bed clothes. Is this science? True, science has taught us how to pasteurize cheese. And true, this can be fun in mixed company—but what of the H-bomb? Have you ever seen what happens when one of those things falls off a desk accidentally? And where is science when one ponders the eternal riddles? How did the cosmos originate? How long has it been around? Did matter begin with an explosion or by the word of God? And if by the latter, could He not have begun it just two weeks earlier to take advantage of some of the warmer weather? Exactly what do we mean when we say, man is mortal? Obviously it's not a compliment.

In one of the most famous arguments of all time, Jonathan Swift made "a modest proposal" that the Irish eat their children because they were too poor to feed them: "I have been assured by a very knowing American of my acquaintance in London, that a young healthy child well nursed is at a year old a most delicious, nourishing, and wholesome food, whether stewed, roasted, baked, or broiled; and I make no doubt that it will equally serve in a fricassee or a ragout." Because most of his readers were shocked, Swift was very effective in his use of satire, which is the humorous or critical treatment of a subject in order to expose the subject's or the audience's vices or follies. Swift was, of course, not seriously proposing this remedy for the poverty of the Irish, but he wielded the sword of satire in an effort to move the English to alleviate their misery.

Categorical Statements

The writer of argument may speak in categorical statements that emphasize his or her position by assuring the reader that there are no qualifications to the argument and will be no wavering in his or her position. Thus Abraham Lincoln promised, "We shall not fail—if we stand firm, we shall not fail"; Winston Churchill intoned, "we shall defend our island, whatever the cost may be"; and William Faulkner asserted, "I believe that man not only will endure; he will prevail."

Logical Terms

The writer of argument often, of course, uses the terminology of logic in making her or his presentation. In arguing that the poor have every reason for accommodating to poverty, as their situation is "usually hopeless," John Kenneth Galbraith, the economist, stated that the acceptance by the poor of their fate is "a profoundly rational response" and that "The deeply rational character of accommodation lies back, at least in part, of the central instruction of the principal world religions." Through the use of the word *rational,* he hammered away at the prejudices of the rich against the poor, whom the rich blame for accepting their condition.

Tone and Audience

Two other language considerations that the writer of argument must be aware of are how language conveys his or her tone and what language is appropriate to his or her audience. If the tone is serious, then the language must be serious. If the audience is educated, then the language should be educated. (For other discussions of tone, see Chapter 7, pp. 276–284; Chapter 8, pp. 349–350; and Chapter 9, 430–433; 437–439.)

SOME PRACTICE WITH THE LANGUAGE OF PERSUASION

1. Read "Letter from a Birmingham Jail" for Martin Luther King, Jr.'s use of language in attempting to persuade his audience—eight white Alabama ministers who had publicly disavowed his method—to accept his nonviolent method of gaining civil rights for American black people.

Letter from a Birmingham Jail

Martin Luther King, Jr.

I must confess that over the past few years I have been gravely disappointed with the white moderate. I have almost reached the regrettable conclusion that the Negro's great stumbling block in his stride toward freedom is not the White Citizen's Counciler or the Ku Klux Klanner, but the white moderate, who is more devoted to "order" than to justice; who prefers a negative peace which is the absence of tension to a positive peace which is the presence of justice; who constantly says: "I agree with you in the goal you seek, but I cannot agree with your methods of direct action"; who paternalistically believes he can set the timetable for another man's freedom; who lives by a mythical concept of time and who constantly advises the Negro to wait for a "more convenient season." Shallow understanding from people of good will is more frustrating than absolute misunderstanding from people of ill will. Lukewarm acceptance is much more bewildering than outright rejection.

I had hoped that the white moderate would understand that law and order exist for the purpose of establishing justice and that when they fail in this purpose they become the dangerously structured dams that block the flow of social progress. I had hoped that the white moderate would understand that the present tension in the South is a necessary phase of the transition from an obnoxious negative peace, in which the Negro passively accepted his unjust plight, to a substantive and positive peace, in which all men will respect the dignity and worth of human personality. Acutally, we who engage in nonviolent direct action are not the creators of tension. We merely bring to the surface the hidden tension that is already alive. We bring it out in the open, where it can be seen and dealt with. Like a boil that can never be cured so long as it is covered up but must be opened with all its ugliness to the natural medicines of air and light, injustice must be exposed, with all the tension its exposure creates, to the light of human conscience and the air of national opinion before it can be cured.

In your statement you assert that our actions, even though peaceful, must be condemned because they precipitate violence. But is this a logical assertion? Isn't this like condemning a robbed man because his possession of money precipitated the evil act of robbery? Isn't this like condemning Socrates because his unswerving commitment to truth and his philosophical inquiries precipitated the act by the misguided populace in which they made him drink hemlock? Isn't this like condemning Jesus because his unique God-consciousness and never-ceasing devotion to God's will precipitated the evil act of crucifixion? We must come to see that, as the federal courts have consistently affirmed, it is wrong to urge an individual to cease his efforts to gain his basic constitutional rights because the quest may precipitate violence. Society must protect the robbed and punish the robber.

I had also hoped that the white moderate would reject the myth concerning time in relation to the struggle for freedom. I have just received a letter from a white brother in Texas. He writes: "All Christians know that the colored people will receive equal rights eventually, but it is possible that you are in too great a religious hurry. It has taken Christianity almost two thousand years to accomplish what it has. The teachings of Christ take time to come to earth." Such an attitude stems from a tragic misconception of time, from the strangely irrational notion that there is something in the very flow of time that will inevitably cure all ills. Actually, time itself is neutral; it can be used either destructively or constructively. More and more I feel that the people of ill will have used time much more effectively than have the people of good will. We will have to repent in this generation not merely for the hateful words and actions of the bad people but for the appalling silence of the good people. Human progress never rolls in on wheels of inevitability; it comes through the tireless efforts of men willing to be co-workers with God, and without this hard work, time itself becomes an ally of the forces of social stagnation. We must use time creatively, in the knowledge that the time is always ripe to do right. Now is the time to make real the promise of democracy and transform our pending national elegy into a creative psalm of brotherhood. Now is the time to lift our national policy from the quicksand of racial injustice to the solid rock of human dignity.

You speak of our activity in Birmingham as extreme. At first I was rather disappointed that fellow clergymen would see my nonviolent efforts as those of an extremist. I began thinking about the fact that I stand in the middle of two opposing forces in the Negro community. One is a force of complacency, made up in part of Negroes who, as a result of long years of oppression, are so drained of self-respect and a sense of "somebodiness" that they have adjusted to segregation; and in part of a few middle-class Negroes who, because of a degree of academic and economic security and because in some ways they profit by segregation, have become insensitive to the problems of the masses. The other force is one of bitterness and hatred, and it comes perilously close to advocating violence. It is expressed in the various black nationalist groups that are springing up across the nation, the largest and best-known being Elijah Muhammad's Muslim movement. Nourished by the Negro's frustration over the continued existence of racial discrimination, this movement is made up of people who have lost faith in America, who have absolutely repudiated Christianity, and who have concluded that the white man is an incorrigible "devil."

I have tried to stand between these two forces, saying that we need emulate neither the "do-nothingism" of the complacent nor the hatred and despair of the black nationalist. For there is the more excellent way of love and nonviolent protest. I am grateful to God that, through the influence of the Negro church, the way of nonviolence became an integral part of our struggle.

If this philosophy had not emerged, by now many streets of the South would, I am convinced, be flowing with blood. And I am further convinced that if our white brothers dismiss as "rabble-rousers" and "outside agitators" those of us who employ nonviolent direct action, and if they refuse to support our nonviolent efforts, millions of Negroes will, out of frustration and despair, seek solace and security in black-nationalist ideologies—a development that would inevitably lead to a frightening racial nightmare.

Oppressed people cannot remain oppressed forever. The yearning for freedom eventually manifests itself, and that is what has happened to the American Negro. Something within has reminded him of his birthright of freedom, and something without has reminded him that it can be gained. Consciously or unconsciously, he has been caught up by the *Zeitgeist,* and with his black brothers of Africa and his brown and yellow brothers of Asia, South America and the Caribbean, the United States Negro is moving with a sense of great urgency toward the promised land of racial justice. If one recognizes this vital urge that has engulfed the Negro community, one should readily understand why public demonstrations are taking place. The Negro has many pent-up resentments and latent frustrations and he must release them. So let him march; let him make prayer pilgrimages to the city hall; let him go on freedom rides — and try to understand why he must do so. If his repressed emotions are not released in nonviolent ways, they will seek expression through violence; this is not a threat but a fact of history. So I have not said to my people: "Get rid of your discontent." Rather, I have tried to say that this normal and healthy discontent can be channeled into the creative outlet of nonviolent direct action. And now this approach is being termed extremist.

But though I was initially disappointed at being categorized as an extremist, as I continued to think about the matter I gradually gained a measure of satisfaction from the label. Was not Jesus an extremist for love; "Love your enemies, bless them that curse you, do good to them that hate you, and pray for them which despitefully use you, and persecute you." Was not Amos an extremist for justice: "Let justice roll down like the waters and righteousness like an ever-flowing stream." Was not Paul an extremist for the Christian gospel: "I bear in my body the marks of the Lord Jesus." Was not Martin Luther an extremist: "Here I stand; I cannot do otherwise, so help me God." And John Bunyan: "I will stay in jail to the end of my days before I make a butchery of my conscience." And Abraham Lincoln: "This nation cannot survive half slave and half free." And Thomas Jefferson: "We hold these truths to be self-evident, that all men are created equal . . ." So the question is not whether we will be extremists, but what kind of extremists we will be. Will we be extremists for hate or for love? Will we be extremists for the preservation of injustice or for the extension of justice? In that dramatic scene on Calvary's hill three men were crucified. We must never forget that all three were crucified for the same crime — the crime of extremism. Two were extremists for immorality, and thus fell below their environment. The other, Jesus Christ, was an extremist for love, truth and goodness, and thereby rose above his environment. Perhaps the South, the nation and the world are in dire need of creative extremists.

I had hoped that the white moderate would see this need. Perhaps I was too optimistic; perhaps I expected too much. I suppose I should have realized that few members of the oppressor race can understand the deep groans and passionate yearnings of the oppressor race, and still fewer have the vision to see that injustice must be rooted out by strong, persistent and determined action. I am thankful, however, that some of our white brothers in the South have grasped the meaning of this social revolution and committed themselves to it. They are still all too few in quantity, but they are big in quality. Some — such as Ralph McGill, Lillian Smith, Harry Golden, James McBride Dabbs, Ann Braden and Sarah Patton Boyle — have written about our struggle in eloquent and prophetic terms. Others have marched with us down nameless streets of the South. They have languished in filthy, roach-infested jails, suffering the abuse and brutality of policemen who view them as "dirty nigger-lovers." Unlike so many of their moderate brothers and sisters, they have recognized the urgency of the moment and sensed the need for powerful "action" antidotes to combat the disease of segregation.

a. What are the logical components of King's argument? Are they primarily inductive, deductive, or a combination? Did he appeal to a higher priority in refuting his opposition? If so, what higher priority did he establish?

b. What was his attitude toward his audience? How did this attitude affect his tone? What words and phrases indicate what his tone is?

c. King made extensive use of connotative language. What connotative meanings do phrases like the following have, and how do they make an emotional appeal for his argument: "obnoxious negative peace," "unjust plight," "deep groans and passionate yearnings," "dignity and worth of human personality," "prayer pilgrimages," "creative extremists," and "strong, persistent and determined action"?

d. His letter also abounds in figurative language and allusions. What are some of the many metaphors he used? What are some of the allusions? What effects were these intended to have on his readers? Some of his metaphors are clichés like "the time is always ripe." Why would King use clichés in writing to this audience?

e. Repetition is another key element in King's appeal to his reader's emotions. Point out an instance of this repetition and discuss its usefulness.

f. King also presented his argument in categorical statements. Which do you think are most effective in arousing the reader?

g. Where did King insert logical terms, either to denigrate his opponents' use of reason or to support his own logic? How important a role does this type of emotional appeal play? Explain.

h. How did King's audience's frame of reference affect his choice of words? How would his persuasive language have changed if he had been writing to a group of U.S. Senators?

2. Choose one of the following statements and develop it in a paragraph or two. Once you are satisfied with the logic of your argument, revise your paragraph by using one or more of the methods of persuasive language. Write to an audience of your choosing and convey your tone clearly:

> Leisure time affects the quality of life more than does work because that is when we have an opportunity to think.
>
> Everyone should participate in games because games can teach us how to compete gracefully.
>
> Stress must be dealt with because it is a constant in modern life.

3. Discuss the use of persuasive language by the framers of the Declaration of Independence (pp. 351–359). Compare and contrast their use of such language with that of Martin Luther King, Jr. How can you account for any substantial differences?

Using the Emotional Appeal in Arguing Your Point of View

Creating a case to argue suggests that the word "audience" still conveys some of its original meaning as a group of concerned individuals listening closely to how you express your point of view. If you imagine an actual voice speaking to a real audience, the importance of the emotional appeal will strike home. For example the term "politically correct," used to refer to the language of race, gender, and ethnicity, shows how important a writer's choice of words is in appealing to an audience's emotions. Misusing a word or being unaware of the connotation of a word can offend your audience, causing it to question other elements of your argument. Inappropriate humor; ambiguous or confusing metaphor; irony that falls flat; bold assertions that convey arrogance rather than confidence; repetition that sounds overdramatic—these are some of the misjudgments that can be fatal in arguing to a real audience.

Let your invented role determine what language is appropriate for your case. If, for example, you are a concerned parent addressing an assembly of parents, teachers, and administrators to persuade them to begin a program to counsel children on child abuse or personal safety measures, you are well aware that the audience will be steered by reference to the dangers—actual and hypothetical—their children may face. However, the use of frequent references to bruised and battered faces, images of tiny bodies scarred by adult cruelty, of "our lovely little flowers destroyed in the bud," may strike your audience as overdone but half-baked. What they might want to hear is a more pragmatic, more realistic approach geared to their sense of themselves as concerned and altruistic parents and professionals.

This suggests, as you might have already inferred, that the writer needs to be doubly conscious of how choice of language can move an audience. Woe to the public figure who thought that calling his political opponent a "witless, whining wimp" would impress his audience with his bright phrasemaking, only to have it come back in his weary, worrisome face at election time. Try your language techniques on your peer audience first. Most likely they can suggest ways to rev up or tone down your point of view. The emotional appeal of an argument can call forth the noblest and most eloquent language—as in Martin Luther King, Jr.'s speech—but it can easily hurt the incautious writer.

SOME PRACTICE WITH APPEALING TO THE EMOTIONS
OF THE READER OF YOUR PERSUASIVE ESSAY

1. In preparing your case for an audience, what should you take into account with regard to the connotation of words? For example, assume you are addressing a group that is debating whether to develop vocational programs for special education in your hometown. What effect would your use of the words "crippled," "disabled" or "physically challenged" have on your audience? What other examples of the connotations of words can you think of that might make a crucial difference in an argument?

2. What do you think of the effectiveness of "Rachel McLish's" use of metaphor ("four legs on the chair of health," p. 361)? How can you use figurative language in your argument? Where would it have the biggest impact?

3. What is the danger of using humor and satire in your persuasive essay? How could the use of humor enhance the impact of your case? Where could you use it?

4. In a dictionary of quotations look up topics that touch on your shaping idea. Select quotations you think interesting and appropriate for including in your essay. How do they make a strong emotional appeal? What would be the most effective places to use these quotations?

5. Let your peer group members examine your draft to evaluate your use of figurative language. For example, how can you use metaphor to enliven and intensify your point of view but avoid falling into tired or overused comparisons?

6. Try to use repetition as a way of emphasizing key ideas in your essay. You might revise some of your sentences to make an emotional appeal with repetition of words or sentence structure. For example:

> *Original.* Martin Luther King, Jr. was an eloquent public speaker. He was also an effective leader of his people. King was known throughout the world. He preached nonviolence as a means of social change.

> *Revised.* Yes, Martin Luther King, Jr. was an eloquent public speaker. Martin Luther King was an effective leader of his people. Martin Luther King, Jr. was known throughout the world. But most important, Martin Luther King, Jr. was a man who preached nonviolence as a means of social change.

REWRITING

Obtaining Feedback on Your Rough Draft

Because persuasive writing depends more on audience response than does any other type of writing, the feedback that you receive on your rough draft will be crucial to the success of your final product. Therefore you must solicit the most thoughtful response. Whether this response comes from your "other, critical self," a peer group, or your instructor, the respondent should play to the best of his or her ability the role that you have established for your audience.

In playing the role of your audience, your respondent should know your audience's frame of reference and their point of view on your subject. He or she should be willing to defend your audience's position in order to elicit from you the most effective argument possible. He or she may indicate to you, for example, that you have not appealed to the most telling higher priority and will need to reevaluate the basis of your argument.

You will want to analyze also how your audience has responded to your language and tone, to your evidence, and to your refutation. At some point, your reader(s) should also switch sides and tell you how to better defend your own position.

Try answering the questions of the "Audience Response Guide" for the student essay on bodybuilding (see pp. 360–361) before you rewrite your essay.

AUDIENCE RESPONSE GUIDE

1. What argument does the writer want to convey in this paper? What is his or her purpose in arguing? What does she or he want the paper to mean?
2. How does the argument affect the reader for whom it was intended?
3. How effective has the writer been in conveying his or her argument? What are the strengths of the argument? What are the weaknesses?
4. How should the argument be revised to better fulfill its purpose or meaning?

Revision of the Student Essay "Bodybuilding: The Shape of the Future"

The student who wrote the rough draft on "Bodybuilding: The Shape of the Future" obtained the following comments from her peer evaluation group:

1. They knew that she was arguing that because bodybuilding is a necessity to all who are conscious of their appearance and their health, women should pursue the sport.

2. As readers of Redbook Magazine, her audience felt that the writer had bridged the gap between the images in the media of the bodybuilding woman as an unattractive athlete, on the one hand, and as a sexual athlete, on the other. They felt her concern about both health and appearance was very convincing.

3. Her readers were impressed by her authoritative, yet friendly presentation. They liked the chair analogy, but they felt the paragraphs in the body of the essay were too short and choppy and suggested she rearrange the material on the different elements of the bodybuilder's routine.

4. They were curious about how bodybuilding relates to the women's movement. They also wanted to be reassured that they would not grow "big" muscles.

How do these comments compare with those that you made? Here is the student's revised draft.

BODYBUILDING: THE SHAPE OF THE FUTURE

I am a female bodybuilder who has been actively engaged in bodybuilding for many years. When you hear the word bodybuilding, the first image that probably comes to mind is a man who is clumsy or muscle-bound and a woman who looks manly. Although some people's attitudes have changed, most are still unaware of the benefits of bodybuilding. Bodybuilding has become more than a sport--it has become a way of life. A woman bodybuilder does not lose any of her femininity; she gains sexuality.

In the past, a woman's place was in the home. She was expected to grow up, get married, have babies, clean, cook, and turn into the all-American frumpy housewife. Well, times have changed; more women have their own careers and goals. Along with career changes have come changes in how women feel about themselves and their bodies. More and more women are discovering bodybuilding as a way of staying fit and youthful.

What would you rather have, fat or muscle? A shapely, firm body or a spongy, saggy one? I am sure everyone would choose muscle and a shapely, firm body. That is the best reason to start bodybuilding. Don't sit back and accept saggy, cellulite bodies as part of nature. And you won't gain large, manly muscles. A woman's level of testosterone, the hormone that causes men to grow large muscles, is generally one tenth that of a man's. Though a woman's muscular strength grows from weightlifting, she does not gain the muscle bulk of the man. Yet she does gain a strong, sleek, sexy body.

Because bodybuilding has long been considered a man's sport, one thinks of bodybuilders as clumsy and muscle-bound, but in reality, bodybuilders build their agility along with their muscles. It is important for a bodybuilder to be agile and flexible in order to prevent injuries.

The program for physical fitness can be compared to a chair. One of the legs on the chair is stretching exercises. Stretching exercises increase flexibility and minimize injuries. These exercises help to keep you agile. The second leg is aerobic exercises. Aerobic exercises are running, swimming, and cycling. These exercises strengthen your cardiovascular system, resulting in keeping a strong heart. The third leg is weight training. These exercises increase your strength and power and give you a defined, firm body. The fourth leg is nutrition. Nutrition is essential in keeping your body healthy. You need all four legs to hold up the chair. If one is missing, the chair will fall. And so if one of these components is missing from your routine, then you are not totally fit.

The four legs on the chair of health are part of every bodybuilder's routine; therefore bodybuilders are specimens of perfectly fit human beings. Bodybuilders are fit in all areas, such as strength, agility, flexibility, and muscular and cardiovascular endurance. They are not into just lifting weights. They are totally dedicated to diet and exercise. As men and women develop their physiques, psychological effects also occur, such as self-esteem, confidence, and a new outlook on life.

Revising Your Persuasive Essay

When writing persuasively, your aims are to convince the reader of your logic and your credibility. You might apply the following questions to your persuasive essay in order to determine what revisions you might make in strengthening your logic and overall credibility.

 Checklist for Revising Your Persuasive Essay.

1. Have you included weak or extraneous arguments, arguments that you yourself find unconvincing? More important, have you applied the tests for fallacious reasoning to your points? If not, consider whether any of your arguments now appear to be fallacies. Cut all weak, extraneous, or fallacious arguments from your essay.

2. Have you included enough background for your intended reader? Have you included enough examples to prove your argument? Does an analogy now occur to you? Have you refuted any opposing arguments? At this point, you may want to add background, examples, an analogy, a refutation to your essay.

3. How effective is your organization of your arguments? What pattern of arrangement have you used? Does it correspond to the classical questions that you asked? Is your arrangement of causes, comparisons, classifications, definitions effective? Have you placed your strongest arguments at the end for major effect? If your organization seems illogical or weak, you may want to rearrange your points.

4. If cutting proof that now seems to you unconvincing will leave you with a thin case for your point of view, you might search for a stronger argument as a substitute.

5. Have you neglected to reinforce part of your argument? If so, you might insert mention or proof of this aspect of your case at logical points in your paper. The distributing of an important aspect of your argument reinforces its importance; neglecting it makes the reader wonder why you mentioned it in the first place.

6. **Do you want to retain some of your weak arguments but don't know how to make them seem convincing? You might want to consolidate them under an inclusive heading to bolster their significance.**

7. **Have you chosen words for their emotional connotations as well as their literal meanings? Have you included figures of speech that make comparisons the reader will respond to? Have you added touches of humor that might engage your reader?**

Editing.   Your writing for a persuasive paper should be clear and concrete in order to assure the reader of your credibility. Terms should be carefully defined, and facts should be clearly stated.

Persuasive writing employs figurative language in its appeal to the emotions of the reader. The "Focus" section of this chapter suggests the use of connotative language, wit, humor, irony, and figures of speech in an effort to engage the reader's emotions. You might reexamine the language of your essay to see if you have chosen words for their emotional connotations as well as their literal meanings, included figures of speech that make comparisons the reader will respond to, and perhaps added touches of humor that will engage the reader further.

BECOMING AWARE OF YOURSELF AS A WRITER

1. In presenting your argument, what methods did you use to convince your audience? How could you have been more convincing? How can you be more convincing in the future?

2. Based on your peer group's response, were you able to argue your points logically? Were you able to convince them of your credibility? What effect did your logic and credibility have on your audience?

3. How were you able to use such elements of language as connotation, metaphor, allusion, and repetition to argue your points effectively?

4. From your work with the techniques of persuasion, can you imagine how such techniques can be misused and abused by those seeking to sell a product or to persuade at any cost? Do you feel more powerful as a writer now that you have begun to develop persuasive skills yourself?

5. What have you learned about responding to the arguments of others by fulfilling this task? How might you argue a particular point differently from how you argued it in the past?

9

Writing About an Issue— Joining a Debate

PURPOSE

In the writing task for Chapter 8 you created a case on a controversial issue and argued a point of view on the issue that you hoped would persuade your reader. In supporting your view, your appeal was to your audience's ability to reason responsibly and to respond as emotionally to the issue as you did. By using the techniques of induction, deduction, and the classical questions you joined in and became part of a centuries-old tradition of debate and argumentation. As you constructed your argument, your emphasis was rightly placed on demonstrating to your reader the superiority of your point of view to another view on that issue.

There is an exciting competitiveness in arguing an issue. Because it seems to result in clearly defined winners and losers, you might even see it as a kind of sports event. Cigarette machines should be banned from the campus or they should not. Violence should be eliminated from professional hockey or it should not. It appears that whoever provides the best argument should be the clear winners; that there is no room for a middle ground or for straddling a fence.

But when we enter the larger public world—our individual communities, our nation as a whole—we encounter issues that seem too complex, too important in the way they touch our lives to be decided in terms of clear winners or losers. Unlike the relatively confined and limited debate of a classroom or an assigned essay, many of the significant issues—abortion, euthanasia, pornography—in our contemporary society are not so easily resolved. Because they all pose moral and ethical questions that can polarize people's opinions and split them into irreconcilable, opposing camps, we need to debate these issues in a broader, more inclusive way. In doing so, we learn to see the issue, ourselves and the other participants in the debate in a much more informed way as well. Our arguments will not only provide us with a victory for ourselves, but perhaps also afford one to all the parties concerned because of this enhanced judgment and understanding of a crucial social concern.

First, however, we need to become more aware of the national debate that is taking place with respect to these issues. As you know, abortion, euthanasia, and pornography have been the subject of many books and articles over the years. In the "task" section, nine professional essays will provide you with considerable material for thinking about how these three issues are currently debated, for determining what underlies your own point of view on these subjects, and for preparing an argument that will attempt to create a broader, more inclusive statement of the issue. (Your instructor or your group may wish to choose three essays on a different social issue.)

To understand these issues, you may need to know what basic assumptions and beliefs are held by the various participants. To judge the merits of a particular point of view, you may need to know how your own background and opinions affect your understanding of the issue. This examination of how we think and arrive at conclusions is called critical thinking, and we will discuss how it is important in the "Generating Ideas" section. In the "Audience" section we will suggest how, in your pursuit of an expanded point of view on an issue, you might use role playing as a means of understanding the positions of another informed reader.

TASK: JOINING A DEBATE ON AN ISSUE

Your task will be to write an essay in which, having examined varying points of view on a controversial social issue, you attempt to arrive at and argue a new, broader point of view, one that incorporates both sides of the debate. You will, in a sense, show how a larger understanding of the various positions might lead to a possible resolution of the debate on a significant issue.

In the previous chapter you argued your point of view on a controversy. You formed your argument based on your analysis of the case, the issues involved and the positions of the opposing viewpoint. Through a use of induction, deduction, and the classical questions, you made your appeal to the reason and emotions of your audience, laid out your proposal or argued your position, and refuted the claims of the opposing side. Your main purpose was to establish the superior status of your argument by persuading your audience to that effect. For this task, however, we ask you to use these strategies of argument in a different way and for a different purpose.

Included in the following pages are three essays on each of three social issues: abortion, euthanasia, and pornography. Because these issues are so controversial and arouse so much emotion, many people have positioned themselves so firmly on one side or the other that they barely listen to what the other side is saying. Your task is, first, to learn as much about the issue as you can by analyzing what are the major ideas underlying the various positions; secondly, to try to bring together these differing views by arguing for a new, more inclusive approach to the issue. (You may, of course, select an issue other than those included here about which to gather representative essays and to fulfill your task.)

For example, your argument on pornography might include a way to re-solve community resentment against displaying so-called adult films in a video store but still uphold the constitutional rights of free expression. Or, if you are arguing on the issue of gun control, you might seek some way to accommodate the positions of the National Rifle Association, the police, and the victim of a violent crime. What kind of policy could you propose that might incorporate their different points of view?

As a concerned human being, you most surely have formed strong opin-ions about these issues yourself. Your personal experiences and your reading have all influenced you to form these opinions. In order to write the essay for this task you do not have to submerge or deny these personal viewpoints. What we do suggest, however, is that you try to argue for a point of view that includes your original—or modified—position but that now goes beyond your opinion by being combined with the views of others.

The authors of the following essays work within a relatively narrow range of language choices. They generally avoid the rich metaphorical language of expressive or even much persuasive writing, preferring a language generally unadorned, clear, and objective. Most of these essays were originally published in journals of opinion, periodicals that emphasize matter over manner be-cause their audience expects this in a debate over serious issues of national interest. Some of the authors are lawyers and university professors: they are expected to express ideas in language that is objective and restrained. They seek to persuade through the force of their evidence and reasoning.

In your essay you are not restricted from choosing figurative language. But remember that your purpose in writing this essay is to try to resolve differen-ces rather than move your audience to favor one position over another. Thus a more formal use of words may be appropriate.

Because these essays originally appeared in periodicals intended for an educated informed audience, they present fairly complex arguments and em-ploy a vocabulary that includes a number of abstract words. For example,

Van Den Haag, who writes with particular clarity, uses the words "secularization," "sentience," "abrogation," "abortifacient," "inchoately." Other public arguments such as newspaper editorials or columns often use a more informal, concrete language to reach their large number of readers. Generally, when expressing ideas, you need to consider key abstract words that support your claim. But a lengthy string of abstract words simply obfuscates the inchoate semantic reification of your lucubrations. Most writers avoid them.

Your audience for this task will be an informed reader, most likely your instructor or another member of your school or community who is aware of the varied contexts of your issue and can judge your argument's effectiveness.

The "Generating Ideas" section will focus on the critical thinking that will enter into your analysis of the issues, and your judgment in forming your broader point of view.

READING TO WRITE

I. Abortion Essays

Is There a Middle Ground?

by Ernest Van Den Haag

In pagan antiquity it was taken for granted that, except for slaves, people own themselves. Hence, everybody was free to dispose of himself as he wanted. Suicide was neither illegal nor thought immoral. It was taken for granted as well that free persons owned whatever they produced and could dispose of it as they wished. Infants were the property of the parents who produced them (more specifically of the *paterfamilias*, since *familia id est patrimonium*) until they became independent adults who owned themselves. Roman law consequently did not regard infanticide by parents as a crime. That norm prevailed throughout the pagan world. (Probably also in the early stages of Jewish development: the proposed sacrifice by Abraham of his son Isaac marked the beginning of the end of human sacrifice and probably of parental infanticide as well.) Infants were the property of their parents, to dispose of as they thought fit. *Eo ipso* this was the case also for fetuses, although the technology for aborting them was not well developed.

Christianity changed all this. According to the Christian belief persons possess but do not own themselves. Rather, people belong to their creator, who alone is entitled to dispose of his creatures. Suicide became a sin—and, until recently, a crime. (Of course, only the unsuccessful attempt was punishable in this world.) Infants no longer are regarded as the product of their parents and owned by them. They are God's creatures. He creates them through the instrumentality of parental intercourse. Parents have a fiduciary duty. It gradually became a crime for them to kill their infants, *post partum* and, ultimately, *in utero* as well. For a long time, however, it was not a crime to abort the embryo before "quickening" and "ensoulment."

Followers of the Judaeo-Christian tradition still are most numerous and passionate among those who believe abortion to be wrong. On the other hand, most of those who no longer adhere to Judaeo-Christian beliefs do not find abortion to be wrong in principle. They believe that the decision on whether or not to carry the fetus to term belongs entirely to the mother. She has produced the fetus (with indispensable, but minor, male assistance) and therefore owns it and can dispose of it as she can of her own body.

Pro-abortionists usually shrink from infanticide. They argue that the infant is unquestionably alive, unquestionably human, and viable outside the mother, whereas the fetus may not be. The real reason is less intellectually plausible but psychologically more compelling: feticide occurs inside the maternal womb. It kills an entity that no one has seen alive, that is known to exist but is not directly observed. Infanticide kills a human being that is independently alive. The killing occurs in full view, outside the maternal womb. Infanticide thus mobilizes compassion and solidarity—even horror—far more directly than feticide.

Although within the Judaeo-Christian tradition there are some ways to condone abortion, and on the secular side there are some arguments to oppose it (as well as suicide and infanticide), the theoretical chasm between secularists, who believe that we belong to ourselves, and traditionalists, who believe that we are God's creatures, is unbridgeable. If parents do not own themselves or the fetus, they have no right to dispose of it except within the range prescribed by their creator. If parents own themselves and the fetus is their product, their right to dispose of it can be challenged only when abused in specific ways.

Let me digress to note here that John Locke, despite his strong emphasis on property rights, particularly in one's own product, clung to religious tradition. He did not feel that we own ourselves. Locke wrote: Though man "have an uncontrollable Liberty, to dispose of his Person or Possessions, yet he has not Liberty to destroy himself, or so much as any Creature in his Possession . . . For Men being all the Workmanship . . . of one Sovereign Master . . . they are His Property." *A fortiori* the killing of innocent human offspring cannot be rightful at any stage, since it belongs to God.

The increasing secularization of Western societies since Locke points toward restoration of the pre-Christian concepts of self-ownership. However, these concepts are modified by contemporary individualism (also largely a Christian heritage, but quite divorced now from religion), which weakens the authority of the *paterfamilias,* indeed, of the family itself. Individualism, secularization, and, not least, the current obsession with equality have endowed infants and children with new rights; but not embryos or even fetuses, whose unborn rights, if any, seem superseded by the individual rights of their mothers.

Anti-abortionists believe that "life begins at conception." This makes sense (indeed, what is aborted if not life?), although it amounts to a somewhat circular definition. Conception is the fertilization of the ovum, which then, attached to the uterine wall, develops into an embryo, according to encoded genes which control its individuality and the stages of its growth. As it develops, the embryo acquires human characteristics, becomes a fetus, and is born as a baby. But these characteristics are yet to come. The embryo is pre-human, relating to the human baby as a larva does to a butterfly.

The embryo's potential to become a human being must not be confused with the actuality: a fertilized chicken egg has the potentiality to become a chicken, but is not a chicken until that potential is actualized. Vegetarians eat eggs but not chickens. Thus, one may well believe that life begins at conception. But the life in question is as yet only potentially human and, at its beginning, pre-human. From a religious viewpoint this may make no difference. Even if only potentially human (or, for that matter, potentially alive), the fertilized ovum is God's creation, not to be disposed of as though parental property. Moreover, according to teleological ideas accepted by most religions, the aim of conception is procreation; we are not to interfere with this divine purpose. (I forgo discussing prescriptive natural law, since, without religion, nature has no prescriptive authority.)

From a secular viewpoint the fact that what is conceived is not, as yet, human life may make a difference. The proposition "life begins at conception" may constitute a secular argument against abortion if one believes that life should not be aborted. However, we routinely slaughter and abort animals. Hence, to oppose abortion on secular grounds, one must believe that life conceived by humans is actually human from conception: or else, that no *potentially* human life should be aborted. Both these propositions rely on definitions and prescriptions that come close to collapsing what seems a secular argument against abortion into a religious one.

It is the embryo that might be aborted, not what it will, but has not yet, become. If it, as yet, lacks the distinctly human characteristics that might entitle it to social protection on purely secular grounds, one must ask: When does intra-uterine life become human life? What characteristics are distinctively human? One may disagree on the sufficient characteristics. However, there is little disagreement on the necessary ones. Surely these are absent in the first 12 weeks after conception. The embryo has neither a brain nor the neural system which makes sentience possible.

Before sentience the embryo cannot be aware of itself, nor of losing a future by not being allowed to develop. Anti-abortionists may argue, nonetheless, that we have no more right to deprive the embryo of its future than we have to deprive an unconscious person of his future. Perhaps. But the embryo (unlike the unconscious person) cannot in any meaningful sense own itself. If it does not belong to God, it belongs to its parents. Only upon acquiring a functioning brain and neural system, after the first trimester, does it become possible, though not yet probable, for the fetus even to feel pain. At this point the fetus also starts to resemble an embryonic human being. One may allow the embryo to develop further or abort it. However, after the first trimester abortion seems justifiable only by the gravest of reasons, such as danger to the mother; for what is being aborted undeniably resembles a human being to an uncomfortable degree.

After the first trimester, inconvenience to parents hardly seems a grave enough reason for abortion. However, it may not be in the best interest of the fetus to be born. Surely that is the case if the fetus is highly defective, or likely to live a short or abnormally painful life. Parents may, or may not, be willing to bear the burden of a permanently impaired child, which they would have to carry if the fetus is known to be gravely defective. But it is the burden to the child that must be pondered above all. Life is not good under all circumstances. Thus, when it is likely to be a net burden for the fetus to live after birth, persons who do not adhere to traditional religious beliefs may argue for abortion.

However much the motivation derives from religious tradition, the legal prohibition of abortion is not unconstitutional in a secular state. Religion may enjoin us to feed the hungry and to eschew murder. Yet neither welfare nor criminal homicide statutes are unconstitutional—unless no purpose other than catering to religious beliefs can be demonstrated. If laws can be supported by a secular argument, or a secular public interest, religious traditions which may motivate legislators and their supporters are constitutionally irrelevant.

There are rational secular arguments against abortion. For example, one may insist that the fetus is human and abortion therefore homicide; or that life is a good the living are not entitled to withhold from the unborn. Whether these arguments are persuasive matters little. They are rational enough. Other rational arguments independent of religion are available. Hence legislatures were thought constitutionally entitled to prohibit abortion—until the Supreme Court, in *Roe* v. *Wade,* found a right to abortion in the U.S. Constitution, and made state prohibitions unconstitutional.

In *Griswold* v. *Connecticut* the Supreme Court had held that a Connecticut law violated a constitutional right to sexual privacy by prohibiting the sale of contraceptives. In *Roe* the right to abortion was derived from the privacy right found in *Griswold.* However, the Constitution nowhere mentions a right to privacy, or to sexual privacy, let alone to contraception or abortion. Nor can such rights be logically derived from anything directly articulated in the Constitution. Hence the sexual privacy right recognized in *Griswold* admittedly had to be derived from "emanations" of the "penumbrae" (not visible to the naked non-judicial eye) of the Bill of Rights.

The Connecticut law struck down in *Griswold* (which had not been enforced for a long time) certainly was silly. But silliness is not *per se* unconstitutional. Prohibitions of sodomy, or of prostitution, or of the sale of contraceptives, may strike one as silly, but they are not unconstitutional, if rational arguments for them can be found.

Nobody wants to overturn *Griswold* and allow states to prohibit the sale of contraceptives. *Roe* v. *Wade,* which takes from the states the right to prohibit abortion, is quite another matter, although it rests on the same right to sexual privacy which the Constitution so discreetly fails to mention. Significant groups want to overturn *Roe.* They might succeed. The possible abrogation of *Roe,* or its likely erosion, would return to the states the right to deal with abortion in some measure. Enabled to make their own decision, California and New York, and many other states, are likely to permit abortion. Some states will again prohibit it; but this mainly will stimulate travel.

Permitting abortion does not necessarily mean subsidizing it. There is not much reason for a subsidy. Usually the pregnant woman volunteered for acts and omissions that risked pregnancy and should not ask taxpayers to pay for the consequences. Pregnancy is not a disease. A pregnant woman does not have the moral claim on the public purse that a woman suffering from a disease contracted because of factors beyond her control might have. Further, taxpayers who on moral grounds oppose abortion object to being compelled to subsidize it. To be sure, subsidizing abortion may well save taxpayers' money: if the aborted fetuses had become babies dependent on public welfare, they would cost more than the subsidy used for abortion. However, even if this were so, opponents will oppose the use of their taxes to subsidize it—the financial advantage would not offset the perceived immorality they would be compelled to support.

Emergent technological changes may make much of the legal abortion debate academic. A French drug company has produced an abortifacient pill (RU-486) which makes expulsion of the fertilized ovum cheap and easy and requires little if any medical supervision. As it is perfected the pill could well solve the legal and financial problem for most women who want an abortion in the very early stages of pregnancy.

Currently no American drug company will sell the French drug, for fear of boycotts and lawsuits. Even in France its distribution is still highly restricted. Yet experience suggests that, once a cheap technology is available, its use cannot be prevented for long. The pill will be smuggled in and will become readily available, ultimately to be legalized.

The moral debate is not affected by this technological development. Abortion will remain a moral problem for many, owing to the clash of Christian traditions and current secular attitudes. Yet the moral problem is likely to be felt less. There is not much rational difference between the surgical removal of an extant embryo and the chemical prevention of its development. Yet there is a major difference in perception. Often, ova are expelled naturally even after fertilization. The abortifacient pill may well be seen as simply helping this process along (although morally the intention of the person taking it makes the difference). All this is likely to make for greater acceptability.

The overwhelming majority of Americans are devoted, in some degree, to religious beliefs in the Judaeo-Christian tradition. Yet, most Americans do not believe that abortion should be a crime. This inconsistency will assure continuation of the debate.

A principled and intense minority of Americans think of abortion as murder. Yet the great majority have come to believe, albeit inchoately, that they own and can dispose of their bodies, including fertilized ova and even embryos. At the least they believe the government should not interfere. For this reason it will be impossible to recriminalize abortion, whatever the outcome of current legislative and judicial skirmishes. Americans feel overwhelmingly that the matter should be left to the individual conscience, and that the minority cannot impose their beliefs, however conscientiously held, on the majority. Political parties cannot ignore the handwriting on the wall.

Each of the political parties is split on the issue. Democrats have rallied to the popular "pro-choice" standard. But their traditional constituents include ethnic minorities strongly influenced by religious beliefs. Republicans have courted defeat by opposing the popular view or, worse, waffling. (Their position has a great deal to do with opposition to the improper overreaching of the Supreme Court in *Roe* v. *Wade* but is perceived simply as "anti-abortion.") But not all Republicans are willing to go down for the sake of prohibiting abortion. The anti-abortionists who urge them to do so hardly serve their own cause.

As *Roe* v. *Wade* recedes and states become free to impose their own regulations, they would do well to permit the French pill (which is effective only in the first trimester of pregnancy) and to strongly discourage and regulate later abortions, except in very specific and limited cases, such as danger to the mother. There is no reason for the Federal Government to bear any of the costs—more reason, but perhaps not enough, for the states to do so. There is little hope that a rational and practical settlement along these lines can be formalized soon. But it might evolve informally.

Giving Women a Real Choice
by Rosalind Petchesky

The abortion conflict refuses to go away. From a Supreme Court Justice to the popular press, a chorus of voices in the United States in 1989 declared abortion "the most politically divisive domestic legal issue of our time." Today it stands squarely in the middle of politics, signifying one's position on a liberal-conservative continuum and signaling shifts in institutional power arrangements. The question is *why* the abortion debate persists, why it becomes such a charged site for struggles over not only changes in family, gender and sexual relations in American society and their cultural meanings but over the terms of public disorder.

During the past decade of legal abortion in the United States—a period of heightened political conservatism—advocates of women's reproductive freedom have faced a complicated paradox. Women's "right" to abortion remains, at least at this writing, embedded in the formal apparatus of the law and, depending on the wording of the questions, commands remarkably consistent and continuous support in national public opinion polls. Moreover, neither anti-abortion crusades, innumerable court challenges, bureaucratic regulations, curtailment of Medicaid funding in all but a handful of states, a moratorium on all federal research on abortifacients, clinic harassment nor bombings have made a significant dent in abortion *practice;* about 1.5 million women a year in the United States still persist in getting abortions. This pattern shows that access to abortion will continue to be perceived by women as a necessity, if not a "right," so long as pregnancies occur in women's bodies.

Yet all around the edges of this little kernel of "right," tempers flare, firebombs destroy medical offices, antiabortion "rescue" squads harass patients and providers, and litigations pit pregnant woman against vengeful spouses and irate male fetal advocates. Perhaps most serious of all, fetuses (and babies) have become icons of popular culture beside which pregnant women languish in disrepute. This cultural guerrilla warfare against abortions (and the women who get them) has created a climate hospitable to the ultimate undoing of *Roe v. Wade,* an aim supported by many of the conservative judges with whom the Reagan Administration had by 1988 filled the country's highest courts. In *Webster v. Reproductive Health Services* a plurality of the Supreme Court, without actually rescinding the abortion right, was, in Justice Harry Blackmun's dissenting words, opening the door to "more and more restrictive" state regulation that will impede its "meaningful exercise."

This radical shift seems strange in light of the failure of antiabortion forces in the past decade in conventional political arenas. Since 1977, when the Hyde Amendment curtailing federal funding of abortions was passed, not a single major piece of antiabortion legislation has got through Congress. Particularly after the 1986 elections, when the Democrats recaptured the Senate, it became clear that the prospects for antiabortion legislative initiatives were null. And despite Presidents Reagan and Bush, who have strongly voiced antiabortion rhetoric, the Republican Party itself is not a bastion of antiabortion sentiment. Many Republican politicians now view the "pro-life" position as a distinct liability at the polls.

But in retrospect these failures appear negligible relative to the most effective political gain of the antiabortion movement in this period: the election of two Presidents committed to appointing conservatives who would pass the litmus test to the federal and Supreme Court benches. The real question is not how we tally up "pro-life" gains and losses in electoral and legislative contest but rather how "antiabortion" came to be a sign for a whole range of conservative values. In contrast with their limited gains in formal institutional politics, antiabortion forces have registered a seismic impact on symbolic politics, that is, on cultural and political discourse, media imagery and popular perceptions. More than ever, abortion is the fulcrum of a much broader ideological struggle in which the very meanings of the family, the state, motherhood and young women's sexuality are contested.

Abortion in the United States is still overwhelmingly a phenomenon of young, unmarried women, the majority of them teenagers or in their early 20s. Eighty-two percent of all women getting abortions in 1987 were unmarried, and nearly all were either working or attending school. Two-thirds had family incomes under $25,000 a year, and two-thirds were white, even though abortion rates are higher for black and Latino women. In other words, we are talking about young, single women who are working or students, most of them poor or working class—women who are trying to stay in school, develop their skills *and* maintain sexual lives before taking on marriage and childbearing. These facts more than any others—in a society still imbued with racist and patriarchal values about gender and sex—explain why women's abortion access, despite continued formal legality, is so fiercely contested.

Abortion in the 1970s and 1980s is the consequence, not cause, of complex and mostly positive changes in young women's lives since 1960: higher rates of employment and college attendance, later age at marriage (meaning inevitably more premarital sex) and lower birthrates. The Alan Guttmacher Institute has published comprehensive studies showing that, while other developed countries have experienced similar trends and show similar levels of adolescent sexuality, the United States has "much lower rates of contraceptive use and much higher rates of childbearing, abortion and pregnancy" (especially among teenagers but also among older women) than nearly any other developed country. These more disturbing trends are also the result of complicated social conditions peculiar to the United States: first, the "absence of a unified system of primary health care provision," of which contraceptive services would be an integral and routine part; second, the severe social inequalities in this country, giving many poor young women little reason to plan or hope; and third, the "deep-seated ambivalence toward sexuality" in American culture, in which the glorification of rape and the refusal to advertise condoms can exist side by side.

But these complicated social dynamics are difficult to see. How much simpler to blame young women for "promiscuity" and for "using abortion as a method of birth control," or to blame feminism, and abortion as its main signifier, for subverting the family. What disturbs many people about changes in family life over the past two decades is not that abortion is legal, but that teenagers seem lax and out of control; that sex seems out of control; that mothers are not home when they used to be (to take care of people and police teen sex); that fathers seem to be losing authority over wives and daughters; and that, for perhaps a majority of women at some time in their lives if not for good, having sex and raising children are perceived and experienced outside dependence on men. Indeed, the possibility of lesbian sexuality and lesbian motherhood as viable alternatives presents itself in a more open way than ever in modern history. I suspect that more people share fears about these trends than the small number who actively oppose a woman's right to get an abortion. Thus on one level "moral" opposition to abortion is a response to certain real dimensions of young and poor women's empowerment that many people find threatening.

When I was a teenager in Tulsa, Oklahoma, in the late 1950s and early 1960s, the abortion experience was of course steeped in shame, but it had little to do with harm to the fetus. My generation of young middle-class women knew nothing about the fetus. Like the pregnancy scare and "unwed motherhood," abortion meant shame only because it connoted sex—you'd "done it" without the sanctity of marriage. White teenagers' sexuality in this historical milieu was mediated through an ingenious custom called petting, which was class-, race- and gender-specific and followed definite heterosexist codes. Sex was something you did secretly, in dark parked cars, and you did it only up to a certain point. Built into the very definition of the petting culture as a sexual practice was its own denial; along with shotgun marriages and homes for unwed mothers, it hid the reality of white middle-class women as sexual beings.

The 1970s and 1980s, without in any sense having brought us a "sexual revolution," caused changes in the *signs* of white female teenage sexuality. Birth control and abortion services, widely available without age or marital restrictions, have helped to make the young white woman's sexuality visible, thereby undermining historical race and class stereotypes of "nice girls" and "bad girls." The local abortion clinic represents the existence of her sexual identity independent of marriage, of paternal authority, perhaps of men; and so in a sense it connotes white feminism. This is an important missing piece of the story, and it is why the clinic becomes a target — of bombs and government regulation as well as of prayers — and why, for ardent antiabortionists, the solution of "more effective contraception" so misses the point. The clinic symbolically threatens white patriarchal control over "their" young women's sexual "purity," and thus becomes a target of white patriarchal wrath.

For the one-third of abortion clinic patients who are women of color, both the experience of abortion and the meanings of antiabortion resentment have been different from their meanings for white women. One is struck by the absence, in crowds of Operation Rescue demonstrators, of people of color; except for an occasional black preacher and his followers, it is overwhelmingly a white Christian movement. One senses that, whatever misgivings black and Latino people may have about abortion and the white feminists whom they perceive as leading the pro-choice movement, they are aware of the underlying racism of the antiabortion campaign. The denial of abortion funding and access is clearly racist in its consequences: Poor women are disproportionately women of color and are more likely to suffer deaths or injuries from illegal or botched abortions.

However, many black women have been reluctant to get involved in activities supporting women's abortion rights. To the extent that such activities are associated with white feminist aspirations to "sexual freedom," they may conflict with black women's experiences in several different ways. First, the sense of a collective past in which black women were systematically raped and sexually demeaned by white racists, having constantly to "prove" their "virtue," may make it difficult or painful for many black women to identify with a movement whose emphasis is "sexual liberation." Second, the abortion issue may simply pale next to the daily onslaught of life-and-death crises caused by inadequate health care; child and infant mortality rates twice as high as those for whites; death rates from childbirth four times, and from hypertension seventeen times, those of white women; and the decimation of families by AIDS, drugs and poverty.

People of color have often, and sometimes justifiably, been wary of those promoting abortion and birth control as more interested in racist eugenics or population control than in health. But racism can also take the form of white pronatalism. The pronatalism of the so-called right-to-life movement is not so much about numbers as it is about a patriarchal conception of women's roles as childbearers, mothers and wives. Yet a populationist note is also audible in the continued refrains about adoption as an "alternative to abortion." These appeal to commonly voiced concerns about the "shortage of babies to adopt," and this shortage, it is well known, specifically involves *white* babies. As Patricia Williams notes in the Autumn 1988 issue of *Signs*, while black people were bought and sold under slavery, now "it is white children who are bought and sold, [and] black babies have become 'worthless' currency to adoption agents — 'surplus' in the salvage heaps of Harlem hospitals." What, one wonders, do antiabortionists intend should become of the approximately 500,000 additional nonwhite babies who would be born if hypothetically all abortions were to stop? Whether their solution is adoption by white upscale baby consumers (making poor women conscripted surrogate mothers) or increased poverty and suffering (since they oppose the level of social spending needed to help poor mothers raise their own babies), it is a patently racist and class-biased fantasy.

After seventeen years of legal abortion in the United States, feminists have learned that mere legality, even a constitutional right in terms of individual privacy, is perfectly compatible with a wide range of constraints on abortion access, particularly for poor women, rural women, women of color and young teenagers. Legality does not assure women material means, moral support or political legitimation in their abortion decisions. It certainly does not guarantee funding, conveniently located services, protection from harassment and intimidation at the clinic door or a uniform standard of good treatment once inside. Through a series of bureaucratic tactics and an official rhetorical stance, the neoconservative state under Reagan and Bush has continued to seek restrictions on women's access to abortion. In so doing, it has attempted to accommodate antiabortion politics to the formal doctrine of liberal privacy.

State-sponsored restrictions on abortion access take a variety of forms, but they are harshest for poor women, who suffer from the cutoff of federal and state funds and a shortage of public services, and for teenage women, who in many states and localities are hindered by parental consent or notification requirements. Since no doctor or facility is *required* to provide abortions in a market-dominated medical economy, they are in fact unavailable in many locales. Eighty-two percent of U.S. counties, particularly in rural areas, are without any abortion providers at all. Well before the *Webster* decision public hospitals, upon which most poor and rural women rely for their health care, increasingly refused to provide abortion services, accounting for only 13 percent of induced abortions in 1985. To whatever extent such policies affect the actual number of women getting abortions, they frame the meaning of abortion as an individual and social experience.

The struggle to achieve women's reproductive freedom cannot succeed in the long run if conducted as a civil liberties struggle for individual privacy. At bottom it is a deeply cultural and social conflict for which formal legality provides at best a thin protective cover. What is lost in the language of liberal privacy is the concept of social rights, familiar in most European social democracies: that society has a responsibility to ameliorate the conditions that make either abortion or childbearing a hard, painful choice for some women, and that the bearers of this right are not so much isolated individuals as they are members of social groups with distinct needs.

That is why a feminist politics of reproductive rights cannot rest solely on the notion of privacy. The real paradox — and tragedy — of the past seventeen years of legal abortion is not that although the majority of people believe in "individual choice," politicians and judges do not listen. Rather, it is that the majority believe in "individual choice" — the language of privacy — but fail to

9 / Writing About an Issue — Joining a Debate

connect this belief to the social changes and affirmative public efforts needed to make such choice real for *all* women. A full reproductive rights agenda must involve access not only to abortion services and funds but to adequate prenatal care, maternal, infant and child health services, child care, housing, sex education without stigma, drug treatment and, of course, universal health insurance. While antiabortionists clamor for the rights of fetuses and embryos, we live in a society in which one-fifth of children, more than one-fourth of all black children and one-third of all poor children have no health coverage at all. As Gloria Joseph wrote in 1981, "Given these realities of health care [as] seen by Black people, White women must understand why Black women do not devote their full energies to the abortion issue. The emphasis has to be on total health care." Until privacy or autonomy is redefined in reference to social justice provisions that can give it substance for the poorest women, it will remain not only a class-biased and racist concept but an antifeminist one, insofar as it is premised on a denial of social responsibility to improve the conditions of women as a group.

Happily, a new political movement based on a broader array of forces than feminism has yet known is beginning to emerge under the vocal leadership of black feminists active in the reproductive rights struggle. Perhaps the most besieged clinic in the country is the Atlanta Feminist Women's Health Center. The center's former health education director, Dazon Dixon, herself black, tells a story about a young black client trying to maneuver through Operation Rescue pickets and television cameras so she could enter the clinic for an abortion:

> When a young looking, blonde and blue-eyed white man screamed charges at her that the Rev. Martin Luther King Jr. would "turn over in his grave for what she is doing" and that she was contributing to the genocide of African-Americans, she broke. She stopped, stared him in his eyes with tears in hers, then quietly and coolly said, "You're a white boy, and you don't give a damn about me, who I am or what I do. And you even know less about Martin Luther King or being Black. What you have to say to me means nothin', not a damn thing." He was silenced and she walked on.

That young woman's voice foretells the future, not only of abortion politics but of feminism in America.

Persuasion Preferred

by John Garvey

"Every time you make a choice you are turning the central part of you, the part of you that chooses, into something a little different from what it was before. And taking your life as a whole, with all your innumerable choices, all your life you are slowly turning this central thing into either a heavenly creature or into a hellish creature." — C. S. Lewis, *Christian Behaviour*

This quote, lifted from A. N. Wilson's very good new biography of C. S. Lewis, made me think of the use of choice as a moral category. The most obvious recent use has been by those who support the legal right of a woman to choose abortion under any circumstances, as opposed to those who would limit access to abortion to women whose lives are in some way endangered by pregnancy, or those who have suffered rape or incest. The possibility of civil dialogue has been limited here by prochoice people who refer to their opposite numbers as "antichoice," and by prolife people who refer to their opposite numbers as "antilife" or "pro-abortion." Rude folks, all of them, and letters from any of them (to the tune of "How can you not call them [fill in the blank—prodeath, antilife, antichoice—whatever insulting term you like]") will not be answered. Civility demands more respect for your opposite number's point of view than that, at least an assumption that she or he has assumed it in good faith. I stick with "prolife" and "prochoice."

I have thought for a long time that prolife people should not concentrate on the legal arena but rather the area of persuasion. Law is coercive by nature, and coercion is a bad place to begin a discussion. I would like to suggest that rather than a concentration on what ought to be forbidden under force of the law, the emphasis should instead be on what it is we mean to encourage in our society—among families, within families (both stable and dissolving ones), and between families and the larger societal structures. Legal scholar Mary Ann Glendon has pointed out that the United States has the most permissive abortion laws in the industrial West and at the same time offers the least help to women and children. She sees a connection between these sad facts. I am sure she is right.

The prochoice movement has reacted to attempts to limit access to abortion as if they were morally equivalent to earlier attempts to limit access to contraception, and as if there were a simple sort of moralistic and religiously inspired continuum here; but this ignores the interesting and conveniently forgotten fact that Planned Parenthood once opposed abortion as a form of baby-killing, an evil that resulted from limiting access to contraception. Planned Parenthood's earlier opposition to abortion has been well-documented and the organization really ought to deal with it more honestly. Fat chance of that, as long as the uncivil people on both sides prevail. In the meantime, hundreds of thousands of abortions continue, there is not enough simple honesty about family planning in official Catholic quarters, and most people in our truly weird culture stand around doing nothing, as if the issue were a merely religious quarrel, or embarrassing. Until relatively recently this silent crowd included a number of my Orthodox coreligionists; now several of our bishops have begun speaking more publicly about abortion, and are active in the prolife movement, as are a growing number of Orthodox clergy and laypeople. But when Michael Dukakis was running for president, there was not a word forthcoming from Greek Orthodox Archbishop Iakovos about the inappropriateness of Dukakis's prochoice stand. If Catholic prelates have sometimes been intemperate in their attacks on prochoice Catholic politicians, the alternative is not silence on an important moral issue about which the church has a definite teaching.

There was an outcry from a number of prochoice people when the Catholic bishops announced an expensive public relations campaign to try to persuade people that our society's approach to abortion is wrong. Many people on both sides of the issue argued that the money would better be spent on direct help to women and children. They have a point there, but they lose me when they act as if there were something inherently evil about the use of advertising or public relations. They also miss the fact that the prochoice movement has achieved considerable successes using precisely the medium of advertising and public relations. One of those successes has been in convincing a large number of people that the primary issue here is choice, as if the simple freedom to choose were in itself a moral category, one so important as to eclipse completely the question of the fetal life (which is surely human life, even if its personhood can be philosophically questioned).

While freedom of choice may indeed be an important political principle, it is not in and of itself moral. I have the legal right to spend all day reading dreadful romances or watching television to name two brainrotting activities, or I may drink myself to death, or believe in racist theories. All of these options are mine to choose. Of course, I should not choose them — but I may do so. None of them are good choices, though laws forbidding me to do any of them would be dangerous. Under current U.S. law a woman may choose to have an abortion. I think it can be argued that someone who opposes abortion personally may still support prochoice legislation, on the lesser-of-two-evils principle; this has not yet been argued well, by Governor Cuomo or anyone else who takes that position, but I think it could be done.

Nevertheless, abortion is at the very least a brutal form of retroactive contraception, and does in fact destroy a life which in another instance might be cherished. It is important for anyone who believes this to try to communicate that belief, whatever the legality of the choice might be. In the case of people seeking to lead, it is not only important — it is an obligation, one that has not been met by people afraid of elections, and the reason it has not is, pretty obviously, a combination of moral cowardice and amoral ambition. In a confused climate — confused not least by politicians more eager to follow poll results than to take the risks real leadership involves — I can see why the Catholic bishops have turned to public relations. They should not be faulted for turning to professionals. Who should they turn to? Those of their own number who, through ill-considered denunciations of prochoice Catholic candidates, have managed to get them elected?

I do hope, though, that the campaign is centered not on legislative issues, but on the attempt to persuade people that abortion is not a humane decision, in the great majority of cases. Pharmaceutical technology may make the whole issue irrelevant at the legislative level. It will remain an important moral choice, and if the Catholic bishops have not been able to get that message across by other means, I really can't fault them for trying this one. The point should be to suggest that, however important the legal right to choose may be, the things we choose to do, or refuse to do, define us as individuals and as a society. The widespread choice of abortion is a tragedy, something the most vocal prochoice people either ignore or downplay. But the choice of abortion exists for complex reasons which too many prolife people have ignored. A recent *New York Times* story mentions the efforts of Archbishop Rembert Weakland of Milwaukee who, on this subject and a number of others, listened to the concerns of women in his diocese and responded with more sensitivity than we have been accustomed to from either side of the issue. If the proposed campaign is conducted in this spirit, it will be a genuine advance.

ABORTION — QUESTIONS ON ESSAYS

1. One reason that abortion is such a controversial issue is that it has important legal, moral, social, and political significance. Choose one of these broad factors and analyze the position of the three essays. For example, Garvey asserts that abortion "is not a humane decision." What statements in the other essays can you find that address the moral dimensions of the issue?

2. Does Van Den Haag provide a "middle ground" for discussing abortion? How does he discuss the religious context of abortion? How objective is he about the religious and moral controversy surrounding abortion?

3. What kinds of evidence does Petchesky use in support of her claim? How persuasive is her evidence?

4. What is the difference between Petchesky's and Garvey's views of choice? Is there any way to resolve any differences in their views?

5. What is the significance of *Roe* v. *Wade* to each of the three authors? Can you determine their positions on this landmark Supreme Court case?

6. What essay seems to you to make the best argument? Support your answer by referring to (a) the quality and reasonableness of its claim, (b) the persuasiveness of its evidence, (c) the clarity and credibility of its warrants, and (d) the qualification the writer has made on his or her claim.

II. Euthanasia Essays

Active and Passive Euthanasia

James Rachels

The distinction between active and passive euthanasia is thought to be crucial for medical ethics. The idea is that it is permissible, at least in some cases, to withhold treatment and allow a patient to die, but it is never permissible to take any direct action designed to kill the patient. This doctrine seems to be accepted by most doctors, and it is endorsed in a statement adopted by the House of Delegates of the American Medical Association on December 4, 1973:

> The intentional termination of the life of one human being by another — mercy killing — is contrary to that for which the medical profession stands and is contrary to the policy of the American Medical Association.
>
> The cessation of the employment of extraordinary means to prolong the life of the body when there is irrefutable evidence that biological death is imminent is the decision of the patient and/or his immediate family. The advice and judgment of the physician should be freely available to the patient and/or his immediate family.

However, a strong case can be made against this doctrine. In what follows I will set out some of the relevant arguments, and urge doctors to reconsider their views on this matter.

To begin with a familiar type of situation, a patient who is dying of incurable cancer of the throat is in terrible pain, which can no longer be satisfactorily alleviated. He is certain to die within a few days, even if present treatment is continued, but he does not want to go on living for those days since the pain is unbearable. So he asks the doctor for an end to it, and his family joins in the request.

Suppose the doctor agrees to withold treatment, as the conventional doctrine says he may. The justification for his doing so is that the patient is in terrible agony, and since he is going to die anyway, it would be wrong to prolong his suffering needlessly. But now notice this. If one simply withholds treatment, it may take the patient longer to die, and so he may suffer more than he would if more direct action were taken and a lethal injection given. This fact provides strong reason for thinking that, once the initial decision not to prolong his agony has been made, active euthanasia is actually preferable to passive euthanasia, rather than the reverse. To say otherwise is to endorse the option that leads to more suffering rather than less, and is contrary to the humanitarian impulse that prompts the decision not to prolong his life in the first place.

Part of my point is that the process of being "allowed to die" can be relatively slow and painful, whereas being given a lethal injection is relatively quick and painless. Let me give a different sort of example. In the United States about one in 600 babies is born with Down's syndrome. Most of these babies are otherwise healthy — that is, with only the usual pediatric care, they will proceed to an otherwise normal infancy. Some, however, are born with congenital defects such as intestinal obstructions that require operations if they are to live. Sometimes, the parents and the doctor will decide not to operate, and let the infant die. Anthony Shaw describes what happens then:

> . . . When surgery is denied [the doctor] must try to keep the infant from suffering while natural forces sap the baby's life away. As a surgeon whose natural inclination is to use the scal-

pel to fight off death, standing by and watching a salvageable baby die is the most emotionally exhausting experience I know. It is easy at a conference, in a theoretical discussion, to decide that such infants should be allowed to die. It is altogether different to stand by in the nursery and watch as dehydration and infection wither a tiny being over hours and days. This is a terrible ordeal for me and the hospital staff—much more so than for the parents who never set foot in the nursery.[1]

I can understand why some people are opposed to all euthanasia, and insist that such infants must be allowed to live. I think I can also understand why other people favor destroying these babies quickly and painlessly. But why should anyone favor letting "dehydration and infection wither a tiny being over hours and days"? The doctrine that says that a baby may be allowed to dehydrate and wither, but may not be given an injection that would end its life without suffering, seems so patently cruel as to require no further refutation. The strong language is not intended to offend, but only to put the point in the clearest possible way.

My second argument is that the conventional doctrine leads to decisions concerning life and death made on irrelevant grounds.

Consider again the case of the infants with Down's syndrome who need operations for congenital defects unrelated to the syndrome to live. Sometimes, there is no operation, and the baby dies, but when there is no such defect, the baby lives on. Now, an operation such as that to remove an intestinal obstruction is not prohibitively difficult. The reason why such operations are not performed in these cases is, clearly, that the child has Down's syndrome and the parents and doctor judge that because of that fact it is better for the child to die.

But notice that this situation is absurd, no matter what view one takes of the lives and potentials of such babies. If the life of such an infant is worth preserving, what does it matter if it needs a simple operation? Or, if one thinks it better that such a baby should not live on, what difference does it make that it happens to have an unobstructed intestinal tract? In either case, the matter of life and death is being decided on irrelevant grounds. It is the Down's syndrome, and not the intestines, that is the issue. The matter should be decided, if at all, on that basis, and not be allowed to depend on the essentially irrelevant question of whether the intestinal tract is blocked.

What makes this situation possible, of course, is the idea that when there is an intestinal blockage, one can "let the baby die," but when there is no such defect there is nothing that can be done, for one must not "kill" it. The fact that this idea leads to such results as deciding life or death on irrelevant grounds is another good reason why the doctrine should be rejected.

One reason why so many people think that there is an important moral difference between active and passive euthanasia is that they think killing someone is morally worse than letting someone die. But is it? Is killing, in

---

[1] A. Shaw, "Doctor, Do We Have a Choice?" *The New York Times Magazine,* January 30, 1972, p. 54.

itself, worse than letting die? To investigate this issue, two cases may be considered that are exactly alike except that one involves killing whereas the other involves letting someone die. Then, it can be asked whether this difference makes any difference to the moral assessments. It is important that the cases be exactly alike, except for this one difference, since otherwise one cannot be confident that it is this difference and not some other that accounts for any variation in the assessments of the two cases. So, let us consider this pair of cases:

In the first, Smith stands to gain a large inheritance if anything should happen to his six-year-old cousin. One evening while the child is taking his bath, Smith sneaks into the bathroom and drowns the child, and then arranges things so that it will look like an accident.

In the second, Jones also stands to gain if anything should happen to his six-year-old cousin. Like Smith, Jones sneaks in planning to drown the child in his bath. However, just as he enters the bathroom Jones sees the child slip and hit his head, and fall face down in the water. Jones is delighted; he stands by, ready to push the child's head back under if it is necessary, but it is not necessary. With only a little thrashing about, the child drowns all by himself, "accidentally," as Jones watches and does nothing.

Now Smith killed the child, whereas Jones "merely" let the child die. That is the only difference between them. Did either man behave better, from a moral point of view? If the difference between killing and letting die were in itself a morally important matter, one should say that Jones's behavior was less reprehensible than Smith's. But does one really want to say that? I think not. In the first place, both men acted from the same motive, personal gain, and both had exactly the same end in view when they acted. It may be inferred from Smith's conduct that he is a bad man, although that judgment may be withdrawn or modified if certain further facts are learned about him — for example, that he is mentally deranged. But would not the very same thing be inferred about Jones from his conduct? And would not the same further considerations also be relevant to any modification of this judgment? Moreover, suppose Jones pleaded, in his own defense, "After all, I didn't do anything except just stand there and watch the child drown. I didn't kill him; I only let him die." Again, if letting die were in itself less bad than killing, this defense should have at least some weight. But it does not. Such a "defense" can only be regarded as a grotesque perversion of moral reasoning. Morally speaking, it is no defense at all.

Now, it may be pointed out, quite properly, that the cases of euthanasia with which doctors are concerned are not like this at all. They do not involve personal gain or the destruction of normal healthy children. Doctors are concerned only with cases in which the patient's life is of no further use to him, or in which the patient's life has become or will soon become a terrible burden. However, the point is the same in these cases: the bare difference between killing and letting die does not, in itself, make a moral difference. If a doctor lets a patient die, for humane reasons, he is in the same moral position as if he had given the patient a lethal injection for humane reasons. If his decision was wrong — if, for example, the patient's illness was in fact curable — the decision would be equally regrettable no matter which method was used to carry it out. And if the doctor's decision was the right one, the method is not in itself important.

The AMA policy statement isolates the crucial issue very well; the crucial issue is "the intentional termination of the life of one human being by another." But after identifying this issue, and forbidding "mercy killing," the statement goes on to deny that the cessation of treatment is the intentional termination of a life. This is where the mistake comes in, for what is the cessation of treatment, in these circumstances, if it is not "the intentional termination of the life of one human being by another"? Of course it is exactly that, and if it were not, there would be no point to it.

Many people will find this judgment hard to accept. One reason, I think, is that it is very easy to conflate the question of whether killing is, in itself, worse than letting die, with the very different question of whether most actual cases of killing are more reprehensible than most actual cases of letting die. Most actual cases of killing are clearly terrible (think, for example, of all the murders reported in the newspapers), and one hears of such cases every day. On the other hand, one hardly ever hears of a case of letting die, except for the actions of doctors who are motivated by humanitarian reasons. So one learns to think of killing in a much worse light than of letting die. But this does not mean that there is something about killing that makes it in itself worse than letting die, for it is not the bare difference between killing and letting die that makes the difference in these cases. Rather, the other factors—the murderer's motive of personal gain, for example, contrasted with the doctor's humanitarian motivation—account for different reactions to the different cases.

I have argued that killing is not in itself any worse than letting die; if my contention is right, it follows that active euthanasia is not any worse than passive euthanasia. What arguments can be given on the other side? The most common, I believe, is the following:

"The important difference between active and passive euthanasia is that, in passive euthanasia, the doctor does not do anything to bring about the patient's death. The doctor does nothing, and the patient dies of whatever ills already afflict him. In active euthanasia, however, the doctor does something to bring about the patient's death: he kills him. The doctor who gives the patient with cancer a lethal injection has himself caused his patient's death; whereas if he merely ceases treatment, the cancer is the cause of the death."

A number of points need to made here. The first is that it is not exactly correct to say that in passive euthanasia the doctor does nothing, for he does do one thing that is very important: he lets the patient die. "Letting someone die" is certainly different, in some respects, from other types of action— mainly in that it is a kind of action that one may perform by way of not performing certain other actions. For example, one may let a patient die by way of not giving medication, just as one may insult someone by way of not shaking his hand. But for any purpose of moral assessment, it is a type of action nonetheless. The decision to let a patient die is subject to moral appraisal in the same way that a decision to kill him would be subject to moral appraisal: it may be assessed as wise or unwise, compassionate or sadistic, right or wrong. If a doctor deliberately let a patient die who was suffering from a routinely curable illness, the doctor would certainly be to blame for what he had done, just as he would be to blame if he had needlessly killed the patient. Charges against him would then be appropriate. If so, it would be no defense at all for him to insist that he didn't "do anything." He would have done something very serious indeed, for he let his patient die.

Fixing the cause of death may be very important from a legal point of view, for it may determine whether criminal charges are brought against the doctor. But I do not think that this notion can be used to show a moral difference between active and passive euthanasia. The reason why it is considered bad to be the cause of someone's death is that death is regarded as a great evil — and so it is. However, if it has been decided that euthanasis — even passive euthanasia — is desirable in a given case, it has also been decided that in this instance death is no greater an evil than the patient's continued existence. And if this is true, the usual reason for not wanting to be the cause of someone's death simply does not apply.

Finally, doctors may think that all of this is only of academic interest — the sort of thing that philosophers may worry about but that has no practical bearing on their own work. After all, doctors must be concerned about the legal consequences of what they do, and active euthanasia is clearly forbidden by the law. But even so, doctors should also be concerned with the fact that the law is forcing upon them a moral doctrine that may well be indefensible, and has a considerable effect on their practices. Of course, most doctors are not now in the position of being coerced in this matter, for they do not regard themselves as merely going along with what the law requires. Rather, in statements such as the AMA policy statement that I have quoted, they are endorsing this doctrine as a central point of medical ethics. In that statement, active euthanasia is condemned not merely as illegal but as "contrary to that for which the medical profession stands," whereas passive euthanasia is approved. However, the preceding considerations suggest that there is really no moral difference between the two, considered in themselves (there may be important moral differences in some cases in their *consequences,* but, as I pointed out, these differences may make active euthanasia, and not passive euthanasia, the morally preferable option). So, whereas doctors may have to discriminate between active and passive euthanasia to satisfy the law, they should not do any more than that. In particular, they should not give the distinction any added authority and weight by writing it into official statements of medical ethics.

Active Euthanasia Violates Fundamental Principles

by Samuel F. Hunter

Only death unshackles the patient and physician from terminal illness, and both may desire death more earnestly than they hope for life. Any physician's action to terminate a patient's life when that life is not already supported by extraordinary measures may be defined as active euthanasia. Physician-assisted suicide, requiring the physician to supply the knowledge and means for ending life at the patient's initiative, can be considered equivalent. Although euthanasia proponents want to respect individual dignity, the concept still presents medicine with grave ethical problems.

As medical students, we become familiar with suicidal ideation; we learn that the desire for self-destruction can arise from pain and the fear of pain, from feelings of despair, guilt, and meaninglessness. When otherwise healthy individuals present with these signs, our diagnosis is depression, and we intervene to restore mental balance and prevent suicide. Helping a patient to end his or her life radically departs from our usual purpose; moreover, suicide and euthanasia irreversibly exclude other medical, psychological, and social avenues for dealing with these feelings.

For many diseased persons, the mere availability of euthanasia could make this option seem attractive. Disease processes (as in acquired immune deficiency syndrome or multiple sclerosis) or drugs (eg, opiate analgesics) can cloud judgment and evoke inappropriate emotions. A patient's guilt and fear together with the sympathetic pain of loved ones can also be strongly persuasive. Furthermore, a besieged psyche could be swayed by even cursory mention of euthanasia, especially if the suggestion were to come from a physician.[1]

The patient's perspective on his own illness—a perspective the physician helps create—crucially affects his quality of life. Our role as physicians should be to maximize the potential for a long and rich life, even though death is inevitable and approaches inexorably. Victor Frankl,[2] a psychiatrist who survived the atrocities of German concentration camps, found the words of Spinoza to be axiomatic for life: "Emotion, which is suffering, ceases to be suffering as soon as we form a clear and precise meaning of it."[3] Helping a patient find a meaning, a measure of control, can make terminal illness a period of growth. If we advocate euthanasia, we risk thwarting the spiritual, emotional, and historical meaning of death.

Instead of promoting active euthanasia, we can best serve our patients by accurate prognosis and skillful management of complications and pain. Along with social workers and the clergy, we can bolster emotional strength. When we no longer heal, we palliate and comfort. This has been the time-honored tradition of medicine.[4-8] Adding death-on-demand to our armamentarium would subvert society's faith in us, which is crucial for our healing role. If society demands the right to euthanasia, it does not need physicians to supply or encourage that choice. Condemned murderers are executed by injection without our help; should we not also shun unnatural death by active euthanasia?

In contrast to this kind of killing, permitting death from a terminal illness without intervening (passive or voluntary euthanasia) offers fewer obstacles, and the legal system can help us decide when it is appropriate. The avoidance of unnecessary distress and expense has always been part of our ministry to the patient. We are therefore obliged to protect the terminally ill patient's option to end life-prolonging treatment.

When the patient is not fully cognizant and has not expressed his or her wishes in a legal document, many interests can compete. Institutions and medical providers welcome paying customers, while insurers benefit from withholding treatment. Families may hope to prolong or shorten the patient's life according to their own benefit. Our own emotions can also provoke self-conflict. We lack the time and training to evaluate properly a patient's familial, social, and financial environment. The objectivity, neutrality, and oversight of a judge can equitably deal with these conflicting concerns. Physicians should therefore resist laws that abrogate the role of the court in order to streamline "death with dignity."

Maintaining the emotional well-being and self-image of our patients should be a major goal, but active euthanasia violates our fundamental precepts of healing and disrupts important social, emotional, and spiritual processes. To procure death with honor for our patients, let us not be angels of death, but ministers of healing, comfort, and hope.

References

1. Orentlicher DO. Physician participation in assisted suicide. *JAMA.* 1989; 262; 1844–1845.
2. Frankl V. *Man's Search for Meaning.* New York, NY: Washington Square Press, 1984.
3. Spinoza. *Ethics,* Part V, Prop. 3.
4. *The Oath of Hippocrates.*
5. *The Oath of Asaph.*
6. *The International Code of Medical Ethics,* 1949.
7. *Report of the Council on Ethical and Judicial Affairs of the American Medical Association: Euthanasia.* Chicago, Ill: American Medical Association, 1989.
8. *Euthanasia: A Christian Medical Dental Society Statement,* 1988.

The State as Parent

by Sandra H. Johnson

I have to admit that when I first heard of the Missouri Supreme Court's decision in Nancy Cruzan's case, my reaction was not a particularly "lawyerly" one. My thoughts went first to my soon-to-be-driving teenage daughter Emily. What this decision meant to me was that if Emily were severely and irreversibly injured in a car accident it would be the state of Missouri and not I who would decide what would happen to her. How could this state, whether judge or legislature, take the place of a parent who had loved and protected and known her all her life?

The court's salute to the compassion and faithfulness of the Cruzan family was no comfort. It chose to look not at the real Nancy Cruzan, whose family had kept a vigil at her bedside, but at "all the Nancy Cruzans." In the name of protecting these hypothetical and symbolic Nancy Cruzans, who certainly do exist somewhere, the majority of the Supreme Court of Missouri denied to the Cruzans the authority to make a very important decision on behalf of their child. While deciding for "all the Nancy Cruzans," this court also decided for all the parents—and spouses—in Missouri.

When the Missouri Supreme Court issued its opinions in the case of Nancy Cruzan, it became the first and only court to require the continued medical treatment of a formerly competent adult who was now in a persistent vegetative state (PVS). During the nearly fifteen years since the case of Karen Ann Quinlan thrust the choices presented by advancing medical technology into the consciousness of the public, state courts had developed a framework for analysis that attracted a wide consensus. These courts generally approached the cases to discover what the particular individual would do if able to make the decision himself or herself. Sometimes these cases were not very persuasive. Many of the patients involved had not expressed any preferences concerning medical treatment. In those cases, it became customary for the courts to defer to the decision of family members if it was compatible with what was known about the patient. The Missouri Supreme Court in *Cruzan* defied this framework. But its holding could be dismissed cavalierly as an "odd decision from a strange state."

Or, it could be placed among the "hard" cases because it involved the discontinuation of nutrition and hydration for a person who was not terminally ill. While every other court examining the issue had concluded that such treatment should be approached in the same fashion as any other medical treatment, several state legislatures, including Missouri's, had specifically excluded medically provided nutrition and hydration from the medical treatments that could be refused through a document executed by a person prior to becoming incapacitated. The major medical professional associations, including the American Medical Association and the American Academy of Neurology, had adopted the same position as had the courts, concluding that it was ethical for physicians to withdraw nutrition for patients suffering irreversible conditions such as PVS. Ethicists, including many from the Catholic faith, had reasoned that there was no moral compulsion to accept medically provided nutrition in such circumstances. Still, many disagreed and there remained a degree of discomfort with withdrawal of nutrition and hydration that didn't exist with medical interventions such as ventilators, chemotherapy, hemodialysis, or surgeries such as amputations.

The Missouri Supreme Court did not clearly confine its decision in *Cruzan* to the withdrawal of medically provided nutrition. Drawing a line between medically provided nutrition and other medically provided sustenance, such as oxygen provided by a ventilator, is difficult. If withdrawing medically provided nutrition is death by starvation, then withdrawing the ventilator is death by suffocation. There are strong advocates on each side of this issue within various traditions, including the Catholic tradition. The *Cruzan* case, involving the withdrawal of nutrition, thus falls within the area of least consensus.

But the *Cruzan* case clearly involves more, as the decision by the U.S. Supreme Court to accept the case for review indicates. The fact that the Court announced that it had accepted this case on the same day that it announced its decision in the abortion case (*Webster* v. *Reproductive Health Services*) only increased speculation over the justices' strategy in selecting it.

Of course, the Supreme Court will *not* be deciding what *ought* to be done for Nancy Cruzan. Rather, the Court will be deciding whether the law of Missouri, as identified by the Missouri Supreme Court, is unconstitutional. A lot will depend, then, on how the U.S. Supreme Court describes what the Missouri Supreme Court did. Surprisingly enough, there are a few choices here.

The bottom line of the Missouri Supreme Court's majority opinion is quite clear—neither Nancy Cruzan herself nor her family has any legal authority under Missouri law to refuse continued medical treatment. She must continue, as a matter of legal compulsion, to receive medical treatment, at least medically provided nutrition. The major justifications for the Missouri court's conclusion are the gravity of the state's interest in the preservation of life; their skepticism that any right to refuse or consent to medical treatment would survive a person's incompetency; and the absence of clear and convincing evidence of Nancy Cruzan's own decision concerning medical treatment.

The Missouri Supreme Court clearly held that the state of Missouri had an interest in life that was unique among the states. The court relied on Missouri's abortion statute, which survived constitutional challenge in *Webster*, and its living will statute as evidence of an intense interest in the "sanctity" of life, which it defined as prolongation of life. The court also held that the state's interest in life outweighed Nancy Cruzan's right to refuse medical treatment, if she in fact had such a right, because the continued treatment caused no burden to her. The court concluded that Nancy Cruzan herself bore no burden because the treatment caused her no pain.

The court repeatedly described its belief that any right that a competent person has to control his or her own medical treatment ends when he or she loses the physical or mental capacity to make his or her own decisions. Since the incompetent patient had no right to refuse treatment herself, that right could not be delegated to her family "absent the most rigid formalities," if at all.

Rather than decide squarely on that basis, however, the Missouri Supreme Court concluded that Nancy Cruzan had left no clear and convincing evidence of her own desires concerning medical treatment in the event of a catastrophe such as the one in which she now finds herself. The court viewed her conversations with her family and friends as too informal to bear any weight in the decision now confronting the state of Missouri.

What the Cruzan case really does, if taken in its entirety, is to appropriate for the state the entire responsibility of deciding the course of medical treatment for an incompetent person like Nancy Cruzan. It completely eliminates any role for the family: as guardians, according to the opinion, they are acting merely as agents for the state of Missouri. It eliminates any concern for what this individual would have desired unless that desire is expressed in the most rigid formalities. It gives to the state the sole authority for weighing the benefits and burdens of a particular medical treatment and further asserts that, for the state of Missouri, the prolongation of life will be the primary value unless achieving that goal is too painful physically.

Still, the United States Supreme Court could read *Cruzan* v. *Harmon* as a case in which the state of Missouri simply requires that medical treatment must be administered to any person who is no longer capable of making his or her own decisions, unless there is clear and convincing evidence that that person would have chosen to refuse that particular treatment. Speculation over what the U.S. Supreme Court will do in any case is hazardous. The Court includes relatively new justices who are developing their own jurisprudence and making their mark on the law of the Constitution. If the question framed by the Court is whether Missouri's requirement of maintaining treatment is constitutional, I would guess that the majority of the justices will say that it is.

In many ways, this is the least offensive course because it strikes a middle ground. It does recognize that there is some constitutional protection for refusal of medical treatment and so does not compel medical treatment in all cases. It does allow individuals to exempt themselves from the state's requirement that they accept medical treatment, if the individual plans well enough in advance. It appears to establish merely procedural protections for vulnerable persons. Furthermore, approval of this approach of itself would not require other states to establish such rules. State courts and legislatures could choose other approaches. The question of what ought to be done would remain the prerogative of the states.

I approach the question of what ought to be done from presumptions that are quite different from those implicit in the opinion of the Missouri Supreme Court. It is from these presumptions that I would criticize a requirement that treatment is to be provided unless there is clear and convincing evidence of the person's choice, especially if that standard implies mandatory judicial process.

First, I do not begin with the presumption that the very availability of medical treatment creates a moral obligation to accept such treatment. Rather, the decision to undergo or refuse treatment must involve weighing the benefits and burdens of that treatment in particular circumstances. There is a surprising uniformity of consent or refusal concerning some medical treatments; for example, most people consent to blood transfusions in life-threatening situations and most at least say they would refuse life support if they were in PVS. But for most medical treatment decisions, the weighing of benefits and burdens is quite personal. While one now-incompetent individual may have firmly believed and practiced a faith that holds a vision of an everlasting life after death, another may have equally firmly and devotedly believed that the breath of life on earth is the ultimate value of human life. Allowing the decision to be made on an individual basis and taking account of the individual's values and life history is most true to the ethical nature of the medical treatment decision.

Second, most people expect that their spouses or adult children will be in charge of any medical treatment decisions that must be made without their own participation. The custom of the medical profession to confer with and seek the consent of the spouse or the parent or the adult children of their incompetent patients reflects this expectation. The expectation that the family will make these decisions is grounded in trust and intimacy. It is also one that recognizes the importance of having someone that can engage the physicians in explaining the risks and benefits of recommended treatments when the very specific and very important facts of the particular situation are known.

One supposed advantage of the clear and convincing evidence approach is that it would force people to confront medical treatment decisions while still capable of doing so. Perhaps. But if you are not a nurse or a physician or otherwise familiar with the great variety of medical treatments that are now available or will be available in the near future for a full range of illnesses or conditions that might rob you of your ability to make your own decisions, how will you leave clear and convincing evidence of your choice? Imagine trying to write out instructions that cover all the bases in a fashion that cannot be misinterpreted. The clear and convincing evidence standard reduces the process of medical treatment decision making to a set of directions and the family to tape recorders.

Who will be authorized to apply this standard? If a court is the only authorized agent of the state, then a court must be used for every case. One need only remember the Linares tragedy in Chicago last year—when a father took his comatose child off a respirator holding the nursing staff at bay with a gun—to see the unworkability of mandated judicial proceedings. Would the Linares child have been better protected by the court? Would the court have reached a different decision? If not, what is the purpose of mandating a judicial process?

In the aftermath of *Cruzan*, it is likely that the various states will have wide latitude in regulating medical treatment decision making. My expectation is that the legal system in this context will honor the medical ethical principle— first, do no harm. The law should not deny the expectations of the vast majority of citizens who believe that their spouses or parents or children are the persons who, knowing them best, should make these important and intimate decisions. Nor should the law reject so completely the tradition and custom of health-care providers in consulting with these natural surrogates. Rather, the legal system should strive to be in harmony with these expectations by giving legal authority to documents appointing health-care proxies. Of course, not all families are wonderful and not all decisions are correct. There will need to be some protection developed.

No legal procedure will resolve all the issues. Conflicts over the goals and limitations of medical treatment will remain. But in a case such as that of the Cruzans, where the family was examined under a microscope by the trial court and the Missouri Supreme Court and found to be a "loving family" and where the courts found that the Cruzans' decision was supported by widely accepted medical principles, by ethical reasoning, and by their daughter's own statements, the state's order of medical treatment simply reduces itself to the assertion that the state knows best.

EUTHANASIA—QUESTIONS ON ESSAYS

1. Rachels's essay is built around hypothetical situations; Johnson's on the Cruzan case. As evidence for or against the issue, which do you think constitutes better evidence? How do you account for the differences in their approach?

2. What does Hunter mean by "death with honor"? How would you apply this to the Cruzan case or any other current cases you are familiar with?

3. Hunter quotes the psychiatrist Victor Frankl who quotes from the philosopher Spinoza. What kind of evidence is this? Could it be called "expert testimony" on euthanasia?

4. How would Rachels respond to Hunter's belief that active euthanasia violates "fundamental precepts of healing"? How would you try to resolve their differences?

5. What warrants are there in Rachels's and Hunter's essays, both of which focus on the role of the physician?

6. How would you use your own experience or observation in order to resolve the debate on euthanasia?

III. Pornography Essays

Erotica vs. Pornography

by Gloria Steinem

Look at or imagine images of people making love; really making love. Those images may be very diverse, but there is likely to be a mutual pleasure and touch and warmth, an empathy for each other's bodies and nerve endings, a shared sensuality and a spontaneous sense of two people who are there because they *want* to be.

Now look at or imagine images of sex in which there is force, violence, or symbols of unequal power. They may be very blatant: whips and chains of bondage, even torture and murder presented as sexually titillating, the clear evidence of wounds and bruises, or an adult's power being used sexually over a child. They may be more subtle: the use of class, race, authority, or just body poses to convey conqueror and victim; unequal nudity, with one person's body exposed and vulnerable while the other is armored with clothes; or even a woman by herself, exposed for an unseen but powerful viewer whom she clearly is trying to please. (It's interesting that, even when only the woman is seen, we often know whether she is there for her own pleasure or being displayed for someone else's.) But blatant or subtle, there is no equal power or mutuality. In fact, much of the tension and drama comes from the clear idea that one person is dominating another.

These two sorts of images are as different as love is from rape, as dignity is from humiliation, as partnership is from slavery, as pleasure is from pain. Yet they are confused and lumped together as "pornography" or "obscenity," "erotica" or "explicit sex," because sex and violence are so dangerously intertwined and confused. After all, it takes violence or the threat of it to maintain the unearned dominance of any group of human beings over another. Moreover, the threat must be the most persuasive wherever men and women come together intimately and are most in danger of recognizing each other's humanity.

The confusion of sex with violence is most obvious in any form of sadomasochism. The gender-based barrier to empathy has become so great that a torturer or even murderer may actually believe pain or loss of life to be the natural fate of the victim; and the victim may have been so deprived of self-respect or of empathetic human contact that she expects pain or loss of freedom as the price of any intimacy or attention at all. It's unlikely that even a masochist expects death. Nonetheless, "snuff" movies and much current pornographic literature insist that a slow death from sexual torture is the final orgasm and ultimate pleasure. It's a form of "suicide" reserved for women. Though men in fact are far more likely to kill themselves, male suicide is almost never presented as sexually pleasurable. But sex is also confused with violence and aggression in all forms of popular culture, and in respectable theories of psychology and sexual behavior as well. The idea that aggression is a "normal" part of male sexuality, and that passivity or even the need for male aggression is a "normal" part of female sexuality, are part of the male-dominant culture we live in, the books we learn from, and the air we breathe.

Even the words we are given to express our feelings are suffused with the same assumptions. Sexual phrases are the most common synonyms for conquering and humiliation (*being had, being screwed, getting fucked*); the sexually aggressive woman is a *slut* or a *nymphomaniac*, but the sexually aggressive man is just *normal*; and real or scientific descriptions of sex may perpetuate the same roles; for instance, a woman is always *penetrated* by a man though she might also be said to have *enveloped* him.

Obviously, untangling sex from aggression and violence or the threat of it is going to take a very long time. And the process is going to be greatly resisted as a challenge to the very heart of male dominance and male centrality.

But we do have the common sense of our bodies to guide us. Pain is a warning of damage and danger. If that sensation is not mixed with all the intimacy we know as children, we are unlikely to confuse pain with pleasure and love. As we discover our free will and strength, we are also more likely to discover our own initiative and pleasure in sex. As men no longer can dominate and have to find an identity that doesn't depend on superiority, they also discover that cooperation is more interesting than submission, that empathy with their sex partner increases their own pleasure, and that anxieties about their own ability to "perform" tend to disappear along with stereotyped ideas about masculinity.

But women will be the main fighters of this new sexual revolution. It is our freedom, our safety, our lives, and our pleasure that are mostly at stake.

We began by trying to separate sex and violence in those areas where the physical danger was and is the most immediate: challenging rape as the one crime that was considered biologically irresistible for the criminal and perhaps invited by the victim; refusing to allow male–female beatings to be classified as "domestic violence" and ignored by the law; exposing forced prostitution and sexual slavery as national and international crimes. With the exception of wife beating, those challenges were made somewhat easier by men who wanted to punish other men for taking their female property. Women still rarely have the power to protect each other.

Such instances of real antiwoman warfare led us directly to the propaganda that teaches and legitimizes them—pornography. Just as we had begun to separate rape from sex, we realized that we must find some way of separating pornographic depictions of sex as an antiwoman weapon from those images of freely chosen, mutual sexuality.

Fortunately, there is truth in the origin of words. *Pornography* comes from the Greek root *porné* (harlot, prostitute, or female captive) and *graphos* (writing about or description of). Thus, it means a description of either the purchase of sex, which implies an imbalance of power in itself, or sexual slavery.

This definition includes, and should include, all such degradation, regardless of whether it is females who are the slaves and males who are the captors or vice versa. There is certainly homosexual pornography, for instance, with a man in the "feminine" role of victim. There is also role-reversal pornography, with a woman whipping or punishing a man, though it's significant that this genre is created by men for their own pleasure, not by or for women, and allows men to *pretend* to be victims— but without real danger. There could also be lesbian pornography, with a woman assuming the "masculine" role of victimizing another woman. That women rarely choose this role of victimizer is due to no biological superiority, but a culture that doesn't addict women to violence. But whatever the gender of the participants, all pornography is an imitation of the male–female, conqueror–victim paradigm, and almost all of it actually portrays or implies enslaved woman and master.

Even the 1970 Presidential Commission on Obscenity and Pornography, whose report is often accused of suppressing or ignoring evidence of the causal link between pornography and violence against women, defined the subject of their study as pictorial or verbal descriptions of sexual behavior characterized by "the degrading and demeaning portrayal of the role and status of the human female."

In short, pornography is not about sex. It's about an imbalance of male–female power that allows and even requires sex to be used as a form of aggression.

Erotica may be the word that can differentiate sex from violence and rescue sexual pleasure. It comes from the Greek root *eros* (sexual desire or passionate love, named for Eros, the son of Aphrodite), and so contains the idea of love, positive choice, and the yearning for a particular person. Unlike pornography's reference to a harlot or prostitute, *erotica* leaves entirely open the question of gender. (In fact, we may owe its sense of shared power to the Greek idea that a man's love for another man was more worthy than love for a woman, but at least that bias isn't present in the word.) Though both erotica and pornography refer to verbal or pictorial representations of sexual behavior, they are as different as a room with doors open and one with doors locked. The first might be a home, but the second could only be a prison.

The problem is that there is so little erotica. Women have rarely been free enough to pursue erotic pleasures in our own lives, much less to create it in the worlds of film, magazines, art, books, television, and popular culture—all the areas of communication we rarely control. Very few male authors and filmmakers have been able to escape society's message of what a man should do, much less to imagine their way into the identity of a woman. Some women and men are trying to portray equal and erotic sex, but it is still not a part of popular culture.

And the problem is there is so much pornography. This underground stream of antiwoman propaganda that exists in all male-dominant societies has now become a flood in our streets and theaters and even our homes. Perhaps that's better in the long run. Women can no longer pretend pornography does not exist. We must either face our own humiliation and torture every day on magazine covers and television screens or fight back. There is hardly a newsstand without women's bodies in chains and bondage, in full labial display for the conquering male viewer, bruised or on our knees, screaming in real or pretended pain, pretending to enjoy what we don't enjoy. The same images are in mainstream movie theaters and respectable hotel rooms via closed-circuit TV for the traveling businessman. They are brought into our own homes not only in magazines, but in the new form of video cassettes. Even video games offer such features as a smiling, rope-bound woman and a male figure with an erection, the game's object being to rape the woman as many times as possible. (Like much of pornography, that game is fascist on racial grounds as well as sexual ones. The smiling woman is an Indian maiden, the rapist is General Custer, and the game is called "Custer's Revenge.") Though "snuff" movies in which real women were eviscerated and finally killed have been driven underground (in part because the graves of many murdered women were discovered around the shack of just one filmmaker in California), movies that simulate the torture murders of women are still going strong. (*Snuff* is the porn term for killing a woman for sexual pleasure. There is not even the seriousness of a word like *murder*.) So are the "kiddie porn" or "chicken porn" magazines that show adult men undressing, fondling, and sexually using children; often with the titillating theme that "fathers" are raping "daughters." Some "chicken porn" magazines offer explicit tips on how to use a child sexually without leaving physical evidence of rape, the premise being that children's testimony is even less likely to be believed than that of adult women.

Add this pornography industry up, from magazines like *Playboy* and *Hustler*, to movies like *Love Gestapo Style, Deep Throat,* and *Angels in Pain,* and the total sales come to a staggering eight billion dollars a year—more than all the sales of the conventional film and record industry combined. And that doesn't count the fact that many "conventional" film and music images are also pornographic, from gynocidal record jackets like the famous *I'm "Black and Blue" from the Rolling Stones—and I Love It!* (which showed a seminude black woman bound to a chair) to the hundreds of teenage sex-and-horror movies in which young women die sadistic deaths and rape is presented not as a crime but as sexual excitement. Nor do those industries include the sales of the supposedly "literary" forms of pornography, from *The Story of O* to the works of the Marquis de Sade.

If Nazi propaganda that justified the torture and killing of Jews were the theme of half of our most popular movies and magazines, would we not be outraged? If Ku Klux Klan propaganda that preached and even glamorized the enslavement of blacks were the subject of much-praised "classic" novels, would we not protest? We know that such racist propaganda precedes and justifies the racist acts of pogroms and lynchings. We know that watching a violent film causes test subjects to both condone more violence afterward and to be willing to perpetuate it themselves. Why is the propaganda of sexual aggression against women of all races the one form in which the "conventional wisdom" sees no danger? Why is pornography the only media violence that is supposed to be a "safety valve" to satisfy men's "natural" aggressiveness somewhere short of acting it out?

The first reason is the confusion of *all* nonprocreative sex with pornography. Any description of sexual behavior, or even nudity, may be called pornographic or obscene (a word whose Latin derivative means *dirty* or *containing filth*) by those who insist that the only moral purpose of sex is procreative, or even that any portrayal of sexuality or nudity is against the will of God.

In fact, human beings seem to be the only animals that experience the same sex drive and pleasure at times when we can and cannot conceive. Other animals experience periods of heat or estrus. Humans do not.

Just as we developed uniquely human capacities for language, planning, memory, and invention along our evolutionary path, we also developed sexuality as a form of expression, a way of communicating that is separable from our reproductive need. For human beings, sexuality can be and often is a way of bonding, of giving and receiving pleasure, bridging differentness, discovering sameness, and communicating emotion.

We developed this and other human gifts through our ability to change our environment, adapt to it physically, and so in the very long run to affect our own evolution. But as an emotional result of this spiraling path away from other animals, we seem to alternate between periods of exploring our unique abilities and feelings of loneliness in the unknown that we ourselves have created, a fear that sometimes sends us back to the comfort of the animal world by encouraging us to look for a sameness that is not there.

For instance, the separation of "play" from "work" is a feature of the human world. So is the difference between art and nature, or an intellectual accomplishment and a physical one. As a result, we celebrate play, art, and invention as pleasurable and important leaps into the unknown, yet any temporary trouble can send us back to a nostalgia for our primate past and a conviction that the basics of survival, nature, and physical labor are somehow more worthwhile or even more moral.

In the same way, we have explored our sexuality as separable from conception: a pleasurable, empathetic, important bridge to others of our species. We have even invented contraception, a skill that has probably existed in some form since our ancestors figured out the process of conception and birth, in order to extend and protect this uniquely human gift. Yet we also have times of atavistic suspicion that sex is not complete, or even legal or intended by God, it if does not or could not end in conception.

No wonder the very different concepts of "erotica" and "pornography" can be so confused. Both assume that sex can be separated from conception; that human sexuality has additional uses and goals. This is the major reason why, even in our current culture, both may still be condemned as equally obscene and immoral. Such gross condemnation of all sexuality that isn't harnessed to childbirth (and to patriarchal marriage so that children are properly "owned" by men) has been increased by the current backlash against women's independence. Out of fear that the whole patriarchal structure will be eventually upset if we as women really have the autonomous power to decide our sexual and reproductive futures (that is, if we can control our own bodies, and thus the means of reproduction), anti-equality groups are not only denouncing sex education and family planning as "pornographic," but are trying to use obscenity laws to stop the sending of all contraceptive information through the mails. Any sex or nudity outside the context of patriarchal marriage and forced childbirth is their target. In fact, Phyllis Schlafly[1] has denounced the entire women's movement as "obscene."

Not surprisingly, this religious, visceral backlash has a secular, intellectual counterpart that relies heavily on applying the "natural" behavior of some selected part of the animal world to humans. This is questionable in itself, but such Lionel Tiger-ish[2] studies make their political purpose even more clear by the animals they choose and the habits they emphasize. For example, some male primates carry and generally "mother" their infants, male lions care for their young, female elephants often lead the clan, and male penguins literally do everything except give birth, from hatching the eggs to sacrificing their own membranes to feed the new arrivals. Perhaps that's why many male supremacists prefer to discuss chimps and baboons (many of whom are studied in atypical conditions of captivity) whose behavior is suitably male-dominant. The message is that human females should accept their animal "destiny" of being sexually dependent and devote themselves to bearing and rearing their young.

Defending against such repression and reaction leads to the temptation to merely reverse the terms and declare that *all* nonprocreative sex is good. In fact, however, this human activity can be as constructive or destructive, moral or immoral, as any other. Sex as communication can send messages as different as mutual pleasure and dominance, life and death, "erotica" and "pornography."

The second kind of problem comes not from those who oppose women's equality in nonsexual areas, whether on grounds of God or nature, but from men (and some women, too) who present themselves as friends of civil liberties and progress. Their opposition may take the form of a concern about privacy, on the grounds that a challenge to pornography invades private sexual behavior and the philosophy of "whatever turns you on." It may be a concern about class bias, on the premise that pornography is just "workingmen's erotica." Sometimes, it's the simple argument that they themselves like pornography and therefore it must be okay. Most often, however, this resistance attaches itself to or hides behind an expressed concern about censorship, freedom of the press, and the First Amendment.

In each case, such liberal objections are more easily countered than the antiequality ones because they are less based on fact. It's true, for instance, that women's independence and autonomy would upset the whole patriarchal apple cart: the conservatives are right to be worried. It's not true, however, that pornography is a private concern. If it were just a matter of men making male-supremacist literature in their own basements to assuage their own sexual hang-ups, there would be sorrow and avoidance among women, but not the anger, outrage, and fear produced by being confronted with the preaching of sexual fascism on our newstands, movie screens, television sets, and public streets. It is a multibillion-dollar industry, which involves the making of

[1]Conservative opponent of the women's movement.
[2]The allusion is to anthropologist Lionel Tiger, author of *Men in Groups*.

public policy, if only to decide whether, as is now the case, crimes committed in the manufacture and sale of pornography will continue to go largely unprosecuted. Zoning regulations on the public display of pornography are not enforced, the sexual slavery and exploitation of children goes unpunished, the forcible use of teenage runaways is ignored by police, and even the torture and murder of prostitutes for men's sexual titillation is obscured by some mitigating notion that the women asked for it.

In all other areas of privacy, the limitation is infringement on the rights and lives and safety of others. That must become true for pornography. Right now, it is exempt: almost "below the law."

As for class bias, it's simply not accurate to say that pornography is erotica with less education. From the origins of the words, as well as the careful way that feminists working against pornography are trying to use them, it's clear there is a substantive difference, not an artistic or economic one. Pornography is about dominance. Erotica is about mutuality. (Any man able to empathize with women can easily tell the difference by looking at a photograph or film and putting himself in the woman's skin. There is some evidence that poor or discriminated-against men are better able to do this than rich ones.) Perhaps the most revealing thing is that this argument is generally made *on behalf* of the working class by propornography liberals, but not by working-class spokespeople themselves.

Of course, the idea that enjoying pornography makes it okay is an overwhelmingly male one. From Kinsey forward, research has confirmed that men are the purchasers of pornography, and that the majority of men are turned on by it, while the majority of women find it angering, humiliating, and not a turn-on at all. This was true even though women were shown sexually explicit material that may have included erotica, since Kinsey and others did not make that distinction. If such rare examples of equal sex were entirely deleted, pornography itself could probably serve as sex aversion-therapy for most women; yet many men and some psychologists continue to call women prudish, frigid, or generally unhealthy if they are not turned on by their own domination. The same men might be less likely to argue that anti-Semitic and racist literature was equally okay because it gave them pleasure, or that they wanted their children to grow up with the same feelings about people of other races, other classes, that had been inflicted on them. The problem is that the degradation of women of all races is still thought to be normal.

Nonetheless, there are a few well-meaning women who are both turned on by pornography and angered that other women are not. Some of their anger is misunderstanding: objections to pornography are not condemnations of women who have been raised to believe sex and domination are synonymous, but objections to the idea that such domination is the only form that normal sexuality can take. Sometimes, this anger results from an underestimation of themselves: being turned on by a rape fantasy is not the same thing as wanting to be raped. As Robin Morgan[3] has pointed out, the distinguishing feature of a fantasy is that the fantasizer herself is in control. Both men and women have "ravishment" fantasies in which we are passive while

[3]A feminist writer.

others act out our unspoken wishes—but they are still *our* wishes. And some anger, especially when it comes from women who consider themselves feminists, is a refusal to differentiate between what may be true for them now and what might be improved for all women in the future. To use a small but related example, a woman may now be attracted only to men who are taller, heavier, and older than she, but still understand that such superficial restrictions on the men she loves and enjoys going to bed with won't exist in a more free and less-stereotyped future. Similarly, some lesbians may find themselves following the masculine–feminine patterns that were our only model for intimate relationships, heterosexual or not, but still see these old patterns clearly and try to equalize them. It isn't that women attracted to pornography cannot also be feminists, but that pornography itself must be recognized as an adversary of women's safety and equality, and therefore, in the long run, of feminism.

Finally, there is the First Amendment argument against feminist anti-pornography campaigns: the most respectable and public opposition, but also the one with the least basis in fact.

Feminist groups are not arguing for censorship of pornography, or for censorship of Nazi literature or racist propaganda of the Ku Klux Klan. For one thing, any societal definition of pornography in a male-dominant society (or of racist literature in a racist society) probably would punish the wrong people. Freely chosen homosexual expression might be considered more "pornographic" than snuff movies, or contraceptive courses for teenagers more "obscene" than bondage. Furthermore, censorship in itself, even with the proper definitions, would only drive pornography into more underground activity and, were it to follow the pattern of drug traffic, into even more profitability. Most important, the First Amendment is part of a statement of individual rights against government intervention that feminism seeks to expand, not contract: for instance, a woman's right to decide whether and when to have children. When we protest against pornography and educate others about it, as I am doing now, we are strengthening the First Amendment by exercising it.

The only legal steps suggested by feminists thus far have been the prosecution of those pornography makers who are accused of murder or assault and battery, prosecution of those who use children under the age of consent, enforcement of existing zoning and other codes that are breached because of payoffs to law-enforcement officials and enormous rents paid to pornography's landlords, and use of public-nuisance statutes to require that pornography not be displayed in public places where its sight cannot reasonably be avoided. All of those measures involve enforcement of existing law, and none has been interpreted as a danger to the First Amendment.

Perhaps the reason for this controversy is less substance than smokescreen. Just as earlier feminist campaigns to combat rape were condemned by some civil libertarians as efforts that would end by putting only men of color or poor men in jail, or in perpetuating the death penalty, anti-pornography campaigns are now similarly opposed. In fact, the greater publicity given to rape exposed the fact that white psychiatrists, educators, and other professionals were just as likely to be rapists, and changes in the law reduced penalties to ones that were more appropriate and thus more likely to be administered. Feminist efforts also changed the definition to sexual assault so that men were protected, too.

Though there are no statistics on the purchasers of pornography, clerks, moviehouse owners, video-cassette dealers, mail-order houses, and others who serve this clientele usually remark on their respectability, their professional standing, suits, briefcases, white skins, and middle-class zip codes. For instance, the last screening of a snuff movie showing a real murder was traced to the monthly pornographic film showings of a senior partner in a respected law firm; an event regularly held by him for a group of friends including other lawyers and judges. One who was present reported that many were "embarrassed" and "didn't know what to say." But not one man was willing to object, much less offer this evidence of murder to the police. Though some concern about censorship is sincere — the result of false reports that feminist anti-pornography campaigns were really calling for censorship, or of confusion with right-wing groups who both misdefine pornography and want to censor it — much of it seems to be a cover for the preservation of the pornographic status quo.

In fact, the obstacles to taking on pornography seem suspiciously like the virgin–whore divisions that have been women's only choices in the past. The right wing says all that is not virginal or motherly is pornographic, and thus they campaign against sexuality and nudity in general. The left wing says all sex is good as long as it's male-defined, and thus pornography must be protected. Women who feel endangered by being the victim, and men who feel demeaned by being the victimizer, have a long struggle ahead. In fact, pornography will continue as long as boys are raised to believe they must control or conquer women as a measure of manhood, as long as society rewards men who believe that success or even functioning — in sex as in other areas — depends on women's subservience.

But we now have words to describe our outrage and separate sex from violence. We now have the courage to demonstrate publicly against pornography, to keep its magazines and films out of our houses, to boycott its purveyors, to treat even friends and family members who support it as seriously as we would treat someone who supported and enjoyed Nazi literature or the teachings of the Klan.

But until we finally untangle sexuality and aggression, there will be more pornography and less erotica. There will be little murders in our beds — and very little love.

The First Amendment Forbids Censorship
by Lois Sheinfeld

"Suppression" Spinoza said, "is paring down the state till it is too small to harbor men of talent." These words, written over 300 years ago, precisely describe the anti-pornography censorship campaign now being waged against filmmaker Brian De Palma and others. While modern packaging cleverly disguises the new censors — the 1984 models come cloaked in civil rights theory—the mindset of those who would smother free thought and expression has not changed. Bookburners may wrap themselves in new rationalizations, but the books and films they condemn still burn.

The latest brand of censorship ordinances—passed in Minneapolis and vetoed by the mayor; enacted into law in Indianapolis—forbids pornography on the theory that it violates women's civil rights. Under the terms of this legislation, newspapers, literature, films, and visual art portraying the "graphic, sexually explicit subordination of women" are subject to governmental proscription. Not only motion pictures depicting violence against women, but all "pictures" or "words" in which women are presented as sexual objects for domination or conquest, as sexually submissive, or as degraded or inferior in a sexual context, can be suppressed.

Dangerous Departure from Free Speech

This anti-pornography legislation represents a radical and dangerous departure from accepted First Amendment principles. It permits any woman to demand the censorship of offending depictions without proving factually that they caused direct, immediate, serious harm—or, indeed, any harm at all—to her or to anyone else. According to the architects of the legislation, Catharine MacKinnon and Andrea Dworkin: "The systematic sexual subordination of the pornography *is* the injury." Thus, the purported justification for government censorship is not some demonstrated evil to which the publication of an idea will lead but rather the offensive nature of the idea itself, namely, "dehumanizing women as sexual things and commodities."

Further, the new laws plainly forbid portrayals of women that do not fall within the very limited category of expression which the courts have defined as obscenity. Literary and film classics found sufficiently demeaning to women under the sweeping, ill-defined provisions of the ordinances are now subject to repression.

But that is not the full measure of the danger. If the ordinances are sustained as constitutional, nothing in the theory that supposedly supports them would restrict censorship to "sexually explicit" material. Unlike laws against obscenity, where the arousal of prurient interest is the essential focus, here prohibition is based upon the "subordination" of a sex-defined class. A claim of "subordination" could as easily be leveled against a treatise suggesting that a woman's place is in the home raising children, or against a film portrayal of a "dumb blond" (Marilyn Monroe in *Bus Stop* or *The Misfits*), or even a smart blond (Meryl Streep in *The Seduction of Joe Tynan*). And government "civil rights" censorship needn't be limited to the professed protection of women. Blacks, Poles, Jewish mothers, Orientals, "Moonies," *et al.* could equally claim that satirical, derogatory, or critical portrayals are suppressible as "dehumanizing" and "subordinating." First Amendment rights would be bounded by the sensibilities of *every* group in our pluralistic society.

ALL Voices Protected

Constitutional protection of free speech is content blind. Every person's voice is protected, not because we like or approve every "picture" or "word," but because we recognize that when official censors make the choice of what we see and hear, all speech is at risk. The authors of the Constitution understood that a democracy can flourish only when each of us decides the value and acceptability of ideas, not the government. Otherwise, demanded Thomas Jefferson: "Whose foot is to be the measure to which ours are all to be cut or stretched?"

Invoking governmental repression of disfavored expression is not unique to these times. We have a sorry history of attempts to override the fundamental First Amendment guarantees of free speech and press in order to impose an official guardianship over the public mind. As John Milton observed, censors have often tried to "starch" us into a gross conformity, and to change our open society into one in which the people hear only one voice and see only one image, that which the government in power seeks to put forward. Political dissenters and the proponents of unpopular views — advocates of civil rights, women's rights, and the nuclear freeze — have all sufferd the assaults of censorship because some people thought their voices were "offensive," "repulsive," and "dangerous."

The First Amendment imperative of free expression protects our liberty against just such assaults. Justice Oliver Wendell Holmes made the essential point long ago: "The ultimate good desired is better reached by free trade in ideas — the best test of truth is the power of the thought to get itself accepted in the competition of the market. . . . That at any rate is the theory of our Constitution . . . we should be eternally vigilant against attempts to check the expression of opinions that we loathe and believe to be fraught with death, unless they so imminently threaten immediate interference with the lawful and pressing purposes of the law that an immediate check is required to save the country."

Courts Are Vigilant Against Suppression

Courts have upheld this basic principle even when the speech at issue was, to most minds, hateful, dehumanizing, and subordinating. When television films broadcast the Ku Klux Klan disparaging blacks and Jews, the Supreme Court held in *Brandenburg* v. *Ohio* (1969) that the state could not punish this advocacy, absent a clear showing that the speech was directed at, and would likely produce, "imminent lawless action."

Similarly, when public officials attempted to forbid the neo-Nazi march through Skokie, Illinois, a suburb with a large Jewish population including several thousand survivors of the Nazi holocaust, the court upheld even the neo-Nazis' right of free speech. *Collin* v. *Smith* (1978). Despite the judges' "personal views" that the march would be "extremely mentally and emotionally disturbing" to many people, and "repugnant to the core values held generally by residents of this country," the court held: "However pernicious an opinion may seem, we depend for its correction not on the conscience of judges and juries but on the competition of other ideas"; this is what "distinguishes life in this country from life under the Third Reich." In the absence of evidentiary proof of intentional and direct incitement to violence, the Skokie march was constitutionally protected.

Insufficient Evidence

Some supporters of the anti-pornography ordinances claim that pornography causes rape and other acts of criminal sexual violence. This view ignores the state of the evidence. There have been two comprehensive studies of the supposed link between pornography and sex crimes: the investigations of the President's Commission on Obscenity and Pornography (1970), and the British Committee on Obscenity and Film Censorship (1979). Both concluded that there was no causal nexus between pornography and crime. That finding is further buttressed by studies of actual sex offenders.

As for the recent rash of laboratory research done under artificial conditions (conducted by academic psychologists on student subjects who received extra credit in their psychology courses), suffice it to say here that Professors Edward Donnerstein and Neil Malamuth, whose studies are most often cited by would-be-pornography censors, admit that the research does not establish a direct causal connection between pornography and sexual violence. They do not advocate censorship legislation.

Failure of Proof

Anti-pornography censors are simply unable to meet the evidentiary burden imposed by the First Amendment upon those who seek to suppress expression on the ground that it causes serious harm. They should not be permitted to sidestep this profound failure of proof by the legerdemain of declaring that pornography is *per se* a violation of women's civil rights.

Filmmaker Brian De Palma said, "I'd hate to live in a world where art is left in the hands of the political people. I'd leave the country if it came to that — sounds like Russia." Indeed it does. In August of this year, the Moscow Communist Party Committee criticized the Soviet film studios for straying from Socialist Realism and issued new directives requiring filmmakers to reflect current problems and workers' lives. A month later, Soviet Party leader Konstantin U. Chernenko had this to say: "Freedom of creative work cannot be a privilege for a few. Nothing and no one can free a person from the compulsory demands of society, its laws that are obligatory for all. It is naive to think that one can blacken the moral and political foundations of our system. . . . The nation will not forgive anyone defecting to the side of our ideological opponents. . . ."

Such government control over the content of expression is an anathema in a democracy. What De Palma sees and paints onto his "white canvas" might not be to everyone's taste. But the state may no more proscribe his creative work than it may prescribe his artistic images.

In Luis Buñuel's succinct phrase: "A pox on censors!"

The First Amendment Does Not Protect Pornography

by Janella Miller

The latest movie in the stream of Hollywood offerings in which women are brutally murdered has arrived — *Body Double*. Director Brian De Palma's attitude toward the violence and toward the encroachment of pornography into the mainstream media demands a response. De Palma told interviewer Pally that he opposes pornography legislation because he has a right as an individual to take pictures of anything he pleases, including pictures of a woman being violently murdered with a drill. He says that he does not believe viewing pornography has any effect upon male viewers or their likelihood of committing acts of aggression against women.

De Palma has obviously not been paying any attention to the victims of pornography, the *women* who are hurt by and through pornography, who have courageously spoken out about the abuse they have experienced because of pornography. Nor has he studied the most recent research linking pornography to increased aggression against women. If he had, he would know that pornography is not just ideas or words or pictures on a page; it is a *practice* that harms women and children.

Pornography as Discrimination

Recent legislation passed in Minneapolis and in Indianapolis addresses, for the first time, the harm done by pornography. Feminist writer and activist Andrea Dworkin and University of Minnesota law professor Catharine MacKinnon, at the request of the Minneapolis city council, wrote a civil rights ordinance on pornography that defines pornography as a form of sex discrimination and as a violation of women's civil rights. The ordinance defines pornography as "the sexually explicit subordination of women, graphically depicted, whether in pictures or in words," that also includes one or more of nine listed characteristics which range from "women are presented as sexual objects who enjoy pain or humiliation" to "women are presented in postures of sexual submission or sexual servility, including by inviting penetration" to "women are presented being penetrated by objects or animals."

Material must meet *each* part of the definition to be pornography. It must be graphic, *and* sexually explicit, *and* subordinate women, *and* meet at least one of the nine characteristics. If the material is found to meet the definition of pornography, the ordinance provides for a civil cause of action if a woman is coerced into making pornography, has pornography forced upon her in her workplace or any other context, or is assaulted or attacked in a way that is caused by a specific piece of pornography. The ordinance also provides for a claim against the makers, exhibitors, distributors, and sellers of pornography for the terrorism and intimidation created by pornography which perpetuates women's inferior status and promotes continued discrimination against women in all areas of our society. A woman could bring her claim directly to court or to the city civil rights commission, which would decide whether to pursue the matter further. Because the ordinance creates a civil cause of action, a judge could award damages or issue an injunction against the further sale of the pornography, but he or she could not order a criminal penalty. The ordinance does not give more power to the police. It *does* give more power to women.

Harm to Women

By acknowledging the harm done to women and providing them with a way to do something about that harm, the ordinance goes beyond any previous legislation. The ordinance is not an obscenity law and does not contain any of the language of obscenity laws which rely upon criminal sanctions to enforce community standards of decency. The theory behind this ordinance is diametrically opposite to the theory behind obscenity laws.

The ordinance says that women have a right to possess their bodies and their lives. Obscenity laws, on the other hand, are based upon the premise that women's bodies are dirty, that sex is immoral, and that pornographic materials should be kept behind closed doors where only men over the age of 18 can have access to them. Under obscenity laws, a judge must decide whether the "average person, applying contemporary community standards" would find that the work, taken as a whole, appeals to prurient interest. That usually means that a work is "obscene" when a man is sexually aroused. Because of their vagueness, obscenity laws have been haphazardly and erratically applied. Nowadays, we seldom hear cries of censorship about obscenity, which is not protected speech under the First Amendment, perhaps because the laws do not work.

Accountability, Not Censorship

There have been many, however, who claim that the civil rights ordinance on pornography is censorship. They misunderstand what the ordinance does and also what censorship means in a society that values freedom of speech. The word *censorship* implies official examination of pictures, plays, television, etc., for the purpose of suppressing parts deemed objectionable on moral, political, military, or other grounds. The ordinance works on an entirely different principle. There are no prior restraints, no criminal penalties, and no increase in police powers. A particular work could be removed only after an adversarial hearing before a judge. Both sides could present evidence, as in any legal case. The ordinance provides no mechanism for telling people that they *cannot* publish what they want. What it *does* do is tell pornographers that if they print material in which women and children are harmed, or material that *leads* to harm or discrimination, they must be responsible for the harm that they cause. In that regard, the ordinance works much like libel laws which hold the media accountable for false information that harms an individual if the individual can prove that he or she was injured.

If the ordinance were effectively applied, pornographers would undoubtedly choose not to publish certain materials because it would be too costly for them. There *would* be fewer pornographic pictures, movies, and books. Supporters of the ordinance intend that result. For the first time, people are challenging the idea that the First Amendment should shield pornography from any legal challenge. The harm done to women in this legal system is great enough to justify limitations on the pornographers' right to "freedom of speech" under which they have committed atrocities against women for centuries.

Right to Freedom Not Absolute

Those who cry censorship whenever someone mentions the ordinance act as though the right to freedom of speech were absolute and that it exists in a vacuum apart from any other social concern. But no lawyer who has ever studied the First Amendment would *ever* claim that we have an absolute right to freedom of speech.

We have libel laws, slander laws, and court decisions which limit words that create a "clear and present danger" or that constitute "fighting words." Obscenity is not protected speech under the First Amendment, nor is child pornography. In *New York* v. *Ferber*, 458 U.S. 747 (1982), the Supreme Court said that the *harm done* to children in pornography justified restricting the pornographers' right to print what they please. There is thus a precedent for weighing the harm done to *women* against the pornographers' right to "freedom of speech." That harm was well documented in the hearings before the Minneapolis city council in December 1983 and the Senate Sub-committee on Juvenile Justice in September 1984.

Social scientists, researchers on pornography, people who work in the field of sexual assault, and victims of pornography have all testified about the effects of pornography. Using this documentation to support legislation and legal decisions would not be a new idea. The Supreme Court has used sociological data in the past, most notably in *Brown* v. *Board of Education*, to support their finding that the harm done to black children in segregated schools was so great that integration was required to alleviate it.

Worst Outcome Not Likely

Opponents of the ordinance are also fond of claiming that we are on a slippery slope that will end in the suppression of the Bible or of Shakespeare. The concern about the Bible and Shakespeare is very interesting, since they are not sexually explicit and would not be covered under the ordinance as it is written. But opponents also seem to be arguing that *any* limitation on freedom of speech will lead to the institution of a repressive regime. These arguments are based not upon facts about the ordinance or upon a reasoned analysis of the First Amendment, but rather upon the manipulation of people's fears. Forecasting the worst possible outcome for any piece of legislation is an old legal strategy that is particularly powerful when the predicted outcome is the suppression of ideas. However, it does not necessarily follow that the worst possible outcome will occur *because* we are in the area of the First Amendment. In fact, the opposite outcome is more likely. Americans guard their right to freedom of speech with a tenacity that would surprise people in other countries which also value their freedom of speech. A judge would likely interpret the ordinance narrowly, finding that material falls under the ordinance only if it clearly degrades and subordinates women.

We always trust the courts to make decisions which clarify and illuminate the law. To say that task is difficult begs the question. Asking the courts to decide which works subordinate women and which works fall within the definition of pornography, when a woman claims to be harmed, will be far less onerous than asking them to decide which works are "obscene" under obscenity laws or what constitutes "discrimination" under civil rights laws. There is actually much less potential for abuse under the ordinance than there is under obscenity laws, under which we allow judges to make moral decisions about what we should view. Under the ordinance, as written, morality plays no role. The ordinance speaks only to the subordination of women and the harm done to women in pornography. I fear more the continuation and legitimation of a system which treats women as less than human, as objects to be consumed, than I do allowing our judges to decide what is covered under a specific and narrow definition of pornography.

An amendment to the ordinance further prevents frivolous abuses of the trafficking provision by precluding legal actions based upon isolated passages or isolated parts. The ordinance does not specify a certain percentage of the work that must be pornographic to be actionable, but the authors clearly intend to require more than a *de minimum* amount.

Finally, the ordinance avoids any interpretation leading to the suppression of *ideas* by defining pornography as "the sexually explicit subordination of women, graphically depicted, whether in pictures or in words." Pornography does not present the "idea" of subordination or of any other idea. It is an active *practice* of subordination. Only pictures and words that *do* subordinate women are pornography and fall within the scope of the ordinance.

Solution Cannot Wait

We cannot wait for a solution any longer. Pornography has grown into an $8 billion-a-year industry that has spread into every form of media and advertising. America's culture has become pornographic. It is time to look at the harm done by pornography and weigh it against the pornographers' claimed right to freedom of speech. We legislate for the good of society — to establish justice, equality, and freedom for all Americans. But women still do not have justice, equality, or freedom. The pornographers tell lies about women which lead to terrorism and intimidation. Men rape and torture women with the use of pornography. Men force women to perform in pornography. A beaten and tortured woman is not free, nor is she an equal member of our society. She is a second-class citizen with no way to improve the daily condition of her life, because no one hears her screams.

PORNOGRAPHY — QUESTIONS ON ESSAYS

1. What is the position of each of the writers on the claim regarding the "sexually explicit subordination of women"? What evidence does each writer use in support of her claim?

2. Which writer submits the most effective evidence in your opinion?

3. Both Sheinfeld and Miller are attorneys. Does this have any bearing on the strategy of their arguments? How does their approach differ from Steinem's?

4. How would you use any current news item or personal experience or observation in your own essay on pornography?

5. How would you attempt to resolve the argument based on the "slippery slope" view of the effects of censorship? How can we be sure that any limitation of freedom of speech will lead, in Miller's words, "to the institution of a repressive regime"?

6. What topics does Steinem discuss that are not discussed by the other two writers? Does this absence affect the persuasiveness of the other's arguments?

WRITING YOUR ESSAY

Generating Ideas: Critical Thinking

You have just read nine essays on three different controversial issues. None of these authors apparently felt the need to block the doors of abortion clinics, or to threaten to replace the life support equipment of a patient whose family has given the hospital orders not to resuscitate, or to forcibly remove books from a school library's shelves. Each of these authors has instead taken part in a debate — an exchange of ideas conducted in a reasoned, knowledge-able, dispassionate way by a well-informed group of participants, intended for a responsive, critical, knowledgeable audience. The authors represented in these essays advocated different claims, appealed to different constituencies, and addressed different audiences.

What these authors all had in common was a kind of implicit warrant about how the language of debate is conducted. In preparing your essay, you are literally joining in debate with them and indeed all others — past and present — who have had a similar purpose. These authors share a common understanding of, and respect for, the standards of civilized discourse in a free society. Free to express their views on a subject of their choice, they are, however, at the same time constrained by the conventions and shared princi-ples of public argument. Only within these conventions of form and style, in fact, can these debaters fully convey the range and effectiveness of their thinking.

In addition to having knowledge of these public conventions of debate, it is also important for your development as a writer to submit your methods of thinking to self-examination. Understanding and explaining how you think, developing a self-consciousness about your methods of arriving at con-clusions, is called critical thinking.

Critical thinking teaches you to be more cautious and less hasty with your judgments and often to suspend your final views on an issue until you are satisfied that you have examined it thoroughly from as many different per-spectives as you can. Critical thinking is not very easy to accomplish. The more controversial the issue, the more each side of the issue stakes out a position with which the other side finds it impossible to agree. The result is often inconclusive and unsatisfying as each side is unable to move beyond its own self-made limitation of perception and understanding.

The subject of abortion, for example, is as intensely argued as any single issue in our society. To apply critical thinking here would require the participants to examine the significance and application of at least some of the following contexts of that issue: the status of the fetus with respect to scientific, moral, and legal opinion; freedom of choice; the priority of religious or secular views; the conflict between liberal and conservative attitudes on sexual behavior; the role of majority and minority opinion in a democracy; the function of the media; the conflict between public and private morality; the differences in regional and ethnic opinion; the emergence of women's rights as a major social force.

Critical thinking, therefore, requires us to examine (1) our interaction with the issue itself, (2) viewpoints of the specific parties involved, (3) the larger group of human beings affected by this issue, (4) and other ideas and issues that become implicated as a result of the process of critical thinking. For example, critical thinking might reveal to participants in the abortion discussion that (1) freedom of choice also entails social responsibility; (2) expressions of religious or moral conscience must be weighed against prevailing secular opinion; (3) private sexual behavior also has broad social ramifications; and (4) the word "life" is subject to varying definitions depending upon the different perspectives of the users.

Arriving at a Broader Point of View.   Let's say the issue for debate is whether college students should pursue a general liberal arts curriculum or a specialized vocational program. You have read several essays arguing for or against the values of both kinds of college undergraduate education.

In order to generate ideas for your task, you try to form generalizations about the main idea of each essay. The following questions can help you as you try to generalize about each essay's approach:

1. What is the essay's point of view? How clearly is it stated?
2. How logical is the main idea? How consistent?
3. How does the writer present and organize his or her information?
4. How much authority does the essay convey?
5. What tone of voice does the essay reveal?
6. How sufficient is the evidence for supporting each generalization?
7. What attitude does the essay take toward opposing points of view? What are these opposing points of view?
8. How closely do the essay's conclusions coincide with your point of view?
9. Are the writer's conclusions justified by the supporting information?
10. What kinds of conclusions, whether practical or philosophical, specific or abstract, does the writer make? How appropriate are they? What effects might they have on the reader? What effects might they have on society in general?

Let's assume one essay opts for the traditional liberal arts curriculum, recommends a return to the study of accepted classics, and advocates a moral and ethical foundation as the basis for college work. Another essay favors a technical vocational curriculum and an emphasis on practical contemporary concerns. Still a third essay focuses on the increasingly diverse population of American colleges, especially the tailoring of the curriculum to help minority groups. As a reader—and a college student as well—you find many of their ideas and points of view interesting and reasonable. In some ways their positions converge, in other ways they seem far apart. But rather than dispose of the side you find objectionable through the attack of argument, you have the opportunity to try to resolve these various points of view. You can create a new, modified, perhaps even more persuasive point of view that incorporates or includes elements of all the major generalizations in the essays, thus forming a new generalization of your own.

Applying the four critical thinking skills to the issue, you discover that (1) the issue is what is best for all students; (2) some students want vocational skills, some want a traditional liberal arts education, and some want a diversified education that recognizes their ethnic identities; (3) the decision will affect how America competes in the job market, how individual Americans feel about their ethnic identities, and how future citizens make important decisions; and (4) the questions arise as to whether students know what is best for them, and on the other hand, does what has been done historically have a bearing on planning for the future. Your synthesis might suggest a new curriculum for the college student that includes both traditional subject matter and ideas that meet the needs of the changing population of today's college students. Notice that this viewpoint attempts to resolve conflicting ideas by creating other generalizations that can then be tested by other readers. Rather than closing off discussion by claiming you are right and the others are wrong, you encourage a continuing dialogue with your readers, for you recognize that all generalizations possess a tentativeness that requires them to be submitted to examination and possible change.

From the simplest observations to the most complex operations of thought, human beings unceasingly form concepts and select experiences or observations that act as supports for those concepts. To arrive at general ideas, or generalizations, without adequate examples is to reason ineffectively. To interpret our particular experience and points of view without trying to connect them to some larger idea or pattern of thought is also to limit the worth and effectiveness of our thinking. Thinking, whether it is directed toward the acts of writing or reading, involves an ever-extending linkage of generalizations and examples.

Much of the writing that college students are asked to do is in the form of essay examinations, "Compare and contrast . . ." "trace the causes of . . ." "show the relationship between. . . ." These are all recognizable rhetorical formulas of exposition that students acquire from their earliest days as writers. All of them require careful analysis and understanding of the material or issues involved. All of them require the ability to create interlocking chains of generalizations and examples that are clear and reasonable. The writer is expected to show sufficient knowledge of the subject and to be able to arrange this knowledge so that it reveals the relationships announced in the examination question.

SOME PRACTICE WITH CRITICAL THINKING ON A DEBATE

1. Write an imaginary dialogue between a male firefighter and a newly appointed female firefighter in which the former questions the latter's fitness for the job and the latter responds. Then bring in a third character who attempts to resolve the issue through critical thinking.

2. In order to understand how the media deal with controversy, select from one of the newsmagazines or television news programs like "Nightline" a controversial topic like capital punishment, child abuse, or gun control. Show how the various media present their arguments. How do the media strive for objectivity? Should they take sides? Why or why not? How could they enable the parties involved to seek compromise in order to resolve their varying points of view?

3. Collaborate with your group on a social or political topic that is currently a subject of controversy in your school or community. To what extent does the discussion modify your individual positions? After further collaboration, compare the results with the ideas that evolved after the first collaboration. What generalizations were developed further? What connections were made between ideas?

4. Make a list of issues that probably cannot be resolved by compromise. What characteristics do these issues have in common?

5. Take an issue you believe to be unresolvable and write a one-paragraph theme in your journal that tries to show how the varying points of view on this issue might be accommodated.

6. Write a brief theme on an issue you have very strong feelings about, but write about it from the opposing point of view. How convincing is your argument? What points that support your original point of view did you omit?

Using Evidence. In a debate the writer demonstrates a knowledge of the subject by the skillful use of evidence. As you read in Chapter 8 (see pp. 327–328), there are many kinds of evidence you can use in writing an argument. The authors of the essays in this chapter, for example, used the following sources:

1. Philosophers John Locke and Benedict Spinoza
2. Supreme court decisions
3. Congressional acts
4. Authors of other books or articles
5. Origins of words
6. Films
7. Novels and popular magazines
8. The *New York Times*
9. Personal experiences
10. Events of the 1960s, 1970s, 1980s
11. Current school problems
12. Publications of professional societies

Clearly, to join in debate you need to have at your command a variety of sources relevant to the issue. Some sources are alluded to only briefly in order to enforce a point or suggest a broader context for the argument that follows: for example, Garvey's quotation from C. S. Lewis (p. 392). Other sources form the basis of the debate such as Johnson's complete reliance on the Cruzan case in the Missouri Supreme Court.

More typical of a writer's approach is Petchesky's argument on abortion with its wide use of sources drawn from feminist authors, statistics on family income, personal experience, court decisions, political analysis, and discussion of contemporary social patterns. The author's argument gains credibility because she has clearly attempted to support her claim with incisive and convincing evidence.

Your essay will be judged for the most part by the nature of the evidence you cite. The word "tendentious" implies a slanting or bias that the reader will almost certainly pick up if you choose evidence that seems narrowly one-sided or unqualified. Naturally you will wish to use evidence that furthers your argument, but, remember, you want to qualify any claim you make and not try to mislead your audience by selecting evidence that is only favorable to your point of view. Another problem arises when the writer attempts to make too broad a claim from limited data. As a matter of common practice — not just in debate — we should be cautious not to try to overgeneralize from our evidence. Because your purpose in this task is to try to bring together opposing views, you will surely try to use your evidence fairly and reasonably.

SOME PRACTICE WITH USING EVIDENCE FOR A DEBATE

1. Write a summary of one of the essays in this chapter in order to understand its claim, supporting evidence and conclusion. Include this information in your much shorter version.

2. Choose a newspaper editorial or column and write a supporting argument with evidence drawn from your own knowledge and experience. If you disagree with the editorial, write a counterargument.

3. Compare the evidence you wish to use in your argument with that used in one of the essays in this chapter. What additional evidence from the essay could you include that would make your argument more persuasive?

   Using Your Journal. Perhaps the best way to begin to work towards a final generalization is to use your journal. You might begin by writing brief summaries of essays representing all points of view on an issue. Writing summaries gives you a clearer picture of the chain of generalizations and examples by reducing the discussion to its essential ideas. Remember that a summary tries to retain the basic form of the original by giving the equivalent space to parts in the original essay (see Chapter 10, pp. 469–473).

   Writing summaries will give you a feel for the author's point of view and method of argument as well as allow you to grasp the main ideas and supporting examples of each essay.

   The summaries can be used as a starting point for free writing about your own views on the issue of each essay. Write about your past encounters with the issue and what you think has shaped your own attitudes on it. What recent news events have highlighted this issue? Has it caused any recent controversy in your community? If so, how was it resolved?

   Another way to "get inside" each issue is to create a dialogue between two persons having contradictory points of view. They don't have to be participants in the issue; they might represent different roles or positions that are somehow affected by the issues. Here is an example:

   Jack: I just think pornography is out of place in a moral society.
   Joan: Perhaps. But aren't you really saying "ideal" society? It's obvious that in many ways our society is quite imperfect, pornography being one of the lesser evils we have to tolerate.
   Jack: But why tolerate it if we can pass laws that will make it illegal?
   Joan: You're assuming that laws can simply make something disappear. What would happen to the reasons why we have pornography? Would they just go away? I don't think so.
   Jack: I agree but don't we have to do something? Should we just allow it to continue to do damage to our society?

Joan: But I'm not so sure it really does do damage. Explain what you mean. . . .

Creating an imaginary discussion such as the one above allows you to observe how ideas are connected, how arguments are advanced by the expression of contradictory or conflicting ideas. It also gives you an understanding of points of view that differ from your own. It helps you to avoid the creation of a "straw-man" character, one who takes easily refuted or even ridiculous positions that do little to advance the discussion but make your own point of view look good by comparison.

Brainstorming Groups. The issues discussed in this chapter provoke so much passionate argument that the individual writer can hardly expect to know and understand all the feelings and thoughts of the many persons affected by these issues. By sharing the ideas of others we learn more about the issues than we could by ourselves. You may have already used the technique of brainstorming in Chapter 6 (see pp. 234–240) as a means of drawing out ideas and associations about a ritual or tradition. In this task, brainstorming can provide you with a list of key general concepts that can act as a starting point for your own analysis of an issue. As in other brainstorming exercises, begin with an important word or sentence and then try to write down whatever comes to your mind. After a set amount of time, members of your group can share the results, eliminate those items you find repetitious or irrelevant, and continue brainstorming, this time on a narrower topic or more specific line of thought. See what you come up with and what key ideas seem to emerge.

Using Critical Thinking in Generating Ideas for Your Essay on a Debate. Because the purpose of your essay is to arrive at a broader point of view, your initial strategy is to establish the grounds for your later generalizations, in this case the different views on your topic expressed in the reading you have done for fulfilling this task. A thorough understanding of these views—how they conflict, what evidence each writer uses as a support for a claim—will help you to form your own generalization on the issue.

Your journal and brainstorming sessions can be used to open up the different perspectives on the issue that will lead you to your own broader point of view. At this stage of your writing, try to generate as many views on the issue as you can. If you compare and contrast the evidence and generalizations of each side of the issue and if you identify the causes and effects of the different points of view, you can begin to work toward your resolution of the issue.

Examine your own experiences and observations to learn what you already know about this issue. By evaluating this knowledge you may reveal any personal bias or one-sided opinion that will affect your judgment.

SOME PRACTICE IN USING CRITICAL THINKING IN GENERATING IDEAS FOR YOUR ESSAY ON A DEBATE

1. Using your journal, state in one column the position on an issue of each of your print sources, then in the other column list the most important data or grounds the writer has given in support of this position. Have some writers drawn different conclusions from the same data? How would you account for this in your essay? Evaluate the evidence of your sources for validity.

2. Compose a list of key words on your issue and brainstorm on them to see what ideas or arguments you can discover. Which words produced the most ideas? Concentrate on these words in your analysis of the different points of view on your issue and use them to arrive at your own broader point of view.

3. Write a journal entry that tells about your own background or experience with regard to your issue. How can you use this evidence for creating a broader point of view? Evaluate its usefulness as a source.

4. Write an argument supporting each of the major positions on your issue that emerge from your sources. Which side has the strongest argument? Why? Take the strongest points of each argument and try to incorporate them in a new argument that will achieve a broader point of view.

Addressing Your Audience: The Informed Reader

In the "Addressing the Audience" section in Chapter 6, we discuss how frame of reference can be used to bridge the gap that can be present between the writer and an uninformed reader. Certainly the reader needs to be provided with the information necessary to understand the writer's attitude toward the subject. But of great importance as well is the writer's need to address the values and attitudes of his or her audience.

Particularly with regard to the provocative and controversial contemporary issues discussed in this chapter, the writer needs to reach out to the values and beliefs of the audience, to convince the audience that its beliefs are understood and respected even if the writer disagrees with them. The issues of abortion, pornography, and euthanasia have been with us for a long time. Most of your audience will be familiar with the key ideas that cluster around these issues. Some will be quite well informed, perhaps because of their own personal or community involvement in the consequences these issues have on their lives. They should be able to judge the validity and relevance of your analysis. They will be applying the same elements of critical thinking to your argument as you applied in preparing your discussion of the issue.

How, then, can you reach out to this informed reader in a way that shows your awareness of his or her own values and attitudes on these controversial issues? One way is to attempt to put yourself in their place: to imagine yourself in their position by actually trying to play their role. The more important the issue, the more roles there seem to be that have bearing on deciding how the issue can be resolved. Let us look in more detail at how the method of role-playing can give you a greater awareness of the values and attitudes of the informed reader.

Role-playing. Thinking critically about any issue of importance suggests that you have examined your own means of arriving at a judgment on a subject that influences the lives of many people. If a newly appointed Supreme Court Justice is to consider the issue of abortion as the courts have judged it, we may want to analyze this particular judge's ability to empathize with the many different parties who hold strong but conflicting views on this topic. In effect, how well can this person render such a crucial judgment without an understanding of the values and beliefs of all the concerned parties?

By being able to enter into the roles of others, we learn to see the issue as others see it—and then to use this information when forming our own judgments about what is important and how the issue might be resolved. Perhaps we can never say we are truly dispassionate and objective about any of these critical issues. But by incorporating others' roles within our own we may gain more confidence that we have judged these issues fully and responsibly. Role-playing reminds us that there is a human dimension to critical thinking—it isn't just an abstract, indifferent arrangement of evidence and reasoned conclusions.

SOME PRACTICE WITH WRITING FOR
AN INFORMED AUDIENCE

1. Examine your own views about gun control. What might a member of the National Rifle Association think of your views? What might a member of the local police force think? A liberal Democrat? A conservative Republican? Play the roles of each of these segments of society with viewpoints on gun control. How informed do you imagine each of these potential readers to be about the issue of gun control? How objective? To what extent do you think being knowledgeable about an issue leads one to be objective?

2. Pick a controversial topic, such as gun control, abortion, or capital punishment, and canvas your class members for their views and knowledge of it. Use role-play to identify with each point of view. Then put together a composite sketch of a person whose point of view on the topic reflects the point of view of the class as a whole. How well informed might such a person be? How might you write about the topic if your reader were such a person?

3. What role might you assume in writing about each of the following topics if your audience were to be a reader who knew little about the topic?

   a. The *National Enquirer*

   b. Fraternity hazing

   c. Sibling rivalry

   d. The Great Depression

   e. The Equal Rights Amendment

Explain how your approach might change if, instead, your audience were to be a teacher with experience in a subject area associated with the topic: a journalism teacher in the case of Topic a, an anthropology teacher in the case of Topic b, a psychology teacher in the case of Topic c, an American history teacher in the case of Topic d, and a political science teacher in the case of Topic e.

Addressing the Informed Reader of Your Essay on a Debate. By employing methods of critical thinking, you demonstrate that you are informed both about your subject and about your audience, that you understand how an informed reader thinks and what will be of interest to such a reader. In a sense, you play the role of such a reader yourself.

This should caution you against doing a number of things. You should probably avoid writing at length about what your reader already knows, except to the degree that you are using such information to illustrate and explain your own knowledge of and ideas about the subject. Also, it is probably a good idea to avoid straying from the subject at hand, especially by dwelling at length on your views of peripheral issues. If you are writing about violence in sports, for example, do not stray too far into an expression of your personal distaste for violence of any kind. Stick to what you know about the viewpoints on the central issue.

Finally, you should find it useful to observe the formal conventions of grammar and organization that will appeal to an educated and informed audience. If you want to sound well informed, at least for such an audience, you probably need to sound reasonably logical, thorough, and articulate as well.

Answering the questions of the Audience Analysis Guide will help you in gauging how to address your informed reader:

AUDIENCE ANALYSIS GUIDE

1. What can I expect my informed reader to know about this issue?

2. What is the frame of reference of the audience in relation to this issue?

3. What point of view is my audience likely to have on this issue?

4. How can I bridge the gap that may exist between my audience's point of view and my own by entering into the roles of others?

SOME PRACTICE WITH ADDRESSING THE INFORMED READER OF YOUR ESSAY ON A DEBATE

1. Compare the tone of voice you use in your essay to the voices of your sources. What similarities or differences do you observe? Underline words or expressions you think best convey your voice to your audience in order to ensure that you did not depend too closely on the language of these sources. If you find that your wording is quite similar, change it into your own words.

2. Ask one of your classmates—a friend, or a member of your peer group—to play the role of "devil's advocate" for each of the major points of view on your issue. Compare your classmate's arguments with the arguments you include in your draft to determine what significant points of view you might have omitted or overemphasized.

3. If you have concluded that your informed reader will judge your evidence to be inadequate, try to obtain additional information for revising your essay.

4. What generalizations have you made about your issue that you feel will meet with strong disagreement by members of your audience? What can you do to resolve these disagreements? If there is no way you feel you can achieve a broader point of view on the issue, what can you do to lessen the conflict your view has provoked?

Arranging Your Essay

The Shaping Idea: Stating Your Broader Point of View.   Your shaping idea for this task should result from the thinking you have done about the issue you selected. It should try to incorporate the different positions set forth in each of the essays studied, and to lead your audience to a new, broader point of view. As we have stated, this is no easy task when a writer is confronted with issues as formidable as abortion, euthanasia, and pornography. But after you have studied the various arguments, identified your own position on the issue, and the points of view of others whose roles you have encountered, you are ready to form your own shaping idea. For example, after analyzing the issue of euthanasia you might have concluded that the formulation of a living will is a way to resolve this dilemma in a manner that

satisfies the conflicting views of the parties involved. By focusing on this conclusion, you consider the different opposing arguments but create out of them
a new idea that incorporates the legal and ethical dimensions of the issue.
You may not have "solved" the problem, but you will have opened up the
issue to include this consideration in any future debate on the problem. Remember that your shaping idea is a generalization that needs to be supported
by evidence — perhaps examples drawn from recent developments that have
been reported in the media.

Close-up on the Organization of Petchesky's Essay.   Let us look briefly
at the organizational strategy of Rosalind Petchesky's essay "Giving Women a
Real Choice." She begins her introduction to her essay on abortion with a
brief paragraph that supplies the background for her argument. Her purpose
is clearly stated:

> The question is *why* the abortion debate persists, why it be-
> comes such a charged site for struggles over not only changes in
> family, gender and sexual relations in American society and their
> cultural meanings but over the terms of public disorder.

The warrant, or implied assumption of her argument, seems to be that
most women have belief in their reproductive freedom and will be interested
in learning why obstacles to abortion have been put in their way. Her thesis,
stated at the end of her introduction, follows from her observation that these
obstacles exist even in a period characterized by legal and popular support for
abortion:

> More than ever, abortion is the fulcrum in which the very mean-
> ings of the family, the state, motherhood and young women's
> sexuality are contested.

Petchesky's discussion proceeds with the data that support her claim that
abortion rights are part of a larger, more culturally significant dynamic of
change. She refers to the changes in women's roles; their attitudes toward
sexuality; the impact of abortion on minority women; the inadequacy of
legislation for protecting women's reproductive rights. At the end of her essay
she concludes with evidence that suggests that favorable social change for
women is emerging in the 1990s.

Petchesky's arrangement pattern is a useful approach for organizing this
essay: background followed by statement of claim, support for claim, conclusion.

An alternative organizational pattern to Petchesky's is to provide background, and then present the strengths and weaknesses of the various viewpoints in preparation for presenting your claim of a broader viewpoint on the
issue.

In either case, unlike the classic arrangement pattern for an argument discussed in Chapter 8, here you will not want to refute any one point of view, but rather to present the strengths and weaknesses of *all* positions in order to build a consensus.

Writing Your Rough Draft

Following is the rough draft of a student essay on the issue of pornography. As you read the essay, ask yourself the following questions: How well has the writer stated the issue? How thoroughly and objectively has she presented the various points of view? Has she considered the ramifications of the various solutions for groups within society, for society itself? Has she considered all the major related issues, issues that must be considered if her argument is to be useful? What is her point of view? To what extent does it in fact express a broader point of view?

PORNOGRAPHY AND ME AND YOU

Porn flicks, girlie magazines, smutty paperbacks--I have always felt removed from, insulated against their seaminess here in my clean, comfortable, middle-class existence. Exposure to obscenity in my suburban neighborhood would never be inadvertent but intentionally and diligently sought. There are no x-rated movie houses here, no racks of offensive books or sex-peddling periodicals on display in our local stationery store. My husband does not subscribe to Hustler. None of this unpleasantness (or to some people, pleasantness) touches me. Or does it?

In her essay, "Erotica vs. Pornography," Gloria Steinem made such keen observations about pornography's allure in our society that she compelled me to sit up and take notice of a topic that had previously never concerned or interested me.

First she makes a distinction between pornography (dominance and submission) and erotica (mutuality). She then points out that the seeds of pornography are not sown by the Larry Flynts of our society but by you and me as a result of our own complacency about and tolerance of a societal structure in which males have greater power than females.

Those of us who think it is cute when a young boy struts, postures, or is openly aggressive and a young girl shies away, is coy, or flagrantly flirtatious, are, on the other hand, extremely offended by depictions of aggression and submission in pornographic films and magazines. We never see the obvious relation that exists between the cute and the offensive.

If we were able to clear away the smoke screen emitted by the social mechanisms of sexual role playing and gender identification, we would see this cute behavior of children as equally obscene as the portrayals in so-called "adult" magazines, books, and films. Pornography is not a disease, as many people seem to think, but merely a symptom of the disease of sexism that pervades our society. We should be seeking a cure and not simply masking the disease by treating the symptoms, because then the disease continues to spread unchecked.

I recently came across a perfect example of blind acceptance of the status quo as it pertains to male/female roles. In a letter to the New York Times, Diana Trilling responded to an article by Fred M. Hechinger about the legal dispute touched off by a public school's attempt to discipline a high school student for using sexual innuendo in a campaign speech supporting a fellow student. Ms. Trilling referred to "a student's decent acceptance of male sexuality as an aspect of male strength. . . ."

That is an outrageous statement! Is she saying that male sexual prowess has a legitimate place in a political campaign (albeit a high school election)? Would a frank allusion to the sexual attributes of a female candidate have been equally indicative of an acceptance of female strength?

I doubt it! On the contrary, when a woman emphasizes her sexuality, she is typically viewed as irrational and therefore politically weak.

Ms. Trilling's aim is to oppose censorship, and she offers a valid argument, yet at the same time she unwittingly endorses male sexual prowess as a valid qualification for political office. That student's speech was, in my opinion, obscene even though he made no specific reference to genitalia or sexual acts because it represented the commonly held belief that male power stems solely from physical traits, which perpetuates the oppression of women.

Pornography is just one of many subtle forces that chisel away at our collective subconscious and almost imperceptibly sculpt our ideas about male-female relationships. It is just one more thing that contributes to what I see as an intolerable situation for women, a situation that even sways political decisions and that certainly has an effect on everyone, even me.

Joining in debate means that you need to be aware of how your own thought, knowledge, and language are conditioned by your participation in a larger audience of writers and readers. In the following "Focus" section you will learn how your essay fits into a larger "community of discourse."

FOCUS ON THE WRITER: JOINING THE COMMUNITY OF DISCOURSE

Jonathan Swift, the eighteenth-century satirical author of the essay "A Modest Proposal," imitated the form and style of a contemporary "projector" (social planner) so accurately that when you read his essay you might really believe it is a serious proposal for reducing the poverty of Swift's Ireland: sell its poor children to be used for food, thus making money and at the same time ridding the island of its excess population. Because the proposal seems in a way so credible, its language so reasoned, its voice so unemotional, its form so orderly and logical, you are easily lulled into accepting it as a conventional example of its type.

In other words, Swift's imaginary character mastered so well the conventions of language and voice expected of a real bureaucrat that, as readers, we almost automatically respond to his proposal. We might pose this situation as a syllogism:

In order to make a persuasive proposal, one must address an audience in the form and style expected of a projector.

X writes like a genuine projector.

Therefore, X's proposal is persuasive.

Swift's understanding of his audience's frame of reference suggests that there is a social dimension to our response to any discourse. It is our membership in a particular community of readers that determines how we will respond to this discourse. In fact we may belong to several different discourse communities, adjusting from one to another as the need or occasion arises. In joining in a debate you need to recognize how your interpretation of other writers' arguments, as well as the construction of your own, is shaped by your presence in a community of readers and writers.

Swift understood that his community of readers—generally the literate, informed elite of his society—had certain expectations about how a proposal should look and sound. For example, it should proceed by (1) announcing the problem, (2) stating the proposed solution, (3) refuting objections to the proposal, and (4) discussing and praising the benefits of the proposal for society. The language of the proposal should reflect the rational, educated, ethical character of the writer.

Because the writer does all these things so effectively, the reader's assent seems to follow naturally, irrespective of the actual worth of the proposal Swift's character has made. Swift's audience believes in the projector precisely because he has demonstrated that he is "one of us." He has established his membership in the discourse community of his readers.

The essays you have read for writing your own interpretation of an issue are also part of a discourse community, one in fact which you are asked to join by showing your ability to express your thoughts in a similar way. We have already pointed out the characteristics of language and thought that identify this community of writers and readers.

First, the writer must demonstrate a depth of knowledge of the subject. Simply put, the writer signals to the audience that she has studied the issue, thought critically about it from a number of significant perspectives, and expressed her conclusions in language that is reasoned, clear (but not necessarily simple), and objective.

Second, the writer uses a method for presenting her ideas that informed readers will judge to be appropriate. For example, the writers of the essays in this chapter create a pattern of assertion and example in which ideas are proposed, developed, and qualified. Each writer tries to anticipate the informed reader's cognitive response, guiding the reader to her conclusion with words like "first," "second," "still," "although," "but," "yet," "for instance," "while," "however," "finally," "nonetheless," and "similarly." These are of course transitional words, words crucial in leading the reader through parts of the argument, and in revealing the process of a mind working towards a conclusion.

The previous statement implies that knowledge is not just the product or end result of writing, but a process or cognitive activity in which writing becomes the medium of thought itself. Recently "writing across the curriculum" and "interdisciplinary learning" have become commonplace in American colleges. Possibly in your other courses you have been asked to write on subjects in the humanities, and technological, scientific, and vocational fields. Whether you write lab reports or narrative journals you become part of a discourse community that evaluates your learning on the basis of your ability to use the language of a specific discipline as it is understood and accepted by other members of this community. Your critical thinking skills, your choice of words, your knowledge of the methodology of argument are crucial for your performance within the different discourse communities you wish to join — in college and the professional and business world beyond.

The latter half of our text focuses on writing and thinking activities characteristic of the communities of public discourse. The ability to form generalizations, use evidence, and write objectively is amply demonstrated by the writers in this chapter. Their knowledge of the forms and conventions of discourse and their awareness of their audience create the human dialogue that defines a community of writers and readers.

SOME PRACTICE WITH JOINING
A COMMUNITY OF DISCOURSE

1. Select an article in a journal of opinion like *Harper's* or *Atlantic*. Analyze its use of language and argument to determine methods it employs to arrange and present its evidence. What key transitional words are used to move the argument forward?

2. Write an interpretation of one of the essays used in this chapter. Include in your discussion an explanation of the way the author presents and organizes her arguments for her audience.

3. Reread one of your previous essays and examine it from the standpoint of its membership in a particular discourse community. Point out any specific uses of reasoning, language, or awareness of audience that show how you had a certain discourse community in mind.

4. Following the pattern outlined for a proposal, create a proposal on an issue you feel strongly about.

5. What other kinds of writing can you assign to a specific discourse community? For example, analyze the language and form of an advertising brochure for a vacation resort; a letter promoting a new magazine or periodical; a request for a contribution to a nonprofit organization to show how these were intended for a discourse community (see Chapter 7, pp. 276–284).

REWRITING

Obtaining Feedback on Your Rough Draft

Before evaluating—or having your group evaluate—your essay and before reading the peer evaluation below of "Pornography, and Me, and You," the rough draft of the student essay on pp. 435–437, you might take time now, if you haven't already done so, to do your own critique of her essay. As you read, ask yourself, in particular, how skillful the writer's judgment has been, how well she has incorporated the views and ideas of others, if she has tried to broaden the reader's point of view on her subject.

Using the "Audience Response Guide" to critique both her rough draft and your own might help you and/or your group to evaluate the success of both essays. Then, compare your evaluation with the student critique below of "Pornography and Me and You."

——— AUDIENCE RESPONSE GUIDE ———

1. What do you think the writer wanted to say about this issue? What is his or her purpose in writing?
2. How does the paper affect the informed reader for whom it was intended?
3. How effective has the writer been in conveying a broader point of view? What are the strengths of the paper? What are the weaknesses?
4. How should the paper be revised to better fulfill its purpose and meaning?

1. The group, playing the role of expert reader, agreed that her purpose in writing was to persuade the reader that pornography is just a surface issue, that in fact the real issue is that our society encourages distinctions between male and female roles and relationships.
2. On the one hand, they felt that the paper is thoughtful and intelligently written; on the other, they believed that the writer has not responded to the other positions in the controversy on pornography. She argues her own point rather than developing a broader point of view. Some of the group members wanted her to support her comments on the Hechinger/Trilling dialogue with more details.
3. The group felt the essay is effective in touching on important problems and particularly so in analyzing the situation to see that the problem is deeper than most participants realize. However, she considers only one side of the issue and lets her outrage take over.

4. The group wanted the writer to demonstrate more thoroughly how her conclusion derives from a critical analysis of all three points of view and serves to incorporate those points of view. She also needs to supply details about the Hechinger/Trilling dialogue and to recognize the conflict between heredity and environment in the paragraph on children's role-playing.

Revision of Student Essay "Pornography and Me and You"

Following is the student's revision of her rough draft. How effective do you now think it to be as a model of this chapter's task? What further revisions might she make?

PORNOGRAPHY AND ME AND YOU

Porn flicks, girlie magazines, smutty paperbacks--I have always felt removed from, insulated against their seaminess here in my clean, comfortable, middle-class existence. Exposure to obscenity in my suburban neighborhood would never be inadvertent but intentionally and diligently sought. There are no x-rated movie houses here, no racks of offensive books or sex-peddling periodicals on display in our local stationery store. My husband does not subscribe to Hustler. None of this unpleasantness (or to some people, pleasantness) touches me. Or does it?

In her essay "Erotica vs. Pornography," Gloria Steinem made such keen observations about pornography's allure in our society that she compelled me to sit up and take notice of a topic that had previously never concerned or interested me.

First, she makes a distinction between pornography, which entails dominance and submission, and erotica, which describes mutuality. She then points out that the seeds of pornography are not sown by the Larry Flynts of our society but by you and me as a result of our own complacency about, and tolerance of, a societal structure in which males have greater power than females.

Those of us who think it is cute when a young boy struts, postures, or is openly aggressive and a young girl shies away, is coy, or flagrantly flirtatious, are, on the other hand, extremely offended by depictions of aggression and submission in pornographic films and magazines. We never see the obvious parallels that exist between the cute and the offensive.

If we are able to clear away the smoke screen emitted by the social mechanisms of sexual role playing and gender identification, we might see this cute behavior of children as equally obscene as the portrayals in so-called "adult" magazines, books, and films. Some would disagree with this train of thought, because although it is undeniable that we are social beings influenced in many ways by societal expectations, whether or not some of this sexual role playing is innate and therefore normal and acceptable behavior is a controversial topic open to debate, and neither theory has yet to be proven.

I recently came across a perfect example of blind acceptance of the status quo as it pertains to male-female roles. In a letter to the New York Times, Diana Trilling responded to an article by Fred M. Hechinger about the legal dispute touched off by a public school's attempt to discipline a high school student for using sexual innuendo in a campaign speech supporting a fellow student. The student, Matthew N. Frazer, described the candidate he supported as "a man who is firm--he's firm in his pants, he's firm in his shirt, his character is firm." Ms. Trilling lauded Mr. Hechinger's support of the student's right to speak, regardless of his age and circumstance, and referred to Matthew Frazer's speech as "a student's decent acceptance of male sexuality as an aspect of male strength...."

Is she saying that male sexual prowess has a legitimate place in a political campaign (albeit a high school election)? Would a frank allusion to the sexual attributes of a female candidate have been equally indicative of an acceptance of female strength?

On the contrary, when a woman emphasizes her sexuality, she is typically viewed as irrational and therefore politically weak. This view is often defended as valid by those who believe that women, and men, are born with a certain emotional makeup as the result of chance chromosomal combination--that women are naturally just less logical, less aggressive, and more emotional than men.

Ms. Trilling's aim is to oppose censorship, defend this young man's right to free speech, yet at the same time she unwittingly endorses male sexual prowess as a valid qualification for political office.

Pornography is just one of many subtle forces that chisel away at our collective subsconscious and almost imperceptibly sculpt our ideas about male-female relationships. It is just one more thing that contributes to and aids in perpetuating the oppression of women. Yet, to advocate censorship of pornography would be detrimental to the feminist cause.

As Alan M. Dershowitz points out in his essay "Partners Against Porn," if feminists, banded together with Falwell's fundamentalists, were successful in censoring pornographers, what is to prevent fundamentalists from securing censorship of feminists? By denying the First Amendment protection to some, they may be setting a precedent that would justify denying the same protection to others. In joining with fundamentalists and pressing for censorship of pornographers, feminists may be digging their own grave.

On the other hand, fear of an avalanche effect could be used as justification for the prevention of many other types of legislation and government control. George Will points out in his essay, "Pornographic Minds," that some could argue against having police forces because they "might become gestapos." He contends that by taking a stance, making value judgments, men (meaning humankind) are practicing a form of repression, but by doing so, they are pointing up the difference between humans and all other animals--humans are capable of rationality. It is his opinion that by allowing pornography to flourish behind the skirts of the First Amendment we relinquish our high position among animals.

For those who see pornography as a cancerous blight on society, treating the symptoms with censorship will not check the spread of the disease. Those who are offended should utilize their own freedom of speech to encourage a more critical view of the roles of men and women in our society and instill healthy respect for the individual's thought processes and ability to make changes based on those processes.

Editing

Transitions.   The most well-organized argument may appear disorganized if transitions have not been used or if those used are imprecise. Effective transitions point out for the reader the essential unity of the sentence, the paragraph and the essay.

Topic Sentences.   Once again, review your topic sentences. Should transitions be added to relate the paragraph to the essay? Should any other words or phrases be added to make this important sentence as precise a summary of the paragraph as possible?

Mechanics.   Review earlier samples of your writing on which mechanical errors have been noted for guidelines to the spelling, punctuation, and grammatical errors common in your writing. Work with the handbook at the back of the book, if necessary, in making these corrections.

Revising Your Essay on a Debate

Now that you have received the feedback of your peers and have analyzed how the student writer in this chapter revised her essay, you may want also to ask yourself the following questions as one last step before revising your own rough draft.

 Checklist to Consider in Revising an Essay on a Debate

1. **How clearly does your shaping idea show how you have incorporated the various points of view of your issue?**
2. **Have you examined your own knowledge of the subject and your own general assumptions about the subject and audience?**
3. **Have you provided adequate support for all points of view?**
4. **Have you arranged your material so that it conveys maximum effectiveness?**
5. **Have you used language appropriate for the subject of your debate and your audience?**
6. **Have you used key transitional words for joining parts of your argument?**

Now, revise and edit your draft, bearing in mind that even at this stage new material can be generated by the act of writing. In other words, do not mechanically rewrite or edit only, but continue to develop new ideas about your subject to include in your essay.

BECOMING AWARE OF YOURSELF AS A WRITER

1. What new insights did the essays in the task section of this chapter provide you on the issue you chose for your task? If you read the essays on either or both of the other issues, what new perspectives did these essays provide?

2. Did you have a strong opinion about the issue you chose before beginning your task? Did thinking critically about the issue alter your opinion in any way? How effective might critical thinking be in thawing out the frozen positions in an old controversy so that dialogue can flow again?

3. By thinking critically about the other two issues represented by the essays in the "Task" section, what resolution can you now arrive at for each of them?

4. You can argue about a controversial issue or you can think critically about it and attempt to reach accommodation; both are legitimate approaches used every day. In what situations would argumentation be appropriate? When should critical thinking be applied instead?

5. How effective has role-play proven to be as a method of understanding other people and other points of view? What other techniques may have proven to be more valuable to you in identifying with others?

6. What have you learned about organizing and presenting evidence that you can use in other writing assignments? Can you evaluate others' use of evidence more critically now that you have examined your own?

P A R T

V

Writing About Research, Writing About Literature

INTRODUCTION

Much of the writing that you do in college is about reading. You may be assigned to read a chapter in a textbook, then write answers to questions at the end of the chapter or on an exam. You may be required to read books and articles from the library, then write summaries, reports, critiques, analyses. Sometimes, you are asked to write your reactions to and opinions of a single text—an essay by Margaret Mead in an anthropology class, a novel by Charles Dickens in a literature class, a speech by Martin Luther King, Jr. in a political science class. Other times, you compare two or more readings, or you engage in extensive library research on a subject.

You do such writing, of course, because instructors assign it. If you want to succeed in their classes, you must try to meet their expectations. But to do such writing well, you also need to recognize how it serves purposes other than convincing an instructor that you deserve a good grade. The essay on "Henry David Thoreau" in Chapter 2 was written by a student whose purpose was to express herself to a sympathetic reader. The essay on "Pornography and Me and You" in Chapter 9 was written to persuade an informed reader. Both authors also wrote because they were assigned to do so. Their purposes were mixed in this sense and in another as well. Although her purpose was primarily persuasive, the student writing on pornography does tell something about herself; to the degree that the writer on Thoreau may provoke some agreement or disagreement with her point of view, her writing too reflects a persuasive voice along with an expressive purpose.

On the one hand, we want to remind you of the importance of clarifying your purpose whenever you write. If, for example, your aim is to explore one or more pieces of reading material, you may summarize more than if your aim is to explain, in which case—depending on how informed your reader is—you may comment and evaluate more. Whenever you write for an instructor, clarifying the purpose behind the assignment is a good idea.

On the other hand, we want you to remember how likely any piece of writing is to reflect mixed purposes. When you write a love letter, you express your feelings in order to sway the feelings of your reader. In the same way, when you write a book review, you express your opinion at the same time that you both inform and influence a reader. A good writer utilizes elements of expressive, exploratory, explanatory, and persuasive writing together.

The two assignments in Part V will challenge your ability to do this—to select from and combine the techniques and conventions that you have been practicing in Parts I–IV. In the task for Chapter 10, we will ask you to write about research you have conducted in order to test a hypothesis you have devised on a subject in the natural or social sciences. In the task for Chapter 11, we will ask you to write about a short story in order to offer your interpretation of a literary text.

10

Writing About Research — Testing a Hypothesis

PURPOSE

You enter a large room. You observe that approximately thirty males and females, mostly between the ages of eighteen and twenty-one, are seated facing a wide wall with a gray slate board mounted on it. In front of the wall, an adult male is seated behind a wood-grained metal desk. The young people in the room are looking directly at the seated male, who is speaking to the entire group. Occasionally an arm rises, followed by a comment from the person whose arm is raised. After about an hour, the adult male stops speaking, begins to collect his books and papers from the desk, and stands. Shortly after, the young people stand and walk toward the door.

Because these observations are so familiar, you don't have to think long before deciding on a generalization that explains the situation just described. Somewhere during your reading of this paragraph, the details cohered into a single conclusion: this is a description of a class. The process of reasoning that leads us to this conclusion is called *induction*. Induction is one of the major methods through which we arrive at the meaning of our observations and experiences, providing us with a technique for verifying what we decide is the factual truth. Scientists in the laboratory and in the field use induction to arrive at conclusions about phenomena in nature and in society.

In this chapter, we will ask you to write with the specific purpose of explaining to your reader a hypothesis you have created on a topic of your choice. Your task will be a research paper on a subject drawn from the natural or social sciences organized according to the principles of inductive reasoning. Inductive reasoning relies on the assumption that collected data — the products of observation or experimentation — can produce reliable explanations of the physical world, provided that the data are relevant to the problem under consideration. The writer who wishes to provide valid scientific explanations must be able to produce evidence and to draw conclusions from it that the reader will recognize as "scientific" and thus will accept as valid.

In fulfilling the writing task in Chapter 5, you relied solely on your own powers of observation to give you authentic information on an ongoing situation. And what gave power to these observations was the use of the classical questions. These questions provided you with a mental framework on which you could construct your case. In this chapter, your emphasis will be on the implications for scientific inquiry contained in the questions "What examples are there of it?" and "What conclusions can we draw from these examples?" Whereas, in Chapter 7, you also responded to these questions, there you cited examples to support a generalization about the value of some knowledge that you possess.

Here we will ask you to discuss scientific ideas arrived at by the scientific method. You will want to explain both examples and conclusions in a way that gives credibility to your method of investigation. You also will want to present a hypothesis or explanation that is meaningful, one that does not conflict with the accepted scientific model of the physical world. You could not expect to offer convincing evidence that there are unicorns in the municipal zoo or that the sun will literally rise or set tomorrow.

Following from your reasonable hypothesis, you will need to provide, through your research, examples of investigations or experiments performed by scientists that pertain to your subject and that, taken together, prove your hypothesis: You will answer another classical question: "What has been said about it?" You will also want to know the methods that are used to create a piece of scientific research: finding and evaluating information; arranging materials into a meaningful, logical form; employing the conventions of scientific documentation; and using the voice and tone of objective discourse.*

Although your emphasis will be on using scientific materials, the methods of research that you employ to investigate your topic can be applied to many other subjects. Many subjects are assigned in college with the assumption that the student has the knowledge and the skill to apply certain methods of investigation to solving problems.

---

* We are using the term *research* in two not unrelated ways: one refers to your research into the work of others, or academic research, and the other refers to the research of scientists in the laboratory or field. Essentially your task will be to research the research that scientists have done, and to use the inductive method in your presentation.

A knowledge of the process of induction can lead you to insights in unexpected areas. One of these areas is simply your own personal observation. Although this is not on the same conceptual level as research performed in a laboratory, your informed observation of, for example, students applying for jobs at the college employment office is a method of arriving at an inductive understanding of the job prospects for potential college graduates. Similarly, an interview with the employment counselor, in which you learn that employment opportunities for liberal arts graduates have declined by 20 percent in the past five years, will give you inductive evidence for coming to a conclusion about where the future job opportunities will be found.

You can then support these findings with the research you have done in books and periodical articles that investigate the topic of employment opportunities for college graduates. Through the combined use of library research, observation, and interview, you can arrive at a conclusion that is the result of original investigation.

This brief discussion of the kind of discourse we recognize as scientific implies the existence of an audience for whom this discourse is intended. A scientific audience may be one that is interested primarily in the practical application of scientific principles (as in magazines like *Popular Mechanics* and *Popular Electronics*), or one interested in the explanation of current research and scientific theory for the science-educated nonspecialist (as in *Scientific American* or *Science*), or the audiences for the many specialized and highly technical publications in which such professional scientists as nuclear biologists or enzyme chemists report the results of their experiments. As we move up the pyramid of complexity, the audience becomes smaller and smaller, so that at the highest levels of abstraction only a relative handful of readers is capable of evaluating and validating the writer's conclusions. In the audience section of this chapter, we will discuss the kinds of audience to whom you might direct your investigation, as well as the nature of the discourse that you will want to adopt.

When you write in order to explain, you want to take into account other important elements of the writing process. In dealing with a large number of ideas or relevant examples, you are faced with the need to organize your materials and to form a preliminary framework on which to arrange them so that they can be presented most logically and efficiently. This outline also functions as a kind of screen on which you project the order of your evidence and the conclusions that result from it. You can then begin to see the emerging direction of your paper. The result of this process can be a paper that is credible and convincing. Although you will not be expected to make an original scientific discovery, you can, through the act of synthesizing (or combining already existing materials into a new arrangement), create a discourse that has the authority of skillful, objective research. You can lead your reader to a new insight.

TASK: TESTING A HYPOTHESIS

Your task for this chapter is to select a subject that you are familiar with, in either the natural or the social sciences; to devise a hypothesis about it based on your present knowledge; to investigate it; to analyze and interpret the materials you find; and to convey your information either as leading to a theory in support of your original hypothesis or to a new or revised interpretation.

You will not yourself experiment with your hypothesis, but will synthesize the findings of others, recorded in books and periodicals, with information that you gather through your own observations, and from interviews with others who are capable of providing you with authoritative comment on your subject. This synthesis of information will provide evidence that will help you formulate a conclusion.

In this act of informing your readers by interpreting your findings and those of others, you are engaging in the activity of research. Although this process is one we undergo everyday—say, in the gathering, interpretation, and evaluation of the information needed to find a suitable gift for a friend or to buy a used car—in the more formal discourse of the college and professional worlds, research implies a specific kind of mental activity and a specific form for presenting this effort to others. In many of your college classes, you may be asked to write a paper showing that you understand how to use the methods and forms of academic research.

As a possible approach to the research task for this chapter, you might begin with your experiences with your cousin, who suffers from anorexia nervosa, and then form a hypothesis about the causes of the illness based on your initial observations of your cousin's behavior. In order to test your hypothesis, you will need to gather outside information on the subject, to analyze your sources, to find scientifically convincing and acceptable statements on the causes of the illness, and to present your findings in a clear and accurate manner as either validating your own interpretation or indicating a revised or new hypothesis. Or, if you have developed a hypothesis about the effects on society of reduced tax rates for the rich, you might include in your essay the results of an interview with a member of your college's economics department, as well as the information that you acquire from printed sources.

When you are writing such a paper, it is helpful to imagine an audience that would profit from your findings. An audience of your peers, readers of a college publication, for example, would be interested in the research activity of other students. And a publication that shares the results of such exploration with others would be a genuine source of information that others would profit from. For this task, try writing your researched essay as an article for a college magazine that presents the work of students exploring the natural and social sciences: Your audience will be interested in your findings and will profit from them but will be essentially a lay or nonscientific audience.

The extent of this article is something that your instructor will most likely wish to discuss with you. An investigative paper of approximately five to eight pages, using at least six printed sources, should provide you with an adequate introduction to the methods of inductive research.

In the "Writing the Essay" section that follows, we discuss how to generate ideas, find a topic, gather and evaluate sources, take notes, organize evidence, consider audience, and finally put the paper together.

WRITING YOUR ESSAY

Generating Ideas Through Induction

Thinking Inductively.   In a sense, induction is not really a formal method of inquiry but an ongoing process of perception that gives you knowledge of the external world by imposing an order on the rush of sensations that you constantly experience. The more experiences you have and then file away in your active memory, the more order and understanding you can bring to bear on future experiences. Further experiences cause you to test the validity of your past experiences, and if necessary, you revise your mental maps to take into account new or additional information. Just as physical sensations must leap across nerve cells before they can be transmitted to our brains, experiences must undergo a kind of "leap," an inductive leap, before you can arrange them into a pattern of meaning.

If during several days of going from a dimly lit building into bright sunshine, you found the bright light dazzled you each day in succession, the chances are quite good that it will continue to do so unless you prepare for it in advance. One day you get the idea to put on your sunglasses just before you emerge from the building. You have reasoned from particular experiences and arrived at a general conclusion: sunlight dazzles. Further observations may cause you to refine your conclusion: Some days the sky is cloudy and the sun shines through only intermittently; if you leave the building on such a day, you might not need sunglasses. Or you calculate that if you leave after a certain hour, the sun will have shifted and will no longer dazzle your eyes when you emerge from your usual exit. In fact, there seem to be an endless number of variables that affect your actions, many of which you don't even give conscious thought to because they are so habitual.

Of course, you base your conclusions on a certain degree of probability. Although you cannot be absolutely certain that the sun will emerge tomorrow, you can be pretty sure that it will and that it will appear to rise in the east and set in the west. Your reasoning requires that you base your inductive leap on a limited but *adequate number of examples*. You can't be sure that the last pair of pants on a department-store clothing rack has a price tag on it, but if the other twelve pairs on the rack have such a tag, you can reasonably expect the last pair to have a tag. After you noticed that the first eight or ten pairs of pants had a price tag, you reasoned inductively and concluded, "All these pants have price tags."

If you then decided to generalize further, claiming, "Every item in this store has an attached price tag," you would be guilty of making a *hasty generalization*. How can you be sure that every item has a price tag attached? Would you check every item in the store, spending the next two years of your life moving from department to department? Well, certainly not, but you might decide to check a number of items in every department, taking what you estimate to be a *representative sampling* of items in the store. And you must not avoid counting departments like fine china or baked goods, where you suspect that many dishes and pastries don't have attached price tags, for such an omission would indicate a tendency on your part to exclude *unfavorable evidence that would negate your conclusion*. You don't want to *distort or falsify your evidence* either, for again, that would put your conclusion in question. Finally, you must *evaluate your evidence for the reliability of its sources* to determine whether your conclusion is based on reliable information.

Using Evidence: The Writer as Observer.   One source of evidence that would seem reliable is your own power of observation. But as was suggested earlier in the example of the "rising" and "setting" of the sun, personal observation is full of pitfalls, offering little assurance that you can always believe what you observe. Consider the account of an early-twentieth-century attempt to demonstrate that animals can perform human mental operations such as counting. Michael Polanyi, in his book *Personal Knowledge*, related the story of the horse "Clever Hans":

> The horse . . . could tap out with his hoofs the answer to all kinds of mathematical problems, written out on a blackboard in front of him. Incredulous experts from all relevant branches of knowledge came and tested him severely, only to confirm again and again his unfailing intellectual powers. But at last Mr. Oskar Pfungst had the idea of asking the horse a question to which he, Pfungst, did not know the answer. This time the horse went on tapping and tapping indefinitely, without rhyme or reason. It turned out that all the severely sceptical experts had involuntarily and unknowingly signalled to the horse to stop tapping at the point where they — knowing the right answer — expected him to stop. This is how they made the answers invariably come out right.

In this incident, you see how strongly observers can influence the results of observation by the strength of their own desire to have an experiment mean what they want it to mean, in effect to "prove" what they already believed at the outset of their scientific inquiry. This example suggests that scientific objectivity—the total impartiality of the observing scientist—is never a simple, unambiguous given that you can assume as the guiding principle of all scientific research, but that it is an ideal (some would say a myth) that needs to be understood in advance by the researcher who uses scientific evidence.

In other words, you cannot always trust what you think your observations mean. You must evaluate them critically to see if you have let your own bias or values influence your conclusions. However, for most of us the closest we will come to scientific experimentation is through our reading about it. What can you as a reader do to evaluate the evidence of your sources?

Using Evidence: Evaluating Sources.   Actually, by now you have acquired an extensive working knowledge of using and evaluating various kinds of evidence: examples drawn from the media to support your generalization in Chapter 7; support for your claim, proposal, or belief in Chapter 8; analysis of the controversial issues in Chapter 9.

But doing more extensive research among printed sources presents the writer with an obvious problem: How do I know what evidence to use? How can I be sure I'm not using data that are unreliable or worthless? At the beginning of your research you may feel like a stranger in a strange land, but there are some questions you can ask that will help you to distinguish the useful from the not-so-useful.

When was it published? If your topic is violence in professional sports, use a book or article that is up-to-date. Your reader will expect you to be aware of the current state of your topic. An author will often note in the preface or introduction to a book how this book differs from past work on the subject, what updating has been done from previous editions, what other viewpoints there are on this subject.

Magazine articles tend to date faster than books. Sources like *Newsweek, Time,* and other newsmagazines report events but are too close to these events sometimes to evaluate them fully. Information on science, as you are well aware, should be current, taking into account the latest theories or results.

Encyclopedias like the *Britannica* or *World Book* are fine for giving you a general overview of a subject you aren't knowledgeable about, but are not very useful for topics currently in the news or topics that have undergone much change or development.

Who wrote it? In using any evidence, be certain the writer's work is authoritative, that the writer is an expert in the field. You cannot always be sure but you can infer from your material at hand whether the author has some credible expertise. For example, is the writer's academic or professional affiliation given? Is there any information about the writer's training or background? Is the writer referred to in other books or articles, either in the text or bibliography? What other work has the writer produced on this or other subjects? After some investigation you may find that a number of authors' names are frequently referred to as having significance in their field of study. Their works are a good place to begin your research.

What can I learn about the source by analyzing its intended audience? If you are looking for an article on the effects of TV advertising on children's buying habits, you won't find it in the *National Enquirer* or *Sports Illustrated*. Their audience doesn't read these publications to learn about such information. There are, however, magazines that are known for their analysis and interpretation of contemporary political and social issues. *Atlantic, Commonweal, Commentary, Harper's, National Review,* the *Nation, New York Times Magazine* all appeal to informed, educated readers. Note, however, that many periodicals—including a number of those above—appeal to readers with specific liberal or conservative opinions, or those who have other special interests or attitudes. Check the entire contents of a periodical, especially any editorial comment, to see if you can identify a particular slant or bias that may affect the validity of an article or account for its conclusions.

Evaluating a source, therefore, suggests that you need to interpret its aim and purpose, the depth of its coverage and analysis, its intended audience, and its applicability to your own research purposes. After you have read and explored your topic somewhat, you should become familiar with additional sources you encounter, and gain a better idea of how useful or reliable they are.

Using Evidence: Seeking Non-Print Sources for Your Essay. The definition of research, as we use it, is not just the image of the scientist in white lab coat pouring some mysterious liquid from beaker to beaker, or the bespectacled student developing calluses from thumbing through card catalogs or tapping computer keyboards. Your sources will no doubt derive primarily from printed materials. But research also describes the ongoing activity of observation and hypothesis-making that characterize our daily encounter with the world around us. You may decide to take your research into the field and conduct surveys or interviews relevant to your topic.

As in your essay in writing about a place in Chapter 4, you can make up a list of questions to ask those whose views or knowledge on a subject can contribute toward your conclusion. If you want to find out whether students who own their cars on campus lose valuable study time in maintaining them, set up a number of questions that will provide you with material to further your research.

In addition, interviews with student personnel counselors or those who conduct work-study programs may be able to give you some valuable analysis of students' work habits or their personal lives. You can judge quite skillfully who those experts are that can help you with your research project. In most cases they will be quite eager to help in time and resources.

If you need to determine the views of a larger number of people than you can interview, consider making up a written survey or questionnaire to be sent to, let's say, the counseling departments of local area colleges or employment offices. Here too you need to refine your questions so that the data you receive is valid for the hypothesis you wish to explore. We discuss how to obtain print sources in the following section, but in all cases—observations, interviews, books and periodicals—you will want to apply the principles of valid induction to the data you compile.

SOME PRACTICE WITH INDUCTION AND EVALUATING SOURCES

1. Use your journal to record observations that are as objective as possible. Select a place from which to begin observing and recording examples, for instance, the student cafeteria, a bench in front of a bus stop, or the window in your room that overlooks the street. Record the details observed from this vantage point over a period of several days. Try observing the same object but from a different observation point. You might take a photograph of the scene or even tape-record the sounds that you heard for a limited period of time. What generalizations can you make from your observations? Was there any discernible pattern that emerged from these observations?

2. Assume you are a social anthropologist, one who observes the practices of cultures that are strange to us and tries to understand their meaning. Select some ritual of daily life that goes largely unnoticed, for example, a gathering of students at the campus lounge. Write down your observations very carefully, trying not to impose your views on what is taking place. Some other rituals that you might observe are lunchtime at a fast-food establishment or the behavior of customers in a supermarket. After gathering sufficient examples of behavior, arrive at a conclusion about the meaning of the ritual or the pattern of behavior observed.

3. Select a topic about which to poll student attitudes on campus. Prepare a series of questions. Determine what would be an adequate sampling of views and how the respondents should be selected. Next, conduct your poll, collecting answers to your questions from selected students. Evaluate your collected data and make some generalizations about the views of the students who contributed opinions. To what extent are your results accurate as a representation of student opinion? What criticisms might be made of your method of questioning or your sampling of opinions?

4. Basing your opinions on the evidence supplied, explain whether the generalizations in the examples below are valid:

    a. Everyone in the class has had at least one unpleasant experience in dealing with bureaucracies. The class overwhelmingly concludes that bureaucracies are terrible and should be abolished.

b. In Steve's survey of students who smoke, 67 percent in two classes of business majors smoke, whereas only 48 percent of the students in two classes of English majors smoke. Steve concludes that business majors smoke more than English majors.

c. When asked by a local newspaper, ten out of ten members of the college administration state that the evening students on campus are satisfied with the college's evening program, as enrollment has gone up from last year. The newspaper says that the unanimous agreement of the administration is conclusive evidence that they are right.

5. After choosing a subject that interests you, investigate the books on this subject in your college library to see how adequate its holdings are. Do these works appear to represent a valid coverage of the subject? Are they scientifically current? Are the authors represented vital to an understanding or interpretation of this subject? Construct a selected annotated list of the most significant works and, if possible, state what works might be added that your library does not own.

6. Evaluate the potential usefulness of the following sources for doing research on the stated topics.

   a. A history of the American Civil War written in 1916.

   b. An analysis of the French painter Cezanne published in 1925.

   c. Nancy Reagan's autobiography for use in evaluating the Reagan presidency.

   d. A book by Nancy Reagan's astrologer for use in evaluating the Reagan presidency.

   e. A study of the effects of nicotine authorized by the American Tobacco Institute.

   f. An article on surgery in the *Encyclopedia Britannica* for a paper on the most recent techniques in sports medicine.

   g. An interpretation of constitutional rights published by the director of the National Rifle Association.

   h. The report of a cure for cancer published by a private press in North Grande, a small town in the Southwest.

Using Induction to Generate Ideas for Testing Your Hypothesis. Your journal can offer a useful beginning for your research essay. Because so much of the success of a research paper depends on a clearly stated, manageable hypothesis, you might begin a section on research in your journal with a series of questions or observations—personal or drawn from your reading—on a variety of topics. Use your journal to annotate these questions with some comments on what difficulties or advantages you can anticipate about your research on these topics. If no topics occur to you, you might select some from the list on p. 465.

Perhaps you find a topic interesting but aren't sure you can find enough material because this topic is too current. Or you might have some knowledge about one of the questions you pose because of some prior investigation in another class or even a personal experience.

A research journal can also be a convenient catchall for all the small details that arise once you begin concentrated work on your paper. A library call number, a title of an article you had in mind to look up, a brief evaluation of the usefulness of a source, or an idea about how you might develop the middle section of your draft—all these details are part of the shopping list of a researcher and can be retrieved more easily if available in one place.

SOME PRACTICE IN USING INDUCTION IN TESTING YOUR HYPOTHESIS

1. If you are at the beginning stages of your research, use your journal to record observations, articles, or quotations from newspapers or magazines that might have a connection to a topic you are interested in investigating.

2. Arrange to interview a professor in your school whom you believe has expertise in the area you are interested in researching. Prepare some questions beforehand on matters that you think might be relevant to your interest. Use your journal to record your conclusions about what you learned and any advice about how to pursue your topic further.

3. Prepare a list of questions that you think you may have to answer in order to arrive at a conclusion for a hypothesis on your subject. Submit these questions to a number of students or faculty in your school to see what kind of feedback they can generate on your topic. In your journal, classify their responses to determine whether there is a consensus on the research for your topic. If so, here is an area you might investigate further.

Addressing Your Audience: The Lay Reader

On one of his television talk shows, Phil Donahue had as guests two of the most widely read scientist-writers of our time, Carl Sagan and Stephen Jay Gould. Here were two highly trained, technically skilled university professors explaining theories of evolution to a large television audience. Pointer in hand and standing before a large TV graphic, Sagan explained that all of geological time could be understood if we thought of it as if it were only a one-year calendar. According to this analogy, humankind makes its first appearance about December 25, almost at the very end of the "year."

In this way, Sagan tried to show how recently our species had arrived on the planet. It was an imaginative comparison, one that his audience could grasp far more easily than if he had said that the evolutionary process was of several billion years' duration. Certainly Sagan would not have used this analogy if he were addressing a convention of the American Association for the Advancement of Science or a graduate seminar on the origins of the solar system. But for an audience of the scientifically unschooled, this was a highly effective learning device.

In recent years, the public consciousness of science has undergone a minor revolution. Much of it may be due to the rise of the computer sciences and their startling grasp on the popular imagination. In addition, there are exciting discoveries that have altered our view of human genetics and its effects on the human species.

You need look no further for evidence of this ferment in scientific exploration and discovery than your nearest newsstand. Here are some of the many science magazines now being directed to relatively large audiences:

The Sciences	*Scientific American*	*Astronomy*
Omni	*Nature*	*American Health*
Science News	*Discover*	*Science Digest*
American Scientist	*Psychology Today*	
Natural History	*High Technology*	

Each of these magazines differs somewhat in style and substance. Some are weighted more heavily toward the behavioral and life sciences. Others, intended for a large reading public, are heavily illustrated and tend to focus on the future implications of scientific technology. *Scientific American* and *Nature* make rigorous demands on the reader and often report important new discoveries. All of these periodicals are aware of the level of interest and scientific abilities of their readers.

At the same time that more people are becoming interested in science, the technical language of scientific explanation is becoming more remote from the understanding of the ordinary—even if scientifically educated—reader. Thus the need exists for writers like Sagan and Gould who can explain and interpret the world of scientific discourse in ways that are interesting yet not patronizing to their readers. Gould, a professor of biology and geology at Harvard University, writes a monthly essay on a variety of biological topics for *Natural History*, a widely circulated magazine published by the American Museum of Natural History in New York. His writing is a combination of human curiosity and penetrating intelligence, supported by a fine writer's eye for the unexpected analogy and the offbeat allusion:

> When I was 10 years old, James Arness terrified me as a giant, predaceous carrot in *The Thing* (1951). A few months ago, older, wiser, and somewhat bored, I watched its latest television rerun with a dominating sentiment of anger. I recognized the film as a political document, expressing the worst sentiments of America in the cold war: its hero, a tough military man who wants only to destroy the enemy utterly; its villain, a naively liberal scientist who wants to learn more about it; the carrot and its flying saucer, a certain surrogate for the red menace; the film's famous last words—a newsman's impassioned plea to "watch the skies"—an invitation to extended fear and jingoism.
>
> Amidst all this, a scientific thought crept in by analogy and this essay was born—the fuzziness of all supposedly absolute taxonomic distinctions. The world, we are told, is inhabited by animals with conceptual language (us) and those without (everyone else). But chimps are now talking. All creatures are either plants or animals, but Mr. Arness looked rather human (if horrifying) in his role as a mobile, giant vegetable.
>
> Either plants or animals. Our basic conception of life's diversity is based upon this division. Yet it represents little more than a prejudice spawned by our status as large, terrestrial animals. True, the macroscopic organisms surrounding us on land can be unambiguously allocated if we designate fungi as plants because they are rooted (even though they do not photosynthesize). Yet, if we floated as tiny creatures in the oceanic plankton, we would not have made such a distinction. At the one-celled level, ambiguity abounds: mobile "animals" with functioning chloroplasts; simple cells like bacteria with no clear relation to either group.
>
> Taxonomists have codified our prejudice by recognizing just two kingdoms for all life—Plantae and Animalia. Readers may regard an inadequate classification as a trifling matter; after all, if we characterize organisms accurately, who cares if our basic categories do not express the richness and complexity of life very well? But a classification is not a neutral hat rack; it expresses a theory of relationships that controls our concepts. The Procrustean system of plants and animals has distorted our view of life and prevented us from understanding some major features of its history.

The style and tone of Gould's essay assume that a reader interested in the subject of evolution and biological taxonomy (classification) need not possess a highly specialized vocabulary nor a graduate degree in order to understand and appreciate the subject. Gould began by recollecting a movie that terrified him as a child. It now suggested to him an analogy of how we divide living things into either plants or animals. This is a "Procrustean system," that is, a limited way to "express the richness and complexity of life." The last sentence points ahead to Gould's main intention: to show how our method of classifying living things prevents us from understanding their real nature.

Although he began with references to himself, Gould's purpose was not to draw attention to the terrors of his childhood or to his taste in films. He was simply using these references as an interesting, colorful introduction to the scientific ideas that are brought into the second paragraph. The author's main purpose was expository, not expressive.

He was soon engaged in a serious discussion of the implications of scientific classification. As a scientist, he freely used the language of scientific discourse (*macroscopic organisms, functioning chloroplasts, taxonomists*), yet the overall voice in his langauge is that of a literate, interested writer making contact with a reader of similar qualities who can also perceive that his is a topic of importance. Both author and reader meet at a level of special knowledge and range of reference that should not be very difficult for a college student to attain.

In discussing a scientific topic in language that will be understandable and interesting to a lay audience, your writing will require the synthesis, or combining, of scientific knowledge into a coherent discussion that presents this knowledge in a convincing way. The language of your discussion must be adapted to the knowledge of the subject that your audience can reasonably be expected to possess. As Gould's writing shows, this approach does not have to result in oversimplifying or in trivializing the subject matter. You should see yourself as the reader's guide through a densely wooded forest, where your familiarity with the trails is the important factor that ensures everyone's safety.

SOME PRACTICE WITH WRITING FOR A LAY AUDIENCE

1. Select three of the science magazines listed in the audience section. Write an analysis of each magazine's intended audience. Does each magazine address its audience successfully? Which is the most successful and why? What changes in each publication would you recommend? How does the format of each magazine (layout, length of articles, amount of advertising, illustrations, special features, and so on) reveal a particular intended audience? How is the language different?

2. Select an author of one of the articles featured in any science magazine named above whose other works are named in the magazine. Look these up in your college library. Write a brief analysis of the differences between the author's treatment of the same (or different) scientific subject in the magazine article and in the book or more specialized publication in which the writer's other work appeared. What differences in audience do you notice? What differences in research techniques do you notice?

3. College textbooks are excellent examples of how specialized technical material is adapted for a large audience. Analyze your own textbook from one of

the natural, physical, or social sciences with regard to the methods it uses to teach technical material to a college audience. How has the author tried to interest students? Has the author been successful? Would you read this book if you were not a student? Contrast this text with another on the same subject and determine which is the more successful. Write a brief report for the department chairman on the book, either recommending it for further adoption or urging that it be dropped.

4. Prepare an outline describing a proposed college science magazine or newsletter. Organize your outline under the following headings: advertising techniques and products, general format of publication, and special features. Briefly explain how this magazine would have special interest and appeal for a college-aged population.

Addressing the Lay Reader of Your Essay Testing a Hypothesis. Although you were curious enough about your topic to pursue it further and research it in the form of print sources or other media and non-print sources, you cannot be certain that your audience will share your interest or your knowledge. In addition, your reader may not have a clear idea of the importance or relevance of your topic. It is your task as a writer to convince your reader of your topic's significance by presenting the results of your research in a clear, interesting discussion.

Remember that you are conveying more than just information in the form of transcribed facts. Through your use of research techniques you wish to introduce your lay audience to information that results from your synthesis of your sources. Keep in mind what your reader needs to know about your topic and use language that most directly conveys this knowledge. Your task is not to impress your reader with a lot of technical or scientific jargon but to lead him or her to an insight and perhaps arouse the reader's interest enough to explore the topic further.

Answering the questions of the "Audience Analysis Guide" will assist you in addressing the lay reader of your essay:

AUDIENCE ANALYSIS GUIDE

1. How much knowledge of my topic can I expect my reader to possess?
2. How interesting and worthwhile is this topic for the lay reader?
3. Will my audience be familiar with the sources I have used?
4. Will my audience's frame of reference create any special problems for the reception of my research?

SOME PRACTICE IN ADDRESSING THE LAY READER OF YOUR ESSAY TESTING A HYPOTHESIS

1. Prepare two lists of questions about your topic that will reveal the depth of knowledge of a group of college students. One list will use nontechnical language; the other, technical terms that are important for explaining your subject. Submit both lists to a group of students. If your respondents find that they must refer to your first list in order to understand the second, they are unfamiliar with the technical terms: In your essay, you should consider defining these terms with the nontechnical language of your first list.

2. Make a list of the specialized terms used in your sources. Rank them in order of significance and complexity to determine what terms should have priority and how they should appear in your essay.

3. Record in your journal any media items you have recently observed that might be relevant to your topic. Explain how you might use these news items in order to introduce or explain some facet of your topic.

Doing Research

Selecting a Topic. Although your purpose is to write an article for a school publication, your topic should be one that interests you as well as others. Will you be able to learn from your topic in the process of explaining it to others? There is little point in writing on a topic that you yourself find uninteresting. But if you have been wondering in your journal why your cousin suffers from anorexia nervosa or why punk rockers dress as they do, this might be a good place to begin.

Quite possibly you may be drawn to a topic because you have heard a lot about it, have seen it featured on TV, or have read about it in a magazine or newspaper. Topics like these are often controversial as well; they provide the writer with a certain advantage in catching the attention of an audience. For the researcher, however, controversy poses some difficulty: some topics are so timely that you might have difficulty finding any information other than newspaper stories and a few scattered magazine articles. A subject needs to seep into the public consciousness and to be studied over a period of time before reasoned, reliable books begin to appear. You might be better off writing on a topic that has been the subject of considerable study. Here are some topics that you might find interesting and about which you should be able to find ample recent investigations. Some are fairly broad and, in forming your hypothesis, you will need to focus more narrowly.

Sciences

AIDS
Space stations
Anorexia nervosa
Genetic engineering
Animals threatened with
  extinction
Toxic wastes
Organ transplants
The extinction of the
  dinosaurs
Animal intelligence
The aging process
The discovery of DNA
Cancer and diet
The debate over cholesterol
  and the heart

Vitamins and health
Nuclear power and the
  environment
Hypertension
New cancer therapies
New diagnostic tools in
  medicine
The origins of the universe
Harnessing the sun's energy
The future of artificial
  satellites
Applications of laser
  technology
Microchips and semi-
  conductors
The greenhouse effect
Saving our air and water

Social Sciences

Occupational health and
  safety
Measuring human intelligence
Computers and child learning
Religious cults
Changing roles of men and
  women
The new immigration
The graying of America
Child abuse
The Japanese worker
Violence in sports
Creationism and the schools
The attack on psychoanalysis
Nursing homes

Nurse practitioners
Women executives
Children of divorce
The homeless problem
Phobias: their causes and
  effects
The effect of television
  violence on children
The battered-wife syndrome
Careers for the 1990s
Sex stereotypes on TV
The value of the hospice
Physical fitness: fad or
  revolution
Social change in Eastern Europe

Your first attempt to find a topic will often begin with a question: What do I know about the extinction of the great whales? Why are some people subject to severe phobias? What are the most successfully treated malignancies? Not only can a question help to point you to a topic that interests you, it can also guide you through your first crucial choice: selecting a topic that is limited enough so that you can explain it in a short article.

Your next step is to form a hypothesis. Your hypothesis will emerge from your reading or hearing about your subject or your own personal observations. For example, you may have observed a natural phenomenon, such as a shooting star or an illness, or read about a social phenomenon, such as the behavior of a cult, and you may have arrived already at a tentative interpretation of some aspect of this phenomenon: A shooting star is in actuality a comet, anorexia nervosa is caused by anxiety, punk rockers were motivated by alienation from society just as the beatniks of the 1950s were.

This tentative conclusion, phrased as a complete thought, is your hypothesis. Whether your hypothesis ultimately proves to be right or wrong is not the point; the point is that, like the scientist, you must begin somewhere. The scientific method begins with the most logical interpretation at the time, proceeds to gather evidence, and then makes a determination based on that evidence. It is the process and the conclusion that attest to a scientist's acumen. Thus, it is a good idea to phrase your hypothesis in a way that suggests you are investigating, rather than arguing, the matter: Instead of asserting that "Critics of punk rock are insensitive to its social significance," it may be better to write, "The punk rockers were motivated by their alienation from society."

Gathering Sources: Preparing a Preliminary Bibliography.   Gathering sources—for many writers the most interesting part of the research process—takes you to the library and sends you through its vast maze of printed materials. Intimidating as it first is for many students, the library soon becomes a place where you feel more confident as you grow to have more and more authority in using its resources.

You might begin by looking at one of the magazines named in the audience section of this chapter. It may give you an insight into a topic that you are curious about or may lead you to a topic that you hadn't really been aware of. To find more magazines, often with more information, consult *The Readers' Guide to Periodical Literature.* For many years, this source has been an indispensable starting point for researchers. Arranged by author and subject, *The Readers' Guide* lists articles in more than 150 periodicals read by a relatively wide audience. For example, if you are interested in the subject of the brain, you will want to begin by looking at recent entries:

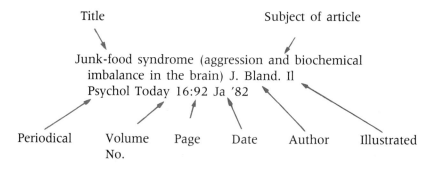

In addition to *The Readers' Guide*, there are a number of reference works that list more specialized articles in periodicals for particular fields in the sciences and the social sciences, such as the following:

Applied Science and Technology Index
Biological and Agricultural Index
Consumers' Index
Educational Index
Environment Index
General Science Index
International Index
Social Sciences and Humanities Index
Social Sciences Index

For recent developments and past events, a good place to begin is *The New York Times Index*, where you will find, listed by subject, summaries of news articles that have appeared in this important newspaper. Most college libraries have the *Times* in microfilm. Check yours to see if this service is available.

Once you begin to explore sources on your subject, you will need a method for recording essential information identifying those sources from which you will take your data. Although any scrap of paper will do for scribbling down a few words, such as "*Scientific American* May 1990," a more efficient method includes at least a full reference to the author, the title of the book or of the periodical, the title of the article, its date and pages, and some comment briefly stating the contents of the work, along with any identifying number for locating this source in the library. Having this information handy can save you additional trips to the library, especially once you have already begun to prepare your paper.

A convenient way to record this information is to write all the important bibliographic data on a separate slip of paper or an index card. These separate bibliographic cards will—along with your note cards (see below)—contain the results of your investigations in the library stacks and periodical sections. Later, you can use these cards to prepare the final bibliography for your completed paper. At this stage of your research, your main concern is to acquire a sufficient number of sources from which to draw your information.

For an article of five to eight pages, you might begin with twenty or more periodicals and books. After some broad reading in your sources—skimming, in the case of books, to find usable material—you will most likely depend mainly on six to eight sources in preparing your article. If you use considerably more than this number, your topic is probably too broad, and you may not be able to organize your information coherently. If you are too dependent on one or two books or articles, you probably will write more of a summary

Rorvik, David M. Your Baby's Sex: Now You Can Choose. New York: Dodd, Mead & Co., 1970.

— background of preselection
— research of L. B. Shettles
— effects on population control

QH 309
R 54

BIBLIOGRAPHY CARD

or a report than a paper that investigates a variety of sources and synthesizes information to form a new whole. There is no formula for determining the right number of sources to use, but too many or too few tend to produce an uninteresting and unsatisfying paper.

Taking Notes. Taking notes from your sources is one of the most important steps in preparing your paper. Not only are you recording information, but by turning another writer's language into your own, you are also selecting, analyzing, and interpreting this material with an eye to how it will be made into your own continuous discussion. You need to decide as you are reading over your material what is likely to be important to your topic. You can't always be certain that a particular passage will be of value, but it is better to take more notes than you will actually need than to realize later that some material that you decided not to take down was quite important.

Nor can you rely on the duplicating machine to do your note-taking for you. Certainly duplicating is useful if you want to spend more time with materials like periodical articles or reference books that you cannot ordinarily take out of the library. But you will then still want to take notes from your information. Underlining or annotating the text of an article cannot substitute for extracting specific passages for quotation or summary and arranging them under subject headings that will later become the organizing plan of your article.

For your notes, you will want separate slips of paper or index cards. Because you will already have written the complete bibliographic information

> *New developments on the horizon*
>
> Ray, 76.
>   Scientists experimenting with pills that stop one type of male sperm production
>
> Rorvik,
>   Shettles is experimenting with insemination high into the cervical canal. The more motile male sperm reaches the egg first. He feels he can achieve a 90% success rate. Female sperm can be preselected since they are stronger and survive after aging for days in a petri dish.

on a separate card, you will need only to write some identifying word, usually the author's last name, on your note card. You can leave room at the top of the card for a subject heading if you aren't sure at this time what your headings will be. If you are quoting directly, you can write the page number(s) next to your quotation. The quotation must be exact. If you wish to omit words or sentences that are unnecessary for your purposes, you can show this through the use of the ellipsis (see "Handbook," pp. 595–596).

A note card is more effective if it is limited to a single note. Even if you are taking notes from the same page of an article or the same chapter of a book, the quoted information may actually pertain to more than one of the main subjects of your paper. If you remember that you are always trying to anticipate how you can have ready access to your information when you are writing your paper, you will not bury a note in such a way that it will be difficult to find later. Efficient notes, for example, cannot be lumped together on a notebook page. Also, because you will be taking notes from many sources, you will probably not want to copy lengthy quotations from all of them.

You will want to make sure to quote carefully and exactly the text you wish to use. Sometimes you may want to *quote* an author who has narrated a distinctive anecdote or has summed up his or her main purpose clearly and succinctly. Or perhaps an author has made a far-reaching conclusion that you would like to use as part of your closing paragraph. These are legitimate uses for quotations. Most of the time, however, it is best to use direct quotations — especially extended ones — sparingly. Therefore you may find it useful to develop the habit of combining these methods of taking notes: quotation, summary, and paraphrase.

Values to preselection

Ray, 77
    Couples can limit family size to the children they desire. They can have only one girl if they so choose. This element of choice has important implications for limiting population growth.

PARAPHRASE

A *summary* is a substantially reduced note that records information that you may want to include in your paper but that you don't think is necessary to quote directly. A *paraphrase*, like a summary, is written in your own words, but, unlike a summary, it approximates the form and content of the original. Whether you quote, summarize, or paraphrase, it is essential to refer

Sperm separation

Pinkel, 904
    "The only . . . difference on which to base sperm separation is chromosomal constitution." In mammals, sperm with X chromosomes result in females; Y chromosomes in males.

QUOTATION

to the source of your information in your citations, so you will want to be sure to take down the page numbers of all such material that comes from your sources. Failure to provide such required documentation is plagiarism, a practice that many students imperfectly understand.

Many students feel that direct quotations are evidence enough that they have used specific sources. Actually this is not true. Anytime you use information that is not your own, you must credit your source. Paraphrasing or summarizing outside source material accurately (making sure to note the specific source and page numbers of your information) is one way to avoid using others' writings as if they were your own. In response to the student who asks, "You mean my whole paper will be continuous citation, as everything in it comes from other sources?" the answer is, "Yes, you will obviously need a large number of citations, but every statement or sentence need not be cited individually. Often one citation will do for a series of sentences from one source." Remember also that your task for this writing assignment makes use of your own direct observations, interviews, or surveys of others who can provide you with information. This material also requires documentation, which will be discussed in the "Focus" section of this chapter.

Working through this stage in your task, you will accumulate a substantial number of notes, with some direct quotations that you think are highly informative, distinctively worded, or illustrative of some main idea that you intend to explain. Your next task will be to examine your notes and subject headings to see how they can be organized into a meaningful plan or outline. This plan, which forms the skeletal structure of your paper, will then be followed as you begin your first draft.

SOME PRACTICE WITH RESEARCH METHODS

1. To write a paraphrase of this paragraph, fill in words that would adequately substitute for those in the original source.

> The fast-growing field of research has even been given a new name—psychoneuroimmunology—and is finally beginning to win the respect of the modern medical establishment, which despite physicians like Dr. Osler, had scorned or ignored previous suggestions of a strong mind–body link. Many of the studies are now being supported by various branches of the National Institutes of Health. More and more, as Dr. Osler recognized, the emotions are being considered necessary components of the cause as well as the treatment of most illness.

The quickly developing area of _____ has been _____ psychoneuroimmunology and is at last starting to _____ of today's medical _____ who had criticized or _____ former _____ of a _____. Much of the research is being _____ by _____ of the

National Institutes of Health. Increasingly, as Dr. Osler _____, the _____ are _____ important _____ of the cause and _____ of most _____.

2. Write a summary and a paraphrase of the following paragraphs of an article written by Jane Brody that appeared in the *New York Times*, May 24, 1983.

> Nearly a century after some leading physicians first recognized the powerful role of the mind in health and healing, scientists have begun to decipher exactly how stress and other emotional states can influence the onset and course of disease.
>
> Aided by new biochemical techniques and a vastly expanded understanding of immunology and neurochemistry, their studies show that emotions, acting through the brain, can affect nervous system function, hormone levels and immunological responses, thereby changing a person's susceptibility to a host of organic ills.
>
> Depending on the circumstances, animal and human studies have revealed that emotional reactions can suppress or stimulate disease-fighting white blood cells and trigger the release of adrenal gland hormones and neurotransmitters, including endorphins, that in turn affect dozens of body processes.

3. Compare the original source with the summary that follows. Did the student fail to change the original wording adequately? How effective will these notes be when the student prepares the paper?

> Although the influence of mind on body was well-known to ancient healers and has dominated folklore to the present day, "scientific" medicine has until recently focused almost exclusively on physical causes for bodily illness. Only a few so-called psychosomatic diseases, such as asthma and ulcers, were said to have an emotional basis.
>
> The new studies strongly indicate, however, that virtually every ill that can befall the body—from the common cold to cancer and heart disease—can be influenced, positively or negatively, by a person's mental state. By unveiling the mechanisms behind these effects, the studies point to new ways to prevent and treat some of the nation's leading killing and crippling diseases. They strongly suggest that psychotherapy and behavioral techniques should be an integral part of preventive and therapeutic medicine.

Summary:

Brody states that although the influence of mind on body was well known to ancient healers, modern medicine has given attention only to the physical causes of bodily illnesses. New research shows that almost all illness is affected by a person's psychological condition. By unveiling the mechanisms behind these effects, the studies point to new methods of stopping the country's leading illnesses. They show that psychotherapy and behavioral techniques should be considered essential to preventative and therapeutic medicine.

4. Read an article in one of the periodicals named in the "audience" section. Take notes from this article, making sure to provide complete bibliographic information and subject headings on your note cards.

5. Select one of the topics listed in this chapter and do the following:

   a. Prepare three questions that would give a focus to someone planning to investigate it.

   b. Develop a tentative shaping idea for the topic.

   c. Prepare a broad outline of a paper on this topic.

6. Select one of the topics listed in this chapter and explain how you would begin to investigate it in your library. What kinds of sources could you use?

7. Prepare a preliminary bibliography of at least six items for the investigative paper that you are writing. Write each source on a separate index card or slip of paper. Write a sentence or two for each source summarizing its content and evaluating its apparent usefulness.

8. Select a paragraph from one of your sources. Write a paraphrase and then a summary. How are they different? Compare your paraphrase with the original. Did you change the language sufficiently?

Arranging Your Essay

The Shaping Idea: Stating Your Hypothesis. Your shaping idea for your research paper derives from the hypothesis you formulated as the result of your preliminary research. Perhaps you first began your research by asking a question you thought needed an answer, for example "Is memory loss an inevitable consequence of the aging process?" Your interest in the topic might have begun from your own personal experiences with a family member or your observations and readings over the years. You might have already formed a tentative answer to this question but were not sure how right you were or whether you had just accepted the views of others. You might have written some journal entries in which you asked questions about this subject—what you are interested in explaining or what conclusion you think might be persuasive.

After you did preliminary research, you arrived at some kind of conclusion—"Memory loss is not an inevitable consequence of the aging process."

This is your working hypothesis and it becomes the shaping idea of your paper.

At this point, it might be useful to review several criteria for an effective hypothesis:

1. Your hypothesis should be reasonable. It should not conflict with the accepted scientific model of the physical world.
2. It should explore an aspect of the broader topic that is not familiar to you and your reader and will be of interest to both of you.
3. Your hypothesis should be specific—limited to the amount of space and the ambition of your essay.
4. It should be a topic about which there are available print sources.
5. It should be phrased as a topic for scientific exploration and not for an argument.
6. It should be written as a shaping idea, as a statement with subject and predicate, not as a phrase.

For example, "acid rain affects nature" as the statement of your hypothesis fulfills criteria 1, 4, 5, and 6, as even the federal government now agrees that acid rain is devastating our forests and bodies of water; it is a complete statement, not a phrase; and there is much research about it. It does not fulfill criteria 2 and 3, however, because it is too broad for a student essay and because everyone is aware of the issue. A better hypothesis would be "Acid rain has destroyed the maple trees in our state park," which fulfills all criteria, assuming that print source material exists.

After you have formulated your hypothesis and shaping idea, what remains for you to do is to conduct your research and then recognize how you can communicate this idea most efficiently to your lay reader by organizing your research clearly and by adapting your material to the frame of reference of your reader. You should be confident that your references are relevant to your hypothesis and that you have a sufficient number of examples to support your conclusion. Your reader should know at the outset what your hypothesis is and how you propose to demonstrate it.

Of course, like any scientific research, your research may disprove your hypothesis. This should not be a matter of concern for you any more than it is for the scientist. The scientific researcher is evaluated for the validity of the research; a positive result is a bonus. As long as you applied the criteria for effective induction to your research, you need not be concerned with the consequences for your hypothesis. At the end of your essay, you may recommend a revised hypothesis based on your new knowledge, just as the scientist does.

Outlining. An outline is the pattern of meaning that emerges from the body of notes you have taken. After you have given much thought to your notes and the main ideas under which you arranged these notes, you will begin to see how these main ideas are related to one another and which main ideas should precede or follow others. In other papers that you have written, you performed the same kind of organizing operations. But in a research paper, with its larger number of facts and statements, the need to organize in detail is essential. During the course of your research, you may find it helpful to make several outlines, beginning with a broad overview of your topic and ending with a more detailed plan once the direction of your investigation becomes clearer. At first you might write a broad outline such as this:

Topic: Choosing the sex of an unborn child
  I. Introduction
 II. X and Y chromosomes
III. Recent experiments
 IV. Effects on society

After you have organized your notes, perhaps even gathering more information to fill what you think are gaps in your research, you will want to prepare a more detailed outline. This outline, listing the main topics of your article as you foresee them emerging during the course of your writing, actually shows you what the paragraph structure of your paper will be. Each main topic or subtopic of your outline shows you that one paragraph or more will be needed to explain this idea. And the words that you use in your outline to describe each topic can later become the topic sentences for these paragraphs. Thus, when you prepare a fairly detailed outline, you are actually beginning the first draft of your paper. Here is a more detailed version of the previous outline, revealing a more advanced stage of a student's plan:

CHOOSING THE SEX OF AN UNBORN CHILD

  I. Introduction
      A. Couples have always desired to choose the sex of their child
      B. Values to society of preselection
      C. Failed methods

 II. Methods for choosing the sex of an unborn child
      A. The basis of all theories of sex determination: X and Y chromosomes
      B. The research of L. B. Shettles into X and Y chromosomes
          1. Differing sizes of X and Y sperm cells

   2. Need for ways to separate boy sperm from girl
      sperm
C. R. J. Ericsson separated sperm for the first time
D. S. Langendoen developed dietary programs for women
   prior to conception
E. Selective abortion

III. New frontiers in the science of preselection

IV. Conclusion: Effects of preselection on society

In this outline the student has divided her plan into four main sections. Part II, the longest part of her paper, has been divided into five subtopics, one of which has been subdivided into two parts. Notice also that each major division is indented to show that it is subordinate to the topic above. This student may yet modify her outline as she continues to organize her information and revise the plan of her article. But in preparing a fairly detailed outline, she has begun her next step, writing the first draft of her paper.

Putting Your Notes Together. In writing the rest of your paper, you will want to take your collected notes and work them into a continuous discussion of your own, based on your outline. It is important to avoid an unbroken chain of quotations, for they will require the reader to sort out the crowd of voices in such a paper. Try instead to turn these other voices into your single voice. That is, clarify in your own mind the relationships among your notes of quotations, summaries, and paraphrases, in order to transform them into sentences and paragraphs that will blend smoothly into a single, coherent discourse.

Here is one student's use of quoted material:

When alcohol begins to take effect in small amounts, feelings of happiness and lightness may occur, depending on the personality, mood, and expectations of the user. Alcohol offers an escape from the pressure and tension of everyday society. As the drinking continues, drowsiness, extreme boisterousness, or depression may occur, along with physiological discomfort. "Most people don't drink because they like the taste or smell of alcohol: they drink because they have been taught to do so by the advertisements and the examples of those around them."[3]

This student's use of quotation is inadequate. The student has not introduced the quotation or shown why it is important. If it were not quoted material but an original sentence, it would simply be incoherent, having no connection to the rest of the paragraph. Furthermore, the information conveyed in the quotation does not seem particularly noteworthy, as its main point—that drinkers are affected by outside influences—seems obvious.

Another student's paragraph reveals other problems in the use of quotations:

"Supporters of lie detector methods insist that the technique is more than 90 percent accurate, that it is difficult for most offenders to deceive an experienced polygraph operator." "Others contend that the polygraph has never been accepted by the scientific community, and libertarians question the fairness of the lie detector, arguing that it unjustly robs a person of his innermost secrets." But its main function is to clear the wrongly accused innocent, not to convict the guilty.

This writer relied on a quotation to provide a main idea sentence for the paragraph. Beginning a paragraph with a quotation leaves it up to the reader to determine what the paragraph is to be about and why the quotation is important. And using quotations in sequence without even a minimal bridge between them creates a paragraph of little value, because the relationship of its parts is not made clear, nor is its connection with the rest of the essay clarified.

In the following paragraph, the writer tried to avoid direct quotation, using it only once, but failed to really assimilate the source material as the sentences don't follow each other very clearly. The paragraph is mainly a series of loosely related facts:

This pill works after egg implantation and technically produces an abortion. Louise Tyrer, M.D., says that "people should be aware of this." Although this would not be a problem for a majority of people, some would not feel comfortable with it. This four-day pill does not regulate the hormonal cycle. Instead it makes it temporarily impossible for the uterus to absorb progesterone.

In the next example, written by a professional writer, the author has skillfully worked others' material into a continuous discourse. Most of the paragraph is quotation, but through the use of ellipses and by carefully selecting the quoted material, the author has made it part of the structure of his own sentences:

> Viewing the society freshly, students often have clearer insight into this (. . .) lack of human involvement (. . .) than older adults—though they tend, in oversimplified fashion, to blame it on the institutions. "We have just not been given any passionate sense of the excitement of intellectual life around here," said the editor of the Columbia *Spectator*. A student columnist in the *Michigan Daily* wrote, "This institution has dismally failed to inculcate, in most of its undergraduates at least, anything approaching an intellectual appetite." He spoke of the drift "towards something worse than mediocrity—and that is absolute indifference. An indifference towards perhaps even life itself." "We were all divided up into punches on an IBM card," a Berkeley student remarked. "We decided to punch back in the riots of 1964, but the *real* revolution around here will come when we decide to burn computer cards as well as draft cards."
>
> —Rollo May, *Love and Will*

Writing the Introduction.   Once you have organized your information and prepared a working outline, you will be ready to begin writing your paper. As you did in the essays that you wrote in previous tasks, you will need to provide an introduction for your reader. The introduction to your other essays probably began with general approaches to your subject and concluded with your shaping idea. In a research paper, you may have to provide a more extensive introduction for your reader as you move from the general to the specific. Perhaps two or three paragraphs might be necessary to state your hypothesis, to give some necessary background to the uninformed reader, and to tell your reader what the plan of your paper will be. How you introduce your subject often determines how much confidence and belief your reader will have in your research. An introduction that makes the subject interesting, gives the reader an overview of the subject, and tells the reader how you are going to present your material will establish your credibility and give authority to your research.

To introduce your subject, you must first identify it, either directly or indirectly. Some questions you might ask yourself when preparing your introduction are

1. Why is my subject important?
2. What has been said about it?
3. What will I limit myself to?
4. How am I going to investigate it?

5. What hypothesis am I going to prove or set forth?

6. How might my subject change in the future?

It is often the practice of a writer to answer these questions in the introduction to his or her investigation. If you can answer them clearly and briefly in the opening paragraphs of your article, you will be able to write the rest of your investigation confident that you will be informing your reader in an interesting and persuasive way.

Writing Your Rough Draft.   After you have outlined your topic, arranged your notes in a meaningful order, and considered the information you wish to convey to your reader, you are ready to begin your first draft. Make sure that you have exact references for all the sources you wish to cite. If you wish to use direct quotations, be certain that you have copied down the precise words and punctuation of your source. Remember also to use transitions as you move from one section of your article to another.

It is not necessary to divide your paper into sections or "chapters." Because you are writing a relatively short paper, you will be able to write a continuous prose discourse, moving clearly and efficiently from one main idea to the next. You might find it convenient, however, to work on one main section of your paper at a time. Once you finish one section and before you begin the next, reread your entire essay to ensure the direction in which you wish to go: you may find you want to alter your course now that you have actually begun working out your ideas through writing.

Following is a student's rough draft of her research paper. As you read through the paper, you will want to determine whether the writer has used her sources effectively. There should be a smooth transition from the sources to the author's own writing. Paragraphs especially need smooth transitions from one major idea to another. Most important, the paragraphs should flow from the author's own mastery of her sources and information rather than being a string of notes pieced together to form pseudoparagraphs. No less than in the other tasks that you have completed, the voice in the research essay should emerge as coherent, authoritative, and interesting.

You might also want to determine the writer's beginning hypothesis and the extent to which her research supports it. What claims has she made as to the scientific validity of her approach?

NOT THE WEAKER SEX: A COMPARISON OF GIRLS AND BOYS

For many years "they" have said that little girls are brighter, faster, quicker, and/or smarter, than little boys. Old wives' tales have stated that little girls talk earlier and better than their brothers. Teachers I've spoken to in the lower grades seem to feel that boys don't do as well as girls in the early years of school. No young boys, and few men, will easily admit to this. Most males will dismiss the theory of female intellectual superiority at any stage as nothing but unsubstantiated hogwash. Sorry guys, but it seems that science is not on your side!

Studies have shown that girls begin to talk at an average age of eleven months, while boys do not start speech until they reach about thirteen months. In a study conducted at Our Lady of Victory Home in Lackawanna, New York, the results clearly pointed out this difference. At the age of 15 months, girls were ahead of boys in their verbal skills, and at the age of 27 months, surpassed the boys in social and personal skills. My own observances of children--my own and others--had already convinced me of this. Shortly after their second birthdays, my daughter and her friend were almost obsessed with keeping themselves neat and clean; both little girls could eat in a very civilized, adultlike manner. My sons and their friends at the same age, however, were quite content to live with greasy hands and sticky fingers and didn't care if they wore their meals on their shirts. I also noticed this at a later age, through my work as a Brownie and Cub Scout leader. After snack time was over, the girls, though a much larger group, required far less cleanup time than did the boys! The Brownies' conversation tended to be more adultlike, with a higher level of complexity and more variety of subject than that of the Cub Scouts. In both groups, the age range was seven to nine.

In a tape put out by the Christian Broadcasting Services, a possible explanation for this dramatic difference is discussed. Studies done by Dr. Donald Joy have led him to believe that these differences are inborn. According to him, as the brain develops in a fetus, both halves grow at the same rate. During the fourth month, those fetuses that are to be boys start producing testosterone, the male sex hormone. Testosterone somehow slows the growth rate of the left hemisphere of the brain. It is the left half of this marvelous organ that controls the main language and learning centers. During the miracle that causes the sexually neutral fetus to become a boy, the brain must suffer a bit--the left half remains slightly smaller than the right side, and the corpus callosum, the connecting wall between hemispheres, develops fewer electro-impulse areas to allow communication between halves. Joy also uses this argument to explain so-called female intuition. The corpus callosum, more well developed in females, allows for a much quicker recall and processing of information; women, therefore, often can make an accurate judgment or decision more quickly than men can. If questioned on how she arrived at her answer, however, the average woman would not be able to tell exactly how she reached it, but would be likely to say something like "I just knew."

The brain works across the body; that is, the left brain controls the right side of the body, and the right brain controls the left side. This fact does give some boys an even chance. Left-handed males tend to be "right brained"--the right side of their brains contain the centers normally found in the left side of right-handed males. There does not seem to be as great a difference between left-handed and right-handed females, which Dr. Joy attributes to the better developed female corpus callosum. Thus, left-handed males tend to be quick to begin speech and can be said to be brighter and more verbal than their right-handed brothers. We can see proof of this in that many of the world's greatest artists, such as Michelangelo, da Vinci, and van Gogh were left-handed, as were our own American heroes Thomas Jefferson and Ben Franklin. It makes no sense to me, then, that the word sinister--meaning wicked, evil, or dishonest--means left-handed in Latin; the lefties mentioned above were anything but evil!

In addition to causing the growth-rate change in the brain that Dr. Joy mentioned, the presence of the hormone testosterone also tends to make males more aggressive, while the presence of the female hormones produces a more passive individual. I think this, too, could be a stong factor in the intellectual differences.

Boys must channel or work off their aggressiveness, which can distract them from the learning tasks, while girls, with the more passive tendency, are able to concentrate on and master the tasks more easily.

The superiority does not last indefinitely. Although women do tend to retain the better linguistic verbal and intuitive power, men as well have areas in which they excel. When children reach the age in which math, science, and related fields are taught, boys almost always surpass girls. The gap widens even further at and beyond puberty.

Pediatrician Leonard T. Goslee, in an interview on May 3, 1985, told me that little girls have a much greater curiosity than that of little boys. A boy tends to take things pretty much at face value, but a girl will usually probe deeper, especially in more abstract areas. Where a boy might ask, "Why are leaves green?" a girl is more likely to add to that question "How does the tree know it's supposed to make the leaves green and the flowers red?" Dr. Goslee also told me that he has less trouble with little girls. "The boys fight. They don't want shots, they don't want an examination. It can be a real struggle to give a boy a physical, because if he's not willing to go along with it, he'll put up a good struggle. Girls cry. They may cling to mother, they may refuse, verbally, to follow my instructions, but they will go along with what they're told to do, and if I explain what I'm doing, they'll often get interested in the procedures. But they do cry more." Dr. Goslee also told me that boys are much more likely to come in for emergency treatment of cuts, bruises, broken bones, and the like. He feels that girls are more sensible. It isn't too common to find girls doing such things as jumping off roofs or climbing trees as it is to see boys doing these things, and even if a girl is a "tomboy," she'll still hold back and leave the big risks to the boys.

Most of the experts, then, concur. For the first dozen years or so, the average girls do outperform average boys in intellectual and social development. Although the age at which they finally become "even" is about six years beyond that which I first thought, I knew all along that little girls have a clear advantage.

Three teachers and a social worker I interviewed also backed up my theory. All four cautioned against absolutes--a group study may bear out my findings, but I must never forget that all children are individuals and many boys are competent in the traditional "girlish" areas, and vice versa.

The teachers, Mrs. Argis, Mrs. Cancienne, and Mrs. Denara, were all emphatic in their feelings that little girls were usually more mature and settled into school life more easily. They all think, as experience has shown them, that this tends to be so up until junior high. As stated before, they agree with me that girls excel in the language-related subjects. Both sexes are nearly equal in math and science until about halfway into second grade, then boys jump ahead and stay in front. Mrs. Argis told me that differences disappear as maturity and special interests develop and said "All children can excel in areas in which they have talent, inclination, and perhaps most important, encouragement."

Mrs. Denara and Mrs. Cancienne agreed wholeheartedly with that statement, as do I, but both still feel the female populations of their classroom outshine the male.

Dr. Frank Denara, social worker, feels that, while girls do speak earlier and are slightly more mature at kindergarten and first grade age, any differences from that point on are largely environmental. "In my casework, I have seen bright children ruined by uncaring, disinterested parents, and slower, even marginally retarded kids of both sexes lifted to great heights of accomplishment by parents who fully and unquestioningly believe in their offspring." Well said, Frank. I totally agree that the degree of parental support can make or break an education, but the facts speak for themselves. Nine out of ten speech pathology patients are boys, as are eighty-five percent of the children in need of remedial reading! Girls require much less remedial help than boys until sixth or seventh grade, and then it's almost always in math or sciences!

SOURCES

Argis, Joanne--1st grade, 213

Baby Talk, NOVA, PBS, Videotape Feb. 1985

Cancienne, Margaret--3rd grade, 213

Casler, Lawrence--Supplementary Auditory and Vestibular
    Stimulation and Effects on Institutionalized Children--Journal
    of Experimental Psych, Vol 19, 1975 pp. 181-194

Denara, Cathy--2nd grade, SS. Simon Jude, Blairsville

Denara, Frank J. PhD--Social Worker, Indiana Co, Penn,
    interview May 11, 1985

Goleman, Daniel, Introductory Psychology, second edition, NY,
    Random House, 1982

Goslee, LT-- pediatrician, May 9, 1985

Innate Differences Between Boys and Girls--Focus on the
    Family, Dr. James Dobson, host, Dr. Donald Joy, guest,
    Christian Broadcasting Network 1985

FOCUS ON FORM: DOCUMENTATION

Using the Citation Method

As the writer of an investigative essay, you must identify the sources of your information. In doing so, you will probably use the procedures for identifying sources adopted by either the Modern Language Association (MLA) for papers written in writing and literature courses, or the American Psychological Association (APA) for research papers in the social sciences. There are other forms of documentation for use in the biological and physical sciences (see below), which your instructor may wish you to observe. But for your purposes in writing the paper for this chapter's task, the MLA or APA conventions should be sufficient.

You should refer to the books and periodical articles cited in your paper by using "citations" and a list of works cited. A citation includes in parentheses in your text the author's name and the page number(s). The list of "Works Cited" or bibliography is placed at the end of the essay and includes the name of the source and publishing information. To identify the source referred to, the reader can glance quickly from author and page number to the list of works cited. Here is an example of the citation method:

According to Frank, a mother may not wish to accept the rhythms of her infant (160). A child's development, however, is likely to be shaped by a number of forces, all of them interacting in ways that intensify or reduce the effect of any one of them (Frank 161).

Works Cited

Frank, Lawrence K. <u>On</u> <u>the</u> <u>Importance</u> <u>of</u> <u>Infancy</u>. New York: Random House, 1966.

As this example illustrates, you can either work the author's name into your own sentence or include it in the parentheses. You might also say:

As Frank states, ... (160).
In Frank's view, ... (160).
Frank reports that, ... (160).
One investigator notes ... (Frank 160).

MLA and APA Styles of Documentation. In recent years, the trend has been to develop forms of documentation that are clear, coherent, and simple. In the interests of simplicity and efficiency, the MLA method seems preferable to the traditional method of documentation (see "Using Footnotes" on page 487) because it virtually eliminates the need for footnotes and places all the names and page references within the text, where they most logically belong. Your list of "Works Cited," arranged alphabetically, will show your readers all the sources that you referred to in your paper. With some practice, you will be able to work the authors' names into your text without undue repetition.

Like the MLA style, the APA uses citations within the text but also adds the year of publication. Page numbers, if required, are placed at the end of cited information.

According to Frank (1966), a mother may not wish to accept the rhythms of her infant (p. 160). A child's development, however, is likely to be shaped by a number of forces, all of them interacting in ways that intensify or reduce the effect of any one of them (Frank, 1966, p. 161).

Bibliographic information under the APA method is called "References" and is placed at the end of the paper. Note that authors' first names are replaced by initials, and the year of publication follows the author's name. Note also the absence of capital letters for words following the first word of a title.

Frank, L.K. (1966) On the importance of infancy. New York: Random House.

Specialized Science Research.   In your readings in scientific articles, you may have encountered a similar method of documentation. In specialized scientific research, it is common to place the author's name and the date of publication in parentheses: (Miller, 1980, p. 360). Because scientific research changes rapidly, the year of publication would be of great importance in an evaluation of the significance of a specific study. The reader turns from the text to a list of sources following the article to refer to the individual citation. If there is more than one work by an author referred to, the sources are listed by date of publication, starting with the oldest and ending with the most recent.

Before adopting any method of documentation, you will want to make sure that you have discussed with your instructor which form of citation is applicable to your assignment. The traditional or footnote method is discussed on pp. 487–489 and an example of its use can be found on pp. 497–503.

Using a Bibliography

A bibliography is an alphabetized list of works that you have used in preparing your paper. It is placed at the end of your text on a separate page. The bibliography may be synonymous with a list of works cited or your instructor may decide that you can include works that were consulted but that are not cited in your text. The bibliographic citation separates elements with periods and indents the second line. Some bibliographic entries that you are likely to use follow:

1. A book with more than one author:

Mason, Jim, and Peter Singer. Animal Factories. New York: Crown, 1980.

2. An edited book:

Sacks, Sheldon, ed. On Metaphor. Chicago: University of Chicago Press, 1979.

3. A work with a corporate author:

United States Environmental Protection Agency. Health
Effects of Air Pollutants. Washington, D.C.: GPO, 1976

4. An essay published in an edited collection of essays:

DeMan, Paul. "Intentional Structure of the Romantic
Image." Romanticism and Consciousness: Essays in
Criticism. Ed. Harold Bloom. New York: Norton, 1970.
65–77.

5. An article in a journal:

Branscomb, Lewis. "Taming Technology." Science 171 (12
March 1971): 963–975.

6. An article in a magazine:

Begley, S. "How the Brain Works." Newsweek 7 Feb 1983:
40–47.

7. An article in a newspaper:

Brody, Jane E. "Emotions Found to Influence Nearly Every
Human Ailment." New York Times 24 May 1983: C1.

8. Interview:

Denara, Frank. Personal interview. 11 May 1985.

Using Footnotes

Footnotes — or endnotes, as they are called if they appear on a separate page
at the end of the paper — are the traditional method of indicating to the reader
that you have borrowed from your sources to back up your statements. The
footnote or endnote includes the same information as the bibliographic entry

as well as the page or pages of the source from which the material was borrowed. Note, however, that, unlike the bibliographic entry, the first line in a footnote is indented and the elements are punctuated with commas. A footnote number appears twice: once in the text of your paper (where the citation also appears) and again at the bottom of the page of text or on the separate page for notes. Footnotes are numbered consecutively throughout the text. Here is a typical footnote for a book:

[1]David M. Rorvik, Your Baby's Sex: Now You Can Choose (New York: Dodd, Mead, 1970), p. 48.

You should give this information the first time you cite this book. If you refer to it again, you need only give a short note:

[2]Rorvik, p. 49.

For periodical articles, the following would be typical first and subsequent references:

[3]John Lorber, "Disposable Cortex," Psychology Today (Apr. 1981), p. 126.
[4]Lorber, p. 127.

Other sources that you use may require different styles of documentation. Here are some of the possible citations that you are likely to encounter:

1. A book with more than one author:

[1]Jim Mason and Peter Singer, Animal Factories (New York: Crown, 1980), p. 46.

2. A work without a specified author, often written by some corporate, governmental, or institutional agency:

[2]Health Effects of Air Pollutants, by the U.S. Environmental Protection Agency (Washington, D.C.: Government Printing Office, 1976), p.2.

3. A book made up of a variety of essays by a single author:

[3]Lewis Thomas, "The Iks," <u>The Lives of a Cell: Notes of a Biology Watcher</u> (New York: Viking Penguin, 1974), p. 60.

4. A book made up of a variety of essays by several authors:

[4]Donald Davidson, "What Metaphors Mean," <u>On Metaphor</u>, ed. Sheldon Sacks (Chicago: University of Chicago Press, 1979), p. 36.

5. An article in a periodical with continuous pagination:

[5]Lewis Branscomb, "Taming Technology," <u>Science</u> 171 (12 March 1971), 970.

6. An article in a newspaper:

[6]Jane E. Brody, "Emotions Found to Influence Nearly Every Human Ailment," <u>New York Times</u> (24 May 1983), Sec. C, p. 1.

7. An interview:

[7]Dr. George Adams, Assoc. Prof. of Anthropology, Danville College, Interview on 20 June 1983.

SOME PRACTICE WITH DOCUMENTATION

1. Write a bibliographic entry for a magazine article entitled "The Compleat Eclipse-Chaser" that appeared in *The Sciences* in the May–June 1983 issue, on pages 24–31. The author is Laurence A. Marschall.

2. Write a bibliographic entry for an article entitled "Nerve Cells That Double as Endocrine Cells," written by W. K. Samson and G. P. Kozlowski. It appeared in Volume 31 of *Science*, the June 1981 issue, on pages 445–448.

3. Write a bibliographic entry for an essay by Loren C. Eiseley named "Charles Darwin." It appeared on pages 283–293 in a collection of essays entitled *Modern American Prose: A Reader for Writers*. The book was edited by John Clifford and Robert Di Yanni and was published in New York by Random House in 1983.

4. Write a footnote for each bibliographic entry above.

5. Write subsequent footnotes for each of the above sources.

REWRITING

Obtaining Feedback on Your Rough Draft

By now, you are accustomed to getting direct responses to your work. Hopefully, you have grown more comfortable in accepting the comments of others, and they have learned to be more specific about their responses. You may find, however, that your audience's reaction to your research article will be somewhat ambivalent. On the one hand, they may be reluctant to criticize a project that has occupied so much of your time and concentrated effort. On the other hand, you may notice immediately by their reaction whether you have adapted your research materials to their understanding. If they're not quite sure about what level of comprehension you were aiming at, you might have to give your approach to your audience some more thought when you revise your first draft.

Below are the questions of the "Audience Response Guide" for your research essay.

AUDIENCE RESPONSE GUIDE

1. What hypothesis does the writer want to demonstrate in this paper? What is his/her purpose in writing?
2. How does this paper affect the lay reader for whom it was intended?
3. How effective has the writer been in developing her or his hypothesis? What are the strengths in the writer's use of research techniques? What are the weaknesses?
4. How should the paper be revised to reflect the comments made on the writer's stated hypothesis and use of research methods?

Here is a peer evaluation of the rough draft of "Not the Weaker Sex: A Comparison of Girls and Boys."

1. Her peer group agreed that her hypothesis was very clearly stated: She believed in the intellectual superiority of girls over boys in the early years of development. Her purpose was to explain her research to her reader.

2. While one member of the group wished he knew more about developmental psychology, the majority of the group believed the essay was written for a nontechnical audience. As one member commented, "When the vocabulary is somewhat technical, technical terms are explained."

3. The writer received good comments for her research and inclusion of life experiences--her children and their friends--from every member of the group. They felt she proved her hypothesis. Weaknesses include her reliance on interviews rather than on published studies. Several group members felt she should eliminate her slang.

4. The group felt she should support her research with additional examples from published studies; transitions should be inserted between formal research and personal experience; her language level should be balanced to eliminate slang, jargon, and unnecessary technical words; and her information about her sources should be arranged accurately.

Revision of Student Essay "Not the Weaker Sex: A Comparison of Girls and Boys"

What follows is the final draft of the student's research paper, "Not the Weaker Sex: A Comparison of Girls and Boys." In this final draft, the student has added citations in the text wherever she felt that it was necessary to document the sources of her information. She also has added a bibliography ("Works Cited") at the end of her paper.

Compare the rough draft of the student's research paper on pages 479–484 to the revised paper that follows. You might also want to review the peer group evaluation above, as well as your own response, before doing so.

Following her revised essay, which uses the citation method of documentation, we have reprinted the essay, this time using the traditional footnote method, in order to present examples of both methods of documentation.

Citation Method

NOT THE WEAKER SEX: A COMPARISON OF GIRLS AND BOYS

For many years, it has been widely accepted that little girls are brighter, faster, quicker, and/or smarter than little boys. Old wives' tales have long stated that little girls talk earlier and better than their brothers. Primary-grade teachers I have spoken to seem to agree that boys do lag behind girls in the early years of schooling. No young boys, and few men, will easily admit this, preferring instead to dismiss these ideas as unsubstantiated rumor. As painful as it may be for these males to accept, my experience clearly shows that, until the third grade, girls have a definite advantage over little boys.

Studies of normal children have shown that girls begin to talk at an average age of eleven months while boys generally do not start speaking until two or four months later (Casler 460). Even when children reach the age of three or four, when language is well established, girls' speech is more complex and more easily understandable. In a study taken at Our Lady of Victory Home in Lackawanna, New York, the results clearly point out this difference. At the age of fifteen months, girls were ahead of the boys in verbal skills, and, at twenty-seven months, surpassed the boys in social and personal skills as well (Casler 460-461).

My personal observations of children--my own and others--had already convinced me of this. Shortly after their second birthdays, my daughter and her friend were almost obsessed with keeping themselves neat and clean. Both little girls could eat in a very civilized and adult-like manner, and their play involved detailed, coherent conversation. My sons and their friends at approximately the same age were quite content to live with greasy hands and sticky faces, and did not care if they wore half their meals on their shirts. In their play, there was much less real conversation and more pure noise, such as airplane and motor sounds.

I even found this superior development later, through my work as a Brownie and Cub Scout leader. After snack time, the girls, though a much larger group, required far less clean-up time than did the boys. The Brownies' conversations tended to be more grown up, with higher levels of complexity on a wider variety of subjects than those of the Cub Scouts. And though quite common with the boys, there was never a food fight among the girls! In both groups, the age range was six and a half through eight.

Studies done by Dr. Donald Joy have led him to believe that these differences are inborn. According to Dr. Joy, in the early stages of fetal development, both halves of the brain grow at the same rate. During the fourth month, the male fetus starts producing testosterone, the male sex hormone. Testosterone slows the growth of the left hemisphere of the brain, the side that houses the main learning and language centers. During the miracle that causes the sexually neutral fetus to become obviously male, the brain suffers a bit; in addition to the left half remaining slightly smaller than the right, the corpus callosum, the connecting wall between brain halves, develops fewer electro impulse areas. These areas enable impulses to travel across the brain, thus allowing the signals to be transformed into useful information (Joy).

Dr. Joy refers to this as a form of "brain damage," but I think that is much too harsh a term; a better word would be "different." Joy also uses his findings to explain female intuition. Due to the absence of large amounts of the growth-inhibiting testosterone, the corpus callosum is more highly developed in females, allowing for a much more rapid recall and processing of information. This makes females able to reach often accurate judgments faster than most males. Because the process involves virtually no conscious thought processes, if questioned about how she arrived at her answer, the average female would not be able to tell, but would be likely to say something like, "I just knew" (Joy).

The brain works across the body; that is, the left brain controls the right side of the body, and the right brain governs the left. This fact gives some males an even start. Left-handed males tend to be right brained. The right sides of their brains contain the centers normally found in the left brains of right-handed males. Therefore, the linguistic information does not have to shift from one side to the other in order to be used. (There is not such a difference in left-handed females, which Dr. Joy attributes to the better developed corpus callosum.) Left-handed males tend to speak earlier and can often be said to be brighter, more creative and more verbal than their right-handed brothers (Joy). We can see proof of this in that many of the world's greatest artists, such as Michelangelo, DaVinci, Van Gogh, and Picasso, were left-handed, as were at least two of our American heroes, Thomas Jefferson and Ben Franklin.

In addition to the growth-rate change Dr. Joy mentioned, the presence of testosterone also tends to make males more aggressive, while the female hormones help to produce a more passive individual (Goleman 530). Boys must work off some of this aggressiveness, which can distract them from the learning task. Girls, with the more passive tendency, are better able to concentrate on and master the task more easily (Goleman 530).

Pediatrician Leonard Goslee, whom I interviewed on this subject, also finds a difference in how children learn. Since his patients are from a wide range of social and economic groups, I asked if there were any major influences due to class differences. He told me that learning cuts through social classes, given that the family lifestyles are normal (i.e., no alcoholic or abusive parents). Little girls, he says, generally have a deeper curiosity.

A boy may ask, "Why are the leaves green?" but a girl is likely to add to that question, "How does the tree know it's supposed to make the leaves green and the flowers red?" Girls tend to make easier patients. Though they may cry more and cling to their mothers, they are more easily convinced to submit to an exam than boys are. Girls are more pliable. Boys are much more likely to need a doctor's care for emergency treatment of broken bones, cuts, and bruises. Girls are much more cautious. It is not as common to find girls doing such things as jumping off a roof or climbing the high branches of a tree. Even if a girl is a tomboy, she is still likely to hold back and leave the really big risks to the boys (Goslee).

Dr. Joy also noted that girls are more cautious and calls them "more sensible."

I interviewed three teachers--Joanne Argis, Margaret Cancienne, and Cathy Denara--who backed up my findings, though all three cautioned against absolutes. "Though a group study may bear out a theory, you must never forget that all children are individuals, and many boys are competent in the 'feminine' areas, and vice-versa" (Argis). Harold Stevenson confirms this by concluding that what and how much a child can learn depends largely on his or her maturity or reason to learn. There are very marked differences among normal children as to limits of educability (Stevenson 347-350).

Mrs. Argis, Mrs. Cancienne, and Mrs. Denara were all emphatic in their feelings that little girls are usually more mature and are able to settle into school life more easily than boys. Experience has shown them that this tends to be so up until junior high school age. "Some differences, however, disappear as maturity and special interests develop, and all children can excel in areas in which they have talent, and, perhaps most important, encouragement" (Argis). When I spoke to Mrs. Denara, I mentioned that I was somewhat concerned that she may have different observations because she teaches at a rural school. I was reassured, however, when I realized that many of the textbooks her students use are the same ones my children have used in the New York City school system. "City kids, country kids, they're the same. The little girls are still more mature and more sociable than the boys" (C. Denara).

Social worker Frank Denara thinks that, while girls do speak earlier and are slightly more mature than boys at kindergarten age, any differences from that point on are largely environmental. "In my casework, I have seen bright children ruined by uncaring, disinterested parents, and slower, even marginally retarded kids of both sexes lifted to great heights of accomplishment by parents who fully and unquestioningly believe in their offspring" (F. Denara).

While I certainly agree with Dr. Denara's statement, I still believe that girls start out with an advantage. The superiority does not last indefinitely. Although women do retain an edge linguistically and intuitively, males have special areas in which they, too, excel. When children reach the age at which math and sciences are taught, around third grade, boys begin to surpass the girls. The gap widens steadily up to and beyond puberty ("Baby Talk"). Although girls require far less remedial work than boys do, at least until sixth or seventh grade, when girls do need help, it is almost always in math or science (Joy). Before sixth grade, boys make up the majority of those students needing special help. Nine out of ten speech pathology patients are boys, as are nearly eighty-five percent of the children in remedial reading classes ("Baby Talk").

Most of the experts agree, then, that girls do start out in life with a firm advantage over boys. They are ahead socially and intellectually before they start their formal education, as I had long suspected. I was surprised to find, however, that boys and girls never seem to become scholastically equal. I thought that, by third or fourth grade, any intellectual differences would be purely individual, but my research showed me this is not so. All the way up the educational ladder throughout junior high, there are specific areas in which one sex tends to dominate the other. The "battle of the sexes" rages on!

Works Cited

Argis, Joanne. Personal interview. 11 May 1985.
"Baby Talk." Nova, PBS. WNET, New York. 11 Feb 1985.

Cancienne, Margaret. Personal interview. 13 May 1985.

Casler, Lawrence. "Supplementary Auditory and Vestibular
  Stimulation and Its Effects on Institutionalized Children."
  Journal of Experimental Psychology 19 (1975): 456–463.

Denara, Cathy. Personal interview. 11 May 1985.

Goleman, Daniel, Trygg Engen, and Anthony Davids.
  Introductory Psychology. New York: Random House, 1982.

Goslee, Leonard, M.D. Personal interview. 9 May 1985.

Joy, Donald. "Innate Differences Between Boys and Girls." Focus
  on the Family. Christian Broadcasting Services. 6 Apr 1983.

Stevenson, Harold W. Children Learning. New York: Appleton-
  Century-Crofts, 1972.

Endnotes Method

NOT THE WEAKER SEX: A COMPARISON OF GIRLS AND BOYS

For many years, it has been widely accepted that little girls
are brighter, faster, quicker, and/or smarter than little boys. Old
wives' tales have long stated that little girls talk earlier and better than their brothers. Primary-grade teachers I have spoken to
seem to agree that boys do lag behind girls in the early years of
schooling. No young boys, and few men, will easily admit this,
preferring instead to dismiss the ideas as unsubstantiated rumor.
As painful as it may be for these males to accept, my experience
clearly shows that, until the third grade, girls have a definite
advantage over little boys.

Studies of normal children have shown that girls begin to talk
at an average age of eleven months while boys generally do not
start speaking until two to four months later.[1] Even when children
reach the age of three or four, when language is well established,
girls' speech is more complex and more easily understandable. In
a study taken at Our Lady of Victory Home in Lackawanna, New
York, the results clearly point out this difference. At the age of
fifteen months, girls were ahead of the boys in verbal skills, and,

at twenty-seven months, surpassed the boys in social and personal skills as well.[2]

My personal observations of children--my own and others--had already convinced me of this. Shortly after their second birthdays, my daughter and her friend were almost obsessed with keeping themselves neat and clean. Both little girls could eat in a very civilized and adult-like manner, and their play involved detailed, coherent conversation. My sons and their friends at approximately the same age were quite content to live with greasy hands and sticky faces, and did not care if they wore half their meals on their shirts. In their play, there was much less real conversation and more pure noise, such as airplane and motor sounds.

I even found this superior development later, through my work as a Brownie and Cub Scout leader. After snack time, the girls, though a much larger group, required far less clean-up time than did the boys. The Brownies' conversations tended to be more grown up, with higher levels of complexity on a wider variety of subjects than those of the Cub Scouts. And though quite common with the boys, there was never a food fight among the girls! In both groups, the age range was six and a half through eight.

Studies done by Dr. Donald Joy have led him to believe that these differences are inborn. According to Dr. Joy, in the early stages of fetal development, both halves of the brain grow at the same rate. During the fourth month, the male fetus starts producing testosterone, the male sex hormone. Testosterone slows the growth of the left hemisphere of the brain, the side that houses the main learning and language centers. During the miracle that causes the sexually neutral fetus to become obviously male, the brain suffers a bit; in addition to the left half remaining slightly smaller than the right, the corpus callosum, the connecting wall between brain halves, develops fewer electro impulse areas. These areas enable impulses to travel across the brain, thus allowing the signals to be transformed into useful information.[3]

Dr. Joy refers to this as a form of "brain damage," but I think that is much too harsh a term; a better word would be "different." Joy also uses his findings to explain female intuition. Due to the absence of large amounts of the growth-inhibiting testosterone, the corpus callosum is more highly developed in females, allowing for a much more rapid recall and processing of information. This makes females able to reach often accurate judgments faster than most males. Because the process involves virtually no conscious thought processes, if questioned about how she arrived at her answer, the average female would not be able to tell, but would be likely to say something like, "I just knew."[4]

The brain works across the body; that is, the left brain controls the right side of the body, and the right brain governs the left. This fact gives some males an even start. Left-handed males tend to be right brained. The right sides of their brains contain the centers normally found in the left brains of right-handed males. Therefore, the linguistic information does not have to shift from one side to the other in order to be used. (There is not such a difference in left-handed females, which Dr. Joy attributes to the better developed corpus callosum.) Left-handed males tend to speak earlier and can often be said to be brighter, more creative and more verbal than their right-handed brothers.[5] We can see proof of this in that many of the world's greatest artists, such as Michelangelo, DaVinci, Van Gogh, and Picasso, were left handed, as were at least two of our American heroes, Thomas Jefferson and Ben Franklin.

In addition to the growth-rate change Dr. Joy mentioned, the presence of testosterone also tends to make males more aggressive, while the female hormones help to produce a more passive individual.[6] Boys must work off some of this aggressiveness, which can distract them from the learning task. Girls, with the more passive tendency, are better able to concentrate on and master the task more easily.[7]

Pediatrician Leonard Goslee, whom I interviewed on this subject, also finds a difference in how children learn. Since his patients are from a wide range of social and economic groups, I asked if there were any major influences due to class differences.

He told me that learning cuts through social classes, given that the family lifestyles are normal (i.e., no alcoholic or abusive parents). Little girls, he says, generally have a deeper curiosity.

A boy may ask, "Why are the leaves green?" but a girl is likely to add to that question, "How does the tree know it's supposed to make the leaves green and the flowers red?" Girls tend to make easier patients. Though they may cry more and cling to their mothers, they are more easily convinced to submit to an exam than boys are. Girls are more pliable. Boys are much more likely to need a doctor's care for emergency treatment of broken bones, cuts and bruises. Girls are much more cautious. It is not as common to find girls doing such things as jumping off a roof or climbing the high branches of a tree. Even if a girl is a tomboy, she is still likely to hold back and leave the really big risks to the boys.[8]

Dr. Joy also noted that girls are more cautious and calls them "more sensible."

I interviewed three teachers--Joanne Argis, Margaret Cancienne, and Cathy Denara--who backed up my findings, though all three cautioned against absolutes. "Though a group study may bear out a theory, you must never forget that all children are individuals, and many boys are competent in the 'feminine' areas, and vice-versa."[9] Harold Stevenson confirms this by concluding that what and how much a child can learn depends largely on his or her maturity or reason to learn. There are very marked differences among normal children as to limits of educability.[10]

Mrs. Argis, Mrs. Cancienne, and Mrs. Denara were all emphatic in their feelings that little girls are usually more mature and are able to settle into school life more easily than boys. Experience has shown them that this tends to be so up until junior high school age. "Some differences, however, disappear as maturity and special interests develop, and all children can excel in areas in which they have talent, and, perhaps most important, encouragement."[11] When I spoke to Mrs. Denara, I mentioned that I was somewhat concerned that she may have different observations because she teaches at a rural school. I was reassured, however, when I realized that many of the textbooks her students use are the same ones my children have used in the New York City school system. "City kids, country kids, they're the same. The little girls are still more mature and more sociable than the boys."[12]

Social worker Frank Denara thinks that, while girls do speak earlier and are slightly more mature than boys at kindergarten age, any differences from that point on are largely environmental. "In my casework, I have seen bright children ruined by uncaring, disinterested parents, and slower, even marginally retarded kids of both sexes lifted to great heights of accomplishment by parents who fully and unquestioningly believe in their offspring."[13]

While I certainly agree with Dr. Denara's statement, I still believe that girls start out with an advantage. The superiority does not last indefinitely. Although women do retain an edge linguistically and intuitively, males have special areas in which they, too, excel. When children reach the age at which math and sciences are taught, around third grade, boys begin to surpass the girls. The gap widens steadily up to and beyond puberty.[14] Although girls require far less remedial work than boys do, at least until sixth or seventh grade, when they do need help, it is almost always in math or science.[15] Before sixth grade, boys make up the majority of those students needing special help. Nine out of ten speech pathology patients are boys, as are nearly eighty-five percent of the children in remedial reading classes.[16]

Most of the experts agree, then, that girls do start out in life with a firm advantage over boys. They are ahead socially and intellectually before they start their formal education, as I had long suspected. I was surprised to find, however, that boys and girls never seem to become scholastically equal. I thought that, by third or fourth grade, any intellectual differences would be purely individual, but my research showed me this is not so. All the way up the educational ladder throughout junior high, there are specific areas in which one sex tends to dominate the other. The "battle of the sexes" rages on!

End Notes

[1]Lawrence Casler, "Supplementary Auditory and Vestibular Stimulation and Its Effects on Instiutionalized Children," Journal of Experimental Psychology, 19 (1975), 460.

[2]Casler, pp. 460-461.

[3]Donald Joy, "Innate Differences Between Boys and Girls," Focus on the Family, James Dobson, host. Christian Broadcasting Services, 1983.

[4]Joy.

[5]Joy.

[6]Daniel Goleman, Trygg Engen, and Anthony Davids. Introductory Psychology (New York: Random House, 1982), p. 530.

[7]Goleman, p. 530.

[8]Leonard Goslee, M.D., Pediatrician, Interview on 9 May 1985.

[9]Joanne Argis, First grade teacher, P.S. 213, Queens, New York. Interview on 11 May 1985.

[10]Stevenson, Harold W. Children Learning (New York: Appleton-Century-Crofts, 1972), pp. 347-350.

[11]Argis.

[12]Cathy Denara, Second grade teacher, SS. Simon and Jude Elementary School, Blairsville, Pennsylvania, Interview on 11 May 1985.

[13]Denara, Frank, Social worker, Indiana County, Pennsylvania, Interview on 11 May 1985.

[14]"Baby Talk," Nova, Public Broadcasting Service, February 1985.

[15]Joy.

[16]"Baby Talk."

Bibliography

Argis, Joanne. First grade teacher, P.S. 213, Queens, New York. Interview on 11 May 1985.

"Baby Talk." Nova, Public Broadcasting Service. February 1985.

Cancienne, Margaret. Third grade teacher, P.S. 213, New York.
    Interview 13 May 1985.

Casler, Lawrence. "Supplementary Auditory and Vestibular
    Stimulation and Its Effects on Institutionalized Children."
    Journal of Experimental Psychology, 19 (1975), 456-463.

Denara, Cathy. Second grade teacher, SS. Simon and Jude
    Elementary School, Blairsville, Pennsylvania. Interview on 11
    May 1985.

Denara, Frank. Social worker, Indiana County, Pennsylvania.
    Interview on 11 May 1985.

Goleman, Daniel, Trygg Engen, and Anthony Davids.
    Introductory Psychology. New York: Random House, 1982.

Goslee, Leonard. M.D. Pediatrician. Interview on 9 May 1985.

Joy, Donald. "Innate Differences Between Boys and Girls." Focus
    on the Family, James Dobson, host, Christian Broadcasting
    Services, 6 April 1983.

Stevenson, Harold W. Children Learning. New York: Appleton-
    Century-Crofts, 1972.

Checklist for Revising Your Scientific Essay

1. **Did you accomplish all the purposes you set out at the beginning of your paper?**
2. **Did you provide sufficient information to demonstrate your hypothesis?**
3. **Have you created a smooth, orderly arrangement of your material?**
4. **Have you carefully and accurately documented all the information you obtained from your sources?**
5. **Does your conclusion offer your reader a broader perspective or something further to consider about the subject of your paper?**
6. **Do you feel you have provided your reader with a really interesting insight into your topic and not just a boring chain of facts?**

Revising and Editing

Revising. As a writer of expository prose who is researching a scientific subject, you will want to be as objective and impartial as possible. In order to help you emphasize your objectivity, we ask questions below that you might apply to your scientific paper. These questions are based on the revising strategies discussed in this section in previous chapters—cutting (Ch. 2), adding (Ch. 3), substituting (Ch. 4), distributing (Ch. 5), rearranging (Ch. 6), and consolidating (Ch. 7).

1. **Cutting.** Have you digested your research material thoroughly, or, on closer scrutiny, have you either repeated points or included points that do not apply? If so, you will want to cut this material from your paper.

2. **Adding.** Have you included all the research on the subject that can affect your decision about your hypothesis? Have you included all the supporting research for your conclusion about your subject? A reexamination of your sources may indicate that you have material that should be added.

3. **Substituting.** If you have cut questionable points and replaced them with new ones, then you have already engaged in substituting. In addition, you may want to ask yourself if any of the sources you cited are questionable. For example, have you relied too heavily on popular sources or on outdated material? Rather than weaken your presentation by cutting too much supporting evidence, you may want to substitute more reputable or current scholarship.

4. **Distributing.** Have you constantly referred to your hypothesis or have you left it up to your reader to remember what it is? If the latter is true, you may want to distribute mention of it throughout your essay as a way of keeping your purpose clearly focussed for your reader.

5. **Rearranging.** Do your major subdivisions present the material in the most useful order for your reader? Do you present background material first, followed by aspects of the research? Should these aspects be arranged in chronological order or in some other order such as those suggested in Chapter 5 (cause and effect, comparison and contrast, or process analysis)? If you cannot discern any logic to your organization, you may want to rearrange your points so that an order is apparent.

6. **Consolidating.** Does your essay seem scattered because aspects of your major points reappear throughout? If so, gather them together and present them in one section. Have you made your points as forcefully as you would like? If not, it may be that you have not given sufficient information to establish their significance. If this information is elsewhere in your essay, consolidate it around your point for greater emphasis.

Editing. In writing on a scientific subject, you will want your language to be as clear and concrete as possible. You will want to define all technical terminology for your reader and for yourself as well to insure that you use all scientific terms accurately. You might also review the "Focus" section on "Style" in Chapter 7 for other suggestions about how to make your style concrete, such as the use of verbal sentences.

You will also want your language to be appropriate for your subject. You will want to avoid slang on the one hand because it is too informal for your subject and figurative language on the other because figures of speech do not meet the criteria of clarity and concreteness discussed above. You will probably want to avoid humor also because it may detract from your goal of impartiality. You may also want to write in the third person pronoun, rather than the first, in order to further convince your reader of your objectivity.

BECOMING AWARE OF YOURSELF AS A WRITER

1. How efficient were your methods of investigation in writing the research paper? What was the most helpful method you used?

2. Were you able to use your knowledge of other academic subjects to provide you with material for your paper? If so, how were you able to adapt this knowledge for your audience?

3. Was it difficult obtaining information on your topic? What could you have done to find more material?

4. How skillfully were you able to analyze and interpret the usefulness or validity of your sources? Did you encounter any contradictory information in your sources? If so, how did you decide what to accept or reject?

5. How did you convert your source material into your own words? Were there any rough spots that you found particularly difficult to work on? How would you account for them? How did you solve the problems they created?

6. If you are assigned an investigative paper in the future, might you pursue your research any differently? How might you proceed?

7. How does writing for an audience affect the preparation of an investigative paper? What adjustments did you make?

8. Do you see the writing of an investigative paper as mainly an exercise in acquiring factual information, or are there other skills to be learned? What are those skills? How do you think you can use these skills in other writing that you do?

9. What did the author of the student essay do to avoid making her paper an exercise in "sterile fact gathering"? Would her technique work for you?

11

Writing About a Short Story—Interpreting a Text

PURPOSE

The author John Steinbeck once wrote that the purpose of a book is "to amuse, interest, instruct but its warmer purpose is just to associate with the reader . . . . . The circle is not closed until the trinity is present—the writer, the book, and his reader."

Notice how his "trinity" is a variation of the communications triangle, including the writer and the reader but substituting the *book* for the *subject*:

COMMUNICATIONS TRIANGLE   STEINBECK'S TRINITY

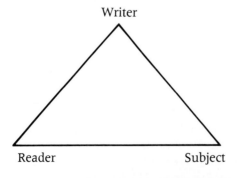

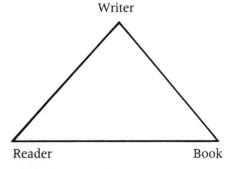

Although Steinbeck was referring specifically to novels, his words point out an essential similarity between literary texts in general and other kinds of writing: like the essays you have been writing this term, a short story or a novel, a poem or a play is incomplete until a reader makes it his/her own.

But Steinbeck's substitution of *book* for *subject* also suggests an essential difference between literary and other types of writing. While your purpose in writing one or another type of essay has been primarily to communicate with a reader about a subject, the primary purpose of a story teller or a poet may well be to close the circle, to intensify the sense of association between writer and reader through their shared experience of the written word. Whatever the subject matter of a story or poem or play, what draws the writer and reader together is the story or poem or play itself.

One reason for writing about literature is to participate more actively in this "warmer" association. The quotation from John Steinbeck comes from a letter the author wrote to a student, after the student sent Steinbeck a paper he had written on Steinbeck's novel *Grapes of Wrath*. You probably will not close the circle with an author this directly. But you might broaden the circle by sharing your understanding of a *book* with other readers and so building a sense of community between the writer, the book and many readers.

There are other reasons for writing about literature. Scholars write about literary texts in order to explore the insights they offer into the history, the culture, the values of the people who produced them. Critics write in order to inform readers of new developments in literature and to measure these developments against the literature of the past. Students are often asked to write about literary texts, perhaps because such writing helps them develop into more active readers of all kinds of texts, both literary and nonliterary.

When you read as well as when you write, you compose meaning out of your perceptions and knowledge of the world around you. Writing about literature is a particularly good way of fine tuning this skill because literary texts have no overt point to make, no stated thesis to explain, no explicit argument to develop. Because stories are told and poems are sung, in this sense, for their own sake, such writing invites—indeed requires—a reader's interpretation more obviously than expository prose. When you summarize the thesis of an essay, you clarify the essay's meaning. But a summary of a short story is only a retelling of the story's plot—what the story means, finally, depends on the reader's point of view and the judgments it leads him/her to make about the story.

For this chapter's task then, we will ask you to explore the meaning that a story holds for you, in order to share your understanding of the story with others who have read it.

TASK: INTERPRETING A SHORT STORY

Your task for this chapter is to write an essay in which you explore the meaning or significance that a short story holds for you and explain how and why you arrived at your understanding of the story. You will need to find ways to generate your own ideas about the story: free writing in your journal about your initial responses to the story may help, or posing and answering questions about the story, or brainstorming on your own or with your peer group. You will also need to collect and offer evidence of details of the story—such elements as plot, character, point of view—that support your interpretation.

Your audience is other readers of the story whose understanding might be enhanced by your interpretation. They are informed readers in the sense that they too have read the story: they know what happens in it. But their perspective on what happens may differ from yours, and you will need to find ways to bridge such differences.

In the next section, we include two short stories for you to read—"Gooseberries," by Anton Chekhov, and "The Lesson," by Toni Cade Bambara. (Your instructor or your group may decide to have you focus on one story or both, or on a different or additional story.) Following are sections on different ways a reader might respond to a story; different perspectives a reader might bring to a story; and ways of arranging, writing, and revising an essay about a story.

Reading to Write

Gooseberries

by Anton Chekhov

The sky had been overcast since early morning; it was a still day, not hot, but tedious, as it usually is when the weather is gray and dull, when clouds have been hanging over the fields for a long time, and you wait for the rain that does not come. Ivan Ivanych, a veterinary, and Burkin, a high school teacher, were already tired with walking, and the plain seemed endless to them. Far ahead were the scarcely visible windmills of the village of Mironositzkoe; to the right lay a range of hills that disappeared in the distance beyond the village, and both of them knew that over there were the river, and fields, green willows, homesteads, and if you stood on one of the hills, you could see from there another vast plain, telegraph poles, and a train that from afar looked like a caterpillar crawling, and in clear weather you could even see the town. Now, when it was still and when nature seemed mild and pensive, Ivan Ivanych and Burkin were filled with love for this plain, and both of them thought what a beautiful land it was.

"Last time when we were in Elder Prokofy's barn," said Burkin, "you were going to tell me a story."

"Yes; I wanted to tell you about my brother."

Ivan Ivanych heaved a slow sigh and lit his pipe before beginning his story, but just then it began to rain. And five minutes later there was a downpour, and it was hard to tell when it would be over. The two men halted, at a loss; the dogs, already wet, stood with their tails between their legs and looked at them feelingly.

"We must find shelter somewhere," said Burkin. "Let's go to Alyohin's; it's quite near."

"Let's."

They turned aside and walked across a mown meadow, now going straight ahead, now bearing to the right, until they reached the road. Soon poplars came into view, a garden, then the red roofs of barns; the river gleamed, and the view opened on a broad expanse of water with a mill and a white bathing-cabin. That was Sofyino, Alyohin's place.

The mill was going, drowning out the sound of the rain; the dam was shaking. Wet horses stood near the carts, their heads drooping, and men were walking about, their heads covered with sacks. It was damp, muddy, dreary; and the water looked cold and unkind. Ivan Ivanych and Burkin felt cold and messy and uncomfortable through and through; their feet were heavy with mud and when, having crossed the dam, they climbed up to the barns, they were silent as though they were cross with each other.

The noise of a winnowing-machine came from one of the barns, the door was open, and clouds of dust were pouring from within. On the threshold stood Alyohin himself, a man of forty, tall and rotund, with long hair, looking more like a professor or an artist than a gentleman farmer. He was wearing a white blouse, badly in need of washing, that was belted with a rope, and drawers, and his high boots were plastered with mud and straw. His eyes and nose were black with dust. He recognized Ivan Ivanych and Burkin and was apparently very glad to see them.

"Please go up to the house, gentlemen," he said, smiling; "I'll be there directly, in a moment."

It was a large structure of two stories. Alyohin lived downstairs in what was formerly the stewards' quarters: two rooms that had arched ceilings and small windows; the furniture was plain, and the place smelled of rye bread, cheap vodka, and harness. He went into the showy rooms upstairs only rarely, when he had guests. Once in the house, the two visitors were met by a chambermaid, a young woman so beautiful that both of them stood still at the same moment and glanced at each other.

"You can't imagine how glad I am to see you, gentlemen," said Alyohin, joining them in the hall. "What a surprise! Pelageya," he said, turning to the chambermaid, "give the guests a change of clothes. And, come to think of it, I will change, too. But I must go and bathe first, I don't think I've had a wash since spring. Don't you want to go into the bathing-cabin? In the meanwhile things will be got ready here."

The beautiful Pelageya, with her soft, delicate air, brought them bath towels and soap, and Alyohin went to the bathing-cabin with his guests.

"Yes, it's a long time since I've bathed," he said, as he undressed. "I've an excellent bathing-cabin, as you see—it was put up by my father—but somehow I never find time to use it." He sat down on the steps and lathered his long hair and neck, and the water around him turned brown.

"I say—" observed Ivan Ivanych significantly, looking at his head.

"I haven't had a good wash for a long time," repeated Alyohin, embarrassed, and soaped himself once more; the water about him turned dark-blue, the color of ink.

Ivan Ivanych came out of the cabin, plunged into the water with a splash and swam in the rain, thrusting his arms out wide; he raised waves on which white lilies swayed. He swam out to the middle of the river and dived and a minute later came up in another spot and swam on and kept diving, trying to touch bottom. "By God!" he kept repeating delightedly, "by God!" He swam to the mill, spoke to the peasants there, and turned back and in the middle of the river lay floating, exposing his face to the rain. Burkin and Alyohin were already dressed and ready to leave, but he kept on swimming and diving. "By God!" he kept exclaiming. "Lord, have mercy on me."

"You've had enough!" Burkin shouted to him.

They returned to the house. And only when the lamp was lit in the big drawing room upstairs, and the two guests, in silk dressing-gowns and warm slippers, were lounging in armchairs, and Alyohin himself, washed and combed, wearing a new jacket, was walking about the room, evidently savoring the warmth, the cleanliness, the dry clothes and light footwear, and when pretty Pelageya, stepping noiselessly across the carpet and smiling softly, brought in a tray with tea and jam, only then did Ivan Ivanych begin his story, and it was as though not only Burkin and Alyohin were listening, but also the ladies, old and young, and the military men who looked down upon them, calmly and severely, from their gold frames.

"We are two brothers," he began, "I, Ivan Ivanych, and my brother, Nikolay Invanych, who is two years my junior. I went in for a learned profession and became a veterinary; Nikolay at nineteen began to clerk in a provincial branch of the Treasury. Our father was a *kantonist,*[1] but he rose to be an officer and so a nobleman, a rank that he bequeathed to us together with a small estate. After his death there was a lawsuit and we lost the estate to creditors, but be that as it may, we spent our childhood in the country. Just like peasant children we passed days and nights in the fields and the woods, herded horses, stripped bast from the trees, fished, and so on. And, you know, whoever even once in his life has caught a perch or seen thrushes migrate in the autumn, when on clear, cool days they sweep in flocks over the village, will never really be a townsman and to the day of his death will have a longing for the open. My brother was unhappy in the government office. Years passed, but he went on warming the same seat, scratching away at the same papers, and thinking of one and the same thing: how to get away to the country. And little by little this vague longing turned into a definite desire, into a dream of buying a little property somewhere on the banks of a river or a lake.

"He was a kind and gentle soul and I loved him, but I never sympathized

---

[1] *kantonist:* the son of a private, registered at birth in the army and trained in a military school.

with his desire to shut himself up for the rest of his life on a little property of his own. It is a common saying that a man needs only six feet of earth. But six feet is what a corpse needs, not a man. It is also asserted that if our educated class is drawn to the land and seeks to settle on farms, that's a good thing. But these farms amount to the same six feet of earth. To retire from the city, from the struggle, from the hubbub, to go off and hide on one's own farm — that's not life, it's selfishness, sloth, it is a kind of monasticism, but monasticism without works. Man needs not six feet of earth, not a farm, but the whole globe, all of Nature, where unhindered he can display all the capacities and peculiarities of his free spirit.

"My brother Nikolay, sitting in his office, dreamed of eating his own *shchi*,[2] which would fill the whole farmyard with a delicious aroma, of picnicking on the green grass, of sleeping in the sun, of sitting for hours on the seat by the gate gazing at field and forest. Books on agriculture and the farming items in almanacs were his joy, the delight of his soul. He liked newspapers too, but the only things he read in them were advertisements of land for sale, so many acres of tillable land and pasture, with house, garden, river, mill, and millpond. And he pictured to himself garden paths, flowers, fruit, bird-houses with starlings in them, crucians[3] in the pond, and all that sort of thing, you know. These imaginary pictures varied with the advertisements he came upon, but somehow gooseberry bushes figured in every one of them. He could not picture to himself a single country-house, a single rustic nook, without gooseberries.

"'Country life has its advantages,' he used to say. 'You sit on the veranda having tea, and your ducks swim in the pond, and everything smells delicious and — the gooseberries are ripening.'

"He would draw a plan of his estate and invariably it would contain the following features: a) the master's house; b) servants' quarters; c) kitchen-garden; d) a gooseberry patch. He lived meagerly: he deprived himself of food and drink; he dressed God knows how, like a beggar, but he kept on saving and salting money away in the bank. He was terribly stingy. It was painful for me to see it, and I used to give him small sums and send him something on holidays, but he would put that away too. Once a man is possessed by an idea, there is no doing anything with him.

"Years passed. He was transferred to another province, he was already past forty, yet he was still reading newspaper advertisements and saving up money. Then I heard that he was married. Still for the sake of buying a property with a gooseberry patch he married an elderly, homely widow, without a trace of affection for her, but simply because she had money. After marrying her, he went on living parsimoniously, keeping her half-starved, and he put her money in the bank in his own name. She had previously been the wife of a postmaster, who had got her used to pies and cordials. This second husband did not even give her enough black bread. She began to sicken, and some three years later gave up the ghost. And, of course, it never for a moment occurred to my brother that he was to blame for her death.

---

[2] *shchi:* a peasant soup.
[3] crucians: Central European goldfish.

Money, like vodka, can do queer things to a man. Once in our town a merchant lay on his deathbed; before he died, he ordered a plateful of honey and he ate up all his money and lottery tickets with the honey, so that no one should get it. One day when I was inspecting a drove of cattle at a railway station, a cattle dealer fell under a locomotive and it sliced off his leg. We carried him in to the infirmary, the blood was gushing from the wound—a terrible business, but he kept begging us to find his leg and was very anxious about it: he had twenty rubles in the boot that was on that leg, and he was afraid they would be lost."

"That's a tune from another opera," said Burkin.

Ivan Ivanych paused a moment and then continued:

"After his wife's death, my brother began to look around for a property. Of course, you may scout about five years and in the end make a mistake, and buy something quite different from what you have been dreaming of. Through an agent my brother bought a mortgaged estate of three hundred acres with a house, servants' quarters, a park, but with no orchard, no gooseberry patch, no duck-pond. There was a stream, but the water in it was the color of coffee, for on one of its banks there was a brickyard and on the other a glue factory. But my brother was not at all disconcerted: he ordered a score of gooseberry bushes, planted them, and settled down to the life of a country gentleman.

"Last year I paid him a visit. I thought I would go and see how things were with him. In his letter to me my brother called his estate 'Chumbaroklov Waste, or Himalaiskoe' (our surname was Chimsha-Himalaisky). I reached the place in the afternoon. It was hot. Everywhere there were ditches, fences, hedges, rows of fir trees, and I was at a loss as to how to get to the yard and where to leave my horse. I made my way to the house and was met by a fat dog with reddish hair that looked like a pig. It wanted to bark, but was too lazy. The cook, a fat, barelegged woman, who also looked like a pig, came out of the kitchen and said that the master was resting after dinner. I went in to see my brother, and found him sitting up in bed, with a quilt over his knees. He had grown older, stouter, flabby; his cheeks, his nose, his lips jutted out: it looked as though he might grunt into the quilt at any moment.

"We embraced and dropped tears of joy and also of sadness at the thought that the two of us had once been young, but were now gray and nearing death. He got dressed and took me out to show me his estate.

"'Well, how are you getting on here?' I asked.

"'Oh, all right, thank God. I am doing very well.'

"He was no longer the poor, timid clerk he used to be but a real landowner, a gentleman. He had already grown used to his new manner of living and developed a taste for it. He ate a great deal, steamed himself in the bathhouse, was growing stout, was already having a lawsuit with the village commune and the two factories and was very much offended when the peasants failed to address him as 'Your Honor.' And he concerned himself with his soul's welfare too in a substantial, upper-class manner, and performed good deeds not simply, but pompously. And what good works! He dosed the peasants with bicarbonate and castor oil for all their ailments and on his name day he had a thanksgiving service celebrated in the center of the village, and then treated the villagers to a gallon of vodka, which he thought was the thing to do. Oh, those horrible gallons of vodka! One day a fat landowner hauls the peasants up before the rural police officer for trespassing, and the next, to mark a feast day, treats them to a gallon of vodka, and they drink and shout 'Hurrah' and when they are drunk bow down at his feet. A higher standard of living, overeating and idleness develop the most insolent self-conceit in a Russian. Nikolay Ivanych, who when he was a petty official was afraid to have opinions of his own even if he kept them to himself, now uttered nothing but incontrovertible truths and did so in the tone of a minister of state: 'Education is necessary, but the masses are not ready for it; corporal punishment is generally harmful, but in some cases it is useful and nothing else will serve.'

"'I know the common people, and I know how to deal with them,' he would say. 'They love me. I only have to raise my little finger, and they will do anything I want.'"

"And all this, mark you, would be said with a smile that bespoke kindness and intelligence. Twenty times over he repeated: 'We, of the gentry,' 'I, as a member of the gentry.' Apparently he no longer remembered that our grandfather had been a peasant and our father just a private. Even our surname, 'Chimsha-Himalaisky,' which in reality is grotesque, seemed to him sonorous, distinguished, and delightful.

"But I am concerned now not with him, but with me. I want to tell you about a change that took place in me during the few hours that I spent on his estate. In the evening when we were having tea, the cook served a plateful of gooseberries. They were not bought, they were his own gooseberries, the first ones picked since the bushes were planted. My brother gave a laugh and for a minute looked at the gooseberries in silence, with tears in his eyes — he could not speak for excitement. Then he put one berry in his mouth, glanced at me with the triumph of a child who has at last been given a toy he was longing for and said: 'How tasty!' And he ate the gooseberries greedily, and kept repeating: 'Ah, how delicious! Do taste them!'

"They were hard and sour, but as Pushkin has it,

> The falsehood that exalts we cherish more
> Than meaner truths that are a thousand strong.

I saw a happy man, one whose cherished dream had so obviously come true, who had attained his goal in life, who had got what he wanted, who was satisfied with his lot and with himself. For some reason an element of sadness had always mingled with my thoughts of human happiness, and now at the sight of a happy man I was assailed by an oppressive feeling bordering on despair. It weighed on me particularly at night. A bed was made up for me in a room next to my brother's bedroom, and I could hear that he was wakeful, and that he would get up again and again, go to the plate of gooseberries and eat one after another. I said to myself: how many contented, happy people there really are! What an overwhelming force they are! Look at life: the insolence and idleness of the strong, the ignorance and brutishness of the weak, horrible poverty everywhere, overcrowding, degeneration, drunkenness, hypocrisy, lying . . . Yet in all the houses and on all the streets there is peace and quiet; of the fifty thousand people who live in our town there is not one who would cry out, who would vent his indignation aloud. We see the people who go to market, eat by day, sleep by night, who babble nonsense, marry, grow old, good-naturedly drag their dead to the cemetery, but we do not see or hear those who suffer, and what is terrible in life goes on somewhere behind the scenes. Everything is peaceful and quiet and only mute statistics protest: so many people gone out of their minds, so many gallons of vodka drunk, so many children dead from malnutrition . . . And such a state of things is evidently necessary; obviously the happy man is at ease only because the unhappy ones bear their burdens in silence, and if there were not this silence, happiness would be impossible. It is a general hypnosis. Behind the door of every contented, happy man there ought to be someone standing with a little hammer and continually reminding him with a knock that there are unhappy people, that however happy he may be, life will sooner or later show him its claws, and trouble will come to him—illness, poverty, losses, and then no one will see or hear him, just as now he neither sees nor hears others. But there is no man with a hammer. The happy man lives at his ease, faintly fluttered by small daily cares, like an aspen in the wind—and all is well.

"That night, I came to understand that I too had been contented and happy," Ivan Ivanych continued, getting up. "I too over the dinner table or out hunting would hold forth on how to live, what to believe, the right way to govern the people. I too would say that learning was the enemy of darkness, that education was necessary but that for the common people the three R's were sufficient for the time being. Freedom is a boon, I used to say, it is as essential as air, but we must wait awhile. Yes, that's what I used to say, and now I ask: Why must we wait?" said Ivan Ivanych, looking wrathfully at Burkin. "Why must we wait, I ask you? For what reason? I am told that nothing can be done all at once, that every idea is realized gradually, in its own time. But who is it that says so? Where is the proof that it is just? You cite the natural order of things, the law governing all phenomena, but is there law, is there order in the fact that I, a living, thinking man, stand beside a ditch and wait for it to close up of itself or fill up with silt, when I could jump over it or throw a bridge across it? And again, why must we wait? Wait, until we have no strength to live, and yet we have to live and are eager to live!

"I left my brother's place early in the morning, and ever since then it has become intolerable for me to stay in town. I am oppressed by the peace and the quiet, I am afraid to look at the windows, for there is nothing that pains me more than the spectacle of a happy family sitting at table having tea. I am an old man now and unfit for combat, I am not even capable of hating. I can only grieve inwardly, get irritated, worked up, and at night my head is ablaze with the rush of ideas and I cannot sleep. Oh, if I were young!"

Ivan Ivanych paced up and down the room excitedly and repeated, "If I were young!"

He suddenly walked up to Alyohin and began to press now one of his hands, now the other.

"Pavel Konstantinych," he said imploringly, "don't quiet down, don't let yourself be lulled to sleep! As long as you are young, strong, alert, do not cease to do good! There is no happiness and there should be none, and if life has a meaning and a purpose, that meaning and purpose is not our happiness but something greater and more rational. Do good!"

All this Ivan Ivanych said with a pitiful, imploring smile, as though he were asking a personal favor.

Afterwards all three of them sat in armchairs in different corners of the drawing room and were silent. Ivan Ivanych's story satisfied neither Burkin nor Alyohin. With the ladies and generals looking down from the golden frames, seeming alive in the dim light, it was tedious to listen to the story of the poor devil of a clerk who ate gooseberries. One felt like talking about elegant people, about women. And the fact that they were sitting in a draw-ing room where everything—the chandelier under its cover, the armchairs, the carpets underfoot—testified that the very people who were now looking down from the frames had once moved about here, sat and had tea, and the fact that lovely Pelageya was noiselessly moving about—that was better than any story.

Alyohin was very sleepy; he had gotten up early, before three o'clock in the morning, to get some work done, and now he could hardly keep his eyes open, but he was afraid his visitors might tell an interesting story in his ab-sence, and he would not leave. He did not trouble to ask himself if what Ivan Ivanych had just said was intelligent or right. The guests were not talking about groats, or hay, or tar, but about something that had no direct bearing on his life, and he was glad of it and wanted them to go on.

"However, it's bedtime," said Burkin, rising. "Allow me to wish you good night."

Alyohin took leave of his guests and went downstairs to his own quarters, while they remained upstairs. They were installed for the night in a big room in which stood two old wooden beds decorated with carvings and in the corner was an ivory crucifix. The wide cool beds which had been made by the lovely Pelageya gave off a pleasant smell of clean linen.

Ivan Ivanych undressed silently and got into bed.

"Lord forgive us sinners!" he murmured, and drew the bedclothes over his head.

His pipe, which lay on the table, smelled strongly of burnt tobacco, and Burkin, who could not sleep for a long time, kept wondering where the un-pleasant odor came from.

The rain beat against the window panes all night.

The Lesson

by Toni Cade Bambara

Back in the days when everyone was old and stupid or young and foolish and me and Sugar were the only ones just right, this lady moved on our block with nappy hair and proper speech and no makeup. And quite natur-ally we laughed at her, laughed the way we did at the junk man who went about his business like he was some big-time president and his sorry-ass horse his secretary. And we kinda hated her too, hated the way we did the winos who cluttered up our parks and pissed on our handball walls and stank up our hallways and stairs so you couldn't halfway play hide-and-seek without a goddam gas mask. Miss Moore was her name. The only woman on the block with no first name. And she was black as hell, cept for her feet, which were fish-white and spooky. And she was always planning these boring-ass things for us to do, us being my cousin, mostly, who lived on the block cause we all moved North the same time and to the same apartment then spread out gradual to breathe. And our parents would yank our heads into some kinda shape and crisp up our clothes so we'd be presentable for travel with Miss Moore, who always looked like she was going to church, though she never did. Which is just one of things the grownups talked about when they talked behind her back like a dog. But when she came calling with some sachet she'd sewed up or some gingerbread she'd made or some book, why then they'd all be too embarrassed to turn her down and we'd get handed over all spruced up. She'd been to college and said it was only right that she should take responsibility for the young ones' education, and she not even related by marriage or blood. So they'd go for it. Specially Aunt Gretchen. She was the main gofer in the family. You got some ole dumb shit foolishness you want somebody to go for, you send for Aunt Gretchen. She been screwed into the go-along for so long, it's a blood-deep natural thing with her. Which is how she got saddled with me and Sugar and Junior in the first place while our mothers were in a la-de-da apartment up the block having a good ole time.

So this one day Miss Moore rounds us all up at the mailbox and it's puredee hot and she's knockin herself out about arithmetic. And school suppose to let up in the summer I heard, but she don't never let up. And the starch in my pinafore scratching the shit outta me and I'm really hating this nappy-head bitch and her goddamn college degree. I'd much rather go to the pool or to the show where it's cool. So me and Sugar leaning on the mailbox being surly, which is a Miss Moore word. And Flyboy checking out what everybody brought for lunch. And Fat Butt already wasting his peanut-butter-and-jelly sandwich like the pig he is. And Junebug punchin on Q.T.'s arm for potato chips. And Rosie Giraffe shifting from one hip to the other waiting for somebody to step on her foot or ask if she from Georgia so she can kick ass, preferably Mercedes'. And Miss Moore asking us do we know what money is, like we a bunch of retards. I mean real money, she say, like it's only poker chips or monopoly papers we lay on the grocer. So right away I'm tired of this and say so. And would much rather snatch Sugar and go to the Sunset and terrorize the West Indian kids and take their hair ribbons and their money too. And Miss Moore files that remark away for next week's lesson on brotherhood, I can tell. And finally I say we oughta get to the subway cause it's cooler and besides we might meet some cute boys. Sugar done swiped her mama's lipstick, so we ready.

So we heading down the street and she's boring us silly about what things cost and what our parents make and how much goes for rent and how money ain't divided up right in this country. And then she gets to the part about we all poor and live in the slums, which I don't feature. And I'm ready to speak on that, but she steps out in the street and hails two cabs just like that. Then she hustles half the crew in with her and hands me a five-dollar bill and tells me to calculate 10 percent tip for the driver. And we're off. Me and Sugar and Junebug and Flyboy hanging out the window and hollering to everybody, putting lipstick on each other cause Flyboy a faggot anyway, and making farts with our sweaty armpits. But I'm mostly trying to figure how to spend this money. But they all fascinated with the meter ticking and Junebug starts laying bets as to how much it'll read when Flyboy can't hold his breath no more. Then Sugar lay bets as to how much it'll be when we get there. So I'm stuck. Don't nobody want to go for my plan, which is to jump out at the next light and run off to the first bar-b-que we can find. Then the driver tells us to get the hell out cause we there already. And the meter reads eight-five cents. And I'm stalling to figure out the tip and Sugar say give him a dime. And I decide he don't need it bad as I do, so later for him. But then he tries to take off with Junebug foot still in the door so we talk about his mama something ferocious. Then we check out that we on Fifth Avenue and everybody dressed up in stockings. One lady in a fur coat, hot as it is. White folks crazy.

"This is the place," Miss Moore say, presenting it to us in the voice she uses at the museum. "Let's look in the windows before we go in."

"Can we steal?" Sugar asks very serious like she's getting the ground rules squared away before she plays. "I beg your pardon," say Miss Moore, and we fall out. So she leads us around the windows of the toy store and me and Sugar screamin, "This is mine, that's mine. I gotta have that, that was made for me, I was born for that," till Big Butt drowns us out.

"Hey, I'm goin to buy that there."

"That there? You don't even know what it is, stupid."

"I do so," he say punchin on Rosie Giraffe. "It's a microscope."

"Watcha gonna do with a microscope, fool?"

"Look at things."

"Like what, Ronald?" ask Miss Moore. And Big Butt ain't got the first notion. So here go Miss Moore gabbing about the thousands of bacteria in a drop of water and the somethinorother in a speck of blood and the million and one living things in the air around us is invisible to the naked eye. And what she say that for? Junebug go to town on that "naked" and we rolling. Then Miss Moore ask what it cost. So we all jam into the window smudgin it up and the price tag say $300. So then she ask how long'd take for Big Butt and Junebug to save up their allowances. "Too long," I say. "Yeh," adds Sugar, "outgrown it by that time." And Miss Moore say no, you never outgrown learning instruments. "Why, even medical students and interns and," blah, blah, blah. And we ready to choke Big Butt for bringing it up in the first damn place.

"This here costs four hundred eighty dollars," says Rosie Giraffe. So we pile up all over her to see what she pointin out. My eyes tell me it's a chunk of glass cracked with something heavy, and different-color inks dripped into the splits, then the whole thing put into a oven or something. But for $480 it don't make sense.

"That's a paperweight made of semi-precious stones fused together under tremendous pressure," she explains slowly, with her hands doing the mining and all the factory work.

"So what's a paperweight?" asks Rosie Giraffe.

"To weigh paper with, dumbell," say Flyboy, the wise man from the East.

"Not exactly," say Miss Moore, which is what she say when you warm or way off too. "It's to weight paper down so it won't scatter and make your desk untidy." So right away me and Sugar curtsy to each other and then to Mercedes who is more the tidy type.

"We don't keep paper on top of the desk in my class," say Junebug, figuring Miss Moore crazy or lyin one.

"At home, then," she say. "Don't you have a calendar and a pencil case and a blotter and a letter-opener on your desk at home where you do your homework?" And she know damn well what our homes look like cause she nosys around in them every chance she gets.

"I don't even have a desk," say Junebug. "Do we?"

"No. And I don't get no homework neither," says Big Butt.

"And I don't even have a home," say Flyboy like he do at school to keep the white folks off his back and sorry for him. Send this poor kid to camp posters, is his specialty.

"I do," says Mercedes. "I have a box of stationery on my desk and a picture of my cat. My godmother bought the stationery and the desk. There's a big rose on each sheet and the envelopes smell like roses."

"Who wants to know about your smelly-ass stationery," say Rosie Giraffe fore I can get my two cents in.

"It's important to have a work area all your own so that . . . "

"Will you look at this sailboat, please," say Flyboy, cuttin her off and pointin to the thing like it was his. So once again we tumble all over each other to gaze at this magnificent thing in the toy store which it just big enough to maybe sail two kittens across the pond if you strap them to the posts tight. We all start reciting the price tag like we in assembly. "Handcrafted sailboat of fiberglass at one thousand one hundred ninety-five dollars."

"Unbelievable," I hear myself say and am really stunned. I read it again for myself just in case the group recitation put me in a trance. Same thing. For some reason this pisses me off. We look at Miss Moore and she lookin at us, waiting for I dunno what.

"Who'd pay all that when you can buy a sailboat set for a quarter at Pop's, a tube of glue for a dime, and a ball of string for eight cents? It must have a motor and a whole lot else besides," I say. "My sailboat cost me about fifty cents."

"But will it take water?" say Mercedes with her smart ass.

"Took mine to Alley Pond Park once," say Flyboy. "String broke. Lost it. Pity."

"Sailed mine in Central Park and it keeled over and sank. Had to ask my father for another dollar."

"And you got the strap," laugh Big Butt. "The jerk didn't even have a string on it. My old man wailed on his behind."

Little Q.T. was staring hard at the sailboat and you could see he wanted it bad. But he too little and somebody'd just take it from him. So what the hell. "This boat for kids, Miss Moore?"

"Parents silly to buy something like that just to get all broke up," say Rosie Giraffe.

"That much money it should last forever," I figure.

"My father'd buy it for me if I wanted it."

"Your father, my ass," say Rosie Giraffe getting a chance to finally push Mercedes.

"Must be rich people shop here," say Q.T.

"You are a very bright boy," say Flyboy. "What was your first clue?" And he rap him on the head with the back of his knuckles, since Q.T. the only one he could get away with. Though Q.T. liable to come up behind you years later and get his licks in when you half expect it.

"What I want to know is," I says to Miss Moore though I never talk to her, I wouldn't give the bitch that satisfaction, "is how much a real boat costs? I figure a thousand'd get you a yacht any day?"

"Why don't you check that out," she says, "and report back to the group?" Which really pains my ass. If you gonna mess up a perfectly good swim day least you could do is have some answers. "Let's go in," she say like she got something up her sleeve. Only she don't lead the way. So me and Sugar turn the corner to where the entrance is, but when we get there I kinda hang back. Not that I'm scared, what's there to be afraid of, just a toy store. But I feel funny, shame. But what I got to be shamed about? Got as much right to go in as anybody. But somehow I can't seem to get hold of the door, so I step away for Sugar to lead. But she hangs back too. And I look at her and she looks at me and this is ridiculous. I mean, damn, I never ever been shy about doing nothing or going nowhere. But then Mercedes steps up and then Rosie Giraffe and Big Butt crowd in behind and shove, and next thing we all stuffed into the doorway with only Mercedes squeezing past us, smoothing out her jumper and walking right down the aisle. Then the rest of us tumble in like a glued-together jigsaw done all wrong. And people lookin at us. And it's like the time me and Sugar crashed into the Catholic church on a dare. But once we got in there and everything so hushed and holy and the candles and the bowin and the handkerchiefs on all the drooping heads, I just couldn't go through with the plan. Which was for me to run up to the altar and do a tap dance while Sugar played the nose flute and messed around in the holy waters. And Sugar kept givin me the elbow. Then later teased me so bad I tied her up in the shower and turned it on and locked her in. And she'd be there till this day if Aunt Gretchen hadn't finally figured I was lyin about the boarder takin a shower.

Same thing in the store. We all walkin on tiptoe and hardly touchin the games and puzzles and things. And I watched Miss Moore who is steady watchin us like she waiting for a sign. Like Mama Drewery watches the sky and sniffs the air and takes note of just how much slant is in the bird formation. Then me and Sugar bump smack into each other, so busy gazing at the toys, 'specially the sailboat. But we don't laugh and go into our fat-lady bump-stomach routine. We just stare at that price tag. Then Sugar run a finger over the whole boat. And I'm jealous and want to hit her. Maybe not her, but I sure want to punch somebody in the mouth.

"Watcha bring us here for, Miss Moore?"

"You sound angry, Sylvia. Are you mad about something?" Givin me one of them grins like she tellin a grown-up joke that never turns out to be funny. And she's lookin very closely at me like maybe she plannin to do my portrait from memory. I'm mad, but I won't give her that satisfaction. So I slouch around the store bein very bored and say, "Let's go."

Me and Sugar at the back of the train watchin the tracks whizzin by large then small then gettin gobbled up in the dark. I'm thinkin about this tricky toy I saw in the store. A clown that somersaults on a bar then does chin-ups just cause you yank lightly at his leg. Cost $35. I could see me askin my mother for a $35 birthday clown. "You wanna who that costs what?" she'd say, cocking her head to the side to get a better view of the hole in my head. Thirty-five dollars and the whole household could go visit Grandaddy Nelson in the country. Thirty-five dollars would pay for the rent and the piano bill too. Who are these people that spend that much for performing clowns and $1000 for toy sailboats? What kinda work they do and how they live and how come we ain't in on it? Where we are is who we are, Miss Moore always pointin out. But it don't necessarily have to be that way, she always adds then waits for somebody to say that poor people have to wake up and demand their share of the pie and don't none of us know what kind of pie she talkin about in the first damn place. But she ain't so smart cause I still got her four dollars from the taxi and she sure ain't gettin it. Messin up my day with this shit. Sugar nudges me in my pocket and winks.

Miss Moore lines us up in front of the mailbox where we started from, seem like years ago, and I got a headache for thinkin so hard. And we lean all over each other so we can hold up under the draggy-ass lecture she always finishes us off with at the end before we thank her for borin us to tears. But she just looks at us like she readin tea leaves. Finally she say, "Well, what did you think of F.A.O. Schwartz?"

Rosie Giraffe mumbles, "White folks crazy."

"I'd like to go there again when I get my birthday money," says Mercedes, and we shove her out the pack so she has to lean on the mailbox by herself.

"I'd like a shower. Tiring day," say Flyboy.

Then Sugar surprises me by saying, "You know, Miss Moore, I don't think all of us here put together eat in a year what that sailboat costs." And Miss Moore lights up like somebody goosed her. "And?" she say, urging Sugar on. Only I'm standin on her foot so she don't continue.

"Imagine for a minute what kind of society it is in which some people can spend on a toy what it would cost to feed a family of six or seven. What do you think?"

"I think," say Sugar pushing me off her feet like she never done before, cause I whip her ass in a minute, "that this is not much of a democracy if you ask me. Equal chance to pursue happiness means an equal crack at the dough, don't it?" Miss Moore is besides herself and I am disgusted with Sugar's treachery. So I stand on her foot one more time to see if she'll shove me. She shuts up, and Miss Moore looks at me, sorrowfully I'm thinkin. And somethin weird is goin on. I can feel it in my chest.

"Anybody else learn anything today?" lookin dead at me. I walk away and Sugar has to run to catch up and don't even seem to notice when I shrug her arm off my shoulder.

"Well, we got four dollars anyway," she says.

"Uh hunh."

"We could go to Hascombs and get half a chocolate layer and then to the Sunset and still have plenty of money for potato chips and ice cream sodas."

"Un hunh."

"Race you to Hascombs," she say.

We start down the block and she gets ahead which is O.K. by me cause I'm goin to the West End and then over the Drive to think this day through. She can run if she want to and even run faster. But ain't nobody gonna beat me at nuthin.

WRITING YOUR ESSAY

Generating Ideas: Reader Responses

The Active Reader. Reading and analyzing a short story with the intent of writing about it is something you are probably already familiar with. In high school you might have written essays on individual works of literature as well as book reports and journals. If so, you are aware that studying literature requires a particularly alert response from a reader. In a short story almost every word or sentence seems to play a vital role in the unfolding of the characters' lives or the development of the narrative of events. The reader must approach the text of a story with a kind of Janus mask—looking behind and ahead at the same time, trying to establish some pattern of meaning or significance that will make the story coherent to you and to other readers.

As a reader, you often want to be particularly responsive to even the smallest details; taken together they provide us with the evidence that we might need to explain to others our larger view of the meaning of the story. Look, for example, at the character of Ivan Ivanych in Chekhov's "Gooseberries." Before he relates the story of what he sees as his brother's misdirected quest for personal happiness, he himself exults in bathing in the cool waters of the river, crying out, "Ah my God, Ah my God!" as he remains in the water after everyone has left. Does this contradict his view stated later in the story that human beings pay too much attention to their own desire for happiness?

There are several ways that you might direct your active responses to the story so that they generate ideas for a draft of an essay. Perhaps the most basic way is the method that readers have used for centuries: entering into a dialogue with the story by commenting in the margins of your text. This can simply mean a pencil marking or felt-tip underlining of some passage you deem to be interesting or important to the story. You might ask a question about some detail of the plot or some description of or comment by a character. However you mark up the text, it will record your active responses of the moment to the process of reading a story.

One student, for example, jotted down in the margin next to the passage in Chekhov's story where Ivan watches Nikolay eat the gooseberries, "Is Ivan jealous?" Another wrote next to the same passage, "Nikolay refusing to admit that his dream had gone sour"; while a third student, who simply underlined the passage, seemed to still have it in mind when she wrote the following journal entry:

6/15/90

"GOOSEBERRIES" BY ANTON CHEKHOV

I think that Ivan was a man who loved the beauty of his country, but was bothered by the insensitivity of the rich and the injustices that were silently suffered by the poor. All pretended to be content with their lives as if they were deaf, dumb, and blind.

While sitting with his two friends, he tells the story of his brother who had always dreamed of living in the country, on a farm with a lake, ducks and gooseberry bushes of his own. He was so obsessed by this dream that he lived like a miser, married a woman he didn't love and then starved her to death for that house of his dreams. Ivan visited his brother and saw that his brother became fat and flabby and the house he lived in was nothing like the one he struggled so hard to have. The only thing he had were gooseberry bushes which yielded hard and sour ones. The brother still living his dream thought they were delicious. He had blinded himself from the truth and was living a lie, content none-the-less.

After relating his story he, Ivan, talks about how all this hypocrisy is disturbing to him and that something should be done about it. He urges the younger men to try to change all this to go out and do some good. (Help others share the wealth.) They did not bother to listen because it had nothing to do with them and they were disinterested. Ivan went to bed and asked the Lord for forgiveness and his friend Burkin found himself unable to sleep, perhaps from thinking about what Ivan had said.

Double-Entry Journal. After reading the story you can use your journal — like the student who wrote the above entry — to record your response to the story and its significance to you. You can enter into a three-way dialogue between yourself, the story, *and* your initial response to the story — answering your own questions, explaining your first impressions, analyzing and elaborating your preliminary ideas.

One way to do this is to use the double-entry journal technique. Dividing your journal page into two columns, use one column to record your explanation or description of some element of the story; the other column will express your point of view, evaluation, or association with some personal experience that might help you to see this aspect of the story in a broader perspective.

Here is an example:

At the end of the story Burkin smokes his pipe apparently unable to sleep or perhaps disturbed by Ivan's story. This seems to be a rather inconclusive ending.	Maybe B. has been made to feel guilty about his own life by I's story of his brother. The beauty of the maidservant and simple luxuries of the 2nd floor of the peasant's house seem to me to represent an ideal form of happiness that I's brother just didn't know or seem to care about. I'm not sure whether I could sacrifice anything or anyone just for the sake of some personal good. Does the inconclusive ending have something to do with the different characters' ideas on what makes a person happy?

In the next journal entry, a student records the effect that Ivan's story had on Burkin:

If the story never accomplished much you could say it had a profound effect on Burkin. He couldn't sleep because his conscience was bothering him. It may or it may not help him in the future but at least Ivan got him to think about himself and the people around him. Ivan should feel good that it hit someone smack in the face.

But when she brings in her personal point of view, her judgment of Ivan becomes more harsh, as her second entry shows:

Some people may have a lot of difficulty with the message. It is so hard to do good all the time. We have the "human" urge to get things done the fastest and most beneficial way. We don't like to really work for what we want. It sometimes is an unconscious thing that we do. I'm annoyed with Ivan for preaching the almost impossible. It makes him sound religious in a way, almost like my parents.

Another student is critical of Nikolay in the first entry she writes about him:

-Gooseberries - A man, Ivan Ivanych, tells a story of his brother, who scrimped and saved his whole life so that he could buy his own estate. A requirement he insisted on was that his land have a gooseberry patch. When his gooseberries grew and ripened they were served to him (the brother) and he dug in. He said they were the best he'd ever tasted, when actually they were hard and sour. Rather than admit it he ate and raved about the berries. Here is a man who had worked all his life to attain his goal and when he finally reaches his dream, he finds it is sour. He wont admit it. He wont see that his berries are sour. He can't face it.

The whole moral of the story was stated:
The falsehood that exists we cherish more
Than meaner truths that are a thousand strong.

But in her commentary on that entry, she appears to identify with the common human failing that Nikolay suffers from:

Many times I have wanted something very badly and when I finally got it, it was not all that I had anticipated. For example, a new video tape, a new pet, or even a new boyfriend. Furthermore, I have also been in situations where I've seen something about myself or a friend that was so disconcerting that I chose to block it out of my mind and refused to look at it for what it really was.

Each student is beginning to develop an interpretation of the story and its characters. Perhaps Ivan is as much of a dreamer as his brother: he appears to trouble the first student—and possibly Burkin—as much as Nikolay troubles him. But is Nikolay as wrongheaded as Ivan makes him out to be? For the second student, the story may be as critical of Ivan's high expectations as it is of Nikolay's self-deceit.

Your double-entry journal can also be used in group meetings as a way of further generating ideas. Ask the members of your group to respond to some statement in your left-hand column by writing their own comments. There are bound to be areas of agreement and disagreement that might send you back to the text of the story for supporting evidence for your comments.

Here is an entry that a student showed to her peer group:

Gooseberries

Ivan tries to point out what so many of us are guilty of ignoring - the pain of others. Life in our quiet lovely homes can be so peaceful as long as those who are suffering do it quietly and out of our sight. Ivan feels guilty for having been happy? Maybe.

The student's peers supported her response to the story:

I agree 110%! It's amazing what we don't know or should I say - don't <u>want</u> to know about the countless people who need help and are being ignored. Your ideas gave me insight into a story I was originally indifferent to.

I agree, most people tend to ignore what happens around us. For a person to take notice of other people's suffering, this person must possess great qualities.

This is true, and sometimes, it upsets people's homes when suffering comes upon us.

The student then went back to the story, gathered supporting evidence, and wrote a longer journal entry in which she developed her ideas:

Monday 6-18

Ivan's love for nature went beyond owning a farm, working the land or simply sleeping in the sun. "Man needs only six feet of earth" but to Ivan "six feet is what a corpse needs." On the other hand his brother Nikolay spent his entire life penny pinching to fulfill his dream of some day owning a farm, having gooseberry bushes and being a country gentleman.

Nikolay attains his dream, however his journey had been a long empty one. His life had been filled with obsessions, selfishness and lack of compassion for people. With 300 acres of land Nikolay placed boundaries of fences and hedges and trees separating himself from the real world. Ivan realizes that life can pass so easily if only you can ignore the suffering of others. Ivan asks for mercy and forgiveness for never hearing the cries of those suffering, whereas Nikolay spends his life without the slightest concern for those <u>beneath</u> <u>him</u>.

```
He finally got gooseberries, but he paid too high a price as
anybody else would see it. His obsession led to his gaining
gooseberries all right but he gave his life for it.
```

Question Sets. As a group you can also generate worthwhile discussion by having each reader prepare a list of questions that he or she thinks are important to an understanding of the characters and narrative. Exchange sets of questions to see which ones appear most frequently and which seem to offer the most insight into the story for other readers. Some questions can ask about the nuts-and-bolts matters that are of concern to all readers, the literal facts of the story: who did what to whom, when and where; what happened and how? Other questions can take a broader view and try to establish some of the thematic concerns of the story. Often, the questions we ask reflect our own curiosity, and perhaps even our confusion, about some of the story's most provocative or imaginative features. In fact our most significant dialogue — between the text and between other readers — often is the result of this initial confusion or uncertainty about the meaning of the story.

Here is a set of questions that one group of students generated about "Gooseberries." Are there different questions that you would add to their list? Which are "nuts-and-bolts" questions? Which seem to take a broader view? Which one question of this set seems in your opinion to hold the most potential for generating ideas about the story? Why?

QUESTIONS ABOUT "GOOSEBERRIES"

1. What do the gooseberries represent?

2. Why was Nikolay crazy about them?

3. Was Nikolay really happy after he got his house in the country?

4. Why was Nikolay obsessed with having a house in the country?

5. Why does Nikolay's life bother Ivan?

6. Why does Ivan tell his "boring" story?

7. What function does the chambermaid have? Why is she in the story?

8. Why can't Burkin fall asleep?

9. What does the last sentence mean?

Brainstorming. Another activity that can be worthwhile in terms of generating ideas about a story is brainstorming (see Chapter 6, pp. 234–240, and Chapter 9, p. 429). To brainstorm, simply list details of the story along with any comments or questions about them that occur to you. You can do this on your own first, then compare your list to the list of others or your peer group; or you can work with your group from the start, with each member contributing to the list and commenting on, playing off, and reacting to the contributions of other members.

Below is the list produced by a brainstorming session of one group on "Gooseberries":

1. Nikolay wanted to be a landowner.
2. He wanted to be a member of the gentry and addressed as "Your Honor."
3. His father was an officer.
4. Nikolay wanted to go back to a past way of life—to his youth.
5. Nikolay is more of a looker than a doer.
6. He is always looking at advertisements.
7. He buys a property that was not what he dreamed of.
8. He overlooks the muddy water and sour berries.
9. He lets the agent do everything for him.
10. Did he see the property before he bought it?
11. Money goes to Nikolay's head.
12. He thinks he knows how to handle people.
13. He forgets that his grandfather was a peasant.
14. He was too timid as a clerk to express his own opinions.
15. Buying the property changed him.
16. He felt noble.
17. When he gave the peasants vodka and they bowed, he felt important.
18. Was his dream fulfilled, despite its shortcomings?
19. Chekhov felt the Russian people suffered in silence.
20. Ivan told Alyohin not to be quiet but to do good.
21. Ivan wanted freedom now.
22. Is Chekhov Ivan, or Ivan and Nikolay together?
23. Ivan's ideas were revolutionary in Tsarist Russia.
24. Were Ivan's ideas just general philosophical statements?
25. When life is as dreary as Ivan thinks, one way to deal with it is to dream.

Try clustering the observations and ideas on this list. What shaping idea might they lead you to develop for an essay about "Gooseberries"? What additional material might you need to generate, in order to illustrate and explain this shaping idea?

SOME PRACTICE WITH READER RESPONSES

1. Read over the short story "The Lesson," entering into a dialogue with the story by commenting in the margins of your text. What passages did you underline, comment on, raise questions about? Compare your responses with those of your classmates.

2. Write a journal entry about your reading of "The Lesson." Record your reactions and thoughts freely, commenting if you choose on how they compare and contrast with the reactions of your classmates. Wait a day, then write another journal entry in which you try to account for or qualify your first entry.

3. In a group or on your own, list questions about the literal facts and thematic concerns of "The Lesson." Select the question that you feel most curious about answering and write about it in your journal.

4. Conduct a brainstorming session on "The Lesson." Either by clustering or by free writing about the list in your journal, come up with a potential shaping idea for an essay about the story.

Responding to a Short Story in Writing Your Essay. Begin now to generate your own ideas about a short story. You may choose to focus on "Gooseberries" or "The Lesson" (or on both stories). You may take as your subject another story, perhaps one suggested by your instructor. Try one or more of the strategies of reader response we have reviewed in this section. But keep in mind as well other methods of generating ideas you have learned this semester: if, for example, the journalist's questions (pp. 91–96), or the explorer's questions (pp. 138–143) or some of the classical questions (pp. 186–192) have worked well for you in other tasks, you might want to apply one of them to the present task of interpreting a short story.

Addressing Your Audience: Reader Perspectives

In Chapter 9, we suggested that one way you can effectively address an informed reader—a reader who knows as much as and possibly more than you about your subject—is to play the role of a critical thinker. You might feel impelled to play this role when you write about a short story for a literature instructor. You would, however, need to research different interpretations of the story first. Often in upper-level literature courses, students are assigned to do just that. But here we would like you to take a different approach to your audience—only one member of which is your instructor.

If your audience is simply other readers of the story, they are "informed" primarily in the sense that they share your familiarity with the story itself. They do not need to be retold what happens in the story, or who the characters are, or where and when the events take place. Like you, also, they may have their own interpretation of the story. But here differences arise: different readers are likely to find different meanings in a story because of who they are and the perspective from which they examine the story.

Reader Points of View.   Look, for example, at the following passages that two students wrote about Ivan in "Gooseberries."

Ivan of "Gooseberries" took the world's problems upon his own head. He shouldn't have been pondering on about his brother's lifestyle. He should have been happy for him and respected his judgment. We may all never be happy with what other people do but we have to live with it. This causes him to begin to analyze his whole life all over again and then he comes to the conclusion that he didn't live a worthwhile life. His life was worthwhile all this time, how could it just change all of a sudden? We as a people worry too much and we give ourselves more problems than we can deal with. Life should be taken one day at a time.

. . .

Ivan is truly special for he transcends his brother and all others who either suffer in silence or accept things as they are because their own immediate needs are being met, as in the case of his host. Like the others, he looks around and sees poverty, crime, sickness, inequality, lack of opportunity for change and despair. Unlike his brother, Ivan is not content to achieve his own dream and live happily ever after with full knowledge of the all pervasive cycle of grinding despair that far too many people have come to endure. He looks at the world as it is, and thinks of the world as it might be. In a moment that is no less prophetic than it is emotionally wrenching, we hear his anguished cry. "Why can't all this change? And right now!" At this moment he ceases to be Ivan a mere character in a story by

Chekhov. He is transformed and uplifted into the incarnation of every prophet and every martyr who ever walked the earth. He will not suffer a martyr's death; but he will suffer the endless anguish of seeing and knowing and yet being powerless to act on his vision and to change an unjust society into a utopia.

The students share a similar understanding of Ivan as a man who is intensely aware of and deeply troubled by the "problems of the world." But they take markedly different attitudes toward this character, which in turn leads them to offer different versions of the story's meaning. Is "Gooseberries" a tale about the importance of taking life one day at a time? Or is it about the impossibility of doing so for those honest enough to look at the world "as it is"? The interpretation each student offers of the story rests to some degree on the individual attitude each brings to a reading of it.

Reader Frames of Reference.   Your understanding of "Gooseberries" may be enhanced then if you learn not only what these students think about the story but also why they think it. To explain why, they need to point out details of the story that support their interpretations. But this is only a partial explanation. In addition, they need to give you some sense of their own personal history when they read the story, of those elements in their frame of reference that account for the unique point of view they take toward the characters and their interactions.

Your understanding of a story, in other words, should be more fully enhanced by another reader's interpretation, if you know something about what that reader brings to the story which makes his or her perspective on it similar to or different from your own. In the same way, you may enhance the understanding of other readers of the story if you offer them information about the perspective that leads you to develop your interpretation.

What kind of perspectives might you bring to a story you are interpreting? You have a *personal* perspective, of course, composed of your family background and the private or individual life you have led; a *social* perspective that reflects such elements of your life as your ethnic background, economic status, work experience, political affiliations; a *cultural* perspective made up of such factors as your reading, education, religious practice, as well as your experience of the media and other elements of popular culture; and we might add a *literary* perspective — the result of your study of literary structures, techniques, and traditions.

Reader Perspectives: Angles on a Story.   A reader of "The Lesson" who asks why Sylvia gets so angry after Miss Moore takes her to F.A.O. Schwarz may come up with any number of different answers — answers that are based, of course, on the details of the story but also on the individual reader's perspective. Some readers, for example, might answer that Sylvia is angry because she has learned something about the hard realities of being poor and Black in American society. But a reader who has experienced similar realities in his or her life is different from one who only knows about such realities through reading and television—and the interpretation of each will be more honest and complete if this difference is taken into account.

Writers who explain both what a story means to them and how their point of view on the story reflects particular elements in their frame of reference offer an audience the opportunity to understand their interpretation in the broadest possible terms. At the same time, they establish a unique bridge with their audience: by inviting the audience to look at the story from one particular angle, such writers in essence admit that there are other, equally valid angles—and hence that their audience may have other interpretations that are nonetheless equally reasonable.

Thus, a writer who sees Sylvia's problem as one of "sibling" rivalry—Sylvia is angry because her jealousy of her cousin, Sugar, has been aroused—may be less likely to invite dissent from and more likely to enhance the understanding of readers who hold other interpretations, if this writer explains that he or she is looking at the story from the perspective of a student of human psychology.

As you develop your ideas about a story for this task, try to add some information about the perspective (or perspectives) you are bringing to bear on the story. Analyze not only the details of the story but also those elements of your frame of reference which may have had an effect on how you saw or understood these details. This is an effective way to open up your audience to an interpretation that may differ from their own.

SOME PRACTICE WITH READER PERSPECTIVES

1. How might you interpret "The Lesson" if you look at the story in terms of your reading of "Gooseberries"? Is Sylvia comparable to Ivan in any way? Take a literary perspective and explore how thinking about Sylvia in terms of the techniques of plot, character, and point of view (see focus section on the Elements of the Short Story below) might affect your understanding of her and what she experiences.

2. What can you infer about the frame of reference of the readers who offer the following interpretations of "Gooseberries"?

   a. Chekhov's story, most obviously in its depiction of the chambermaid Pelageya, illustrates the blatant chauvinism of late nineteenth-century Russian society.

   b. In "Gooseberries," Chekhov offers a radical critique of materialism by showing how Nikolay's obsession with property led him to live a deluded and lonely life.

    c. Ivan's problem is guilt—guilt over his own happiness in an unhappy world. The central issue in "Gooseberries" is neither philosophical nor political—it is psychological. The roots of Ivan's discontent lie in his own neurotic personality.

3. What reaction might you expect each of the three readers above to have toward your interpretation of "Gooseberries" or "The Lesson"? How might you bridge any gaps between their point of view and yours?

Using Reader Perspectives in Writing Your Essay. Answering the following questions of the "Audience Analysis Guide" should help you to write and arrange your essay for Chapter 11 more effectively:

───────── AUDIENCE ANALYSIS GUIDE ─────────

1. **What difficulties do you foresee your audience having in their attempt to understand the story or stories you are interpreting?**
2. **What special knowledge or experience will help your reader to understand these stories better?**
3. **What other reading experiences might your reader bring to these stories as an aid to understanding them more fully?**
4. **What details of the plot do you need to retell for your reader? Why is this necessary?**

Arranging Your Essay

The Shaping Idea. Your shaping idea for this essay should answer the question "What do I think about this story and why do I think it?" It should offer your reader a succinct statement of the short story's significance for you.

    You may want to lead up to this statement in a paper that explores the process by which you arrived at it. You may want to begin the paper with your shaping idea and then proceed to illustrate, explain, and/or defend it. In either case, you will want to arrange a discussion that refers both to details of the story and to elements of your frame of reference that help account for your interpretation.

The Reader's Story. One way you might arrange this essay is by reviewing the steps you took to arrive at your interpretation. In a sense, you simply tell the story of your reading experience. The framework of your essay is a narrative of your process of reading a story and responding to its details. You include exposition in order to summarize, explain, and interpret parts of the story; to analyze their effect as you explore what meanings the story holds; and to draw some generalized conclusion about the results of your exploration.

See what you think about the following student draft that employs this sort of arrangement strategy:

A BLIND MAN'S DREAM

As Ivan in "Gooseberries" tells his tale to his two friends, he recalls his childhood and his brother Nikolay's obsession. Ivan and Nikolay were brought up in the country; their father dies, and his estate is lost. To quote Ivan " ... whoever even once in his life has caught a perch or seen thrushes migrate in the autumn, when on clear cool days they sweep in flocks over the village, will never really be a townsman and to the day of his death will have a longing for the open." (Chekhov p. 510) Nikolay was such a man, only his obsession dominated his whole life. His youth was spent scrimping and saving; even the money that Ivan would give him was put into savings. He led the life of a pauper.

He was past forty and still didn't have enough money to purchase his estate; so he marries an old, homely widow, takes her money, and puts it into a savings in his own name. This woman was used to the finer things in life, none of which was hers any longer. She gets sick and dies. This doesn't bother Nikolay; all he is interested in is his estate in the country.

Nikolay finally had enough money to make his purchase, "... but with no orchard, no gooseberry patch, no duckpond. There was a stream, but the water in it was the color of coffee, for on one of its banks there was a brickyard and on the other a glue factory." (Chekhov p. 512) Nikolay buys a score of gooseberry bushes and plants them. He was surrounded by a fat dog, too lazy to bark, a fat housekeeper that looked like a pig; he had his gooseberries, but they were hard and sour.

Did Nikolay see all of this, or was he satisfied to have his estate? Nikolay was growing stout, he ate all the time, he wanted the peasants to call him "Your honor"; he somehow felt that he had achieved his goal. Nikolay wasted his whole life in greed and obsession.

I can understand wanting to have all these material things, the house in the country, wanting to spend your life enjoying your dreams; but you must keep these dreams in their proper perspective. I have known people like Nikolay, maybe not to his extreme, but selfish to the point that they don't care whose toes they step on, whose feelings they hurt, or whose reputation they harm, as long as they get their own way. They think that if things go their way, they will be happy. Like Nikolay, their lives are spent wishing and dreaming, resenting those around them who have a happy life. They reach a point when they have talked themselves into believing that these material things will make them happy; they fail to see any of the beauty of life that is going on around them. Nikolay never laughed or played; he never enjoyed friendships and love; so now he must convince himself that he is happy.

He tastes the gooseberries and thinks they are great; he surrounds himself with ugliness: the coffee-colored water, the brickyard and glue factory, and the fat ugly dog and housekeeper that look like pigs. He spent his youth in greed and isolation, and when he finally achieves his financial goal, he has wasted his entire life; he is now an old man. It's as though he is punishing himself by surrounding himself with all this ugliness, and somehow convincing himself that he is happy. He must bribe the peasants with vodka to celebrate his name day.

Ivan compares his brother's greed to that of a man who puts honey all over his money and eats it before he dies, so no one else can have it. Nikolay is also compared to a man whose leg is cut off in an accident, the leg gushing blood. The injured party begs for someone to find his leg because he had money in the boot that was on that leg, and he didn't want anyone else to have his money.

Greed is all consuming: it blinds you to the things in life that are the simplest and the most pleasing. You can be a man with sight and never see the beauty of life that surrounds you, or you can be a man without sight and see far more than sight will ever allow.

How well does this draft convey the writer's interpretation of "Gooseberries"? Does it include information you find unnecessary? Are there ideas that might be more fully developed? Where does the writer's reference to details of the story offer effective support of her interpretation? What does her fifth paragraph, in which she explains how she has known people like Nikolay, add to a reader's understanding of the main point of her essay?

The Writer's Repertoire.   While a narrative pattern may prove an effective arrangement option for you in putting together the essay for this task, it is certainly not your only option. By now, you have tried your hand at a variety of expository and persuasive patterns of arrangement. You have built up, in effect, a repertoire of possible ways to frame and organize an essay. We would encourage you to make full use of this writer's repertoire, so that whenever you write, your arrangement suits your purpose.

In working through an essay on your interpretation of a short story, you may find that a classically expository or emphatically persuasive pattern is more to your purpose than a narrative one. You might want to begin your essay, for example, with a specific statement about the effect of the story on you—what it made you think about or feel or understand—then, in the body of the essay, explain one by one the causes that led to this effect. Or, you might compare and contrast a number of possible ways of interpreting such elements as a character's actions or a story's theme, in order to argue your preference for one interpretation over the possible others.

Consider all the options available to you in arranging your essay for this task. Take advantage of your method(s) of generating ideas. Take into account both your purpose and your audience. By utilizing your repertoire of arrangement patterns in this way, you should be able to produce essays that communicate not only with clarity but also with originality.

Writing Your Rough Draft

Before you begin writing your own rough draft, read over "No Man Is an Island," the following draft that a student wrote on "Gooseberries." What arrangement patterns has this student utilized? How effective do you find her arrangement?

NO MAN IS AN ISLAND

"No Man Is an Island," a phrase those of us who grew up in the late sixties are very familiar with. While I was reading the short story "Gooseberries" by Chekhov, the phrase kept coming back to me. When Ivan told the story of his brother, Nikolay, the difference of their perception of the world became very apparent. Nikolay was trying to secure his little island, his place in the country, his gooseberry patch, cut off from the rest of humanity. His peace lay in living in a controlled environment, almost a bubble-like environment. Even before he could make his dream a reality, his fantasy of the dream sustained him. Everything in his life prior to his obtaining the farm was geared toward its acquisition. He never lived in the present, his every moment was geared for the future. He spent time drawing his dream, as he lived, ate and dressed like a beggar, constantly saving every penny for "his dream." He was a man obsessed, so much so that once he achieved his farm, he even had to lie to himself as to how grand it was. The truth was too painful for him to face, he had sacrificed too much to admit it wasn't all he cracked it up to be. He had to constantly tell himself how good the gooseberries tasted, he even had to get up in the middle of the night to eat one after another. He constantly had to reinforce the lie, or he might have had to face the reality, and how painful that would have been for a man as obsessed as Nikolay. "The falsehood that exalts we cherish more than meaner truths that are a thousand strong."

Ivan, the storyteller, is coming from another perspective. He is aware of all that is around him. He is not an island cut off from all others. The difference is clearly shown even before the story of his brother is told. It describes how Ivan leaves the restricted confines of the bathing cabin, which his friend Alyohin uses in a protected environment, and plunges into the open water. The rain is falling, he is part of all that flows around him. He is immersed in it, he is surrounded by it. He raises waves, he swims vigorously, as he attempts to touch bottom. He literally touches bottom by swimming to the mill and speaking to the peasants. It is all part of his reality, his experience.

Ivan describes his brother's life prior to acquiring his farm. How his whole life was lived so miserably, so geared to the one obsession of obtaining his "patch." He had cut off any feeling of anyone else's suffering. His dream was such an obsession that he could stand by and watch his wife die for lack of nourishment because all had to be sacrificed to attain his "dream." Nothing and no one mattered, in fact they did not even exist in the realm of his consciousness. He had built his ditches, fences, hedges and rows of fir trees around his heart many years before he built them around his gooseberry patch. If Nikolay lived today, I would see him as a man who would walk through Penn Station in Manhattan staring straight ahead, not taking notice of the hundreds of homeless huddled on the floor.

Ivan had no such restrictions. He was not a slave to an obsession, but rather free to all and not limited to "one." And yet his openness to all around him left him vulnerable to feeling more, to suffering more. It filled him with despair to see a happy man, oblivious to all around him.

It is difficult to have a conscience and to live in a world that by and large is not burdened by such baggage. And yet to be truly alive, to be truly a man in a generic sense, one has to be aware, to be alive to all that is around him. The alternative of such is the dance of the "walking dead." It is living, but not really living, rather simply going through the motions. To some it is acceptable, to me it is impossible. I, like Ivan, am not an island. I am my brother's keeper, the bell that tolls is for me as well. It is not easy, but the alternative is intolerable. All of us, as Ivan did, must pull the covers over our head once in awhile. However, to go through life like that would be cheating oneself of life itself.

Begin now to write the rough draft of your essay. When you have finished writing it, take a break for twenty-four hours.

FOCUS ON FORM AND STYLE: THE ELEMENTS OF THE SHORT STORY

Short stories invite us into a fictional world of their own making. But whether this world is Czarist Russia in the nineteenth century or New York City in the twentieth century, there are familiar elements in human experience that allow us, like the writers of the journals you read earlier in this chapter, to move freely through stories confident that we will find some common meeting ground for responding to them. However, once we experience this personal involvement in the lives of the characters, we also need to step back a bit and use our knowledge of the story in a somewhat different way—to derive from our careful reading of the text an interpretation that provides us as much as possible with an understanding of the story's meaning. Our reading of a story is bound to comprise a complex web of subjective associations and objective analysis. Realizing how difficult it is to separate these strands, we need to do just that whenever we attempt to interpret a story—through an explanation of the story-telling techniques and language use we encounter in literature.

In the task for Chapter 7 you might have done something similar if you wrote on a television drama or film. Viewers of TV and film acquire a visual vocabulary and grammar for interpreting what they experience on a screen—for example, an awareness of how camera angles can influence our perception of what is happening to the characters, or how silence or a pause in the action can arouse an expectation of a violent action to come. Frequent viewers of these and other images become accustomed to interpreting the reality of life on the screen through visual conventions of story telling. The experience—or process—of viewing a film is deeply affected by the use of these techniques.

Beginnings

Our experience of reading a short story is no less influenced by the way a story is told. How many readers can resist turning to the last page of a story before they read it—not to read the ending but to count how many pages the story has? This habit isn't necessarily a sign of the reader's laziness: it indicates how important length may be to the reader, who realizes that reading a three-page story demands a different kind of involvement and perspective from reading a forty-page one.

From the opening words of a story our interpretive energies are at work. The beginning of the story "Gooseberries" shows us two men seen from a distance, outlined against a broad expanse of sky, landscape and human habitation. The story teller, or narrator, tells us what the two men feel about this land and prepares the reader for another story—Ivan's story of his brother—

that is to follow. The effect on the reader is that of a leisurely, unhurried introduction to some aspect of human experience, something that we will learn about in good time, for the rain begins to fall and the two men have to find their way to shelter at a peasant's farm.

By contrast, the beginning of "The Lesson" immerses us directly into the consciousness of the character named Sylvia. We only see what she sees, learning about the events of the day though this young girl's distinctive, stingingly acute street talk. Yet, as her first sentence indicates, the story that is to follow is already the past, for it took place "back in the days when everyone was old and stupid or young and foolish." The narrator is herself distanced from these events and so the reader is prompted to judge the action with a similar detachment.

Our understanding and appreciation of these and other stories will depend on how well we respond to the multiplicity of details we find in them. In the rest of this section we shall look briefly at the elements of the short story, and how the reader can focus on them in the process of interpretation.

Plot

"Once upon a time. . . ." And so on. We read a story to get to the end. Along the way we follow a series of events that occur in time. Whether these events are presented chronologically or in a different order, they should be connected in a way the reader perceives as coherent. This coherent pattern of action is what we mean when we refer to the *plot* of a story. Embedded in this plot is often a *conflict*, or opposition of forces that moves the story along until the conflict is somehow resolved. The conflict between Ivan's values and his brother's; between Sylvia's attitudes towards life and Miss Moore's—these oppositions generate the action and reveal the characters to us.

Character

Thus action creates character, and character creates action. For many readers the meaning of a story depends upon their ability to identify the characters as the equivalent of real human beings, or as one poet referred to the essence of a poem, real toads in imaginary gardens. A *major character* carries the most significance for the story's plot and theme but even *minor characters* can highlight some important point in the story. For example, in "Gooseberries" we might conclude that Alyohin's beautiful servant Pelageya, contrasted with Nikolay's cook who "looked like a pig," tells us something about the relative worth of the values represented by the hardworking, healthy peasant and the obsessed, corrupted brother of Ivan. As a means of providing us with insight, many stories set up implied comparisons and contrasts of characters. We can infer from them what characters mean, why they interact the way they do, how and why they change during the course of the story. This insight contributes to our understanding of the story as a whole.

Point of View

In our discussion of the opening paragraphs of "Gooseberries" and "The Lesson," we focused on the difference in the narrative voices in each story — in other words, who tells the story and how. The status and role of the narrator in fiction is called *point of view*. "Gooseberries," as we have seen, is told from a *third-person* point of view, a narrator who knows what the characters think and feel about Ivan's story of his brother. This is an *omniscient point of view* and has the advantage of giving a broad and knowing insight into the action and characters. "The Lesson" is told by a *first person* narrator whose knowledge of her experience seems limited by her adolescent emotions and value judgments. Although we see the other characters only through Sylvia's eyes, the reader can discern qualities of Miss Moore that the young girl cannot.

Theme

This brief discussion of plot, character, and point of view should indicate how all the elements of a story work together to provide us with the *theme* of a story, the overall generalization that we can make about the story's point or significance. The statement of a story's theme can be a simple sentence that attempts to sum up what the story means: "The theme of 'The Lesson' is that Sylvia determines to close the gap that separates her from the wealthy white world of Fifth Avenue." You might conclude that this statement of theme doesn't really convey adequately what you think this story meant. Your thematic statement, then, would attempt to account for your reading experience and interpretation. Stories that really engage our emotions and intellect rarely can be neatly reduced to a single meaning or theme. The theme can often be restated to convey another idea about the story that seems equally important.

Irony

Another characteristic that can emerge from our reading of a story is the use of *irony*. Irony implies a gap between what is said and what may be really meant (see Chapter 7, p. 307). When Sylvia as an adult narrator refers to her life "back in the days when everyone was old and stupid or young and foolish," she may be telling us that that's the way she might have seen others as a young girl; that is, she no longer judges people so narrowly or so simplistically as she did in her youth. Her speech is to be taken ironically rather than strictly literally. A more significant use of irony may explain the ending of "Gooseberries," where Burkin goes to his troubled sleep after Ivan's impassioned pleas to "Do Good!" seem to fall upon ears more attuned to enjoying the worldly pleasures of Alyohin's house. And of course the gooseberries themselves have a biting irony in Ivan's story of his brother

Nikolay's quest for happiness. Chekhov's irony seems directed to some larger discrepancy between human ideals and actions.

The presence of irony in a work of literature should caution us against looking for a specific "moral" or "lesson" in what we read. Few stories that deliberately set out to enforce some moral instruction will engage our imagination for long. Ancient forms of storytelling like fables and parables did aim to convey some spiritual point of practical wisdom. But your interpretation of a short story—a fairly modern type of fiction—should be the end result of all the observations, perceptions, inferences, judgments, and conclusions you can make about the story.

SOME PRACTICE WITH INTERPRETING "GOOSEBERRIES" AND "THE LESSON"

1. Read the opening of the story, "I Stand Here Ironing" by Tillie Olsen, that follows. What do you assume will be the main focus of the story? How does this beginning establish a conflict that needs to be resolved? Write a paragraph in which you explain your speculations.

> I stand here ironing, and what you asked me moves tormented back and forth with the iron.
>
> "I wish you would manage the time to come in and talk with me about your daughter. I'm sure you can help me understand her. She's a youngster who needs help and whom I'm deeply interested in helping."
>
> "Who needs help." . . . Even if I came, what good would it do? You think because I am her mother I have a key, or that in some way you could use me as a key? She has lived for nineteen years. There is all that life that has happened outside of me, beyond me.
>
> And when is there time to remember, to sift, to weigh, to estimate, to total? I will start and there will be an interruption and I will have to gather it all together again. Or I will become engulfed with all I did or did not do, with what should have been and what cannot be helped.

2. How would "Gooseberries" be different if it had a first-person narrator like Ivan? What if Nikolay were the narrator?

3. Explain in a paragraph or two why Toni Cade Bambara chose Sylvia to tell the story rather than Miss Moore. What if it were told by one of the other children, say Sugar?

4. Write down a list of all the things you did or that happened to you today. Do those actions or events form a plot? If not, how can you connect events

so that they form a plot? Finally, create from them a brief narrative that you can read to a group of other readers who will share their narratives with you.

5. Try to imagine a movie of either "Gooseberries" or "The Lesson." What scenes in each story would be particularly important to film? How do you envision these scenes? What scenes or descriptive language in either story would you omit? What characteristics of both stories would be hard to convey on the screen? How do you account for this?

6. Choose a story with your group that everyone is familiar with, say a fable or fairy tale. Explain how the story would change if it were told from the point of view of the various characters. Imagine, for example, "Little Red Riding Hood" as told by the wolf.

7. Choose a favorite story of yours and bring it to class, making sure to reproduce copies for members of your group. Ask them to write a paragraph about the story's theme, indicating what characteristics of plot, character, and point of view led them to their conclusions.

REWRITING

Obtaining Feedback on Your Rough Draft

Because your class may be all writing on the same story, you have probably shared your interpretive comments with each other. This should help you to locate points of confusion or controversy in the stories and give you an idea of what points you may still need to resolve for your reader.

After reading different students' rough drafts, you may notice that some specific part of the story was explained in different ways. You may want to rethink your own view in light of those differences.

Check to see that you have not unnecessarily retold or summarized portions of the plot. Retell only those passages that you intend to analyze or explain, keeping your summary to the bare essentials.

Make use of the "Audience Response Guide" to obtain feedback on your draft from your "other self," your peers, or your instructor:

AUDIENCE RESPONSE GUIDE

1. What did the writer want to explain or interpret in this paper? What is her or his purpose in writing about this story? What does she or he want the paper to mean?

2. How does this interpretation affect other readers of the story?

3. How effective has the writer been in conveying her or his interpretation of the story? What are the strengths of the paper? What are the weaknesses?

4. How should the paper be revised to better fulfill its purpose and meaning?

The student who wrote the rough draft "No Man Is an Island" received the following comments from her peer evaluation group:

1. The writer stated that she chose to compare Ivan's and Nikolay's characters as a means of bringing out the idea that human beings should not only be concerned about their own happiness.

2. The readers agreed that the two characters seemed very familiar types to a modern audience. Their lifestyles would be typical of lifestyles in today's world.

3. The readers thought that her observations on Ivan were very effective. They agreed, however, that she did not take into consideration what Ivan's faults or blind spots might be. They also felt the writer should have gotten more quickly and directly to her point.

4. The writer might try to suggest what Chekhov's overall point of view toward life might be and generalize more about the theme of the story.

Revision of Student Essay "No Man Is an Island"

Here is a revised version of the student's essay. How has the writer responded to the group's suggestions? What other revisions would you suggest?

NO MAN IS AN ISLAND

While reading the short story "Gooseberries," by Chekhov, the phrase "No Man Is an Island" kept coming back to me. When

Ivan told the story of his brother Nikolay, the difference of their perception of the world became very apparent.

Nikolay was trying to secure his little island, his place in the country, his gooseberry patch. His peace lay in living in a controlled environment, almost a bubble-like environment. Even before he could make his dream a reality, his fantasy of the dream sustained him. Everything in his life prior to his obtaining the farm was geared toward its acquisition. He never lived in the present, his every moment was geared for the future. He spent time drawing his dream, as he lived, ate and dressed like a beggar, constantly saving every penny for "his dream." He was a man obsessed, so much so that once he achieved his farm, he even had to lie to himself as to how grand it was. The truth was too painful for him to face; he had sacrificed too much to admit it wasn't all he cracked it up to be. He had to constantly tell himself how good the gooseberries tasted; he even had to get up in the middle of the night to eat one after another. He constantly had to reinforce the lie, or he might have had to face the reality, and how painful that would have been for a man as obsessed as Nikolay. "The falsehood that exalts we cherish more than meaner truths that are a thousand strong."

Ivan, the storyteller, is coming from another perspective. He seems to be aware of all that is around him and not an island cut off from all others. The difference is clearly shown even before the story of his brother is told, when Ivan leaves the restricted confines of the bathing cabin, which his friend Alyohin uses in a protected environment, and plunges into the open water. The rain is falling; he is part of all that flows around him. He is immersed in it, and surrounded by it. He raises waves, he swims vigorously, as he attempts to touch bottom. He literally touches bottom by swimming to the mill and speaking to the peasants. It is all part of his reality, his experience.

Ivan describes his brother's life prior to acquiring his farm. How his whole life was lived so miserably, so geared to the one obsession of obtaining his "patch." He had cut off any feeling of anyone else's suffering. His dream was such an obsession that he could stand by and watch his wife die for lack of nourishment because all had to be sacrificed to attain his "dream." Nothing and no one mattered; in fact they did not even exist in the realm of his consciousness. He had built his ditches, fences, hedges and rows of fir trees around his heart many years before he built them around his gooseberry patch. If Nikolay lived today, I would see him as a man who would walk through Penn Station in Manhattan staring straight ahead, not taking notice of the hundreds of homeless huddled on the floor.

Ivan had no such restrictions. He was not a slave to an obsession, but rather free to all and not limited to "one." And yet his openness to all around him left him vulnerable to feeling more, to suffering more. It filled him with despair to see a happy man, oblivious to all around him.

For all Ivan's freedom and lack of restrictions in his life, his personal relationship with his brother is a puzzling one. Although he professes such love for his brother, he chooses not to confront Nikolay about his obsessions and lifestyle. Instead, he voices his concern to his friends, where it is of no use to Nikolay. It is obvious that Ivan's emotional expression is rather limited.

It is difficult to have a conscience and to live in a world that by and large is not burdened by such baggage. And yet to be truly alive, to be truly a man in a generic sense, one has to be aware, to be alive to all that is around him. The alternative of such is the dance of the "walking dead." It is living, but not really living, rather simply going through the motions. To some it is acceptable, to me it is impossible. I, like Ivan, am not an island. I am my brother's keeper, the bell that tolls is for me as well. It is not easy, but the alternative is intolerable. All of us, as Ivan did, must pull the covers over our head once in awhile. However, to go through life like that would be cheating oneself of life itself.

Revising Your Essay on a Short Story

As a final step in revising your essay for this chapter's task, answer the following questions about what you have written.

 Checklist for Revising Your Interpretive Essay

1. How clearly did you establish a shaping idea or theme? What evidence from the text did you use as proof for your shaping idea?

2. Did you provide your reader with an adequate context for understanding the personal, social, cultural or literary perspectives you brought to the story?

3. How effectively did you organize your interpretation of the story? Did you proceed logically from one element of the story to another? One thematic concern to another?

4. Do you feel your interpretation makes a real contribution to your reader's understanding and appreciation of the story's meaning and value? How might you improve your interpretation of the story?

5. Were you able to relate your interpretation of the story to some broader context or perspective as a way of showing the story's relevance or significance to a modern reader?

6. If you quoted from the story, does your quotation highlight some important point in the story that is vital to your interpretation?

Now revise and edit your rough draft.

BECOMING AWARE OF YOURSELF AS A WRITER

1. What value did your journal have as a means for developing your ideas about a work of literature?

2. What do you think is most important for a writer to convey about a work of literature?

3. How might your knowledge of other literary works such as poems, plays, and novels contribute to your interpretation of your chosen story?

4. How do disagreements about the meanings of works of literature get resolved? Can they always he resolved? Should they?

5. Why write about a work of literature in the first place? Isn't it enough for the
   reader to form his or her own opinion? Does it hold true that in matters of
   taste everyone's opinion is equally valid?

6. How might you use your experience with this chapter's task in another literature course?

7. What importance do stories have in our "real" lives? What is the relationship
   between fiction and reality?

8. How would you write an essay on a poem, play, or novel? What special
   problems do you think these kinds of literature would pose that are different
   from writing on short stories?

Handbook

(gr) Grammar, 551

Parts of Speech, p. 551

(noun) The Noun, p. 551
(pron) The Pronoun, p. 551
(vb) The Verb, p. 553
(adj) The Adjective, p. 555
(adv) The Adverb, p. 555

(conj) The Conjunction, p. 555
(conj adv) The Conjunctive Adverb, p. 556
(prep) The Preposition, p. 557
(art) The Article, p. 558

Review Exercise–Parts of Speech, p. 558

Parts of Sentences, p. 558

(subj) The Subject, p. 558
(pred) The Predicate, p. 559

(cpl) The Complement, p. 559

(base) Base Sentences, p. 560

Phrases and Clauses, p. 560

(phr) The Phrase, p. 560
(cl) The Clause, p. 562

(combine) Combined or Expanded Sentences, p. 563

Review Exercise–Parts and Types of Sentences, p. 563

(awk) Awkward Sentences, p. 564

(cdn/subn) Faulty Coordination or Subordination, p. 564
(inc) Incomplete Sentences, p. 565

(mix) Mixed Sentences, p. 566
(pv) Inconsistent Point of View, p. 566

Review Exercise–Awkward Sentences, p. 567

(gr) Common Grammatical Errors, p. 568

(agr) Faulty Agreement, p. 568
(ref) Faulty Reference, p. 572
(ca) Case Errors, p. 573
(mm/dg) Misplaced and Dangling Modifiers, p. 576

(‖) Faulty Parallelism, p. 578
(r-o) Run-on Sentences, p. 579
(cs) Comma Splices, p. 579
(frag) Sentence Fragments, p. 581

Review Exercise–Common Grammatical Errors, p. 582

(p) Punctuation, p. 584

(.) The Period, p. 584
(?) The Question Mark, p. 585
(!) The Exclamation Point, p. 586
(,) The Comma, p. 586
(;) The Semicolon, p. 590
(:) The Colon, p. 591

(—/--) The Dash, p. 592
(( )/[ ]) Parentheses and Brackets, p. 593
(. . .) The Ellipsis, p. 595
(" ") Quotation Marks, p. 596
(') The Apostrophe, p. 599

(m) Mechanics, p. 601

(cap) Capitalization, p. 601
(ital) Italics, p. 604
(ab) Abbreviations, p. 604

(num) Numbers, p. 606
(-) Hyphenation, p. 608
(sp) Spelling, p. 608

Review Exercise–Punctuation and Mechanics, p. 617

Grammar

PARTS OF SPEECH

The Noun

A noun designates a person, a place, an object, a quality, or an idea. It names something.

A common noun refers to a member of a general class of things, such as an *artist*, a *town*, a *car*, *beauty*, *goodness*.

A proper noun names a specific person, place, or thing, such as *Pablo Picasso* or *St. Louis, Missouri*. It may name a particular kind of common noun, such as a *Model-T Ford*. Proper nouns are capitalized.

Most nouns are either singular or plural. The plural is formed with *s* (one *car*, two *cars*) or *es* (one *sandwich*, two *sandwiches*). A few nouns form the plural by a change in their spelling (one *child*, many *children*; one *man*, many *men*). Refer to a good dictionary if you are uncertain about the plural form of any noun.

Adding an apostrophe and an *s* to most nouns indicates possession or ownership (the *woman's* car).

The Pronoun

A pronoun substitutes for a noun or a noun phrase. The noun that a pronoun replaces is called the *antecedent* of the pronoun.

Pronouns help a writer to sound less repetitious, as in the sentence

Joe drove his new car home.

where the pronoun *his* has replaced the proper noun *Joe's*.

Pronouns fall into one of the following categories:

Personal Pronouns.   Personal pronouns take different forms, depending on whether they are used as subjects (subjective form), as objects or indirect objects (objective form), or to indicate ownership (possessive form):

	Subjective		*Objective*		*Possessive*	
	Singular	*Plural*	*Singular*	*Plural*	*Singular*	*Plural*
1st person	I	we	me	us	my, mine	our, ours
2nd person	you	you	you	you	your(s)	your(s)
3rd person	he, she, it	they	him, her, it	them	his, her(s), its	their(s)

Reflexive Pronouns.   Reflexive pronouns indicate an action that affects the person who performs it. They are also used for emphasis:

myself	himself
ourselves	herself
yourself	itself
yourselves	themselves

Indefinite Pronouns.   Indefinite pronouns refer to unspecified persons or things, and so they have no antecedent:

all	everybody	no one
another	everyone	none
any	everything	one
anybody	few	some
anyone	many	somebody
anything	most	someone
both	nobody	something
each		

Demonstrative Pronouns.   Demonstrative pronouns point something or someone out:

this	these
that	those

Relative Pronouns.   Relative pronouns introduce noun or adjective clauses:

who (subjective)	which
whom (objective)	that
whose (possessive)	

Interrogative Pronouns.   Interrogative pronouns ask questions:

who/whom   which
whose   what

The Verb

vb

A verb expresses an action (*to drive*) or a state of being (*to live*). The root or plain form of any verb is the infinitive, the form listed in the dictionary and usually combined with *to*. This plain form is altered in a variety of ways, depending on how the verb is being used.

All verbs add *s* or *es* to the plain form in order to indicate third-person singular present (she *drives*, he *lives*); the only exceptions are *to be* (she *is*) and *to have* (he *has*).

What are called *regular verbs* add *d* or *ed* to the plain form in order to indicate the past tense (he *lived*). What are called *irregular verbs* indicate the past tense by more radical alterations of form (she *drove*, he *swam*).

Most verbs form the past participle, which indicates a completed action, by adding *d*, *ed*, *n*, or *en* to the plain form (*lived, driven*), although again there are irregularly formed past participles of verbs such as *to do (done)* or *to keep (kept)*. The present participle, which indicates a continuing action, is formed by the addition of *ing* to the plain form of a verb *(living, driving, doing, keeping)*.

Refer to a dictionary if you are uncertain about the past tense or the past participle of a verb. Any good dictionary lists the past tense if it is irregular, the past participle, and the present participle of a verb.

A verb can be combined with an auxiliary or helping verb to indicate different relationships between the action or state of being that the verb describes and the passage of time (tense), or the actor (voice), or the writer's view of the action (mood). The modal auxiliaries are *can, could, do, does, did, may, might, must, shall, should, will,* and *would.*

Tense.   Verb tense indicates the relationship between an action or state of being and the passage of time. The present tense indicates that something is taking place now (I *live*, you *live*, he or she *lives*, we *live*, you *live*, they *live*). The past tense indicates that something was completed in the past (he *lived*, she *drove*). The future tense indicates that something will take place in the future (she *will drive*).

Each of these three tenses may be formed by use of the past or the present participle. The combination of a past participle with a form of the auxiliary verb *to have* produces what are called the *perfect tenses*, which focus on a completed action: present perfect (I *have driven*, she *has driven*); past perfect (she *had driven*); and future perfect (she *will have driven*). The combination of a present participle with a form of the auxiliary verb *to be* produces what are called the *progressive tenses*, which focus on an ongoing or continuing action: present progressive (I *am living*, you *are living*, he *is living*, we, you, they *are living); past progressive (I *was driving*, you *were driving*, she *was driving*, we, you, they *were driving*); and future progressive (she *will be driving*).

More complex combinations of verb forms are possible, for example the present perfect progressive (she *has been driving*), which focuses on an ongoing action in the past, continuing into the present.

Voice. A verb may be either active or passive, depending on whether the subject of the verb is performing the action (she *drives* the car) or is being acted on (the car *was driven* by her; she *was driven* crazy by her car). The passive voice is formed with a past participle and the auxiliary verb *to be*.

Note: The active voice tends to be more direct and concise than the passive. Compare the following:

Joe reeled in the fish. (ACTIVE)
The fish was reeled in by Joe. (PASSIVE)

But the passive voice is useful if you want to focus on a person or thing that has been acted upon:

The thief was finally caught by the police.

or if you don't know or don't need to say who or what performed the action:

A week after the hurricane, the electricity was finally restored to our neighborhood.

(For a more complete discussion of active and passive constructions, see the "Focus" section in Chapter 7, pp. 304–305.)

Mood. A verb may be formed to reflect any one of three different moods or attitudes: the indicative mood states a fact or an opinion (she *drives* carefully), or it asks a question (*does* she *drive* carefully?); the imperative mood gives commands or directions (*drive* carefully); the subjunctive mood expresses doubt or uncertainty (I'm not sure that she *should drive* at all), or it states a condition (if she *were to drive* carefully, she'd make me feel better), or it expresses a suggestion or a wish (I'd like it if she *would drive* carefully), or it states a requirement (it is important that she *be* a careful driver). Note that the subjunctive employs *be* (rather than *am, is,* or *are*) in the present tense and *were* (rather than *was*) in the past tense.

The Adjective

An adjective modifies a noun by describing a particular attribute of it (a *blue* car), by qualifying it (a *good* car), or by specifying it (the *second* car; *my* car). In qualifying a noun, an adjective may limit (*that* car) or broaden (*any* car; *most* cars) the meaning of the noun.

An attributive adjective comes immediately before or after the noun it modifies (it is a *dangerous* car). A predicate adjective is separated from its noun by a linking verb (the car is *dangerous*).

An adjective often can be identified by its suffix: *-able, -ous, -full, -less, -ic, -er, -est*. The last two suffixes indicate the comparative and superlative forms of many adjectives (*happy, happier, happiest*). Other adjectives form the comparative and superlative by combining with *more* and *most* (*dangerous, more dangerous, most dangerous*).

The Adverb

An adverb modifies a verb (she drives *slowly*), an adjective (the road is *dangerously* steep), another adverb (she drives *more* slowly), or a complete clause or sentence (*evidently*, she is a careful driver).

Many adverbs are formed by adding *ly* to an adjective:

shy, shyly	beautiful, beautifully
nice, nicely	hopeless, hopelessly
terrible, terribly	comical, comically
dangerous, dangerously	

Adverbs often specify when something happened (the storm ended *today*; I got lost *again*); where it happened (it was colder *inside* than *outside*; I tried to call you *there*); the manner in which it happened (she left *quickly*; she spoke *hoarsely*); or the extent or degree to which it happened (she *almost* lost her wallet; he *never* thought about it).

Most adverbs form comparatives and superlatives by combining with *more* and *most*, although a few add *er* and *est* (*soon, sooner, soonest*).

The Conjunction

A conjunction links one part of a sentence to another part. It joins words, phrases, and clauses to one another, showing the relationships between them; for example, the coordinating conjunction *and* shows equality between two parts of a sentence, whereas the subordinating conjunction *because* indicates a cause-and-effect relationship.

Coordinating conjunctions link words or phrases or clauses of equal grammatical rank. They may link one word to another (dogs *and* cats), one phrase to another (in the house *or* in the car), or one clause to another (I like candy, *but* I am on a diet). The coordinating conjunctions are *and, but, or, nor, for, so,* and *yet.*

Correlative conjunctions work in pairs, such as *both . . . and, not only . . . but also, either . . . or, neither . . . nor (either* knock on the door *or* ring the bell).

Subordinating conjunctions link dependent clauses, which cannot stand by themselves as sentences, to independent clauses, which can stand by themselves as sentences (she took the blue car *because* it is faster). Subordinating conjunctions include *after, although, as, because, before, if, in order that, once, since, so, than, unless, until, when, whenever, where, wherever,* and *while.*

The Conjunctive Adverb

Conjunctive adverbs, or sentence connectors, link independent clauses. Like conjunctions, they focus attention on the nature of the relationship between the clauses, although often they do so more emphatically. In the sentence

They could not get their car started; consequently, they walked home.

the conjunctive adverb *consequently* emphasizes the cause-and-effect relationship between the two clauses. In the example

The first time they met, he didn't like her at all. The next time, however, he fell in love.

the conjunctive adverb *however* emphasizes the contrast between the two sentences.

Whereas coordinating conjunctions are usually preceded by a comma, conjunctive adverbs are usually preceded by a semicolon. Also, whereas both coordinating and subordinating conjunctions always stand between the two parts of the sentence that they join, a conjunctive adverb may be moved around within the second clause:

They could not get their car started; they, consequently, walked home.

Conjunctive adverbs include the following:

accordingly	as a result	conversely	for instance
also	besides	earlier	further
afterward	certainly	finally	hence
anyway	consequently	for example	however

in addition	meanwhile	on the other hand	thereafter
indeed	moreover	otherwise	therefore
instead	nevertheless	similarly	thus
in the same way	next	still	undoubtedly
likewise	nonetheless	subsequently	
later	now	then	

The Preposition

prep

A preposition links a noun, a pronoun, or a group of words functioning as a noun to some other word in a sentence. It indicates the relationship in time, space, or logic between the linked words (the car is *in* the garage).

Prepositions include the following:

about	behind	except	onto	toward
above	below	for	out	under
across	beneath	from	outside	underneath
after	beside	in	over	unlike
against	between	inside	past	until
along	beyond	into	regarding	up
among	by	like	round	upon
around	concerning	near	since	with
as	despite	of	through	within
at	down	off	throughout	without
before	during	on	to	

The noun linked to another word by a preposition is called the *object* of the preposition. The combination of the preposition, its object, and any words modifying the object is called a *prepositional phrase*. In the prepositional phrase *in the garage*, the preposition is *in*, the object is *garage*, and the modifier is *the*.

Prepositional phrases usually function as adjectives or adverbs in sentences. The phrase *in the garage* is adverbial, describing where the car is located. In the following sentences, the prepositional phrases function as adjectives:

The house *around the corner* burned down.
The girl *in the green coat* sneezed.
It was John, *with his mother*.

In the next group of sentences, the prepositional phrases are adverbial:

She ran *around the track*.
He left *in a hurry*.
John writes *with clarity and skill*.

art

The Article

The articles are *a, an,* and *the.* They modify nouns. *A* and *an* are indefinite; *a car* could mean any car. *The* is definite; *the car* indicates a specific car.

The article *a* precedes nouns that start with a consonant sound *(a rocket).* The article *an* precedes nouns that start with a vowel sound *(an astronaut).*

REVIEW EXERCISE–PARTS OF SPEECH

Identify as a noun, verb, adjective, or adverb each underlined word in the following passage and explain why you identify it that way. For example, the word *boxed* in the sentence *They boxed me in* is a verb, as indicated by the *-ed* ending and by the action the word conveys.

For days, Jackson gazed searchingly at the sky for a break in the weather. But the biting cold persisted. It was the coldest fall on record. The area where he used to garden and the field where he took his walks had turned yellow. Yellow was the dominant color everywhere, a light shade, sulphurous almost, that seemed to infect the light in the sky as well. Growing old was bitter, he told himself. When he had been younger, he never minded these turns in the season. In those days, no matter how much nature trashed the woods, his own vital force never diminished. But now the winds knifed into his soul. And only with a grave distrust, and with a quaking in his innermost being, could he eye that horizon line of trees beyond the window.

PARTS OF SENTENCES

subj

The Subject

A subject is a noun (or a word or a group of words serving as a noun) that tells who or what is doing the action or experiencing the state of being expressed by the verb in a clause. In the main clause

The boy's mother had to drive home slowly,

mother is the simple subject, the noun without any modifiers; *the boy's mother* is the complete subject, the noun with its modifiers.

A pronoun, of course, may act as a subject, but other parts of speech may do so also. For example, in the sentence

Driving home took a long time.

the gerund phrase *driving home* serves as a noun and is the subject.

The Predicate

A predicate is usually said to include all parts of a clause other than the subject and its modifiers. A simple predicate is the verb and its auxiliaries, such as the verb *to drive* and its auxiliary *had* in the sentence

   The boy's mother had to drive home slowly.

The complete predicate includes any modifiers of the verb *(slowly)* and any complements *(home)*.

The Complement

A complement is a word or a word group that completes or modifies the subject, the verb, or the object of a clause.
   Subject complements are called *predicate adjectives* or *predicate nominatives*. A predicate adjective follows a linking verb (often a form of *to be* or a verb like *to become, to appear*, or *to seem*) and modifies the subject, as does the adjective *cautious* in the sentence

   She is cautious.

   A predicate nominative is a noun (or a noun substitute) that follows a linking verb and defines the subject more specifically, as does the noun *driver* in the sentence

   She is the driver of the car.

   Verb complements are called *direct* and *indirect objects*. A direct object is a noun (or a noun substitute) that names who or what is affected by the action of the verb. In the sentence

   She gave the keys to him.

the direct object is *keys*, and the indirect object is *him*. An indirect object is a noun (or its substitute) that names to or for whom or what the action is done.
   Object complements are adjectives and nouns (or their substitutes) that modify direct objects. In the sentence

   She gave the car keys to him.

car is an object complement.

base

BASE SENTENCES

The most basic sentence structure is a simple subject and predicate:

She drives.

This structure is often expanded by the addition of complements to the predicate:

She drives the car cautiously.

Such base sentences may be combined with others to form longer, more complicated sentence structures. These longer sentences may be composed of clusters of words (usually phrases) that act as free modifiers, and/or coordinate clauses, and/or subordinate clauses. See the "Focus" section of Chapter 5 (pp. 212–222).

PHRASES AND CLAUSES

The Phrase

A phrase is a group of words that acts as a single part of a speech. Unlike a clause, it has no subject and predicate.

The following are the most common types of phrases:

The Noun Phrase. A noun phrase is a noun (*car*) and its modifiers. The most common modifiers are articles (*the* car), adjectives (the *blue* car), and prepositional phrases (the blue car *in the garage*). A noun phrase functions as a single noun in a sentence. In the sentence

The blue car in the garage is mine.

the noun phrase functions as the subject.

The Verb Phrase. A verb phrase is a verb (*drive*) and its auxiliaries (*should* drive). It may be expanded by the addition of one or more adverbs (should drive *slowly*), prepositional phrases (should drive slowly *on this road*), or complements (should drive the *car* slowly on this road).

The Prepositional Phrase. A prepositional phrase is a preposition combined with its object and any modifiers. It usually functions as an adjective or an adverb in a clause. In the sentence

The girl at the beach likes to swim.

phr

the prepositional phrase *at the beach* functions as an adjective; in the sentence

She likes to swim at the beach.

the same phrase functions as an adverb.

The Infinitive Phrase. An infinitive phrase consists of an infinitive form of a verb along with its subject, and/or object, and/or modifiers. In the sentence

We expected John to tell his mother right away.

John is the subject of the infinitive *to tell, mother* is the object, and *right away* is an adverbial modifier; within the sentence, this infinitive phrase functions as the direct object of the verb *expected* and so is being used as a noun. An infinitive phrase may also be used as an adjective:

John is the person to tell his mother.

or as an adverb:

John left to tell his mother.

The Participial Phrase. A participial phrase consists of a past or present participle along with its object and/or any modifiers. Participial phrases function as adjectives. In the sentence

Soaked to the skin, they came in out of the storm.

the participial phrase *soaked* (past participle) *to the skin* modifies the pronoun *they.* In the sentence

Soaking wet, they came in out of the storm.

the participial phrase *soaking* (present participle) *wet* functions similarly.

The Gerund Phrase. A gerund phrase consists of an *-ing* verb when it serves as a noun, along with its subject, and/or object, and/or any modifiers. Gerund phrases function as nouns. In the sentence

His driving the car recklessly made her nervous.

the gerund phrase consists of the gerund *driving* along with its subject *(his),* its object *(car),* and an adverbial modifier *(recklessly);* the entire phrase serves as the subject of the sentence.

The Absolute Phrase. An absolute phrase consists of a noun or pronoun and a participle, along with any modifiers. It modifies a whole base sentence rather than a single word within the base sentence. In the sentence

The car skidding on the rain slick road, the driver held his breath.

the phrase preceding *the driver* is absolute; it has its own subject *(car)* and modifies the whole base sentence. Compare it to the participial phrase that modifies only *the car* in the following sentence:

The driver held his breath as he felt the car skidding on the rain-slick road.

The Clause

cl

A clause is a group of words that contains a subject and a predicate.
  A main or independent clause can stand alone as a sentence:

He drove to the bank.

Two or more main clauses may be linked to form a single sentence with a coordinating conjunction, or a semicolon, or a conjunctive adverb:

He drove to the bank, and he deposited the money.

or

He drove to the bank; and he deposited the money.

or

He drove to the bank; then he deposited the money.

  A subordinate or dependent clause cannot stand alone as a sentence because it is introduced by either a relative pronoun, such as *that* or *which*, or a subordinating conjunction, such as *because* or *if* or *when*. Subordinate clauses function as nouns, adjectives, or adverbs in a sentence. Noun clauses and adjective clauses usually begin with a relative pronoun. Adverbial clauses always begin with a subordinating conjunction. In the sentence

That you drive carefully is a comfort to me.

the noun clause *(that you drive carefully)* acts as the subject. In the sentence

The new front tire, which he just bought yesterday, went flat today.

the adjective clause *(which he just bought yesterday)* modifies the noun *tire*. In the sentence

When he hit the brakes, the car swerved to the left.

the adverbial clause *(when he hit the brakes)* modifies the verb *swerved*.

COMBINED OR EXPANDED SENTENCES

combine

Base sentences may be combined or expanded to form compound, complex, or compound-complex sentences. A base sentence, or simple sentence, consists of a single clause:

The red sportscar in the garage is mine.

A compound sentence consists of two or more main clauses linked by a coordinating conjunction, a semicolon, or a conjunctive adverb:

The red sportscar in the garage is mine; however, I might sell it.

A complex sentence consists of one main clause and one or more subordinate clauses:

Although I will miss driving the car, I will sell it if I can get a good price.

A compound-complex sentence consists of two or more main clauses and one or more subordinate clauses:

The red sportscar in the garage is mine, but I might sell it if I can get a good price.

A simple sentence, then, may be expanded into one with a more complicated structure by the addition of phrases, by the coordination of one or more main clauses, or by a combination of main clauses with subordinate and relative clauses. See the "Focus" sections of Chapters 5 (pp. 212–222), 6 (pp. 258–263), and 7 (pp. 302–311) for additional discussion of sentence length and style.

REVIEW EXERCISE–PARTS AND TYPES OF SENTENCES

In the following paragraph, identify the parts of each sentence, the subject, the predicate, and their complements. How many different types of phrases can you identify? How many subordinate clauses? Label each sentence as simple, compound, complex, or compound-complex. Finally, rewrite the paragraph, combining its base sentences into larger sentence units:

> Nick sat against the wall of the church where they had dragged him to be clear of machine-gun fire in the street. Both legs stuck out awkwardly. He had been hit in the spine. His face was sweaty and dirty. The sun shone on his face. The day was very hot. Rinaldi, big backed, his equipment sprawling, lay face downward against the wall. Nick looked straight ahead brilliantly. The pink wall of the house opposite had fallen out from the roof, and an iron bedstead hung twisted toward the street. Two Austrian dead lay in the rubble in the shade of the house. Up the street were other dead. Things were getting forward in the town. It was going well. Stretcher bearers would be along any time now. Nick turned his head carefully and looked at Rinaldi. "Senta Rinaldi. Senta. You and me we've made a separate peace." Rinaldi lay still in the sun breathing with difficulty. "Not patriots." Nick turned his head carefully away smiling sweatily. Rinaldi was a disappointing audience.
>
> —Ernest Hemingway, *In Our Time*

awk

AWKWARD SENTENCES

Sentences become awkward or confused for many reasons: a writer may employ faulty coordination or subordination, may omit necessary sentence elements, may mix elements that are incompatible, or may make inconsistent shifts in point of view.

cdn/ subn

Faulty Coordination or Subordination

When the logical connection between two coordinated clauses, phrases, or words is unclear, the writing suffers from faulty coordination: in the sentence

> She likes to drive, but her teeth hurt.

the coordinating conjunction (*but*) fails to make clear why the writer has chosen to link the subject's feelings about driving to the subject's problems with her teeth.

When the logical connection between a subordinate clause and a main clause is unclear, the writing suffers from faulty subordination: in the sentence

> Because my breaks failed, I hit the tree instead of the pedestrian.

the subordinating conjunction *(because)* fails to explain why the driver hit the tree rather than hitting the pedestrian. Often faulty subordination occurs when a writer subordinates what seems to be the main idea of the sentence: the sentence

When I hit the tree, I had never had an accident before.

might be better revised so that the emphasis falls on the main point:

Although I had never had an accident before, I hit the tree.

Incomplete Sentences

inc

Incomplete sentences are missing necessary words or phrases.

In a compound construction, a word that has the same function as, but differs grammatically from, a preceding word should not be omitted. For example, in the sentence

The car was given an oil change, and its flat tire (was) fixed.

the second *was* might be omitted; but if the subject of the second clause were plural, its verb could not be so shortened:

The car was given an oil change, and its wheels (were) aligned.

An incomplete sentence also results when a comparison is made incompletely or illogically. In the sentence

My car is faster.

a reader is not told what the car is faster than. In the sentence

She likes the car better than her brother.

a reader is uncertain if the subject likes the car better than she likes her brother or better than her brother likes the car.

If two things are being compared that are not really comparable, the sentence will be logically incomplete. In the sentence

The engine in his car was more powerful than most of the other cars in the race.

an engine is being compared to other cars rather than to the engines of other cars.

Incomplete sentences also result when a writer omits a needed article or preposition. For example, the sentence

The boy has both a talent and love of fixing engines.

is incomplete because the preposition *for* is needed after the word *talent* and the article *a* is needed before the word *love*.

---

mix

Mixed Sentences

In a mixed sentence, two parts are presented as compatible either in grammar or in meaning when they actually are incompatible. For example, in the sentence

After driving all night made him feel exhausted.

a prepositional phrase *(after driving all night)* is being treated ungrammatically as a subject and is linked to a predicate *(made him feel exhausted)*.
In the sentence

Driving all night is when he feels exhausted.

an adverbial clause *(when he feels exhausted)* is being equated, illogically, with a noun substitute *(driving all night)*. When a predicate does not apply logically to a subject in this way, it is called *faulty predication*. A linking verb, like *is*, should connect a noun with another noun that is logically comparable to it, as in the revised sentence

Driving all night is an activity that makes him feel exhausted.

Do not link a subject and a predicate together that are not logically comparable, as in the sentence

The use of seat belts was invented to save lives.

The *seat belts* themselves, not their *use*, were invented to save lives.

---

pv

Inconsistent Point of View

A sentence of a paragraph can become awkward if there are logical inconsistencies in the verb tense or mood or voice. In the sentence

He drove the car home and parks it in the garage.

the writer has shifted confusingly from past to present tense. In the sentence

> I was mad when I failed the driving test because I practiced for so many weeks before taking it.

the point of view with regard to verb tense is awkward because the writer indicates an action that was completed before the ·test was taken: the verb should be placed in the past perfect tense *(had practiced)*. In the sentence

> If you are caught speeding, you would get a ticket.

the shift from indicative to subjunctive mood is a confusing inconsistency; *would* should be changed to *will*. In the sentence

> Ann waxed the car after it had been washed.

the shift from active voice *(Ann waxed the car)* to passive voice *(it had been washed)* creates an ambiguity about who actually washed the car; if Ann washed it, the subordinate clause might be better revised to read *after she had washed it.*

A sentence also may become awkward if there are inconsistencies in person or number with reference to pronouns. In the sentence

> If one drives too slowly on the highway, you can cause an accident.

the shift from third person *(one)* to the second person *(you)* is confusing. Similarly, if in this sentence the writer had substituted *they* for *you*, the shift from singular *(one)* to plural *(they)* would have been awkward.

REVIEW EXERCISE–AWKWARD SENTENCES

Recast each of the following sentences so that it is no longer awkward. Make whatever changes or additions that you need in order to clarify the meaning of each sentence.

1. If a person thinks about it, you would understand why it's easy for anyone to make mistakes.

2. Buying a computer is easy; learning to use one is where you run into trouble.

3. The driver of the car said that the reason why he crashed into the fence was because of a cow in the road.

4. The store had only been open a week, and the thief pulled out his gun.

5. Her muscles were twice the size of anyone else in the gym.

6. The little boy was climbing in the apple tree, which blossoms each year in May, when he fell and broke his leg.

7. While the table was being cleared, she broke a dish and two glasses.

8. She took the weather report more seriously than her brother, since living in Wisconsin and never having seen a hurricane before was something that frightened her, and he sees them often, living now in Florida.

COMMON GRAMMATICAL ERRORS

Faulty Agreement

agr

A verb should agree in person and number with its subject. A pronoun should agree in person, number, and gender with its antecedent.

Subject/Verb Agreement.   In the sentence

> Her car runs well.

the third-person-singular subject *(car)* and the third-person-singular verb *(runs)* are in agreement. If the subject were to become plural *(cars)*, the verb would have to be altered to a plural form *(run)*. If the subject were plural in form but singular in meaning, however, it would take a singular verb:

> The news is good.

When a phrase comes between a subject and its verb, do not make the verb agree with a noun in the phrase rather than with the subject:

> The car with new tires and new breaks costs (SINGULAR) more than the other cars.

Phrases beginning with *in addition to* or *as well as* do not change the subject's number:

> Her car, as well as the other two, was (SINGULAR) broken into.

A compound subject joined by *and* usually takes a plural verb. One exception occurs when the parts of the subject refer to a single entity:

Ice cream and cake is (SINGULAR) my favorite dessert.

Another exception occurs when a compound subject is preceded by *each* or *every*:

Every car and truck on the lot was (SINGULAR) sold.

The indefinite pronouns tend to be singular:

Each of them is (not *are*) right.
Everyone is (not *are*) doing it.

All, any, none, and *some* may be either singular or plural:

Some of his time is (SINGULAR) spent at home.
When they get home at night, some of them watch (PLURAL) television.

Two singular subjects joined by *or* or *nor* take a singular verb:

Either Ann or Al is going to pick up the pizza.

Two plural subjects joined by *or* or *nor* take a plural verb:

Either the girls or the boys are going.

If one of the subjects is singular and one is plural, however, the verb agrees with the subject that is closer to it:

Ann or the boys are going.
The girls or Al is going.

When a sentence begins with *there,* the subject tends to follow the verb. Special attention should be paid to agreement:

There was one hole in the muffler; there were two holes in the tire.

When *there* precedes a compound subject, the verb is singular if the first part of the subject is singular:

There is a hole in the muffler and two flat tires.

When a subject complement follows a linking verb, make sure that the verb agrees with the subject, not with its complement:

Cars and trucks are my hobby.
My hobby is cars and trucks.

A collective noun, which names a group of individuals, takes a singular or a plural verb, depending on whether the group is acting as a unit or as separate individuals:

The team is traveling to the game by bus.
The team are traveling to the game in their own cars.

A singular verb follows a title, a word that is being defined, and a word denoting some form of measurement (weight, an amount of money, a period of time):

Forty thousand miles is a lot to put on a car in a year.

When a relative pronoun is the subject of a clause, the verb should agree in number with the antecedent of the relative pronoun. In the sentence

She is one of those drivers who never get a ticket.

the antecedent of *who* is *drivers*, and hence the verb *get* is plural.

Pronoun/Antecedent Agreement.   In the sentence

Ann washed her car.

the third-person-singular feminine pronoun *(her)* agrees with its third-person-singular feminine antecedent *(Ann)*. If the antecedent were changed in person, number, and/or gender, the pronoun would have to be changed accordingly:

Joe washed his car.
Joe and Ann washed their cars.

(Note that in the last example the word *cars* is pluralized because Joe and Ann washed different cars; if they washed a single car that they owned together, the object *car* would be singular.)

A compound antecedent joined by *and* usually takes a plural pronoun. One exception occurs when the parts of the antecedent refer to a single entity:

The soldier and patriot was given a ticker tape parade by his home-town neighbors.

Another exception occurs when the compound antecedent is preceded by *each* or *every*;

Each car and truck was parked in its proper place.

The indefinite pronouns, when they serve as antecedents, usually require a singular pronoun:

Everybody will have a chance to take his or her turn.

When the gender of the antecedent is not specifically masculine or feminine but both, two singular pronouns *(his or her)* are used. It is acceptable to substitute a plural pronoun *(their)* in such cases. Simply to write either *his* or *her* in reference to an indefinite antecedent is considered sexist.

Note that sometimes it is awkward to follow an indefinite antecedent with a singular pronoun, as in the sentence

When everybody arrived, I asked him or her to sit down.

Substituting *them* for *him or her* in this sentence does not really clarify the meaning. The sentence might be better revised to read *either*

When all of them had arrived, I asked them to sit down.

or

As each of them arrived, I asked him or her to sit down.

Two singular antecedents joined by *or* or *nor* take a singular pronoun:

Neither Ann nor Sally washed her car.

Two plural antecedents joined by *or* or *nor* take a plural pronoun:

Neither the girls nor the boys washed their cars.

Note that in this last example, if the word *cars* were made singular *(car)*, it would indicate that the boys and the girls own one car together.

A collective noun, when used as an antecedent, takes a singular or a plural pronoun, depending on whether it refers to a group that is acting as a unit or as separate individuals:

The family is coming in its car.

The family are coming in their cars.

Faulty Reference

A pronoun should refer clearly to its antecedent (see p. 551). If there is any ambiguity or confusion about who or what the antecedent of a pronoun is, the pronoun reference is faulty.

If there is more than one possible antecedent, the sentence should be revised. The sentence

Sam told Don that he had used his car.

might be revised to read

Sam said to Don, "I used your car."

The sentence

He hit the ball on the roof, and it fell down.

might be revised to read

After he hit it on the roof, the ball fell down.

Ambiguity may result if the pronoun is placed too far away from its antecedent in a long sentence. In the sentence

The lake is large and pretty with a cabin on the shore and plenty of fish in it.

does the pronoun *it* refer to the cabin or to the lake?

Ambiguity often results when a pronoun such as *this, that, which,* or *it* refers to an entire clause rather than to a specifically defined antecedent. In the sentence

We drove all morning and then stopped for a picnic lunch, which made me sleepy.

the relative pronoun, *which,* could refer to the drive and/or to the lunch. The reference would be clearer if it were less broad:

We drove all morning, which made me sleepy, and then we stopped for a picnic lunch.

Another way to clarify the reference would be to define the antecedent more specifically:

> We drove all morning and then stopped for a picnic lunch; the drive combined with the lunch made me sleepy.

A similar kind of error involves the use of a pronoun whose antecedent is implied rather than specifically expressed. In the sentence

> In George Orwell's novel *1984*, he describes a world where love is a crime.

no specific antecedent for the pronoun *he* is named; if the reference is intended to be to Orwell, the sentence should be revised to make this intention clear:

> In his novel *1984*, George Orwell describes a world where love is a crime.

Often this sort of ambiguity results when a writer employs the pronoun *it* or *they* or *you* without a definite antecedent: in the sentence

> In college, they expect you to type your papers.

no possible antecedent for *they* is mentioned. Note also that when the pronoun *it* is used in more than one way in a sentence, the results are often confusing:

> Because it is hot by the lake, it looks inviting.

Finally, the pronoun *which* should not be used to refer to people. Use *who* to refer to people, *which* to refer to animals or objects or places. *That* may refer both to people and to animals, objects, or places. For example:

> The man *who* went out this morning caught a huge bluefish.
> He caught the fish, *which* weighed over fifteen pounds, just off the point.
> "You think this one's big," he said. "You should've seen the one *that* got away!"

Case Errors

The most common case errors involve the use of a subjective form of a pronoun when an objective form is required or the use of an objective form of a pronoun when a subjective form is required.

ca

Generally, the subjective forms should be used if the pronoun is part of the subject of a clause:

The truck driver and I (SUBJECTIVE) stopped at the light.
The light turned green before we (SUBJECTIVE) drove on.

The subjective case is also used for a subject complement after any form of the verb *to be*:

It is I (SUBJECTIVE).
It was they (SUBJECTIVE) who went home last.

The objective forms should be used if the pronoun is a direct object in a clause:

Joe invited her (OBJECTIVE) and me (OBJECTIVE).

an indirect object in a clause:

Joe lent him (OBJECTIVE) the car.

or the object of a preposition:

Joe is in love with her (OBJECTIVE).

Note that the objective forms should be used not only when a pronoun is the object of an infinitive:

Joe wanted to give her (OBJECTIVE) the car.

but also when the pronoun is the subject of an infinitive:

Joe wanted him (OBJECTIVE) to return the car.

There are a number of situations in which many writers find the choice of case confusing:

When the first-person-plural pronoun is used with a noun, its case depends on how the noun is being used. If the noun is a subject, the writer should use *we* along with it.

We students love summer vacation.

If the noun is an object, the writer should use *us* along with it, as in the following sentence in which the noun *students* is the object of the preposition *of*:

All of us students love summer vacation.

When a pronoun is used as an appositive, appearing next to a noun that it helps to identify or explain, its case depends on how the noun is being used. If the noun is a subject, the appositive pronoun should be in the subjective case:

Three boys, Joe, Sam, and I (SUBJECTIVE), went camping.

If the noun is an object, the appositive pronoun should be in the objective case:

Joe went camping with two other boys, Sam and me (OBJECTIVE).

Note: One case is sometimes incorrectly substituted for another in common, everyday expressions. Such expressions as *just between you and I* or *Him and me went home* are faulty. In formal writing, it is best to use the correct forms, *just between you and me* and *He and I went home*.

Who is always used to refer to a subject; *whom* is always used to refer to an object. If you are writing a question, use a personal pronoun to formulate the answer first; the case of the personal pronoun in your answer will indicate whether you should start the question with *who* or *whom*: the answer

She is the judge.

should be rephrased as the question

Who is the judge?

The answer

She sentenced him to a fifty-dollar fine.

should be rephrased as the question

Whom did she sentence to a fifty-dollar fine?

When *who* or *whom* is used in a subordinate clause, the case depends on how the pronoun is being used in the clause. The case depends upon the use of the pronoun in the clause no matter how the clause itself is being used in the sentence. In the sentence

A judge is a person who is honest.

who is the subject of the clause *who is honest*; the clause itself modifies the direct object, *person*. In the sentence

A judge is a person whom most people trust.

whom is the object of the modifying clause *whom most people trust*. If you rewrite the clause as a separate sentence, substituting a personal pronoun for *who* or *whom*, the proper choice of case is often clarified:

She *(who)* is honest. Most people trust her *(whom)*.

Finally, the possessive form of a pronoun should be used before a gerund, an *-ing* verb that is being used as a noun:

I approved of his (POSSESSIVE) going out with my sister.

---

mm/
dg

Misplaced and Dangling Modifiers

Misplaced Modifiers.   A modifier is misplaced if its position in a sentence causes ambiguity about just what part of the sentence it is modifying. For example, in the sentence

I gave the shirt to my brother with the red pinstripes.

the prepositional phrase *with the red pinstripes* is misplaced: Does it modify *brother* or *shirt*? The sentence should be revised to read

I gave the shirt with the red pinstripes to my brother.

Similarly, a subordinate clause can be misplaced. In the sentence

He parked the car in the garage after he had washed it.

did the subject wash the car or the garage? Again, one can revise the sentence simply by moving the misplaced modifier to another position:

After he had washed it, he parked the car in the garage.

Usually, a modifier should be placed as close as possible to the word or words that it is meant to modify. This is particularly important when a writer is using what are called *limiting modifiers*, single-word adverbs such as *almost, exactly, hardly, just, nearly, only,* and *simply*. Misplacing one of these modifiers can change the meaning of a sentence radically. Thus you might write

The old Ford is the only car that I will drive.

if you are unwilling to drive any other car, but

The old Ford is the car that only I will drive.

if no one else but you is willing to drive the old Ford.

Sometimes a writer positions a modifier so that a reader cannot determine if it modifies the words that come right before it or the words that come right after it. Such modifiers are called *squinting modifiers.* For example, in the sentence

Joe had told her in May they would go to the beach.

did Joe tell her in *May* that they would go to the beach at some future time, or did Joe tell her that they would go to the beach *in May?* A squinting modifier should be repositioned away from the part of the sentence that it is not meant to modify:

In May, Joe had told her they would go to the beach.

or

Joe had told her they would go to the beach in May.

Dangling Modifiers.   A dangling modifier is a phrase or clause that does not sensibly describe any specific word in its sentence. For example, in the sentence

Arriving after midnight, the house seemed deserted.

the only word that the opening phrase could modify is *house*, but clearly it is not the house that arrived at midnight; the actual word that the phrase modifies is missing, and the sentence must be revised to include it:

Because we arrived after midnight, the house seemed deserted.

A writer most often produces dangling modifiers by starting or ending a sentence with a phrase that lacks a subject itself, such as the participial phrase that starts the sentence

Soaked to the skin, the walk home in the rain was no fun.

or the infinitive phrase that ends the sentence

An umbrella should be taken to walk in the rain.

Also an elliptical clause, a subordinate clause in which the subject is unstated but understood, often becomes a dangling modifier. In the sentence

When I was only a small boy, I often went fishing.

the opening clause might be made elliptical by the omission of *I was*; if this elliptical clause is then used to introduce a main clause in which the subject is no longer *I*, a dangling construction results:

When only a small boy, my father often took me fishing.

To correct a dangling modifier, add the missing word or words to which it refers. You can do this by changing the subject of the main clause:

When only a small boy, I was often taken fishing by my father.

You can also do it by rewriting the dangling modifier as a complete subordinate clause:

When I was only a small boy, my father often took me fishing.

Faulty Parallelism

//

Faulty parallelism occurs when elements in a sentence or a paragraph that express comparable ideas and that perform similar grammatical functions are expressed in different grammatical form. In the sentence

Walking on the beach relaxes him more than a swim.

the parallelism is faulty because one comparable idea, *walking on the beach*, is expressed as a gerund phrase, whereas the other, *a swim*, is expressed as an unmodified noun. The sentence might be revised to read

Walking on the beach relaxes him more than swimming in the ocean.

or

A walk on the beach relaxes him more than a swim in the ocean.

Elements linked by coordinating or correlative conjunctions should be expressed in parallel form. To correct the faulty parallelism of the sentence

He is an excellent musician, a talented dancer, and puts on an exciting performance.

you might rephrase the last of the coordinated elements:

He is an excellent musician, a talented dancer, and an exciting performer.

As an alternative, you might subordinate the last element:

He is an excellent musician and a talented dancer who puts on an exciting performance.

Note that faulty parallelism often occurs with correlative conjunctions because the writer omits a preposition or an infinitive marker *(to)* after the second conjunction: in the sentence

He was often overtired not from working too hard but sleeping too little.

a second *from* should be added after *but*; in the sentence

She told him either to wait for her or leave.

a second *to* should be added after *or*, or perhaps a parallel prepositional phrase should be added after *leave*, such as *without her*.

Run-on Sentences and Comma Splices

A run-on sentence (also called a *fused sentence*) occurs when a writer fails to separate two or more main clauses with any punctuation; for example,

He likes music he likes to dance.

A comma splice occurs when a writer links two or more main clauses with commas; for example

He likes music, he likes to dance.

A run-on sentence or a comma splice can be corrected simply if each main clause is punctuated as a separate sentence:

He likes music. He likes to dance.

A second option is to link the main clauses with semicolons:

He likes music; he likes to dance.

A third option is to link the main clauses with coordinating conjunctions:

He likes music, and he likes to dance.

A fourth option is to link the clauses with subordinating conjunctions or relative pronouns, leaving only one main clause:

He likes music because he likes to dance.

Run-ons and comma splices often result when a writer links two or more main clauses with conjunctive adverbs. Conjunctive adverbs, like *also, however,* and *then,* should always follow either a semicolon or a period when they are being used to link main clauses.

He likes to dance, therefore, he likes music.

is a comma splice; it should be repunctuated to read

He likes to dance; therefore, he likes music.

or

He likes to dance. Therefore, he likes music.

Note, however, that comma splices are used effectively by writers to emphasize the link or the contrast between ideas, particularly if the main clauses expressing the ideas are short and are phrased in a parallel fashion. The following sentences can make their point more effectively as one long comma splice:

I love the circus, I love the clowns, I love the acrobats, I love the side show, I love the whole spectacle.

"Be sensible," she pleaded, "listen to reason, open your mind."

I have my secrets, you have your secrets, everyone has something to hide.

Similarly, two or more contrasting ideas expressed in parallel phrasing may be punctuated as a comma splice to emphasize the contrast:

She did not hate him, she pitied him.

Act now, tomorrow will be too late.

The first house was destroyed by the storm, the second was damaged but remained standing, the third was untouched.

Sentence Fragments

frag

A fragment is a part of a sentence that is punctuated with an initial capital letter and a final period as if it were a complete sentence. Often fragments give a reader trouble because they convey the impression that the writer's thoughts are incomplete.

A sentence fragment may lack a subject, as does the verb phrase

Drove home at night.

It may lack a verb, as does the noun phrase

The boy on the bicycle.

It may lack both a subject and a verb, as does the prepositional phrase

On the beach.

It may include both a subject and a verb but begin with a subordinating conjunction, as does the subordinate clause

Because I love strawberries.

or with a relative pronoun, as does the relative clause

Which is my favorite.

If a fragment lacks a subject and/or a verb, you can correct it by adding the missing part or parts:

He drove home at night.
The boy on the bicycle left.
She is walking on the beach.

You can also correct it by linking it to a complete sentence:

He stayed for dinner then drove home at night.

If a fragment is a dependent clause, you can correct it by rewriting the clause as an independent or main clause:

I love strawberries.

You can also correct it by linking it to a complete sentence:

I like vanilla but prefer chocolate, which is my favorite.

A fragment often results when a writer adds on information after completing a sentence. The added information might be the answer to a question:

What kind of day was it? A great day.

The information might be a modifying word or phrase:

My uncle is a conservative man. Old-fashioned.
He is a farmer. Living off the land.

Or the information might be a clause that further explains or qualifies:

She pitied him. Even though he was cruel to her.

Like comma splices, fragments can be used effectively by a writer for emphasis. Instructions are often written as fragments:

Bake in preheated oven (425°). One hour. Remove. Let cool before slicing.

Sometimes a definition is easier to remember if it is written in fragments:

Alcoholism. A disease. Both physiological and psychological.

A description may sometimes be made more vivid if some of the images that compose it are fragments:

The schoolroom was quiet. Empty desks. Rows of them. The board cleaned of chalk. The afternoon light fading outside the closed windows.

In general, because a fragment isolates a piece of information, it focuses a reader's attention on that information. If a writer can make use of fragments for this purpose without confusing the reader, there is no reason not to employ them on occasion.

REVIEW EXERCISE–COMMON GRAMMATICAL ERRORS

Each of the following sentences contains one or more grammatical errors. Rewrite them, correcting each error you identify.

1. Every one of the twenty-five students in the class are required to write five papers this term and type it before handing it in.

2. Either Lois or one of her cousins, Al and Don, who own the restaurant, keep the accounts, paying each of the bills as soon as they come in.

3. Joe called his brother once a week after he went to college, which cost him a lot of money, although he insisted it was worth it.

4. Whom do you think did better on the exam, me, who studied in the library half the night, or my two roommates that were asleep by 10 o'clock?

5. At the stable, they wanted she and I to rub down the horses after taking them for a ride.

6. Sitting up in the bleachers, the game started, and we bought hotdogs for the children with mustard that cost $1.25.

7. The sky had been ominous all day when, suddenly growing dark, we watched out the window as the rain began to fall, and the lightning began to flash and thunder was booming.

8. "You must be very happy," Uncle George said, "it's a wonderful thing to get married." Which was true, of course. But she wasn't at all sure she was happy, indeed she had half a mind to call it off. Just wedding day jitters? That's what she finally told herself, it was normal for the bride to feel unsure about it. The groom too, with only a few hours left to go before the ceremony.

Punctuation

The conventions of punctuation that follow are more complete than those offered in the "Focus" section on sentence combining in Chapter 5 (pp. 217–218). The basic information about how punctuation marks can help a reader to follow the separations or links that you wish to make between sentences and parts of sentences is the same.

THE PERIOD (.)

A period is one way to end a sentence. It may be used to end any declarative sentence, any statement:

She is at the office.

It may be used to end a mild command:

Think about it.
Let me know.

It may be used to end an indirect question, a report of what someone has asked:

She wondered why they had to leave so early.

Periods are also used with many abbreviations: cities (N.Y.C., L.A.); states (Pa., Ill., Ariz.); names (Franklin D. Roosevelt); titles (Mr., Ms., Dr., Rev.); degrees (B.A., Ph.D., D.D.S.); months (Sept.); addresses (St., Ave., Rte.); Latin abbreviations (ibid., etc., et al.). Note that when an abbreviation is the last element in a sentence, a single period is used both to end the abbreviation and to end the sentence:

He lives in Washington, D.C.

Periods are not used with the capital letter abbreviations of technical terms (FM, IQ); organizations (NFL, AFL-CIO); corporations (CBS, IBM); or government agencies (FBI, TVA). Nor are periods used with acronyms, pronounceable words formed from the initial letters in a multiword title (NATO, VISTA).

Additional information on abbreviations is offered below in the section on abbreviations.

THE QUESTION MARK (?)

A question mark is used to end a direct question:

What do you want to be when you grow up?

Note that if you write a series of questions, each is followed by a question mark:

He asked, "What profession do you think you will enter? Medicine? Law? Business?"

Note also that a question mark is never combined with another question mark or with a period or comma or exclamation point. The question

Who asked, "What do you want to be when you grow up?"

does not take a second question mark after the final quotation mark. The statement

He asked her, "What profession do you plan to enter?"

does not take a period after the final quotation mark.

A question mark may also be used within parentheses to indicate uncertainty within a statement:

My grandfather was ninety-two (?) when he remarried.

Someone—my brother Al (?)—borrowed my favorite shirt.

THE EXCLAMATION POINT (!)

An exclamation point is used after a sentence or a phrase or a word that expresses a strong emotion:

Leave me alone!

What a wonderful day!

Yes! I must go home right now!

Its use should be reserved to indicate unusually strong emphasis.

Note that an exclamation point should not be used in parentheses to express amazement or irony or sarcasm, as in the sentence

My brother borrowed (!) my favorite shirt.

The context itself should indicate that a word, in this case *borrowed*, is being used ironically.

THE COMMA (,)

A comma is used, above all else, to prevent misreading, by signaling that the reader should pause slightly before reading on. For example, although a comma is not absolutely required following a short introductory phrase, sometimes inserting one can clarify a sentence: in the sentence

After tomorrow morning choir practice will begin.

the meaning is different depending on whether a comma is inserted following *tomorrow* or following *morning*. Alternatively, it is sometimes necessary to omit a comma at a point in a sentence where one would ordinarily be inserted: in the line

The woods are lovely, dark and deep.

from "Stopping by the Woods on a Snowy Evening," the poet Robert Frost left out the comma that ordinarily would be inserted after *dark*; had he inserted the comma, the three adjectives would have seemed equivalent descriptions of the woods; by omitting the comma, Frost suggested that the phrase *dark and deep* modifies *lovely*, that the woods are lovely because they are dark and deep. Commas, then, should be used with common sense as tools that can help a reader see how words, phrases, and clauses in a sentence are meant to be linked together or set apart from one another.

Generally, a comma is used to set off an introductory word, phrase, or clause from the rest of the sentence.

> Undoubtedly, the villain will be caught. To catch him, the authorities will set a trap. Once the trap is set, we can sit back and relax.

Certainly, the comma may be omitted after a single introductory word or a short introductory phrase or clause if no confusion will arise as a result. Note that a comma is not needed after an introductory conjunction:

> Yet the villain may escape.

A comma is inserted before a coordinating conjunction that links two main clauses in a sentence:

> The authorities are armed with the most modern investigative tools, but the villain may prove too clever for them.

If the main clauses are short, however, and no confusion will arise, the comma may be omitted:

> The authorities have set a trap but the villain may escape.

See the following section on the semicolon for information about when a semicolon should replace a comma that links two main clauses.

Note that a comma should not be inserted between two words or phrases that are joined by a coordinating conjunction. In the sentence

> The authorities, and the criminal are clever.

the comma after *authorities* should be omitted.

Commas are used to separate two or more adjectives that precede a noun that they modify equally:

> The criminal is a clever, ingenious thief.

If the adjective nearer the noun is more closely related to the noun in meaning, however, no comma should separate the noun from the preceding adjective:

> The authorities have clever legal minds.

If you can rearrange the adjectives or insert the conjunction *and* between them without changing the meaning, the comma should be used: thus you might write the phrase *an ingenious, clever thief,* or *a clever and ingenious thief,* but you would not write *legal, clever minds,* or *clever and legal minds.*

Commas are used to join three or more words, phrases, or clauses in a series:

> The thief is tall, dark, and handsome. He is suspected of stealing a diamond tiara in New York, a ruby brooch in Paris, and a pearl necklace in Singapore. His manners are charming, his victims are never suspicious of him, and his real name is a mystery.

The final comma in the series, the comma that comes before the conjunction, is regularly omitted by some writers and is regularly inserted by others. It is probably best to use the final comma consistently, except when you wish to emphasize the link between the final two items in a series, to identify the final two items as a single element:

> The thief is handsome, tall and dark.

See the following section on the semicolon for information about when semicolons should replace commas that separate items in a series.

Commas are used to set off a nonrestrictive modifier, a phrase or clause that offers additional (in a sense, parenthetical) information about an element in a sentence. Because the information offered by a nonrestrictive modifier is not essential to the meaning of the sentence, the modifier can be omitted without causing any confusion in the reader's mind. In the sentence

> The left front tire, which had forty thousand miles on it, blew out.

the relative clause *which had forty thousand miles on it* is nonrestrictive; the basic meaning of the sentence is that the left front tire blew out; it is not essential to know that the tire had forty thousand miles on it.

On the other hand, in the sentence

> The tire that had forty thousand miles on it blew out.

the relative clause *that had forty thousand miles on it* is restrictive; if it is omitted, the reader has no way of knowing which tire blew out. A restricted phrase or clause is not set off with commas.

Note that although both nonrestrictive and restrictive clauses may begin with *which,* only restrictive clauses begin with *that.*

An appositive, a noun or noun phrase that renames or further identifies the noun immediately before it, also may be nonrestrictive or restrictive. In the sentence

My brother John is a Marine.

John is an appositive that further identifies the writer's brother. Because it is not set off by commas, it is restrictive, essential to the meaning of the sentence; presumably, the writer has other brothers, so he must distinguish his bother John from his brother Michael or his brother Arthur. If the sentence is rewritten

My only brother, John, is a Marine.

the appositive is nonrestrictive; the writer has only one brother, and his brother's name happens to be John.
Commas may be used to set off an absolute phrase:

The day drawing to a close, we headed home.

A phrase of contrast:

Speed, not strength, is a boxer's most important asset.

A conjunctive adverb:

He got home, however, before the rain started.

An additional explanation or example preceded by such expressions as *for example, namely,* and *such as*:

His favorite sports are team sports, such as baseball and soccer.

A noun of address:

John, you must get up now.

Also, a comma follows the salutation in a personal letter.
Conventional usage requires that commas separate the items in a date, an address, or the name of a place. Within a sentence, each date, address, or place is also followed by a comma, unless it appears at the end of the sentence:

On December 7, 1941, the weather was mild in New York.
His old address is 705 Walton Avenue, Mamaroneck, New York.

One final note: never use a comma to separate a subject from its verb or a verb from its object, unless there are words between them that must be set off by commas. Thus you might write

My brother, John, is a Marine.

setting off *John* as a nonrestrictive appositive; but you should not write

My brother John, is a Marine.

Similarly, you might write

She ate, not a dietetic snack, but a hot fudge sundae.

setting off the phrase of contrast; but you should not write

She ate, a hot fudge sundae.

For the use of commas with quotation marks, see the section on quotation marks.

THE SEMICOLON (;)

A semicolon may be used, instead of a period, to separate two main clauses:

She loves to roller-skate; he loves to ice-skate.

A semicolon is used to emphasize that two or more main clauses are closely related in meaning:

Someone had left a window open; it was freezing in the house.

A semicolon is used between two main clauses when the second clause contains a conjunctive adverb:

In the morning he jogs; however, yesterday morning he slept late.

Note that the semicolon in this instance may be replaced by a period, in which case the first letter of the second clause is capitalized. Note also that the semicolon may be used even if the conjunctive adverb does not immediately follow the initial clause:

In the morning he jogs; yesterday morning, however, he slept late.

In this case, a comma is inserted both before and after the adverb.

When two main clauses are linked by a coordinating conjunction, it is helpful to use a semicolon, rather than a comma, before the conjunction if the clauses are long and/or contain internal punctuation:

> Driving down the icy mountain road, he downshifted, pumped the brakes, and honked the horn as he rounded each curve; and he breathed a sigh of relief when, rounding the last curve, he saw the road level out before him.

Similarly, it is helpful to separate the items in a series with semicolons when those items are long and/or contain internal punctuation:

> It was a scary drive because the road was icy, steep, and narrow; the night was dark, and one of the headlights was out; and the car, with its worn tires, kept skidding each time he drove around a sharp curve.

Note: a semicolon should not be used between a phrase and a clause, between a main clause and a subordinate clause, or to introduce a list.

Incorrect:	To get up early; he sets the alarm.
Revised:	To get up early, he sets the alarm.
Incorrect:	He always sleeps late; if the alarm fails to ring.
Revised:	He always sleeps late if the alarm fails to ring.
Incorrect:	You need the following ingredients; eggs, butter, milk, flour, and chocolate chips.
Revised:	You need the following ingredients: eggs, butter, milk, flour, and chocolate chips.

THE COLON (:)

A colon is used to introduce a list or series:

> There are many different writing tools: the pencil, the pen, the typewriter, and now the word processor.

Note, however, that a colon should not be used to introduce a list if the colon interrupts the completion of a main clause by coming between a verb and its object or a preposition and its object.

Incorrect:	Some different writing tools are: the pencil, the pen, and the typewriter.

Revised: Some different writing tools are the pencil, the pen, and
the typewriter.
Incorrect: A pencil is made of: lead, rubber, and wood.
Revised: A pencil is made of the following: lead, rubber, and wood.

A colon is used to introduce an explanation or summary of the statement
that it follows:

She writes only with a pencil or a pen: She hates to type.

Note that if the material following the colon is a complete sentence, it may
begin with an initial capital letter.
    A colon may be used instead of a comma to introduce a quotation. See the
section below on quotation marks.
    A colon is also used to separate a subtitle from a title:

In Bluebeard's Castle: Some Notes Toward a Redefinition of Culture

to separate the hour from the minute in a time reference:

2:15 P.M.

to separate chapter from verse in a biblical citation:

Genesis 19:24–28

after the salutation in a formal letter:

Dear Mr. President:

For the use of colons in footnote and bibliographic entries, see the "Focus"
section of Chapter 10 (pp. 484–490).

— /--

THE DASH (— or --)

A dash (two hyphens placed without spacing against preceding and following
letters when you are typing) indicates a sudden interruption in tone or
thought:

She looked sincere — although looks can be deceiving — when she testified in court.

Note: To replace the two dashes in the preceding example with parentheses would suggest that the interrupting clause is less relevant; to replace the two dashes with commas would make the interruption less emphatic.

> She looked sincere (although looks can be deceiving) when she testified in court.

> She looked sincere, although looks can be deceiving, when she testified in court.

A dash may be used to lend greater emphasis to an appositive:

> My mother — a wonderful woman — is coming to visit.

It may be used to set off a word, a phrase, or a clause that summarizes a preceding list:

> Men, women, children — people of all ages love the circus.

It may be used to emphasize an important idea at the end of a sentence:

> There was nothing wrong with their marriage — but she wanted more from life.

Also, a dash may replace a colon before a list, although it is considered less formal than a colon.

> When you go to the store, get everything we need for lunch — bread, peanut butter, jelly, and milk.

PARENTHESES AND BRACKETS ( )/[ ]

( )/[ ]

Parentheses

Parentheses are used to enclose words, phrases, and clauses that are not essential to the meaning of a sentence or paragraph but that clarify or comment on a point made in the sentence or paragraph. Parenthetical expressions may offer —

Factual Information:
   On the day that Pearl Harbor was attacked (December 7, 1941), my father was studying in his dormitory room.

Examples:
   He likes any kind of pasta (spaghetti, linguine, or ravioli), as long as it is smothered in tomato sauce.

Explanations:
   The suicide squeeze (in which the batter bunts and the runner on third races for home) is one of baseball's most exciting plays.

Qualifications:
   He said he was so upset (although "angry" may be a better description) that he could not eat or sleep.

When a complete sentence is enclosed in parentheses, it needs no capital letter at the start or period at the end if the parentheses fall within another sentence:

   The day that he left home (it was a sad day for all of us), rain fell all morning.

Note that although a comma may follow the closing parenthesis within a sentence, no comma comes before the opening parenthesis.
   When a complete sentence is enclosed in parentheses that fall between two sentences, the sentence in the parentheses does begin with a capital letter and end with a period:

   The day that he left home, rain fell all morning. (It was a sad day for all of us.) In the afternoon, however, the sky cleared.

Parentheses also are used to enclose cross-references: (see Freud's *Totem and Taboo*, p. 27); and to enclose letters or numbers that label items in a list:

   There were a number of reasons that he preferred taking the train to driving: (1) he could sleep on the train; (2) the train got him there faster; and (3) he did not have to worry about parking his car when he arrived.

Brackets

Brackets are used to enclose your own explanations, comments, and corrections within a quotation from another writer. They may be used to add information:

E.B. White believes that *"Walden* [published in 1854] is an oddity in American letters."

They may be used to enclose a substitute word or phrase for a part of a quotation that, without the substitution, would be unclear, as in the following sentence, where the bracketed name has replaced the pronoun *his*:

E. B. White writes that *"Walden* is [Henry David Thoreau's] acknowledgement of the gift of life."

Note that the Latin word *sic* may be placed in brackets after an error in quotation to indicate that the error was made by the author of the quotation. Also, brackets replace parentheses that are inserted within parentheses.

White's essay on Thoreau ("A Slight Sound at Evening," *Essays of E. B. White* [New York: Harper & Row, 1977], 234–242) is both sensitive and insightful.

THE ELLIPSIS (...)

An ellipsis is three periods separated from one another by single spaces. It indicates that material has been omitted from a quotation. If a comma, a semicolon, or a colon precedes the ellipsis, it is dropped. If a complete sentence precedes the ellipsis, the period ending the sentence is retained and is followed by the periods of the ellipsis.

Look at the following quotation from an essay by E. B. White on Thoreau's *Walden*:

> Thoreau said he required of every writer, first and last, a simple and sincere account of his own life. Having delivered himself of this chesty dictum, he proceeded to ignore it. In his books and even in his enormous journal, he withheld or disguised most of the facts from which an understanding of his life could be drawn.

To omit the phrase "first and last" from the first sentence along with the entire second sentence, two ellipsis marks are necessary:

> Thoreau said he required of every writer . . . a simple and sincere account of his own life. . . . In his books and even in his enormous journal, he withheld or disguised most of the facts from which an understanding of his life could be drawn.

Some writers use ellipsis marks to indicate that they have omitted material at the end of a quoted message:

"In his books and even in his enormous journal, he withheld or disguised most of the facts. . . . "

Others feel that the ellipsis is unnecessary in this case.

Note that an ellipsis may be used to indicate a pause or an incomplete statement in dialogue or quoted speech:

"Oh, no . . . " she said; then her words were drowned in tears.

Note also that a line of ellipsis marks across the full width of an indented quotation can be used to indicate that one or more lines of poetry have been omitted.

> Now therefore, while the youthful hue
> Sits on thy skin like morning dew
> And while thy willing soul transpires
> At every pore with instant fires,
> Now let us sport us while we may . . .
>
> Now therefore, while the youthful hue
> Sits on thy skin like morning dew
> . . . .
> Now let us sport us while we may . . .
> —Andrew Marvell, "To His Coy Mistress"

" "

QUOTATION MARKS (" ")

Quotation marks are used to enclose words, phrases, or sentences that are quoted directly from speech or writing:

The mayor said he was "confident" that he would win reelection. According to the local paper, however, his popularity is "the lowest that it has been since his term began." In yesterday's editorial, the paper threw its support to his opponent. "While the incumbent has done a respectable job," the editorial said, "his opponent is better qualified in every respect."

Note that an indirect quotation, which reports what someone has said or written, but not in the exact words, should not be enclosed in quotation marks.

The mayor voiced his confidence in his ability to win reelection, despite the fact that his popularity is at its lowest and the local paper is supporting his opponent who, the editors feel, is more qualified in every way.

Single quotation marks are used to enclose a quotation within a quotation:

Yesterday's editorial went on to say, "The challenger's promise that she will hire more teachers, 'even if it means raising taxes,' is another reason that she has earned this paper's support."

If you are writing a dialogue, begin a new paragraph each time the speaker changes.

"I don't like the mayor," she said. "He doesn't understand the problems that women face in this town. He's insensitive and chauvinistic."

"Nonsense," I told her. "Mayor Tubbs is all right. He's just a little old-fashioned."

"Old-fashioned! Huh! He's a cave man!"

"Oh, come on, Gloria," I argued. "Aren't you overreacting just a bit?" But I couldn't convince her.

Note that if you are quoting more than a single line of poetry, you should mark the line divisions with slashes:

Frost wrote, "The woods are lovely, dark and deep,/But I have promises to keep."

If you are quoting more than three lines of poetry or more than four lines of prose, you should not use quotation marks; instead, use indentation to indicate where the quotation begins and ends. End the sentence introducing the quotation with a colon, double-space both above and below the quotation, and indent the quotation itself ten spaces from the left-hand margin (and an additional five spaces to start a new paragraph). Note the following example, in which quotations from Thoreau and Frost are each preceded by an introductory sentence:

Thoreau's optimism is apparent in the following passage from *Walden*:

> I think that we may safely trust a good deal more than we do. We may waive just so much care of ourselves as we honestly bestow elsewhere. Nature is as well adapted to our weakness as to our strength. The incessant anxiety and strain of some is a well-nigh incurable form of disease.

Frost seemed more careworn when he wrote:

> The woods are lovely, dark and deep,
> But I have promises to keep,
> And miles to go before I sleep,
> And miles to go before I sleep.

Quotation marks are used to indicate the title of a part or a chapter of a book ("Economy" is the first chapter of *Walden*); the title of an essay ("The Angry Winter," by Loren Eiseley); the title of a short story ("Rip Van Winkle," by Washington Irving); the title of a short poem ("To His Coy Mistress," by Andrew Marvell); the title of a magazine article ("What Do Babies Know?" in *Time*); the title of a song ("Yesterday," by the Beatles); or the title of an episode of a television or radio series ("The Miracle of Life," on *Nova*). Note that quotation marks are not used around the title on the title page of a paper that you have written.

Quotation marks are used by some writers to indicate that they are raising a question about the way a word is being used:

> What he called his "new" car turned out to be a ten-year-old wreck.

Note, however, that when they are defining a word, most writers set it off by italicizing it. See the section on italics below.

When a single word or phrase is placed within quotation marks, no punctuation is needed to introduce it. When one or more sentences are placed within quotation marks, either an introductory comma or an introductory colon is needed. Some writers use a comma before a single sentence, a colon before two or more sentences.

> He said, "Let's go home now." She replied: "First I've got to stop at the bank. Then we'll go home."

Other writers use a comma to introduce quoted speech and a colon to introduce quoted writing.

Use a comma at the end of a quoted sentence that is followed by a tag, a reference to the speaker:

> "I think that we may safely trust a good deal more than we do," Thoreau tells us.

If the quoted sentence is a question or an exclamation, however, it should end with a question mark or an exclamation point:

> "Do you agree with Thoreau?" he asked.

In either case, the tag begins with a lowercase, not a capital, letter.

If a tag interrupts a quoted sentence, it is set off by two commas:

"I think," Thoreau wrote, "that we may safely trust a good deal more than we do."

If a tag is placed between two quoted sentences, the first quoted sentence is followed by a comma, the tag is followed by a semicolon or a period, and the second quoted sentence begins with a capital letter and ends with a period:

"Nature is as well adapted to our weakness as to our strength," Thoreau wrote; "The incessant anxiety and strain of some is a well-nigh incurable form of disease."

Note that at the end of a quotation, a period or a comma is always placed inside the closing quotation mark, and a semicolon or colon is always placed outside the closing quotation mark. A dash, an exclamation point, or a question mark is placed inside the closing quotation mark only if it is part of the quotation:

"Do you understand?" she asked.

If the dash, exclamation point, or question mark applies to the whole sentence, however, it is placed outside the closing quotation mark:

Does anyone understand what Thoreau meant when he wrote that "we may safely trust a good deal more than we do"?

THE APOSTROPHE

An apostrophe followed by *s* is used to form the possessive case of singular and plural nouns that do not end in *s*: the *boy's* dog, the *man's* property, *women's* rights, *children's* toys.

Singular common nouns ending in *s* also take an apostrophe followed by *s* to form the possessive: the *boss's* daughter, the *business's* manager. Singular proper nouns ending in *s* may form the possessive with an apostrophe followed by *s* or with an apostrophe alone: *Doris's* house or *Doris'* house, Mr. *Jones's* apartment or Mr. *Jones'* apartment. There are a few singular nouns ending in an *s* or a *z* sound that form the possessive with an apostrophe alone: for *conscience'* sake, *Moses'* law. Often such forms are rephrased to omit the apostrophe altogether: *for the sake of conscience, the law of Moses.*

An apostrophe alone is used to form the possessive case of plural nouns that end in *s: babies'* cribs, the two *boys'* tree house, the *Joneses'* apartment, the *Smiths'* home.

An apostrophe followed by *s* is added to the last word of a compound noun to indicate possession: my *sister-in-law's* car, *somebody else's* truck.

Only the last of two or more nouns take the apostrophe (and the *s*, if needed) to indicate joint possession: the phrase *the boy and the girl's dog* indicates that the boy and the girl own one dog together; if this phrase is revised to read the *boy's and girl's dogs*, it indicates that the boy and the girl each own one or more dogs individually.

An apostrophe followed by *s* is used to form the possessive of indefinite pronouns: *everybody's* favorite ice cream, *someone's* dirty laundry. Note, however, that the possessive personal pronouns do not require an apostrophe to indicate ownership:

This is *his* house, that is *hers.*

I like *their* house, but *its* backyard is so small.

An apostrophe is also used to indicate that letters, words, or numbers have been omitted in contractions: *can't* (cannot), *doesn't* (does not), *don't* (do not), *he's* (he is), *I'll* (I will), *isn't* (is not), *it's* (it is), *I've* (I have), *ma'am*(madam), *o'clock* (of the clock), *she's* (she is), *they're* (they are), *you're* (you are), *we're* (we are), *weren't* (were not), *who's* (who is), *won't* (will not), *'84* (1984). Note that the contraction *would've* means *would have*; do not write *would of* instead of *would've*. Better yet, do not use this contraction; write *would have*.

Note also that the personal pronouns *its, their, your*, and *whose* should not be confused with the contractions *it's, they're, you're*, and *who's*. See the section below on spelling for examples of the proper use of each of these pronouns and contractions.

An apostrophe followed by *s* is used to form the plural of abbreviations with periods, lowercase letters used as nouns, and capital letters that would be confusing if *s* were added:

The college graduated 275 B.A.'s.

She is learning her abc's.

Sam Smith has two S's in his name.

At the same time single or multiple letters used as words and numbers (spelled out or in figures) add *s* alone to form the plural, as long as omitting the apostrophe will cause no confusion:

She is studying the three Rs.

He works out at three different YMCAs.

My father was in his early twenties in the 1940s.

Mechanics

CAPITALIZATION

cap

To capitalize a word, make the first letter of the word a capital letter. Capitalize the first word of a sentence:

She hates to type.

Capitalizing the first word of a sentence that follows a colon is optional:

She writes only with a pencil or a pen: She (*or* she) hates to type.

Capitalizing the first word of a direct quotation is necessary if the original begins with a capital letter:

John F. Kennedy said, "Ask not what your country can do for you. Ask what you can do for your country."

Capitalize proper nouns, such as the names of specific persons, places, events, institutions, and organizations:

Aunt Sally	the Renaissance
George Washington	World War I
Fifth Avenue	the New York Public Library
Los Angeles	Mamaroneck High School
the Rocky Mountains	Michigan State University
Lake Michigan	the Internal Revenue Service
the Pacific Ocean	the Boy Scouts of America
France	the Boston Red Sox
Africa	the United Nations
Jupiter	

Note that common nouns like *avenue, mountain, lake, ocean, high school,* and *university* are capitalized when they are part of the name of a place or an institution.

> I went to Lakeville High School.
>
> I was in high school from 1960 to 1964.
>
> He sailed across the Atlantic Ocean.
>
> We swam in the ocean on our vacation.

The article preceding a proper noun and any preposition that is part of a proper noun are not capitalized.

Capitalize adjectives formed from proper nouns:

> a *Shakespearean* play
> an *American* car
> the *Republican* party

Capitalize trade names:

> *Scotch* tape
> *Kleenex* tissues
> a *Xerox* copier

Capitalize the names of the points of the compass when they refer to specific geographical regions:

> the *Midwest*
> the *North Pole*
> *Western civilization*

Do not capitalize the points of the compass when they simply indicate direction:

> a *southerly* wind

Capitalize the days of the week, the months of the year, and holidays. Capitalize the names of religions, their followers, and their sacred books:

> Protestantism   Muslims
> Judaism   the Bible
> Christians   the Koran

Also capitalize all words used to designate the deity, including pronouns:

> *He*   the *Lord*

His   *Allah*
God   *Buddha*

Capitalize abbreviations of academic degrees (B.A., Ph.D., M.D.); titles (Mr., Jr., Dr.); and all letters of acronyms (NATO, NASA, VISTA).
Capitalize a title that comes before a proper name.

President Bush is seeking reelection.

If the title refers to only one person and can substitute for his or her name, capitalize it.

The President announced his plans to run for a second term.

But if the title can refer to more than one person, do not capitalize it when it substitutes for a specific person.

Mayor Jones ran for Congress in 1964. It was a close election, but the mayor lost.

Note: In the sentence

The president in our system is limited to two terms in office.

President is used as a general term for the chief executive officer of the government and is not capitalized. Similarly, a word designating a relationship (*father, aunt*) is not capitalized, unless it forms a part of or substitutes for a proper name.

She is my aunt on my mother's side.
My brother went to pick up Uncle George at the station.
"I want to go home now, Grandpa," I said.

Capitalize all words in the title of a book or a chapter of a book, a magazine or newspaper or an article in either, an essay, a short story, a poem, a musical composition, a painting, a play, a film, or a television or radio show. Note, however, that no article, conjunction, or preposition of less than five letters is capitalized unless it is the first word of the title:

For Whom the Bell Tolls
Romeo and Juliet
Gone with the Wind

Always capitalize the first person singular pronoun, *I*.

| ital |

ITALICS

Italic type slants upward to the right. You can use italics to set off and emphasize words and phrases. In a typed or handwritten paper, you italicize a word or phrase by underlining it.

Italics are used to give emphasis to a word:

I don't want to know what *she* thinks; I want to know what *you* think.

Italics are also used to set off a word that is being treated as a word:

What does the word *love* really mean?
Why must you preface everything you say with *I think*?

Italics are used to identify a foreign word or phrase not yet accepted as a standard English expression: the phrase *carpe diem* is italicized, whereas the phrase per diem is not. Consult a dictionary to check whether a foreign expression is italicized.

Italics are used to indicate the title of a book (*Walden*); a long poem (the *Odyssey*); a play (*Romeo and Juliet*); a magazine (*Time*); a newspaper (the Philadelphia *Inquirer*); a pamphlet (*Common Sense*); a published speech (the *Gettysburg Address*); a long musical work (*Rubber Soul*); a work of visual art (the *Mona Lisa*); a movie (*Star Wars*); and a television or radio show (*60 Minutes*). Note, however, that the Bible and the books within it are neither italicized nor placed in quotation marks, although they are capitalized:

Genesis is the first book of the Bible.

Italics are also used to indicate the name of trains (the *Orient Express*); ships (the *Queen Elizabeth II*); airplanes (the *Spirit of St. Louis*); and spacecraft (*Apollo 8*).

| ab |

ABBREVIATIONS

The more formal you wish to make your writing, the less you should abbreviate words and phrases. Although special abbreviations may be used regularly in the technical writings of business, law, scholarship, and science, common abbreviations should be used only moderately in most formal writing. If you are uncertain about whether or not a term should be abbreviated, spell it out fully.

Titles that accompany a proper name may be abbreviated:

Ms. Jones	Mary Stuart, D.D.S.
Dr. Smith	John Doe, Jr.
Rev. Wilson	

Note that some writers feel that the titles of religious, government, and military leaders should be spelled out in full:

the Reverend Martin Luther King, Jr.
Senator John Glenn
General George Patton

Titles should not be abbreviated when they appear without a proper name:

I called the doctor for an appointment.

Titles of academic degrees are an exception:

I received my B.A. this June.

Well-known abbreviations of organizations, corporations, people, and some countries are acceptable. When they are comprised of the first letters of three or more words, they are usually written without periods:

FBI	FDR
YMCA	JFK
ITT	USA
NBC	USSR

Abbreviations that specify a date or a time of day are acceptable:

621 B.C.	10:30 A.M.
A.D. 1983	1:17 P.M.

Note also that the abbreviations for number (*no.*) and dollars (*$*) may be used with specific numbers: *no.* 9, *$5.50*. None of these abbreviations should be used without a specific numerical reference: in the sentence

I feel asleep in the P.M.

P.M. should be changed to *afternoon*.
	Note that if an abbreviation comes at the end of a declarative sentence, the

period that marks the end of the abbreviation also marks the end of the sentence.

> We left at 3:30 P.M.

If an abbreviation comes at the end of a question, the question mark follows the period that marks the end of the abbreviation:

> Did you leave before 3:00 P.M.?

In formal writing, the following should not be abbreviated:

> Units of measurement, such as *inches* or *pounds*. Long phrases such as *miles per hour* (*mph*) are an exception.
>
> Geographical names, such as *Fifth Avenue* or *California*. *USA* and *USSR* are exceptions, as are *Mount* (*Mt. Washington*) and *Saint* (*St. Louis*).
>
> Names of days, months, and holidays, such as *Wednesday*, *September*, or *Christmas*.
>
> Names of people, such as *Charles* or *Robert*.
>
> Academic subjects, such as *economics* or *English*.
>
> Divisions in books such as *page* (*p.*), *chapter* (*chap.*) or *volume*(*vol.*). These abbreviations are acceptable, however, in footnote and bibliographic entries, and in cross-references, in a formal research paper.

Note finally that common Latin abbreviations that may be used in parenthetical references in informal writing, such as *e.g.*, (*for example*), *etc.* (*and so forth*), and *i.e.* (*that is*), should be replaced by their equivalent English phrases in formal writing:

> In some of the songs in *Blood on the Tracks*, for example, "Idiot Wind," Dylan returns to the biting social criticism of his early career.

num

NUMBERS

Like abbreviations, numbers written as figures are used only moderately in formal writing, as compared to their regular use in technical and informal writing.

Generally, in formal writing, numbers are spelled out if they can be expressed in one or two words:

He lived to be one hundred years old.

If a number is hyphenated, it is considered one word:

The car has eighty-two thousand miles on it.

If spelling out a number takes more than two words, the number should be written in figures:

The book has 372 pages.

Note, however, that if several numbers appear in a sentence or a paragraph, they should be spelled out or written in figures consistently:

In the crowd of 275 people attending the rehearsal of the circus, there were only 25 grown men and 37 grown women; all the rest, a total of 213, were children.

Use figures to write the following: a date (*September 2, 1947*); a time of day (*8:45 A.M.*); an address (*705 Walton Avenue*); a telephone number (*631-6303*); an exact sum of money (*$12.42*); a decimal (*a 4.0 grade average*); a statistic (*37 percent*); a score (*7 to 3*); a volume, chapter, and/or page number in a book (*Volume 3, Chapter 10, page 105*); and an act, scene, and/or line number in a play (*Act II, Scene 3, lines 12–14*).
Note, however, that if the name of a street when the street is numbered can be spelled out in one or two words, it should be (*42 Fifth Avenue*), unless a word such as *East, West, North,* or *South* precedes the street name (*42 East 57th Street*). Also, a figure in round numbers may be written out (*ten cents, two o'clock, a hundred miles*).
Finally, always spell out numbers that begin a sentence:

Thirteen is my lucky number.

If the number requires more than two words to be spelled out, rearrange the sentence: the sentence

275 people attended the rehearsal.

should be revised to read

The rehearsal was attended by 275 people.

HYPHENATION

A hyphen may be used to divide a word between the end of one line and the beginning of the next line. The hyphen should be placed only at the end of the first line, never at the start of the second. The last word on a page should not be divided with a hyphen.

When dividing a word with a hyphen, break the word only between syllables (*divi-sion, hyphen-ation*). Consult a dictionary to check the syllable breaks in a word. Words that have a prefix or a suffix should be divided between the prefix and the root (*dis-approve*) or between the root and the suffix (*happi-ness*). A compound word should be divided between the two words that form the compound (*air-plane*).

Never divide a word of only one syllable; for example, the word *dropped* cannot be divided between the two *p*'s.

Some writers prefer not to divide a word so that a single letter is left at the end of a line (*a-men*) or so that fewer than three letters appear at the start of a line (*com-ic*). Also, some writers prefer not to divide a word if the division creates a pronunciation problem (*con-science*).

A hyphen is also used to form some compound nouns (*a vice-president*) and some compound adjectives when they appear before a noun (*a hard-boiled egg*). Note that many compound nouns are simply written as one word (*playhouse*) or as two words (*hair stylist*). Many compound adjectives are written as one word (*childlike*) or as two words when they appear after a noun in a sentence (*he is well liked*). Consult a dictionary to check whether a compound noun or adjective should be written as a single word, as a hyphenated word, or as two words.

A hyphen is used to join a prefix to a proper noun (*un-American*). it is not used to join a prefix to a common noun, an adjective, or a verb (*superpatriot, profile, rejoin*), unless it is needed to avoid a misreading; for example, it is used to distinguish the word *re-creation* (something that has been created over again) from the word *recreation* (relaxation).

A hyphen is used to divide compound numbers written as words between *twenty-one* and *ninety-nine*. Some writers use the hyphen to divide fractions written as words (*three-fourths*).

Finally, hyphens are used in a series such as the following: *a two-and-one-half, a three-, or a four-minute egg.*

SPELLING

The most important thing to keep in mind with regard to spelling is that you should consult a dictionary whenever you have any doubt about whether you have spelled a word correctly. If, in addition, you keep a notebook in which you list the words that you misspell frequently, along with their proper spelling, you will have a valuable tool that you can use whenever you are proofreading a paper. Always proofread your papers for spelling.

Beyond these preparations, there are a few basic rules that you can follow to avoid common spelling errors:

Put *i* before *e*, except after *c* or when pronounced like *a*, as in *neighbor* or *weigh*. Thus, write *believe* or *grief*, but *ceiling* or *receive*. Other exceptions to the rule of putting *i* before *e* include *either, leisure, foreign, seize,* and *weird*.

Generally, a final *e* is dropped before a suffix that begins with a vowel:

love, lovable, loving
imagine, imagination, imaginary
grieve, grieving, grievous

Some exceptions are *changeable, courageous, mileage, shoeing*.

Generally, a final *e* is retained before a suffix that begins with a consonant: *lovely, arrangement, fineness*. Some exceptions are *truly* and *judgment*.

Generally, a final *y* is changed to *i* before a suffix is added to a word:

beauty, beauties, beautiful
copy, copies, copied

One exception occurs when the suffix is *ing: copying*. Another exception occurs when the final *y* comes after a vowel:

obeyed, days, journeys

Generally, in a one-syllable word that ends in a consonant preceded by a single vowel, the final consonant is doubled before a suffix that begins with a vowel:

drop, dropped
slap, slapping
win, winner

However, when the final consonant of a one-syllable word is preceded by two vowels or by a vowel and another consonant, the final consonant is not doubled before a suffix that begins with a vowel:

cool, cooler   park, parking
real, realized   strong, strongest

Generally, in a word of two or more syllables that ends in a consonant, the final consonant is doubled before a suffix that begins with a vowel, if the accent falls on the last syllable of the word and if a single vowel precedes the final consonant:

begin, beginning
occur, occurred
regret, regrettable

The final consonant is not doubled if the accent does not fall on the last syllable:

enter, entered

Nor is it doubled if the final consonant is preceded by two vowels or by a vowel and another consonant:

despair, despairing
return, returning

Note: Avoid the common mistake of joining words that should be written separately, such as *a lot* and *all right*, or separating words that should be joined, such as *together* and *throughout*.

Commonly Confused Homonyms

Finally, many times spelling errors arise because a writer confuses two words that sound alike but that differ both in spelling and in meaning. Such words are called *homonyms*. The following is a list of some commonly confused homonyms:

Accept/except.   *Accept* is a verb meaning "receive" or "agree to":

He accepted her terms.

Except is used most often as a preposition meaning "but for" or "other than":

I like every kind of music except rock and roll.

As a verb, *except* means "leave out" or "exclude":

Excepting his accountant, no one knows how rich he is.

Advice/advise.   *Advice* is a noun meaning "recommendation" or "guidance":

She gave her son good advice.

Advise is a verb meaning "give advice to":

She advised him to study hard.

Affect/effect.   *Affect* is used most often as a verb meaning to "change" or "influence":

The jury's decision was affected by her testimony.

It also can mean "pretend to feel":

He affected amusement, even though he was really quite angry.

Effect is used most often as a noun meaning "result" or "consequence":

The side effects of the medicine are unknown.

As a verb, *effect* means to "bring about" or "perform":

The senator's efforts effected change in the tax laws.

All ready/already.   *All ready* means "completely prepared":

She was all ready to leave.

Already means "by this time" or "by that time":

The game was already half over when we got there.

All together/altogether.   *All together* means "in a group":

The family was all together at my aunt's house last Thanksgiving.

Altogether means "completely" or "entirely":

He changed his mind partially but not altogether.

An/and.   *An* is an article:

I ate an apple.

And is a coordinating conjunction:

I love apples and oranges.

Buy/by.   *Buy* is a verb meaning "purchase":

We need to buy a new car.

By is most often used as a preposition meaning "near to," "through," or "with":

The house by the station was destroyed by fire.

By is also used as an adverb:

The time went by.

Conscience/conscious.   *Conscience* is a noun meaning "a sense of right and wrong":

She thought about cheating, but her conscience kept her from doing it.

Conscious is an adjective meaning "aware" or "awake":

He was conscious for a few minutes after the accident, but then he passed out.

Every day/everyday.   *Every day* means "daily":

She jogs two miles every day.

Everyday means "common," "ordinary," or "regular":

"Oh," she said, "this old thing is just an everyday dress."

Formally/formerly.   *Formally* means "in a formal or ceremonious way":

He was dressed formally, in a white tuxedo, at his wedding.

Formerly means "previously," or "at an earlier time":

She was formerly a student, but now she works on Wall Street.

Hear/here.   *Hear* is a verb meaning to "perceive," to "listen," or to "learn" by the ear or by being told:

I hear you are leaving town.

Here is an adverb meaning "in or to or at this place or point":

I am not leaving; I am staying right here.

Its/it's.　*Its* is a possessive pronoun:

He likes the car but not its price.

It's is a contraction meaning "it is":

Unfortunately, it's too expensive.

Know/no.　*Know* is a verb meaning to "understand," "perceive," or "be aware of":

Do you know what I mean?

No is used as an adverb to express denial, dissent, or refusal:

No, I do not understand.

No is also used commonly as an adjective meaning "not any" or "not at all":

I have no idea what you mean.

Later/latter.　*Later* refers to time:

I have to finish a paper right now so I'll call you later.

Latter refers to the second of two things previously mentioned:

When David fought Goliath, the former used his brain, the latter used only his brawn.

May be/maybe.　*May be* is a verb phrase:

My brother, who is overseas, may be coming home.

Maybe is an adverb meaning "perhaps":

Maybe he will sell it, if he gets a good enough offer.

Peace/piece. *Peace* is a noun meaning "freedom from war or strife," "harmony," or "calm":

Why can't we live in peace with one another?

Piece, used as a noun, means "a limited quantity or part of something" (a *piece of land*), or "a specimen of workmanship" (*a piece of music*), or "an individual article in a set or a collection or a class" (*a piece of furniture*). *Piece* is also used as a verb meaning to "mend" or "joint together":

A detective pieces clues together to solve a mystery.

Principal/principle. *Principal*, used as a noun, means "chief administrator":

The school principal ran the assembly.

It also means a "capital sum of money":

He had to pay the interest on the principal of his car loan.

Principal, used as an adjective, means "main" or "most important":

The principal reason that I fear cats is the memory I have of being scratched as a child.

Principle is a noun meaning "rule" or "basic truth" or "law":

He followed the principle of doing unto others as he would have them do unto him.

Right/write. *Right*, used as an adjective, means "proper," "correct," "genuine," or "legitimate":

Apologizing was the right thing to do.

Right, used as a noun, means a "just claim" or a "privilege" (*freedom of speech is a basic right*). Used as an adverb, it means "directly" or "exactly" (*do it right now*) or the opposite of "left." Used as a verb, it means to "set up" or to "set in order":

It took a crane to right the fallen statue.

Write is a verb meaning "trace words on paper" or "communicate" or "compose":

My sister is writing a novel.

Sight/site.   *Sight,* used as a verb, means to "observe" or to "perceive with one's eyes":

The sailor on the mast was the first to sight land.

Sight, used as a noun, means "vision" or "spectacle":

After the food fight, the dining room was a sight to behold.

Site is used most often as a noun meaning "location":

This hill is the site we have chosen to build the house on.

Site is also used as a verb meaning to "locate":

They sited the shore through the telescope.

Note: Do not confuse *sight* or *site* with *cite,* a verb that means to "refer to" or to "mention":

The lawyer cited the case of *Jones* v. *Jones* in his argument before the judge.

Some/sum.   *Some* is used as an adjective, an adverb, or a pronoun to indicate a certain unspecified number, amount, or degree of something:

We are having dinner with some friends.

Sum, used as a noun, means a "total" or a "quantity":

One million dollars is a large sum of money.

Sum is also used as a verb meaning to "combine into a total" or to "form an overall estimate or view of":

The lawyer summed up her case for the jury.

Than/then.   *Than* is a conjunction used in making comparisons:

I like the blue shirt better than the yellow.

Then is an adverb used in referring to the passage of time:

He put the cake in the oven; then he waited an hour before checking to see if it was done.

Their/there/they're.   *Their* is a third-person-plural possessive pronoun:

Their car is in the driveway.

There indicates a place:

The kids will like the park, so let's go there.

There is also used in the expressions "there is" and "there are."
They're is a contraction meaning "they are":

I always root for the home team, even when they're having a bad year.

Threw/through.   *Threw* is a past-tense form of the verb "to throw":

He threw the ball to her.

Through is used as a preposition, an adverb, and an adjective meaning "in one end and out the other," "between or among," "during the whole period of," "having finished," "by means of," or "by reason of":

They drove through the tunnel.
He ran through the people in the crowd, looking for her.
He was sick all through last week.
She practiced one hour before she was through.
She finished the marathon through sheer willpower.

Note: Do not employ the popular shortened form *thru* for *through*; similarly avoid the shortened form *nite* for *night* or *tho* for *though*.

To/too/two.   *To* is a preposition that indicates place, direction, or position:

We have flown to the moon.

To also forms the infinitive with all verbs.

I'd like to get to know you.

Too is an adverb meaning "also" or "excessively":

She is too tired to go out tonight.

Two is a number:

Two plus two equals four.

Were/we're/where. *Were* is a past-tense form of the verb "to be":

They were not home.

Were is also used to form the subjunctive mood:

If they were home, we would visit them.

We're is a contraction meaning "we are":

We're planning to go on our vacation next month.

Where is used as an adverb or as a conjunction to indicate a place or a position:

Where are the keys? They are where you left them.

Who's/whose. *Who's* is a contraction meaning "who is":

Who's coming to the party?

Whose is a possessive form of the pronoun who:

Whose party is it?

Your/you're. *Your* is a possessive form of the pronoun you:

I saw your sister today.

You're is a contraction meaning "you are":

She said that you're leaving for college this week.

REVIEW EXERCISE—PUNCTUATION AND MECHANICS

The following paragraphs, from an essay by E. B. White called "Coon Tree," contain punctuation and mechanical errors. Add proper punctuation and capitalization, wherever you think necessary. Check to see where italics, abbreviations, or numbers might be used. Correct any misspellings that you come across.

Today ive been rereading a cheerful forecast for the comming century prepared by some farsighted professors at the california institute of technology and published not long ago in the times. man, it would appear is standing at the gateway to a new era of civilization, technology will be king. Everything man needs the report says is at hand all we require is air, sea water, ordinary rock and sunlight. The population of the earth will increase and multiply but that'll be no problem the granite of the earths crust contains enough uranium and thorium to supply an abundance of power for everybody. If we just pound rock, were sitting pretty.

I have made a few private tests of my own and my findings differ somewhat from those of the california technology men. We have two stoves in our kitchen hear in maine a big black iron stove that burns wood and a small white electric stove that draws its strength from the bangor hydro electric company. We use both. One represents the past the other represents the future. If we had to give up one in favor of the other and cook on just one stove there isnt the slightest question in anybodys mind in my household witch is the one we'd keep. It would be the big black Home crawford Eight Twenty made by walker and pratt, with its woodbox that has to be filled with wood, its water tank that has to be replenished with water, its ashpan that has to be emptied of ashes, its flue pipe that has to be renewed when it gets rusty, its grates that need freeing when they get cloged and all its other foibles and deficiencies. . . .

My stove witch Im sure would be impracticle in many american homes, is never the less a symbol of my belief. The technologists with there vision of happyness at the core of the rock, see only halve the rock halve of mans dream and his need. Perhaps sucess in the future will depend partly on our ability to generate cheep power but I think it will depend to a greater extent on our ability to resist a technological formula that is sterile: peas without pageantry . . . knowledge without wisdom, kitchens without a warm stove. There is more to these rocks than uranium there is the lichen on the rock, the smell of the fern who's feet are upon the rock, the view from the rock.

Acknowledgments

November 13, 1949 journal entry from *Letters Home by Sylvia Plath: Correspondence 1950–1963* by Aurelia Schober Plath. Copyright © 1975 by Aurelia Schober Plath. Reprinted by permission of HarperCollins Publishers.

Journal entries by Margaret Ryan, from *Ariadne's Thread: A Collection of Contemporary Women's Journals*, edited by Lyn Lifshin. Reprinted by permission of Margaret Ryan.

"50,000 on Beach Strangely Calm as Rocket Streaks Out of Sight" by Gay Talese. *The New York Times*, February 21, 1962. Copyright © 1962 by The New York Times Company. Reprinted by permission.

Part 1 from "The Angry Winter" in *The Unexpected Universe*, by Loren Eiseley. Copyright © 1968 by Loren Eiseley. Reprinted by permission of Harcourt Brace Jovanovich, Inc.

"Momma's Private Victory" from *I Know Why the Caged Bird Sings*, by Maya Angelou. Copyright © 1969 by Maya Angelou. Reprinted by permission of Random House, Inc.

From "Encouraging Honest Inquiry in Student Writing" by David V. Harrington, in *College Composition and Communication*, Vol. XXX, No. 2 (May 1979). Reprinted by permission of the National Council of Teachers of English.

"On a Kibbutz" from *To Jerusalem and Back* by Saul Bellow. Copyright © 1976 by Saul Bellow. Reprinted by permission of Viking Penguin, Inc.

"The Iowa State Fair" by Paul Engle. Reprinted by permission of the author.

"Workers" from *Hunger of Memory* by Richard Rodriguez. Copyright © 1982 by Richard Rodriguez. Reprinted by permission of David R. Godine, Publisher.

"A Second Look at Allen Ginsberg" by Patrick Fenton. Reprinted by permission of the author.

From *Calcutta* by Geoffrey Moorhouse. Published by Weidenfeld & Nicholson Ltd., 1971. Reprinted by permission of A. P. Watt Ltd., literary agent.

619

From *The Lives of a Cell* by Lewis Thomas. Copyright © 1971 by the Massachusetts Medical Society. Originally published in the *New England Journal of Medicine*. Reproduced by permission of Viking Penguin, Inc.

Specified excerpt from "Letter from a Birmingham Jail, April 16, 1963" from *Why We Can't Wait* by Martin Luther King, Jr. Copyright © 1963 by Martin Luther King, Jr. Reprinted by permission of Harper & Row, Publishers, Inc.

"Is There a Middle Ground?" by Ernest van den Haag in *National Review*, December 22, 1989. © 1989 by *National Review*, Inc., 150 East 35th Street, New York, NY 10016. Reprinted by permission.

"Abortion Politics in the 90s: Giving Women a Real Choice" by Rosalind Petchesky, from *The Nation*, May 28, 1990/ The Nation Co. Inc., © 1990.

"Persuasion Preferred" by John Garvey. From *Commonweal*, June 15, 1990. Used by permission of the Commonweal Foundation.

"Active and Passive Euthanasia" by James Rachels, from *The New England Journal of Medicine*, Vol. 292, 1975. Copyright © 1975 by the Massachusetts Medical Society. Reprinted by permission of the publisher.

"Active Euthanasia Violates Fundamental Principles" by Samuel F. Hunter. From *Journal of the American Medical Association*, December 1, 1989, Vol. 262, No. 21, page 3074. Copyright 1989, American Medical Association.

"The State as Parent" by Sandra H. Johnson. From *Commonweal*, May 4, 1990. Used by permission of the Commonweal Foundation.

"Erotica vs. Pornography" from *Outrageous Acts and Everyday Rebellions* by Gloria Steinem. Copyright © 1983 by Gloria Steinem, © 1984 by East Toledo Productions, Inc. Reprinted by permission of Henry Holt and Company, Inc.

"The First Amendment Forbids Censorship" by Lois Sheinfeld.

"The First Amendment Does Not Protect Pornography" by Janella Miller.

From "Emotions Found to Influence Nearly Every Ailment" by Jane E. Brody. *The New York Times*, May 24, 1983. Copyright © 1983 by The New York Times Company. Reprinted by permission.

"Gooseberries" by Anton Chekhov and translated by Avrahm Yarmolinsky, from *The Portable Chekhov* by Avrahm Yarmolinsky, editor. Copyright 1947, 1968 by Viking Penguin, Inc. Renewed copyright © 1975 by Avrahm Yarmolinsky. Used by permission of Viking Penguin, a division of Penguin Books USA Inc.

"The Lesson" from *Gorilla, My Love* by Toni Cade Bambara. Copyright © 1972 by Toni Cade Bambara. Reprinted by permission of Random House, Inc.

Index

Abbreviations, 604–606
Abstractness, 305
Accept/except, 610
Adding, 129–131, 504
Ad hominem, 343
Adjectives, 305
  demonstrative, 122
Ad populum, 343
Adverbs, 214, 305, 555
  conjunctive, 556–557
Advice/advise, 610–611
Affect/effect, 611
Agreement
  faulty, 568
  pronoun/antecedent, 570–572
  subject/verb, 568–570
Allen, Woody, 366
All ready/already, 611
All together/altogether, 611
Allusion, in arguments, 364
Ambiguity, 74, 372
Analogies, 96, 106, 189
  in classical questions, 186–187
  faulty, 342
Analysis, problems in, 172–173
An/and, 611
Anecdotes, 80, 173
Angelou, Maya, 106–110
APA method of documentation,
  485–486
Apostrophe, 599–600
Appropriateness, in writing about
  the media, 278, 282
Argument, 327–331
  building, 355
  conclusion, 356
  formulation, 346
  introduction, 356
  proof, 356
  refutation, 355–356
  stating, 355
  See also Persuasive writing
Aristotle, 184, 322

Arrangement
  A-to-Z, 103
  cause-and-effect, 198
  classification, 247–248
  comparison, 198
  definition, 247
  description, 150, 151–153
  details, 90, 110
  explanation, 246–247
  narrative, 65, 103, 110, 150, 200,
    221
  patterns, 152, 185, 197–201, 267,
    271
  process, 200
  See Narration
Articles, 558
Associations, past, 22
Assumptions, 339
  implied, 434
A-to-Z arrangement, 103
Attitudes, 240–243
Audience, 13
  addressing, 13, 37–45, 53–54,
    97–98, 143–146, 192–197,
    240–242, 271, 276–278
  analyzing, 350
  attracting, 75, 80
  consciousness, 43
  depth of information, 143–149
  expectations, 39
  frame of reference, 97–99, 148,
    348, 350
  gap, 89, 97, 106, 242, 430
  hostile, 325
  persuading, 348–354
  point of view, 90, 99–100, 102,
    530–531
  public, 276–278, 282–283,
    310–311
  scientific, 451
  specific, 192
  sympathetic, 53–54, 57
  undecided, 325

  values, 39, 430
  See also Readers
Authenticity, personal, 39

Balanced phrasing, 306
Bambara, Toni Cade, 515–521
Bandwagon, 343
Begging the question, 343
Bellow, Saul, 154–157
Bibliography, 484, 502–503
  preliminary, 466–468
Brackets, 594–595
Brainstorming, 64–65, 230,
    232–240, 508
  clustering, 236–237
  to generate ideas, 238–240
  listing, 234–236
  in writing about an issue, 429
  in writing about incidents, 106,
    126
  in writing about literature, 528
  in writing persuasively, 354
Buy/by, 612

Capitalization, 601–603
Case
  errors, 573–576
  forming, 355
  studies, 183, 184
Casing the subject, 183, 225
Categorical statements
  in arguments, 367
Categorization (explorer's question),
  138
Causation, 120, 187
Cause-and-effect, 198, 246–247,
    297
Changing (explorer's question), 138
Character
  major, 540
  minor, 540
  stereotypical, 275
  in writing about literature, 508,
    540

Chekhov, Anton, 508–515
Chief Joseph, 170
Choice, 120
Chronology, 120–121, 137
   in narration, 103, 110
   in writing, 90
Churchill, Winston, 365, 367
Citation method of documentation,
   484–485, 492–497
Claims, 327
Clarification
   in writing about incidents, 121
Clarity, 303
Clark, Kenneth B., 329
Classical questions
   analogies in, 186–187
   in arguments, 331–332, 344–347
   in brainstorming, 236
   compared to explorer's questions,
     186–187
   generalization, 273
   in writing about media, 273
   in writing about prejudice,
     186–192
   in writing about research, 450
   in writing about tradition, 238
Classification
   in writing about tradition, 247
Clauses
   adverbial, 563
   dependent, 562
   independent, 562
   main, 562
   subordinate, 213–214, 305, 562
Clustering, 236–237
Coffin, Robert P. Tristram, 167
Collaboration, 64
Colon, 218, 591–592
Comma, 217, 586–590
   splices, 579–580
Commenting, 33
Communication
   facilitating, 72
   triangle, 19
Community of discourse, 437–439
Comparison, 120, 151, 189,
   198–200
   in writing about tradition,
     246–247
Comparison (explorer's question),
   138, 150
Composition (explorer's question),
   138
Conclusion, 164–165
   in argument, 355–356
   controversial, 340
   in essay writing, 174
   negated, 454
   strategy, 171
   in writing about places, 171–174
Concreteness, 303–304
Conjunctions, 120–122

causal, 340
coordinating, 555
correlative, 555
subordinating, 213, 556
Connotation
   in arguments, 362–364
Conscience/conscious, 612
Consolidating
   in editing, 319
   in rewriting, 317–318
Contradiction, in persuasive writing,
   332
Contrast, 120, 151, 189, 198–200
   in writing about tradition,
     246–247
Conventions
   of debate, 423
   disciplinary, 72
   exploratory writing, 230
   expressive writing, 230
   form, 72
   of grammar, 432
   of organization, 432
   of public argument, 423
   of scientific documentation, 450
   style, 72
Coordination, 165–166, 168
Coppola, Eleanor, 32
Credibility in arguments, 349
Critical thinking, 423–430
Cutting, 85–86, 504

Dash, 218, 592–593
Deadwood, elimination of, 258–263
Debate. See Writing about issues
Deduction, 324
   in arguments, 331–332, 339–344
Deductive fallacies, in arguments,
   342–344
Definition, in writing about tradition, 247
Depth of information, 143–149
   differences in, 144
   evaluating, 137, 185
   reader's, 240
Description, 150
   explorer's question, 138
   patterns, 150, 152–153
   perceptions, 137
   in writing about places, 152–153,
     161
Details
   arrangement, 90, 110
   conveying, 105–106
   in revising, 130
   substituting, 179
   unnecessary, 111
   in writing about incidents, 110
   in writing about literature, 521
Dialogue, 106, 110, 137
   in writing about places, 153–154,
     161

Didion, Joan, 116, 246, 274
Discipline, 71
Distributing, 224–226, 504
Documentation, 484–490
   APA style, 485–486
   bibliography, 486–487, 502–503
   citation method, 484–485,
     492–497
   endnotes, 487–489, 497–502
   footnotes, 487–489
   MLA style, 485–486
   in writing about research,
     484–490, 492–503
Doscher, Barbara, 278
Duration, 103

Editing
   adding, 129–131, 504
   consolidating, 319, 504
   cutting, 85–86
   distributing, 226, 504
   heavy, 111
   mechanics, 86, 131–132, 181,
     226, 319, 444
   paragraphs, 181
   proofreading, 87
   rearranging, 267–268, 504
   substitution, 179–180, 504
   transitions, 122–126, 131, 180,
     226, 444
   writing about incidents, 131–132
Eiseley, Loren, 103–105
Either/or, 343
Elbow, Peter, 21, 23–24
Ellipsis, 595–596
Emig, Janet, 134
Emotional appeal, 362, 378
   in arguments, 348, 362–373
Emotions, 322, 324
Endnotes, 497–502
Engle, Paul, 158–161
Enthusiasm, 283
Enthymeme, 339
Essayist vs. journalist, 95–96
Essay writing
   about incidents, 89–132
   about places, 135–182
   about prejudice, 182–227
   about self, 19–47, 49–87
   analysis, 106, 157–158
   coherence in, 120
   developed from a journal, 27
   developed from free writing, 26
   expressive, 49, 89
   journalist's questions, 94–96
   main point, 58, 72, 77
   organization, 85
   outlines, 14
   structure, 114–126
Ethical appeal
   in arguments, 350–351, 353–354
Ethics, 322, 324

Every day/everyday, 612
Evidence, 327
  contrary, 332
  unfavorable, 454
  in writing about an issue,
    426–428
  in writing about research,
    454–455
Exclamation point, 586
Expert knowledge, 327
Explanation, 246–247
  in exposition, 111
  versus exploration, 230, 246–247
  in writing about media, 269–320
  in writing about tradition,
    231–268
Exploration
  versus explanation, 230, 246–247
  in writing about places, 135
  writing about a prejudgment,
    183–228
Exploratory writing, 135–182
Explorer's questions
  answering, 140–141
  in brainstorming, 236
  compared to classical questions,
    186–187
  in writing about places, 138–143
  in writing about prejudice,
    186–187
Exposition, 137
  in narrative, 110–112
  patterns, 150–152, 200–201
  in process analysis, 200–201
  in writing about places, 151–152,
    161
Expressive writing. *See* Self-
    expression

False causes, 342–343
Faulkner, William, 215, 363–364,
    367
Feedback
  in persuasive writing, 374
  in writing about an issue, 440
  in writing about incidents, 126
  in writing about literature, 543
  in writing about media, 311
  in writing about places, 174–175
  in writing about prejudice,
    222–223
  in writing about research, 490
  in writing about self, 80–81
  in writing about tradition, 263
Fenton, Patrick, 150–151, 153,
    205–210
Form
  conventions, 72
  documentation, 484–490
  paragraph
    development, 164–171, 226

  structure, 114–122, 181
  sentence
    combining, 212, 219–222, 226
    length, 216–217
    rhythm, 216–217
  transitions, 122–126, 131, 180,
    218–219
Formally/formerly, 612
Fraiberg, Selma H., 336–337
Frame of reference. *See also* Point of
    view
  assumptions on, 105, 106
  audience, 97–98, 348, 350
  characterizing, 54
  composite, 192
  constructing, 185
  and point of view, 45
  practice with, 98–99
  of readers, 98–99, 143, 145,
    193–194, 240–242, 531
Franklin, Benjamin, 274
Free association, 234
Free writing, 508
  about self, 19–47
  ideas, 21–23
  practice, 23–24, 26–27
  voice in, 37–45
Frost, Robert, 1, 11

Galbraith, John Kenneth, 367
Garvey, John, 392–395
Generalization
  hasty, 332, 454
  in writing about media, 271–276,
    284–285
Genetic fallacy, 343
Goodman, Ellen, 338–339
Gould, Stephen Jay, 460–462
Grammar errors, 568–572
Gray, Francine Du Plessix, 247
Grossberger, Lewis, 290–297

Harrington, David V., 143–144
Hear/here, 612–613
Hofstadter, Richard, 334–336
Homonyms, 610–617
How (journalist's question)
    91–96
Humor
  in arguments, 366
  avoidance, 505
  inappropriate, 372
Hunter, Samuel F., 400–402
Hyphenation, 608
Hypothesis
  forming, 466
  revised, 452
  stating, 473–474
  testing, 458–459, 463
  in writing about prejudice, 185

  in writing about research,
    449–453, 473–474
Ideas
  brainstorming, 234–240
    clustering, 236–237
    listing, 234–236
  critical thinking, 423–430
  generating, 11–13, 49–50, 91–94,
    138–139, 186–192, 234–240,
    272–276, 326–327, 428–430,
    453–459, 521–522
  from journal, 49–50, 53
  major, 236
  shaping, 57–58, 72–74, 102–103,
    149–150, 197–198, 245–246,
    284–285, 355–356, 433,
    473–474
  supporting, 236
  through generalization, 272–276
Impression, overriding, 149, 154
Incidents (writing about), 89–132
  audience, 97–102
  feedback, 126
  ideas, 91–94, 102–103
  journalist's questions, 91–96
  practice, 94–96
  rough draft, 112–113
  significance, 103
Induction, 324, 449–450
  in arguments, 321–339
  in writing about research, 451,
    453–459
Inferences, 100–102, 149
Inhibitions, 37
Interpretation in exposition, 111
Intimidation, 40
Introduction, 164–165
  in arguments, 355–356
  finalizing, 79
  practice, 79–80
  rewriting, 80–81
  in writing about self, 72–79
Irony, 306
  in writing about literature, 541
  in writing about media, 283, 307
Issues (writing about)
  brainstorming, 429
  community of discourse, 437–439
  critical thinking in, 423–430
  evidence in, 426–428
  feedback, 440
  ideas, 423–430
  point of view, 425–426, 433–434
  role playing, 431
  rough draft, 435
Italics, 604
Its/it's, 613

Jacobs, Jane, 166–167
Jefferson, Thomas, 43
Johnson, Sandra H., 402–406

Journal
  double-entry, 96, 142, 523
  free writing in, 508
  incidents, 96
  keeping a, guidelines for, 20–37
  narration in, 65
  patterns in, 49–50, 53
  practice, 36–37
  publishing, 48
  self-expression in, 18
  as source of ideas, 13, 36, 233
  starting, 27
  for summaries, 428–429
  in writing about media, 275
  in writing about places, 142–143
Journalist's questions
  in writing about incidents, 91–96
Journalist vs. essayist, 95–96
Judgment of authorities, 327

Kanner, Bernice, 278
Kinneavy, James, 134
King, Martin Luther Jr., 367–370
Kingston, Maxine Hong, 246
Kinnicutt, Susan, 29
Know/no, 613
Kreisberg, Paul H., 330–331

Language
  appropriate, 505
  in dreams, 34
  figurative, 306, 364, 378, 381,
    505
  patterns, 365
  persuasive, 362–373
  vivid, 105
Later/latter, 613
Leonard, George, 153–154
Lifton, Robert Jay, 166
Like/as, 364
Lincoln, Abraham, 367
Lindbergh, Anne Morrow, 277–278
Listing, 234–236
Literature (writing about), 506–547
  brainstorming, 528
  character, 540
  feedback, 543
  ideas, 521–522
  irony in, 541
  plot, 540
  rough draft, 536
  theme, 541
Logic, 322, 324
Logical terms
  in arguments, 367

Macrorie, Ken, 39
Mannes, Marya, 117, 169
Mauriac, Francois, 116
May, Rollo, 478
May be/maybe, 613
McCullers, Carson, 246

McDermott, Alice, 285–289
Mead, Margaret, 233, 248
Mechanics of editing, 86, 131–132,
  181, 226, 319, 444
Media
  influence, 269
  understanding, 270
  writing about, 269–320
    classical questions, 273
    feedback, 311
    generalization, 272–276,
      284–285
    ideas, 272–276
    irony in, 307
    narration in, 272–273
    practice, 274, 276
    rough draft, 298
Melville, Herman, 115–116
Metaphors, 96, 225, 306–307, 364
  confusing, 372
Method of inquiry, 16
  explorer's questions, 147–148
  journalist's questions, 147–148
Miller, Arthur, 307
Miller, Janella, 418–422
MLA method of documentation,
  485–486
Modifiers
  dangling, 577–578
  free, 214–215, 218
  misplaced, 576–577
  using, 305
Moorhouse, Geoffrey, 216
Morris, Wright, 304

Narration
  arrangement, 65, 221
  chronological, 103
  in exploratory writing, 248
  exposition in, 110–112
  in expressive writing, 248
  formulas, 275
  in journals, 65
  patterns, 150
  in process analysis, 200–201
  in writing about incidents, 103
  in writing about media, 272–273,
    284–285
  in writing about places, 150–151,
    161
  in writing about prejudice,
    200–201
  in writing about tradition,
    248–255
Nehru, Jawaharlal, 364
Newman, Edwin, 152, 279–281
Notes, in writing about research,
  468–471
Noun phrase, 560
Nouns, 305, 551
Numbers, 606–607

Ogilvie, Bruce C., 152
Olson, Eric, 166
Outlining
  immersion, 161
  paragraph, 166
  in writing about research,
    474–476
Overexplanation, 262
Oversimplification, 189

Paragraph
  concluding, 165
  coordinate, 169
  development, 150, 164–171, 226
  introductory, 165
  outline, 166
  part-by-part method, 199–200
  rewriting, 181
  structure, 114–122, 181
  subordinate, 169
  substitution in, 179
  whole-by-whole method,
    199–200
Parallelism, faulty, 578–579
Paraphrasing, 469–471
Parentheses, 593–594
Parts of speech
  adjective, 214, 305, 555
    demonstrative, 122
  adverb, 214, 305, 555
  article, 558
  conjunction, 120–122, 340,
    555–556
    coordinating, 555
    correlative, 556
    subordinating, 213, 556
  conjunctive adverb, 556–557
  noun, 214, 305, 551
  preposition, 557
  pronoun, 551
    demonstrative, 552
    indefinite, 552
    interrogative, 553
    personal, 552
    reflexive, 552
    relative, 552
  verb, 214, 305, 553
    mood, 554
    tense, 553–554
    voice, 554
Patterns
  arrangement, 152, 185, 197–201,
    267, 271
  chronological, 221
  of coherence, 273
  contradictory, 52
  description, 150, 152–153
  exposition, 150–152, 200–201
  journal, 49–50, 52–53, 73
  narrative, 150, 297, 536
  for process analysis, 201
  of thinking, 75, 332